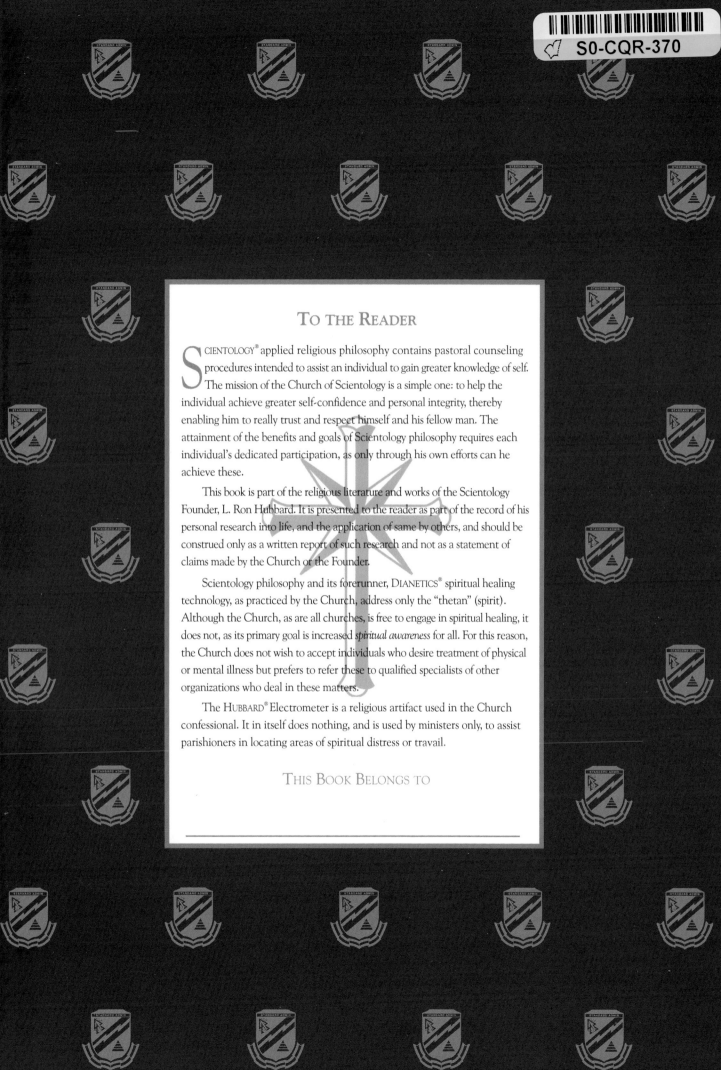

TO THE READER

SCIENTOLOGY® applied religious philosophy contains pastoral counseling procedures intended to assist an individual to gain greater knowledge of self. The mission of the Church of Scientology is a simple one: to help the individual achieve greater self-confidence and personal integrity, thereby enabling him to really trust and respect himself and his fellow man. The attainment of the benefits and goals of Scientology philosophy requires each individual's dedicated participation, as only through his own efforts can he achieve these.

This book is part of the religious literature and works of the Scientology Founder, L. Ron Hubbard. It is presented to the reader as part of the record of his personal research into life, and the application of same by others, and should be construed only as a written report of such research and not as a statement of claims made by the Church or the Founder.

Scientology philosophy and its forerunner, DIANETICS® spiritual healing technology, as practiced by the Church, address only the "thetan" (spirit). Although the Church, as are all churches, is free to engage in spiritual healing, it does not, as its primary goal is increased *spiritual awareness* for all. For this reason, the Church does not wish to accept individuals who desire treatment of physical or mental illness but prefers to refer these to qualified specialists of other organizations who deal in these matters.

The HUBBARD® Electrometer is a religious artifact used in the Church confessional. It in itself does nothing, and is used by ministers only, to assist parishioners in locating areas of spiritual distress or travail.

THIS BOOK BELONGS TO

_____

THE
MANAGEMENT
SERIES

VOLUME 2

PUBLICATIONS, INC.

THE
MANAGEMENT
SERIES

VOLUME 2

THE PERSONNEL SERIES
THE ORG SERIES
THE ESTABLISHMENT OFFICER SERIES

L. RON HUBBARD

FOUNDER OF DIANETICS AND SCIENTOLOGY

Bridge Publications, Inc.
4751 Fountain Avenue
Los Angeles, California 90029

ISBN 1-57318-260-5

IMPORTANT NOTE

In reading this book, be very certain you never go past a word you do not fully understand.

The only reason a person gives up a study or becomes confused or unable to learn is because he or she has gone past a word that was not understood.

The confusion or inability to grasp or learn comes after a word that the person did not have defined and understood.

Have you ever had the experience of coming to the end of a page and realizing you didn't know what you had read? Well, somewhere earlier on that page you went past a word that you had no definition for or an incorrect definition for.

Here's an example. "It was found that when the crepuscule arrived the children were quieter and when it was not present, they were much livelier." You see what happens. You think you don't understand the whole idea, but the inability to understand came entirely from the one word you could not define, *crepuscule,* which means twilight or darkness.

It may not only be the new and unusual words that you will have to look up. Some commonly used words can often be misdefined and so cause confusion.

This datum about not going past an undefined word is the most important fact in the whole subject of study. Every subject you have taken up and abandoned had its words which you failed to get defined.

Therefore, in reading this book be very, very certain you never go past a word you do not fully understand. If the material becomes confusing or you can't seem to grasp it, there will be a word just earlier that you have not understood. Don't go any further, but go back to BEFORE you got into trouble, find the misunderstood word and get it defined.

We have administrative tech.

And it is all published and there for use.

*And further, when it **is** known and used,*

proven times without number now,

production and prosperity occur AND show up

as statistics which INDICATE that production

and prosperity are occurring.

L. Ron Hubbard
HCO PL 20 Sept. 76

INTRODUCTION

When, after twenty years of organizational experience, L. Ron Hubbard developed what he called *The Management Series*, top administrators around the world found in their hands an extraordinarily powerful tool: the ultimate reference for executive success. Since then, in many countries and on all continents, these administrators have conclusively proven that this revolutionary technology provides the means to establish, operate and expand any activity or group — and guarantee its total success.

The Management Series consists of eleven managerial subjects that LRH isolated and then codified, each as a complete subject series — 434 policy letters in all. To understand this accomplishment, one must realize that each series contains key principles of organization never before known to man, let alone codified. And that together they represent unprecedented administrative breakthroughs that form the only precise technology anyone anywhere can use to recognize and handle organizational problems and situations.

This new edition of Volume Two of *The Management Series* includes the Personnel, Org and Establishment Officer Series — the technology which brings staff rapidly and stably to high levels of competence. Here is all the policy necessary to establish, organize and expand any endeavor.

In all, this is the most complete compilation of the Management Series in history, containing all the policies of each series and every fundamental policy letter referred to in them — the full body of data for any executive.

These volumes contain the very laws and principles governing organization — third dynamic technology which mirrors exactly the precision of auditing technology, providing standard handlings for any organizational situation. The most powerful and needed management technology man has ever known, these materials, correctly applied, mean expansion and planetary clearing. Thus, an executive with a full knowledge of *The Management Series* has the tools to organize, establish and operate any organization and take it to the stars.

—*The Editors*

THE ORG SERIES

THE ESTABLISHMENT OFFICER SERIES

ABOUT THE AUTHOR

INDEX

THE
PERSONNEL
SERIES

HUBBARD COMMUNICATIONS OFFICE
SAINT HILL MANOR, EAST GRINSTEAD, SUSSEX

HCO POLICY LETTER OF 29 AUGUST 1970
ISSUE I

REMIMEO
DEPT 1 HAT
HCO AREA HAT
EXEC SEC HATS
DEPT 13 HAT
DEPT 14 HAT
QUAL SEC HAT

PERSONNEL SERIES 1
PERSONNEL TRANSFERS CAN DESTROY AN ORG

It is an observation that Personnel, by critical definition, is "that function which creates havoc in one place in an org by trying to solve a personnel mess in another."

Example: We have just gotten in our Div 6. It has two people. The org has been suffering for lack of Div 6 actions. Now we've finally got two people there and they are being trained up. Meanwhile there is a shortage of staff in CF. Personnel "solves" the CF problem by transferring those in Div 6 to CF in Div 2. There goes any progress on Div 6.

By solving one problem, another is created.

Also there is the fact that it takes a while to train someone on a post and get the post in order. So rapid transfers defeat any post training or competence.

We call this action "musical chairs." That is a game in which people rapidly change positions.

So these transfers defeat not only the org on the third dynamic but also the individual on the first dynamic.

An earlier action similar to this went on. Then whenever Tech got an auditor trained up, Personnel would transfer the auditor to an admin post.

As the auditor was *tech* trained and not OEC trained, you began to find auditors in charge but they didn't have any admin training, thus shattering, by ignorance, the org form and defeating the org's production.

I've just seen a case where a staff member went on full-time training Class VI (very expensive) and was made HCO ES on his return. *But* had never had an OEC.

Using the Tech Divs as a "personnel pool" and taking tech people for admin posts thus defeats twice — defeats the org as a producing activity and defeats its form by not training people in admin (OEC) when they are going to be used in admin.

3

These personnel errors (or crimes) cause every staff member to suffer in terms of lowered income, lowered pay, lowered facilities, lower success. I doubt there is any org where these errors (or crimes) are not current at this writing.

To give the HCO ES candidate full-time training on the OEC or FEBC would make sense. Not Class VI! If you reverse it, you'll see what I mean: we give a new staff member an OEC only and put him onto auditing. Of course that would be disastrous. It's just as disastrous the other way around — taking an auditor who is a Class VI but not an OEC grad and making him the HCO Area Sec!

There is an optimum executive who is *both* an experienced, trained administrator (OEC and time on org posts) and an auditor. But an org would have to be in high production with *lots* of auditors before *that* could happen.

ERRORS

These errors are of long duration. They happen over and over. And they do more to destroy an org than any other action.

A. Making a hole in one place to remedy a hole in another.

B. Training a person for tech but not admin and putting him in admin.

C. Using the Tech Divs as personnel pools from which to man other divs.

D. Rapid shifts of post.

E. Leaving areas in an org unmanned.

SOLUTIONS

The reason why these things are done all come under the heading of failures to recruit and properly train.

Org expansion often gets pinned by false economy in personnel. "If we hired anyone else, we would get less pay." This completely overlooks the fact that if the org doesn't hire more people it will go broke. An org has to be of a certain size to be solvent; it has certain basic expenses such as rent which makes it cost just so much to run. Yet personnel can be so poorly thought out that the org is kept at starvation level.

I heard one not long ago which takes a prize, "But we don't need an Advance Registrar. We can't afford one anyway. You see we have pcs booked in advance for ten weeks already as we don't have enough auditors so why should we have any further promotion?" An idiot smile went with this of course. Backlog became "advance registration."

Orgs in various ways fix their income and prevent its increase. First and foremost of these is personnel.

In every org where I have acted as Executive Director, I have had a personnel procurement problem. In each case the problem was *internally* created. First I would get, "Well, units are low . . ." or "Nobody ever applies." I would take it from there.

I finally became very clever at these impasses. "What," I would ask the Receptionist, "do you tell people who come looking for a job?" Cunning. "Oh them!" I would get, "I tell them we aren't hiring, of course." I would set up a line from a specially appointed Personnel person to me only and would shortly have enough people. I have run an org from 8 people to 63 in 30 days and its GI from £50 to £3,000 in 60 days. Just by doing the usual. It created *awful* problems of course, like auditing rooms, classrooms, hand grooving people onto posts — it was busy. The favorite graveyard calm, so adored there before that, got shattered to hell!

I concluded many times then and conclude now that it is a characteristic of an org to refuse new personnel and to keep them off. In approaching this problem in an org, I am afraid experience has taught me to begin with that assumption and handle it from that viewpoint.

So I normally set up a line that can't be stopped and get people on post. Then I force in training on posts. And I personally inspect and talk to every section every day about what they need and how it's going and keep up their section production.

LRH Comms tell me they *can't* get execs to inspect their areas daily. And personnel shortages show that others do not blow the lines open on recruiting and even prevent handling.

So here is one area where I do some things in managing a production org that not many others do:

1. Force recruitment.

2. Train on post.

3. Daily inspection and comm with everyone in the place in his post area.

4. Concentrate on section and individual production.

5. Let people finish the job they are on.

The result of all this has uniformly been sky-high stats, sky-high pay, huge reserves and excellent tech produced.

So these are the magic solutions.

I do NOT empty out tech to fill admin. I do NOT encourage transfers. I do NOT create problems in one area by transferring to another. I will NOT accept that no one applies for jobs. And I don't wreck one project by grabbing people off it to start another. I FIND NEW PEOPLE.

IMPOSSIBILITIES

Behind every "impossibility" lies some great big WHY which if not found, keeps things messed up. One area that "couldn't get any auditors" had expelled 60 percent of the field from the Church! Another area had dismissed 50 percent of staff every time the income dropped. Another area cut the staff's pay very low and then made it go lower each time the gross income fell. Another "never could find the right people."

Sometimes internal squabbles are given a much higher importance than the org itself.

Some areas use "social acceptability" instead of stats to handle personnel.

Whatever the reason an org isn't getting on, it is *internal*. It isn't some other org or some senior management body. It's right inside that org. Further it has to do with personnel mishandling.

Any org at any time has *not* given as much quantity of service as the public demanded. If you continued to expand at the rate of demand, giving very high quality of service mind you, the org would expand to hundreds or even thousands of staff members.

Somewhere, when that doesn't happen, personnel mishandling has cut off the expansion.

So when we look this over, we find that quality of delivered product determines how much it will be in demand and that the only thing which will limit an expansion to meet that demand is personnel procurement, training and stability on post, getting the staff to produce and holding the form of the org and making it go.

When personnel commits the errors (or crimes) mentioned here and when management fails to do the (1) to (5) listed above that I do in an org, there will be a halt.

True, an org is complex. True, quality is hard to maintain. True, one has to work. But unless personnel procurement and handling is IN, all else will fail. So that's the weak spot.

An undermanned division will empty.

An undermanned org will pay badly and go down.

The point to handle is personnel.

L. RON HUBBARD
FOUNDER

HCO POLICY LETTER OF 29 AUGUST 1970
ISSUE II

REMIMEO
DEPT 1 HAT
HCO AREA HAT
HCO ES HAT
DEPT 13 HAT

PERSONNEL SERIES 2
PERSONNEL PROGRAMING

If personnel are not programed, you get chaos.

The subject of personnel carries with it always the subjects of training and experience and suitability.

Dept 13 has been created to permit personnel to be "enhanced" or improved.

This is done by programing.

HCO should make known what it will need in the org in the next year. How many of what kind it now has.

Dept 13 must work out what programing is now needed. It posts a board, puts the names on it and sees that part-time study will occur and be followed for the *next* post. It sees that this will be made.

HCO by looking back over some period of expansion will be able to forecast what will be needed more easily. Anyone in the org is usually aware of the undermanned points that exist and the unfilled posts, as they get hit with them continually. So if HCO doesn't know what these points are by record, it is easy to do a survey.

With an inefficient HCO which has not recruited and programed, the org is already starting well behind the gate and is already howlingly undermanned and undertrained. Yet to solve all this by instantaneous transfers will unmock the lot.

The RIGHT way to do it is to:

1. Count up what you have.

2. Figure out where they will be promoted to.

3. Program them on part-time training and

4. Recruit.

5. When recruits are on, get them genned in fast on the lower posts so they can operate.

6. Shift the programed people to the posts for which they have been programed.

7. Begin to train up the recruits with part-time programing.

8. Recruit.

This does not mean you shift every post in the org. It does mean your more experienced people are the ones that go up.

Various rules go with this:

TRY TO KEEP TECH TRAINED PEOPLE IN TECH.

TRY TO TRAIN ADMIN PEOPLE FULLY FOR ADMIN.

There are ways to waste enough training time to crash your org. Train a person to Class VI, put him in Public Divs. Train up a PES and transfer him to tech training. All sorts of goofs can be made in programing, all of them costly to the org, all of them defeating the objects of Personnel Dept 1 and Enhancement Dept 13. One obvious way is to train somebody up with no contract or note. But the main one is not to program at all and just rattle around as a total effect.

Part of the action by Dept 1 is to beat down all the reasons why we can't hire anyone. I recently reviewed an area where personnel problems were desperate. Five to ten people a week were applying. Only one to two were "suitable," whatever that meant. That ratio is wrong. Eighty percent unsuitable? Ten percent maybe, not 80 percent.

The area Dept 13 has to beat down is arranging work so no part-time study can occur. Only about 20 percent of a staff won't study. Nearly 90 percent will handle their post if it's overloaded rather than study, which is okay. But putting somebody on Day *and* Foundation and putting one man on a 10,000 name Address Section to keep it up and in use are the usual reasons for no study time.

This comes together between Dept 1 and Dept 13 AND IS AN INDICATOR THAT DEPT 1 IS GOOFING ITS RECRUITING ACTIONS.

Dept 3, Inspections, or the Executive Secretaries or Secretaries can also foul up both Dept 1 and Dept 13. By not inspecting and not running on and by stats, these salt the org down with idling people. So you see Dept 22, let us say, with six people and no production while the Treasury Sec has to work every night to handle an undermanned Dept 8.

The answer is *stats,* honest stats for everyone.

You can get a situation where you have enough people in the whole org to run an org but a third are overloaded and the rest dev-ting around. That's where there is no stat watching and no daily area inspections or executive interest.

I know of one org that has 44 on staff doing the work and potential service load of about 75. Naturally they can't take time off to study so they can't be programed. *Yet* the stat situation is not watched or used nor is the place inspected so the production is about a 20 person org and no funds exist to pay 44 much less 75. The clue is that it's all manned except for Tech! The customers are there in droves. They can't get service. So no pay.

It is silly situations like this that occur when personnel are not programed. Two years ago the above org did not train anyone, worked as a clinic and would not even audit staff. All its auditor contracts expired. HCO and the OES sat there in a fog and let it happen. There was no Dept 13 to program anyone.

So here is a new angle to the recruitment problem. HCO is faced with the vital necessity of recruiting trained auditors NOW. Yet at this writing hasn't even sent around a bulk mailing to ask field auditors to drop in.

DEPT 14

So this is where Dept 14 gets into the act. It is a problem in org correction. If even Qual is empty, it's all an OES function. The correct solution is to force recruitment of trained auditors, force recruitment of ordinary applicants and program it in Dept 13 to train up new auditors as well.

THE REMEDY

You should realize that no matter how rough the problem looks, it involves *recruitment* and *programing*. Instant transfers can utterly wreck an org. Yet inevitably "transfer!" is all you hear when a solution is required to org production failures.

I think this comes in from the world of "psychology." Maybe labor unions. If a man isn't doing well on a post, you transfer him. It assumes that each person has "aptitude." It never changes so you fit the post to the person by finding a new post. That's really nonsense. You can actually more profitably fit the person to the post.

Only when programing has failed (or doesn't exist) does one resort to transfers to solve personnel problems. Of course experienced, able people get promoted. But unless they are programed and trained, watch out! He was a fine CF clerk and a lousy Dissem Sec. Why? It *isn't* his personality. It's that nobody trained him to be a Dissem Sec. He wasn't programed.

It's cruel to promote a person and let the guy fall on his head.

Transferring because somebody doesn't do well is discipline, it is not "adapting people to jobs they can handle."

There is quite an awful jolt in losing one's post. Never think there isn't.

Promote–demote occurs when the person is not programed. Therefore the new Dept 13.

Therefore this Personnel Series.

L. RON HUBBARD
FOUNDER

HCO POLICY LETTER OF 29 AUGUST 1970
ISSUE III

REMIMEO
DEPT 1 HAT
HCO AREA SEC HAT
EXEC SEC HATS
DEPT 13 HAT
DEPT 14 HAT
QUAL SEC HAT

PERSONNEL SERIES 3
RECRUIT IN EXCESS

I have always followed a doctrine of hiring or recruiting in excess.

There is a heavy turnover in personnel. There are many stresses in human society.

You lose people from all ranks, particularly toward the top. Early on, for instance, I never could keep a secretary. Because she'd been *my* secretary she could get a big-pay job (one of them $10,000 a year) from a bigwig. Or some young man had to marry her (and divorce her when she was no longer so glamorously placed). Anyway she *was* trained and had become an executive secretary. The only one I know of who didn't go UP had a commie husband making sure she went down.

So the higher they go:

A. The more altitude they have that has market value, and

B. The more stress that hits them and blows them apart.

This is true of auditors. You'll lose three times as many Class VIIIs as you lose Class VIs. You'll lose three times as many Class VIs as you do Class IVs. Etc. And you'll lose more auditors than you will admin people.

Therefore you have to be very careful indeed who you send for full-time, expensive technical training. You have to ask these questions:

A. Is the candidate a uniformly good HDC auditor?

B. Is the candidate scheduled for a technical post?

C. Is the candidate a fast study by record?

D. Is the candidate uninvolved with anti-Scientology or non-Scientology connections such as wife or family?

E. Is the candidate out of personal debt?

F. Does the candidate have a good record of keeping his promises?

G. Is the candidate willing to sign a new contract and note?

H. Have the candidate's stats been high on post or especially in auditing?

I. Does the candidate stay with the org and not go into a mission?

If the answer to all these is emphatically *yes* there is a chance that the org will benefit. If any of these are no, or if any are even maybe, then *don't do it*. Find somebody who *will* be able to get a YES on every one. They are more numerous than you suppose.

This is also true for highly specialized admin training. The same list, except for B (and is scheduled for an admin post and is a candidate for higher org admin training), applies rigorously.

Failing to establish these things first and getting it all understood, you can find yourself with all such funds expended and no highly trained personnel either.

LOSSES

The percentage of loss or incompetence discovered is hard to establish but is remarkably high. In the decade from 1960 to 1970 personnel turnover was quite heavy even in orgs that were booming.

During that time staff staff auditing was at a minimum. The orgs were jittery under psychiatric inspired attacks. Dianetic tech was not in use until mid-1969. From 1966 to 1970 Scientology tech was quickie and the Grade and Class Chart not followed. Pay after I ceased to be Executive Director was low. Therefore you can make a list of things that have to be in hand to reduce heavy turnover.

1. Audit staffs well and train them for staff status.

2. Keep PRO area control in in areas and in the org.

3. Use Dianetics heavily and teach it well.

4. Keep all Scientology tech materials in action with tapes and all materials and books in full use, well used, well taught.

5. Keep personal and sectional, departmental and divisional stats high.

6. Keep the org recruited up.

7. Keep personnel programed.

8. Hold the form of the org.

9. Deliver an excellent, flubless product.

10. Work for volume of training and processing as the org's product.

As recruitment was also neglected and as contracts expired without being filled, we can add:

11. Over-recruit always.

If you have an idea you will need 20 people in the next 6 months, you had better take on at least 40 and you will have your 20. And double is a low figure.

LINEAR RECRUITING

A firm hires a girl to write their letters. After 60 days they find she doesn't do her job. So they get rid of her and hire another. And in 90 days find she can't do her job. So they fire her and hire another. . . . That's 150 days of no correspondence. It's enough to ruin any firm. It's costly.

SIMULTANEOUS HIRING

A firm hires 3 girls feeling they need 1.

At the end of 150 days they have 1 girl.

But they had 150 days of correspondence. And a profit.

The economical answer in terms of saved profit is *keep up the production*. Don't fixate on personnel. Always do multiple personnel procurement.

In actual practice when you do this, you seldom fire anyone. They blow off or they were actually needed.

If people *are* let go, you don't just brush your hands of it. You in an organization can let them continue being programed while they hold an outside job, fix them up, get them trained and hire them later.

Modern society is *very* loose-footed. The state pays them not to work (apparently only). The society is suppressively oriented. The push and pull of personal relationships is poor.

You are edged in upon a society of dying cultural values, encroaching drugs, threatened annihilation.

No one out there feels very safe.

This insecurity leaks into the org and people get pushed around or push people around.

Real or fancied wrongs occur.

People are rather timid really.

And the more the society buys the idea it's a world of tooth and claw, the more it becomes so.

All this reflects into the picture of personnel.

You have to really work to keep orgs manned and trained up.

You do this by:

A. Running a very good org,

B. Delivering an excellent product,

C. Keeping a steady inflow of new personnel,

D. Training and processing well those you have.

If the (1) to (11) are in in the org then EXPANSION occurs and losing hardly anyone you have to scramble to keep up.

As the INCOME OF THE ORG DEPENDS WHOLLY ON ITS GDSes (Gross Divisional Statistics) and as these are wholly *under the control of the org,* then it's obvious that the only finance trouble or pay trouble an org can have is by undermanning, undertraining and underproducing.

No great international GI slump has ever occurred unless there has been a long GDS slump. So it's obvious that an undermanned org is asking for a cave-in.

Much of this has been learned in recent years.

At this writing there is little or no recruitment by HCOs and training of staffs could be better.

But the lessons we learn, we learn and apply.

And so it is with personnel.

L. RON HUBBARD
FOUNDER

HCO POLICY LETTER OF 30 AUGUST 1970

REMIMEO
DEPT 1 HAT
HCO AS HAT
ES HATS
DEPT 13 HATS
DEPT 14 HATS

PERSONNEL SERIES 4
RECRUITING ACTIONS

The first thing one has to handle in recruiting is the willingness of an org staff to have new people as staff members.

New people tend to cut pay down, they stretch internal staff services thinner, they are not yet "with it" and create a lot of dev-t. Ethics problems rise. Deadwood goes overlooked. Staffs have a certain esprit and élan and aren't all that willing to confer it.

Some orgs plug along on a fixed inadequate gross income, refusing to recruit, losing old staff by contract expiry or graduating to higher orgs or general wear and tear.

They have a sort of horror of green staff members. One can't blame them — files get upset, comms vanish, body interruptions go high, one gets overloaded just handling the dev-t generated.

BUT THERE IS A WAY TO HANDLE ALL THIS.

HCO PL 4 Jan. 66, PERSONNEL, STAFF STATUS, and Staff Status 0, I, II and III take care of these faults.

All this is programed in LRH ED 121 Int, 29 Aug. 70, STAFF TRAINING PGM No. 2, which is a part of this series.

Taking on new staff has to be done. Otherwise the org will not expand; that which stays the same shrinks and the org faces collapse.

So recruitment is a vital necessity.

To overcome any objections, one makes sure that HCO PL 4 Jan. 66, PERSONNEL, STAFF STATUS, is IN. Otherwise the place becomes a maelstrom. It is gotten in by the LRH ED, STAFF TRAINING PGM No. 2.

RECRUITING POOLS

HCO PL 24 June 70 II, PERSONNEL POOLS, lists proper personnel pools for a Dianetics or Scientology organization.

This covers areas for recruitment and gives ways to do it.

The main thing, the most important thing, is that IT HAS TO BE DONE. It doesn't just happen.

Any organization or activity has to recruit and it has to train.

The dream of the industrialist and even the modern agriculturalist is an activity which is totally automated (automatically run by machinery not people). The more "overpopulated" the world becomes, the more the bigwigs dream about automation. I had a psycho editor once (cured him of being psychotic but never cured him of being an editor) who used to dream up civilizations where the machines were even repaired by machines.

The lovely part of machines is that they are supposed to be invariable in action. Each part meshes smoothly with every other part.

If you conceive of a machine made out of human beings instead of metal parts, you see at once that the parts are not exact nor are they perfectly adapted to each other.

This is the fact about beings that dismays the industrialist. The parts don't fit, they vary, they have ideas of their own.

The "parts" also drop out of the "machine."

Any old-time personnel system seeks to fit the people into the "machine" composed of people or fit the "machine" to the people.

All these systems were based upon a psychological principle that no person ever changed or got better.

Also the idea was that people's social order as it existed was the basic social order. (That the existing departure from the ideal scene *was* the ideal scene. See the Data Series policy letters.)

Thus it was conceived that an organization composed of human beings required perfect human beings or it wouldn't run at all. But there are no perfect human beings.

In "straightening an organization up" there is a belief that one must get rid of all its imperfect beings.

And this can go so far as to refuse to try out or let in any beings who are not perfect.

When things get to this pass, one is looking at the probable death of an org.

In real life only a small percentage of people are "unsuitable." They come in four general classes:

a. Those who are destructively antisocial (suppressive persons).

b. Those who are connected with the destructively antisocial outside the org (potential trouble sources).

c. Those ill, diseased or in some way unable to function.

d. Those who are active enemies sent in by active enemies to harm the org.

Anyone hiring should be familiar with the HCOBs covering suppressive persons and HCOBs and policy letters concerning potential trouble sources.

He should also be familiar with testing procedures: (1) E-Meter tone arm position and needle manifestation (HCO PL 26 Aug. 65, ETHICS E-METER CHECK), (2) IQ tests, (3) Aptitude tests, (4) Leadership score, (5) Oxford Capacity Analysis, (6) The Chart of Human Evaluation (*Science of Survival*).

These skills and procedures are part of the Hubbard Consultant (HC) Checksheet.

Using this technology, one minimizes the entrance onto staff of persons who will upset the place.

If no reasonableness (faulty explanations) enters into this, the 10 percent who would enter disturbance into the place are eliminated.

If this barrier is put up and held up, then the people brought in on staff will not upset anything.

Following the Staff Status procedure, one grooves them in.

And all is well.

If this procedure is NOT followed rigorously, the org will become educated into resisting new staff or recruiting. The place will not smoothly expand.

BEGINNING HIRING

To begin a cycle of recruitment one must first apply all the test procedures to *all* on the existing staff and compare it to production records.

This is important. In one case where scores of green personnel were recruited, the place was *very* upset. The whole organization blamed the new recruits. BUT THE TROUBLE WAS COMING FROM THREE PERSONS ALREADY THERE — two were on drugs, the third was a suppressive of a classic kind and these three blocked all training and processing of the new recruits! The three eventually blew off, people got trained and processed and the whole org went upstat. There were no undesirables amongst the new people! They were just so battered around and left so untrained that they were made to look bad!

Any org which has lost a lot of staff and has failed to recruit had hidden in it someone who should have been screened out!

So one is looking for a small percentage. He is NOT trying to find perfect people!

With that small percentage screened out one can make recruits into valuable staff members.

Whenever I see "80 percent were unsuitable" I really raise an eyebrow. Wrong percentage. When I see "we dismissed 50 percent" I raise the other eyebrow. Wrong percentage. Ten percent yes. Fifty to 80 percent no.

So when I see figures like that, I know that the screening is taking place in the wrong area. Somebody already IN is blocking others out and getting rid of them.

The test is not PAST. The test is what the E-Meter reads (no questions, just what *is* the read). What's the IQ, Leadership, Aptitude and Oxford? Where does he sit on the Chart of Human Evaluation?

If that's all okay and the personnel is IN now, what's his stat of production? What's his study stat? What's his case gain?

And that handles that. Without much trouble. Without opinion. Without any oppression or threats.

THE CHARACTER OF MAN

You see, man is not a savage beast at all. He is rather timid. He is easily alarmed.

His symptoms of revenge grow out of his fears.

His basic nature is social, not antisocial. He is not an animal. He likes to communicate. He actually would like to be friends. Rebuffs and upsets and failures to understand him and efforts to harm him can make him hide under a mask of aggression. And this, when it gets too bad and is wrong, is apt to drive him crazy.

If he isn't crazy, he is decent and tries to do his best.

That he put a foot wrong is unimportant. Will he put his foot right? is all I ever care about.

Discipline and punishment and threats can go far too far and can upset him very badly rather than crowd him "into line."

When madmen are amongst him he responds badly, is upset and becomes turbulent. Protected, he acts well and behaves well and is constructive.

A lot of experience is talking. I've even made great crews out of people the government had made into convicts.

A very few have gone so wrong that only huge amounts of processing would ever repair. In *personnel* recruiting and training they have to be audited so long that they are only cases, not personnel. They cause upsets for too long a period before they are handled as cases to be trusted.

They are not even natively bad. They think they are psychiatrists or wolves or vultures or something. They are crazy and think they have to kill or destroy.

People closely connected to them are a bit psycho as they go into terror.

When any weeding out goes further than this, it is a bad mistake, upsets an organization, blows people off and is itself oppressive.

THE TOOLS

You have to realize that we have precision tools. If we lose them or don't use them we get into trouble.

For a long while the E-Meter as a personnel instrument was out of use in the test battery. The Chart of Human Evaluation was laid aside. The Oxford Capacity Analysis was not used.

And personnel errors almost destroyed several orgs.

The tools we have tell the story well. They can be disregarded; opinion, police record, social acceptability, etc., get put into use instead and we are for it. Those are the OLD tools that failed.

But to use the tools we have, one has to realize they are precise tools. One doesn't get a bad needle on a personnel and explain it away. It's a bad needle (a rock slam or a dirty needle or a stuck needle or a stage four needle). It means we are dealing with dynamite.

We *can* handle it in processing. We *can* bring the person up to a valuable person IF WE ARE PROCESSING THE PERSON AS A PC.

But we are discussing *staff members*. We are discussing PRODUCTION. We are discussing hiring personnel.

Only about 10 percent fall into an unacceptable category. And they too can be saved. BUT WE DON'T WANT THEM AS PART OF AN ORG STAFF.

You see, there are two different things here. One is CASES. The other is PERSONNEL.

When a person knows he can handle offbeat cases, he tends to get careless about cases being offbeat as personnel. AND IT'S A NEAR FATAL ERROR.

It costs the org its calm, staff members their pay and deprives the area of full use of the product.

So it's quite an overt to overlook the niceties and technology of personnel and goof it up.

A very bad-off case on staff can actually cause enough trouble to blow off and bar out all good staff.

Bad recruits can make a whole org allergic to *any* recruits.

It's up to those in charge of Personnel to get trained as HCs and act accordingly.

L. RON HUBBARD
FOUNDER

HCO POLICY LETTER OF 10 SEPTEMBER 1970

REMIMEO

PERSONNEL SERIES 5

TRANSFERITIS

A survey of personnel on posts who would ordinarily be considered for transfer brings to light certain factors which underlie WHY they are failing on post even while seeming to work at it.

People on Personnel posts in companies have followed a nineteenth-century psychological approach that if a person can't do one post he can be transferred to another post to which he is better "adapted." "Talent," "native skill," all sorts of factors are given. But if a person with all things considered in the first place is then found to do badly on that post, the second think of nineteenth-century Personnel was to transfer him to another post and yet another and another. The third think when *again* he fails is then to fire him.

Transferring under these circumstances is usually not only wrong for the person but strews the error all through the org.

The HCO PL 24 June 70 I, MANAGEMENT CYCLE, gives an answer to "has to be transferred."

CAMOUFLAGED HOLES

A "camouflaged hole" means a hole in the org lineup that *appears* to be a post. Yet it isn't a held post because its duties are not being done. It is therefore a *hole* people and actions fall into without knowing it is there. It can literally drive an org mad to have a few of these around. *Camouflaged* means "disguised" or made to appear something else. In this case a hole in the lineup is camouflaged by the fact that somebody appears to be holding it who isn't.

Let's take a Receptionist who doesn't receive and route people. You will find the people in the org being fouled up by this. They all have to act *after* the fact of no-reception. This makes them handle reception in the midst of a mess of reception goofs. But there *appears* to be a Receptionist. If there were NO pretended-Receptionist, people would at least know this and keep an eye out. But as there "is a Receptionist" who isn't a Receptionist, all reception actions have to be handled by others each time *after* there has been a goof! Guaranteed to mess up the environment and strain tempers more than somewhat.

An executive post is much harder to detect. Those below it are not aware of the skills the post needs and are only aware of trouble. Yet it easily can be just a camouflaged hole.

Given the fact that one is not dealing with a sick person or a scoundrel (any post requires that a person be fairly healthy and with a clean ethics record), for a person to be on a post and not doing it, he or she must be suffering from one or more of the following conditions:

1. Never trained up for the post in the first place (per Management Chart),

2. Never grooved in on the post purpose,

3. Unreality or unfamiliarity with the ideal scene in its practical aspects, resulting in omitted data or a missing scene.

Furthermore, for a person to *remain* on a post under these conditions he/she must:

a. Be unaware of their lack of knowledge,

b. Blame it on another or

c. Have considerations about status (i.e., it would be damaging to their reputation for it to be found out that they didn't know).

This last point, status, puts any post flub onto a WITHHOLD basis resulting in continuously deteriorating performance each time it occurs.

In actual fact in each one of the cases examined, one or more of the above points were evident in greater or lesser degree. My suggested remedy would be:

1. *Thorough* training as deputy before putting any person on a major post. The purpose being to familiarize the person with actual working conditions.

2. A clear, approved statement of post purpose must be written in the front of the post hat write-up, which is easily comprehensible and simple. This post purpose is then cleared to F/N in Qual before the person can be considered fully on post.

3. Once on post the person must constantly maintain and increase their working knowledge of their appointed areas of responsibility and study and familiarize themselves with old and new HCOBs and PLs as they apply.

   That they undergo a competent examination from time to time on the duties and actions of their post as they exist or are extended.

4. That to this end any poor performance on post be reported to Div 5, Dept 13 for investigation and correction by examining the above points and putting in those found out.

5. That within the framework of Cases and Morale policy letter that priority be given to those posts in the org that most likely would be expected to collect a "status value" so that the integrity of those holding such posts be maintained.

6. That in any case, notwithstanding the above paragraph, persons on such posts should make every attempt to keep themselves clean of O/Ws, including making it known to the proper terminals when they find they have misunderstoods or missing data on post.

If there is any trouble in training a person up for a post, it will be traced ordinarily to LACK OF ADEQUATE MATERIAL about that post and no checksheet to be thoroughly checked out on.

This should be checked as a point.

It is common not to have a pack of data or checksheet for a post and, if so, one must be made.

SUMMARY

Given a person on post not producing, TRANSFER is almost never the right answer. Yet it is the one most frequently done.

If a person is morally unfit, a criminal or mad, it is obvious that "transfer" is the wrong answer.

So this leaves us with these actions to do:

As given in the Management Cycle, HCO PL 24 June 70 I.

L. RON HUBBARD
FOUNDER

HCO POLICY LETTER OF 12 SEPTEMBER 1970

REMIMEO

PERSONNEL SERIES 6
TRAINING

By actual test and practical experience, a fully trained, on-policy executive will raise the stats of an org.

An untrained executive will depress the stats.

An officer trained on the Flag Executive Briefing Course will send stats up where an equivalent officer not so trained will send them down.

This appears so obvious that it can be missed.

It means that it costs an org thousands upon thousands to use an untrained executive who has not done an FEBC. It costs personnel their pay, their facilities and their security.

If an FEBC cost $30,000 (which it does not), the org would make it back in a few weeks.

If an untrained executive is placed in charge of an org, it can prepare for losses and can succumb.

This is a very simple lesson. It is a matter of actual fact, not of PR.

This is shown up well when a fully trained executive is placed in charge of a whole org.

It is less visible but just as decisive regarding ANY post.

An untrained person on a post will be at best somebody not too destructive and at worst a camouflaged hole.

These facts are facts.

When you do not know this, be prepared to have lots of trouble, losses and dev-t.

It costs money not to spend money pretraining for a post. It also costs money not to train a person *on* a post to familiarize him with it.

Training is of course a relative word. The materials taught must be practical and useful and must apply to the job to be held.

Given this, a Personnel Officer who does not advise or provide for full prepost training will be found to be very costly.

One who insists on full pretraining and on-post training will be found to be a very valuable asset.

This data is *not* theoretical. It is the living truth.

L. RON HUBBARD
FOUNDER

HCO POLICY LETTER OF 13 SEPTEMBER 1970
ISSUE I

REMIMEO

PERSONNEL SERIES 7
HATS — VITAL DATA

I can prove conclusively and utterly that any down statistic traces at once to two points:

1. Failure to *hire* or recruit.

2. Failure to *train* people on their hats.

Regarding training, the failure of any executive is traceable to three points:

A. Not making up a checksheet for the posts of juniors under him.

B. Not making up a pack for the checksheet and a hat for each junior.

C. Not fully training his juniors up on their hats as per A & B.

To do all this an executive must himself be trained.

HAT — means the duties of a post. It comes from the fact that jobs are often distinguished by a type of hat as fireman, policeman, conductor, etc. Hence the term HAT.

A "hat" is really a folder containing the write-ups of past incumbents on a post plus a checksheet of all data relating to the post plus a pack of materials that cover the post.

One also has a "staff hat" which is to say a folder containing all his duties as a staff member, the org itself and its lines and purposes.

There is also a hat folder for general or technical directives issued to all the staff regardless of post.

So there is a:

Post Hat

Staff Hat

Tech Hat

for every staff member.

Before Personnel transfers and begins a musical-chair parade, it is well to inspect and see if:

a. the post has all these hats and knows them,

b. the post's senior has actively provided them and checked them out or had them checked out on the junior.

If (a) and (b) are not true then I can assure you Personnel will be replacing and musical-chairing forever.

It well may be that the executive is the trouble, not the incumbent.

A senior who does not see to full hats in the possession of juniors and does not see they are fully checked out is a liability.

ANY ORG'S TROUBLES CAN BE TRACED TO THESE TWO POINTS.

Therefore one must be very sure that seniors take responsibility for the hats, checksheets, packs and know-how of juniors.

A successful executive is one who understands:

1. Organization,

2. His own hat, has a checksheet and pack for it and knows these,

3. That he is at extreme risk if he does not enforce hat, checksheet and pack checkouts on his juniors.

ANYONE WHO HAS JUNIORS UNDER HIM IS A TRAINING OFFICER FOR THOSE JUNIORS AS A VITAL ADDITIONAL DUTY.

So really, Personnel, if you want to know who your executives are, find one who:

i. Has been trained,

ii. Who produces well himself,

iii. Who enforces hats, checksheets and packs on his juniors, and

iv. Trains his juniors as per (iii).

There you have an excellent executive, if not an Executive Director.

———

It is a cruel, vital, total truth that you normally can trace the reason for inefficient areas in an org or company to:

1. Lack of hiring or recruiting,

2. Lack of trained executives,

3. Lack of executives who will assemble hats for and train their juniors.

An organization is a third dynamic technology.

When the hats aren't known or worn, it's a mob.

A division which blows up or unmocks is usually:

1. Undermanned,

2. Unorganized,

3. Untrained.

Whenever a senior on the line of command fails to see to the hats and full training of his juniors you have a total breakdown.

Personnel sees this in terms of hiring and firing and transfers.

Look into any area that can't keep its people and you find not enough people or untrained people. And you for sure will also find an executive who WILL NOT train his people, see that they have post hats and checkouts.

The solutions are pretty obvious.

L. RON HUBBARD
FOUNDER

HCO POLICY LETTER OF 16 SEPTEMBER 1970
ISSUE I

REMIMEO
PERSONNEL HATS
ETHICS HATS

PERSONNEL SERIES 8
ETHICS AND PERSONNEL

(Applies to E/Os)

Personnel can be harassed by utilization failures.

Demands *for* personnel are usually met by an inspection of the area (dept or div or activity) that is demanding the personnel.

A personnel demand received by Personnel is properly routed to the Ethics Officer with the following request:

"Dept (or activity) _____ is asking for personnel.

"Please check these points.

"A. Are existing personnel there busy? _____

"B. Have there been recent blows from that area? _____

"C. Are their MEST and comm lines in good condition? _____

"D. Do the personnel in that area each have HATS, FULL
CHECKSHEETS FOR POST AND AREA? _____

"E. Does the senior officer of that area have and support a
program for training and grooving in his personnel? _____

"F. Have the personnel now on post been ill (PTS)? _____

"G. Is there an SP in the area by meter check? _____

"H. Is study and auditing time arranged for? _____

"Please note by HCO PL 16 Sept. 70 I, ETHICS AND PERSONNEL, that if D and E above are out and no vigorous action is in progress to get these two points in, a Comm Ev should be convened.

"Please let me have a report on this area so that I can expedite needful personnel or demand utilization of existing personnel.

"Personnel I/C"

UTILIZATION

An area which does not make hats, checksheets and packs for its staff members and does not vigorously groove in and get personnel on purpose lines and knowledgeable will cause endless trouble for Personnel Recruitment Officers and Personnel Control Officers.

An area can get into this hideous cycle:

> Recruit
> Don't train
> Don't groove in
> Don't utilize
> Apply heavy ethics
> Lose personnel
> Demand personnel
> Don't train
> Don't groove in
> Don't utilize
> Apply heavier ethics
> Lose personnel

It will just keep on and on and on.

The staff member who goofs is NOT the proper Ethics target. The correct Ethics target is the divisional officer or department head who does not hat, checksheet and pack and train on them and groove in on post every personnel he has.

In some areas this failure is not sloth or "no time," but a solid great big WON'T TRAIN.

As the area subjected to this is downtone and poor imaged and overloaded, the job of recruitment is made nearly impossible.

PURPOSE AND CRIME

A breakthrough in the know-how of civilization is that a thetan evidently considers any beingness better than no beingness.

This would explain how people cling to an even painful existence and why even a slave or prisoner does not just drop a body.

Beingness is valuable.

A post or job is enormously valuable. Even the most minor post has a status value.

The only quality that is critical about a job is can it be held at all. By heavy overload and harassment a job can be made untenable. But a "blow" or departure is only occasioned by hope of a better one elsewhere in this same life. A workload can be heavy. But when it gets impossible, one gets a blow.

An overloaded division will empty.

The most common way to overload an area is to fail to hat, checksheet and pack the personnel and not train them. Then they work badly as a team with lots of friction as the jobs are not meshed with one another. Dev-t results. An apparency of hard work ends up in poor or little production.

Then personnel begin to make goofs which absorb the time of other personnel.

Not only this but A PERSONNEL WITHOUT PURPOSE CAN COMMIT CRIMES.

The secret of a turbulent society is contained in these facts.

A welfare state pays people not to work. It is paying to have people without purpose or hats. Therefore it gets crime. There is NO surer way to beget an insurgent society than to deny purpose and posts to its members.

Knowingly or unknowingly, welfare statism is aimed at disenfranchising citizens. From Rome on forward, every welfare state has eventually erupted in revolt and civil war. And every state which denied jobs or status has blown up in revolt. The French and Russian revolutions were fully concerned with breaking a monopoly of status.

However you view it or however it was done, FAILURE TO PROVIDE JOBS, PURPOSE AND TRAINING ON JOBS BEGETS REVOLT.

Unhappiness, social misery are not answered by denying in any way actual useful jobs.

The sense of belonging and purpose in living can be strangled in many ways.

Whenever it is done, it is done by some mechanism (like the dole or relief or plain unemployment) which prevents participation.

Participation is only achieved by the worthwhileness of the activity, the factualness and understanding of the activity, explained purpose and an exact and trained-in set of duties.

Crime stems totally and entirely from lack of belonging and understanding that to which one belongs. The criminal or juvenile gang is a substitute for society. It is an outlaw pack at the throat of that which forced it not to belong.

Preventing youthful participation, permitting airy-fairy education, unreal values and lack of understanding turns youth against the state.

Politicians and financiers have been too deficient in imagination to provide real jobs, real training, real objectives. It is easier to toss contemptuous starvation handouts to the multitude. Or lock them out entirely.

The wages of such action are revolt and social decline.

There is work and thought needful in providing:

A. A worthwhile cause,

B. Valuable production,

C. Jobs and status,

D. Real education for the posts held,

E. Perpetuation of a valuable activity.

Any businessman for various reasons tries to do this. He is usually overburdened by the state.

In Russia, where there is only the cynical state, police duress is all that holds the rickety framework together.

Thus there is a direct coordination between (a) social disorder and (b) no-job or no-hat or no-training on it.

ETHICS AND HATS

Wherever Ethics has to be heavy you find:

1. No real hats,

2. No checksheet or pack,

3. No thorough grooving in.

Given a worthwhile cause, Personnel can be made a near impossible post by neglect of grooving in.

When a person is unable to wear a hat, *processing* can trace back *the cycle of attaining status and losing it* until the person can have a hat.

Personnel placement is far less important than on-the-job hats, checksheets and packs grooved in.

Promotion follows any good production in due course.

———————

This is how Ethics and Personnel work together or conflict.

If Ethics does not target those who fail to train rather than those who aren't trained or processed and goof or commit crimes, Ethics and Personnel both will come a resounding cropper.

In support of what I say, Ethics can trace any trouble in an area back to a failure to recruit and fully realistically train on posts.

And Personnel can trace any trouble in an area to past failures to recruit and fully realistically train on posts.

You have here in an org what has been destroying all of man's civilizations — denying jobs and status, failing to groove in and train. Man has only had force and Cossacks to remedy these lacks when what he really needed was imagination, jobs and training.

———————

A full appreciation of this solves many riddles regarding social planning and societies.

In our own sphere we must use this understanding well and drive the social aberrations out of our orgs and keep them out by recruiting, hats, checksheets, packs and full training for every post and the sweeping removal of all blocks and barriers which prevent it.

A man wants to belong. He can't if he does not know the purpose of that to which he belongs and *all* the duties and actions of his post.

So make it so by recruiting, training and processing that he *can* belong and be valuable.

And by having upstat orgs, make it so the public can come in, get service and also belong by membership.

If you understand this fully, we can triumph for it is a know-how few other men have.

L. RON HUBBARD
FOUNDER

HUBBARD COMMUNICATIONS OFFICE
Saint Hill Manor, East Grinstead, Sussex

HCO POLICY LETTER OF 22 SEPTEMBER 1970

Remimeo
Exec Hats
Personnel Hats
Ethics Hats

AN URGENT IMPORTANT AND STAR–RATE PL

Personnel Series 9
Org Series 4
HATS

HAT — A term used to describe the write-ups, checksheets and packs that outline the purposes, know-how and duties of a post. It exists in folders and packs and is trained in on the person on the post.

HAT TECHNOLOGY

"Hats" developed in 1950 for use in Dianetic orgs as a special technology. The term and idea of "a hat" comes from conductors or locomotive engineers, etc., each of whom wears a distinctive and different type of headgear. A "hat" therefore designates particular status and duties in an organization.

A "hat" is a specialty. It handles or controls certain particles in various actions and receives, changes and routes them.

A "hat" designates what terminal in the organization is represented and what the terminal handles and what flows the terminal directs.

Every hat has a product.

The product can be represented as a statistic.

Any job or position in the world *could* have its own hat. The reason things do not run well in a life, an org, a group, nation or the world is an absence of hats.

The reason why an org runs well when it does is hats.

Any protest of anyone against things not running right can be traced to lack of hats.

Any slump an org goes through can be traced directly and at once to an absence of one or more hats being worn.

HAT CONTENT

A hat must contain:

A. A *purpose* of the post.

B. Its relative position on the org bd.

C. A write-up of the post (done usually by people who have held it before relief and when so done it has no further authority than advice).

D. A checksheet of all the policy letters, bulletins, advices, manuals, books and drills applicable to the post. (As in a course checksheet.)

E. A full pack of the written materials or tapes of the checksheet plus any manuals of equipment or books.

F. A copy of the org bd of the portion of the org to which the post belongs.

G. A flow chart showing what particles are received by the post and what changes the post is expected to make in them and to where the post routes them.

H. The product of the post.

I. The statistic of the post, the statistic of the section, the statistic of the department and division to which the post belongs.

STAFF HAT

There is also a general staff hat.

This hat contains:

a. The overall purpose of the org, its aims, goals and products.

b. The privileges or rewards of a staff member such as auditing, training on post, general training availability, pay, vacations or leave, etc.

c. The penalties involved in nonproduction or abuse of post privileges or misuse of the post contracts.

d. The public relations responsibilities of a staff member.

e. The interpersonal relations amongst staff members including courtesy, cleanliness, attitudes to seniors and juniors, office etiquette, etc.

f. The MEST of posts generally, its papers, despatches, files, equipment.

g. The comm and transport system of the org.

GRADIENT SCALE OF HATS

A "gradient scale" means "a gradual increasing degree of something." A non-gradient scale would be telling someone to enter a skyscraper by a 32nd-story window.

Thus there is a gradient scale of organizing.

A key to this is found in the *Problems of Work*'s theory of confusion and the stable datum.

One in actual practice has to cope while organizing.

COPE means to handle whatever comes up. In the dictionary it means "to deal successfully with a difficult situation." We use it to mean "to handle any old way whatever comes up, to handle it successfully and somehow."

IF YOU *REMAIN* IN COPE, THE DEMAND TO COPE INCREASES.

In that you have the key to "exhausted executives" or staff members. You have why the president of the US ages about 20 years in one term of office as you can see by comparing dated photographs of past presidents. He is totally on cope. His government has an org board that looks like a pile of jackstraws. He has no hat. His staff have no hats. His government departments have no hat. The technologies of economics, law, business, politics, welfare, warfare, diplomacy have been neglected or lost (they *do* exist to some extent).

The guy is on total cope. And the post has been on total cope since it was created as an afterthought by the Constitutional Congress that began the post in the eighteenth century. Even what it says in US civics textbooks is not found in practice.

So "difficult situations" are the order of the day and are handled by special actions and appointments.

The people who *should* handle them haven't got real hats.

This is all catching up with the country at this writing to such a degree that the citizen cannot benefit from a stable society or social order. The country looks more like a war of insurgency.

In other words departures from hats has led into total cope and it is steadily worsening.

Any organization put in by one political party is knocked out by the next incumbent, and who could totally organize a country in 4 years? (The term of a president.)

Yet it is hanging together some way and some way meeting increasing demands and pressures.

I have stated this in a large example so that it can be seen in a smaller unit.

To handle this one would first have to want to straighten it out and then assemble the tech of admin to straighten it out. And then one would have to begin on a gradient scale of org bd and hats.

A cope sort of hat would be tossed-off orders to some other people on staff who have some title of some sort.

Along with this would be a posted org bd that has little to do with duties actually performed and used by a staff that doesn't know what it is.

One begins to move out of cope (as given in other series) by putting an org board together that labels posts and duties and getting people on them to handle the types of particles (bodies, mailings) of the org.

The next action would be brief write-ups of the posts and their duties and checking people out on them.

Actually if you only got to the middle of the last paragraph with an org the executives would remain in cope. So much know-how would be missing in the org's staff that every rough bit would shoot up to the executive for special handling. And that is *cope*.

Hats only in this far is not good enough as it still takes a genius to run the place.

The next gradient scale is to get the hat to contain:

i.   The post write-up itself,

ii.   The theory and practical necessary to run it.

This is done by a preparation of checksheets of data and a pack matching it for key posts.

Naturally the org bd now has to become more real and staff has to be checked out on it.

Then hats as post checksheets and packs are extended to the rest of the staff.

The mechanisms of training have to exist by this time.

Seniors have to be made responsible that every junior below them has a hat consisting of write-up, checksheet and pack.

Meanwhile one continues to cope.

Gradually, gradually staff begin to know (through checkouts) their hats.

New staff coming on are grooved in better.

Cope begins to diminish and the organization tends to smooth out.

Here and there competent handlings begin to show up brightly.

Now we find a new situation. With everyone throwing together checksheets and packs for staffs we find nonstandard checksheets. Some messenger has to do the full checksheet of the HCO Division pages and pages long. The HCO Sec has a checksheet with just 10 items on it.

So a central authority has to standardize post checksheets and survey and put in overlooked bits of data.

But that is way up the line. The org long since has become smooth and prosperous.

So that is the gradient scale of getting in hats.

EXPERTS

Here and there you find an area of special expertise in an org where the expertise is so expert in itself that it obscures the fact that the person does not also have a full post hat.

A lawyer would be a case in point. It takes so long to learn law in some law school that an org executive can overlook the fact that the *post* hat is missing. Org policy on legal matters and staff hat remain unknown to this legal post AND JAM IT UTTERLY. This came to light when a whole series of cases was being neglected because the legal staff member, an excellent lawyer, did not know how to make out a purchase order or that one could or should. Investigation found *no* post or staff hat. Only a legal degree.

Orgs continually do this with auditors. They are technical experts in *auditing*. So they get assigned to posts in the HGC WITH NO HAT. Backlogs occur, things goof up. Tech fails. All because it is overlooked that they are PART OF AN ORG and need staff and post hats and need to be trained on them.

Worse than that, a highly classed auditor is often put on an admin post without hat or training for it.

You would not take an admin trained person and without further training tell him to audit. So why take an auditor and tell him to handle an admin division?

Without his post write-up, checksheet and pack FOR THE POST and without training on it, the person just isn't qualified for it no matter what *other* line he is expert in.

It is great to have an expert who has been specially trained in some profession. But lawyer, engineer or public relations, he must have his hat for the *org* post and be trained on it or he will goof! Yet one won't suspect why that area is goofing because "he's a Class VI isn't he?"

UTILIZATION

Personnel can recruit madly, answering every frantic demand for personnel and yet HAVE THEM ALL WASTED for lack of full hats and full training on those hats.

An investigation of blows (desertions) from orgs shows that lack of a grooved-in hat was at the bottom of it.

People come on a job. It is at once a great mystery or an assumption of total know — one or the other.

Either one continued leads them into a state of liability to the org.

People who don't know what they are doing and people who don't but think they do are both NONUTILIZED PERSONNEL.

Pay and prosperity for the rest of the staff will go down unless this is remedied.

The whole org can sag and even vanish under these conditions.

So Personnel has a vested interest in hats being complete and staff trained on them. For Personnel people cannot possibly cope with "no pay so can't hire anyone" and "no people so can't produce."

The answer is H-A-T-S.

And a hat is a write-up, a checksheet and a pack.

And the staff member trained on them.

ETHICS

When a person has no hat he lacks purpose and value.

When he has no purpose and value he not only goofs, he will commit crimes.

It is apparently easier to hit with ethics than to program and give someone a full hat and get him trained on it.

Police action is not a substitute for having purpose and value.

This is so fundamental that one can even trace the unrest of a nation to lack of purpose and value. A huge welfare program guarantees crime and revolt because it gives handouts, not hats.

Even a field Scientologist should have a hat.

By doing only this over the world we would own the planet as in an expanding population individual purpose and value are the most vital and wanted commodities.

If there are no real hats there will soon be no money of any value and no bread!

SUMMARY

ANY HAT IS BETTER THAN NO HAT according to the way a thetan seems to think.

But be that as it may, the downfall of any org can be traced directly and instantly to no recruiting or no org board, no hats or unreal hats or no training on hats.

The sag of an org can be traced directly to lack of hats and lack of training on hats.

The overload of any post can be traced directly to lack of an org bd and lack of hats and no training on hats.

The way out is to organize the org board and hats while you cope.

If you do not, your cope will become an overwhelm. If you do, your burden will lighten and your prosperity increase.

It took 13 months of hard work and 20 years of org experience to learn that given a product lack of HATS was *the* WHY of departures from the ideal scene and that working toward providing full complete HATS was the way to get back toward the ideal scene.

L. RON HUBBARD
FOUNDER

HCO POLICY LETTER OF 6 OCTOBER 1970
ISSUE II

REMIMEO

PERSONNEL SERIES 10
"MOONLIGHTING"

Staff members of an org who also have other jobs outside the org are said to be MOONLIGHTING.

Day staff with an evening or weekend job or Foundation staff with a day job have been accused unjustly in the past of injuring an org.

An org only gets injured when its doors get closed and it ceases to promote and deliver good service.

If a whole staff of a Day org decided to close the org all day and open it only in the evening, "moonlighting" would have destroyed the Day org. This would be heavily frowned upon.

If a Foundation staff closed the Foundation to get evening work, it would be a highly nonsurvival act and injurious.

An org which is just starting up or which has been so un-org boarded and unhatted that it fell into such a slump that staff could not live on its pay, the staff would be remiss not to moonlight while they built the org back up. Built up, org boarded and hatted, the org could pay its staff adequately.

To forbid the practice of moonlighting would be to force a staff member to blow in self-defense.

INFLATION

As money inflates (purchases less) and as the cost of operating rises and fees remain unchanged, an org can get into a situation where it is inefficient and pays low salaries.

"Moonlighting on the government" would be quite permissible. With governments anxious to hand out welfare, in some depressed area it would be quite all right to go on the dole or relief and work as a church volunteer in the org.

The higher unemployment rises, the less money will buy, the more finance trouble there is.

Org staffs under such duress can even live as monasteries for food, shelter and pocket money and keep an org going.

SUBSIDY

At this writing the only subsidies available from governments are for those who kill people. The money the government should be spending to support our orgs goes to special interest groups like psychiatry who pocket it and deliver nothing.

Up the years this may change.

Until it does we have to keep our heads up financially.

That also applies to an org staff member. There is no reason he should lose his staff job because he also has to moonlight to live.

A well-run, well-recruited, well-org boarded, well-hatted, well-trained org delivering high-quality training and auditing makes very adequate income and pays well. But it sometimes takes time to build up from a mismanaged slump to an ideal scene again.

There is no policy against MOONLIGHTING where it does not injure the org.

L. RON HUBBARD
FOUNDER

HCO POLICY LETTER OF 9 OCTOBER 1970

Remimeo
Personnel Hats
PR Checksheets

Personnel Series 11
PR Series 4

THE PR PERSONALITY

A public relations personnel has to be spot on in:

a. Confronting,

b. Organizing,

c. Working.

CONFRONT

In confronting, a shy or retiring PR is not about to handle suppressive persons or situations. A PR must be able to stand up to and handle the more wild situations easily and with composure. When he does not, his confront blows and any sense of presentation or organization would go up in smoke. A PTS (potential trouble source) person or one who roller-coasters casewise or one who tends to retreat has no business in PR. His connections that make him PTS and his case would have to be handled fully before he could make good on PR lines.

ORGANIZE

In organizing, a PR has to be able not only to organize something well but to organize it faultlessly in a flash.

Every action a PR takes concerns groups and therefore has to be organized down to the finest detail; otherwise it will just be a mob scene and a very bad presentation.

A PR who can confront, can "think on his feet" and grasp and handle situations rapidly and who can organize in a flash will succeed as a PR.

WORK

The last essential ingredient of a PR is the ability to WORK.

When appointing people to PR training, the person's *work record* is very, very important.

The ability to address letters, push around files, haul furniture into place, handle towering stacks of admin in nothing flat are all PR requisites.

To be able to tear out to Poughkeepsie before lunch and set up the baby contest and build a scene for a press conference on catfish before two and get dressed, meet the governor by six is WORK. It takes sweat and push and energy.

A PR should be able to get out a trade paper in hours where an "editor" might take weeks.

The ability to work must be established in a potential PR before wasting any training time, as a PR who can't work fails every time.

DELUSORY REQUIREMENTS

People *think* a PR must be charming, brilliant, able to inspire, etc., etc.

These are fine if they exist. But they are actually secondary qualities in a PR.

Lack of the (a), (b), (c) qualities is why you see PRs begin to hit the bottle, get sick, fail.

If a PR is *also* charming, brilliant, able to inspire, he is a real winner. Possibly one is born with all these qualities every few generations.

Personnel in appointing and training PR must look for the wish to be a PR and (a), (b) and (c).

And anyone taking up PR who does so to escape hard work will fail as it IS hard work.

A real top PR wants to be one, has the abilities of (a), (b) and (c) and is trained hard and well in the subject. Then you have a real stat raiser, a real winner, a real empire builder.

L. RON HUBBARD
FOUNDER

HUBBARD COMMUNICATIONS OFFICE
SAINT HILL MANOR, EAST GRINSTEAD, SUSSEX

HCO POLICY LETTER OF 20 NOVEMBER 1970
(Also issued as an HCOB, same date and title)

REMIMEO

PERSONNEL SERIES 12
ORG SERIES 15
WORD CLEARING SERIES 18

ORGANIZATION MISUNDERSTOODS

By Scientology study technology, understanding ceases on going past a misunderstood word or concept.

If a person reading a text comes to the words "Felis domesticus" and doesn't know it simply means HOUSE CAT, the words which appear thereafter may become "meaningless," "uninteresting" and he may even become slightly unconscious, his awareness shutting down.

Example: "Wind the clock and put out the Felis domesticus and then call Algernon and tell him to wake you at 10:00 A.M.," read as an order by a person who didn't bother to find out that "Felis domesticus" means "house cat" or "the variety of cat which has been domesticated" will not register that he is supposed to call Algernon, will feel dopey or annoyed and probably won't remember he's supposed to wake up at 10:00 A.M.

In other words, when the person hit a misunderstood word, he ceased to understand and did not fully grasp or become aware of what followed after.

All this applies to a sentence, a book, a post or a whole organization.

Along the time track a crashing misunderstood will block off further ability to study or apply data. It will also block further understanding of an organization, its org board, an individual post or duties, and such misunderstoods can effectively prevent knowledge of or action on a post.

ALL THIS IS THE MOST COMMON CAUSE OF AN UNACCEPTABLE POST PRODUCT, OR NO PRODUCT AT ALL.

The difficulties of an organization in functioning or producing stem from this fact.

Personal aberration is the cause of products that are in fact overt acts.

Scientology technology today easily handles the personal aberration part of the problem, IF IT IS USED AND PROPERLY APPLIED. Leaving an org unaudited or being unable to figure out how to run a viable org so that it can afford to audit its staff members is asking for post or org products that are overt acts.

Employing persons of the Leipzig, Germany, death camp school (psychologists, psychiatrists) to handle personal aberration is like throwing ink in water to clean it up. Governments stupidly do this and wonder why their final product as an organization is riot, war and a polluted planet. The point is not how bad psychology and psychiatry are, but that one does have to *handle* personal aberration in an organization, and these schools were too vicious and incompetent to do so.

Those who are personally very aberrated are not about to produce anything but an overt act. They are difficult to detect as they are being careful not to be detected. Things "just sort of go wrong" around them, resulting in a product that is in fact an overt act. But these constitute only about ten or twenty percent of the population.

The remaining eighty percent or ninety percent where they are nonfunctional or bungling are so because they do not understand what it's all about. They have in effect gone on by a misunderstood such as what the org is supposed to do or the admin tech they use on their posts or where they are or what their product is.

Earth organizations like governments or big monopolies get a very bad repute because of these factors:

1. Personal aberration of a few undetected and unhandled,

2. Inadequate or unreal basic education technology and facilities.

3. Inadequate or unknown organization technology.

4. Noncomprehension of the individual regarding the activities of which he is a part.

5. Noncomprehension of the basic words with which he is working.

6. Purposes of the post uncleared.

7. Admin of the post not known or comprehended.

8. Technology in use not fully understood.

9. A lack of comprehension of products.

Out of these nine things one gets organizational troubles and the belief that it takes a genius to run one successfully. Yet all the genius in the world will fail eventually if the above nine things are not handled to some degree.

The common methods currently in use on the planet to handle these things are very crude and time-consuming as the items themselves are either dimly comprehended or not known at all.

1A. Personal aberration is met by torture, drugs or death when it is detected. Yet only the very serious cases who are obviously screaming, muttering or unconscious are singled out, whereas the dangerous ones are neither detected nor handled at all and become with ease generals or presidents or dictators, to say nothing of lesser fry. Ten percent to 20 percent of any organization is stark staring mad, doing the place in so adroitly that only their actual product betrays them.

2A. Basic education as well as higher general education has become a mass-produced area crawling with bad texts and noncomprehension and used mainly by hostile elements to overturn the state or pervert the race and its ideals.

3A. Organizational technology is so primitive as to change national maps and leading companies many times a century, an extremely unstable scene for a planet.

4A. Very few individuals on the planet have any concept of the structure of entities such as their country or state or company. Persons surveying the public in the US, pretending to advise acceptance of "new measures" already in the Constitution, were threatened for being revolutionaries. Hardly anyone knew the basic document of the nation's organization much less its rambling structure.

5A. The basic words of organization are glibly used but not generally comprehended, words like "company," "management," "policy." Vocabularies have to be increased before comprehension and communication occur and misunderstoods drop out.

6A. Post purposes are often glibly agreed with while something entirely different is done.

7A. Administrative actions involving posts are often only dimly comprehended and seldom well followed; but in this matter of communication, despatches, etc., the planet is not as deficient as in others except that these functions, being somewhat known, can become an end-all — tons of despatches, no actual product. In some areas it is an obsession, an endless paper chain, that is looked on as a legitimate product even when it leads to no production.

8A. The planet's technology is on the surface very complex and sophisticated but is so bad in actual fact that experts do not give the planet and its populations thirty years before the smoke and fumes will have eaten up the air cover and left an oxygenless world. (The converters like trees and grass which change carbon dioxide to oxygen are inadequate to replace the oxygen and are additionally being killed by air impurities coming out of factories and cities.) If the technology destroys the base where it is done — in this case the planet — it is not adequate and may even be destructive technology.

9A. The whole idea of "product" is not in use except in commercial industry where one has to have a car that sells or a washing machine that actually washes.

THE HARD ROAD

It is against this primitive background that one is trying to run an organization.

If it were not for improvements made on each one of these points, the task could be hopeless.

I have gone to some length to outline the lacks in order to show the points where one must concentrate in (a) putting an org together and (b) keeping it viable.

In these nine areas we are dealing with the heart of it in running orgs.

Enthusiasm is a vital ingredient. It soon goes dull when insufficient attention is paid to resolving and getting in these nine points.

Bluntly, if they are not gotten in and handled, the task of living and running a post or an org will become so confused that little or no production will occur and disasters will be frequent.

THE WORDS

The by no means complete list of words that have to be fully cleared and understood just to talk about organization as a subject, and to intelligently and happily work in an org EVEN AS ITS LOWEST EMPLOYEE is:

A company
A board of directors
Top management
Policy
Management
Programs
Targets
Orders
Technology
Know-how
Org bd
Post
Hat
Cope
Purposes
Organize
Duties
A checksheet
A checklist
A comm channel
A command channel
A relay point
A stable terminal
Double-hatted
A product
Aberration
VIABILITY

This is key vocabulary. One could draw up a whole dictionary for these things and no one studying it would be any wiser since it would become salted with other words of far less importance.

The way to do this list is sweat it out with a meter until one knows each can't mean anything else than what it does mean.

Out of a full understanding of what is implied by each, a brilliantly clean view is attained of the whole subject of organization, not as a fumble but as a crisp usable activity.

Unless one at least knows these words completely so that they can be used and applied, they will not buffer off confusions that enter into the activity.

Glibness won't do. For behind these words is the full structure of an activity that will survive and when the words aren't understood the rest can become foggy.

We *do* know all these needful things. We must communicate them and use them successfully.

L. RON HUBBARD
FOUNDER

HCO POLICY LETTER OF 6 DECEMBER 1970

REMIMEO
DEPT 14 HATS

PERSONNEL SERIES 13
ORG SERIES 18

THIRD DYNAMIC DE–ABERRATION

The exact mechanism of 3rd dynamic (group or organization) aberration is the conflict of COUNTER–POLICY.

Illegal policy set at unauthorized levels jams the actions of a group and IS responsible for the inactivity, nonproduction or lack of team spirit.

Counter-policy independently set jams the group together but inhibits its operation.

Out-reality on org bds, hats, etc., is to a large degree caused by disagreements and conflicts which are caused by illegal policy.

If we had a game going in which each player set his own rules, there would be no game. There would only be argument and conflict.

VARIETIES OF COUNTER–POLICY

At the start it must be assumed or effected that there is someone or some body to set authorized policy for the group. Absence of this function is an invitation to random policy and group conflict and disintegration. If such a person or body exists, new proposed policy must be referred to this person or body and issued, not set randomly at lower levels or by unauthorized persons.

Policies so set by the policy authority must be informed enough and wise enough to forward the group purpose and to obtain agreement. Ignorant or bad policy even when authorized tends to persuade group members to set their own random policy.

When no policy at all exists random policy occurs.

When policy exists but is not made known, random policy setting will occur.

Ignorance of policy, the need or function of it, can cause random policies.

Hidden not stated random policies can conflict.

Correct policy can be relayed on a cutative basis — a few words left off or a qualifying sentence dropped which makes policy incorrect or null. "Children may not go out" can be made out of "Children may not go out after midnight."

Altered policy can be limitless in error.

Attributing a self-set policy to the authorized source can disgrace all policy as well as pervert the leadership purpose.

Policy can be excluded from a zone of a group that should be governed by it. "Pipe-making policy does not apply to the *small* pipe shop."

Such masses of unnecessary policy can be issued that it cannot be assimilated.

Policy can exist in large amounts but not be subdivided into relevant subjects as is done in hat checksheets.

Disgrace of policy can occur in a subsequent catastrophe and render any policy disgraceful, encouraging self-set policy by each group member.

CLEARING A GROUP

All authorized policy must be set or made available in master books and adequate complete policy files. This makes it possible to compile hats and checksheets and issue packs.

Group surveys of "What policy are you operating on?" can reveal random policy.

All bugged (halted) projects can be surveyed for illegal policy and cleaned up and gotten going again.

Other actions can be taken all of which add up to:

1. Get existing policy used.

2. Get areas without policy crisply given policy from the authorized source.

3. Debug all past projects of false policy.

4. De-aberrate group members as per the Organization Misunderstoods PL and other materials.

5. Educate the group members concerning policy technology.

6. Set up systems that detect, isolate and report out-policy and get it corrected and properly set, issued and known.

7. Monitor any new policy against statistics and include policy outnesses as part of all statistical evaluations.

ADMIN SCALE

I have developed a scale for use which gives a sequence (and relative seniority) of subjects relating to organization.

GOALS
PURPOSES
POLICY
PLANS
PROGRAMS
PROJECTS
ORDERS
IDEAL SCENES
STATS
VALUABLE FINAL PRODUCTS

This scale is worked up and worked down UNTIL IT IS (EACH ITEM) IN FULL AGREEMENT WITH THE REMAINING ITEMS.

In short, for success, all these items in the scale must agree with all other items in the scale on the same subject.

Let us take "golf balls" as a subject for the scale. Then all these scale items must be in agreement with one another on the subject of golf balls. It is an interesting exercise.

The scale also applies in a destructive subject. Like "cockroaches."

When an item in the scale is *not* aligned with the other items, the project will be hindered if not fail.

The skill with which all these items in any activity are aligned and gotten into action is called MANAGEMENT.

Group members only become upset when one or more of these points are not aligned to the rest and at least some group agreement.

Groups appear slow, inefficient, unhappy, inactive or quarrelsome only when these items are not aligned, made known and coordinated.

Any activity can be improved by debugging or aligning this scale in relation to the group activity.

As out-reality breeds out-comm and out-affinity, it follows that unreal items on the scale (not aligned) produce ARC breaks, upsets and disaffection.

It then follows that when these scale items are well aligned with each other and the group there will be high reality, high communication and high affinity in the group.

Group mores aligned so and followed by the group gives one an ethical group and also establishes what will then be considered as overts and withholds in the group by group members.

This scale and its parts and ability to line them up are one of the most valuable tools of organization.

DEBUG

When orders are not complied with and projects do not come off, one should DETECT, ISOLATE and REPORT and handle or see that it is handled, any of the scale items found random or counter.

If any item below POLICY is in trouble — not moving — one can move upwards correcting these points, but certainly concentrating on a discovery of illegal or counter-policy. Rarely it occurs some old but legal policy needs to be adjusted. Far more commonly policy is being set by someone, verbally or in despatches, or hidden, that is bugging any item or items below the level of policy.

So the rule is that when things get messed up, jammed up, slowed or inactive or downright destructive (including a product as an overt act) one sniffs about for random or counter-policy illegally being set in one's own area or "out there."

Thus in the face of any outness one DETECTS — ISOLATES — REPORTS and handles or gets handled the out-policy.

The *detection* is easy. Things aren't moving or going right.

The isolation is of course a WHAT POLICY that must be found and WHO set it.

Reporting it would mean to HCO.

Handling it is also very easy and would be done in Qual.

This admin tech gives us our first 3rd dynamic de-aberrater that works easily and fast.

Why?

Well, look at the Admin Scale. *Policy* is just below *purpose*.

Purpose is senior to policy.

The person who is setting random or counter illegal policy is off group purpose. He is other-purposed to greater or lesser degree.

From 1960 to 1962 I developed a vast lot of technology about goals and purposes. If we define a goal as a whole track long long-term matter and a purpose as the lesser goal applying to specific activities or subjects we see clearly that if we clean up a person's purposes relating to the various activities in which he is involved and on the eight dynamics we will handle the obsession to set random or counter-policies!

So it is an auditing job and the tech for it is extensive. (The African ACC was devoted to this subject. Lots of data exists on it.)

It happens however that around 20 percent (probably more) of any group's members are actively if covertly antigroup and must be handled at a less profound level under "personal aberration" in the Org Misunderstoods policy letter before you can begin to touch purpose.

Thus any group member, since this tech remedy helps them all, would be handled with:

1. General case de-aberration (called L10s on Flag),

2. Purpose handling for posts,

3. Org bd, hatting and training.

Those setting random or counter-purpose later detected would get further no. 2 and no. 3.

———————

As the universe is full of beings and one lives with them whether he likes it or not, it would be to anyone's interest to be able to have functioning groups.

The only way a group jams up and (a) becomes difficult to live in and (b) impossible to fully separate from is by random and counter-purposes.

If one thinks he can go off and be alone anywhere in this universe he is dreaming.

The first impulse of a hostile being is "to leave" a decent group. What a weird one.

The only reason he gets in jams is his inability to tolerate or handle others.

There's no road out for such a being except through.

Thus all we can do to survive even on the first dynamic is to know how to handle and be part of the third or fourth dynamic and clean it up.

Probably the reason this universe itself is considered by some as a trap is because their Admin Scale is out regarding it.

And the only reason this universe is sometimes a trial is because no one published its Admin Scale in the first place.

All this is very fundamental first dynamic tech and third dynamic tech.

It is the first true group technology that can fully de-aberrate and smooth out and free within the group every group member and the group itself.

Thus, combined with auditing tech, for the first time we can rely wholly on technology to improve and handle group members and the group itself toward desirable and achievable accomplishment with happiness and high morale.

Like any skill or technology it has to be known and done and continued in use to be effective.

The discovery, development and practical use of this data has made me very, very cheerful and confident and is doing the same thing on the test group.

I hope it does the same for you.

L. RON HUBBARD
FOUNDER

———

HUBBARD COMMUNICATIONS OFFICE
SAINT HILL MANOR, EAST GRINSTEAD, SUSSEX

HCO POLICY LETTER OF 14 DECEMBER 1970

REMIMEO

PERSONNEL SERIES 14
ORG SERIES 19
GROUP SANITY

The points of success and failure, the make and break items of an organization are:

1. HIRING

2. TRAINING

3. APPRENTICESHIPS

4. UTILIZATION

5. PRODUCTION

6. PROMOTION

7. SALES

8. DELIVERY

9. FINANCE

10. JUSTICE

11. MORALE

These eleven items MUST AGREE WITH AND BE IN LINE WITH THE ADMIN SCALE (HCO PL 6 Dec. 70, Pers Series 13, Org Series 18, THIRD DYNAMIC DE–ABERRATION).

Where these subjects are not well handled and where one or more of these are very out of line, the organization will suffer a third dynamic aberration.

This then is a SANITY SCALE for the third dynamic of a group.

The group will exhibit aberrated symptoms where one or more of these points are out.

The group will be sane to the degree that these points are in.

Internal stresses of magnitude begin to affect every member of the group in greater or lesser degree when one or more of these items are neglected or badly handled.

The society at large currently has the majority of these points out.

These elements become aberrated in the following ways:

1. HIRING

The society is running a massive can't-have on the subject of people. Automation and employment penalties demonstrate an effort to block out letting people in and giving them jobs. Confirming this is growing unemployment and fantastic sums for welfare — meaning relief. Fifty percent of America within the decade will be jobless due to the population explosion without a commensurate expansion in production. Yet production by US presidential decree is being cut back. War, birth control, are two of many methods used to reduce population. THIS THIRD DYNAMIC PSYCHOSIS IS A *REFUSAL TO* EMPLOY *PEOPLE.* EXCLUSION OF OTHERS IS THE BASIC CAUSE OF WAR AND INSANITY.

2. TRAINING

Education has fallen under the control of one-worlders, is less and less real. Data taught is being taught less well. Less data is being taught. School and college unrest reflect this. Confirmation is the deteriorated basic education found in teenagers such as writing. Older technologies are being lost in modern rewrites. THIS THIRD DYNAMIC PSYCHOSIS IS A *COVERT REFUSAL TO TRAIN.*

3. APPRENTICESHIPS

The most successful industries, activities and professions of earlier centuries were attained by training the person as an apprentice, permitting him to understudy the exact job he would hold for a long period before taking the post. Some European schools are seeking to revive this but on a general basis not as an apprentice system. A THIRD DYNAMIC PSYCHOSIS IS A *DENIAL OF* ADEQUATE *EXPERIENCE TO SUCCEED.*

4. UTILIZATION

In industries, governments and armed services as well as life itself, personnel are not utilized. A man trained for one thing is required to do something else. Or his training is not used. Or he is not used at all. A THIRD DYNAMIC PSYCHOSIS IS *FAILURE TO UTILIZE PEOPLE.*

5. PRODUCTION

Modern think is to reward downstats. A person is paid for not working. Governments who produce nothing employ the most people. Income tax and other current practices penalize production. Countries which produce little are given huge handouts. War which destroys attains the largest appropriations. A THIRD DYNAMIC PSYCHOSIS IS *TO PREVENT PRODUCTION.*

6. PROMOTION

Promotion activities are subverted to unworthy activities. True value is seldom promoted. What one is actually achieving gets small mention while other things are heavily promoted. Reality and PR are strangers. A THIRD DYNAMIC PSYCHOSIS IS *UNREAL OR NONFACTUAL PROMOTION.*

---

7. SALES

Sales actions are unreal or out of balance. Clumsy or nonfunctioning sales activities penalize producers and consumers. In areas of high demand, sales actions are negligible even when heavy advertising exists. This is proven by the inability to sell what is produced even in large countries so that production cutbacks are continual threats to economies and workers. A population goes half-fed in times of surplus goods. With curtailed car factories a nation drives old cars. With a cut-back construction industry people live in bad houses. Sales taxes are almost universal. A THIRD DYNAMIC PSYCHOSIS IS *THE IMPEDING OF PRODUCT DISTRIBUTION TO POTENTIAL CONSUMERS*.

8. DELIVERY

Failure to deliver what is offered is standard procedure for groups in the humanities. Commercially it is well in hand.

9. FINANCE

One's own experience in finance is adequate to demonstrate the difficulties made with money. A THIRD DYNAMIC PSYCHOSIS IS *THE PERVERSION OF FINANCE*.

10. JUSTICE

Under the name of justice, aberrated man accomplishes fantastic injustices. The upstat is hit, the downstat let go. Rumors are accepted as evidence. Police forces and power are used to ENFORCE the injustices contained in 1 to 9 above. Suppressive justice is used as an ineffectual but savage means of meeting situations actually caused by the earlier listed psychoses. When abuses on (1) to (9) make things go wrong, the social aberration then introduces suppressive injustices as an effort to cure. Revolt and war are magnified versions of injustices. Excess people — kill them off in a war. A THIRD DYNAMIC PSYCHOSIS IS *THE SUBSTITUTE OF VIOLENCE FOR REASON*.

11. MORALE

A continuous assault on public morale occurs in the press and other media. Happiness or any satisfaction with life is under continuous attack. Beliefs, idealism, purpose, dreams, are assaulted. INSANITY IS A REFUSAL TO ALLOW OTHERS TO BE, DO OR HAVE.

Any action which would lead to a higher morale has to be defended against the insane few. A THIRD DYNAMIC PSYCHOSIS IS *A DETESTATION OF HIGH MORALE*.

The COMMON DENOMINATOR of all these insanities is the desire to SUCCUMB.

Insanities have as their end product self or group destruction.

These eleven types of aberration gone mad are the main points through which any group SUCCUMBS.

THEREFORE, these eleven points kept sane guarantee a group's SURVIVAL.

EXAMPLES

Seeing all this in one example permits one to see that these third dynamic insanities combine to destroy.

A. Believing it impossible to obtain money or make it, a firm cannot hire enough people to produce. So has little to sell, which is badly promoted and is not sold so it has no money to hire people.

B. Needing people for another job the firm robs them from a plant which then collapses and fails to make money so no new people can be hired. This reduces production so people have to be dismissed as they can't be paid.

C. Persons are in the firm but are kept doing the wrong things so there is little production and no promotion or sales so there is no money to pay them so they are dismissed.

D. A new product is put in. People to make it are taken from the area already making a valuable product which then collapses that area and there is not enough money to promote and selling fails so people are dismissed.

The examples are many. They are these same eleven group insanities in play upon a group, a firm, a society.

SANITY

If this is a description of group aberration, then it gives the keys to sanity in a group.

1. HIRING

Letting people INTO the group at large is the key to every great movement and bettered culture on this planet. This was the new idea that made Buddhism the strongest civilizing influence the world has seen in terms of numbers and terrain. They did not exclude. Race, color, creed, were not made bars to membership in this great movement.

Politically the strongest country in the world was the United States, and it was weakened only by its efforts to exclude certain races or make them second-class citizens. Its greatest internal war (1861–65) was fought to settle this point and the weakness was not resolved even then.

The Catholic Church only began to fail when it began to exclude.

Thus *inclusion* is a major point in all great organizations.

The things which set a group or organization on a course of *exclusion* are (a) the destructive impulses of about 10 or 15 percent of the society (lunacy) and (b) opposition by interests which consider themselves threatened by the group or organization's potential resulting in infiltration, (c) efforts to mimic the group's technology destructively and set up rival groups.

All these three things build up barriers that a group might thoughtlessly buy and act to remedy with no long-range plans to handle.

These stresses make a group edgy and combative. The organization then seeks to solve these three points by exclusion, whereas its growth depends wholly upon *in*clusion.

No one has ever solved these points successfully in the past because of lack of technology to solve them.

It all hinges on three points: (1) the sanity of the individual, (2) the worthwhileness of the group in terms of general area, planetary or universal survival and (3) the superiority of the group's organization tech and its use.

Just at this writing, the first point is solved conclusively in Scientology. Even hostile and destructive personalities wandering into the group can be solved and, due to the basic nature of man, made better for the benefit of themselves and others.

The worthwhileness of the organization is determined by the assistance given to general survival by the group's products and the actual factual delivery of those valid products.

The superiority of a group's admin tech and its application is at this current writing well covered in current developments.

Thus *in*clusion is almost fully attainable. The only ridges that build up are the short-term defense actions.

For instance, Scientology currently must fight back at the death camp organizations of psychiatry whose solution is a dead world, as proven by their actions in Germany before and during World War II. But we *must* keep in mind that we fully intend to reform and salvage even these opponents. We are seeking to *include* them in the general survival by forcing them to cease their nonsurvival practices and overcome their gruesome group past.

There are two major stages then of *including* people — one is as paid organization personnel and one as unpaid personnel. BOTH are in essence being "hired." The pay differs. The wider majority receive the pay of personal peace and effectiveness and a better world.

The org which *excludes* its own field members will fail.

The payment to the org of money or the money payment to the staff member is an internal economy. Pay, the real pay, is a better personal survival and a world that can live.

Plans of INclusion are successful. They sometimes contain defense until we *can* include.

Even resistance to an org can be interpreted as a future inclusion by the org. Resistance or opposition is a common way point in the cycle of inclusion. In an organization where everyone wins eventually anyway the senselessness of resistance becomes apparent even to the most obtuse. Only those who oppose their own survival resist a survival producing organization.

Even in commercial companies the best organization with the best product usually finds competitors merging with it.

2. TRAINING

Basic training, hats, checksheets and packs MUST exist for every member of a group.

Criminal or antisocial conduct occurs where there is no hat.

Any type of membership or role or post in the whole organization or its field requires individual and team training. Only where you have a group member who will not or cannot bring himself to have and wear a hat will you have any trouble.

This is so true that it is the scope of Personal Enhancement.

Ask yourself "Who isn't trained on his post and hatted?" and you can answer "Who is causing the trouble?"

Basic training, slight or great, is vital for *every* member of a group, paid or unpaid.

A field auditor must have a hat. A student needs a student hat, etc., etc.

This requires training.

Training begins in childhood. Often it has to be reoriented.

Training as a group member must be done.

Training in exact technology or in the precise tech of admin is not the first stage of training. Basic training of group members, no matter how slight, must exist and be done.

Otherwise group members lack the basic points of agreement which make up the whole broad organization and its publics.

Training must be on real materials and must be rapid. The technology of how to train is expressed in speed of training.

The idea that it takes 12 years to make a mud pie maker is false. TIME in training does not determine quality of training. Amount of data learned that can be applied and skills successfully drilled determine training.

That the society currently stresses *time* is an aberrated factor.

The ability to learn and apply the data is the end product of training. Not old age.

The rate of training establishes to a marked degree the expansion factor of a group and influences the smoothness of the group during expansion.

If training is defined as making a person or team into a part of the group then processing is an influencing factor. The facilities for processing and quantity available are then a determining factor in group expansion.

3. APPRENTICESHIP

Training on post is a second stage of any training — and processing — action.

This is essentially a familiarization action.

To have a person leave a post and another take it over with no "apprenticeship" or groove-in can be quite fatal.

The deputy system is easily the best system. Every post is deputied for a greater or lesser period before the post is turned over and the appointment is made. When the deputy is totally familiar he becomes the person on the post.

Rapid expansion and economy on personnel tend to injure this step. Lack of it can be *very* destructive.

Optimally there should be one or two deputies for every key post at all times. This is a continual apprenticeship system.

Economically it has limitations. One has to weigh the *losses* in not doing it against the cost in doing it. It will be found that the losses are *far* greater than the cost, even though it increases personnel by at least a third for a given organization.

When an organization has neglected it as a system (and has turned over too many posts without deputy or apprenticeship action) its economics may decay to where it can never be done. This is almost a death rattle for an organization.

In a two-century-old highly successful industry, *only* the apprentice system was and is used (Oporto wine industry). The quality of the product is all that keeps the product going on the world market. If the quality decayed the industry would collapse. Apprenticeship as a total system maintains it.

Certainly every executive in an organization and every technical expert should have a deputy in training. Only then could quality of organization be maintained and quality of product guaranteed.

The total working organization should be on this system actually. And whenever a person is moved up off a post, the deputy taking over, a new deputy should be appointed. The last step (appointment of a new deputy) is the one that gets forgotten.

Failure to recruit new people over a period will very surely find the whole organization declining soon solely because there is no apprentice system of deputies. The organization expands, singles up the posts, promotes some unapprenticed people and begins to lose its economic advantage. Low pay ensues, people blow off and then no one can be hired. It's a silly cycle, really, as it is prevented easily enough by hiring enough soon enough when the org is still doing well.

The rule is DEPUTY EVERY POST AND NEWLY DEPUTY THEM WHEN PROMOTIONS OCCUR.

The most covert way to get around this is just to call each person's junior a deputy even though he has other duties. This makes it all look good on an org board. "Do you have each post deputied?" "Oh yes!" But the deputies are just juniors with posts of their own.

A deputy is *used* to run the same post as it is deputied for. This means a double posting pure and only.

You'd be amazed at how much production an executive post can achieve when it is also deputied and when the principal holder of the post will use the deputy and gen him in, not get him to cover an empty lower post.

4. UTILIZATION

People must be utilized.

Equipment must be utilized.

Space must be utilized.

Learning to USE is a very hard lesson for some. Untrained people, bad organization, poor machinery, inadequate space all tend to send one off utilization.

The rule is, if you've got it use it; if you can't use it get rid of it.

This most specifically applies to people. If you've got a man, use him; if you can't use him get him over to someone who can use him. If he isn't useful, process and train.

Anyone who can't figure out how to use people, equipment and spaces to obtain valuable final products is not worthy of the name of executive.

Reversely we get what an executive or foreman is — an executive or foreman is one who can obtain, train and use people, equipment and spaces to economically achieve valuable final products.

Some are very skilled in preparing people, systems, equipment, property and spaces to be used. But if these then go to someone who does not USE them you get a bad breakdown.

The welfare state and its inflation is a sad commentary on "executive ability."

An executive whose people are idle and whose materiel is decaying is a traitor to his people and the org, just that, for he will destroy them all.

UTILIZATION requires a knowledge of what the valuable final products are and how to make them.

Action which doesn't result in a final product that adds up to valuable final products is destructive, no matter how innocent it seems.

Man has a planet as a valuable final product. Improper *use* of the countries and seas, air and masses which compose it will wind up with the destruction of man, all life on it and the usefulness of the planet. So *proper* utilization of anything is a very real factor.

The nineteenth-century industrialist, like the mad kings who built great structures, used up men; they didn't properly use men.

And not using them at all, the current fad, is the most deadly of all.

UTILIZATION is a big subject. It applies to resources, capabilities and many other factors.

The question being asked in all cases is, "How can we USE this to economically obtain a valuable final product?"

Failing to answer that question gives one the "mysteries of life."

5. PRODUCTION

One may be prone to believe there is no sense in any production at all. Such a one would also be likely to say, "There is no sense at all." Or "If they keep on producing it will become impossible to destroy it all."

Production of some final valuable product is the chain of all production sequences.

Even the artist is producing a *reaction*. The reaction's service in a wider sphere to enforce it is what gives art its sense. A feeling of well-being or grandeur or light-heartedness are legitimate valuable final products, for instance.

The production areas and activities of an org that produce the valuable final products are the most important areas and activities of the org.

6. PROMOTION

The acceptance of valuable final products and of their value depends in a large degree upon (a) a real value and (b) a desire for them.

Promotion creates desire for the valuable final product.

The old saw that the man who builds a better mousetrap will have the whole world coming to his door is a total falsity.

Unless the value is made known, and the desire created, the mousetraps are going to go unsold.

Promotion is so important that it can stand alone. It can have limited success even when there is no product! But in that case it will be of short duration.

Promotion must contain reality and the final product must exist and be deliverable and delivered for promotion to be fully successful.

Public relations and advertising and all their skills cover this area of promotion.

7. SALES

It is hard to sell what isn't promoted and can't be delivered.

Economics greatly affect selling.

Anything must be sold for a price comparable to its value in the eyes of the purchaser.

COSTING is a precise art by which the total expenses of the organization administration and production must be adequately covered in the PRICING allowing for all losses and errors in delivery and adequate to produce a reserve.

PRICING (the amount being asked) cannot be done without some idea of the total cost of the final valuable product.

The sale price of one final valuable product may have to cover the cost of producing other products which are delivered without price.

PRICING however does not necessarily limit itself to only covering immediate cost of a product. A painting with a dollar's worth of paint and canvas may have a price of half a million dollars.

Also a painting used in promotion may cost two hundred dollars and be displayed at no cost at all to the beholder.

These relative factors also include the SKILL of the salesman himself and there is much technology involved in the act of selling something to someone and the world abounds in books on the subject.

Therefore sales (once promotion is done) are bound up really in COSTING, PRICING AND SELLING.

The value in the eye of the purchaser is monitored by the desire created in him for it. If this is also a real value and if delivery can occur then SELLING is made very easy — but it is still a skilled action.

The production of a valuable final product is often totally determined by whether or not it can be sold. And if it can be sold at a price greater than the cost of delivering it.

That it *gets* sold depends on the salesman.

The skill of the salesman is devoted to enhancing the desire and value in the eyes of the buyer and obtaining adequate payment.

8. DELIVERY

The subject and action of DELIVERY is the most susceptible to breakdown in any organization. Any flaw on the sequence of actions resulting in a valuable final product may deteriorate it or bar off final delivery.

There are many preparatory or hidden-from-public-view steps on a production line. When any of these break down, delivery is imperiled.

Given the raw materials and wherewithal to make some valuable final product, the valuable final product should occur.

WHEN A VALUABLE FINAL PRODUCT DOES NOT GET PRODUCED AND CANNOT BE DELIVERED, REPAIR THE EARLIER STEPS OF ITS PRODUCTION.

Example: An auditing result is not delivered. Don't just repair the pc. Repair training of auditors and C/Ses. Repair the assembly line *before* the valuable final product. The subproducts are less visible. Yet they add up to the valuable final product.

THE LAW OF THE IRREDUCIBLE MINIMUM occurs in all delivery problems. Someone is trying to produce only the visible end product of a post or production line and neglects the earlier contributory actions and products as these are not plainly visible.

When an organization or its posts operate only on an irreducible minimum, production goes bad and DELIVERY crashes.

Take a cook who has his post at an irreducible minimum. Food is appearing on the table. If he reduced just one bit more the food would no longer be edible at all. He neglects purchasing, menus and preparation. That these occur is invisible to the diners. That food appears on the table is visible to the diners. If the cook operates at any less level than he is, no edible food would be visible — hence, irreducible minimum. The food served will be bad. But it will be visible. Invisible-to-the-diners actions aren't being done.

To improve the food, get the less visible actions *done*. Get the sequence of actions all done. The result will be improved food.

Take training. The final valuable product is a trained auditor. The Course Supervisor who runs his post on an irreducible minimum is simply there, appearing to supervise.

His final product may be horribly unskilled. The teaching may take "forever."

To improve this one goes earlier on the assembly line — materials, packs, tapes, student tech services, recorder repair, scheduling — dozens of actions including getting the Course Supervisor trained.

The visibility is still a Course Supervisor and students being taught. But with the *whole* earlier line in, the final valuable product is excellent!

A being hopes lazily for instantaneous production. It doesn't happen this way in the MEST universe. Things are produced in a sequence of subproducts which result in a final valuable product. Hope all you want to. When you omit the subproducts you get no valuable final product.

When the people in an organization do not know the valuable final products of the org and when a person on a post does not know the final products of his post, a condition arises where no org DELIVERY will occur, or if it does occur it will be poor or costly. It is vital that a person knows what his post final products are and what his unit, section, department and division subproducts are and how his own and each of these contribute to the valuable final products of the organization for actual delivery to occur.

Delivering other than valuable final products or useless final products or final products that need constant correction also adds up to nondelivery.

A whole civilization can break down around the point of DELIVERY. So can an organization.

Since money can be looked upon as too valuable a final product it can actually prevent DELIVERY.

Failure to deliver is the one point beings do not forgive. The whole cycle hangs upon DELIVERY.

DELIVER WHAT IS PROMISED when it is expected, in sufficient volume and adequate quality is the first maxim even of a group in politics or the humanities.

9. FINANCE

Finance too often disregards the other factors in this scale or the other factors in this scale too often disregard finance for organizations to long remain viable.

Financing must be in agreement with all the other factors of this scale and all the other factors must be in agreement with finance for viability to occur.

Because money is interchangeable for commodities then people can confuse it with too many things.

If you regard money like so many beans, as a commodity in itself, you open the door to understanding it.

Money is so many beans in to get so many beans out.

When you can master this you can handle FINANCE.

The FINANCE persons of an org, a civilization, a planet should put so many beans in and expect more beans out than they put in. This is quite correct as a viewpoint for finance.

The difference of beans in and beans out for a planet is made up by adding beans enough to those already in existence to cover new commodity.

When finance people fail to do this beans cease to be in pace with production and inflation and deflation occur.

In an org or any of its parts, industriousness of the staff makes the difference between the beans in and beans out.

An org has to have income greater than outgo. That is the first rule of finance. Violating it brings bankruptcy.

Now if the FINANCE people of an org apply the same rule remorselessly to all *its* transactions (financial planning) with each person and part of an org, finance becomes real and manageable.

So many beans in to support the first division means so many beans out of the org back to finance because of the cooperative work of the first division.

A hectic effort to work only with production products will wind finance up in a knot.

One has to estimate (cost) the contribution of each part of an org to the valuable final product to know what to allow what part of an org.

Finance has to have a full reality on the valuable final products and the subproducts and post products of the whole org to intelligently allocate funds.

This person, that division, each contributes some part of the action that results in the money received for the valuable final products.

So finance can extend so much money for each and expect that and an additional amount back.

If this occurs, so will expansion.

Finance comes unstuck when it fails to "cost" an organization and fails to support valuable final product production.

Finance must not only practice "income greater than outgo" for the org, it must practice it for each part of the org as well.

Then solvency becomes real.

The greatest aberration of finance is that it seeks to *save* things into solvency. The real losses in an org are the sums never made. These are the most important losses for finance to concentrate upon.

An org that makes 500 pounds a week that should make 5,000 pounds a week in potential is losing the finance people 4,500 pounds a week!

Finance can force production along certain lines by putting in funds and getting more back.

Finance becomes too easily the management of an org but it only does that when it ceases to deal in its own commodity — money.

An org which has executives unfamiliar with finance will fall at once into the control of the finance people in the org. And these finance people, if they don't really know money, will fall at once under the control of outside finance people.

One has to know finance in any organization anywhere, even in a socialism. Sooner or later the books get balanced in any society.

10. JUSTICE

Without justice there can be no real organization.

Even a government owes its people an operating climate in which human transactions and business can occur.

Where insane and criminal individuals operate unchecked in the community, justice is uncertain and harsh.

The society in which the insane rise to positions of power becomes a nightmare.

Justice is a difficult subject. Man handles it badly.

Justice cannot occur until insanity can be detected and cured.

The whole task of justice is to defend the honest man. Therefore the target of justice is the establishment of a sane society.

The inability to detect or cure the insane destroys civilizations.

Justice is an effort to bring equity and peace. When one cannot detect and cure insanity then sooner or later justice actions will become unjust and be used by the insane.

To us, justice is the action necessary to restrain the insane until they are cured. After that it would be only an action of seeing fair play is done.

11. MORALE

When all factors balance up in an org and give the group a common direction and mutual viability, morale can be expected to be good.

When the Admin Scale and the ten elements described are out of balance (without proper importance given to each) and when one or many of these (Admin Scale and the elements herein described) are not in agreement one with another, then morale will be poor.

Morale is not made of comfort and sloth. It is made of common purpose and obstacles overcome by the group.

When the Admin Scale and these elements are not held together by similar aims, then morale has to be held up artificially.

The most ghastly morale I have ever seen was amongst "the idle rich."

And the highest morale I've ever seen was amongst a furiously dedicated common-purposed group working under fantastic stresses with very little against almost hopeless odds.

I used to observe that morale in a combat unit would never materialize before they had been through hell together.

All drama aside, morale is made up of high purpose and mutual confidence. This comes from the Admin Scale items and these elements of organization being well aligned, one with the next, and honest sane endeavor to achieve a final goal for all.

L. RON HUBBARD
FOUNDER

HCO POLICY LETTER OF 30 DECEMBER 1970

REMIMEO
SO MEMBER HAT
STAFF MEMBER HAT

PERSONNEL SERIES 15
ORG SERIES 20

ENVIRONMENTAL CONTROL

The differences between a competent person and an incompetent person are demonstrated in his environment (surroundings).

A person is either the effect of his environment or is able to have an effect upon his environment.

The nineteenth-century psychologist preached that man had to "adjust to his environment." This false datum helped begin a racial degeneration.

The truth is that man is as successful as he adjusts the environment to him.

Being competent means the ability to control and operate the things in the environment and the environment itself.

When you see things broken down around the mechanic who is responsible for them, he is plainly exhibiting his incompetence — which means his inability to control those things in his environment and adjust the environment for which he is responsible — motors.

When you see the mate's boats broken up, you know he does not have control of his environment.

Know-how, attention and the desire to be effective are all part of the ability to control the environment.

One's "standards" (the degree of rightness one is trying to establish and maintain) are directly related to one's desire to have a controlled environment.

The attainment of one's *standards* is not done by criticism (a human system). It is done by exerting control of one's environment and moving things effectively toward a more ideal scene.

Control of the environment begins with oneself — a good case state, a body that one keeps clean and functioning. This extends to one's own gear, his clothing, tools, equipment. It extends further to the things one is responsible for in the environment. Then it extends out into the whole environment, the people and the MEST.

One can get pretty dirty fixing things up. That's okay. But can one then also clean oneself up?

The ability to confront MEST is a high ability. After that comes the ability to handle and control it.

The ability to confront people is also a high ability. After that comes the ability to get along with them and to handle and control them.

There is the supreme test of a thetan — the ability to make things go right.

The reverse of this is the effort to make things go wrong.

Incompetence — lack of know-how, inability to control — makes things go wrong.

Given some know-how or picking it up by observation, sane people make things go right.

The insane remain ignorant intentionally or acquire know-how and make things go wrong.

Insane acts are *not* unintentional or done out of ignorance. They are intentional, they are not "unknowing dramatizations." So around insane people things go wrong.

One cannot tell the difference really between the sane and insane by behavior. One can tell the difference only by the product. The product of the sane is survival. The product of the insane is an overt act. As this is often masked by clever explanations, it is not given the attention it deserves. The pretended good product of the insane turns out to be an overt act.

A large percentage of this planet's population (undetermined at this time for the "general public" but in excess of 20 percent) are insane. Their behavior looks passable. But their product is an overt act. The popularity of war confirms this. The products of existing governments are mainly destructive. The final product of the human race will be a destroyed planet (a contaminated air cover rendering the planet unable to sustain life, whether by radiation or fumes).

Thus, due to the inability to detect and handle the insane, the sane majority suffers.

The hidden actions of the insane can destroy faster than an environment can be created UNLESS one has the know-how of the mind and life and the tech of admin and the ability and know-how to handle MEST.

An area or activity hit by an influx of new recruits or new customers tends to unsettle. Its MEST gets abuse, things go out of control.

Gradually, working to put in order, the standards are again being attained. The minority insane get handled, the know-how of groups and orgs becomes more generally known, the tech of MEST gets used again.

As an organization expands it goes through cycles of lowered condition and raised condition. This is normal enough since by taking on more and more area one is letting in more and more insane even though they are in a small proportion to the sane.

Order is reestablished and survival trends resumed to the degree that the sane begin to reach out and handle things around them and as the insane are made sane.

Thus one gets downtrends and uptrends. As soon as a group begins to feel cocky, it takes on more area. This includes more unhandled people, admin and MEST and a downtrend begins. Then the sane begin to handle and the insane begin to be sane and the uptrend starts.

This is probably even the basis of national economic booms and depressions.

This is only bad to the degree that the insane are put in charge. As soon as this happens the downtrend becomes permanent and cultural decay sets in.

A group expanding rapidly into a decadent culture is of course itself subjected to the uptrend–downtrend cycles and has to take very special measures to counteract the consequences of expansion in order to maintain any rate of growth.

The individual member of a group can measure his own progress by increased ability to handle himself, his post and environment and the degree of improvement of the group itself because of his own work within it.

A group that is messing up its gear and environment worse than it did a while ago and is not improving it of course has to be reorganized before it perishes.

No group can sit back and expect its high brass to be the only ones to carry the load. The group is composed of individual group members, not of high brass.

The survival of a group depends upon the ability of its individual members to control their environment and to insist that the other group members also control theirs.

This is the stuff of which survival is made.

A sane group, knowing and using their technologies of handling men and MEST, cannot help but control their environment.

But this depends upon the individual group member being sane, able to control his MEST and those around him and using the tech of life, the tech of admin, the tech of specific types of activity.

Such a group inevitably inherits the culture and its guidance.

L. RON HUBBARD
FOUNDER

HCO POLICY LETTER OF 27 DECEMBER 1970

REMIMEO
HCO AREA SEC
DIR RAP
HATS OFFICER

PERSONNEL SERIES 16
HATS PROGRAM
PITFALLS

The main outnesses about hats are:

1. Personnel having a hat and title but doing some *other* job or jobs.

2. Personnel falling between two divs or posts and being in neither.

3. Personnel having no hat at all.

4. Personnel unable to even cope because people around them don't have hats.

5. Hats matching an org board but the org board itself is disorganized.

6. Personnel holding a part-time hat but no other hat even though full time.

7. Hats lost in post turnovers and no complete hat file.

8. The only other copy in the hat file issued and *also* lost.

9. Org pattern changes which make hats unreal.

10. Juniors trying to wear their hats but a senior, being unaware of them, issuing different orders.

11. Seniors trying to wear their hats but juniors unaware of them and making different demands.

12. Personnel moving off not replaced, leaving others in the organization to carry a load for which they have no hat.

13. Missing ideal scene for hat.

14. Missing general ideal scene for division.

15. No concept of the scene at all.

16. A person just not doing his hat.

17. Checksheet and/or pack missing or incomplete for post.

18. Missing any part of full hat content per HCO PL 22 Sept. 70, Personnel Series 9, Org Series 4, HATS.

19. Hat checksheet contains (a) omissions (too short); (b) highly irrelevant data; (c) doesn't belong to the post.

20. Counter-policy present in hat write-up.

21. Seniors issue counter-policy in despatches or verbally.

22. Senior not grooving personnel in on post or seeing to proper hat study.

23. Valuable final product missing for hat.

24. Purpose and/or valuable final product missing in hat for group's whole activity.

25. An *earlier* or more basic hat is out such as a top executive not knowing the basic staff hat fully.

26. Nonutilization in any of its various forms such as a personnel trained for one thing is required to do something else. Or his training is not used. Or he is not used at all.

If the Hats Officer can do his job and not get caught up in these pitfalls, we'll really soar.

L. RON HUBBARD
FOUNDER

HCO POLICY LETTER OF 19 JANUARY 1971

REMIMEO

PERSONNEL SERIES 17
ORG SERIES 21

DUPLICATING FUNCTIONS

All you have to do to run out of personnel, finance and get no production is to duplicate the same functions that give the same product in an org.

Take three orgs side by side under the same management. Only if each division of each org had entirely different products would this be possible.

Now let's do it wrong. Each of these three orgs has an HCO and full personnel duties. Each separately promotes. Each has its own finance office, each has its production div producing the same products. Each has its own correction div — the place in general would be very overmanned, yet each div would be undermanned for its full functions. The product would be terrible if it existed at all. Morale would be ghastly, interorg collisions continual.

The right way would be to work out the different products and then assign them to one or another of these orgs. One org would have to be the source org that produced the other two. One org would have all the finance with liaison only in the other two orgs. One org would have to hire, hat and train with only liaison in the other two. The orgs would have org boards which *had* the function but under it would be the note "Liaison with _____," source org.

In the impatience and emotion of organizing one org tends to individuate and establish a duplicate function because "it can't get service." This begins the catastrophe. Now they'll all begin to go broke while having men bulging out of the windows.

In looking over potential insolvency, look over duplicate functions.

L. RON HUBBARD
FOUNDER

HUBBARD COMMUNICATIONS OFFICE
Saint Hill Manor, East Grinstead, Sussex

HCO POLICY LETTER OF 10 FEBRUARY 1971
Issue II

Remimeo
CO Hat
HAS Hat
Dept 1 Hats
Dept 3 Hats
HCO Checksheets
E/O Hat

PERSONNEL SERIES 18

Adds to Personnel Series 8,
HCO PL 16 Sept. 70 I,
ETHICS AND PERSONNEL
(Applies to E/Os)

An I&R Form 1 (HCO PL 6 Oct. 70 I, INSPECTION OF LOW STATS) must be done by Inspections and Reports on the dept or div or activity that is demanding personnel, at the request of Personnel, Dept 1.

When the I&R Form 1 is done by the Inspector (be it the Ethics Officer or another) the *additional* questions on Personnel Series 8, A–H, are covered by the Ethics Officer who personally gets the answers to them.

His answers are added to the I&R Form 1, together with any ethics actions proposed.

In this case the routing of the I&R Form 1 is Inspector to E/O to Personnel.

Personnel adds his recommendations regarding either (a) to expedite needful personnel or (b) to demand utilization of existing personnel.

The I&R Form 1, with the E/O's added report and Personnel's added recommendations then follows the routing as laid down on the form, and the standard procedure for the form is carried out.

WITHOUT THE AUTHORIZATION OF THE EXEC DIR OR HCO ES FOR THE ACTIONS RECOMMENDED ON THE I&R FORM 1, NO TRANSFER OR ASSIGNMENT MAY TAKE PLACE AT ALL. THE EXEC DIR OR HCO ES MAY ORIGINATE ORDERS ON THE PERSONNEL REQUEST BUT SUCH ORDERS MUST BE BASED ON THE COMPLETED I&R FORM 1 WITH E/O REPORT AND

PERSONNEL RECOMMENDATION TO HAND AND THESE DOCUMENTS MUST ACCOMPANY SUCH ORIGINATED ORDERS BEFORE THE HCO AREA SEC IS EMPOWERED TO ISSUE AND ENFORCE THEM.

No more than 24 hours should be allowed from the receipt in Dept 3 of Personnel's request for I&R Form 1 to the receipt of the completed action by the HCO Area Sec.

L. RON HUBBARD
FOUNDER

Assisted by
LRH Pers Comm

HUBBARD COMMUNICATIONS OFFICE

Saint Hill Manor, East Grinstead, Sussex

HCO POLICY LETTER OF 16 MARCH 1971

Issue III

Remimeo

Personnel Series 19
Org Series 25

LINES AND HATS

It will be found that in organization there are *MANY* major factors involved.

The following three, however, give the most problems:

1. Personnel

2. Hats

3. Lines

Technology is a subdivision of both personnel (who may have to be specially trained before they can be considered personnel) and hats (which are mainly admin technology and line functions).

To solve any problem, one has to recognize what the problem is. One cannot solve problem A by trying to solve problem B or C. Example: Problem: broken-down car. You cannot fix the car by repairing the kitchen lino. Example: You cannot floor the kitchen by fixing the car.

All this may seem obvious when obliviously stated. But there is a more subtle version. ANY PROBLEM THAT DOES NOT SOLVE IS NOT THE PROBLEM. There must be some other problem.

Locating and isolating situations (problems) in an organization is the technique of the Data Series. That technology will find for one the problem that should be solved.

As there are three major organizational factors these then also form the core of all organizational situations (or problems, same thing).

Each one of these is its own zone — personnel, hats, lines.

Each one has its own problems. There are situations in personnel. There are situations in hats. There are situations in lines.

They *are* related. They are not identical.

You will find you cannot wholly solve a problem in lines by solving personnel. You cannot wholly solve a problem in hats by solving lines. You cannot wholly solve a problem in personnel by solving the other two.

Example: Production hours are down. Fifteen new personnel are added to the area. Production stays down. It was a problem in lines.

Example: Confusion reigns in the pipe shop. The lines are carefully straightened out. Confusion still reigns. It was a problem in hats.

Example: Broken products are wrecking org repute. Hats are carefully put on. Products continue to be broken. It was a problem in personnel.

Example: The org stays small. Executives work harder. The org stays small. It was a series of problems in personnel, hats *and* lines, none addressed at all.

You will see symptoms of all this in various guises. The test of whether or not the right problem was found is whether or not production increased in volume, quality and viability.

In actual practice one works on all three of these factors constantly — personnel, hats and lines — when one is organizing.

You will find with some astonishment that failure to have or know or wear or do a *hat* is the commonest reason why *lines* do not go in. That personnel is hard to procure and train because hats and lines are being knocked out. That hats can't be worn because lines or personnel are out.

Situations get worsened by solving the wrong problem instead of the real problem. In the Data Series this is called finding the right *Why*.

Organizational problems center around these three things in the broadest general sense. More than one can be present in any situation.

Production problems are concerned with the particles which flow on the lines, changed by the hatted personnel, with consumption and general viability. So to make a full flow from organization through to distribution, one would add raw materials, changed state of materials and their consumption. Organization is not an end-all. To have value it must result in production.

But when personnel, hats and lines are not solved, production is very difficult. Therefore to get production one must have an organization to back it up. And personnel, hats and lines must exist and be functional. If these exist, the rest of the factors of establishment can be brought into being.

It goes without saying that organization involves other problems like space, materiel, finance, etc. These and many more also enter into "Whys" of no production. But dominating others are problems in personnel, hats and lines. Others tend to solve if these are handled and organized.

L. RON HUBBARD
FOUNDER

HCO POLICY LETTER OF 19 MARCH 1971R

Issue I

Revised 21 January 1991

Remimeo

Personnel Series 20

PERSONNEL PREDICTION

Sudden and unauthorized transfers of personnel for whatever reason disrupt hats and lines. Every such transfer is a failure to predict concerning personnel.

By a few transfers ("musical chairs"), an area can be totally unmocked.

Personnel people tend to undervalue the time and care necessary to train, hat and apprentice people.

Even a small unit is a "working installation" if it produces. An order to "turn over the hat this morning and take another post" is quite unreal.

Prediction is the button that is usually out in personnel handling.

How many will we need in _____ weeks or months? is the key question. It is the one Personnel should *continually* work on. Stressing only "Who can we assign to _____?" shows a lack of prediction.

Man tends to run in today and seldom in tomorrow much less next week or year. The fault will someday destroy him as a species. He is even unable to predict the fate of his habitat, the planet.

Thus Personnel should be very wary of this fault.

Recruiting for tomorrow instead of yesterday, people in full-time training, future executives being sorted out by today's performance all add up to good prediction by Personnel people.

One must catch up the backlog of yesterday's needs by gradual moving up into the future.

Every key post should have a deputy in training or in apprenticeship for the post. By key post is meant one that has urgent responsibility and great expertise.

Personnel will see where it stands by just listing their *current* answers to these questions:

1. What are the key posts of the org or activity that require *great* expertise and *training?* From top to bottom list them out.

2. How many of the above list have people in training or apprenticeship for them?

3. What will be the personnel scene on these posts in one year?

4. What plans did you have *yesterday* to do this?

5. What plans can be made now to do this?

Having actually done the above questions, one will see what prediction consists of regarding personnel and a sample of what it means to predict.

This should be done at full org level and then at divisional level and then at department level.

Then one will see that sudden transfers done without training or apprenticeship can be avoided in the future at key levels IF ONE PROGRAMS IT *NOW*. And then ACTS to make the program work out.

Where prediction is out, expansion becomes impossible to do without collapse.

For one has to predict expansion as well.

An action on expansion would be:

1. To increase the org's stats five times (GDSes and GI) how many more trained, hatted people would be needed:

    a. In the CO or ED Office?

    b. In HCO?

    c. In Div 2?

    d. In Div 3?

    e. In Dept of Training?

    f. In the HGC?

    g. In Qual?

    h. In the Distribution Division?

    i. In the LRH Comm Office?

    j. In the Estate area?

    k. In the Dept of Special Affairs?

    l. In space?

m. In furniture?

n. In equipment?

o. In decoration?

p. Finance?

q. Personnel care (food, shelter, clothes)?

While the last (l to q) are not properly "Personnel" the personnel action would collide with them so hard that personnel action would be *stopped.* "Do not hire anyone else!" "Do not _____." "Do not _____."

So somebody says, "We are going to boost the GI from $100 to $50,000."

Well, to do that one would have to promote and deliver as well as make money.

So, when such a prediction is made, what does a good Personnel Officer do?

He does the computations outlined in this policy letter and any other that seem indicated and says, "There you are, chums. This is my part of the deal and (presenting a plan) this is how I'll go about it, to hire, recruit, get trained and apprenticed the needful personnel. Now what are YOU doing about (l) to (q) in this PL so you don't stop *my* progress doing *my* job of getting you eighty additional, functional, useful, nongoofing, producing staff?"

This wakes up the prediction elsewhere so Personnel's prediction doesn't fall down plop.

Once the action is begun, part of the prediction is that it will require continuous guiding, handling and pounding to make it come true.

For instance it can be predicted that as Personnel loads them in there will be failures to program, hat, train, apprentice and utilize. One Personnel loaded an org full and a month later *fifty-seven* nonutilized, nonassigned people were combed out of the debris. "But they are so new . . ." "But you can't assign . . ." etc., etc. And Personnel got blamed for recruiting "unsuitable people." Because the hatting, training, apprenticing actions were neglected! You can *only* recruit untrained people, really.

So Personnel regards unutilized people as a backlog on his lines. Recruited not utilized means he still has them as they have not "fed into the org."

"Prove you have used what I got. Show me the programing of their training. How many have hats? How many are apprenticed?" These are legitimate Personnel questions. And they are demands.

Until utilized, personnel are regarded as still on Personnel's plate no matter where they've gotten to in the org.

Otherwise, Personnel is pounded, pounded for people, people, people when the halls are impassable with nonutilized personnel.

Yet I've never heard a Personnel man say, "What'd you do with the guys I got you last week?" It would produce some blushes.

Personnel aren't personnel really until they are utilized.

Hectic transfers from working posts, "musical chairs," all come from lack of personnel programs based on predictions.

When programs *are* made and are in action, a failure to predict probable failures to hat, train, apprentice, post is a legitimate prediction and should be watched carefully and corrected by Personnel.

L. RON HUBBARD
FOUNDER

Revision assisted by
LRH Technical Research
and Compilations

HCO POLICY LETTER OF 8 NOVEMBER 1971RA
Issue II
Revised 1 June 2000

Remimeo

Personnel Series 20-1
COMPLEMENT

(Originally written by LRH for the *Apollo* OODs
of 8 Nov. 71. Issued as an HCO PL on 24 June 73.)

Some recent personnel troubles became explained when it was found that the basic complement of an org had never been filled.

The concept of what is a "complement" has been misunderstood in HCO and is probably generally misunderstood. This means the officially allowed number of persons and the officially designated posts for an activity, whether an org or a ship.

Without these basic complements orgs get misposted. Instead of ten auditors they have one auditor and nine admin personnel somewhere else.

This general concept of complement is generally missing and underlies the reason why org boards are, to some degree, in disuse.

In any org which is not doing well you may find not enough personnel and too many personnel. You may also find that the personnel there are not posted onto the post necessary to be held.

Designating the post necessary to be held is what is meant by "assigning a complement."

I never realized the concept was hard to get across until recently. In the dictionary it says that a complement is simply a full list of the officers and men of a ship. This falls so far short of the actual definition that it generates confusion.

A complement is the full list of posts and where they belong on the org board, which must be held. This gives you a slightly different idea of what is meant by "complement."

Two orgs, for instance, didn't have a standard complement. They simply had all possible posts which could be held in the org. This does not tell you what posts should be held in the org.

Therefore, personnel control is not possible.

In the case of another org there was a maximum allowed complement but it was never filled up.

There is a complement for every separate and individual org.

Until the complement of an org is laid out, known and filled, there will be continual trouble with personnel and difficulties in handling it.

The sooner this is straightened out, the easier time there will be for all.

L. RON HUBBARD
FOUNDER

Revision assisted by
LRH Technical Research
and Compilations

HCO POLICY LETTER OF 29 JULY 1971
ISSUE I

REMIMEO

PERSONNEL SERIES 21
ORG SERIES 28

WHY HATTING?

A few days ago when I found that musical chairs and flubbed hatting had unstabilized some areas, I wondered whether or not this might stem from some social aberration that was very general in the societies in which we are working.

And it seems to have been the case. I worked on it a bit and found this:

LAW: THE POWER OF A THETAN STEMS FROM HIS ABILITY TO HOLD A POSITION IN SPACE.

This is quite true. In *Scientology 8-80* the base of the motor is discussed. It holds two terminals in fixed positions. Because they are so fixed, power can be generated.

If a thetan can hold a position or location in space he can generate POWER.

If he cannot, he cannot generate power and will be weak.

We have known this for nineteen years. It applies here.

Observation: MODERN SOCIETY TENDS TO CONFUSE AND UNSTABILIZE PERSONS WITH ITS HECTIC PACE.

Observation: BEINGS WHO ARE AFRAID OF STRONG PEOPLE TRY TO WEAKEN THEM.

Observation: PERSONS WHO ARE PUSHED AROUND FEEL THEY CANNOT HOLD A POSITION IN SPACE.

Observation: PEOPLE HATE TO LOSE THEIR POSTS AND JOBS. THEY FIND IT DEGRADING.

In processing, picking up this chain of lost positions achieves very good gains and rehabilitates a person's ability to hold a job.

LAW: BY GIVING A PERSON A POST OR POSITION, HE IS SOMEWHAT STRENGTHENED AND MADE MORE CONFIDENT IN LIFE.

LAW: BY LETTING A PERSON RETAIN HIS POST, HE IS MADE MORE SECURE.

LAW: BY HATTING A PERSON, HE IS GREATLY STRENGTHENED AS HE IS HELPED TO HOLD HIS POST.

A basically insecure person who feels he is unable to hold his position in space is sufficiently strengthened by hatting to feel secure enough to do his job.

LAW: HAVING A HAT, BEING HATTED AND DEMONSTRATING COMPETENCE MAKES A PERSON FEEL CAPABLE OF HOLDING HIS POSITION IN SPACE AND HE BECOMES MORE STABLE, CONFIDENT IN LIFE AND MORE POWERFUL.

LAW: UNHATTED PERSONS ON A POST CAN BECOME CRIMINAL ON THE POST BECAUSE THEY FEEL INSECURE AND BECOME WEAK.

When a person is secretly afraid of others, he instinctively will not hat them or hats them wrongly and tends to transfer or move them about.

When a person is insecurely posted and insufficiently hatted, he can try to weaken others by trying to prevent their hatting and trying to get them transferred or even dismissed.

This is apparently the social aberration at work.

The answer to a sane org and a sane society is not welfare and removal. It is:

Recruit them,

Train them,

Hat them,

Apprentice them,

Give them a post.

This is so strong in truth it would de-aberrate the bulk of the crime out of a society.

And it sure will put an org in POWER.

L. RON HUBBARD
FOUNDER

83

HCO POLICY LETTER OF 11 AUGUST 1971
Issue II

Remimeo

Personnel Series 22
DON'T UNMOCK A WORKING INSTALLATION

The stable rule of a good HAS or HCO Cope Officer is NEVER UNMOCK A WORKING INSTALLATION.

It takes a lot of executive time and effort to build up a section or dept or division.

For someone to then come along and scramble it up with transfers is a criminal action.

If a unit, section, dept or division is operating well, *don't unmock it.*

Strengthen it. Hat it better. Put apprentices in it opposite to its posts to learn. Give it help.

But DON'T SCRAMBLE IT.

The work of years can be destroyed overnight by "urgent," "vital" personnel action.

Such crazy actions are only done by people too lazy to recruit and train new people or by unreal financial planning or a failure to get it to produce.

THE MAIN REASON WE HAVE EVER HAD SLUMPS HAS BEEN UNMOCKING ORGS OR UNITS.

Firing people, too heavy ethics, putting off people as "PTS" when all you needed was to pull their withholds, a thousand reasons can be given for unmocking an org or its parts.

They are all coverups for execs who won't keep the place busy and for HCO failures to recruit, train and hat.

To do so is a sign of insanity.

People like their jobs.

DON'T UNMOCK A WORKING INSTALLATION.

L. Ron Hubbard
FOUNDER

HCO POLICY LETTER OF 2 OCTOBER 1971

REMIMEO

PERSONNEL SERIES 23
HCO PUZZLES

There are some fundamental problems in HCOs that make puzzles.

NO STAFF

A. When an HCO is nonfunctional, *it* needs new people.

B. As it is not getting in any new staff, it of course cannot be restaffed or replaced.

These two circumstances (A and B) add up to a total impasse.

Until this impasse is broken the situation will remain impossible.

A way to break it is to take *any* existing staff, put a Dept 1 there and get people in.

If an HCO is so blocked, the normal staff losses will in time unmock the org.

BACKLOGS

When *any* part of an org — or HCO — backlogs in despatches, situations, pcs, the amount of dev-t which will *then* occur will make the place look frantic and busy but not one bit of production will actually occur.

All the effort is being spent fending off the traffic caused by the backlog itself!

An HCO for instance can furiously generate dev-t by calling everything it gets dev-t.

In this way it can spread chaos through the org.

"I want to report _____," "I'm sorry we're busy" will add up at last to nothing *but* dev-t in the whole org.

A hurricane of "activity" is visible because the area has not handled anything to begin with. These unhandled matters recoil on the area as new traffic.

Result, very busy but no production.

The answer is studiously handle or make the area handle everything that comes its way at once—backlogs get caught up. The area gets calm and production occurs.

BASIC ACTIONS

An HCO only begins to function when it has an up-to-date, *in use* org board and an up-to-date, in-use staff list.

If those two things aren't in, a puzzle results almost at every turn consisting of WHO and WHERE, and WHO isn't WHERE, and what's empty.

One org couldn't for the life of it figure out why it got no customers.

When a common paper org board (just paper with lines on it and written with a felt pen) was put up, it turned out that they had no Registrar! Fact. An HCO Expeditor was at the Registrar desk but "couldn't be hatted" "because he was an HCO Expeditor." He was not able to registrar because he "was not the Registrar." As soon as an org board went up, the post was seen to be empty.

OMITTED DATA

The reason HCO or other divisions in the org become puzzles which won't resolve is:

THE MOST COMMONLY OVERLOOKED WHY IS AN OMITTED DATA, TERMINAL OR ACTION.

Because it isn't there to *see* it did not get put down as an outpoint. One had to know the *scene* to be able to know it *should* be there.

Thus, lack of staff or lack of hats or lack of an apprentice for a key post is almost never noted.

AN ETHICS CYCLE

When HCO doesn't function or form or do its job, parts of the org begin to overload.

Duties don't get done by overload. Mistakes begin to be made because of duress.

Ethics moves in.

Almost all harsh ethics periods trace back to HCO failures to function in the first place.

The answer is to make HCO get ethics in on itself and do its job before it starts pounding heavy ethics into the rest of the org it overloaded or improperly manned to begin with.

The first target of Ethics must be any outness in HCO itself.

Dept 1's (Personnel) failures to act will inevitably get expressed as Dept 3 (Ethics) overreaction on the rest of the org.

———————

HCO must solve puzzles, not make them.

A smooth, producing HCO can and must exist in every org.

Some of the above tips can help bring it about.

L. RON HUBBARD
FOUNDER

HCO POLICY LETTER OF 22 JANUARY 1972
ISSUE II

REMIMEO
PERSONNEL
    PROGRAMER

PERSONNEL SERIES 24
PERSONNEL PROGRAMING

(Cancels and replaces HCO PL
20 Jan. 72 of the same title.)

A program can be defined as:

"A plan of study for an individual student over a given period."

"A plan of procedure; a schedule or system under which action may be taken toward a desired goal. The keynote is a sequence of actions."

"To work out a sequence of operations to be performed by a person or computer."

The root words associated are *programme* (French), "a public notice," and *prographein* (Greek), "to write before" (*Webster's 7th Collegiate Dictionary*).

A Personnel Programer works with individual staff members and draws up workable personnel programs and sees that they are fully executed.

The purpose of a Personnel Programer is to help LRH to expertly program each staff member to a point of real success on his own post so he can operate well as a member of the group and attain higher and higher levels of skill, knowledge and ability through full use of the technology of Scientology and Dianetics.

L. RON HUBBARD
FOUNDER

Assisted by
Qual Aide

HCO POLICY LETTER OF 12 MAY 1972R
REVISED 27 OCTOBER 1982

REMIMEO
INT FINANCE NETWORK
  FOR ENFORCEMENT

ETHICS

EXECUTIVE SERIES 13
PERSONNEL SERIES 25
FINANCE SERIES 12

PTS PERSONNEL AND FINANCE

PTS means Potential Trouble Source. This is a person who is connected to a suppressive person, group or thing. (For further data on PTSness see HCOB 24 Nov. 65, SEARCH AND DISCOVERY, and HCO PL 27 Oct. 64, POLICIES ON PHYSICAL HEALING, INSANITY AND SOURCES OF TROUBLE.)

NCG means No Case Gain despite good and sufficient auditing.

A chronically ill person, whether the person is known to be connected to a suppressive or not, is always found to have been so connected and PTS.

IT IS UNSHAKABLE POLICY HEREAFTER THAT NO PERSON WHO IS PTS OR CHRONICALLY ILL OR WHO GETS NO CASE GAIN MAY BE ON FINANCE OR REGISTRAR LINES OR IN TOP COMMAND POSTS OR AS HAS OR ETHICS OFFICER OR MAA.

TECHNICAL FACT

A person who is connected to a suppressive person, group or thing will dramatize a "can't-have" or an "enforced overt-have" on an org or staff members.

A "can't-have" means just that — a depriving of substance or action or things.

An "enforced overt-have" means forcing upon another a substance, action or thing not wanted or refused by the other.

The technical fact is that a PTS person got that way because the suppressive *was* suppressive by depriving the other or enforcing unwanted things upon the person.

The PTS person will dramatize this characteristic in reaction to the suppression.

Therefore, a PTS person as an ED, CO, product officer, org officer, Treasury Sec, Cashier or Body Reg will run a can't-have on the org and its staff by:

a. Refusing income,

b. Wasting income made,

c. Accepting wrong customers (like psychos) and forcing them on the org,

d. Fail to provide staff or service,

e. Advocate overt products.

HISTORICAL

When staffs went on proportionate pay in the late 1950s, so long as I ran the orgs directly the staffs made more money than before.

When I moved off these lines directly, the staffs began to receive less money personally.

At that time it seemed to me that proportionate pay served as an excuse to some in an org to run a can't-have on the staff.

We knew that some Registrars could take money in easily and others never seemed to be able to.

The technical reason for this has just emerged in another line of research entirely.

In completing materials and search on Expanded Dianetics, I was working on the mechanism of how a PTS person remained ill.

I found suppressives became so to the person by running a "can't-have" and "enforced overt-have." This pinned the PTS person to the suppressive.

Working further I found that a PTS person was a robot to the suppressive. (See HCOB 10 May 72, ROBOTISM)

This research was in the direction of making people well.

Suddenly it was apparent that a PTS person, as a robot to SPs, will run "can't-haves" and "enforced overt-haves" on others.

Checking rapidly, it was found that where finance lines were very sour a PTS person was on those lines.

RECOVERY

PTS tech, Objective Processes, PTS Rundowns, Money Processes and Expanded Dianetics will handle the condition.

However, one cannot be sure that it has been handled expertly in orgs where a money "can't-have" has been run as its tech quality will be low due to an already existing lack of finance.

Only stats would tell if the situation has been handled fully.

Thus the policy stands. Handled or not handled, no person who is PTS or who has no case gain will be permitted in top command or any lines that influence finance.

Any org which has consistently low income should be at once suspect of having PTS or NCG persons on the key finance posts, and an immediate action should be taken to discover the PTS or NCG condition and replace such persons with those who are not connected to suppressives or who do get case gain.

Nothing in this policy letter permits *any* PTS person to be in an org or cancels any policy with regard to PTS.

This policy letter *requires* direct check, close investigation and handling of PTS or SP situations on these posts that may go undetected otherwise.

NOTHING IN THIS POLICY LETTER PERMITS ANY KEY ORG POST TO REMAIN EMPTY.

NATIONAL

As a comment on something that may impinge on orgs and might affect them, the FOREMOST reason for a failing national prosperity and inflation is a personal income tax agency. This runs a vicious can't-have on every citizen and makes them PTS to the government. Individuals even begin to run a can't-have on themselves and do not produce. This IS the cause of a failing national economy. It can be a factor in an org and must be handled on the individuals so affected.

L. RON HUBBARD
FOUNDER

*Revision written
at the request of the
Church of Scientology
International*

HCO POLICY LETTER OF 23 JULY 1972RB
REVISED 11 JANUARY 1991

REMIMEO

EXECUTIVE SERIES 15
PERSONNEL SERIES 26
ORG SERIES 31
ESTABLISHMENT OFFICER SERIES 23

THE VITAL NECESSITY OF HATTING

On a graph analysis of past stats, my campaign on hatting where a hat was a checksheet and pack apparently introduced a steady rise of the International Gross Income.

Studying this further I discovered a new basic, simple fact:

HATTING = CONTROL

A person who is hatted can control his post.

If he can control his post he can hold his position in space — in short, his location. And this is power.

When a person is uncertain, he cannot control his post, he cannot control his position. He feels weak. He goes slow.

If he can control his post and its actions he feels confident. He can work effectively and rapidly.

The key is CONTROL.

Control is the ability to START, CHANGE and STOP.

When he is hatted he knows the tech of HANDLING things. Thus he can control them. He is at CAUSE over his area.

If you have an org composed only of weak wobbly posts, they tend to collapse in on each other. There is no POWER.

The org then cannot be CAUSE over its environment because it is composed of parts which are not cause. The whole is only the sum of its parts.

If all the parts are each one at cause, then the whole will be at CAUSE over its environment.

Only an org at CAUSE can reach and CONTROL.

Thus a fully hatted org can be at cause over its environment, can reach and control its fates and fortunes.

THUS THE PRIMARY TARGETS OF AN ESTO ARE:

A. ESTABLISHED ORG FORM and

B. FULLY HATTED PERSONNEL.

BASIC SEQUENCE OF HATTING

1. Recruited or hired. Signs contract.

2. Instant-hatted for the job assigned as an HCO Expeditor.

3. Staff Status 0.

4. Basic Study Manual (if the staff member has not previously done the Student Hat or Primary Rundown).

5. Staff Status I.

6. Staff Status II.

7. Posting as other than an HCO Expeditor.

8. Full hatting with a checksheet and pack fully done with M6, M7, M9, M3 and M4 Word Clearing.

9. Eligibility for study and auditing (OR for staff service or study).

10. Must have a stat and demonstrated he has produced on post.

11. Purification Rundown.

12. Objective Processes: CCHs, 8-C, SCS, Havingness, etc.

13. Scientology Drug Rundown (if required).

14. Method One Word Clearing, Student Hat.

15. Administrative or tech training (OEC or auditing).

Flag Orders in the Sea Org may change this lineup slightly but it is basically the same.

No one should have any other training, much less full-time training, before step 12 in the above.

After a staff member has completed Staff Status 0 he may receive PTS handlings and study the PTS checksheet and may have emergency assists. He may also be audited by students and TTC if he has rising stats.

There are time limits placed on how long it takes to do SS I and SS II. A person who can't make it is routed to Qual where he is offloaded with advice on how to get more employable. (In the SO it is Fitness Board.)

TIME–TESTED

The above is the route that has been tested by time and found good.

Other approaches have NOT worked.

Granting full-time training at once is folly. The person may get trained but he'll never be a staff member. This is the biggest failure with auditors—they don't know the org. Admin training with no org experience to relate it to is a waste of time.

This was how we built every great org. And when it dropped out the org became far less powerful.

Old-timers talk of these great orgs in their great days. And they will tell you all about the org boarding and hatting that went on. How the Hatting Officer in HCO and the Staff Training Officer in Qual worked as a team. And how fast the lines flew.

The above steps have stood the test of time and are proven by stats.

RECRUITING AND HIRING

You *never* recruit with a promise of free courses or free auditing. Not even HASes or HQSes. You recruit or hire somebody to be part of the team.

OPEN GATE

If *any* opinion or selection is permitted as to who is going to be let on staff, *all* recruitment and hiring will fail.

By actual stats when you let *anyone* say, "No! Not him! Not her!" the gate shuts, the flow stops. And you've had it.

Requirements and eligibility *fail*. The proof is that when they have existed in orgs, the org wound up with only PTSes and no-case-gains!

The right answer is FAST FLOW hiring. Then you have so many that those who can't make it drift low on the org board or off. You aren't trying to hold posts with unqualified people "who can't be spared."

In a short-staffed org "looking only for the best people" the guy nobody will have gets put in an empty "unimportant" department. He's now a Director!

It only happened because you didn't have dozens.

The answer is NOT lock the gate or have requirements. The answer is HAT.

An org that isn't hatted goes weak and criminal.

Don't be selective in hiring or recruiting. Open the gates and *HAT!*

Follow the steps given above and you have it.

Don't spend coins like training or auditing (or travel) on people until they have proven their worth. No bonuses or high pay for anyone until they have reached and attained step 10 (a good stat). The cost of such fast flow hiring is not then a big factor.

The only trouble I ever had with this was getting div heads to UTILIZE their staff. A FIRST JOB FOR AN EXECUTIVE IS TO GET THINGS FOR HIS PEOPLE TO DO. AND KEEP THEM BUSY AT PRODUCTIVE THINGS.

So I used to have to go through the org that did FAST FLOW HIRING regularly and get people to use their new people. And to move off those who could not work.

This was ALL the trouble I had with the system.

And until I enforced FAST FLOW HIRING there was always some effort by someone to close the gate.

ALL the great executives in Scientology came up in such orgs.

With a *flow* of people the best move on up. The worst, if any, drop off.

Only orgs with restricted hiring or recruiting give trouble.

IN A FAST FLOW HIRING ORG THE HAS AND ESTOs *MUST* BE ON THE BALL. THE BREAKDOWN OCCURS WHEN THEY DO NOT *HAT* AND KEEP ON TOP OF THE PERSONNEL SCENE.

Fast flow hiring only breaks down and gets protested where HCO and Estos are not doing a top job. They have to really *handle* the personnel, post them, hat them, keep the form of the org.

A fully formed org in a heavily populated location would need hundreds of staff. It would make hundreds of thousands.

But only if it is fast flow hiring, hatting, holding the form of the org, and only then could it produce.

L. RON HUBBARD
FOUNDER

Revision assisted by
LRH Technical Research
and Compilations

HCO POLICY LETTER OF 2 SEPTEMBER 1974RB
Revised 23 March 1989

Remimeo
Applies to
 Scn and SO Orgs

IMPORTANT

Personnel Series 27

RECRUITING AND HIRING

Refs:
Vol 1 OEC policies regarding personnel hiring and status
Flag Orders on Sea Org recruit training

ANY DIVISIONAL SECRETARY MAY RECRUIT OR HIRE STAFF FOR HIS OWN DIVISION.

The divisional secretary may use the staff in his own division.

Representatives of networks in an org or a continental office may also take advantage of this policy letter. Bureau heads of CLOs are included.

The org that hires or recruits staff may retain that staff.

It is only required that:

a. The person be placed on a routing form for new personnel in his org.

b. That any unusual pay arrangement or any pay arrangement be passed by FP and that the findings of FP are superior to or senior to any verbal or written promise to the person by the divisional secretary.

c. That HCO PL 4 Jan. 66RA V, PERSONNEL STAFF STATUS, is followed.

d. To become "Permanent" and be entitled to training or auditing and post protection a person must have signed a 2½-year contract and passed the Staff Status II checksheet. For full-time training, a 5-year contract must be signed in advance with the beginning date at the completion of his training.

SEA ORG

A. The person signs an SO contract.

B. At the end of 45 days he must pass a fitness board and have a recommendation by his divisional secretary.

C. He must attain the status of a Product 0 before he receives other training or auditing on a part-time basis.

D. He may not receive full-time auditor or admin training until he is a Product 2.

E. He may not hold any rating or rank other than "Swamper" until he is a Product 2.

If a divisional secretary does not have his staff on individual stats, if his staff is not busy actually producing viable products, he may lose such staff by transfer ordered by the HES or Supercargo:

i.   By published order.

ii. When the divisional stats are downtrending, Emergency or lower, for 3 consecutive weeks.

iii. When the divisional secretary has neglected the rules of this PL, such as not getting his staff to Provisional — Staff Status I or Product 0 in a reasonable time or not having them on individual stats or routing them for org boarding.

All these conditions (i) to (iii) must be present for a divisional secretary to have staff he recruits transferred out of his division.

In the case of an ORG, it may have staff transferred out of it only when it is in Emergency by trend of six weeks on paid completions or GI, when it is found to have falsified its stats, if it does not have an active Qual Cramming doing an honest job OR when its cash-bills tend toward insolvency.

Nothing in this PL restrains the ordering of a veteran to Flag as Flag furnished the veterans in the first place, but there must be adequate replacement.

No person recruited by a divisional secretary may be sent at org expense to a higher org for training or grades. But if trained, may replace a fully contracted staff member who has been reliably producing at the org to do so.

ANY DISPUTES ARISING BY REASON OF THIS PL ARE TO BE RESOLVED BY THE CONTINENTAL LRH COMM.

Nothing in this PL relieves the HAS or Flag Personnel Procurement Officers or any Recruiter of his duties or responsibility for recruiting.

L. RON HUBBARD
FOUNDER

Revision assisted by
LRH Technical Research
and Compilations

HUBBARD COMMUNICATIONS OFFICE
Saint Hill Manor, East Grinstead, Sussex

HCO POLICY LETTER OF 14 NOVEMBER 1976

Remimeo
Flag Bu
All Orgs
Ext HCO FB

Admin Know-How Series 36
Executive Series 18
Personnel Series 28
Org Series 36

MANNING UP AN ORG

THE SEQUENCE OF POSTING DEPTS AND DIVS

You need an org board first and an allocation board.

The sequence in which an org is manned up is roughly:

- Dept 1

- Dept 11

- Reg and Body Routers and Intro people in Div 6

- Dept 12 (enough auditors and C/Ses to approach 2 admin to 1 tech in org)

- Dept 6

- Dept 7

- Dept 3

- SSO and Supers in Qual to train staff

- Dept 5 for CF, Address and Letter Reges

- Dept 4 for promo

- Dept 21 (LRH Comm)

- Dept 10

- Dept 20

- FR and execs

- Full Div 6

- Full Div 1

- Full Div 4

- Full Div 2

- Full Div 5

- Full Div 7

- Full Div 3

(Note, an AO always mans up the AO Dept or Div along with the SH one in each case.)

Wrong sequence of manning is Dept 6, Dept 12, Dept 6, Dept 12, Dept 6, Dept 12, as you wind up with a stuck clinic that won't expand.

Wrong sequence will contract an org while trying to expand it, as the org will go out of balance, bad units, noisy and unproductive.

If manned in a correct sequence, its income has a chance to stay abreast of its new staff additions.

Emphasis on GI without comparable emphasis on delivery and organization can throw an org into such a spin only a genius can run it.

Manned in proper sequence, and hatted as it goes, an org almost runs itself.

Single handing from the top comes from long-standing failures to man or man in sequence, from earlier noncompliance with explicit orders or from not understanding orgs in the first place.

An unhappy org that doesn't produce has usually been manned only partially and out of sequence.

The trick is planned manning, ignoring the screams of those who know best or demand personnel; just manning by posting those who have been screamed for the loudest is a sure way to wind up with no people and total org problems instead of a total org that is prosperous and producing.

Incidentally, this is a rough approximation of the sequence of hats the ED gradually unloads as his org takes over.

L. RON HUBBARD
FOUNDER

HCO POLICY LETTER OF 6 JANUARY 1977

REMIMEO
HASES
LRH COMMS
DIRECTORS OF ROUTING
   & PERSONNEL
PPOS
PCOS
SSOS

PERSONNEL SERIES 28-1

INCOMPLETE COURSES CAUSED BY RIP–OFFS

Refs:

HCO PL	29 Aug. 70 I	Personnel Series 1 PERSONNEL TRANSFERS CAN DESTROY AN ORG
HCO PL	29 Aug. 70 II	Personnel Series 2 PERSONNEL PROGRAMING
HCO PL	19 Mar. 71 I	Personnel Series 20 PERSONNEL PREDICTION
HCO PL	11 Aug. 71 II	Personnel Series 22 DON'T UNMOCK A WORKING INSTALLATION
HCO PL	28 Mar. 71 II	PERSONNEL TROUBLES

IT IS A COMM EV OFFENSE TO TRANSFER ANYONE IN AN ORG WHEN THE RECRUITING AND HATTING STATS ARE NOT MORE THAN ADEQUATE FOR THE ORG, and

IT IS A COMM EV OFFENSE TO FAIL TO RECRUIT AND USE THIS AS AN EXCUSE FOR NO TRANSFERS.

In one org it was discovered that they lacked the necessary technical personnel to deliver all of the auditing rundowns available at their org even though teams of auditors had previously been trained on this tech. It was further discovered that the currently posted technical personnel had many incomplete courses, preventing their training on these rundowns and the full delivery of the tech to their public.

Further investigation revealed rampant musical chairs as having both unmocked previous working installations and prevented course completions with new courses begun each time a transfer occurred.

The solution, of course, lies in good application of HCO policy on recruitment in Division 1.

L. RON HUBBARD
FOUNDER

Compilation assisted by
LRH Technical Research
and Compilations

HUBBARD COMMUNICATIONS OFFICE
SAINT HILL MANOR, EAST GRINSTEAD, SUSSEX

HCO POLICY LETTER OF 29 NOVEMBER 1978

ADMIN KNOW-HOW SERIES 37
PERSONNEL SERIES 29

HOW YOU HANDLE DEMANDS FOR PERSONNEL

Refs:
HCO PL   15 Sept. 59 II   HATS AND OTHER FOLDERS
HCO PL   1 July 65 III   HATS, THE REASON FOR
HCO PL   22 Sept. 70   Personnel Series 9
                            Org Series 4
                            HATS

HCOs get continual demands for personnel from all areas of an org. To keep an HCO from going mad with all these demands, they must, on every request, (1) have the Dir of I&R do a full utilization survey on the division, dept or section requesting personnel and (2) do a full hat inspection on all personnel in that division, dept or section.

Only if these two steps are done for *each* personnel request will sanity reign in HCOs on the subject of personnel.

HCO PL 15 Sept. 59 II, HATS AND OTHER FOLDERS (Vol 0), HCO PL 1 July 65 III, HATS, THE REASON FOR (Vol 0) and HCO PL 22 Sept. 70, Personnel Series 9, Org Series 4, HATS (Vol 0) must be well known by all staff in Depts 1 and 3.

Personnel can recruit madly, answering every frantic demand for personnel, and yet HAVE THEM ALL WASTED for lack of full hats and full training on those hats.

The whole org can sag and even vanish under these conditions.

So Personnel has a vested interest in hats being complete and staff trained on them. For Personnel people cannot possibly cope with "no pay so can't hire anyone" and "no people so can't produce."

So for every demand for personnel, *ALWAYS* demand a utilization survey *AND* an inspection of hats in that area.

L. RON HUBBARD
FOUNDER

HCO POLICY LETTER OF 29 MARCH 1982

REMIMEO

PERSONNEL SERIES 30
ESTABLISHMENT OFFICER SERIES 43
PERSONNEL POLICY

We are building strongly for the future.

Scientology is going to go on for a VERY long time.

The way to build a strong future is to build a strong organization.

Internally, the only way we have been held back is by out-ethics and nonproduction. This does not build a strong organization or a strong future.

Therefore, we have no room on staffs for those who do not produce — or worse, are extravagant and produce overt products — or (which goes with poor production) are out-ethics.

We need productive people who keep their ethics in.

Individuals, and above all execs, are the building blocks of organizations.

To build strongly for the future, keep the above points in mind where appointing, promoting or handling personnel.

Personnel of that caliber belong outside orgs — they are the pcs and cases. Do not recruit them, appoint them or leave them on post when found.

One can mend people. But one cannot build a new world with broken straws.

It takes the ethical few to handle the many. And these are what our orgs must be built with now. The strong within only then can handle the weak outside.

Make it easy in the future for all of us. We have a long way to go. The speed we get there is measured by the ethical quality of persons on exec posts and on staffs. It is fine to be big brother to all the world — so long as we keep our staffs the top people. Be them.

L. RON HUBBARD
FOUNDER

HCO POLICY LETTER OF 20 AUGUST 1982R

Issue II

Revised 15 December 2000

Remimeo

Personnel Series 31

MOONRIPPING

Ref: HCO PL 6 Oct. 70 II   Personnel Series 10
"MOONLIGHTING"

"Moonripping" is a contraction formed from the words "moonlight" (the act of working on a job outside an org) and "rip-off" (the act or action of stealing or cheating; exploiting or taking advantage of another or others, especially financially).

In HCO PL 6 Oct. 70 II, "MOONLIGHTING," the last sentence is the operative line, "There is no policy against MOONLIGHTING where it does not injure the org." However, it is another matter where there is active depression of org stats so that staffs have to moonlight for the fellow who is depressing the org stats. Persons depressing org stats to enrich themselves personally by employing staff or promoting moonlighting for self-enrichment are of course committing a suppressive act.

The following are some of the varieties of moonripping:

1. Using the org as an employment agency and hiring people into the org and getting them somewhat trained and processed to use them in an outside business.

2. Holding an executive position on staff so that one can run a business that employs staff.

3. Arranging staff schedules so they can work in the private business.

4. Making people replace themselves in a private business (before going on staff in an org).

5. Concentrating on the outside job to a point where they do not look to the org for support and so don't care at all what happens to it.

6. Using the org and its connections but actually working in a mission and shunting org public to it.

The dividing line is where moonlighting is done in any way to damage or erode org income or staff involvement in their own post.

For instance, an evaluation was done on an org that persisted in staying small. Now most orgs that stay small do so because they neglect to apply policy, but this was a different case: The org in question was kept poor so that the staff would have to moonlight in a business run by a leading executive of that org for his own personal profit. By overtly and knowingly preventing the org from making money (cutative, giveaway prices, refusing to sign up pcs, etc.) the amount available for salaries in the org was kept very low. As their "best friend" this executive then "let them" work in his own company, which he ran on the side and from which he was getting quite well-to-do.

There was another version of this: A nearby business "befriended staff" by getting them to moonlight to the exclusion of their org duties and of course the org made no money. But the staff reasoned that they could not live on their pay while not realizing that their moonlighting was cutting their own pay. They didn't make much working for their "friend" either.

Another version of this was found: The staff auditing which the org owed to their staff was cut off and they were told they had to moonlight and make enough money to personally pay two auditors very high fees to audit them after org hours.

In all these cases the org was being used as a sort of employment agency for the personal profit of someone inside or outside the org.

The crime in these cases amounted to a SUPPRESSIVE ACT.

Anybody having any information leading to the use of org staff as an employment agency, convincing staff the org can't make money, persuading the staff to moonlight, using staff to further their own business, and so forth, must report the matter outside the org to the Inspector General Network.

L. RON HUBBARD
FOUNDER

Revision assisted by
LRH Technical Research
and Compilations

HCO POLICY LETTER OF 19 DECEMBER 1982
ISSUE I

ALL ORGS
ALL EXECS
ALL STAFF
ALL DIV HEADS
LRH COMMS
HCO
DEPT 1 HATS
DEPT 3 HATS

PERSONNEL SERIES 32
ORG SERIES 44

"DOING A QUICKSILVER" FORBIDDEN

Refs:

HCO PL	19 Mar. 71 I	Personnel Series 20 PERSONNEL PREDICTION
HCO PL	24 June 70 II	PERSONNEL POOLS
HCO PL	7 Jan. 66 I	LEAVING POST, WRITING YOUR HAT
HCO PL	20 Apr. 69 II	HATS, NOT WEARING
HCO PL	20 Aug. 71 III	MUSICAL CHAIRS
HCO PL	11 Aug. 71 II	Personnel Series 22 DON'T UNMOCK A WORKING INSTALLATION
HCO PL	7 Mar. 65 III	OFFENSES AND PENALTIES
HCO PL	13 July 74 II	Org Series 34 WORKING INSTALLATIONS

There is a condition that can exist in orgs which differs slightly from "musical chairs" (the rapid transfer of personnel from post to post) but is akin to that and every bit as deadly.

We could call it a "quicksilver personnel" scene.

("Quicksilver" is another name for mercury, the silvery-white metallic element, liquid at room temperature, which is used in thermometers, barometers and similar instruments.)

Used figuratively, the term "quicksilver" means something that is quick-moving, unpredictable and as elusive as mercury, or "mercurial." Something that is mercurial is changeable, variable, volatile.

To anyone who has ever observed a drop of quicksilver, or mercury, in an open container or placed on a slab of glass, this will be real. One second it's here, the next second it's there. Just about all you have to do is breathe on it and it changes its position. And where it *was* a second ago there's now nothing.

It is miserable (if not impossible) for an executive or management body trying to run things with staff doing a quicksilver. One can hit up against some nasty surprises.

For example, an org's personnel scene may look great on the board, with posts filled, hats existing and known, production occurring and on the rise — all is looking good when suddenly the stats crash.

An initial check may show there haven't honestly been any post transfers, per se. But dig a bit further and you're likely to find a quicksilver personnel scene. The top delivery auditor is off on a two-week vacation. The Qual Sec has been fired on a recruitment tour. The Reg has gone out-ethics and been suspended, unreplaced, pending some ethics handling. The Chief Officer is off on maternity leave and the CO, holding her post from above, is being the guest speaker at an event in the next city.

It happens and it happens not only in Class IV orgs but in the higher service orgs and management units where tours are essential and missions need to be fired and other situations can crop up requiring personnel.

It has shown up drastically at times in several large orgs. In one, the head of a vital network went off on mission and, with no one left being the senior, the stats in the area crashed. In another, the sales manager took his leave, his routine functions were ignored and sales suffered severely. And in still another org, no less than *six* key delivery terminals were all found to be out on regging tours in one week, some of them over a period of several weeks, at a time when delivery of paid-in-full services was backlogged!

None of these terminals had been removed or transferred or promoted. And one could say the actions being done are all covered in some way in policy, are needed, and therefore justified. But these terminals were all off post unreplaced, weren't they?

That's a quicksilver personnel scene. It's unstable.

CONTRIBUTING FACTORS

Executives who issue orders that unmock working installations where production is occurring at "A" to get something done at "X" bring about such scenes.

Personnel who, like quicksilver, accommodatingly move off their assigned posts unreplaced to do something else at the first invitation or order, help to generate and sustain such scenes.

Seniors who permit or condone this are also a party to them.

Personnel can do a quicksilver for any of a number of reasons. For some, the chance to go off and see other people and new places may be an alluring prospect. Some are too timid to refuse a destructive order and so they comply, under protest. For others there is financial gain involved — there are often commissions or a bonus at stake.

Tours have been used by some, apparently condoned by executives, to take longer leaves (more time off on leave per year) by combining 4 to 6 or even 8 weeks of a "regging tour" with a "leave," with the org paying both the person's fare and living expenses and no clear distinction made between the period of "tour" and the period of the "leave." (While this is part of an unstable personnel scene, it is also a situation requiring a separate ethics handling in itself.)

Sometimes a staff member is made to feel, by a very convincing exec, that the action which calls for his suddenly going off post with no or inadequate replacement is actually more important than his job. Where this threatens production and there is no adequate replacement, this is almost always a falsehood.

It is true that missions need to be fired. Tours are vital to income and delivery. Staff sometimes do need to go off post temporarily for handling of one type or another. Events are valuable in terms of promotion, goodwill, PR and sign-ups, and for certain types of these, key personnel or trained tech delivery personnel may be required. Emergencies do arise. Personnel are entitled to annual leave. And speed of operations is important.

On the plus side, we do have capable and versatile staff who are willing to extend themselves, when needed, to make things go right. We have demanding, fire-breathing executives who are out to handle situations and open up new fields for delivery which, in itself, is a good thing. And many of these go about it standardly.

But the senior or exec at any level who endangers ongoing delivery and production and/or unstabilizes a producing personnel scene to get these things done is simply advertising to one and all that he can't predict and plan and organize or get others to do so. Control is lacking here as well as just plain common sense. The kindest thing one could say about such an exec is that he is shortsighted. And "quicksilver" is a rather mild term for the staff member who steps so easily off his post and leaves a hole in the lineup with no thought of the consequences.

One could say that everyone has personnel problems. BUT that is no Why.

HANDLING "QUICKSILVER PERSONNEL" SCENES

The first policies *missing in application* are those covering replacements and hat turnovers.

BECAUSE IT IS A *"TEMPORARY"* ABSENCE, NO ONE IS DEMANDING REPLACEMENT AND TURNING THE HAT OVER TO SOMEONE WHO CAN COVER THE POST *COMPETENTLY*.

But policies exist in abundance on this subject. HCO PL 29 Aug. 70 I, Personnel Series 1, PERSONNEL TRANSFERS CAN DESTROY AN ORG, points up the outnesses which can destroy an org faster than any others. HCO PL 7 Jan. 66 I, LEAVING POST, WRITING YOUR HAT, covers the staff member's responsibility for a post he is vacating under *any* circumstances. HCO PL 20 Apr. 69 II, HATS, NOT WEARING, emphasizes the staff member's responsibility for knowing that he *is* the Qual Sec, or Reg, or the post title for the post and functions he has accepted. HCO PL 11 Aug. 71 II, Personnel Series 22, DON'T UNMOCK A WORKING INSTALLATION, cites the main reason we have ever had slumps in orgs.

The personnel policies are there. But very often, where a "quicksilver personnel" scene is permitted, BECAUSE SOMEONE PULLS OFF A SUCCESS IN ONE AREA, EVEN THOUGH STATS IN HIS OWN AREA MAY CRASH, THE EXISTING ETHICS

POLICIES THAT COVER SUCH A CRASH OR THE COLLAPSE OF AN AREA MAY BE OVERLOOKED OR DELIBERATELY IGNORED.

So how do we handle "quicksilver personnel" scenes?

The answer is to add some teeth to the existing policies:

1. AN ABSENCE FROM POST FOR EVEN A TEMPORARY PERIOD OF AS LITTLE AS HALF A WEEK IS AN ETHICS OFFENSE, UNLESS SOMEONE IS NAMED AND THERE AS A REPLACEMENT WHO HAS HAD THE POST PROPERLY TURNED OVER TO HIM AND WHO CAN COVER THE POST *COMPETENTLY*.

2. IF SUCH ABSENCE WITHOUT COMPETENT REPLACEMENT OCCURS *AT ALL*, AN IMMEDIATE COURT OF ETHICS MUST BE CALLED ON THE STAFF MEMBER WHO LEAVES HIS POST UNFILLED OR INADEQUATELY COVERED, AS WELL AS ON THE SENIOR OR EXECUTIVE ORDERING, CONDONING OR PERMITTING IT.

3. IF IT OCCURS AND RESULTS IN STATS CRASHING IN A COURSE, A DIVISION, DEPARTMENT, SECTION, UNIT, AREA, ZONE OR ORG, A COMMITTEE OF EVIDENCE MUST BE CALLED WITH *ALL* INVOLVED NAMED AS INTERESTED PARTIES.

The charges are:

CONDONING OR CONTRIBUTING TO CIRCUMSTANCES OR OFFENSES CAPABLE OF BRINGING A COURSE, SECTION, UNIT, DEPARTMENT, ORG, ZONE OR DIVISION TO A STATE OF COLLAPSE

and

NEGLECT OF RESPONSIBILITIES RESULTING IN A CATASTROPHE EVEN WHEN ANOTHER MANAGES TO AVERT THE FINAL CONSEQUENCES.

––––––––––

With this policy made known and enforced, there *is* a cure for those who do a "quicksilver" and for executives and seniors whose out-planning and out-prediction bring about quicksilver personnel scenes.

L. RON HUBBARD
FOUNDER

HCO POLICY LETTER OF 28 MARCH 1984
ISSUE II

REMIMEO
EXECS
HCO
QUAL

EXECUTIVE SERIES 28
PERSONNEL SERIES 33

EXECUTIVE POSTING QUALIFICATIONS

Scientology organizations and their staffs in the past have been subjected to considerable financial losses by appointing to executive positions persons of poor ethics and production records. Therefore this firm policy regarding new appointments to and promotions within Scientology organizations and activities is set and is not to be departed from. Omission of one or more of these in the past has factually cost millions of dollars.

It is expressly forbidden hereafter to propose or post any person to any executive post (Departmental Director or above) without the following:

1. Actual production stats of the proposed person relating to the subject of the post he is being proposed for be found, established and verified.

2. That investigation reveals an acceptable ethics record.

3. Before being posted the person must be checked for any PTSness and any found must be handled.

4. The person must be rolled back for any participation in any black PR activity.

5. The person must be sec checked for false considerations or evil purposes.

6. The person must be false data stripped in relation to the activity he has been or is about to be engaged upon in the organization.

7. In keeping with the policy that any person posted in an executive position in a Scientology organization must be able to achieve, maintain and increase a high level of production and income in his area, the stats found and verified must prove extreme productiveness on the part of the proposed person in the area of the post he is being proposed for. This applies to any executive post. (With the technology and administrative know-how available in Scientology, any exec should, through production and exchange of high quality products, be capable of generating on the order of a million dollars a year for his organization.)

The above requirements are quite in addition to requisite executive status and training certificates held by the person and/or required for the post for which he is being considered. (Ref: HCO PL 29 Dec. 82R II, Rev. 30 July 83, THE TOOLS OF MANAGEMENT)

APPLICATION FOR ACTING STATUS

Before a candidate for an executive posting may assume more than Temporary status, a full CSW covering points 1–7 above and prepared by the Personnel Control Officer must be approved on established executive posting approval lines. The Estab Exec International is responsible for issuing directives setting these approval lines, and for updating them as needed.

Approval lines set up are to include approval of all exec postings by an authorized representative of the Office of Senior C/S Int and an authorized representative of the Inspector General Network.

On receipt of written approval, the candidate is granted "Acting _____" status, and a personnel order to this effect can be issued.

Executive posting CSWs may NOT be allowed to staledate at any point on the approval line.

Establishment and maintenance of approval lines is the responsibility of the Senior HAS International.

REQUIREMENTS FOR PERMANENT STATUS

The following additional requirements are established for *permanent* posting at the level of Departmental Director or above:

8. No person may be permanently posted in a Scientology organization without a thorough apprenticeship under competent supervision before any turnover or permanent posting can occur.

9. No full posting in a Scientology organization can occur until the actual stats of the person achieved during that apprenticeship period have been found to be correct and excellent.

10. No person so assigned as an apprentice on a post may draw a bonus until he is fully Post Purpose Cleared, TIPed, his TIP complete, and he is fully hatted.

APPLICATION FOR PERMANENT STATUS

Once the (Acting) exec has successfully fulfilled the requirements listed in points 8, 9 and 10 above, application is made for Permanent posting. This application follows the same routing as for Acting status. The application consists of a new CSW, with verified evidence of requirements 8–10 above having been met.

Upon receipt of written confirmation of the posting from the Inspector General Network, a personnel order may be issued appointing the executive permanently to that post.

NETWORKS

This policy applies fully to the posting of executives in any of the various management networks, including FBOs, D/FBOs for MORE, Flag Reps, LRH Comms and any other networks.

L. RON HUBBARD
FOUNDER

HCO POLICY LETTER OF 21 AUGUST 2000

REMIMEO
ORG OFFICER HAT
HCO HATS
EXEC HATS
FEBC CHECKSHEET

PERSONNEL SERIES 34
RAPID POSTING

(Originally written by LRH on 5 Jan. 71.)

Refs:

HCO PL	24 Apr. 72 I	Esto Series 16
		HATTING THE PRODUCT OFFICER
		OF THE DIVISION
HCO PL	31 Oct. 71	FULL HATTING

The speed with which a person can be placed on a post and hatted is consistently underestimated.

An organizing officer who cannot transfer, post and hat a staff member in an hour is little help. The idea that it takes months is an org stopper.

I speak from years of experience. That it would take three days to procure a personnel and several weeks to hat one assaults my reality. People are not that unwilling.

L. RON HUBBARD
FOUNDER

THE

ORG

SERIES

HCO POLICY LETTER OF 13 SEPTEMBER 1970
ISSUE II

REMIMEO
EXEC DIR HAT
HES HAT
HAS HAT

ORG SERIES 1
BASIC ORGANIZATION

What is organization?

Most people have so many associated ideas with the word "organization" that they think of one as an identity or a being, not as a dynamic activity.

Let's see what one really is.

Let us take a pile of red, white and blue beads. Let's organize them.

Now let us draw the org board.

Let us dump them all on top of in-charge, all mixed up in a confusion.

Obviously in-charge must *route* them to dig himself out. So we get:

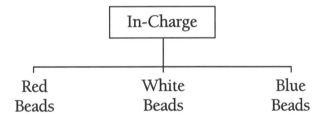

Thus we find out much of what an in-charge does. He routes. He separates into types or classes of thing or action.

This so far is a motionless org.

We have to have products. Let's say its products are drilled beads, strung beads, boxed beads.

We would get:

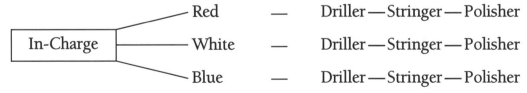

Or we would get:

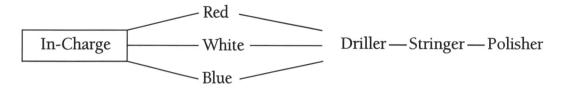

Or we would get:

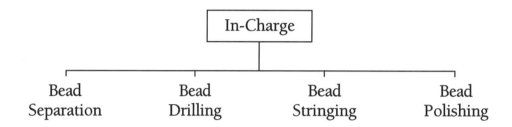

It is not particularly important which pattern of org board we use so long as it handles the volume of beads.

If we only have one person in this "org," he would still have to have some idea of organization and a sort of org board.

If we have any volume to handle we have to add people. If we add them without an org board we will also add confusion. The organization without an org board will break down by overload and cross-flows and currents. These in conflict become confusion.

All a confusion is, is unpatterned flow. The particles collide, bounce off each other and stay IN the area. Thus there is no product as to have a *product* something must flow OUT.

We can now note two things. We have some stable items. These are posts or locations. And we have flow items. These are things undergoing change.

So an org's positions change flowing particles.

Particles flow *in sequence.*

Things enter an org, get changed, flow out of an org.

An org with one type of item only (red beads) is less complex than one with several types of items.

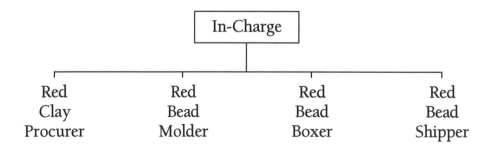

Any activity has a *sequence* of actions. It has to have stable points which do *not* flow in order to handle things which do flow.

It is not necessary to have a stable terminal do only one thing. But if so then it also has a correct sequence of actions.

All this is true of an engine room or a lawyer's office or any organization.

In an engine room fuel flows in and is changed to motion which flows out. Somebody runs the machines. Somebody repairs the machines. It may all be done by one person but as soon as volume goes up one has to plan out the actions, classify them and put them on an org board which the people there know and abide by or the place will not operate well.

This is done by dividing operation and repair into two actions, making two activities on the same org board.

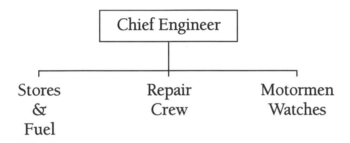

The Chief keeps the flows going and the terminals performing their actions.

In a lawyer's office we get different actions as a flow.

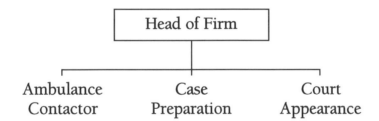

would be a flow pattern, possibly with a different person (with a different skill) on each point.

Or we could have a sort of motionless org board.

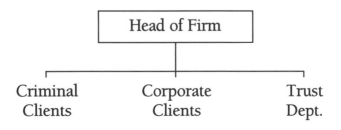

But if we did that we would have to put the motion in vertically so that flow would occur.

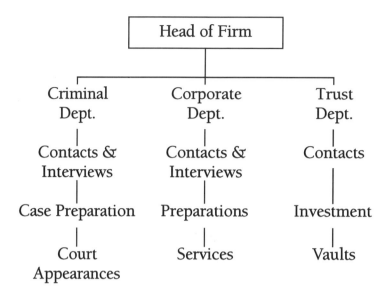

Org boards which only give terminals usually will not flow.

A typical army org board of yesteryear was:

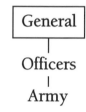

When they got into a lot more men they had to have a *flow* board.

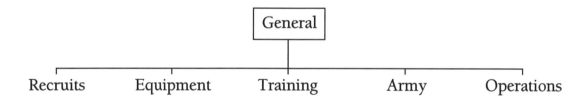

So one *organizes* by:

1. Surveying the types of particles.

2. Working out the changes desired for each to make a product.

3. Posting the terminals who will do the changing along the sequence of changes.

The board also must include a *recognition* of the types in (1) which *routes* the types to the *terminals* who *change* them and to a further *routing out* as *products*.

To be practical an org board must also provide for pulling in the materials, disposing of the product and being paid for the cycle of action and its supervision.

A company has various actions.

It is essentially a collection of small org boards combined to operate together as a large org board.

The basic principles you have to know to organize anything are contained in this policy letter.

To plan out *any* action one has to be able to visualize its sequence of flows and the changes that occur at each point. One has to be able to see where a particle (paper, body, money) comes in and where it leaves.

One has to be able to spot any point it will halt and mend that part of the flow or handle it.

A proper org board is a perpetual combination of flows which do not collide with one another and which do enter and do experience the desired change and which do leave as a product.

L. RON HUBBARD
FOUNDER

HCO POLICY LETTER OF 14 SEPTEMBER 1970
ISSUE I

REMIMEO
EXEC DIR HAT
HES HAT
HAS HAT
EXECUTIVE HAT

ORG SERIES 2

COPE AND ORGANIZE

It's perfectly all right to cope. One always must.

But one MUST organize things while he copes.

The mounting overload and overwhelm in an area comes entirely from cope-cope-cope without organizing also.

Example: You have to handle something for which there is no planned organization. Like a mob at a congress. You *can* cope. But if you don't take the first available instant to grab three guys and give them specific duties right then to mind doors and tickets, it all just gets worse and worse and the cope catches up as overwhelm.

Any old org bd is better than no org bd at all.

A good org bd well grooved in, duties well apportioned, permits things to smooth out and increase in volume without strain.

In a flood if you can channel the water you can handle the flood. If you just batter at water you drown.

ORGANIZATIONAL GENIUS IS COMPOSED ONLY OF ARRANGING SEQUENCES OF ACTION AND DESIGNATING CHANNELS FOR TYPES OF PARTICLES. THAT'S ALL IT IS.

Then you can handle flows and prevent stops.

So you must always organize as you cope.

National riots are just the inability of leaders to arrange sequences of action and designate channels for types of particles.

One area which was never organized became just an anthill of do-less useless motion.

If your in-basket is too high you cope and handle it AND ORGANIZE YOUR LINES for the future.

"I'm absolutely drowning . . ." is the same as saying "I can't organize worth a damn!"

ORG BD

Every exec has his own personal org bd. Really it's at least 21 depts.

But you don't have to go that fancy.

I had an org bd once that was 8 folders, each representing traffic from a major org, reports placed in it latest on top, a communicator who did the placing, a greeter who handled bodies and an inspector that was me. Just myself and one other. But it was an org. With that "org bd" I handled all the Scientology in the world at that time, lectured, researched and had ample time left over. It reduced full-time cope to a part-time job. Later 100 staff members (WW) replaced me as Exec Dir and I moved off post. They were all very busy but they didn't even know they had an org bd they were on, no individual operated his own personal org bd. Their cope and ignorance took the stats right on down. But they sure were busy coping!

The antithesis (opposite) of an org bd is confusion. The amount of confusion present doesn't add up to production, even though it is totally exhausting. The end product one wants is not exhaustion. The amount of energy expended does not measure production. Production is solely the amount of completed cycles that occur. The more they are planned in sequence and the better the different types are channeled the more production will occur.

So cope by all means but don't forget to organize a little each time you get a chance.

The end product of cope is drown.

The end product of organize is freedom.

L. RON HUBBARD
FOUNDER

HCO POLICY LETTER OF 21 SEPTEMBER 1970

REMIMEO

ORG SERIES 2-1
COPE

(Originally written by LRH for the *Apollo* OODs of
21 Sept. 70. Issued as an HCO PL on 12 Oct. 80.)

I've had an insight into what "cope" really is. It is the process of finding and correcting outpoints without ever discovering a WHY and without organizing any return to the ideal scene.

A coper goes "outpoint found—correct it; outpoint found—correct it; outpoint found—correct it." This perpetual cycle never finds or corrects WHY these outpoints. So it just gets worse and worse and worse.

If all one ever did was handle despatches one would really get into a mountain of overwork while stats stayed down.

The WHY we face now is absence of recruiting, lack of full hats with checksheets and packs.

The Why of that was failure to make the materials filed accessible and collatable. So it's a snake eats its tail. No hats then brought a condition of no data available in files. A true dwindling spiral.

And no hats traces to the introduction of ethics into HCOs and that it is easier to assign a condition than to compile or check out a hat. Hats went out when ethics came strongly in. Without ethics in HCO, HCO can only make stats recover by org form and hats.

Ethics has a role—after all else fails.

L. RON HUBBARD
FOUNDER

HCO POLICY LETTER OF 14 SEPTEMBER 1970
ISSUE II

REMIMEO
EXEC DIR HAT
HES HAT
HAS HAT

URGENT

ORG SERIES 3

HOW TO ORGANIZE AN ORG

Let us assume that you have an org to run (or any part thereof).

How would you organize it and get it to function?

1. You would count up and name the different vital actions necessary to functioning.

2. You would count up the persons needed for each function and give them the post names.

3. You would do a checksheet for each post to include its vital data.

4. You would collect the material of each checksheet into a pack.

5. You would recruit the minimal number to begin it, keeping in mind finance and solving that.

6. You would show one of them how to check the others out to get them trained.

7. You would then get the org running.

8. You would expand it by single hatting vital posts.

9. All the while you would cope with things as they came up.

10. You would add to checksheets and packs things learned while operating.

11. You would add posts as they were found needful.

12. You would never drop out the actions of recruiting, checksheets, packs and training.

Naturally the org would have to have a function that was valuable and would have to execute it or produce and be paid or it would not be viable (able to live).

All right. All that seems straightforward enough.

Now let's see how it could go wrong.

Foremost would be a failure to function or produce and a failure to get paid for it. This would cripple the activity and bring in inadequate operating funds, curtailing facilities and pay and making it undermanned, hurting its image and shutting off recruitment.

Recruiting to fill a new function could be incorrectly (destructively) done by using the production area as the recruitment pool. Also each time a portion was operating well, it could be used as a recruitment pool and emptied out and unmocked. This would destroy all training effort and injure the viability and reverse organization back to cope.

Or no recruitment could be done at all.

There could be no checksheets or packs.

There could be no training done even when checksheets and packs existed.

The checksheets or packs could be too short or unreal for the post. Or they could be too long or relate to another post.

The head of the org could fail to check out the heads of portions.

The heads of portions could fail to get their juniors hatted and checked out.

The org staff could be unaware of their belonging to the org and be unaware of its purpose and general products.

The problems as listed above could remain obscured and ethics could be substituted as an effort to get up production.

There are ten basic points that could go out. These are (1) recruiting (2) training (3) training on post (4) utilization (5) production of product (6) promotion of product (7) sale of product (8) finance (9) justice (10) morale.

It is assumed that the activity is worthwhile and the potential production valuable. Given that, the remaining ten points are the points where organization breaks down as these areas are the most aberrated in the society.

The fundamental outnesses, however, would be failure to recruit, to have checksheets and packs for each post, get training done on them and have new people on post serve on it in-training.

Let us suppose the head of an org or division never checked any junior out on anything.

Looking at standard functions, everyone would be posting and routing people except Dept 1, intended for that. Everyone would be handling comm except Dept 2, intended for that. Everyone would be inspecting and handling stats except Dept 3. And so on down the line. The place would be a dog's breakfast of total cope.

All right, let us say one *does* have a dog's breakfast instead of an org. How would one straighten it out?

One would cope to maintain some semblance of viability.

One would throw together an org board and post it and drill people on it.

One would throw together hats and get them worn.

One would continue to cope but now also force others to help the coping and cope themselves as semispecialists on their own posts.

Finally one would get checksheets and packs together for each post covering all its actions.

One would then get these checksheets and their packs trained in for each post fully.

Thereafter one would insist that executives made sure their juniors had checksheets and packs as their hats.

And one would continue to recruit as by this time the org would be expanding and it would become upset by undermanning and go downhill again.

One would watch the ten aberrated points as they go out very easily.

———————

People gather up all sorts of weird solutions to running a disorganized org. "We need more experienced people"; "We can't produce so should be subsidized," are two common ones.

———————

When people on post do NOT have grooved in hats they do goofy things. The goofiness is not confined just to their job functions. Lacking a purpose and not conceiving the org purpose they can go utterly astray and do things that are quite mad. Like tearing things up. Like breaking things. Like getting involved in goofy relationships.

You can detect an org where posts are not grooved in by the number of oddball things happening.

The way to put *this* sort of situation right is to start organizing as given in this rundown.

Working on organization as you cope, it will eventually make it come out right.

When it sags just come back to this rundown and it will all straighten out again.

L. RON HUBBARD
FOUNDER

———————

HCO POLICY LETTER OF 22 SEPTEMBER 1970

REMIMEO
EXEC HATS
PERSONNEL HATS
ETHICS HATS

AN URGENT IMPORTANT AND STAR–RATE PL

PERSONNEL SERIES 9
ORG SERIES 4

HATS

HAT — A term used to describe the write-ups, checksheets and packs that outline the purposes, know-how and duties of a post. It exists in folders and packs and is trained in on the person on the post.

HAT TECHNOLOGY

"Hats" developed in 1950 for use in Dianetic orgs as a special technology. The term and idea of "a hat" comes from conductors or locomotive engineers, etc., each of whom wears a distinctive and different type of headgear. A "hat" therefore designates particular status and duties in an organization.

A "hat" is a specialty. It handles or controls certain particles in various actions and receives, changes and routes them.

A "hat" designates what terminal in the organization is represented and what the terminal handles and what flows the terminal directs.

Every hat has a product.

The product can be represented as a statistic.

Any job or position in the world *could* have its own hat. The reason things do not run well in a life, an org, a group, nation or the world is an absence of hats.

The reason why an org runs well when it does is hats.

Any protest of anyone against things not running right can be traced to lack of hats.

Any slump an org goes through can be traced directly and at once to an absence of one or more hats being worn.

HAT CONTENT

A hat must contain:

A. A *purpose* of the post.

B. Its relative position on the org bd.

C. A write-up of the post (done usually by people who have held it before relief and when so done it has no further authority than advice).

D. A checksheet of all the policy letters, bulletins, advices, manuals, books and drills applicable to the post. (As in a course checksheet.)

E. A full pack of the written materials or tapes of the checksheet plus any manuals of equipment or books.

F. A copy of the org bd of the portion of the org to which the post belongs.

G. A flow chart showing what particles are received by the post and what changes the post is expected to make in them and to where the post routes them.

H. The product of the post.

I. The statistic of the post, the statistic of the section, the statistic of the department and division to which the post belongs.

STAFF HAT

There is also a general staff hat.

This hat contains:

a. The overall purpose of the org, its aims, goals and products.

b. The privileges or rewards of a staff member such as auditing, training on post, general training availability, pay, vacations or leave, etc.

c. The penalties involved in nonproduction or abuse of post privileges or misuse of the post contracts.

d. The public relations responsibilities of a staff member.

e. The interpersonal relations amongst staff members including courtesy, cleanliness, attitudes to seniors and juniors, office etiquette, etc.

f. The MEST of posts generally, its papers, despatches, files, equipment.

g. The comm and transport system of the org.

GRADIENT SCALE OF HATS

A "gradient scale" means "a gradual increasing degree of something." A non-gradient scale would be telling someone to enter a skyscraper by a 32nd-story window.

Thus there is a gradient scale of organizing.

A key to this is found in the *Problems of Work*'s theory of confusion and the stable datum.

One in actual practice has to cope while organizing.

COPE means to handle whatever comes up. In the dictionary it means "to deal successfully with a difficult situation." We use it to mean "to handle any old way whatever comes up, to handle it successfully and somehow."

IF YOU *REMAIN* IN COPE, THE DEMAND TO COPE INCREASES.

In that you have the key to "exhausted executives" or staff members. You have why the president of the US ages about 20 years in one term of office as you can see by comparing dated photographs of past presidents. He is totally on cope. His government has an org board that looks like a pile of jackstraws. He has no hat. His staff have no hats. His government departments have no hat. The technologies of economics, law, business, politics, welfare, warfare, diplomacy have been neglected or lost (they *do* exist to some extent).

The guy is on total cope. And the post has been on total cope since it was created as an afterthought by the Constitutional Congress that began the post in the eighteenth century. Even what it says in US civics textbooks is not found in practice.

So "difficult situations" are the order of the day and are handled by special actions and appointments.

The people who *should* handle them haven't got real hats.

This is all catching up with the country at this writing to such a degree that the citizen cannot benefit from a stable society or social order. The country looks more like a war of insurgency.

In other words departures from hats has led into total cope and it is steadily worsening.

Any organization put in by one political party is knocked out by the next incumbent, and who could totally organize a country in 4 years? (The term of a president.)

Yet it is hanging together some way and some way meeting increasing demands and pressures.

I have stated this in a large example so that it can be seen in a smaller unit.

To handle this one would first have to want to straighten it out and then assemble the tech of admin to straighten it out. And then one would have to begin on a gradient scale of org bd and hats.

A cope sort of hat would be tossed-off orders to some other people on staff who have some title of some sort.

Along with this would be a posted org bd that has little to do with duties actually performed and used by a staff that doesn't know what it is.

One begins to move out of cope (as given in other series) by putting an org board together that labels posts and duties and getting people on them to handle the types of particles (bodies, mailings) of the org.

The next action would be brief write-ups of the posts and their duties and checking people out on them.

Actually if you only got to the middle of the last paragraph with an org the executives would remain in cope. So much know-how would be missing in the org's staff that every rough bit would shoot up to the executive for special handling. And that is *cope*.

Hats only in this far is not good enough as it still takes a genius to run the place.

The next gradient scale is to get the hat to contain:

i.   The post write-up itself,

ii. The theory and practical necessary to run it.

This is done by a preparation of checksheets of data and a pack matching it for key posts.

Naturally the org bd now has to become more real and staff has to be checked out on it.

Then hats as post checksheets and packs are extended to the rest of the staff.

The mechanisms of training have to exist by this time.

Seniors have to be made responsible that every junior below them has a hat consisting of write-up, checksheet and pack.

Meanwhile one continues to cope.

Gradually, gradually staff begin to know (through checkouts) their hats.

New staff coming on are grooved in better.

Cope begins to diminish and the organization tends to smooth out.

Here and there competent handlings begin to show up brightly.

Now we find a new situation. With everyone throwing together checksheets and packs for staffs we find nonstandard checksheets. Some messenger has to do the full checksheet of the HCO Division pages and pages long. The HCO Sec has a checksheet with just 10 items on it.

So a central authority has to standardize post checksheets and survey and put in overlooked bits of data.

But that is way up the line. The org long since has become smooth and prosperous.

So that is the gradient scale of getting in hats.

EXPERTS

Here and there you find an area of special expertise in an org where the expertise is so expert in itself that it obscures the fact that the person does not also have a full post hat.

A lawyer would be a case in point. It takes so long to learn law in some law school that an org executive can overlook the fact that the *post* hat is missing. Org policy on legal matters and staff hat remain unknown to this legal post AND JAM IT UTTERLY. This came to light when a whole series of cases was being neglected because the legal staff member, an excellent lawyer, did not know how to make out a purchase order or that one could or should. Investigation found *no* post or staff hat. Only a legal degree.

Orgs continually do this with auditors. They are technical experts in *auditing*. So they get assigned to posts in the HGC WITH NO HAT. Backlogs occur, things goof up. Tech fails. All because it is overlooked that they are PART OF AN ORG and need staff and post hats and need to be trained on them.

Worse than that, a highly classed auditor is often put on an admin post without hat or training for it.

You would not take an admin trained person and without further training tell him to audit. So why take an auditor and tell him to handle an admin division?

Without his post write-up, checksheet and pack FOR THE POST and without training on it, the person just isn't qualified for it no matter what *other* line he is expert in.

It is great to have an expert who has been specially trained in some profession. But lawyer, engineer or public relations, he must have his hat for the *org* post and be trained on it or he will goof! Yet one won't suspect why that area is goofing because "he's a Class VI isn't he?"

UTILIZATION

Personnel can recruit madly, answering every frantic demand for personnel and yet HAVE THEM ALL WASTED for lack of full hats and full training on those hats.

An investigation of blows (desertions) from orgs shows that lack of a grooved-in hat was at the bottom of it.

People come on a job. It is at once a great mystery or an assumption of total know — one or the other.

Either one continued leads them into a state of liability to the org.

People who don't know what they are doing and people who don't but think they do are both NONUTILIZED PERSONNEL.

Pay and prosperity for the rest of the staff will go down unless this is remedied.

The whole org can sag and even vanish under these conditions.

So Personnel has a vested interest in hats being complete and staff trained on them. For Personnel people cannot possibly cope with "no pay so can't hire anyone" and "no people so can't produce."

The answer is H-A-T-S.

And a hat is a write-up, a checksheet and a pack.

And the staff member trained on them.

ETHICS

When a person has no hat he lacks purpose and value.

When he has no purpose and value he not only goofs, he will commit crimes.

It is apparently easier to hit with ethics than to program and give someone a full hat and get him trained on it.

Police action is not a substitute for having purpose and value.

This is so fundamental that one can even trace the unrest of a nation to lack of purpose and value. A huge welfare program guarantees crime and revolt because it gives handouts, not hats.

Even a field Scientologist should have a hat.

By doing only this over the world we would own the planet as in an expanding population individual purpose and value are the most vital and wanted commodities.

If there are no real hats there will soon be no money of any value and no bread!

SUMMARY

ANY HAT IS BETTER THAN NO HAT according to the way a thetan seems to think.

But be that as it may, the downfall of any org can be traced directly and instantly to no recruiting or no org board, no hats or unreal hats or no training on hats.

The sag of an org can be traced directly to lack of hats and lack of training on hats.

The overload of any post can be traced directly to lack of an org bd and lack of hats and no training on hats.

The way out is to organize the org board and hats while you cope.

If you do not, your cope will become an overwhelm. If you do, your burden will lighten and your prosperity increase.

It took 13 months of hard work and 20 years of org experience to learn that given a product lack of HATS was *the* WHY of departures from the ideal scene and that working toward providing full complete HATS was the way to get back toward the ideal scene.

L. RON HUBBARD
FOUNDER

HCO POLICY LETTER OF 26 SEPTEMBER 1970

REMIMEO
EXECUTIVE HATS

ORG SERIES 5
ORG BOARD CUTATIVES

The most serious blunder in *re*-doing org boards is losing past functions off them.

"Cutative" is an invented word to mean the impulse to shorten or leave out or the thing left out.

THE RULE IS: ANY MAJOR FUNCTION, ACTION OR POST LEFT OFF AN ORG BOARD WILL WRAP ITSELF AROUND THE IN–CHARGE LIKE A HIDDEN MENACE.

As the function is not *expressed* it is not recognized. But it forces itself upward and can swamp an activity if not done.

Thus we get the laws:

1. Activity functions must all be expressed on the org board.

2. All functions below a personnel on an org bd are the responsibility of that personnel, no matter what size the staff may be.

3. Functions omitted will act as invisible overloads.

EVOLUTION OF ORG BDs

Usually the first org board ever done for an activity is a dream-up. It is seldom real but better than no org bd at all.

Experience then refines it.

Some functions on it are not related to it, are unreal.

Some functions not on it rise up to haunt and overload the in-charge.

Actions done by an executive that are not on the org board in departments get posted like small flags opposite the executive's name. (Like legal, VIP greeting, etc.)

After a while these little flags are too many.

A reorganization occurs and the flags are put down into departmental functions. This gets them off the executive's neck and gets them manned up.

So far so good. Now what happens is a catastrophe. A new executive who has no experience with this org bd DREAMS UP A NEW ONE. This is out of sequence in evolution. He is treating the place as though it had NO org bd simply because he doesn't know the existing board.

This gives us the *cutative*. He drops functions off the board. These now wrap around his neck. The place stalls.

YOU HAVE TO KEEP EVERYTHING ON THE ORG BD THAT WAS EVER ON THE ORG BD EVEN IF IT WAS 3,000 YEARS.

SALVAGE

It often occurs that one has to do a full, complete salvage of an org bd.

There is absolutely no reason except the org bd writer's laziness not to put everything on an org bd!

There is a rule about posting an org bd. You don't post a name for every post. That is folly. You post by workload.

All the functions below a person are handled by that person. If they are too much you put in a new name and person on a heavy load function.

So why do a cutative? It means no more people. It just means more space and tape. What's saved but elbow grease? What's lost? The whole org can be lost and become nonviable.

Example: SH original board had ten major divisions on it. They were just functions really. They were the ten sources of income *before* SH trained or processed anyone. Some years ago I tore the place apart looking for that old org bd. It was evidently thrown away. Today SH does not have but *one* of those income functions! Nine have been lost! It added training and processing, it lost nine functions capable of supporting it. They should be looked up in the 1959–1960 accounts records, the old invoices analyzed and gotten back and put on the WW org bd and manned. This is regardless of what is already on the org bd.

Other functions lost off that and the SH org bds should be posted back on them and at least held from above or double- or triple-hatted.

Example: DC which had the original six-dept org bd should recover those posts and put them on the nine-div org bd so early policy would make sense.

Example: London should recover its earliest org bds and put their posts and functions on its current org bd.

There comes a time when early org bds have to be salvaged and reposted on existing org bds.

BECAUSE THOSE FUNCTIONS ARE STILL THERE AND MOST OF THEM GONE INVISIBLE.

Example: A Division 2 org bd asked to be redone threw away 50 percent of its functions and posts, was dreamed up brand-new off a division already caved in by loss of performance. The excuse was "other activities now do these." Published, this org bd would have driven its executive mad with omitted duties that would come to him as invisible overloads.

The "We don't do that now" is like what once happened to tech. One could say, "Maybe you think you don't do it now but the function is still there hidden. It was found once. Now you've lost it again."

OLD EMPIRES

The Egyptian, Greek and Roman Empires still try to operate! I've checked it. The late British Empire may be gone on the British org bd but it will still function without expression until it kicks England's head in. The British public shovels money out by the scoopful to an empire that doesn't exist!

Trying to kill an org takes years and years and years and it still tries to survive.

When one takes responsibility for a function or area it still tends to persist.

It is an odd phenomenon. The third dynamic track is that way. Changes later on the track (short of auditing individuals) do not change earlier circumstances.

A thetan's intentions get very pale perhaps but a thetan never really gives up.

All this expresses itself on the subject of org bds.

One can also willfully disregard an existing board, dream up a new board that does not express the functions and get into real trouble.

A NEW LOOK

Examining this subject of org bds in the light of very current experience with asking people to redo them, these facts have emerged.

It gives us a new look.

The next full Scn org bd issue you see will have on it all functions of which we have any trace *and* the nine-division board we are using.

The new board will have nine divisions. It will also include all past titles and functions in addition to all current titles and functions with the past titles in parentheses.

Many org bds of other activities have never become expressed at all and have left a tangled history. The US still hangs flags around the Office of the President and one hears "The Executive Branch is usurping the power of Congress." Congress once had all those functions but didn't put them on its org bd. They still do them but lost the titles to the president. Thus an appointee despotism rises in place of a democracy. It all goes back to a lost congressional org bd.

It is necessary for a people or a staff to:

a. Have an org bd,

b. Know the org bd,

c. Have the org bd express the total functions and duties that have ever been held by any post even including the flags of yesteryear duly dated.

Don't cut functions off an org bd. If they have become known they have been found. Why lose them?

One can rearrange flow patterns.

One cannot abandon living functions on an org bd.

It's only the unknowns on an org bd that get anyone overloaded, confused or in trouble.

So why not keep it visible?

L. RON HUBBARD
FOUNDER

HCO POLICY LETTER OF 27 SEPTEMBER 1970

REMIMEO
CASHIERS
DIV 3S
PUB DIV HATS
DIV 2 HATS
FSMS
MISSIONS

ORG SERIES 6
CUTATIVE PRICES

HCO PL of 27 Apr. 65 II, PRICE ENGRAM, is fully valid and must be followed. It explains why price cuts damage orgs.

Price cuts are forbidden under any guise.

1. PROCESSING MAY NEVER BE GIVEN AWAY BY AN ORG.

   Processing is too expensive to deliver.

2. BOOKS MAY NEVER BE GIVEN AWAY BY AN ORG OR BY PUBS ORG.

   They are too expensive to manufacture.

3. FSM COMMISSIONS MAY NEVER BE PAID ON DISCOUNTED OR CUT–RATE ITEMS.

   If an FSM can't sell for full value he does not rate any commission.

4. SCHOLARSHIPS FOR COURSES ARE LIMITED TO INTERNSHIPS, HSDC AND ACADEMY LEVELS.

5. COURSE SCHOLARSHIPS ONLY MAY BE OFFERED FSM ON CONTEST AWARDS.

6. SCHOLARSHIPS ARE ONLY AVAILABLE TO WORKING FSMs OF PROVEN SELECTEE SUCCESSES.

7. ALL SCHOLARSHIPS AND AWARDS OUTSTANDING TERMINATE IF NOT TAKEN BEFORE 1 JANUARY 1971.

8. FSM COMMISSIONS ARE PAID ONLY ON THE ARRIVAL OF A STUDENT OR PC, NOT ON RECEIPT OF THE FEE.

   Advance payments are sometimes refunded.

9. ONLY FULLY CONTRACTED STAFF IS AWARDED FREE SERVICE, AND THIS IS DONE BY INVOICE AND LEGAL NOTE WHICH BECOMES DUE AND PAYABLE IF THE CONTRACT IS BROKEN.

10. FSM BONUS AWARDS TO ORGS MAY ONLY BE DELIVERED TO CONTRACTED STAFF MEMBERS OF THAT ORG.

L. RON HUBBARD
FOUNDER

HCO POLICY LETTER OF 1 OCTOBER 1970

REMIMEO
HC CHECKSHEET

ORG SERIES 7

HATS AND COUNTER–EFFORT

When you are trying to get somebody to do something he should do, you are in effect trying to get him to wear his hat.

In trying to get things done, you often feel you are running into "counter-effort" (contrary action or effort to your action or effort).

The most usual counter-effort is NOT willfulness or mutiny or out-ethics. Most people consider these are the reasons they get opposition to worthwhile actions.

The most usual counter-effort is *lack of a hat,* defining a hat as a write-up, checksheet and pack on which the person is trained.

It looks like willful stupidity, waywardness, laziness, mutiny, antagonism or what have you and can amount to any or all of these.

Whatever the reason for it may be, it must include lack of a hat.

The variations are enormous, almost infinite.

Example: Mr. A is trying to get Mrs. A to be a good wife. Mrs. A is in outright mutiny. Now, it could be that Mr. A does not have or know his husband hat or Mrs. A has no wife hat or the neighbors or friends don't have neighbor or friend hats or Mr. B has no social hat and is trying to estrange Mrs. A or he has no husband's hat of his own; but whatever it is, it is a matter of hats. SOMEBODY (or all of them) in this is not wearing their hat.

I had someone in marital trouble look at me thoughtfully once and say, "I don't have *any* idea what *are* the rights or duties OF a wife."

Example: A Course Supervisor having trouble getting a student to study. He pleaded and argued and wore himself out.

He never realized this student DID NOT HAVE A STUDENT HAT. He could have saved all his energy spent in arguing and applied it to making up a student hat and getting *it* assembled and studied and would have gotten somewhere.

ORG BD

So we draw up an org board for an activity for several people.

It is all correct as to function and flows.

We put the names of the several people on it where they seem to be fitted.

The activity doesn't go.

So we explain and drill the org board on the people.

It comes up to a flubby sort of cope.

The missing point now is HATS. Each one has to have and know his own hat and something about the hats of others.

Things will promptly get much better! The activity and the interpersonal relations and the lives of these people are greatly improved.

Personally they are running into much less cross-flow and confusion. So they have a happier time, less effort and more production.

A badly organized, badly hatted, badly trained group is at each other's throats continually. To get anything done at all they have to operate at the level of correction instead of production.

Any ripple of emergency in such a group operates as a major impact.

PROGRAMS

There is still a missing element when one has org boarded and hatted and specialist trained an activity. This is PROGRAMS.

The sequence of flows and the changes or actions at each point plotted against time are in fact the major sequences and programs of a group.

MANAGEMENT SUCCESS

Given a desired product a fully successful management can only be founded on the actions inherent in:

1. A good org board,

2. Hats as write-ups, checksheets and packs,

3. Hats trained in,

4. Sequences and programs known and followed.

IT IS FAR, FAR EASIER TO WORK ON AND ACCOMPLISH THOSE FOUR THINGS THAN IT IS TO COPE AGAINST THE COUNTER–EFFORT GENERATED WITHOUT THEM.

Naturally, while getting this done, anyone has to cope to keep things going.

SINGLE-HANDING

"Single-handing" means to handle things by yourself.

You can single-hand when you are all alone or you can single-hand in a large group that is supposed to be working or helping.

When only one man, senior or junior, is doing all the controlling and work of an activity, he is said to be "single-handing."

The term derives from the sea (like so many English words). Single means "one only" and "hand" means a sailor. "Hand*ing*" is the verb form of "single-hand."

No other activity expresses so well the idea of "one man working" or "one man controlling."

It is of course derogatory to others who are around and not working.

The phenomenon comes about by having non-org boarded, unhatted and untrained people.

Now the oddity of it is that it can occur (a) when there are other people who are also supposed to be working, (b) when there is an org board, (c) when there are hats and (d) when programs exist.

This of course looks like "bad morale," "apathy," even "mutiny."

The missing elements usually are:

a. The other people don't know the purpose of the activity or what's really going on.

b. The org bd is unknown to them even when it exists.

c. The hats are not checksheets and packs and have not been trained in.

d. The sequences or programs that should occur are not drilled in and if they were the no-hat situation would wreck them.

The point is even more amazing when a group with a purpose and an excellent potential product WILL BE POOR AND WILL FAIL if org bd, hats and sequences and programs are not fully known and drilled.

Groups are like that.

This is why man and his activities succeed only in the presence of huge affluences or extraordinary personal leadership.

Lacking org bds, hats, training, programs *that he knows and can do,* man flounders.

UNHATTED LEADERS

Leaders who are not org boarded, hatted and trained and programed can make a fantastic mess out of a formerly well-organized group.

It takes some doing. But no one can knock the known org board apart faster than a senior. No one can knock off hats easier than someone in authority who does not himself know they exist.

Nero and his ilk destroyed the whole Roman Empire. That civilization was about as well org boarded and hatted as any civilization on the planet in recent millennia. Nero thought he was a lute player and composer and charioteer. These were the only hats he ever wore aside from that of murderer.

A few emperors like him and that was that.

The Christians had an org board, member hats and staff hats, post hats of a sort and constant training. And that was the end of the Roman Empire and the beginning of the *Holy* Roman Empire.

Way up in Pope Alexander the Sixth's time (the days of Lucrezia Borgia) when bishoprics were for sale and the member hats were forgotten, the Holy Roman Empire failed.

So there is plenty of history and example, even though the full tech was not even developed. You can see the dim counterparts of org boards and hats weaving their way through all man's yesterdays.

The history of the world is not written by wars and violence. It is written against an unseen background of beneficial products, org board, hats and programs.

The fantastic administrative skill of Arthur Wellesley (the Duke of Wellington) and the rigid org bd of Nicholas of Russia defeated Napoleon whose only skills were military genius and personal leadership and luck.

So when the head of something does not know about org bds and hats and programs, he can single-hand things perhaps into temporary power but will wear himself out with cope and soon decline.

One can't just run things. One has to put something there and the something is a desirable product and org bd, hats and programs and see they are grooved in properly.

And looking over history the most valuable product of an executive is holding the form of his org and providing his staff members with hats and programs well grooved in.

It takes so much more time and effort to build up an org in terms of org bd and hats and get it to hold its form that one might not at once see its benefit. Trying to get a result without also building an organization inevitably winds up in single-handing, coping, overwhelm and eventual defeat.

The *right* answer is single-hand while you train up your people.

For one will wind up single-handing any post he has not org boarded and hatted and programed.

And that is true of even a junior member of a staff. If HE doesn't hammer away to get in org bds and hats and sequences and programs, HE will wind up single-handing all his section — while they stand around making life miserable with inefficiency, goofs and flubs and obvious counter-effort.

It isn't labor against management or the people against government. One or the other or both aren't on org bds and aren't wearing their hats.

And in an interdependent society or a complex activity the final result of no org bd, no hats, no programs known is chaos. And very unpleasant chaos as well.

L. RON HUBBARD
FOUNDER

HCO POLICY LETTER OF 8 OCTOBER 1970

Remimeo
Executives

Org Series 8

ORGANIZING AND PRODUCT

Disorganization gives a poor product.

Organization (providing tech exists to make the product) will produce a good product.

If a product is poor or spotty one must:

a. Organize

b. Make the tech available and known.

You can literally have mobs of people working and excellent production tech and get a horrible product.

The missing ingredient is organization.

Organization consists of a real and functional org board, hats consisting of checksheets, packs and manuals and training of this material.

The most used org board is the "hey you! org board." In other words just tag anyone to do anything.

This guarantees bad production and a lousy product.

One can have an org board that isn't real and get a "hey you! org board."

Or one can have a good org board that isn't known and get a "hey you! org board" in actual practice.

A whole org can be org boarded and hatted and trained and yet shatter when an untrained senior turns it into a "hey you! org board." This is easily the commonest cause of org collapse.

LOSING AN ORG BOARD

When an org board leaves out known vital functions these tend to wrap around the neck of the in-charge as unknown items of irritation.

The commonest fault in re-drawing an org board is throwing the old one away and without looking at or getting a full inspection of the actual functions being done, dreaming up a brand-new board. This produces a delusory situation. It is in fact a disassociation of the real work and the org board delusion.

MINIMUM FUNCTION

A post tends to dwindle down to the "irreducible minimum function."

A mail clerk will distribute mail as that is visible to others. Logging it is less visible. Properly sorting it is less visible.

If "receiving, logging, sorting and distributing" are left off the org board and "mail distribution" is all that is left on it, the other functions tend to vanish and the post slides to "irreducible minimum" of just grabbing and slinging out mail.

A galley org board can be deficient and carry only "food," or "cook," you'll get "food" and that's all. It will possibly be very lousy food as the org board is down to an irreducible minimum. Says "food" so they just sling out food any old way of any old kind. Bad product. The answer is to organize it. What *are* the steps in sequence that it takes to get good food served and the place cleaned up? If they are *all* on the org board as functions you have the SEQUENCE of actions expressed as functions which can be posted and delegated as duties.

OUT SEQUENCE and OMITTED HATS are the commonest fault in programs and org boards. (See Data Series.)

One person may have 35 separate hats.

If so, he needs 35 hat folders, checksheets and packs and 35 baskets or compartments for the flows.

Further, the hats must be in sequence of flow where they relate to one type of particle.

Thirty-five hats is large but many an executive unknowingly wears more. And the ones he doesn't see are his areas of upset.

The smaller the number of people in an activity, the more hats each has.

One girl holding down seven branches of an office finally got untangled just by having seven baskets, one for each branch, and working a stated time on each one each day. She sorted the inflow into the baskets by branches and then did them in rotation. That made an org board of baskets. She suddenly got production where she had had just despair and chaos.

SUMMARY

To improve an existing product, ORGANIZE.

L. RON HUBBARD
FOUNDER

HCO POLICY LETTER OF 28 OCTOBER 1970

REMIMEO

ORG SERIES 9

ORGANIZING AND HATS

"Org bd" is actually an abbreviation not for an organization (noun) board but an organiz*ing* (verb) board.

The org bd shows the pattern of organizing to obtain a product.

A board then is a flow chart of consecutive *products* brought about by terminals in series.

We see these terminals as "posts" or positions.

Each one of these is a hat.

There is a flow along these hats.

The result of the whole board is a product.

The product of each hat on the board adds up to the total product.

WORKING IT OUT

When asked to work out an org bd (or when the board there is doesn't work) one might think the task very difficult.

In studying this subject so as to be able to communicate it, I made several small breakthroughs in the subject itself.

Several questions on this can be very easily answered now.

Does an org bd have any value?

Yes. Without an org bd there is no group product, there is only a mob.

Yes. When there is no org bd there is much greater effort involved in getting anything done.

Yes. The waste of people involved in no org bd and the loss of product justify any amount of effort to work out, make known and use a proper org bd.

Man instinctively uses an org bd and protests the lack of one. The rawest recruit walking aboard a ship assumes the existence of an org bd, if not a posted one, at least a known one. He assumes there will be somebody in charge and that different activities will be under different people. When there is no known org bd he protests. He also feels insecure as he doesn't know where he fits into this organization.

Almost all revolts are manned by people who have been excluded out and are not on the country's org bd. This is so true that the ridiculous circumstance recently occurred in the US. The president found he had "professional relief receivers." Certain people had assumed the status of "government dependent" and were giving this as their profession. It was of course a post of sorts. And because it wasn't admitted as a post by the government there were some riots.

The effort to belong or to be part of is expressed by an org bd. A person with no post is quite miserable. A person with an unreal post feels like a fraud or a mistake.

Morale then is also considerably affected by the quality of an org bd or its absence.

The overall test for the group, however, is its viability. Viability depends on having an acceptable product. Groups which do not have an acceptable product are not likely to survive.

The volume and acceptability of a product depends in no small measure on a workable known org bd. This is true even of an individual product.

An individual or small group, to get anywhere at all, requires a very exact org bd. The oddity is that the smaller the group the more vital the org bd. Yet individuals and small groups are the least likely to have one. Large groups disintegrate in the absence of an org bd and go nonviable in the presence of a poor one.

The quality of a product, usually blamed on individual skill only, depends to an enormous extent upon the org board. For example, one disorganized mob that was trying to make a certain product was worked to death, harassed, angry at one another and had a wholly unacceptable product at about twice the usual cost; when organized to the degree of a third, still without proper schedules, still largely untrained, they began to turn out an acceptable product at about half the effort—so even *some* organization worked.

The product volume and quality depends utterly and totally upon the org board and hats and their use. You can train individuals endlessly but unless they are operating on a workable org bd they will still have a poor or small volume product.

The traditional reliance of British intelligence on star agents instead of organization cost them (along with misused PR) their empire.

Lack of a known and real org bd can spell failure. And lack of knowledge of the *subject* of organization has to be substituted for by pure genius at every point.

Thus to make anything at all, to improve any product, sustain morale and distribute work equitably and make it count, one has to have a real and a known org bd.

So how do you make one?

HATS

An org bd is made up of hats.

The definition of a hat is the "beingness and doingness that attains a product."

Let us take a train:

The engineer wearing his engineer hat has the title of engineer. That's the beingness.

He accepts orders, watches signals and general conditions, operates levers and valves to regulate the operation of his engine and to start, change and stop. That's the doingness.

He safely and on schedule moves the train passengers and/or freight from one location to another. A moved train and load is the product.

So how do we find out there is a hat called engineer?

As people are continually accepting or viewing already existing posts, when you ask them to dream up an org bd they at first may not realize that you are asking them to *invent* the correct posts.

They don't have to invent "engineer." Everybody knows "an engineer runs a train."

So if you didn't know this? You'd have to figure it out.

One would do it this way. One would have to think along these lines:

The idea comes about because of a concept that people and goods have to be moved over distances on land. Or that a new area building up has to have transport of people and goods from and to it.

Ah. This will be viable in an economic framework because people will pay to be moved and pay for their goods to be moved.

Trains do this.

So let's use trains.

Arranging finance (or by prepayment) and obtaining a franchise for a right of way, track is laid, rolling stock and stations and roundhouses are built.

Now it emerges that somebody has to drive the train. So somebody had better be hired to drive the train.

So there comes into view the *post* of engineer.

How do we know this? Because we have to have a *product* of moved people and goods. That was what we were trying to do in the first place.

Therefore, the engineer hat.

So supposing now we did not have any org bd at all.

The engineer hat would be the only hat. So he collects fares, runs stations, fixes his engine, buys fuel, loads the cars, sells stock . . .

Wait a minute. If the engineer did all that the following would happen:

1. He would be exhausted.

2. His temper would be bad.

3. He would have machinery breakdowns.

4. He might have wrecks.

5. The railroad property otherwise unhandled would disintegrate.

6. He would have a low volume of product.

7. His product would be uneven and bad as he could maintain no schedule.

8. There would shortly be no railroad.

Now let's go wog and "solve" this.

Let's appoint a person for each station and say "There we are!"

Well, it would still be a mess.

So let's hire more engineers and more station agents and more engineers and more station agents . . . and wind up with a confused mess, a huge payroll and a lousy product. That's how governments do it. And it is notable that current governments have no product but disaster.

No, we have to solve this in quite another way.

We do not get anywhere and we will not get a sensible org bd and nothing will work or be viable unless WE COUNT THE PRODUCTS CORRECTLY AND DEVELOP HATS TO ATTAIN THEM.

When we have done this we can arrange the hats on an org bd so there is a *flow* and command channels and communication channels and we've got an org bd.

You cannot work out an org bd until you have counted products!

As volume increases you estimate the products before the final product and hat those.

Quality of final product depends on a real org bd and hats, both complete, real and trained in and the functions DONE.

Let us see now how you break down a *final* product into the products which, put together, comprise it.

We have the final product of a railroad — viably moved loads. How many lesser products go into the big product?

There is a matter of machinery here. Any machine has *two* products: (a) the machine itself in good operating condition, (b) the product of the machine. A repairman and machine shop man and a roundhouse keeper each has a product under (a). That is just for the machine, the engine.

Under (b) we have what the machine itself produces (hauled trains in the case of an engine).

Here we have then two major products—and these break down into lesser products, earlier in sequence to the final product.

There is even an earlier product to these—bought engines. And an earlier product to that—finance for equipment.

As for the load itself, a delivered load, accepted by a consignee at the end, as you back up the sequence you will find a product—stored freight. And before that—unloaded freight. And before that—moved freight. And before that—loaded freight. And before that—freight assembled for shipment. And before that—freight contracts procured. And before that—advertising placed in public view. And before that—surveys of public freight requirement. And before that—survey for activities requiring freight service.

Each one of these products is a hat.

Surveying this again we see there's no charges or money involved so no economic viability. Thus we have a product, money made. This has earlier hats of course. The bewilderment of some people (and a lot of executives) who gape at a no-dough situation is laughable. They aren't product-minded. They think money falls into a company's lap or out of a TV set. They can't think the product sequence necessary to obtain money. So they go broke and starve. There are always a lot of prior products to the product MONEY. Fixated people just fixate on money itself, have no product sequence and so go broke or are poor.

Someone has to have a desirable product that is sold for more than it cost to produce and has to sell it and deliver it to have money. Money even makes money. And even a pool of money has to have a product sequence or it vanishes.

Even in socialism or communism the how does it support itself question must be understood, answered, its product sequence identified, org boarded and hatted. In such a moneyless society the org boarding has to be much tighter as money adds flexibility and lack of it as a working factor makes problems that are hard to solve.

ORGANIZING

In order to organize something one only has to:

1. Establish what is the final product.

2. Work backwards in sequence to establish the earlier products necessary to make each next product and which all in a row add up to the final product.

3. Post it in terms of vertical greater and greater completeness of product to get command channels.

4. Adjust it for flows.

5. Assign its comm sequence.

6. Work out the doing resulting in each product. Write these as functions and actions with all skills included.

7. Name these as posts.

8. Post it.

9. Drill it to get it known.

10. Assemble and issue the hats.

11. Get these known.

12. Get the functions done so that the products occur.

This is what is called "organizing."

As a comment, because railroads *didn't* fully organize, their viability decayed and they ceased to be so used.

Railroads think it's the government or airplane rivalry or many other things. It isn't. They had too many missing hats, were actually too disorganized to keep pace with the society's demands, ceased to fully deliver and declined. In fact there has never been a greater need of railroads than today. Yet, disorganized, badly org boarded and hatted, they do not furnish the service they should and so are opposed, government regulated, union hammered and caved in.

To have a quality product, organize!

To raise morale, organize!

To survive, organize!

L. RON HUBBARD
FOUNDER

HCO POLICY LETTER OF 29 OCTOBER 1970
ISSUE I

REMIMEO
EXEC HATS

ORG SERIES 10

THE ANALYSIS OF ORGANIZATION BY PRODUCT

The different products involved in production are:

1. Establishing something that produces. (Product 1)

2. Operating that which produces in order to obtain a product. (Product 2)

3. Repairing or correcting that which produces. (Product 3)

4. Repairing or correcting that which is produced. (Product 4)

Example: A typewriter is manufactured and located on a desk. This is establishing something that produces as in (1). A typist operates or runs the typewriter which thus produces typed sheets, stencils, etc., which are the product produced. This satisfies (2) above. The typewriter from various causes eventually requires repair in order to continue to produce. This satisfies (3). The correction of things typed would satisfy (4).

These are the four basic PRODUCTS involved in production.

Thus there are really four basic products necessary to a production activity. These are:

1. The established machine

2. The machine's product

3. The corrected machine

4. The corrected product

That makes a minimum of four products for any production cycle.

Three major factors govern every product. These are:

A. Quantity

B. Quality

C. Viability

Quantity would be an acceptable, expected or useful volume.

Quality would be the degree of perfection of a product.

Viability would be the longevity, usefulness and desirability of the product.

As *each* product in the four listed above has *three* factors in each product, there are then twelve major points (4 x 3) regulating production.

Product 1 — Establishing the typewriter, contains:

i.   The quantity of typewriters established

ii.   The quality of the typewriters established

iii. The viability of the typewriters established

Product 2 — The product of the typewriter (typed things) also has three:

iv.   The quantity of the typed things

v.   The quality of the typed things

vi.   The viability of the typed things

Product 3 — The repair of the typewriter itself also has three factors:

vii. The quantity (amount) of the repair

viii. The quality of the repair

ix.   The viability of the repair

Product 4 — The correction of the thing produced.

x.   The quantity (amount) of the corrected product

xi.   The quality of the corrected product

xii. The viability of the corrected product

Thus to get a product "typed things" there are actually twelve separate factors.

This applies to all machinery. For instance, there is the generator that produces and there is the thing (electricity) produced by the generator. There is the repaired generator. And there is the corrected electricity (such as reducing its voltage or converting it).

Now if you did not know that you were handling twelve factors in producing electricity the tendency would be to "just run the generator" and ignore the actual factors governing production.

The results of this would be total operation only. The generator would soon go to pieces. The electricity furnished would vary all over the place and blow out other equipment. There would be no funds to repair or replace the generator when it broke down. By paying little attention to products (as the wog world often does) or by shifting their importances — giving total importance to running it — there would soon be *no* viability at all. The end result would be two wrong products—scrap metal that was once a generator and no electricity.

Now, surprise, surprise! An organization composed of people is influenced by these same things!

Org Product 1 is putting it there.

Org Product 2 is what the org produces.

Org Product 3 is the repair of the org.

Org Product 4 is the correction of the org's product.

If we do not know these products and factors exist, continual mistakes can be made just as bad as just running a generator. Instead of the desired final product which is offered and sold and delivered, we get scrap paper and insolvency.

To establish an org one has to put one there. This requires a desirable and economic product of the org envisioned, the technology of making the final product, the technology of making and handling the org, the procurement of a location, recruitment, an org bd, hats, and training and the equipment and materiel needed to produce the final product and the obtaining of the raw material to make the final product. Thus established, it must be done so that:

i.   The amount of org is created proportionate to its final product demand.

ii. The quality of the org itself—shabby, posh, active or lazy, etc.

iii. The viability of the org (how long will it last economically, how will it expand, does income exceed outgo, etc.).

The product of the org itself is regulated by:

iv. The quantity of product produced (which must be of sufficient volume to satisfy demand).

v.   The quality of the org's product or products (which must be adequate to satisfy those requiring and paying for the production).

vi. The viability of the org's product (how long does it last and is it adequate for its value).

The repair of the org itself must be:

vii. The quantity or amount of repair necessary to make the org functional (which may amount to simply giving it a new letterhead or rebuilding the whole place, nearly the establishing product again).

viii. The quality or expertness of the repair (a bad one could destroy the place).

ix. The viability of the repair (if the right Why is handled the repair as a product will last a long time and if a wrong reason for decline is handled the place will just cave in again).

The correction of the org's product to obtain a uniformly satisfactory product:

x.   The quantity (proportion) of the org's product that has to be corrected (which might require, if too high, the repair of some part of the org itself).

xi.   The quality of the correction (expert and can be afforded and itself nondestructive).

xii. The viability of the product corrected. (Will it last and be nearly as good as the better produced product?)

All these factors must be consulted.

ANALYSIS

If one understands these factors and realizes they are all present in running an eggbeater or the world's biggest oil company, one will not be groping around in rags.

A checklist of the twelve factors influencing the four major products can be made up and each point as it relates to an org can be studied about a particular org.

One has here the basics. From these there can arise a near infinity of lesser items.

When one does not know these basics one flounders endlessly while attempting to handle a post, a portion of an org or the whole org. One gets into a frantic correct the errors and outpoints or goes into apathy as he has no guidelines.

However, using these basics, one can easily check them off and so see what he has to do to more closely approach the ideal.

In Dianetics and Scientology, for example, the final pc product of Flag auditors trained on the same HCOBs as field auditors, on *rougher* pcs, is infinitely better than the pc product elsewhere. This is a puzzle. The clue is not in auditing at all. It lies in an earlier product — training. A Class VI or a Class VIII Auditor on Flag was trained (a) more rapidly (amounting to as little as $\frac{1}{6}$th of the time in an org) and (b) more honestly and (c) the Flag auditor is expertly corrected as a product when he begins to audit until the auditing product is perfect. The training (quantity, quality and lasting quality) on the course is better and the training extends to training on post until the auditor's product (the auditing of the pc and the pc) need little or no product correction. The equivalent used to be required HGC training — on-post training — for a staff auditor to become a *staff* auditor. In no org did auditors go fresh from school into auditing with no further training. This went out in some orgs. The product "corrected auditor" became a missing product. Thus Flag auditing produces a better product as *that* product — corrected auditor — exists on Flag.

This is given to show the *use* of the product factors.

Where any of these products or factors are missing, the viability of the whole is shaken. By using them the whole becomes viable.

L. RON HUBBARD
FOUNDER

HCO POLICY LETTER OF 1 NOVEMBER 1970
ISSUE I

REMIMEO

ORG SERIES 11
ORGANIZATION AND MORALE

Morale is a large factor in organizing.

An executive is utterly dependent upon the willingness of those who work for him.. (*How to Live Though an Executive*)

Willingness, while it is also a factor in morale, is also a manifestation of morale.

Morale, the tone of a group, is the target of "do-gooders," the "one-worlders," the labor agitator, the commie agent, the local minister and a general mixed company of often well-meaning but nevertheless deadly people.

"You poor fellow. They treat you so badly . . . we will take up this great injustice . . . workers should have everything free . . . communist imperialist aggressors against poor working people . . . You poor fellow, God will make you welcome in his heaven from this earthly toil . . . Kill the managers . . . Down with law and order . . ."

Well, it all winds up in revolution eventually and mounds of dead workers and a few dead managers.

So let's look this over.

If you can do something about an ill situation you do. If you can be effective, you can at least make the situation easier. If you can't do that you can sympathize.

Sympathy with the abused apparently not only does no good but winds up in revolt!

How?

You have this young girl, see. She is wearing last year's dress. No new clothes. So you say, "You poor thing wearing last year's dress." Up to now she wasn't worried about it. Now she says, "I wish I had some new clothes." And you say, "You poor thing. Doesn't your mother ever buy you new clothes?" "No." "The beast!" She goes home and revolts.

Get it?

The UN says, "Every woiker, he got to have job, house, lotsa dough." Worker says, "Who? Me?" "Yes you poor downtrodden sod." And the UN says, "United States. You

---

rich. You pay!" US pitches out the foreign aid. The countries take the dough and revolt and elect a military junta that chops off heads every hour on the hour.

The one-world do-gooders in the US say, "US, you pay poor fired woikers!" US puts out sixty-three billions. You can't walk down a street. Riot and insurrection.

Why?

Sympathy. But not one brain cell worth of organization.

People want to be part of things, part of life.

If the clodheads that pass for modern politicians had the ability to organize and handle an economy (in big countries or small) people could easily be part of things and build the place up. It is in fact a highly skilled activity. And currently quite beyond the heads of nations. Or they wouldn't have unemployment, riots, inflation and future death.

Take Russia. (You take her, I don't want her.) She had half a century of growing revolt. The oatmeal-brained Romanoffs spent their rubles on war and secret police. Up jumped Lenin, "You poor woikers!" Revolt. Dead czar. Dead Russia. Their "workers' paradise" can't feed itself. The czars were supremely awful. Their commissars weren't even that good. One secret policeman per worker was about the ratio in Stalin's day.

Let's be practical. Who is going to build this UN house for the poor worker? Who is going to pay the billions except the worker?

And if, as we so glaringly see, the end product of all this "poor worker" is riot and civil commotion, insurrection and piles of dead workers then mightn't there be something a bit awry with its morale value?

Sympathy is a morale depressant. And knowingly or not, a morale destroyer.

If the person who sympathized was good enough to do something about it he would.

There's nothing at all wrong with righting evil conditions. Far from it.

But if you want to better things KNOW HOW TO ORGANIZE.

Don't just stir up a revolt that will get workers machine-gunned.

If the chronic moaner knew how to throw together an organizing board and groove in the lines, as part of the state or the opposition, he could certainly change things for the better.

Organizing is the know-how of changing things.

Good morale is the product of good organization!

If you organize something well and efficiently you will have good morale. You will also have improved conditions.

Wherever morale is bad, organize!

A very careful survey of people shows that their basic protests are against lack of organization. "It doesn't run right!" is the reason they protest things.

Inequalities of workload, rewards unearned, no havingness, these are some of the things that are snarled about.

They are cured by organizing things.

Russia Siberiaed or shot all her managers, thinking managers and capitalists were the same thing. Then she couldn't feed her people.

And you can't even discuss morale as a subject when a country has to be held together with barbed wire frontiers to hold in its own secret policed people!

The only thing I really have against communists is that they know how to make a revolt but not how to make a country.

And the only thing I have against the capitalist do-gooder is that all the corn and games in the world will not make a viable country.

Neither system winds up in happiness or high morale.

The physical universe is no rose bed. But it can be confronted and can be lived in by a group.

Wherever you see bad morale, behind it you will see chaotic disorganization.

A nation or an org follow the same laws.

Disorganization from any cause deprives people of wanted beingness, doingness and havingness.

When you deprive people of those things you're going to have pretty awful morale.

And only organization and very good organization will bring about beingness, doingness and havingness.

All three factors must be served. And purpose and reason must exist.

A bum with a handout sandwich is a bum with a handout sandwich. You can't change anyone upward with sympathy. It is a witch's weapon, a devil's curse. But you *can* change someone upward with organization.

Bad organization = bad morale.

Good organization equals good morale.

And good organization is something worked on by a group, not ordered under pain of death.

The only tops that get blown when effective organization starts going in are those who don't want others to have things and take delight in suppression—in other words, good organization is only opposed by those who have reason to fear others. For in organization lies the secret of a group's strength.

A small group thoroughly organized can conquer the disorganized billions. And have excellent morale while they're doing it!

L. RON HUBBARD
FOUNDER

HUBBARD COMMUNICATIONS OFFICE
SAINT HILL MANOR, EAST GRINSTEAD, SUSSEX

HCO POLICY LETTER OF 2 NOVEMBER 1970
ISSUE I

REMIMEO

ORG SERIES 12
THE THEORY OF
SCIENTOLOGY ORGANIZATIONS

This "HCO Bulletin" 21 Sept. 58 explains how a Scientology organization differs from "the industrial ideal."

The industrial idea of organization is a cogwheel-type organization with each member of it totally fixed on post, doing only exact duties, with all cogwheels intending to mesh. The industrial idea does not differentiate between a *machine* and a human or live organization.

The product laws (Products 1, 2, 3 and 4 as given in this Org Series) apply to both a live organization and a machine organization and any organization. Since a live and a machine organization hold these laws in common, the industrialist confuses the live organization and the machine organization.

HCO PL 29 Oct. 70 I, Org Series 10, THE ANALYSIS OF ORGANIZATION BY PRODUCT, also carries a mention of this difference between a live and a machine organization.

As the industrial idea has already been mentioned in this Org Series, and as this Org Series mainly applies to live (not machine) organizations, and as people tend to fall into a machine organization pattern (and also to use a live organization to *not* know their own specialty best) this earlier issue on live organization is published in full:

HUBBARD COMMUNICATIONS OFFICE
LONDON (ISSUED AT WASHINGTON)

HCO BULLETIN OF 21 SEPTEMBER 1958

FOR ALL STAFF
MEMBER HATS

THEORY OF SCIENTOLOGY ORGANIZATIONS

An organization is a number of terminals and communication lines united with a common purpose.

The actions of an organization can all be classified under the heading of particle motion and change. To analyze a post or a department or an organization, make a list of each particle it handles (whether types of bodies, types of comm or any other item) and follow each item from the point it enters the post or department or organization to the point it exits. If a particle isn't handled *properly* and passed along *properly* there is a confusion or a dead end. To organize an organization requires more than theory. One has to inspect and list the particles and get their routes and desired changes of character en route. Then he has to see that terminals and comm lines exist to receive, change and forward the particle. All types of particles belong to somebody, are handled some way, come from somewhere and go somewhere. There are no confusions when lines, terminals and actions exist for each type of particle.

Judgment and decision are needed in every staff post. If the handling of items are just "petty details" then so is your fellow man a "petty detail."

There are no laborers in a Scientology organization. We are all managers of these particles.

Routes of handling are not orders to handle but directions to go. A route is not necessarily correct for all cases. It is only correct for most cases. Robots can't handle livingness. Robot organizations and robot civilizations fail. They only *seem* to work — like the commie empire *seems* to work until you find out everyone is starving to death in it. A *perfect* organization is not a machine but a pattern of agreements. A route is only the *agreed upon* procedure. It is not only occasionally broken, it now and then should be. The terminals involved make the agreement or the route doesn't work. A route along terminals that never agreed is no route but a labyrinth. People agree to postulates they can understand and appreciate. Hence, a route and handling begins with a particle, develops with a theory, comes to life with an agreement and continues to work because of judgment and decision.

The routing, the comm lines, the pattern of an organization do not do the work. The work is done by living beings using good sense and skill. The organizational pattern only makes their work easier and lessens confusion and overburden. Governments, armies, big research bureaus reduce themselves down to routes and titles. They don't work. They don't do work. They allow for no human equation. Therefore, slave societies (composed only of routes and unthinking terminals) are always beaten eventually by free peoples. There is a point where routes and exact procedures become unworkable, just as there is a point, facing a volume of work, that individuality and no teamwork becomes unworkable. An optimum organization is never severely either one. Total individualism and total mechanization alike are impossible. So if you or your department or your organization seem to be too heavily inclined to either one, *yell* don't talk. A bad organization will fire you and you can do something more profitable. A good organization will listen. BUT — always have a *better* idea than the one in use. Grumbling, refusing to work don't work. A better idea, talked over with the terminals on either side of you, put down in concise writing, submitted, will be put into action in a good organization. Of course, there's always a chance that the new proposed handling throws something out of gear elsewhere. If it does, you have the right to know about it.

An "organization" doesn't get the work done. As an orderly plan it helps its terminals get the work done. The staff as individuals do the work. An organization can help or hinder getting the work done. If it helps, it's good. If it hinders, it should be examined thoroughly.

An organization can work wholly at "taking in its own laundry." All the work that gets done is the work generated inside the shop by unreal routes and weird changes of particles. This is a government circa mid-twentieth century. Its highest skill is murder which in its profundity it makes legal.

A totally democratic organization has a bad name in Dianetics and Scientology despite all this talk of agreement. It has been found by actual experiment (LA 1950) that groups of people called on to select a leader from among them by nomination and vote routinely select only those who would kill them. They select the talkers of big deeds and ignore the doers. They seem to select unerringly the men of average skill. That is never good enough in a leader and the people suffer from his lack of understanding. If you ever have occasion to elect a leader for your group, don't be "democratic" about it. Compare records as follows: Take the person who *is* a good auditor, not just says he is. Take the person who has a good, not necessarily the highest, profile and IQ. Take the person who can grant beingness to others. And look at the relative serenity and efficiency of any past command he may have had. And even then you're taking a chance. So always elect temporarily and reserve the right of recall. If his first action is to fire people, recall him at once and find another leader. If the organization promptly prospers, keep him and confirm the election by a second one. If the abundance of the organization sags in a month or so, recall and find another. Popularity is some criteria—but it can be created for an election only, as in the US. Select in an election or by selection as an executive the person who can get the work done. And once he's confirmed, obey him or keep him. He's rare. But beware these parliamentary procedure boys and girls who know all the legal and time wasting processes but who somehow never accomplish anything except chaos. A skilled, successful leader is worth a million impressive hayseeds. Democracies *hate* brains and skill. Don't get in that rut. In the US War between the States militia companies elected their officers with great lack of success in battle. They finally learned after tens of thousands of casualties that it was skill not popularity that counted. Why be a casualty—learn first. Democracy is only possible in a nation of Clears—and even they can make mistakes. When the majority rules, the minority suffers. The best are always a minority.

WHAT IS YOUR JOB?

Anything in an organization is your job if it lessens the confusion if you do it.

Your being exactly on post and using your exact comm lines lessens confusion. *But* failure to wear another hat that isn't yours now and then may cause more confusion than being exactly on post.

The question when you see you will have to handle something not yours is this: "Will it cause less confusion to handle it or to slam it back onto its proper lines?"

Example: A preclear wandering around looking for somebody to sell him a book. You see him. The book sales clerk isn't there. The books are. Now what's the answer? You'll create a little confusion if you hand him a book, take his money and give it to the book sales later. You'll create confusion for your own post and the organization if you go chasing around trying to find "book sales terminal." You'll create a feeling of unfriendliness if you don't help the preclear get his book. Answer it by deciding which is less confusing. You'll find out by experience that you can create confusion by handling another's particles *but* you will also discover that you can create confusion by not handling another's particles on occasion.

The only real error you can make in handling another's particles is to fail to tell him by verbal or written comm *exactly* what you did. You stole his hat for a moment. Well, always give it back.

Remember, in a Scientology organization every *Scientologist* on staff potentially wears not just his own but *every* hat in the organization. He has to know more jobs than his own. Particularly jobs adjacent to his post. He often has to do more jobs than his own because those jobs have to be done and he sees it. A non-Scientology member of an organization is only limited in what he can do in the organization by lack of know-how. But the limitation is applicable only to instruction and auditing. But a Scientologist: he may find himself wearing any hat in the place including mine. And others may now and then wear his hat.

A staff member gets the job done of (1) his own post, (2) his department and (3) the whole organization.

People who are *always* off-line and off-post aren't doing their own jobs. When we find somebody always off-post and in our hair, we know if we look at *his* post we'll find a rat's nest. So there are extremes here as well.

HOW TO HOLD YOUR JOB

Your hat is your hat. It is to be worn. Know it, understand it, do it. Make it real. If it isn't real, it is *your fault* since you are the one to take it up and get it clean with an executive. If he doesn't straighten it up so you can do it, it's still your fault if it's not done.

You hold a job in a Scientology organization by doing your job. There are no further politics involved — at least if I find out about it there aren't. So do your job and you've got a job. And that's the way it is.

But on post or off, we only fail when we do not help. The "public" only objects to us when we fail to help or when we fail to answer their questions. So we have two stable data on which we operate whether we're on post or not:

HELP PEOPLE!

ANSWER PEOPLE'S QUESTIONS EXACTLY!

When you don't you let everybody down.

NEATNESS OF QUARTERS

— THE PUBLIC KNOWS US BY OUR MEST —

A part of everyone's hats is keeping a good mock-up in people, offices, classrooms, quarters.

Keep your desk and your MEST neat and orderly. It helps.

And when you see things getting broken down or run down or dirty, fix them or clean them or if you can't, yell like hell on the right comm line.

THE DESPATCH SYSTEM

The despatch system is not there to plague you but to help you.

Except when you've got to have speed, *never* use an interoffice phone to another terminal. And never write a despatch and present it and *you* at some other point at the same time. That's "off-line" just as a phone is "off-line." A good use of the organization's lines reduces confusion. The other guy is busy, too. Why interrupt him or her unnecessarily with routine that should go on the lines? You'll usually get an answer in the same day or at least in 24 hours. The organization's comm lines are pretty good. They make it possible for this small handful of us to get more things done in this society than any other organization on Earth in terms of actual accomplishment.

A comm line can be jammed in several ways. Principal of these is *entheta*. Ask yourself before it goes on the lines — it's bad news but is it necessarily important? Another is *overburden*. Too much traffic jams a line. Too long a despatch doesn't get read. Another is *too little* data. That can jam a line but thoroughly. It takes more despatches to find out what goes. Another way is to bypass the line itself — this jams the terminal. The final way, in broad classes, to jam a comm line is to *put erroneous data* on it.

The last is a pet hate of Scientology people. Generally its form is "everybody knows." Example: "They say that George is doing a bad job," or "Nobody liked the last newsletter." The proper rejoinder is "Who is Everybody?" You'll find it was one person who had a name. When you have critical data omit the "everybody" generality. Say who. Say where. Otherwise, you'll form a bad datum for somebody. When our actions are said to be unpopular, the person or persons saying so have names.

IN SUMMARY

A post in a Scientology organization isn't a job. It's a trust and a crusade. We're free men and women — probably the last free men and women on Earth. Remember, we'll have to come back to Earth someday no matter what "happens" to us. If we don't do a good job *now,* we may never get another chance.

Yes, I'm sure that's the way it is.

So we have an organization, we have a field we must support, we have a *chance.*

That's more than we had last time night's curtain began to fall on freedom.

So we're using that chance.

An organization such as ours is our best chance to get the most done. So we're doing it!

L. RON HUBBARD
FOUNDER

HCO POLICY LETTER OF 13 NOVEMBER 1970

REMIMEO

ORG SERIES 13
PLANNING BY PRODUCT

One of the cycles or correct sequences of action is:

BE — DO — HAVE

This sequence is often altered in orgs and even in individuals. Be is first in the physical universe, Do is second, Have is third.

By getting it out of sequence a considerable confusion can be generated.

A lot of riddles of human behavior can be solved by realizing this goes out of sequence or gets omissions.

The Spanish peasant and the Spanish officials go to war at the drop of a straw. Their history is jammed with revolts. The peasant knows that if he is a peasant (be) and does his work (do) he should have. The Spanish official is stuck in BE. He *has* so he can *be* and he doesn't have to *do* anything. Also a degree or title in Spain is a BE and there is no *do*. So there is no *have* unless it comes from the peasant. The two altered cycles collide.

Juvenile delinquency and shattered lives in the West stem directly from corruptions of this cycle.

Children in the West are commonly asked, "What are you going to BE when you grow up?" It is a silly question and can drive any child up the wall. Because it's the wrong question — hits the wrong end of the cycle. He can't work out his personal org bd easily.

He is also asked, "What are you going to DO in life?" That's just as bad. It is quite difficult to answer.

You have to do an org bd backwards — establish the product (have), find out what to *do* to achieve it and only then really can you accurately discover what one has to BE to accomplish this.

A lot of people and businesses fail because they don't do this. A beingness taken first all too often winds up in a doingness without any havingness resulting.

If we asked children, "What do you want to PRODUCE in life?" we could probably get a workable answer. From *that* he could figure out what he'd have to do to produce that and from that he could know what he had to BE. Then, with a little cooperation, he would be able to lead a happy and valuable life.

Concentrating on BE? one finds him ready to BE all right, but then he stands around the next fifty years waiting for his havingness to fall out of the sky or slide to him via a welfare state.

The above data, missing in society, contributes to juvenile delinquency, crime, the welfare state and a dying civilization.

It is a wrong personal org bd to BE only.

So it is with an activity or company.

What is the desired product that will also be desired by others? is the first question one asks in organizing. It must be answered before one can adjust or arrange finance or any org bd.

Then one asks what has to be *done* to produce that? And there may be a lot of dones figured out and put in sequence.

Now one can work on BE.

Thus you would have the basic ingredients of an org bd.

Here is a common altered cycle:

Mr. A has a truck — HAVE. He tries to figure out what to DO with it. He works it around to try to make money. He would usually go broke. As he supposes he already has a product — a truck, and he needs a product — "money," he rarely backs it up to a BE.

Some people's "think" gets all involved in altered sequences or omissions of the BE — DO — HAVE cycle.

An activity has several final products. All of them must be worked out and considered. Then one can work out the sequence of DOs (each with a product) in order to accomplish the final products. Only then can one work out the BE.

By omission or fixations on one of these points a person or an org can fail or perhaps never even get started.

Fixation on DO without any product in view leads to bored wandering through life.

Mothers even know this one. "Mama, what shall I do?" is a long-drawn refrain. Smart mamas often say "Make a cake" or "Make mud pies" or "Make a house." Dumb ones say "Go and play and stop bothering me!"

Armies, with guard or death "products," get obsessed with DO to a point where officers and noncoms will state "Get those men busy!" No product. Meaningless, often frantic and useless DO.

It could be said that any developed traffic (dev-t) comes from people who have no product.

Immense bureaucracies can build up where there are no realized or stated products.

Target policies and practice are successful because they state the desired product.

Unless one organizes from the final product the organization can get unreal and useless.

Even Russia could learn this one. Their "workers" are all trying to get to the university where they can BE. The Russian government was recently pleading with young people to become workers. But of course that's just another BE that implies DO. Russia has yet to realize her product was and is revolution. It's no wonder their main problem is how to feed and clothe and house their people.

Unless an org or a person knows exactly what the final product is for the org or a post, there'll be a lot of busyness but not very much havingness for anyone.

The answer is to figure out the final product and work back through the do of subprojects and you will then materialize a real org, a real beingness.

L. RON HUBBARD
FOUNDER

Org Series 14
THE PRODUCT AS AN OVERT ACT

When a product is nonexistent or bad it can be classified as an overt act against both the org and any customer.

You can estimate what the existing scene of a post really is by looking at its product.

When a flubby product is observed, you can at once approximate the existing scene.

The time it takes to achieve the product is also an estimation. A long time to achieve a small flubby product gives one a good idea of the existing scene.

This also estimates the amount of "noise" in an area.

Example: Post X is supposed to sort ruddy rods. There are no sorted ruddy rods ready. That's an omitted action. The post has to be ordered to sort ruddy rods. That's ordering someone to wear his hat which is altered sequence as he should have been wearing it already. The post must be a false terminal as it isn't wearing its hat. The product so far is no sorted ruddy rods. You order them sorted. You get bent tangled ruddy rods furnished after a long time period filled with dev-t. Estimate of existing scene—psychotic and an awful long way from any ideal scene. Actual quality of product—an overt act.

When several org members are furnishing a poor individual product, the org becomes difficult to handle as the person in charge is operating as correction not as establishment and org product.

Wherever an org's product is low in quantity and quality one must recognize that it contains several members who unconsciously furnish overt acts in the guise of post products and begin to straighten things out accordingly.

The road to sanity for such a person or org is a good grasp of organizing and products, making known the technology needed to produce a product, getting it properly done so that the person can then wear his hat.

If this still doesn't occur, personal processing is necessary as the personnel may well be dramatizing overt acts (harmful acts) by turning out a bad product.

The final product of an org is the combined products of all the members of that org directed to accomplish the final products of that org.

Stupidity, lack of a worked out org bd, lack of recognition of what the final org products should be, lack of training, lack of hats can produce poor final products. In an activity not doing well, the poor final product or its lack of any product is the compound errors in subproducts. An org where the product is pretty bad or nonexistent contains many elements — posts — in it which have as *their* individual "post products" not products at all but overt (harmful) acts.

Pride of workmanship is pride in one's own product.

Every post has some product. If the products of all posts in an activity are good and the product sequence is good then the final products of the org will be good.

L. RON HUBBARD
FOUNDER

HCO POLICY LETTER OF 20 NOVEMBER 1970

(Also issued as an HCOB, same date and title)

REMIMEO

PERSONNEL SERIES 12
ORG SERIES 15
WORD CLEARING SERIES 18

ORGANIZATION MISUNDERSTOODS

By Scientology study technology, understanding ceases on going past a misunderstood word or concept.

If a person reading a text comes to the words "Felis domesticus" and doesn't know it simply means HOUSE CAT, the words which appear thereafter may become "meaningless," "uninteresting" and he may even become slightly unconscious, his awareness shutting down.

Example: "Wind the clock and put out the Felis domesticus and then call Algernon and tell him to wake you at 10:00 A.M.," read as an order by a person who didn't bother to find out that "Felis domesticus" means "house cat" or "the variety of cat which has been domesticated" will not register that he is supposed to call Algernon, will feel dopey or annoyed and probably won't remember he's supposed to wake up at 10:00 A.M.

In other words, when the person hit a misunderstood word, he ceased to understand and did not fully grasp or become aware of what followed after.

All this applies to a sentence, a book, a post or a whole organization.

Along the time track a crashing misunderstood will block off further ability to study or apply data. It will also block further understanding of an organization, its org board, an individual post or duties, and such misunderstoods can effectively prevent knowledge of or action on a post.

ALL THIS IS THE MOST COMMON CAUSE OF AN UNACCEPTABLE POST PRODUCT, OR NO PRODUCT AT ALL.

The difficulties of an organization in functioning or producing stem from this fact.

Personal aberration is the cause of products that are in fact overt acts.

Scientology technology today easily handles the personal aberration part of the problem, IF IT IS USED AND PROPERLY APPLIED. Leaving an org unaudited or being unable to figure out how to run a viable org so that it can afford to audit its staff members is asking for post or org products that are overt acts.

Employing persons of the Leipzig, Germany, death camp school (psychologists, psychiatrists) to handle personal aberration is like throwing ink in water to clean it up. Governments stupidly do this and wonder why their final product as an organization is riot, war and a polluted planet. The point is not how bad psychology and psychiatry are, but that one does have to *handle* personal aberration in an organization, and these schools were too vicious and incompetent to do so.

Those who are personally very aberrated are not about to produce anything but an overt act. They are difficult to detect as they are being careful not to be detected. Things "just sort of go wrong" around them, resulting in a product that is in fact an overt act. But these constitute only about ten or twenty percent of the population.

The remaining eighty percent or ninety percent where they are nonfunctional or bungling are so because they do not understand what it's all about. They have in effect gone on by a misunderstood such as what the org is supposed to do or the admin tech they use on their posts or where they are or what their product is.

Earth organizations like governments or big monopolies get a very bad repute because of these factors:

1. Personal aberration of a few undetected and unhandled,

2. Inadequate or unreal basic education technology and facilities.

3. Inadequate or unknown organization technology.

4. Noncomprehension of the individual regarding the activities of which he is a part.

5. Noncomprehension of the basic words with which he is working.

6. Purposes of the post uncleared.

7. Admin of the post not known or comprehended.

8. Technology in use not fully understood.

9. A lack of comprehension of products.

Out of these nine things one gets organizational troubles and the belief that it takes a genius to run one successfully. Yet all the genius in the world will fail eventually if the above nine things are not handled to some degree.

The common methods currently in use on the planet to handle these things are very crude and time-consuming as the items themselves are either dimly comprehended or not known at all.

1A. Personal aberration is met by torture, drugs or death when it is detected. Yet only the very serious cases who are obviously screaming, muttering or unconscious are singled out, whereas the dangerous ones are neither detected nor handled at all and become with ease generals or presidents or dictators, to say nothing of lesser fry. Ten percent to 20 percent of any organization is stark staring mad, doing the place in so adroitly that only their actual product betrays them.

2A. Basic education as well as higher general education has become a mass-produced area crawling with bad texts and noncomprehension and used mainly by hostile elements to overturn the state or pervert the race and its ideals.

3A. Organizational technology is so primitive as to change national maps and leading companies many times a century, an extremely unstable scene for a planet.

4A. Very few individuals on the planet have any concept of the structure of entities such as their country or state or company. Persons surveying the public in the US, pretending to advise acceptance of "new measures" already in the Constitution, were threatened for being revolutionaries. Hardly anyone knew the basic document of the nation's organization much less its rambling structure.

5A. The basic words of organization are glibly used but not generally comprehended, words like "company," "management," "policy." Vocabularies have to be increased before comprehension and communication occur and misunderstoods drop out.

6A. Post purposes are often glibly agreed with while something entirely different is done.

7A. Administrative actions involving posts are often only dimly comprehended and seldom well followed; but in this matter of communication, despatches, etc., the planet is not as deficient as in others except that these functions, being somewhat known, can become an end-all — tons of despatches, no actual product. In some areas it is an obsession, an endless paper chain, that is looked on as a legitimate product even when it leads to no production.

8A. The planet's technology is on the surface very complex and sophisticated but is so bad in actual fact that experts do not give the planet and its populations thirty years before the smoke and fumes will have eaten up the air cover and left an oxygenless world. (The converters like trees and grass which change carbon dioxide to oxygen are inadequate to replace the oxygen and are additionally being killed by air impurities coming out of factories and cities.) If the technology destroys the base where it is done — in this case the planet — it is not adequate and may even be destructive technology.

9A. The whole idea of "product" is not in use except in commercial industry where one has to have a car that sells or a washing machine that actually washes.

THE HARD ROAD

It is against this primitive background that one is trying to run an organization.

If it were not for improvements made on each one of these points, the task could be hopeless.

I have gone to some length to outline the lacks in order to show the points where one must concentrate in (a) putting an org together and (b) keeping it viable.

In these nine areas we are dealing with the heart of it in running orgs.

Enthusiasm is a vital ingredient. It soon goes dull when insufficient attention is paid to resolving and getting in these nine points.

Bluntly, if they are not gotten in and handled, the task of living and running a post or an org will become so confused that little or no production will occur and disasters will be frequent.

THE WORDS

The by no means complete list of words that have to be fully cleared and understood just to talk about organization as a subject, and to intelligently and happily work in an org EVEN AS ITS LOWEST EMPLOYEE is:

A company
A board of directors
Top management
Policy
Management
Programs
Targets
Orders
Technology
Know-how
Org bd
Post
Hat
Cope
Purposes
Organize
Duties
A checksheet
A checklist
A comm channel
A command channel
A relay point
A stable terminal
Double-hatted
A product
Aberration
VIABILITY

This is key vocabulary. One could draw up a whole dictionary for these things and no one studying it would be any wiser since it would become salted with other words of far less importance.

The way to do this list is sweat it out with a meter until one knows each can't mean anything else than what it does mean.

Out of a full understanding of what is implied by each, a brilliantly clean view is attained of the whole subject of organization, not as a fumble but as a crisp usable activity.

Unless one at least knows these words completely so that they can be used and applied, they will not buffer off confusions that enter into the activity.

Glibness won't do. For behind these words is the full structure of an activity that will survive and when the words aren't understood the rest can become foggy.

We *do* know all these needful things. We must communicate them and use them successfully.

L. RON HUBBARD
FOUNDER

HCO POLICY LETTER OF 25 NOVEMBER 1970

REMIMEO

ORG SERIES 16
POLICY AND ORDERS

Probably the greatest single confusion that can exist in the subject of organizing is the reversal of "policy" and "orders."

When definitions of these two things are not clearly understood they can be identified as the same thing or even reversed.

When they are not understood plainly then staff members set their own policy and demand orders from top management, totally reversing the roles.

Confusion thus generated can be so great as to make an organization unmanageable. It becomes impossible for staff to do its job and management cannot wear its hat.

People in an organization obsessively demand orders from policy source and then act on their own policy. This exactly reverses matters and can be a continual cause of disorganization.

As policy is the basis of group agreement, unknown policy or policy set by the wrong source leads to disagreement and discord.

Demanding or looking for orders from policy source and accepting policy from unauthorized sources of course turns the whole organization upside down. The bottom of the org board becomes the top of the org board. And the top is forced to act at lower levels (order issue) which pulls it down the org board.

But this is not strange as we are dealing here with principles rather new in the field of organization, principles which have not been crisply stated. THERE IS NO EXACT ENGLISH WORD for either of these two functions.

POLICY as a word has many definitions in current dictionaries amongst which only one is partially correct: "A definite course or method of action to guide and determine future decisions." It is also "prudence or wisdom," "a course of action" and a lot of other things according to the dictionary. It even is said to be laid down at the top.

Therefore the word has so many other meanings that the language itself has become confused.

Yet, regardless of dictionary fog, the word means an exact thing in the specialized field of management and organization.

POLICY MEANS THE PRINCIPLE EVOLVED AND ISSUED BY TOP MANAGEMENT FOR A SPECIFIC ACTIVITY TO GUIDE PLANNING AND PROGRAMING AND AUTHORIZE THE ISSUANCE OF PROJECTS BY EXECUTIVES WHICH IN TURN PERMIT THE ISSUANCE AND ENFORCEMENT OF ORDERS THAT DIRECT THE ACTIVITY OF PERSONNEL IN ACHIEVING PRODUCTION AND VIABILITY.

POLICY is therefore a principle by which the conduct of affairs can be guided.

A policy exists, or should exist, for each broad field or activity in which an organization is involved.

Example: The company has a lunchroom for its employees. Top policy concerning it might be "To provide the employees cheaply with good food and clean fast service." From this the lunchroom manager could plan up and program how he was going to do this. With these approved they form the basis of the orders he issues.

Now let us say the manager of the lunchroom did not know organization and that he did not try to get a policy set or find if there was one and made up his own policy and planned and programed and issued his orders on that. Only the policy *he* makes up is "To make dough for the company."

Now the wild melee begins.

Top management (the lunchroom manager's highest boss) sees stenos eating cold lunches brought from home at their desks. And begins to investigate. How come? Stenos then say, "We find it cheaper to eat our own lunches." Top management finds coffee in the lunchroom is terrible and costs several shillings. Dried-out sandwiches cost a fortune. There is no place to sit . . ., etc. So top management issues *orders* (not policy). "Feed that staff!" But nothing happens because the lunchroom manager can't and still "make dough for the company." Top management issues more *orders*. The lunchroom manager thinks they must be crazy at board level. How can you make dough and still feed the whole staff? And top management thinks the lunchroom manager is crazy or a crook.

Now you multiply this several times over in an organization and you get bad feeling, tension and chaos.

Let us say top management had issued policy: "Establish and run a lunchroom to provide the employees cheaply with good food and clean fast service." But the lunchroom manager hired knew nothing of organization, heard it, didn't realize what policy was and classified it as a "good idea." Idealistic, probably issued for PR with employees. "But as an experienced lunchroom man I know what they really want. So we'll make a lot of dough for the company!"

He thereafter bases *all* his orders on this principle. He buys lousy food cheap, reduces quality, increases prices, cuts down cost by no hiring and does make money. But the company gets its income from happy customers who are handled by happy staff members. So the lunchroom manager effectively reduces the real company income by failing to cater to staff morale as was intended.

UNPREDICTABLE

It is a complete fact that no top management can predict WHAT policy will be set by its juniors.

The curse of this is that top management depends on "common sense" and grants greater knowledge of affairs to others at times than is justified. "Of course anybody would know that the paper knives we make are supposed to cut paper." But the plant manager operates on the policy that the plant is supposed to provide employment for the village. You can imagine the squabble when the paper knives which do NOT cut paper fail to sell and a threatened layoff occurs.

Nearly all labor–management hurricanes blow up over this fact of ignorance of policy. It is not actually a knowing conflict over different policies. It's a conflict occurring on the unknown basic of unknown or unset policy of top management and the setting of policy at an unauthorized level.

ORDERS

"Order" takes up two small print columns of the two-ton dictionaries.

The simple definition is:

AN ORDER IS THE DIRECTION OR COMMAND ISSUED BY AN AUTHORIZED PERSON TO A PERSON OR GROUP WITHIN THE SPHERE OF THE AUTHORIZED PERSON'S AUTHORITY.

By implication an ORDER goes from a senior to juniors.

Those persons who do not conceive of an organization larger than a few people tend to lump all seniors into order-issuers, tend to lump anything such a senior says into the category of order and tend to lump all juniors into order-receivers.

This is a simple way of life, one must say.

Actually it makes all seniors bosses or sergeants and all juniors into workers or privates. It is a very simple arrangement. It does not in any way stretch the imagination or sprain any mental muscles.

Unfortunately such an organized arrangement holds good for the metal section of the shop or a platoon or squad. It fails to take into account more sophisticated or more complex organizations. And it unfortunately requires a more complex organization to get anything done.

Where one has squad mentality in a plant or firm, one easily gets all manner of conflict.

Few shop foremen or sergeants or chief clerks ever waste any time in trying to tell the "rank and file" what the policy is. "Ours was not to reason why" was the death song of the Light Brigade. And also the open door to communism.

Communism is unlikely to produce a good society because it is based on squad mentality. Capitalism has declined not because it was fought but because it could not cope with squad mentality. The policies of both are insufficiently embracive of the needs of the planet to achieve total acceptability.

An order can be issued solely and only because its issuer has in some fashion attained the right to issue the instruction and to expect compliance.

The officer, the chief clerk, the shop steward, the sergeant, each one has a license, a warrant, a "fiat" from a higher authority which entitles him to issue an *order* to those who are answerable to him.

So where does this authority to issue orders come from?

The head of state, the government, the board of directors, the town council, such bodies as one could consider top management in a state or firm, issues the authority to issue orders.

Yet such top persons usually do not issue authority to issue orders without designating what the sphere of orders will be and what they will be about.

This is the policymaking, appointment making level at work.

All this is so poorly and grossly defined in the language itself that very odd meanings are conceived of "policy" and "orders."

Unless precise meanings are given, then organization becomes a very confused activity.

Understood in this way, the following sentence becomes very silly: "The board of directors issued orders to load the van and the driver was glad to see his policy of interstate commerce followed."

Yet a group will do this to its board of directors constantly. "You did not issue orders . . ." "We were waiting for orders . . ." "I know we should have opened the doors but we had no order from the council . . ."

The same group members, waiting for orders to sit or stand by special board resolution, will yet set policy continually. "We are trying to let others do their jobs without interference." "I am now operating to make each member of my department happy." "I am running this division to prevent quarrels."

Ask officers, secretaries, in-charges, "What policy are you operating on?" and you will get a quick answer that usually is in total conflict or divergence from any board policy. And you will get a complaint often that nobody issues their division orders so they don't know what to do!

————

The fact is that POLICY gives the right to issue orders upon it to get it in, followed and the job done.

A group of officers each one issuing policy madly while waiting for the head of the firm to give them orders is a scene of mix-up and catastrophe in the making.

Policy is a long, long-range guiding principle.

An order is a short-term direction given to implement a policy or the plans or programs which develop from policy.

"People should be seated in comfortable chairs in the waiting room" is a policy.

"Sit down" is an order.

If policy is understood to authorize people to issue orders, the picture becomes much clearer.

"Clearing post purpose" is another way of saying "Get the policy that establishes this post and its duties known and understood."

Unless an organization gets this quite straight, it will work in tension and in internal conflict.

When an organization gets these two things completely clear, it will be a pleasant and effective group.

L. RON HUBBARD
FOUNDER

HCO POLICY LETTER OF 1 DECEMBER 1970

REMIMEO

ORG SERIES 17
REALITY OF PRODUCTS

The character of the VALUABLE FINAL PRODUCTS OF AN ACTIVITY is something which must be established EXACTLY.

Example: Ajax Ball Bearings Ltd. did well for a while and then went into a decline. The exact change point into the decline coincided with a change to new stockholders and considerable executive and staff turnover. At first glance the Why would have seemed to be so many transfers — musical chairs. However, a complete survey shows that the definitions of Ajax valuable final products were changed from "useful ball bearings sold in quantity at a profit" to "world acceptance of Ajax." The big ad campaigns, internal shop and accounting policy shifts to accomplish this, the new fuzzy ideas about it and failure to spot the Why took Ajax down. Traced further it was found that the new advertising manager had originated this policy and the new board had only a foggy notion of its duties and knew nothing of "valuable final products." The whole company started "manufacturing" acceptance instead of ball bearings. The production shop got more and more idle, more and more neglected, had fewer and fewer men in it. Admin got more and more people and down, down, down went the stats.

A survey of any activity, requesting a list from each member of the company answering the question, "What are the valuable final products of this company?" can reveal much and can show that many are setting policies and doing things in the company name which have no real relation to what the company is doing and therefore drive the activity in contrary and conflicting directions.

After all it is the crew, staff members and workers who do the work. When they have to set their own policy and use their own ideas of the valuable final products, you can get a lot of conflicts and upsets which should never exist.

Make no mistake: An activity can be totally unmanageable and become nonviable over just these points. Possibly all labor–management upsets come from them.

1. Policy is set by top management after experience and agreed upon by others. Where policy is needed it should be requested from the top, not set independently by the supervisors or workers.

2. The valuable final products of an activity must be *very* carefully surveyed, established and clearly released at policy level AS POLICY.

Anarchy appears to fail (as it did before the Spanish revolution 1936) and strong central management succeeds around this one point of policy. Everyone sets his own in an anarchy. Businesses succeed only on that point and the precise establishment of valuable final products.

When the exact valuable final products are known and agreed upon, only then does successful group action become possible.

The car industry looks easy. The valuable final product is a car. But automotive labor and unions have not agreed to that. Their "valuable final product" is "a big paycheck." This one point damaged and may have irreparably destroyed the US economy in 1970 when General Motors, the country's largest industry, had a walkout and layoff. Failing to handle this one point GM management was failing duty as management (they lost their general manager last year due to a Ford maneuver of hiring him over, then firing him). Labor in this case ruined their future paychecks and lost thousands of jobs.

Forty years ago a similar inability to set policies and establish valuable final products began to wipe out the coal industry in the US. Under a John L. Lewis, the miners made coal mining economically impossible. Management, mostly absentee and careless, half a century before that had begun to make errors, run unsafe mines and look on an appearance in society pages as a valuable final product. Today "Appalachia" is a ruined poverty area. And oil is the fuel — of which there is little compared to US domestic coal.

So do not discount these two points. They are capable of wicked backlashes when not done right. They are the Why of not only organization failures but also the failures of civilizations.

PRECISE WORDING

The valuable final products of any activity small or large must be very precisely and totally listed and totally continually posted.

The valuable final products of a division should be on the org board under the division and the valuable final products of the org should be on the org board in a glaring red list.

Let us take a college. US colleges and others are so clouded up with "government projects" and "scientific findings" and "published papers" and "sport wins" and "general public awe of their greatness" that they have pretty well forgotten a "well-trained and successful student in the field of his major." So the student body product becomes "revolt." And the college product becomes "???" in the public mind. I do not speak idly. The very last thing a college wants in a student is one who is an individual success. A downtrodden anonymous member of some industrial team or an underpaid professor is about as high as a college will tolerate from their student bodies according to surveys. For several hundred years, since Francis Bacon (1561–1626) in fact, there has been no renowned philosopher who had not been eased carefully out of his college long before graduation. The list exceptions are tame sellouts like Dewey, part of the Leipzig death camper crew.

So here is civilization at risk. The valuable final product of its educational institutions is not stated and is neglected in favor of a multitude of false or valueless products. They are not known by their students but by their arrogance and political connections. This is not idle data. Failure to understand this fact of valuable final products began around 1862, the downfall of imperial Russia, spearheaded by its college students. Having no real valuable final product, clearly stated and agreed upon, opens the door to conflict not only in the company but in the state and the entire civilization. (Granted, imperial Russia stank, which is my exact point. So did Stalinism.)

Studying back and forth over history, poking about in old ruins, remembering, adding it up, the apparent causes of organizational decay are:

a. Failure to have an informed, trained top management capable of setting real policy in accordance with the need of the organization.

b. Failure of top management to set policy.

c. Company members, supervisors and workers setting their own policy out of agreement with or in ignorance of the needs of the organization and themselves.

d. Failure of top management to wisely, completely and precisely establish the valuable final products of the activity.

e. Ignorance of or disagreement with the valuable final products by workers and company members.

In a much more general sense we would have:

A. Unwise or unset policy.

B. Unreal or unstated or undone valuable final products.

These apply to any organization of any size. The most flagrant offenders are governments. I have never met a political leader or police officer who had a clue about valuable final products of the state. You or I might feel that "public safety" was a valuable final product of police, but the police don't say so.

In amongst psychiatry I have worked for hours trying to make numerous psychiatrists state what they were trying to accomplish. I have never even gotten one to hazard even a suggestion of why he was doing what he was doing, much less say "a cured patient" or "a safeguarded society."

The confusion on these points of valid policy and valuable final product is so great in the world of this writing as to be intolerable.

So do not feel strange that in our early organizations it has been hard to handle things — they were cheek by jaw with a society that believed itself a jungle and where "moral" standards were being set by the psychiatrists who gave the world Hitler and twelve million exterminated Germans.

When the society goes in this direction (war, murder, psychiatry) it conceives its valuable final product to be dead men.

Thus it is very, very important for us to get these hitherto obscure or unidentified principles up into the light where they belong and to USE them.

1. The beings of top management must be fully informed and capable of setting or knowing and publishing policy according to the need (including viability) of the organization which will be agreed upon by the whole activity. This means an informed, trained top management and includes org management.

2. Top management and managers must KNOW policy and be able to set or request policy where it is unknown or nonextant.

3. All members (top management, managers, supervisors, technicians, workers) must understand the mechanisms of setting policy, how to get it set, know policy that is set and know what is valid policy and who sets it.

4. The valuable final products of an organization must be known to, precisely and completely established and defined by top management.

5. The valuable final products of an activity must be known fully to and agreed upon by all beings in the organization including why and the abandonment of random products which are being done but which do not in any way add up to valuable final products.

ECONOMICS

The economics of any group is such that it cannot tolerate offbeat products and remain sound. This is true of any political group or commercial company.

All of the activities of a group in some way must add up to known valuable final products of a group or it will, as an entity, shatter.

Even in a "moneyless state," a barter economy, this remains factual.

Western civilization and Eastern alike have decayed on the altars of war gods. Diplomatic and political incompetence have squandered their efforts and brought them to inflation and then dust. A socialism where the population goes unshod or a capitalism where a barrowload of bucks will not buy a loaf of bread are paying for ignorance of their actual valuable final products and the squandering of funds and effort on side issues.

One cannot appropriate or apportion funds without an intimate knowledge of the valuable final products of the activity.

One cannot handle property unless one knows the valuable final products of the activity.

One cannot assign personnel without huge waste of manpower unless one knows the valuable final product.

Therefore *one must* be able to list and know the valuable final products of an activity before one can:

i.   Do financial planning.

ii.   Arrange, buy or sell property.

iii.   Allocate spaces assigned for different functions.

iv.   Assign personnel.

If one tries to do these things first and discover final products later, all efforts to organize will be cancelled.

CENTRAL AUTHORITY

The valuable final products must be agreed upon and issued as policy and additions to the list must be referred to the policymaking level of the group before being confirmed as valid.

The aimless meanderings of contemporary societies show the absence of such lists. It some time ago began to be stated and believed that society "just took in each other's washing"; and the joke, Parkinson's Law, in which bureaucracy multiplies automatically, both give evidence that society is believed not to have any valuable final products even as faint as "a good life."

Individual members of a group or society must know the valuable final products of the activity and must be in some agreement with them to have a successful group.

SURVEYS

Surveys of what should be the valuable final products show mainly the spirit of the matter. It should not be believed for a moment that a standard survey would apply: a standard survey being the adding up of the answers and taking the majority as useful.

Such a survey measures willingness concerning types or directions of activity.

Given this, setting the exact *things* the group can or should produce and wording them exactly requires a lot of looking and a lot of work.

What products of the group are economically *valuable?* This is the key point that will be overlooked. What, in short, can this group exchange with other groups or society that will obtain things the group does *not* produce? This is the heart of economics. The law of supply and demand applies.

This is too hardheaded an approach for a whole group to decide upon without a great deal of personal work.

If the group has a past to assess, then it will previously have produced products from time to time that did demonstrate economic value. A search for and a list of these is of primary value.

If the group has no past, it has some experience available from the society which it can employ.

183

It can be taken as a rule that group members will not identify or phrase the valuable final products. And it can be taken as another rule that it will in the course of time lose those products from its production that were valuable.

Final is another word that will probably escape grasp. Subproducts leading to final products will be given equal billing with the final product.

So three surveys have to be done.

What does the group think its final product should be? This gives willingness and direction.

What have been the previous valuable final product successes of the group? (That did exchange with other groups so the producing group can obtain things it does not produce.) This in a new group would be a survey of what similar groups have produced.

There would then be a period of intense and expert work by or for central policy authority where questions like: Have times changed? Were these items ever thoroughly offered? What was the relative value in light of their cost? Is recosting necessary due to money value changes? Which ones really brought value back to the group from others? Can we still produce these? Thus a list is drawn up, precisely worded.

Then the final (3rd) survey can occur. This is the issue of the reworked list above to the group to get them to look at it from their viewpoint and see if it is feasible and any points missed and any expert opinion taken amongst the experts in the group.

The final list of valuable final products could then be drawn and issued as policy.

A special watchdog production tally officer could then be appointed to make sure *these* valuable final products are being prepared for and produced.

Yes, it would take all that to get the list of valuable final products of an activity.

The valuable final product list does not come wholly from top management.

The list does not come only from the group.

Major social and business catastrophes occur when (a) no list is set, (b) top management only sets the list or (c) the group sets the list up.

Phrases like "a better world" or "a big car" or "lots of customers" are quite incomplete and unreal. Even the words "an auditor" or "a release" are correct but are not fully enough described to be good statements of a valuable final product.

A notable example of all this occurred in the car industry when Edsel Ford, ten years ago, did not survey past products and current demands and produced "The Edsel." Henry Ford half a century earlier had established the company products as a cheap, small, rugged automobile that would put America on wheels and a big, expensive car to hold up the company image. "The Edsel" went in between and millions were lost and scores of dealers were wiped out. No survey. No precise product.

If all this seems commercial, remember that in any civilization a group has to buy or acquire those things it does not produce. This is true in capitalism, communism or tribal barter. There is no Santa Claus and even a corn and games welfare state can go broke and always has.

Thus the *valuable* final product of a group must be valuable to another group or individuals in society around it and sufficiently so that it can receive in return things it wants or needs but does not produce. And it must DELIVER its valuable final product, a point most often missed.

A group of knights in a castle on a hill had protection for the peasant as a valuable final product. When they ceased to deliver and used only threat and robbery the peasant eventually invented a longbow whose arrow could penetrate armor and knighthood was no longer in flower.

All this is really quite simple. It is even in the Factors.

L. RON HUBBARD
FOUNDER

HCO POLICY LETTER OF 6 DECEMBER 1970

REMIMEO
DEPT 14 HATS

PERSONNEL SERIES 13
ORG SERIES 18

THIRD DYNAMIC DE–ABERRATION

The exact mechanism of 3rd dynamic (group or organization) aberration is the conflict of COUNTER–POLICY.

Illegal policy set at unauthorized levels jams the actions of a group and IS responsible for the inactivity, nonproduction or lack of team spirit.

Counter-policy independently set jams the group together but inhibits its operation.

Out-reality on org bds, hats, etc., is to a large degree caused by disagreements and conflicts which are caused by illegal policy.

If we had a game going in which each player set his own rules, there would be no game. There would only be argument and conflict.

VARIETIES OF COUNTER–POLICY

At the start it must be assumed or effected that there is someone or some body to set authorized policy for the group. Absence of this function is an invitation to random policy and group conflict and disintegration. If such a person or body exists, new proposed policy must be referred to this person or body and issued, not set randomly at lower levels or by unauthorized persons.

Policies so set by the policy authority must be informed enough and wise enough to forward the group purpose and to obtain agreement. Ignorant or bad policy even when authorized tends to persuade group members to set their own random policy.

When no policy at all exists random policy occurs.

When policy exists but is not made known, random policy setting will occur.

Ignorance of policy, the need or function of it, can cause random policies.

Hidden not stated random policies can conflict.

Correct policy can be relayed on a cutative basis — a few words left off or a qualifying sentence dropped which makes policy incorrect or null. "Children may not go out" can be made out of "Children may not go out after midnight."

Altered policy can be limitless in error.

Attributing a self-set policy to the authorized source can disgrace all policy as well as pervert the leadership purpose.

Policy can be excluded from a zone of a group that should be governed by it. "Pipe-making policy does not apply to the *small* pipe shop."

Such masses of unnecessary policy can be issued that it cannot be assimilated.

Policy can exist in large amounts but not be subdivided into relevant subjects as is done in hat checksheets.

Disgrace of policy can occur in a subsequent catastrophe and render any policy disgraceful, encouraging self-set policy by each group member.

CLEARING A GROUP

All authorized policy must be set or made available in master books and adequate complete policy files. This makes it possible to compile hats and checksheets and issue packs.

Group surveys of "What policy are you operating on?" can reveal random policy.

All bugged (halted) projects can be surveyed for illegal policy and cleaned up and gotten going again.

Other actions can be taken all of which add up to:

1. Get existing policy used.

2. Get areas without policy crisply given policy from the authorized source.

3. Debug all past projects of false policy.

4. De-aberrate group members as per the Organization Misunderstoods PL and other materials.

5. Educate the group members concerning policy technology.

6. Set up systems that detect, isolate and report out-policy and get it corrected and properly set, issued and known.

7. Monitor any new policy against statistics and include policy outnesses as part of all statistical evaluations.

ADMIN SCALE

I have developed a scale for use which gives a sequence (and relative seniority) of subjects relating to organization.

GOALS
PURPOSES
POLICY
PLANS
PROGRAMS
PROJECTS
ORDERS
IDEAL SCENES
STATS
VALUABLE FINAL PRODUCTS

This scale is worked up and worked down UNTIL IT IS (EACH ITEM) IN FULL AGREEMENT WITH THE REMAINING ITEMS.

In short, for success, all these items in the scale must agree with all other items in the scale on the same subject.

Let us take "golf balls" as a subject for the scale. Then all these scale items must be in agreement with one another on the subject of golf balls. It is an interesting exercise.

The scale also applies in a destructive subject. Like "cockroaches."

When an item in the scale is *not* aligned with the other items, the project will be hindered if not fail.

The skill with which all these items in any activity are aligned and gotten into action is called MANAGEMENT.

Group members only become upset when one or more of these points are not aligned to the rest and at least some group agreement.

Groups appear slow, inefficient, unhappy, inactive or quarrelsome only when these items are not aligned, made known and coordinated.

Any activity can be improved by debugging or aligning this scale in relation to the group activity.

As out-reality breeds out-comm and out-affinity, it follows that unreal items on the scale (not aligned) produce ARC breaks, upsets and disaffection.

It then follows that when these scale items are well aligned with each other and the group there will be high reality, high communication and high affinity in the group.

Group mores aligned so and followed by the group gives one an ethical group and also establishes what will then be considered as overts and withholds in the group by group members.

This scale and its parts and ability to line them up are one of the most valuable tools of organization.

DEBUG

When orders are not complied with and projects do not come off, one should DETECT, ISOLATE and REPORT and handle or see that it is handled, any of the scale items found random or counter.

If any item below POLICY is in trouble — not moving — one can move upwards correcting these points, but certainly concentrating on a discovery of illegal or counter-policy. Rarely it occurs some old but legal policy needs to be adjusted. Far more commonly policy is being set by someone, verbally or in despatches, or hidden, that is bugging any item or items below the level of policy.

So the rule is that when things get messed up, jammed up, slowed or inactive or downright destructive (including a product as an overt act) one sniffs about for random or counter-policy illegally being set in one's own area or "out there."

Thus in the face of any outness one DETECTS — ISOLATES — REPORTS and handles or gets handled the out-policy.

The *detection* is easy. Things aren't moving or going right.

The isolation is of course a WHAT POLICY that must be found and WHO set it.

Reporting it would mean to HCO.

Handling it is also very easy and would be done in Qual.

This admin tech gives us our first 3rd dynamic de-aberrater that works easily and fast.

Why?

Well, look at the Admin Scale. *Policy* is just below *purpose*.

Purpose is senior to policy.

The person who is setting random or counter illegal policy is off group purpose. He is other-purposed to greater or lesser degree.

From 1960 to 1962 I developed a vast lot of technology about goals and purposes. If we define a goal as a whole track long long-term matter and a purpose as the lesser goal applying to specific activities or subjects we see clearly that if we clean up a person's purposes relating to the various activities in which he is involved and on the eight dynamics we will handle the obsession to set random or counter-policies!

So it is an auditing job and the tech for it is extensive. (The African ACC was devoted to this subject. Lots of data exists on it.)

It happens however that around 20 percent (probably more) of any group's members are actively if covertly antigroup and must be handled at a less profound level under "personal aberration" in the Org Misunderstoods policy letter before you can begin to touch purpose.

Thus any group member, since this tech remedy helps them all, would be handled with:

1. General case de-aberration (called L10s on Flag),

2. Purpose handling for posts,

3. Org bd, hatting and training.

Those setting random or counter-purpose later detected would get further no. 2 and no. 3.

As the universe is full of beings and one lives with them whether he likes it or not, it would be to anyone's interest to be able to have functioning groups.

The only way a group jams up and (a) becomes difficult to live in and (b) impossible to fully separate from is by random and counter-purposes.

If one thinks he can go off and be alone anywhere in this universe he is dreaming.

The first impulse of a hostile being is "to leave" a decent group. What a weird one.

The only reason he gets in jams is his inability to tolerate or handle others.

There's no road out for such a being except through.

Thus all we can do to survive even on the first dynamic is to know how to handle and be part of the third or fourth dynamic and clean it up.

Probably the reason this universe itself is considered by some as a trap is because their Admin Scale is out regarding it.

And the only reason this universe is sometimes a trial is because no one published its Admin Scale in the first place.

All this is very fundamental first dynamic tech and third dynamic tech.

It is the first true group technology that can fully de-aberrate and smooth out and free within the group every group member and the group itself.

Thus, combined with auditing tech, for the first time we can rely wholly on technology to improve and handle group members and the group itself toward desirable and achievable accomplishment with happiness and high morale.

Like any skill or technology it has to be known and done and continued in use to be effective.

The discovery, development and practical use of this data has made me very, very cheerful and confident and is doing the same thing on the test group.

I hope it does the same for you.

L. RON HUBBARD
FOUNDER

HUBBARD COMMUNICATIONS OFFICE
SAINT HILL MANOR, EAST GRINSTEAD, SUSSEX

HCO POLICY LETTER OF 14 DECEMBER 1970

REMIMEO

PERSONNEL SERIES 14
ORG SERIES 19
GROUP SANITY

The points of success and failure, the make and break items of an organization are:

1. HIRING

2. TRAINING

3. APPRENTICESHIPS

4. UTILIZATION

5. PRODUCTION

6. PROMOTION

7. SALES

8. DELIVERY

9. FINANCE

10. JUSTICE

11. MORALE

These eleven items MUST AGREE WITH AND BE IN LINE WITH THE ADMIN SCALE (HCO PL 6 Dec. 70, Pers Series 13, Org Series 18, THIRD DYNAMIC DE–ABERRATION).

Where these subjects are not well handled and where one or more of these are very out of line, the organization will suffer a third dynamic aberration.

This then is a SANITY SCALE for the third dynamic of a group.

The group will exhibit aberrated symptoms where one or more of these points are out.

The group will be sane to the degree that these points are in.

Internal stresses of magnitude begin to affect every member of the group in greater or lesser degree when one or more of these items are neglected or badly handled.

The society at large currently has the majority of these points out.

These elements become aberrated in the following ways:

1. HIRING

The society is running a massive can't-have on the subject of people. Automation and employment penalties demonstrate an effort to block out letting people in and giving them jobs. Confirming this is growing unemployment and fantastic sums for welfare — meaning relief. Fifty percent of America within the decade will be jobless due to the population explosion without a commensurate expansion in production. Yet production by US presidential decree is being cut back. War, birth control, are two of many methods used to reduce population. THIS THIRD DYNAMIC PSYCHOSIS IS A *REFUSAL TO* EMPLOY *PEOPLE*. EXCLUSION OF OTHERS IS THE BASIC CAUSE OF WAR AND INSANITY.

2. TRAINING

Education has fallen under the control of one-worlders, is less and less real. Data taught is being taught less well. Less data is being taught. School and college unrest reflect this. Confirmation is the deteriorated basic education found in teenagers such as writing. Older technologies are being lost in modern rewrites. THIS THIRD DYNAMIC PSYCHOSIS IS A *COVERT REFUSAL TO TRAIN*.

3. APPRENTICESHIPS

The most successful industries, activities and professions of earlier centuries were attained by training the person as an apprentice, permitting him to understudy the exact job he would hold for a long period before taking the post. Some European schools are seeking to revive this but on a general basis not as an apprentice system. A THIRD DYNAMIC PSYCHOSIS IS A *DENIAL OF* ADEQUATE *EXPERIENCE TO SUCCEED*.

4. UTILIZATION

In industries, governments and armed services as well as life itself, personnel are not utilized. A man trained for one thing is required to do something else. Or his training is not used. Or he is not used at all. A THIRD DYNAMIC PSYCHOSIS IS *FAILURE TO UTILIZE PEOPLE*.

5. PRODUCTION

Modern think is to reward downstats. A person is paid for not working. Governments who produce nothing employ the most people. Income tax and other current practices penalize production. Countries which produce little are given huge handouts. War which destroys attains the largest appropriations. A THIRD DYNAMIC PSYCHOSIS IS *TO PREVENT PRODUCTION*.

6. PROMOTION

Promotion activities are subverted to unworthy activities. True value is seldom promoted. What one is actually achieving gets small mention while other things are heavily promoted. Reality and PR are strangers. A THIRD DYNAMIC PSYCHOSIS IS *UNREAL OR NONFACTUAL PROMOTION*.

7. SALES

Sales actions are unreal or out of balance. Clumsy or nonfunctioning sales activities penalize producers and consumers. In areas of high demand, sales actions are negligible even when heavy advertising exists. This is proven by the inability to sell what is produced even in large countries so that production cutbacks are continual threats to economies and workers. A population goes half-fed in times of surplus goods. With curtailed car factories a nation drives old cars. With a cut-back construction industry people live in bad houses. Sales taxes are almost universal. A THIRD DYNAMIC PSYCHOSIS IS *THE IMPEDING OF PRODUCT DISTRIBUTION TO POTENTIAL CONSUMERS.*

8. DELIVERY

Failure to deliver what is offered is standard procedure for groups in the humanities. Commercially it is well in hand.

9. FINANCE

One's own experience in finance is adequate to demonstrate the difficulties made with money. A THIRD DYNAMIC PSYCHOSIS IS *THE PERVERSION OF FINANCE.*

10. JUSTICE

Under the name of justice, aberrated man accomplishes fantastic injustices. The upstat is hit, the downstat let go. Rumors are accepted as evidence. Police forces and power are used to ENFORCE the injustices contained in 1 to 9 above. Suppressive justice is used as an ineffectual but savage means of meeting situations actually caused by the earlier listed psychoses. When abuses on (1) to (9) make things go wrong, the social aberration then introduces suppressive injustices as an effort to cure. Revolt and war are magnified versions of injustices. Excess people — kill them off in a war. A THIRD DYNAMIC PSYCHOSIS IS *THE SUBSTITUTE OF VIOLENCE FOR REASON.*

11. MORALE

A continuous assault on public morale occurs in the press and other media. Happiness or any satisfaction with life is under continuous attack. Beliefs, idealism, purpose, dreams, are assaulted. INSANITY IS A REFUSAL TO ALLOW OTHERS TO BE, DO OR HAVE.

Any action which would lead to a higher morale has to be defended against the insane few. A THIRD DYNAMIC PSYCHOSIS IS *A DETESTATION OF HIGH MORALE.*

———————

The COMMON DENOMINATOR of all these insanities is the desire to SUCCUMB.

Insanities have as their end product self or group destruction.

These eleven types of aberration gone mad are the main points through which any group SUCCUMBS.

THEREFORE, these eleven points kept sane guarantee a group's SURVIVAL.

EXAMPLES

Seeing all this in one example permits one to see that these third dynamic insanities combine to destroy.

A. Believing it impossible to obtain money or make it, a firm cannot hire enough people to produce. So has little to sell, which is badly promoted and is not sold so it has no money to hire people.

B. Needing people for another job the firm robs them from a plant which then collapses and fails to make money so no new people can be hired. This reduces production so people have to be dismissed as they can't be paid.

C. Persons are in the firm but are kept doing the wrong things so there is little production and no promotion or sales so there is no money to pay them so they are dismissed.

D. A new product is put in. People to make it are taken from the area already making a valuable product which then collapses that area and there is not enough money to promote and selling fails so people are dismissed.

The examples are many. They are these same eleven group insanities in play upon a group, a firm, a society.

SANITY

If this is a description of group aberration, then it gives the keys to sanity in a group.

1. HIRING

Letting people INTO the group at large is the key to every great movement and bettered culture on this planet. This was the new idea that made Buddhism the strongest civilizing influence the world has seen in terms of numbers and terrain. They did not exclude. Race, color, creed, were not made bars to membership in this great movement.

Politically the strongest country in the world was the United States, and it was weakened only by its efforts to exclude certain races or make them second-class citizens. Its greatest internal war (1861–65) was fought to settle this point and the weakness was not resolved even then.

The Catholic Church only began to fail when it began to exclude.

Thus *inclusion* is a major point in all great organizations.

The things which set a group or organization on a course of *exclusion* are (a) the destructive impulses of about 10 or 15 percent of the society (lunacy) and (b) opposition by interests which consider themselves threatened by the group or organization's potential resulting in infiltration, (c) efforts to mimic the group's technology destructively and set up rival groups.

All these three things build up barriers that a group might thoughtlessly buy and act to remedy with no long-range plans to handle.

These stresses make a group edgy and combative. The organization then seeks to solve these three points by exclusion, whereas its growth depends wholly upon *inclusion*.

No one has ever solved these points successfully in the past because of lack of technology to solve them.

It all hinges on three points: (1) the sanity of the individual, (2) the worthwhileness of the group in terms of general area, planetary or universal survival and (3) the superiority of the group's organization tech and its use.

Just at this writing, the first point is solved conclusively in Scientology. Even hostile and destructive personalities wandering into the group can be solved and, due to the basic nature of man, made better for the benefit of themselves and others.

The worthwhileness of the organization is determined by the assistance given to general survival by the group's products and the actual factual delivery of those valid products.

The superiority of a group's admin tech and its application is at this current writing well covered in current developments.

Thus *inclusion* is almost fully attainable. The only ridges that build up are the short-term defense actions.

For instance, Scientology currently must fight back at the death camp organizations of psychiatry whose solution is a dead world, as proven by their actions in Germany before and during World War II. But we *must* keep in mind that we fully intend to reform and salvage even these opponents. We are seeking to *include* them in the general survival by forcing them to cease their nonsurvival practices and overcome their gruesome group past.

There are two major stages then of *including* people — one is as paid organization personnel and one as unpaid personnel. BOTH are in essence being "hired." The pay differs. The wider majority receive the pay of personal peace and effectiveness and a better world.

The org which *excludes* its own field members will fail.

The payment to the org of money or the money payment to the staff member is an internal economy. Pay, the real pay, is a better personal survival and a world that can live.

Plans of INclusion are successful. They sometimes contain defense until we *can* include.

Even resistance to an org can be interpreted as a future inclusion by the org. Resistance or opposition is a common way point in the cycle of inclusion. In an organization where everyone wins eventually anyway the senselessness of resistance becomes apparent even to the most obtuse. Only those who oppose their own survival resist a survival producing organization.

Even in commercial companies the best organization with the best product usually finds competitors merging with it.

2. TRAINING

Basic training, hats, checksheets and packs MUST exist for every member of a group.

Criminal or antisocial conduct occurs where there is no hat.

Any type of membership or role or post in the whole organization or its field requires individual and team training. Only where you have a group member who will not or cannot bring himself to have and wear a hat will you have any trouble.

This is so true that it is the scope of Personal Enhancement.

Ask yourself "Who isn't trained on his post and hatted?" and you can answer "Who is causing the trouble?"

Basic training, slight or great, is vital for *every* member of a group, paid or unpaid.

A field auditor must have a hat. A student needs a student hat, etc., etc.

This requires training.

Training begins in childhood. Often it has to be reoriented.

Training as a group member must be done.

Training in exact technology or in the precise tech of admin is not the first stage of training. Basic training of group members, no matter how slight, must exist and be done.

Otherwise group members lack the basic points of agreement which make up the whole broad organization and its publics.

Training must be on real materials and must be rapid. The technology of how to train is expressed in speed of training.

The idea that it takes 12 years to make a mud pie maker is false. TIME in training does not determine quality of training. Amount of data learned that can be applied and skills successfully drilled determine training.

That the society currently stresses *time* is an aberrated factor.

The ability to learn and apply the data is the end product of training. Not old age.

The rate of training establishes to a marked degree the expansion factor of a group and influences the smoothness of the group during expansion.

If training is defined as making a person or team into a part of the group then processing is an influencing factor. The facilities for processing and quantity available are then a determining factor in group expansion.

3. APPRENTICESHIP

Training on post is a second stage of any training — and processing — action.

This is essentially a familiarization action.

To have a person leave a post and another take it over with no "apprenticeship" or groove-in can be quite fatal.

The deputy system is easily the best system. Every post is deputied for a greater or lesser period before the post is turned over and the appointment is made. When the deputy is totally familiar he becomes the person on the post.

Rapid expansion and economy on personnel tend to injure this step. Lack of it can be *very* destructive.

Optimally there should be one or two deputies for every key post at all times. This is a continual apprenticeship system.

Economically it has limitations. One has to weigh the *losses* in not doing it against the cost in doing it. It will be found that the losses are *far* greater than the cost, even though it increases personnel by at least a third for a given organization.

When an organization has neglected it as a system (and has turned over too many posts without deputy or apprenticeship action) its economics may decay to where it can never be done. This is almost a death rattle for an organization.

In a two-century-old highly successful industry, *only* the apprentice system was and is used (Oporto wine industry). The quality of the product is all that keeps the product going on the world market. If the quality decayed the industry would collapse. Apprenticeship as a total system maintains it.

Certainly every executive in an organization and every technical expert should have a deputy in training. Only then could quality of organization be maintained and quality of product guaranteed.

The total working organization should be on this system actually. And whenever a person is moved up off a post, the deputy taking over, a new deputy should be appointed. The last step (appointment of a new deputy) is the one that gets forgotten.

Failure to recruit new people over a period will very surely find the whole organization declining soon solely because there is no apprentice system of deputies. The organization expands, singles up the posts, promotes some unapprenticed people and begins to lose its economic advantage. Low pay ensues, people blow off and then no one can be hired. It's a silly cycle, really, as it is prevented easily enough by hiring enough soon enough when the org is still doing well.

The rule is DEPUTY EVERY POST AND NEWLY DEPUTY THEM WHEN PROMOTIONS OCCUR.

The most covert way to get around this is just to call each person's junior a deputy even though he has other duties. This makes it all look good on an org board. "Do you have each post deputied?" "Oh yes!" But the deputies are just juniors with posts of their own.

A deputy is *used* to run the same post as it is deputied for. This means a double posting pure and only.

You'd be amazed at how much production an executive post can achieve when it is also deputied and when the principal holder of the post will use the deputy and gen him in, not get him to cover an empty lower post.

4. UTILIZATION

People must be utilized.

Equipment must be utilized.

Space must be utilized.

Learning to USE is a very hard lesson for some. Untrained people, bad organization, poor machinery, inadequate space all tend to send one off utilization.

The rule is, if you've got it use it; if you can't use it get rid of it.

This most specifically applies to people. If you've got a man, use him; if you can't use him get him over to someone who can use him. If he isn't useful, process and train.

Anyone who can't figure out how to use people, equipment and spaces to obtain valuable final products is not worthy of the name of executive.

Reversely we get what an executive or foreman is — an executive or foreman is one who can obtain, train and use people, equipment and spaces to economically achieve valuable final products.

Some are very skilled in preparing people, systems, equipment, property and spaces to be used. But if these then go to someone who does not USE them you get a bad breakdown.

The welfare state and its inflation is a sad commentary on "executive ability."

An executive whose people are idle and whose materiel is decaying is a traitor to his people and the org, just that, for he will destroy them all.

UTILIZATION requires a knowledge of what the valuable final products are and how to make them.

Action which doesn't result in a final product that adds up to valuable final products is destructive, no matter how innocent it seems.

Man has a planet as a valuable final product. Improper *use* of the countries and seas, air and masses which compose it will wind up with the destruction of man, all life on it and the usefulness of the planet. So *proper* utilization of anything is a very real factor.

The nineteenth-century industrialist, like the mad kings who built great structures, used up men; they didn't properly use men.

And not using them at all, the current fad, is the most deadly of all.

UTILIZATION is a big subject. It applies to resources, capabilities and many other factors.

The question being asked in all cases is, "How can we USE this to economically obtain a valuable final product?"

Failing to answer that question gives one the "mysteries of life."

5. PRODUCTION

One may be prone to believe there is no sense in any production at all. Such a one would also be likely to say, "There is no sense at all." Or "If they keep on producing it will become impossible to destroy it all."

Production of some final valuable product is the chain of all production sequences.

Even the artist is producing a *reaction*. The reaction's service in a wider sphere to enforce it is what gives art its sense. A feeling of well-being or grandeur or light-heartedness are legitimate valuable final products, for instance.

The production areas and activities of an org that produce the valuable final products are the most important areas and activities of the org.

6. PROMOTION

The acceptance of valuable final products and of their value depends in a large degree upon (a) a real value and (b) a desire for them.

Promotion creates desire for the valuable final product.

The old saw that the man who builds a better mousetrap will have the whole world coming to his door is a total falsity.

Unless the value is made known, and the desire created, the mousetraps are going to go unsold.

Promotion is so important that it can stand alone. It can have limited success even when there is no product! But in that case it will be of short duration.

Promotion must contain reality and the final product must exist and be deliverable and delivered for promotion to be fully successful.

Public relations and advertising and all their skills cover this area of promotion.

7. SALES

It is hard to sell what isn't promoted and can't be delivered.

Economics greatly affect selling.

Anything must be sold for a price comparable to its value in the eyes of the purchaser.

COSTING is a precise art by which the total expenses of the organization administration and production must be adequately covered in the PRICING allowing for all losses and errors in delivery and adequate to produce a reserve.

PRICING (the amount being asked) cannot be done without some idea of the total cost of the final valuable product.

The sale price of one final valuable product may have to cover the cost of producing other products which are delivered without price.

PRICING however does not necessarily limit itself to only covering immediate cost of a product. A painting with a dollar's worth of paint and canvas may have a price of half a million dollars.

Also a painting used in promotion may cost two hundred dollars and be displayed at no cost at all to the beholder.

These relative factors also include the SKILL of the salesman himself and there is much technology involved in the act of selling something to someone and the world abounds in books on the subject.

Therefore sales (once promotion is done) are bound up really in COSTING, PRICING AND SELLING.

The value in the eye of the purchaser is monitored by the desire created in him for it. If this is also a real value and if delivery can occur then SELLING is made very easy — but it is still a skilled action.

The production of a valuable final product is often totally determined by whether or not it can be sold. And if it can be sold at a price greater than the cost of delivering it.

That it *gets* sold depends on the salesman.

The skill of the salesman is devoted to enhancing the desire and value in the eyes of the buyer and obtaining adequate payment.

8. DELIVERY

The subject and action of DELIVERY is the most susceptible to breakdown in any organization. Any flaw on the sequence of actions resulting in a valuable final product may deteriorate it or bar off final delivery.

There are many preparatory or hidden-from-public-view steps on a production line. When any of these break down, delivery is imperiled.

Given the raw materials and wherewithal to make some valuable final product, the valuable final product should occur.

WHEN A VALUABLE FINAL PRODUCT DOES NOT GET PRODUCED AND CANNOT BE DELIVERED, REPAIR THE EARLIER STEPS OF ITS PRODUCTION.

Example: An auditing result is not delivered. Don't just repair the pc. Repair training of auditors and C/Ses. Repair the assembly line *before* the valuable final product. The subproducts are less visible. Yet they add up to the valuable final product.

THE LAW OF THE IRREDUCIBLE MINIMUM occurs in all delivery problems. Someone is trying to produce only the visible end product of a post or production line and neglects the earlier contributory actions and products as these are not plainly visible.

When an organization or its posts operate only on an irreducible minimum, production goes bad and DELIVERY crashes.

Take a cook who has his post at an irreducible minimum. Food is appearing on the table. If he reduced just one bit more the food would no longer be edible at all. He neglects purchasing, menus and preparation. That these occur is invisible to the diners. That food appears on the table is visible to the diners. If the cook operates at any less level than he is, no edible food would be visible — hence, irreducible minimum. The food served will be bad. But it will be visible. Invisible-to-the-diners actions aren't being done.

To improve the food, get the less visible actions *done*. Get the sequence of actions all done. The result will be improved food.

Take training. The final valuable product is a trained auditor. The Course Supervisor who runs his post on an irreducible minimum is simply there, appearing to supervise.

His final product may be horribly unskilled. The teaching may take "forever."

To improve this one goes earlier on the assembly line — materials, packs, tapes, student tech services, recorder repair, scheduling — dozens of actions including getting the Course Supervisor trained.

The visibility is still a Course Supervisor and students being taught. But with the *whole* earlier line in, the final valuable product is excellent!

A being hopes lazily for instantaneous production. It doesn't happen this way in the MEST universe. Things are produced in a sequence of subproducts which result in a final valuable product. Hope all you want to. When you omit the subproducts you get no valuable final product.

When the people in an organization do not know the valuable final products of the org and when a person on a post does not know the final products of his post, a condition arises where no org DELIVERY will occur, or if it does occur it will be poor or costly. It is vital that a person knows what his post final products are and what his unit, section, department and division subproducts are and how his own and each of these contribute to the valuable final products of the organization for actual delivery to occur.

Delivering other than valuable final products or useless final products or final products that need constant correction also adds up to nondelivery.

A whole civilization can break down around the point of DELIVERY. So can an organization.

Since money can be looked upon as too valuable a final product it can actually prevent DELIVERY.

Failure to deliver is the one point beings do not forgive. The whole cycle hangs upon DELIVERY.

DELIVER WHAT IS PROMISED when it is expected, in sufficient volume and adequate quality is the first maxim even of a group in politics or the humanities.

9. FINANCE

Finance too often disregards the other factors in this scale or the other factors in this scale too often disregard finance for organizations to long remain viable.

Financing must be in agreement with all the other factors of this scale and all the other factors must be in agreement with finance for viability to occur.

Because money is interchangeable for commodities then people can confuse it with too many things.

If you regard money like so many beans, as a commodity in itself, you open the door to understanding it.

Money is so many beans in to get so many beans out.

When you can master this you can handle FINANCE.

The FINANCE persons of an org, a civilization, a planet should put so many beans in and expect more beans out than they put in. This is quite correct as a viewpoint for finance.

The difference of beans in and beans out for a planet is made up by adding beans enough to those already in existence to cover new commodity.

When finance people fail to do this beans cease to be in pace with production and inflation and deflation occur.

In an org or any of its parts, industriousness of the staff makes the difference between the beans in and beans out.

An org has to have income greater than outgo. That is the first rule of finance. Violating it brings bankruptcy.

Now if the FINANCE people of an org apply the same rule remorselessly to all *its* transactions (financial planning) with each person and part of an org, finance becomes real and manageable.

So many beans in to support the first division means so many beans out of the org back to finance because of the cooperative work of the first division.

A hectic effort to work only with production products will wind finance up in a knot.

One has to estimate (cost) the contribution of each part of an org to the valuable final product to know what to allow what part of an org.

Finance has to have a full reality on the valuable final products and the subproducts and post products of the whole org to intelligently allocate funds.

This person, that division, each contributes some part of the action that results in the money received for the valuable final products.

So finance can extend so much money for each and expect that and an additional amount back.

If this occurs, so will expansion.

Finance comes unstuck when it fails to "cost" an organization and fails to support valuable final product production.

Finance must not only practice "income greater than outgo" for the org, it must practice it for each part of the org as well.

Then solvency becomes real.

The greatest aberration of finance is that it seeks to *save* things into solvency. The real losses in an org are the sums never made. These are the most important losses for finance to concentrate upon.

An org that makes 500 pounds a week that should make 5,000 pounds a week in potential is losing the finance people 4,500 pounds a week!

Finance can force production along certain lines by putting in funds and getting more back.

Finance becomes too easily the management of an org but it only does that when it ceases to deal in its own commodity — money.

An org which has executives unfamiliar with finance will fall at once into the control of the finance people in the org. And these finance people, if they don't really know money, will fall at once under the control of outside finance people.

One has to know finance in any organization anywhere, even in a socialism. Sooner or later the books get balanced in any society.

10. JUSTICE

Without justice there can be no real organization.

Even a government owes its people an operating climate in which human transactions and business can occur.

Where insane and criminal individuals operate unchecked in the community, justice is uncertain and harsh.

The society in which the insane rise to positions of power becomes a nightmare.

Justice is a difficult subject. Man handles it badly.

Justice cannot occur until insanity can be detected and cured.

The whole task of justice is to defend the honest man. Therefore the target of justice is the establishment of a sane society.

The inability to detect or cure the insane destroys civilizations.

Justice is an effort to bring equity and peace. When one cannot detect and cure insanity then sooner or later justice actions will become unjust and be used by the insane.

To us, justice is the action necessary to restrain the insane until they are cured. After that it would be only an action of seeing fair play is done.

11. MORALE

When all factors balance up in an org and give the group a common direction and mutual viability, morale can be expected to be good.

When the Admin Scale and the ten elements described are out of balance (without proper importance given to each) and when one or many of these (Admin Scale and the elements herein described) are not in agreement one with another, then morale will be poor.

Morale is not made of comfort and sloth. It is made of common purpose and obstacles overcome by the group.

When the Admin Scale and these elements are not held together by similar aims, then morale has to be held up artificially.

The most ghastly morale I have ever seen was amongst "the idle rich."

And the highest morale I've ever seen was amongst a furiously dedicated common-purposed group working under fantastic stresses with very little against almost hopeless odds.

I used to observe that morale in a combat unit would never materialize before they had been through hell together.

All drama aside, morale is made up of high purpose and mutual confidence. This comes from the Admin Scale items and these elements of organization being well aligned, one with the next, and honest sane endeavor to achieve a final goal for all.

L. RON HUBBARD
FOUNDER

HCO POLICY LETTER OF 30 DECEMBER 1970

REMIMEO
SO MEMBER HAT
STAFF MEMBER HAT

PERSONNEL SERIES 15
ORG SERIES 20

ENVIRONMENTAL CONTROL

The differences between a competent person and an incompetent person are demonstrated in his environment (surroundings).

A person is either the effect of his environment or is able to have an effect upon his environment.

The nineteenth-century psychologist preached that man had to "adjust to his environment." This false datum helped begin a racial degeneration.

The truth is that man is as successful as he adjusts the environment to him.

Being competent means the ability to control and operate the things in the environment and the environment itself.

When you see things broken down around the mechanic who is responsible for them, he is plainly exhibiting his incompetence — which means his inability to control those things in his environment and adjust the environment for which he is responsible — motors.

When you see the mate's boats broken up, you know he does not have control of his environment.

Know-how, attention and the desire to be effective are all part of the ability to control the environment.

One's "standards" (the degree of rightness one is trying to establish and maintain) are directly related to one's desire to have a controlled environment.

The attainment of one's *standards* is not done by criticism (a human system). It is done by exerting control of one's environment and moving things effectively toward a more ideal scene.

Control of the environment begins with oneself — a good case state, a body that one keeps clean and functioning. This extends to one's own gear, his clothing, tools, equipment. It extends further to the things one is responsible for in the environment. Then it extends out into the whole environment, the people and the MEST.

One can get pretty dirty fixing things up. That's okay. But can one then also clean oneself up?

The ability to confront MEST is a high ability. After that comes the ability to handle and control it.

The ability to confront people is also a high ability. After that comes the ability to get along with them and to handle and control them.

There is the supreme test of a thetan — the ability to make things go right.

The reverse of this is the effort to make things go wrong.

Incompetence — lack of know-how, inability to control — makes things go wrong.

Given some know-how or picking it up by observation, sane people make things go right.

The insane remain ignorant intentionally or acquire know-how and make things go wrong.

Insane acts are *not* unintentional or done out of ignorance. They are intentional, they are not "unknowing dramatizations." So around insane people things go wrong.

One cannot tell the difference really between the sane and insane by behavior. One can tell the difference only by the product. The product of the sane is survival. The product of the insane is an overt act. As this is often masked by clever explanations, it is not given the attention it deserves. The pretended good product of the insane turns out to be an overt act.

A large percentage of this planet's population (undetermined at this time for the "general public" but in excess of 20 percent) are insane. Their behavior looks passable. But their product is an overt act. The popularity of war confirms this. The products of existing governments are mainly destructive. The final product of the human race will be a destroyed planet (a contaminated air cover rendering the planet unable to sustain life, whether by radiation or fumes).

Thus, due to the inability to detect and handle the insane, the sane majority suffers.

The hidden actions of the insane can destroy faster than an environment can be created UNLESS one has the know-how of the mind and life and the tech of admin and the ability and know-how to handle MEST.

An area or activity hit by an influx of new recruits or new customers tends to unsettle. Its MEST gets abuse, things go out of control.

Gradually, working to put in order, the standards are again being attained. The minority insane get handled, the know-how of groups and orgs becomes more generally known, the tech of MEST gets used again.

As an organization expands it goes through cycles of lowered condition and raised condition. This is normal enough since by taking on more and more area one is letting in more and more insane even though they are in a small proportion to the sane.

Order is reestablished and survival trends resumed to the degree that the sane begin to reach out and handle things around them and as the insane are made sane.

Thus one gets downtrends and uptrends. As soon as a group begins to feel cocky, it takes on more area. This includes more unhandled people, admin and MEST and a downtrend begins. Then the sane begin to handle and the insane begin to be sane and the uptrend starts.

This is probably even the basis of national economic booms and depressions.

This is only bad to the degree that the insane are put in charge. As soon as this happens the downtrend becomes permanent and cultural decay sets in.

A group expanding rapidly into a decadent culture is of course itself subjected to the uptrend–downtrend cycles and has to take very special measures to counteract the consequences of expansion in order to maintain any rate of growth.

The individual member of a group can measure his own progress by increased ability to handle himself, his post and environment and the degree of improvement of the group itself because of his own work within it.

A group that is messing up its gear and environment worse than it did a while ago and is not improving it of course has to be reorganized before it perishes.

No group can sit back and expect its high brass to be the only ones to carry the load. The group is composed of individual group members, not of high brass.

The survival of a group depends upon the ability of its individual members to control their environment and to insist that the other group members also control theirs.

This is the stuff of which survival is made.

A sane group, knowing and using their technologies of handling men and MEST, cannot help but control their environment.

But this depends upon the individual group member being sane, able to control his MEST and those around him and using the tech of life, the tech of admin, the tech of specific types of activity.

Such a group inevitably inherits the culture and its guidance.

L. RON HUBBARD
FOUNDER

HCO POLICY LETTER OF 19 JANUARY 1971

REMIMEO

PERSONNEL SERIES 17
ORG SERIES 21

DUPLICATING FUNCTIONS

All you have to do to run out of personnel, finance and get no production is to duplicate the same functions that give the same product in an org.

Take three orgs side by side under the same management. Only if each division of each org had entirely different products would this be possible.

Now let's do it wrong. Each of these three orgs has an HCO and full personnel duties. Each separately promotes. Each has its own finance office, each has its production div producing the same products. Each has its own correction div — the place in general would be very overmanned, yet each div would be undermanned for its full functions. The product would be terrible if it existed at all. Morale would be ghastly, interorg collisions continual.

The right way would be to work out the different products and then assign them to one or another of these orgs. One org would have to be the source org that produced the other two. One org would have all the finance with liaison only in the other two orgs. One org would have to hire, hat and train with only liaison in the other two. The orgs would have org boards which *had* the function but under it would be the note "Liaison with _____," source org.

In the impatience and emotion of organizing one org tends to individuate and establish a duplicate function because "it can't get service." This begins the catastrophe. Now they'll all begin to go broke while having men bulging out of the windows.

In looking over potential insolvency, look over duplicate functions.

L. RON HUBBARD
FOUNDER

HCO POLICY LETTER OF 25 JANUARY 1971

REMIMEO

ORG SERIES 22
SQUIRREL ADMIN

When a squirrel is given a circular wheel he will run in it 'round and 'round and 'round. He gets nowhere.

When persons in an organization do not know organizing or their org board or hats, they go 'round and 'round and 'round and get nowhere.

There is no valuable production. There is no money.

When you have an organization that has no valuable production you know that the people there go 'round and 'round and 'round and get nowhere.

They are squirrel administrators.

STANDARD ADMIN

There are right ways to handle a group. This is the single fact which most often escapes people attempting to handle groups.

Also, for every correct solution there can be an infinity of wrong solutions.

The right way is a narrow trail but strong. The wrong ways are broad but all lead into a bog.

You could "fix" a radio by hitting it with a sledgehammer, putting a hand grenade in it or throwing it out of a 155th-story window. The number of wrong ways you could "fix" it would be infinite.

Or you could find out what was wrong with it and replace the part or properly correct it.

The difference between the wrong way and the right way is that the radio, wrongly "solved," doesn't work. The radio correctly solved works.

So the test of the wrong way or the right way is whether or not the radio then worked.

This is the basic test of *all* administrative solutions. DID THEY WORK?

When experienced persons, working from basic theory, have evolved a technique for handling a situation which routinely now handles that situation, we have now a STANDARD ADMINISTRATIVE ACTION.

When that situation appears, we apply *that* solution and the matter gets handled.

The test is, did the solution work?

Solutions that work and are therefore routinely used to handle the situation to which they apply are then called STANDARD ADMIN.

A multitude of these correct solutions are used in STANDARD ORGANIZING. The org board, the hats, comm lines, comm centers, comm baskets, despatch forms, routing forms, inspection actions, promotion actions, central filing, customer or visitor handling, selling, collecting income, paying bills, inventorying, doing finance reports, handling raw materials, training persons to handle and properly change materials, correcting or improving staff competence, correcting organizational form, inspecting, reviewing and handling failed products, handling contacting and converting the publics, establishing and using field distributors and salesmen, providing public services, maintaining contact with the original and basic technology, handling rivals and opposition, and running the organization in general *all* have standard actions.

Now, glancing over the above rough list, you see we have hit the high spots of a 21-department, 7-division org bd.

Each *is* a standard solution to continuing and recurring problems.

Each contains numerous standard solutions to the recurring problems associated with them.

Underneath all this is basic theory and around it is survival and potential success.

USE OF STANDARD ACTIONS

The difference between a successfully viable organization with cheerful and cared for staff and a limping scene is standard and squirrel administration.

If standard admin is successful then why is it sometimes not used?

First the data has to exist, be available and known.

Next the data has to be used.

At first glance this may seem so clear-cut that it cannot go wrong. But one must look a bit further.

One is dealing with a variable called man. One is working in a world full of noise and conflict.

Certain personalities do not want the group or the organization to succeed (see HCOB 28 Nov. 70, C/S Series 22, PSYCHOSIS). This problem has been so great amongst men that every historical culture—each one an organization—has died. About 10 to 20 percent of mankind, at a broad guess, fit into this category.

In this universe it is easier to destroy than to construct. Yet the survival of life forms depends on construction.

To overcome this, man has developed technology and the cooperative effort known as organization.

The forces of the physical universe can be channeled and used only with technology.

The forces inherent in life forms can succeed only when channeled and aligned with one another.

Therefore to succeed a group must have the technology it uses available and known to it. And then use it.

From this, one obtains the agreement and alignment necessary to generate the group action and production which brings about success.

NONCONFRONT

When a group member has the data, the bar to his using it would be his own disagreement with the group succeeding or, more frequently, his inability to confront things.

EXAMPLE: Two group members are quarreling. A third group member seeks to handle it. Even though he knows the technique (third party law), his own inability to confront people makes him fail to use the correct solution and he backs off.

In backing off he thinks of some nonconfront, nonstandard "solution" such as firing them.

He has become a squirrel administrator.

EXAMPLE: The plant machinery is in bad shape. It is deteriorating to such an extent that it soon will cease to run. The mechanics plead for money to repair. The plant manager unfortunately cannot confront machinery—he not only "doesn't know about it" but it frightens him. He does not financially plan its full repair on a gradient back to an ideal scene. He simply dreams up the vague hope a new type will be invented. He does nothing. The machinery now costs more to run than it produces. The plant fails. The plant manager was a squirrel administrator.

So we have various causes of failure:

1. A secret desire to destroy,

2. The nonexistence of technology,

3. Nonavailability of the technology,

4. Ignorance of the technology even when available,

5. Failure to apply the technology even when available and known because the being cannot or does not confront the people or the portions of the physical universe concerned.

The existence of any of these things brings a group toward squirrel administration.

Natural cataclysms or political or social catastrophes or upheavals are the other two points which can bring about a failure, but even these can be planned for and to some degree handled. The future possibility of these must also be confronted in order to be circumvented.

Any successful organization will be fought by the society's fancied rulers or enemies. This is something which should be taken in stride. The ability to confront these discloses that standard administrative actions exist for these two.

DRILLS

Thus an administrator or staff member, even when the group's tech is available and known, must be able to confront and handle the confusions which can occur and which invite a turn-away and a squirrel solution.

Even this situation of the inabilities to confront and handle can be solved by third dynamic (group) drills and drills on the sixth dynamic (physical universe).

The drills would be practices in achieving general awareness and confronting and handling the noise and confusions which make one oblivious of or which drive one off and away from taking standard actions.

COMPETENCE

Competence is increased in the individual and the group by successes.

Successes come from anticipating the situation and handling it.

Standard admin is the key to competence and successes in an organization.

L. RON HUBBARD
FOUNDER

HCO POLICY LETTER OF 16 FEBRUARY 1971

REMIMEO

ORG SERIES 23
LINES AND TERMINALS

There is a scale concerning lines and terminals.

ASSOCIATED TERMINALS
    Handling flows and correctly changing particles.

GROUPED TERMINALS

LINES

PARTICLES

SIGNIFICANCES

FALSE TERMINALS

MISDIRECTED LINES

WRONG PARTICLES

FALSE SIGNIFICANCES (RUMORS)

MYSTERIOUS TERMINALS

CHAOTIC LINES

MENACING PARTICLES

DANGEROUS IMPRESSIONS

NONEXISTENT TERMINALS

NONEXISTENT LINES

NONEXISTENT PARTICLES

UNCONSCIOUS IMPULSES

THE CHAOS OF UNHAPPY NOTHINGNESS

Any organization and any individual staff member thereof is somewhere on this scale.

The trick of the scale is the awareness factor. At a position on the scale, the being or org is NOT AWARE of the scale levels above him.

Thus an organization *at* "Mysterious Terminals" is unaware of "False Significances" or anything else above "Mysterious Terminals." Thus an org or individual at "Mysterious Terminals" is unaware of any falsity or any oddity in significances or ideas.

Any level is the effect of any level ABOVE IT.

Any level is slightly at cause over any level below it.

Thus a well-organized group is not at effect and can make an effect upon any group below it in awareness on the scale.

CAUSES

There are several causes for lower positions on the scale.

The first cause is degree of *personal aberration* where a personnel is willfully throwing the terminals, lines, particles and significances into disarray. Show me how he regards terminals, handles particles or routes and I will know how sane or crazy he is. The significances given to terminals, handling particles and lines is a direct index of sanity.

The second cause is *unawareness*. Drills on lines and terminals were once thought to *improve* awareness. This is no longer held to be true. Drills have to be done to BRING ABOUT awareness. People are not naturally aware of other people, lines, various particles or ideas. Due to a century of psychological instruction from childhood that they are animals and after thousands of years of the "upper classes" regarding them as such, people tend to favor a dangerously low or nonexistent awareness. A sort of jurisprudence has been in effect that it is safer to be unaware as then one is "not guilty." A humanoid who has just run over a child has a first response of "I didn't see him." This is highly nonsurvival. If one never notices safes about to fall on him he is soon dead. And painfully so. Unawareness is a sort of blindness where the person looks like he is looking but sees nothing. Degrees of this exist. One can make a terrible lot of errors with this. Mr. A appears to the observer to be noticing, smelling things and hearing whereas he *registers* no sights, has a blind nose and tunes out all sound. "Did you read it?" "Yes." "What did it say?" And you hear a lot of things then that weren't on the paper. There are even degrees of registry. A person appears to see and yet doesn't. A person appears to see and on being asked will say what he saw but can be unaware of seeing, registering or saying he saw! This drives teachers quite mad. One has the glib student who can parrot but cannot apply. This is a surface registry without awareness. Thus drills such as the Admin Training Drills or dummy runs on lines are needed to bring about awareness. A few very sane fortunate fellows can see, register, understand and handle correctly without any drills at all. Others need drills to bring about awareness below a superficial response. To unaware people, terminals, lines, particles and significances just don't exist.

The third general category is *delusion*. One sees A and believes it to be G. This is a lower band of self-protection. Some workers (an awful lot of them) will only take jobs which are mechanical "so they can daydream." Their concept of a terminal is an altered terminal. A line goes somewhere else. A particle is something else. And an idea is really another idea. Such people are incapable of duplication. Say "I see the cat," they hear "Cars are dangerous." They aren't really crazy. They just register alterations of what they perceive.

The person who can attain the state of awareness of terminals as they are, lines as they should be, particles as they exist and significances that are the intended significances are very valuable people. An ideal group can be made up of such people.

CONSTRUCTIVE ACTIONS

An organization consists of terminals, lines, particles and significances.

An AGREEMENT factor has to be established and the group has to be aware of it and use it.

This agreement factor would consist of:

1. Purposes of the group,

2. A list of the hats including a short statement of the purpose and function of each post,

3. A full list of the particles handled by the group and the changes expected at each point of flow,

4. The flow lines of the particles being handled and changed,

5. The significances (technologies) of the group to form, flow and change particles.

If an org officer does not compile these five things and make them fully known and agreed to by all in the group, no organization will form or work.

Thus the PLAN of the group has to be laid out and drilled and known or no organization will form.

One will just have a group of individuals colliding with each other with no production.

The greatest source of confusion in a group are intermediate seniors who knock hats off faster than they can be gotten on and lines out before they can flow, all simply out of ignorance of the general plan of the organization.

Those who cannot perceive one or more of the above five points or bodies of data have to be drilled into awareness of them and dummy run.

Those who are quite crazy will frantically fight the hatting, stringing of lines and changing of particles and will inject mad significances into it all.

So the answer to how to make a group into an organization is to handle the insane one, prepare the five layouts named above, drill and dummy run *everyone* in the group on its *entire* pattern and expertly hat the specialist actions required at each point of change.

Then one has an organization that can produce and be viable.

L. RON HUBBARD
FOUNDER

215

HCO POLICY LETTER OF 26 FEBRUARY 1971
ISSUE II

REMIMEO

ORG SERIES 23-1
DRILLS

(Originally written by LRH for the *Apollo* OODs
on 26 Feb. 71. Issued as an HCO PL on 3 Nov. 80.)

Refs:

HCO PL	25 Jan. 71	Org Series 22 SQUIRREL ADMIN
HCO PL	16 Feb. 71	Org Series 23 LINES AND TERMINALS

Drills have several purposes. To groove in a team action is a principal one. To test a system fully. To groove in lines.

Whenever postings are changed, the new post holders have to be grooved in on their posts (hatted and on-post trained) and then the team itself must be drilled.

The two steps are always needed.

This applies to org lines as well. Dummy runs and dummy bullbait runs serve as the drill.

L. RON HUBBARD
FOUNDER

HCO POLICY LETTER OF 6 MARCH 1971

REMIMEO
PROD–ORG HATS
TECH HATS
QUAL HATS

ORG SERIES 24

LINE DESIGN
HGC LINES, AN EXAMPLE

The present lines for the HGC in any org are the subject of HCOB 5 Mar. 71, Auditor Admin Series 10, C/S Series 25, THE FANTASTIC NEW HGC LINE, which is to be considered part of this policy letter.

This modifies early Tech org boards to some extent.

The old line in '65 policy did not include a Case Supervisor as such and shunted failed pcs to Qual Review.

Today Tech does its own pc repairs and Qual concentrates on cramming HGC auditors as well as students. Qual can also cram the Tech C/S.

It is completely amazing that a statistic ceiling on well done auditing hours delivered could not have exceeded 250–300 well done hours a week no matter how many auditors were hired or posted. The post of the C/S overloaded and the D of P post could not function well without overload.

The new line is capable of a statistic ceiling of 600 to 800 well done hours a week. After that a new second HGC is manned fully and given new space.

The importance of a properly formed line, traveling in correct sequence is then driven home.

An improper line will reduce the statistic ceiling by $\frac{1}{2}$ to $\frac{1}{3}$ of what can be achieved by the same number of people.

The overload of seniors usually occurs because of improperly set up lines.

Lines are invisible to most people and they are unable to conceive of them until given full drills.

Unless this new C/S line is used you will not be able to average more than 250 well done hours a week no matter how many auditors you put in the HGC. The auditors will be idle, confused and causing upsets.

If an org cannot get more than 250 well done hours a week, it will find that it cannot really make money from processing.

Thus the new line will give volume, quality and viability in processing pcs.

Advantages of the line are that one HSST can handle up to 30 auditors. The earlier ceiling was 8 or 10 auditors.

With higher volume, backlogs vanish rapidly.

The admin personnel in the line can be afforded.

Line design, then, is a strong and unsuspected cause of low statistic ceilings.

Product and org officers must be intimately familiar with this HGC line. And they must be aware of the fact that faulty line design can cripple an org's income and overload its posts and excellent line design can double the stat ceiling in any department while lightening the load.

L. RON HUBBARD
FOUNDER

HUBBARD COMMUNICATIONS OFFICE
SAINT HILL MANOR, EAST GRINSTEAD, SUSSEX

HCO POLICY LETTER OF 16 MARCH 1971
ISSUE III

REMIMEO

PERSONNEL SERIES 19
ORG SERIES 25
LINES AND HATS

It will be found that in organization there are *MANY* major factors involved.

The following three, however, give the most problems:

1. Personnel

2. Hats

3. Lines

Technology is a subdivision of both personnel (who may have to be specially trained before they can be considered personnel) and hats (which are mainly admin technology and line functions).

To solve any problem, one has to recognize what the problem is. One cannot solve problem A by trying to solve problem B or C. Example: Problem: broken-down car. You cannot fix the car by repairing the kitchen lino. Example: You cannot floor the kitchen by fixing the car.

All this may seem obvious when obliviously stated. But there is a more subtle version. ANY PROBLEM THAT DOES NOT SOLVE IS NOT THE PROBLEM. There must be some other problem.

Locating and isolating situations (problems) in an organization is the technique of the Data Series. That technology will find for one the problem that should be solved.

As there are three major organizational factors these then also form the core of all organizational situations (or problems, same thing).

Each one of these is its own zone — personnel, hats, lines.

Each one has its own problems. There are situations in personnel. There are situations in hats. There are situations in lines.

They *are* related. They are not identical.

You will find you cannot wholly solve a problem in lines by solving personnel. You cannot wholly solve a problem in hats by solving lines. You cannot wholly solve a problem in personnel by solving the other two.

Example: Production hours are down. Fifteen new personnel are added to the area. Production stays down. It was a problem in lines.

Example: Confusion reigns in the pipe shop. The lines are carefully straightened out. Confusion still reigns. It was a problem in hats.

Example: Broken products are wrecking org repute. Hats are carefully put on. Products continue to be broken. It was a problem in personnel.

Example: The org stays small. Executives work harder. The org stays small. It was a series of problems in personnel, hats *and* lines, none addressed at all.

You will see symptoms of all this in various guises. The test of whether or not the right problem was found is whether or not production increased in volume, quality and viability.

In actual practice one works on all three of these factors constantly — personnel, hats and lines — when one is organizing.

You will find with some astonishment that failure to have or know or wear or do a *hat* is the commonest reason why *lines* do not go in. That personnel is hard to procure and train because hats and lines are being knocked out. That hats can't be worn because lines or personnel are out.

Situations get worsened by solving the wrong problem instead of the real problem. In the Data Series this is called finding the right *Why*.

Organizational problems center around these three things in the broadest general sense. More than one can be present in any situation.

Production problems are concerned with the particles which flow on the lines, changed by the hatted personnel, with consumption and general viability. So to make a full flow from organization through to distribution, one would add raw materials, changed state of materials and their consumption. Organization is not an end-all. To have value it must result in production.

But when personnel, hats and lines are not solved, production is very difficult. Therefore to get production one must have an organization to back it up. And personnel, hats and lines must exist and be functional. If these exist, the rest of the factors of establishment can be brought into being.

It goes without saying that organization involves other problems like space, materiel, finance, etc. These and many more also enter into "Whys" of no production. But dominating others are problems in personnel, hats and lines. Others tend to solve if these are handled and organized.

L. RON HUBBARD
FOUNDER

HCO POLICY LETTER OF 25 MARCH 1971

ORG SERIES 26
VALUABLE FINAL PRODUCTS

By definition, a valuable final product is something that can be exchanged with other activities in return for support. The support usually adds up to food, clothing, shelter, money, tolerance and cooperation (goodwill).

On an individual basis this is easy to grasp. The individual produces a product or products which, flowed into the dept, div, org, company, community, state, nation or planet, then returns to him his pay and goodwill or at least sufficient goodwill to prevent his abandonment or destruction.

Long-range survival of the individual is attained in this fashion.

A valuable final product (VFP) is valuable because it is potentially or factually exchangeable.

The key word in this sense is EXCHANGEABLE. And exchangeability means outside, with something outside the person or activity.

A valuable final product could as easily be named a VALUABLE EXCHANGEABLE PRODUCT.

Sanity and insanity are matters of *motive*, not rationality or competence. The sane are constructive, the insane are destructive.

Thus insanity on the part of the potential receiver of a VFP can prevent an exchange of a final product the receiver should be able to use and for which he should be willing to give active support and goodwill to the producer. Example: Man starving; you try to sell him good food at reasonable price for which he has money to pay. He tries to shoot you and destroy the food. This is insanity since he is trying to destroy the product he needs and can afford.

Crime is the action of the insane or the action of attempting seizure of product without support. Example: Robbers who do not support a community seek to rob from it supporting funds.

Fraud is the attempt to obtain support without furnishing a product.

Sanity and honesty then consist of producing a valuable final product for which one is then recompensed by support and goodwill, or in reverse flow, supporting and giving goodwill to the producer of the product.

Ethical basics, morale, social subjects, law, all are based on this principle of the valuable final product. Previously it has been "instinctive" or "common sense." It has not before been stated.

Civilizations which facilitate production and interchange and inhibit crime and fraud are then successful. Those that do not, perish.

Persons who wish to destroy civilizations promote departures from these basic rules of the game. Methods of corrupting fair interchange are numerous.

The FACTORS are the first appearance of these principles.

The theory of the valuable final product is an extension of the FACTORS.

Parts of organizations or organizations, towns, states and countries all follow the principles which apply to the individual.

The survival or value of any section, department, division or org is whether or not it follows these principles of interchange.

The survival or value of any town, state or country follows these principles of interchange.

You can predict the survival of any activity by confirming its interchange regularities or can predict its downfall by irregularities in this interchange.

Therefore it is vital that a person or a section, department, division or part of an org or an org figure out exactly what it is interchanging. It is producing something that is valuable to the activity or activities with which it is in communication and for that it is obtaining support.

If it is actually producing valuable final products then it is entitled to support.

If on the other hand it is only organizing or hoping or PRing and is not producing an interchangeable commodity or commodities in VOLUME or QUALITY for which support can be elicited and even demanded, it will not be VIABLE.

It doesn't matter how many orders are issued or how well org boards are drawn or beautiful the plans to produce are made. The hard fact of production remains the dominant fact.

How well organized things are *increases* production volume and *improves* quality and thus can bring about viability.

But it is the valuable final product there and being interchanged that determines basic survival.

Lack of viability can always be traced to the volume and quality of an actual valuable final product.

Hope of a product has a short-term value that permits an activity to be built. But when the hope does not materialize, then any hoped-for viability also collapses.

One then must organize *back* from the actually produced product.

For instance, a technical subject is capable of producing an exact result.

IF persons are trained to actually produce the result AND THE RESULT IS PRODUCED then one can exchange the technicians with the community for support.

If the result is produced (by training the technicians well) then the result can be interchanged with an individual for support and goodwill.

Where any of these factors suffer in volume or quality then an interchange is difficult and viability becomes uncertain.

As individuals, communities and states are not necessarily sane, upsets can occur in the interchange even when production is occurring.

Therefore the producer has a stake in maintaining the sanity of the scene in which he is operating, and one of his valuable final products is a scene in which production and interchange can occur.

The basics of valuable final products are true for any industrial or political or economic system.

Many systems attempt to avoid these basics and the end result would be disaster.

The individual, section, department, division, org or country that is not producing something valuable enough to interchange will not be supported for long. It is as simple as that.

L. RON HUBBARD
FOUNDER

HCO POLICY LETTER OF 7 JULY 1971

REMIMEO
HASes STAR-RATE
FEBC GRADS
   STAR-RATE
FEBC CHECKSHEET
   STAR-RATE

ORG SERIES 27

HCO ESTABLISHMENT FUNCTIONS

HCO means HUBBARD COMMUNICATIONS OFFICE.

The elementary and very simple actions of HCO are contained in this:

It is really hCo.

C = Communications.

To have Communications you have to have TERMINALS.

Flows can ONLY occur when terminals are rock steady and STABLE. There can be NO flows and NO power without steady terminals. Hence, comm cannot occur without stable terminals.

The ORG BOARD is the pattern of the terminals and their flows. So you have to have an org bd. And the org bd must in truth be a representation of what is in the org.

The org bd shows where what terminals are located in the org so flows can occur.

HCO has recruitment which means it gets people from OUTSIDE the org to be placed as terminals in the org = posts.

HCO has the posting of the org bd and designating the spaces in the org so that flows can occur.

Hatting is a prime function of HCO because otherwise the terminals won't know what they are supposed to be doing or what flows they handle or how.

HCO has INSPECTION to see that the flows are going right and that terminals are functioning.

Ethics exists to handle gross outnesses in flows.

Then routing can occur.

Then production can occur.

In essence that is ALL there is to an HCO.

If it realizes its key is C for Communications and that comm requires terminals and an org bd so that flows can occur then HCO will function.

This action of putting in terminals is called ESTABLISHING.

Thus HCO is the establishing division.

DIS–ESTABLISHING

If HCO does not know this and if it makes numerous errors or alters importances away from this, it DIS–ESTABLISHES the org.

DIS = Take apart.

ESTABLISH = Put there.

DISESTABLISH = Take apart what is put there.

Thus dis-establish means to take out terminals and tear things up.

In using the org itself as a source of personnel, then an "HCO" tears things up far faster than it puts things there.

HAS

The HCO Area Secretary, HAS, has the function of ESTABLISHING THE ORG.

That means to find, hat, train, apprentice persons from OUTSIDE the org, to locate them in the org and on the org bd and then route the raw materials (public people in this case) along the line for production, which means changing particles into a final product.

If HCO *establishes* the org then all will be well.

If it fails to recruit or hat or org bd or route or distribute comm or police the lines, the org will stagger or fail.

The HAS is responsible for seeing that HCO establishes the org.

An HAS who is doing anything else is DIS–ESTABLISHING.

HCO EXTERNAL

HCO has the incoming and outgoing flow lines as well.

This gives it Address. This means the *location* of the terminals OUTSIDE the org that the org contacts.

This in itself is an org bd.

The HAS must insist that the outside terminals are also established.

This gives an international network of flows amongst terminals.

WHAT is produced and WHAT flows on the lines is the business of other terminals outside HCO unless these threaten the functions of HCO.

SIMPLICITY

Now if you think there is anything more to it than this, work and work and work to do it in clay, clean up the misunderstood words and become thus able to envision and handle it.

Many policies exist about HCO. There is a lot of admin tech connected with an HCO but ALL OF IT is entirely and completely concerned with *how* to establish an HCO and an org.

This PL should be known, known, known and any further confusion would be plainly the result of personal aberration such as an inability to conceive of a terminal or a space or a thirst for confusion only found in very batty places.

The functions of an HCO and the duties of an HAS are so elementary and so plain that they cannot be misunderstood even by experts.

HCO establishes the org.

That is the basic thing to know.

The techniques of how it is done are well recorded and broadly issued.

HCO does NOT disestablish the org.

HCO does NOT leave an org un-established.

HCO ESTABLISHES THE ORG.

L. RON HUBBARD
FOUNDER

HCO POLICY LETTER OF 8 MARCH 1971R
ISSUE II
REVISED 22 APRIL 1982

REMIMEO

ORG SERIES 27-1
ORG OFFICER

(Originally written by LRH for the *Apollo* OODs
of 8 Mar. 71. Issued as an HCO PL on 27 Sept. 80.)

Org officers think they approach HASes to organize. They don't.

HCO has not formed because org officers keep making demands on it instead of doing their job. The organization it takes to get out a specific product is instant stuff. HCO is a long-term build of the establishment. Entering instant organization into HCO of course defeats its purposes and prevents it from the long-haul actions necessary to form a whole org.

If an org officer considered himself the product officer's expeditor he would begin to get the idea.

We have a product officer–org officer mission going in to expedite FEBCs. The product officer will get the product—a competent graduated FEBC on an airplane going home—being made and fired. The org officer will push the materiel and lines into shape to back up the product officer. Now, what's *that* have to do with HCO? Nothing.

The org officer makes sure there *is* a pack or tape or recorder or gets them (not by despatch) and the product officer checks out, verifies, grooms, solves FEBC problems, pushes cases.

The Course Super goes on supervising, Course Admin goes on admining. What they're doing right with the student gets pushed and done more of. And what organization there is gets more of from the org officer.

For instance, here is a CO-type prod officer action that was done.

SITUATION: Course numbers building up. You see this in orgs.

HANDLING: Put on a prod–org mission to get numbers completed and fired.

The CO found three who could be made ready to fire at first glance and gave the order GO-GO-GO, to Action.

The cope was fire three, NOW. The medium range was get a mission on it.

That is uptight production.

A prod–org team works in *hours* and *days*. Save an hour, save a day. Do it in hours, do it in days.

By doing it they learn line and materiel outnesses and their reform CSWs of lines and actions are written up when they're completed and that's their first contact with the HAS and HCO.

Now with these reforms the general org action will be easier and faster and a product backlog peak won't occur so fast again.

A prod–org team that writes despatches and harasses HCO just doesn't know THAT THE PROD–ORG SYSTEM IS TO HANDLE BACKLOGS AND OMISSIONS IN PRODUCTS. *Having handled* they can advise or order or get approval for line changes and new recruitment, etc. These, the HAS can get in for the long haul.

Prod–orgs WORK, they don't just order.

L. RON HUBBARD
FOUNDER

HCO POLICY LETTER OF 29 JULY 1971
ISSUE I

PERSONNEL SERIES 21
ORG SERIES 28
WHY HATTING?

A few days ago when I found that musical chairs and flubbed hatting had unstabilized some areas, I wondered whether or not this might stem from some social aberration that was very general in the societies in which we are working.

And it seems to have been the case. I worked on it a bit and found this:

LAW: THE POWER OF A THETAN STEMS FROM HIS ABILITY TO HOLD A POSITION IN SPACE.

This is quite true. In *Scientology 8-80* the base of the motor is discussed. It holds two terminals in fixed positions. Because they are so fixed, power can be generated.

If a thetan can hold a position or location in space he can generate POWER.

If he cannot, he cannot generate power and will be weak.

We have known this for nineteen years. It applies here.

Observation: MODERN SOCIETY TENDS TO CONFUSE AND UNSTABILIZE PERSONS WITH ITS HECTIC PACE.

Observation: BEINGS WHO ARE AFRAID OF STRONG PEOPLE TRY TO WEAKEN THEM.

Observation: PERSONS WHO ARE PUSHED AROUND FEEL THEY CANNOT HOLD A POSITION IN SPACE.

Observation: PEOPLE HATE TO LOSE THEIR POSTS AND JOBS. THEY FIND IT DEGRADING.

In processing, picking up this chain of lost positions achieves very good gains and rehabilitates a person's ability to hold a job.

LAW: BY GIVING A PERSON A POST OR POSITION, HE IS SOMEWHAT STRENGTHENED AND MADE MORE CONFIDENT IN LIFE.

LAW: BY LETTING A PERSON RETAIN HIS POST, HE IS MADE MORE SECURE.

LAW: BY HATTING A PERSON, HE IS GREATLY STRENGTHENED AS HE IS HELPED TO HOLD HIS POST.

A basically insecure person who feels he is unable to hold his position in space is sufficiently strengthened by hatting to feel secure enough to do his job.

LAW: HAVING A HAT, BEING HATTED AND DEMONSTRATING COMPETENCE MAKES A PERSON FEEL CAPABLE OF HOLDING HIS POSITION IN SPACE AND HE BECOMES MORE STABLE, CONFIDENT IN LIFE AND MORE POWERFUL.

LAW: UNHATTED PERSONS ON A POST CAN BECOME CRIMINAL ON THE POST BECAUSE THEY FEEL INSECURE AND BECOME WEAK.

When a person is secretly afraid of others, he instinctively will not hat them or hats them wrongly and tends to transfer or move them about.

When a person is insecurely posted and insufficiently hatted, he can try to weaken others by trying to prevent their hatting and trying to get them transferred or even dismissed.

This is apparently the social aberration at work.

The answer to a sane org and a sane society is not welfare and removal. It is:

Recruit them,

Train them,

Hat them,

Apprentice them,

Give them a post.

This is so strong in truth it would de-aberrate the bulk of the crime out of a society.

And it sure will put an org in POWER.

L. RON HUBBARD
FOUNDER

HCO POLICY LETTER OF 11 AUGUST 1971
ISSUE III

REMIMEO

ORG SERIES 29
INFINITE EXPANSION

There is no reason whatever to ever contract or reduce the size of an org except covert destruction.

In theory there is no limit to the size of an org.

The 1967 org board is capable of expanding to 200,000 staff members!

For our purposes, there is no real limit to expansion.

So long as property purchase does not commit future income dangerously and so long as HASes keep the admin staff in a ratio of two to one technical staff, there is no limit to expansion.

So long as cash-bills is kept more cash than bills there is no limit to expansion.

So long as the staff produces what their posts call for there is no limit to expansion.

So long as you DELIVER in quality what you SELL there is no limit to expansion.

So long as you keep standard on admin and keep standard on tech, there is no limit to expansion.

So don't get frightened, don't fire people, don't cut back. Understand the above and the *whole* of this policy letter. And there is no limit to expansion.

So EXPAND.

L. RON HUBBARD
FOUNDER

HUBBARD COMMUNICATIONS OFFICE

SAINT HILL MANOR, EAST GRINSTEAD, SUSSEX

HCO POLICY LETTER OF 10 NOVEMBER 1971

REMIMEO

ORG SERIES 29-1

ORGANIZATION AND SURVIVAL

(Originally written by LRH for the *Apollo* OODs
of 10 Nov. 71. Issued as an HCO PL on 11 Sept. 80.)

Well-organized activities survive. The survival of individuals in those organizations depends on the highly organized condition of the activity.

A small group, extremely well organized, has excellent chances of survival.

Even a large group, badly organized, hasn't a prayer.

The essence of organization is org boarding, posting with reality and, in keeping with the duties being performed, training and hatting.

To this has to be added the actual performance of the duties so that the activity is productive.

The outward signs of a badly organized group are slovenliness and fumbles.

Another ingredient that goes hand in hand with organization and survival is toughness. The ability to stand up to and confront and handle whatever comes the way of the organization depends utterly on the ability of the individuals of the organization to stand up to, confront and handle what comes the individual's way. The composite whole of this ability makes a tough organization.

An individual who is not properly posted, isn't performing the duties of the post, is not trained or hatted is soft. He has no position to hold, therefore he goes down at the first fan of a feather.

Confidence in one's teammates is another factor in organization survival. Confidence in one's self is something that has to be earned. It is respect. This is a compound of demonstrated competence, being on post and being dependable.

After an individual has failed, confidence in him on the part of his teammates sinks. He has lost face and is not respected. This, then, shows itself up in numerous ways. It is up to that individual to earn back confidence so that his teammates will again trust him. The way to do this is to get properly org boarded, trained, hatted and to confront and handle, with competence, whatever that post is supposed to control.

The ultimate in no confidence by a group in a team member is no post at all. Reports from those who have no post or from those who are between posts stress the horrors of having no post.

Our survival depends fully on becoming entirely and completely organized. This will happen to the degree that every separate unit, department and division in an org is properly org boarded, properly performing the duties of the post, is trained and fully hatted.

L. RON HUBBARD
FOUNDER

HCO POLICY LETTER OF 14 JULY 1972

REMIMEO

EXECUTIVE SERIES 14
ORG SERIES 30
ESTABLISHMENT OFFICER SERIES 22

ESTO FAILURES

For several months I have been studying the Esto system in operation and have finally isolated the exact points of any failures so they can be turned to successes.

PUTTING IN THE SYSTEM

An Esto returning to an org can crash it.

The exact reasons for this are:

A. The execs who heretofore did organizational work say, "Ah, here's the Esto system at last," and promptly drop their organizational and personnel actions.

Yet here is this lone E Esto, no divisional Estos, no one trained to support him.

The right answer is when an E Esto goes into an org where there are no Estos or only a TEO or QEO, he must gather up the execs and tell them it will take him weeks to recruit and train Estos and that THEY MUST CONTINUE ANY ORGANIZATIONAL ACTIONS THEY ARE DOING and that the HAS IS STILL ESTABLISHING THE ORG.

Otherwise they let go their lines.

B. The new E Esto takes key production personnel from the divisions to be Estos and they crash.

The answer to this is to RECRUIT the new Estos.

This is easier than it looks if you recruit idle area *auditors* to be Estos.

If you do this, remember that they went idle as auditors because they had out-ethics, were PTS, had misunderstoods and out-TR 0. To get them you do a 3 May 72 (ETHICS AND EXECUTIVES) PL, a 5 Apr. 72 (PTS TYPE A HANDLING) PL, Method 4 on their courses and make them do *real* TRs, especially zero. And they'll be ready.

You get a list of area auditors and contact them and do the above on them and you'll have Estos who are half-trained already.

Failing this or in addition to it just plain recruit.

C. The first post a new E Esto should take is Dept 1.

He does NOT "hat the HAS" or "just do programs." He rolls up his sleeves and WORKS as director of Dept 1.

He recruits, he posts up Dept 1. He hats the hell out of Dept 1.

He makes a Department 1 that really, really flows in personnel, puts up org boards and hats.

WHEN he has a Department 1 FUNCTIONING he can begin to recruit Estos as well as other org staff.

If he can't get a Dept 1 whizzing he has no business being an Esto, does he?

He does NOT put in Dept 2 or act as Dept 3. He makes the HAS handle these.

With a *strong working* Dept 1, an Esto system can then go in.

D. Musical chairs is the commonest reason any org collapses.

A "new broom sweeps clean" complex will wreck any org.

An E Esto on arrival, taking over Dept 1, FREEZES ALL PERSONNEL TRANSFERS. He does not permit even one transfer.

The only exception would be where a musical chair insanity has just occurred. If this was followed by a stat crash then one REVERTS THE ORG TO THE UPSTAT PERIOD and *then* FREEZES PERSONNEL TRANSFERS.

But before one reverts one must evaluate the earlier period by stats to be sure it WAS the upstat period.

By freezing personnel one protects what he is building.

Almost all musical chairing is the work of a suppressive except when it is the work of an idiot.

E. Anyone trying to hold Dept 1 in a personnel starved org is holding a hot seat as any HAS or Personnel Director can tell you.

Body traffic to this dept in any medium-sized org defies belief.

It looks like Grand Central Station at the rush hour.

"I have to have _____," "Where is my Course Super _____?" etc., etc., etc., is the constant chant.

You can spend the whole day interviewing staff execs and get nothing done.

There is a right way to do all these things and a billion wrong ways.

Obviously the answer to all their problems is to get and train new people. Yet how can one in all the commotion.

Ninety percent of these requests are from people who are not hatting and using the people they already have.

The right way is on any new personnel demanded one gets Dept 3 to do an Inspection and Report Form for people in the area of the exec doing the demanding. You will find very often unhatted, untrained and wasted personnel and many outnesses.

You hold the line on personnel by saying: "Handle these unutilized or half-working staff or these outnesses. You are here on my procurement board as entitled to the (give priority, 3rd, 8th) person we hire or recruit."

And get industrious in recruiting, using all standard actions, for that is the only way things can be solved.

Most orgs would run better on less people because the personnel are not hatted or trained. One org, two years before this writing, made *four* times as much money on *half* the personnel it now has.

Unhatted, the staff is slow and uncertain. Unproducing, the div heads demand little.

But they sure can scream for more personnel!

No org ever believes it is overmanned.

F. Some divisions (like the usual Treasury or Dissem) can be undermanned. Key income posts most often are empty.

When one mans up an org one sets priorities of who gets personnel.

This is done by PRODUCTION paralleling. One mans up against production.

New people come in through Div 6. They are signed up by Div 2. Delivery is done by Div 4. Money is collected by Div 3. That gives you a sequence of manning up.

You man income and delivery posts with new hirings.

The E Esto is trying to get in a Dept 1 so of course he gives this a priority as well.

Until the income is really rolling in and the delivery rolling out, one does very little about other areas.

Having gained VOLUME, one now begins to man up for quality. This means a Cramming and a W/C Section in Qual. It means more HCO.

One now hits for future quantity by getting auditors in training, more upper execs in training.

When the org is so built and running and viable it is time the whole Esto system got manned up.

G. Every 5th person hired on an average should be put in Dept 1 as a *Dept 1* extra personnel who does Dept 1 duties and trains part time as an Esto.

This gives the E Esto additional personnel in Dept 1.

It also begins an Esto right.

His most essential duties as an Esto *are* Dept 1 type duties.

You eventually have a bulging Dept 1. You have a basic Dept 1 that functions well and will continue so. You have the Esto trainees who are working in Dept 1 as Dept 1 personnel. And you have of course some new people who are HCO Expeditors until they get in enough basics for real regular posting.

This makes a fat Dept 1 and proves one can Esto!

SUCCESS

If an E Esto introduces the Esto system exactly as above and in no other way, he will be a success.

Like an auditor varying processes or altering HCOBs, a new E Esto who varies the above will bring about disaster.

Where E Estos have gone into orgs other ways or where the system has been varied, stats have crashed.

By going in this way, as above, it can be a wild success.

How fast can you put in an Esto system? It takes months of hard work. It depends really on how good the E Esto is at recruiting, org boarding and hatting.

If he's good at these things the time does not stretch out to forever.

For comparison, it took half a year each to build DC, Johannesburg and SH to their highest peaks. They were all built from a Dept 1 viewpoint of recruiting, org boarding and hatting hard enough to get production.

So this is the oldest pattern we have — Dept 1 evolves the org.

When the org gets too big Dept 1 loses touch. You extend it into each div and you have the Esto system. And you have Estos.

L. RON HUBBARD
FOUNDER

237

HCO POLICY LETTER OF 23 JULY 1972RB
Revised 11 January 1991

Remimeo

Executive Series 15
Personnel Series 26
Org Series 31
Establishment Officer Series 23

THE VITAL NECESSITY OF HATTING

On a graph analysis of past stats, my campaign on hatting where a hat was a checksheet and pack apparently introduced a steady rise of the International Gross Income.

Studying this further I discovered a new basic, simple fact:

HATTING = CONTROL

A person who is hatted can control his post.

If he can control his post he can hold his position in space — in short, his location. And this is power.

When a person is uncertain, he cannot control his post, he cannot control his position. He feels weak. He goes slow.

If he can control his post and its actions he feels confident. He can work effectively and rapidly.

The key is CONTROL.

Control is the ability to START, CHANGE and STOP.

When he is hatted he knows the tech of HANDLING things. Thus he can control them. He is at CAUSE over his area.

If you have an org composed only of weak wobbly posts, they tend to collapse in on each other. There is no POWER.

The org then cannot be CAUSE over its environment because it is composed of parts which are not cause. The whole is only the sum of its parts.

If all the parts are each one at cause, then the whole will be at CAUSE over its environment.

Only an org at CAUSE can reach and CONTROL.

Thus a fully hatted org can be at cause over its environment, can reach and control its fates and fortunes.

THUS THE PRIMARY TARGETS OF AN ESTO ARE:

A. ESTABLISHED ORG FORM and

B. FULLY HATTED PERSONNEL.

BASIC SEQUENCE OF HATTING

1. Recruited or hired. Signs contract.

2. Instant-hatted for the job assigned as an HCO Expeditor.

3. Staff Status 0.

4. Basic Study Manual (if the staff member has not previously done the Student Hat or Primary Rundown).

5. Staff Status I.

6. Staff Status II.

7. Posting as other than an HCO Expeditor.

8. Full hatting with a checksheet and pack fully done with M6, M7, M9, M3 and M4 Word Clearing.

9. Eligibility for study and auditing (OR for staff service or study).

10. Must have a stat and demonstrated he has produced on post.

11. Purification Rundown.

12. Objective Processes: CCHs, 8-C, SCS, Havingness, etc.

13. Scientology Drug Rundown (if required).

14. Method One Word Clearing, Student Hat.

15. Administrative or tech training (OEC or auditing).

Flag Orders in the Sea Org may change this lineup slightly but it is basically the same.

No one should have any other training, much less full-time training, before step 12 in the above.

After a staff member has completed Staff Status 0 he may receive PTS handlings and study the PTS checksheet and may have emergency assists. He may also be audited by students and TTC if he has rising stats.

There are time limits placed on how long it takes to do SS I and SS II. A person who can't make it is routed to Qual where he is offloaded with advice on how to get more employable. (In the SO it is Fitness Board.)

TIME–TESTED

The above is the route that has been tested by time and found good.

Other approaches have NOT worked.

Granting full-time training at once is folly. The person may get trained but he'll never be a staff member. This is the biggest failure with auditors — they don't know the org. Admin training with no org experience to relate it to is a waste of time.

This was how we built every great org. And when it dropped out the org became far less powerful.

Old-timers talk of these great orgs in their great days. And they will tell you all about the org boarding and hatting that went on. How the Hatting Officer in HCO and the Staff Training Officer in Qual worked as a team. And how fast the lines flew.

The above steps have stood the test of time and are proven by stats.

RECRUITING AND HIRING

You *never* recruit with a promise of free courses or free auditing. Not even HASes or HQSes. You recruit or hire somebody to be part of the team.

OPEN GATE

If *any* opinion or selection is permitted as to who is going to be let on staff, *all* recruitment and hiring will fail.

By actual stats when you let *anyone* say, "No! Not him! Not her!" the gate shuts, the flow stops. And you've had it.

Requirements and eligibility *fail*. The proof is that when they have existed in orgs, the org wound up with only PTSes and no-case-gains!

The right answer is FAST FLOW hiring. Then you have so many that those who can't make it drift low on the org board or off. You aren't trying to hold posts with unqualified people "who can't be spared."

In a short-staffed org "looking only for the best people" the guy nobody will have gets put in an empty "unimportant" department. He's now a Director!

It only happened because you didn't have dozens.

The answer is NOT lock the gate or have requirements. The answer is HAT.

An org that isn't hatted goes weak and criminal.

Don't be selective in hiring or recruiting. Open the gates and *HAT!*

Follow the steps given above and you have it.

Don't spend coins like training or auditing (or travel) on people until they have proven their worth. No bonuses or high pay for anyone until they have reached and attained step 10 (a good stat). The cost of such fast flow hiring is not then a big factor.

The only trouble I ever had with this was getting div heads to UTILIZE their staff. A FIRST JOB FOR AN EXECUTIVE IS TO GET THINGS FOR HIS PEOPLE TO DO. AND KEEP THEM BUSY AT PRODUCTIVE THINGS.

So I used to have to go through the org that did FAST FLOW HIRING regularly and get people to use their new people. And to move off those who could not work.

This was ALL the trouble I had with the system.

And until I enforced FAST FLOW HIRING there was always some effort by someone to close the gate.

ALL the great executives in Scientology came up in such orgs.

With a *flow* of people the best move on up. The worst, if any, drop off.

Only orgs with restricted hiring or recruiting give trouble.

IN A FAST FLOW HIRING ORG THE HAS AND ESTOs *MUST* BE ON THE BALL. THE BREAKDOWN OCCURS WHEN THEY DO NOT *HAT* AND KEEP ON TOP OF THE PERSONNEL SCENE.

Fast flow hiring only breaks down and gets protested where HCO and Estos are not doing a top job. They have to really *handle* the personnel, post them, hat them, keep the form of the org.

A fully formed org in a heavily populated location would need hundreds of staff. It would make hundreds of thousands.

But only if it is fast flow hiring, hatting, holding the form of the org, and only then could it produce.

L. RON HUBBARD
FOUNDER

Revision assisted by
LRH Technical Research
and Compilations

HCO POLICY LETTER OF 28 JULY 1972

Remimeo

Executive Series 16
Org Series 32
Establishment Officer Series 26

ESTABLISHING
HOLDING THE FORM OF THE ORG

If a person who could not play a piano sat down at a piano and hit random keys, he would not get any harmony. He would get noise.

If the head of a division gave orders to his staff without any regard to their assigned posts or duties, the result would be confusion and noise.

That's why we say a division head "doesn't know how to play the piano" when he knows so little about org form that he continually violates it by giving his various staff members duties that do not match their hats or posts.

But even if one could play the piano, one would have to have a piano to play.

SPECIALISTS

Each org staff member is a specialist in one or more similar functions. These are his specialties.

If he is fully trained to do these he is said to be HATTED.

The combined specialties properly placed and being done add up to the full production of an org.

The org form is then the lines and actions and spaces and flows worked out and controlled by specialists in each individual function.

These specialists are grouped in departments which have certain actions in common.

The departments having similar functions are grouped into divisions.

The divisions combine into the whole org form.

It is *far* less complex than it looks. It would be very complicated and confusing if there weren't divisions and departments and specialized actions. Without these you would get noise and very limited production and income, and at great strain.

Take a theater as an example. There are people who advertise it; these are the public relations people; they are hatted to get publicity and make people want to come to the play; call them the PR Division. There are the producers and directors; they are hatted to present a performance and make it occur; call them the Production Division. There are the actors and musicians; call them the Artists Division. There are the property men; they are hatted to get costumes and items needed; call them the Property Division. There are the stagehands and electricians and curtain and set men; call them the Stage Division. There are the ticket sellers and money handlers and payroll and bills payers; they are hatted on money and selling; call them the Finance Division. There are the people who clean the theater and show people to seats and handle the crowds; call them the House Division. And there are the managers and playwrights and score writers and angels (financiers); call them loosely the Executive Division.

Now as long as they know their org board, have their flows plotted out, are hatted for their jobs and do a good job, even a half-good play can be viable.

But throw away the org board, skip the flows, don't hat them and even a brilliant script and marvelous music will play to an empty house and go broke.

Why? Because an org form is not held. Possibly an untrained unhatted producer will try to make the stagehands sell tickets, the actors write the music, the financiers show people to their seats. If he didn't know who the people were or what their hats were he might do just that.

And there would be noise and confusion even where there was no protest. People would get in one another's road. And the general presentation would look so ragged to the public they'd stay away in droves.

ESTO ACTION

Now what would an Esto (or an Executive Director) have to do with, let us say, an amateur, dilettante theatrical company that was about to bog.

Probably half the people had quit already. And even if there were people in the company they would probably need more.

The very first action would be to Esto Series 16 the top men to make money quick.

The first organizing action would be to kick open the hiring door. This would begin with getting out hiring PR and putting someone there to sign people up who came to be hired (not to test and audition and look at references, but just to sign people up).

The next action would be to do a flow plan of public bodies and money. So one sees where the org form reaches. Then a schedule.

Next action would be to do an org board. Not a 3-week job. (It takes me a couple hours to sketch one with a sign pen for posting.) AND GET IT POSTED.

One then takes the *head* of each of these divisions and *hats* him on what his division is supposed to do and tell him to *do* it. NOW.

You make and post the flow plan, org bd and terminal locations plan where the whole company can see them.

Chinese drill on a flow plan to show them what they're doing and what has to be done.

Chinese drill on the org board including introducing each person named on it and getting it drilled, what he does and who he is.

You Chinese drill the terminal locations where each of these persons (and functions) is to be found.

You get agreement on schedules.

You now have a group that knows who specializes in what and what's expected of each.

You get the head of the whole company to work with and hat the heads of his divisions.

Now you get the heads of divisions to hat their own staffs while you help.

And you get them busy.

You then put the polishing touches on your own Dept 1 (personnel PR, personnel hiring, personnel placement, org bds, hat compilations, hat library and hatting, hatting, hatting).

And by hatting and insisting on each doing his specialized job and getting seniors to HOLD THE FORM OF THE ORG by ordering the right orders to the right specialists and targeting their production and MAGIC! This amateur theatrical company gets solvent and good enough to wind up on Broadway. It's gone professional!

You say, yes, but what about artistic quality? What about the tech of writing music and acting . . .

Hey, you overlooked the first action. You kicked the door open on hiring and you hatted and trained. And you let go those who couldn't get a stat.

Eventually you would meet human reaction and emotion and would put in a full HCO and a full Qual particularly Cramming. But you'd still do that just to be sure it kept going.

Yessir, it can't help but become a professional group IF you, the Esto, established and made them HOLD THE FORM OF THE ORG and produce while they did it.

An Executive Director can do all this and produce too. The great ones do things like this. But here it is in full view.

A Scientology org goes together just like that. Which could be why, when we want to get something started, we say:

"Get the show on the road!"

But there is no show until it is established and the FORM OF THE ORG is held.

You are luckier than the amateur theatrical company's Esto. You have policy for every post and a book of it for every division and all the tech besides.

So there is no valid reason under the sun you cannot establish and then hold the form of the org.

L. RON HUBBARD
FOUNDER

HCO POLICY LETTER OF 13 JULY 1974
ISSUE I

REMIMEO

ORG SERIES 33
PRODUCTION BUGS

An analysis of failures to produce in several fields showed this fault:

EXPERIMENTING ON A
STANDARD PRODUCTION LINE.

Example: A cook can cook 30 dishes of various types successfully. Instead of retaining these as they are and seeking on the side to create or find new dishes, the cook experiments with and changes her 30 standard dishes. The result is failed production.

Example: A musical group has 15 finished pieces of repertoire. Instead of developing totally new pieces, they rewrite their existing repertoire. The result is a failure to do good shows.

Example: An org is doing well with a standard CF letter writing campaign. This personnel is pulled off onto phones only as an experiment. The org stats crash. The correct action would be a pilot phone program using new personnel and leaving the standard actions in.

In all cases the right thing to do is maintain without variation the standard production line and if experimenting or change is to be done: pilot it on the side with people or actions that do NOT impede standard production.

There is always a better model in the research lab than there is on the production line. The only bug occurs when the incomplete and unknown model is shoved over *as* the standard production.

If on test and experience a new action, properly piloted, is better, then and only then is it *added* to the standard line.

L. RON HUBBARD
FOUNDER

HCO POLICY LETTER OF 13 JULY 1974

ISSUE II

REMIMEO

ORG SERIES 34

WORKING INSTALLATIONS

Never unmock (take down or destroy) working installations.

A working installation is something that is operational.

The most flagrant violation of this is tearing up Div A to create Div B.

Division A is working. Somebody orders Division B to be strengthened.

A stupid or suppressive personnel person will tear up Div A to get personnel for Div B.

The correct action is to find extra or new people for the new action.

MUSICAL CHAIRS (transfers of persons around an org) is THE SINGLE MOST DESTRUCTIVE ACTION TO AN ORG'S STATS.

A failure to recruit and train new people leads one toward the destruction of working installations.

Whenever a new unit has to be made up, the failure to recruit and train shows up vividly. Essential people are ripped off their posts to form the new unit and the destruction of working installations by this action shows up at once in production stats.

It takes a great deal of work to find, hat and post people and get them experienced enough to produce. It takes a lot of work to make a working installation. But in one swoop some irresponsible personnel transfer can destroy it.

In mechanical matters the same thing applies. It takes a lot of work to make something operational. If for a while it is not used, a mechanic may rob its parts to set up something else instead of getting new parts for the something else. Then when the working installation is needed, it doesn't function and a great deal of trouble and expense is put in setting it up again. The trouble and expense is far more costly than getting the parts elsewhere.

NEVER UNMOCK A WORKING INSTALLATION.

It will be far more costly than going to a lot of trouble and expense to get the people or parts elsewhere.

L. RON HUBBARD
FOUNDER

HCO POLICY LETTER OF 20 SEPTEMBER 1976

REMIMEO
ALL STAFFS

EXECUTIVE SERIES 17
ORG SERIES 35

THE STAT PUSH

WHAT exactly is a stat push?

The danger in talking about this subject at all is that someone can do an immediate make-wrong by saying, "This means don't try to raise any stats."

So to understand this subject at all, one must have a pretty clear idea of exactly what is meant by "Don't push stats."

First of all one has to know precisely that STATISTICS ARE AN INDICATOR, THEY ARE NOT AN OBJECT.

WHEN YOU PUSH THE INDICATOR YOU DO NOT OBTAIN THE OBJECT IT REPRESENTS.

PRODUCTION IS COMPLETED CYCLES OF ACTION, NOT JUST NUMBERS.

The figure "1" in "1 apple" is not the apple.

Therefore pure, raw, naked stat pushing is an outpoint called "wrong target."

Pushing a stat without doing anything to bring about the stat is therefore an aberration.

Demanding a stat without doing anything to see that it occurs or putting anything there to make it or correcting anything that is preventing it is an aberration built out of either psychosis or ignorance of what should really be done.

It is quite true that stats must be kept up. But unless they are kept up by putting something there or correcting something that is there and getting all the cycles of actions done by all those who should do them, the stats will DECREASE and eventually vanish.

An order, a telex, a yell to the effect "GET THE STATS UP" is so much wasted time.

Further, such an order or telex or yell in any form has a very deteriorating effect. Individuals or staffs look at it in a properly weird light. They are there, they are doing what they can, they have problems and tangles and barriers. And telling them to "Get the stats up" causes various reactions, none of them very good. Essentially, it gives them neither help nor direction and even subtly informs them that the person ordering either does not know or does not care what is going on and is not about to help. The eventual reaction can become an ignoring of that command channel.

There are some specialized actions in stat pushing. Chief amongst them is the "GI push."

The usual indicator of this is a neglect or abandonment of staff or caring about staff. One sees no real effective attention on recruitment, training, apprenticing, hatting, future execs. And when one sees this it usually follows that there is a "GI push" going on somewhere in the executive strata. Why this indicator? Well, you see, it only takes a small handful of people to get in GI, and where executive attention is fixated on a "GI push," the various production staff, HCO and the rest of the org aren't "necessary." You find this with EDs who reg instead of getting Registrars and putting an org there, with EDs who go for credit unions and odd financial deals. And you will also find they have the biggest number and amount of refunds and the biggest backlogs AND a shrinking and unhappy org. Unfortunately, they soon also get a crashing GI, for none of the support actions are being done across the divisions.

The reason "GI pushing" happens so often is the structure of the society itself. The only real crime for which one can be punished by the governments of today is lack of money. In other crimes if one has the huge sums necessary to hire lawyers, one can often get off. But the crime of having no money is the only crime one cannot get out of. There are even laws which cause the arrest on the street of persons who do not have so much money in their pockets or wallets: it is called "vagrancy." So with the whole aberrated society on a big "GI push," with Wall Street measuring values only in how much something costs, with wages and prices soaring, at this writing, to total social disaster, it is no wonder that shortsighted and untrained or even aberrated executives get into a "GI push."

The answer to not having money is, of course, to make more money. And there is nothing whatever wrong with that. BUT that is *not* done with a "GI push." It is done with putting a whole org there, every part of it functioning and delivering, with all the bugs out of its lines, *and* making a lot, lot, lot more money. Fifty trained staff producing everything an org is supposed to produce will make far more money than five guys concentrating on GI only and letting the rest of the org go to blazes. The GI made by the fifty will go on increasing. The GI made by the five (and not backed up by the rest of the org) will decrease week by week and then crash.

Let us take some examples of "stat pushing":

The room is cold and the staff is wearing overcoats and using blankets. Mr. Stat Pusher walks over to the thermometer on the wall and sees that it reads very low. So he yells at the thermometer, "Get the stat up!" Nothing happens of course, it still says 15 degrees, so he yells at the staff, "Get that stat up!" Now, in this instance, having a stat pusher around, the org has no Treasury Div and so there was nobody to pay the bills and the fuel company has refused to deliver further fuel. The janitor is missing because there is no HCO to hire one or keep one on post so there's no one to light the furnace even if it had fuel. And due to an unhatted Financial Planning Committee, that also doesn't meet or exist, no new boiler was ordered when the old one blew up last year. The stat pusher seems incapable of observing these facts, and is too unskilled to bring them to rights. So he continues to yell "Get the stat up" and the staff wears more and more coats and blankets until at last it is just a quiet scene of solid ice.

If the letters out stat is down, this is a bad INDICATOR. It is vital that one keeps stats and observes when one goes down. It is extremely hard to manage on one's post or in an org unless one has a stat. But, in going down, WHAT is being indicated? A lack of letters out. So what does one do? Does he yell "Get the letters stat up"? Or does he look into this? If he looked into it, he could find the real Why, handle it and the letters stat would go up. He might find that the Letter Reges were all sacked so as to increase the unit pay one week and that he has somehow gotten a nut onto a personnel or finance post (whose R/Ses make even his head jerk back and forth). He might find that the typewriters had broken down. He might find that Dept 5 people were all being used by Div 5 to handle their files. At the very least he will find something aberrated or ignorant going on which has to be handled before the letters can be flooded out again. WHEN this is found and handled, THEN the letters out stat will go up.

So Mr. Stat Pusher is essentially operating on a short circuit. He cannot or will not look.

And there is another variety of stat aberration which comes about after a lot of "Get the stat up" has failed. This is Mr. Stat Ignorer.

Mr. Stat Ignorer is driving along in a car and he looks at the speedometer. It says 15 mph. He glares at the needle for a moment and then handles it. He pastes a piece of paper over it so it can't be seen. And sits back and drives contentedly. If he'd looked, he would have found he had three flat tires and an engine about to run out of oil and explode.

Then there is also Mr. Stat Faker. He knows that he will get in trouble if his STAT is down. So he simply dreams up a figure and puts it on graph paper. He is encouraged and rendered confident in this because he is sure that no senior will come around and notice the towers of unanswered letters or the huge backlogs of cramming orders or the mobbed waiting room of unhandled public or the mountain of uncorrected and unfiled address plates. He is confident because no senior has in the last year or two. And he can say "I'm an upstat" when the Ethics Officer tries to hit him for keeping the front door to the org obstructed with his motorcycle. And he is recognizable by a caved-in case, low morale and a hunted look of glee as he creeps through the org.

There is one common denominator the stat pusher, the stat ignorer and the stat faker have. And that is AN ABSENCE OF SKILLED MANAGEMENT.

We have investigatory tech. It is there for use. We have the Data Series evaluation tech. It is there for use. We have administrative tech. And it is all published and there for use. And further, when it *is* known and used, proven times without number now, production and prosperity occur AND show up as statistics which INDICATE that production and prosperity are occurring.

Yes, it is very, very true that an org or a manager or an auditor or file clerk gets in trouble if their stats are down.

Yes, it is true that stats should exist and be used.

But it is equally true that the way to get a stat is to put something there that can get something done and get the lines debugged and the scene handled.

The fate of the stat pusher, the stat ignorer and the stat faker is to look around one day and find no org.

It's a very long way between yelling or telexing or writing "Get the stat up" and handling things and getting production cycles completed so that the stat WILL go up.

The stat, properly stated and honestly kept, IS a vital indicator of the scene. If you know how to use them you can get the areas that have to be handled. And if you know your policy and tech you can find the real Whys and get real handlings and get things whizzing.

We mean to have all the stats going up because this INDICATES a bettering state of affairs for everyone.

The job of the product officer is NOT to yell "Get the stats up." The product officer is there to notice and order things like "Get those letters answered so they get answers." And the job of the org officer is to carry out the handlings the product officer finds necessary to get production rolling.

A fire-breathing product officer is worth his weight to every staff member IF he is trying to get and is getting production which results in bettered conditions, better products, better prosperity and THIS will incidentally show up in the stats.

It's a world of things that have to be done and coordinated before the stats go up.

We are in the business of people, we are in the business of a bettered world. We have to have completed cycles of action. And these are shown in stats.

We are also in a world of exchange and would be no matter what ideology we lived under. We have to "make GI" and we have to have "the stats up."

But our success is measured in terms of the ACTIONS we do, for only those show up in the indicators called statistics.

So, okay. Let's go about it the right way. And find what is holding the stats down and handle and correct those things and so, honestly and swiftly become upstat.

L. RON HUBBARD
FOUNDER

HUBBARD COMMUNICATIONS OFFICE
SAINT HILL MANOR, EAST GRINSTEAD, SUSSEX

HCO POLICY LETTER OF 20 SEPTEMBER 1976-1
ADDITION OF 17 APRIL 1977

REMIMEO
ALL STAFFS

EXECUTIVE SERIES 17-1
ORG SERIES 35-1
STAT PUSH CLARIFIED

This policy letter is revised. The second paragraph of the original said that it was dangerous to talk about the subject because somebody could do an immediate make-wrong by saying, "This means don't try to raise any stats."

Well, exactly that happened. There was a heavy campaign run into all Flag Operations Liaison Offices and to orgs designed to discredit asking for raises in stats. (The person who did it and failed to push production quotas is suspended and under Comm Ev.)

The whole point seems to have been missed. It was this: You can't ask for a NUMBER; you CAN and MUST ask for a SOMETHING.

That something is a *product*. It is a thing, a tangible item.

Right this minute, as a result of a mission, HCO PL 16 Nov. 76, Exec Series 19, Org Series 37, PRODUCTION QUOTAS, has now been provided with thoroughly researched subproducts one has to push in order to get the PRODUCTS. These are the real tangible actions you have to take to get a number of actual products. In other words, by getting many exact minor products, you then can achieve the valuable final product.

STATISTICS are those numbers which simply count the products attained or obtained.

Stat management is the only kind of management you can do on a production scene. Management by statistics was brought to a fine art in Scientology admin tech. To discredit it is, of course, to court failure.

Abusing statistical management is also something of a crime. It has been done by some managers who said "Get the stats up" without ever saying what subproducts you had to get that would then make up the product.

Stat management is a valuable tool and has gotten us over the years. To discredit it first by saying first just "Get the stats up" without saying how or what or why was one side of the pendulum. Then the pendulum swung clear to the extreme and people were being made guilty for even watching stats or demanding or working to raise them.

So let's get a little middle swing of the pendulum now.

It is perfectly all right to demand that stats rise so long as one says what subproducts and products make up those stats and gives some indication of what people should do to get the stats rising.

It is perfectly all right to do stat management.

And it is perfectly okay to come down hard on people or orgs who fail to get their stats in viable range.

So long as you give them some idea of what small products (subproducts) they have to get to make up the real products, you are NOT doing a stat push.

So long as you give people some direction and guidance, you can yell for stat increases all you want.

And you better.

L. RON HUBBARD
FOUNDER

HUBBARD COMMUNICATIONS OFFICE
SAINT HILL MANOR, EAST GRINSTEAD, SUSSEX

HCO POLICY LETTER OF 14 NOVEMBER 1976

REMIMEO
FLAG BU
ALL ORGS
EXT HCO FB

ADMIN KNOW-HOW SERIES 36
EXECUTIVE SERIES 18
PERSONNEL SERIES 28
ORG SERIES 36

MANNING UP AN ORG

THE SEQUENCE OF POSTING DEPTS AND DIVS

You need an org board first and an allocation board.

The sequence in which an org is manned up is roughly:

- Dept 1

- Dept 11

- Reg and Body Routers and Intro people in Div 6

- Dept 12 (enough auditors and C/Ses to approach 2 admin to 1 tech in org)

- Dept 6

- Dept 7

- Dept 3

- SSO and Supers in Qual to train staff

- Dept 5 for CF, Address and Letter Reges

- Dept 4 for promo

- Dept 21 (LRH Comm)

- Dept 10

- Dept 20

- FR and execs

- Full Div 6

- Full Div 1

- Full Div 4

254

- Full Div 2

- Full Div 5

- Full Div 7

- Full Div 3

(Note, an AO always mans up the AO Dept or Div along with the SH one in each case.)

Wrong sequence of manning is Dept 6, Dept 12, Dept 6, Dept 12, Dept 6, Dept 12, as you wind up with a stuck clinic that won't expand.

Wrong sequence will contract an org while trying to expand it, as the org will go out of balance, bad units, noisy and unproductive.

If manned in a correct sequence, its income has a chance to stay abreast of its new staff additions.

Emphasis on GI without comparable emphasis on delivery and organization can throw an org into such a spin only a genius can run it.

Manned in proper sequence, and hatted as it goes, an org almost runs itself.

Single handing from the top comes from long-standing failures to man or man in sequence, from earlier noncompliance with explicit orders or from not understanding orgs in the first place.

An unhappy org that doesn't produce has usually been manned only partially and out of sequence.

The trick is planned manning, ignoring the screams of those who know best or demand personnel; just manning by posting those who have been screamed for the loudest is a sure way to wind up with no people and total org problems instead of a total org that is prosperous and producing.

Incidentally, this is a rough approximation of the sequence of hats the ED gradually unloads as his org takes over.

L. RON HUBBARD
FOUNDER

HCO POLICY LETTER OF 16 NOVEMBER 1976

REMIMEO
ALL STAFFS

EXECUTIVE SERIES 19
ORG SERIES 37

PRODUCTION QUOTAS

Ref: HCO PL 8 Feb. 72   Exec Series 7
TARGETING OF DIVISIONAL
STATISTICS AND QUOTAS

In a recent pilot, executed at my orders by the Staff Captain, it was found that:

WHERE A STAFF MEMBER DOES NOT KNOW THE SUBPRODUCTS WHICH GO TO MAKE UP A GROSS DIVISIONAL STATISTIC THE GDS WILL SUFFER AND FALL.

And it was also found:

WHERE SUBPRODUCTS ARE NOT GIVEN A QUOTA, QUOTAING A GDS FAILS.

The report on the pilot follows and is given in full as it is an excellent example of what a product officer or executive runs into and how it is solved.

"During the last two weeks, while running the FSO, I've had a lot of experience with the above subject, and thought that the data that I have on it might be useful to you.

"When first going into the org I pushed for actual products along with quotaing of the GDSes.

"This went over very well, however, the day you sent a telex *to quota the products that make up the stat,* things really started moving much better.

"Your telex really opened the door for me as to how to go about getting an org to work on products and get stats up.

"Here is the best example. The week before last on Monday or Tuesday the student points were heading for bad down stats for the week. The D of T was more or less tearing her hair out about how she could meet her quota. She and the Tech Sec were trying to figure out what had changed.

"This was right after I had read your telex referred to above, so what I did was to tell them how they had to work on the products that make up the stat.

"The next step was *to list out what the subproducts were that made up the stat*. I just made a very simple list, not necessarily a complete one, of: (1) course starts, (2) F/Ning students, (3) students that are on target, (4) students that increase their production daily. Then made sure the D of T would understand how these made up the stat.

"The next step after that was to change 1–4 above into 'number of.'

"This brought about what one could call instant sanity and exclamations of realizations of how the area could be handled.

"This was followed up by making the D of T work on each of these products. It took a lot of work and figure out how to do, as far, far from all students were F/Ning, etc. It took actions like finding every bogged student and debugging him on a flat-out basis.

"The end result was that the stat did not crash, but went up some, and this week went up even more.

"Other actions were required in the area, such as the Qual Sec and Chief Off sorting out the TRs Course, the D of T doing TRs, and more, but it worked for sure.

"After this, we made this the pattern for the dept heads to follow: i.e., work on the products and subproducts that make up the stat, list them out, quota them, make the quotas, make your GDS quotas.

"It has also been put in on Dept 18 lines, so that Tours and external Reges are no longer pushed on GI and bodies only. There is a pilot project with Flag Service Consultant WUS since a few days which puts in a whole subproduct system and quotaing and reporting on it, which was very well received.

"However, what I also wanted to tell you, is that *this does not go in automatically*, we're still catching bugs on it.

"These are the bugs that have been run across:

"1. Dir Reg had a bunch of subproducts and products beautifully quotaed, but when asked what his quotas were for 'closes' and 'completed Reg cycles,' he dropped his jaw as he had not thought about that.

"He immediately quotaed these and production increased right away.

"2. The Dir Procurement (Dissem Sec HFA) had not set any quotas for CF/Address as she stated that 'that area would not be possible to quota.' Her MU was that she thought she had to quota every single area of Addresso, rather than the part they were working on at the moment. She had a major win on this.

"She also kept her quotas in her head as she 'hated to have papers lying around.' She since has them all in a book and is very happy.

"3. The Dist Sec could not think of the subproducts that would produce NNCF.

"4. The Dir Income was working on subproducts in such a way that they did not add up to his GDS, or rather, that they did not result in his GDS quota being met, and tried to justify this.

"Several others required close personal contacts to list out what the products would be that made up their stat.

"MUs are still coming up, but it sure works! It's brilliant, Sir.

"My picture of an org that operated on this basis with every staff member should be incredible.

"Now, I have looked at the trouble an executive would run into implementing the order to quota products that make up stats, and I can see lots, unless you know exactly how to do it.

"This is what I see on it:

"You would have to keep the GDS quota there and in mind constantly, as if you don't, things can slack off too easily.

"You would have to bring the terminals concerned to an understanding of the cycle of working on products that make up the stat.

"You would have to get a list of what the products and subproducts are, without making it miles long.

"You would have to make sure that the list is complete, per policy and actually makes up the stat.

"You would then have to make sure that the list is quotaed.

"You would then have to make sure that the quotas are met, and you would have to watch out for anyone using it wrongly so the GDS quota is not met.

"On most of these you would have to make sure that there are proper 'figure out how to do's,' on how to go about getting the products.

"The above actually, now that I look at it, fits in exactly with your PLs on Name, Want and Get the Products.

"I think also what is of importance is that you really break down what it takes to get the products: i.e., if the DTS here was told to get 10 fully paids into the org, she would be 'blank,' until you broke it down into—make up the list of them, make so many contacts, get so many ETAs, etc.

"Pressure is still required to get a momentum and keep it going.

"Another example is getting out over 100,000 pieces of promo in one week. It takes incredible detailed planning that covers everything; when what has to be through I/A and on to the assembly line, what checks have to be gotten when, what has to be addressed when and franked, what all hands are needed and when, etc. I had to force through exact planning on this with targets assigned, etc., and then push like mad.

"The use of HCO PL 8 Feb. 72, Exec Series 7, TARGETING OF DIVISIONAL STATISTICS AND QUOTAS, is also very important in all this."

Therefore these conclusions can be considered valid and vital:

EVERY GDS MUST BE BROKEN DOWN INTO SUBPRODUCTS AND THE STAFF MEMBERS MUST KNOW THEM IN ORDER TO ATTAIN A GDS.

And:

EVERY SUBPRODUCT MUST BE QUOTAED FOR A GDS QUOTA TO BE ATTAINED.

L. RON HUBBARD
FOUNDER

HCO POLICY LETTER OF 24 JULY 1978

REMIMEO

EXECUTIVE SERIES 19-1
ORG SERIES 37-1
SUBPRODUCTS
HOW TO COMPILE A SUBPRODUCT LIST

If you take any VFP and trace it backwards step by step, using a BE–DO–HAVE breakdown of what it took to create it and then wrote up the list as preliminaries, you would have a subproduct list.

Let us take a cup of coffee as the VFP. The minimum subproducts list would divide into what you had to be, what you had to do and what you had to have to wind up with a cup of coffee.

Be: Somebody who wanted a cup of coffee, somebody hatted to make coffee.

Do: Boil water, add coffee, put coffee in a cup, put it someplace where it could be drunk, let it cool until it was drinkable.

Have: Money to buy the necessary, or the ability to make money so you can buy the necessaries or the skill to create the necessaries: water, a pot to boil water in, fuel to make a fire, a fire to put a pot on, time to boil the water, coffee, the skill to make a cup of coffee, a cup to pour it in when made, a place to put it or drink it.

Now when you put this into a sequence of actions you will see that it looks like a doingness list. So you would have to add the havingness list and there would be no point in it unless you brought about the beingness list.

Now, from the above you could work out the subproduct list of a cup of coffee. Now, if at some future date you found out there was something wrong with the coffee valuable final product all you would have to do is assess this list and find out how come no VFP. The subproduct omits and wrong targets would leap at you and, if handled, could result in the VFP of a cup of coffee quite promptly.

And if you yourself were not involved in making the cup of coffee you would be able to debug how come no cups of coffee.

And if other departments or people had to be convinced there was valid reason for no cup of coffee you would use the list.

So as an exercise why don't you compile the subproduct lists for a cup of coffee.

When you get into anything as vast and complex as an org you can see that subproduct lists are vital to the understanding and accomplishment of VFPs.

And you would not be asking do you have to have one staff member for making each step of making a cup of coffee.

Now, as a second exercise take a valuable final product and break it down yourself, just like we broke down the cup of coffee, and searchlights will play against the sky, bands will strike up and understanding will reign everywhere and so will VFPs.

Not getting pcs audited? Not getting students trained? Not getting mobs of people walking in the front door? Not buying new buildings? Not having a highly trained expert staff? Do some subproduct lists and assess them and you'll know all about it.

USE AS ORDERS

If a valid subproduct list is used as a basis for issuing orders to a staff member, a section, department, division or org, they will be right targeted and valuable final products result.

It will greatly increase org efficiency and show up holes.

When the orders are issued and VFPs do not appear you will know what you are getting and what you are dealing with: Noncompliance? Sabotage? Overload? No recruitment? No hatting? R/Sers? Misguided staff? or what? Well that would be up to you to investigate and you have a guide of the subproduct list and what didn't or couldn't occur and get busy and do something about it.

USE AS QUOTAS

Subproducts can be quotaed and should be but they can only be quotaed in view of what can be done with what one has.

When you quota just one subproduct in a long line-up of other unquotaed subproducts, you can get into a situation where the subproduct or the quotaed subproduct is lacking support and so won't occur. In this case you can see that the subproduct gets the support while being obtained on a cope basis.

You can't just chant a lot of figures at a staff.

It is safer to quota the doable and then gradually add quotas to new doables as your facilities and capacity expand.

You can quota an HGC on pcs gotten into session. But remember you will also have to quota Tech Services phone calls and letters.

To do quotaing you have to know how to "play the piano" and have to be totally knowledgeable of existing scenes at any given moment. It is not an ivory tower job.

You can quota 500 file folders filed but remember you had better quota, for that time only, 500 file folders if there are none.

Quotaing does result in subproducts which result in VFPs and should be done.

But it is a highly educational process. The response can be anything from "They don't make them anymore" to "The auditors have no pens" or "It's busted" but the point is whatever turns up on quotaing, you can handle it.

If you don't quota you probably won't have anything to handle and the result is a nice soft idle life of total poverty for one and all.

Subproduct lists are made for those who are not dedicated to the cult of poverty and destitution.

So quota and very soon you will find out more about playing the org piano than ever before and you may even get some VFPs too which is after all the label of the game. If you misquota too often and don't learn in the process you'll probably get a mutiny.

It's fairly certain that if you quota nothing you won't ever get a cleared area. So quota away and quota intelligently.

DEBUG USE

A major use of subproduct lists is debugging the absence of high quantity, high quality valuable final products or no product at all.

As it is VFPs which keep an org going, not promises or hope you can see that a subproduct list is vital to straighten out an area.

By assessing the subproduct lists against a direct inspection of the area to which it applies one can see the major things that are missing. It is these missing things which are preventing the attainment of the valuable final product of the area, so vital to the org's survival.

UNDERSTANDING

A subproduct list enormously assists an understanding of what an area is supposed to be doing.

It will be found that staffs in a section or department or even division don't really know what it is supposed to be doing.

By simply taking up the subproduct lists with them point by point, they will suddenly envision the VFP and see what it really is.

PRODUCTION

People can be very busy without producing anything. The busyness of people can sometimes be rather misdirected.

By having an exact list of subproducts, a staff gets a very good reality on what productive busyness is. They will coordinate their busyness and drop out nonproductive busyness and real org VFPs will begin to appear.

ORGANIZATION

As an org is compartmented, staff members in one part of an org or even in one part of a department have no view of other areas and don't know what they are supposed to be doing. A subproduct list is highly informative to them. What *is* supposed to be coming out of that other area?

Also a staff member is a part of a flow line. If he has no idea what the point earlier on the line is supposed to be doing and what the point later on the line is supposed to be doing, he sometimes can't see the value of what he is supposed to be doing and does not take adequate responsibility for it as he may not conceive how important it is to the VFP.

A case in point of this — you won't believe it — was where a Division 2 could not understand why they got no re-signs until they found out that F/Ning students were a subproduct of the Academy. When they discovered this — and that there were no F/Ning students in the Academy but an awful lot of high TA students — they couldn't do anything about their own plight. (Needless to say the fur flew at the staff meeting.) Thus, using subproduct lists, a part of an org can improve itself and its own VFP by knowing what subproduct another part is supposed to be producing.

INCOMPLETE LISTS

Where you have incomplete subproduct lists — and probably no subproduct lists are perfect — you can get a false sense of security.

An incomplete list does not operate well as a debug list. Thus subproduct lists have to be intelligently used and often recompiled. They also have to be suitable to the activity for which they are compiled.

WRONG LISTS

Where a subproduct list is wrongly worked out the staff in that area can be mistargeted and can be made very busy again with no VFP.

The test of any subproduct list is: Is it resulting in VFPs? If not, somebody has been busy making a staff busy.

The test of a correct subproduct list is does it result in good VFPs when used.

And knowing all this, you can now act and the VFPs will now magically appear.

It's all just magic after all isn't it.

L. RON HUBBARD
FOUNDER

263

HCO POLICY LETTER OF 20 JULY 1978

REMIMEO

ORG SERIES 38

HELD FROM ABOVE
DOUBLE–HATTING

There are two types of double-hatting.

One of these, we all know about and is very common and quite permissible. This is what might be called *"level"* double-hatting. In this, for example, Mimeo Files is also Mimeo Files Equipment. So long as one does not have a hat in each of separate divisions and the hat is all in one division (and in a large org all in one department) not too much strain and trouble will result.

The other type of double-hatting can be called *"vertical"* double-hatting. In this, the head of an area *also* holds an I/C hat in his own area.

We see this in "HFA" on org boards. "Held from above" is very common. A Tech Sec is also D of P.

Well, in a small org that isn't making any money and isn't delivering, this would be usual. Probably the Tech Sec would also be the only auditor.

But we are talking here about busy areas that produce where we condone too much "HFA."

Vertical double-hatting is a sure way to be under stress.

Example: The Artillery Officer, I/C of all artillery, takes on the hat of "Ammunition Inventory I/C." Well, he's so tied up in counting shells he omits to notice — as he should as Artillery Officer I/C — that they just lost their guns. Result — lost battle, court-martial. And all because he was vertical double-hatted.

When a person occupies two points of different level on a command channel he is asking for trouble. He is busy on the lower point, usually because it is a full-time doingness, and so neglects many other sectors that should be supervised from the higher point.

When I see "D of P" marked as HFA by the ED, I don't have to look at stats or future Ethics Orders for that org. I know exactly what they will be. The D of P post might be being done but the org will be in a shambles for lack of active supervision. The ED will soon be the subject of a mission.

Yes, one can do it for a week—even a month at times. BUT if one does not straighten it out he'll be on the aspirin route.

Advice to any I/C who is vertical double-hatted is:

1. Recruit

2. Train

3. Hat

the lower post quick and see that it produces.

CRAWL BACK UP THE ORG BOARD.

L. RON HUBBARD
FOUNDER

HCO POLICY LETTER OF 9 AUGUST 1979RA
ISSUE II
REVISED 31 DECEMBER 2000

REMIMEO
ALL ORGS
ALL STAFF

ADMIN KNOW-HOW SERIES 38
ORG SERIES 39
ESTABLISHMENT OFFICER SERIES 37

SERVICE PRODUCT OFFICER

Refs:

Taped Lectures		The Flag Executive Briefing Course tape lectures
HCO PLs		The Org Series
HCO PLs		The Establishment Officer Series
HCO PL	9 Aug. 79 I	CALL–IN: THE KEY TO DELIVERY AND FUTURE INCOME
HCO PL	7 Aug. 76 I	AKH Series 33 Esto Series 31 PRODUCT–ORG OFFICER SYSTEM NAME YOUR PRODUCT
HCO PL	7 Aug. 76 II	AKH Series 34 Esto Series 32 PRODUCT–ORG OFFICER SYSTEM WANT YOUR PRODUCT
HCO PL	7 Aug. 76 III	AKH Series 35 Esto Series 33 PRODUCT–ORG OFFICER SYSTEM TO GET YOU HAVE TO KNOW HOW TO ORGANIZE
HCO PL	20 Nov. 65RB I Rev. 13. 3. 99	THE PROMOTIONAL ACTIONS OF AN ORGANIZATION
HCO PL	28 May 72	BOOM DATA PUBLICATIONS BASIC FUNCTION
HCO PL	15 Nov. 60R I Rev. 4. 2. 91	MODERN PROCUREMENT LETTERS
HCO PL	14 Feb. 61 II	THE PATTERN OF A CENTRAL ORGANIZATION
HCO PL	21 Nov. 68 I	SENIOR POLICY
HCO PL	28 Feb. 65 I	DELIVER
HCO PL	23 Aug. 79R I Rev. 23. 8. 84	Esto Series 38 Product Debug Series 1 DEBUG TECH
HCO PL	23 Aug. 79R II Rev. 24. 6. 88	Esto Series 39 Product Debug Series 2 DEBUG TECH CHECKLIST
HCO PL	9 Aug. 79 III	AKH Series 39 SERVICE CALL–IN COMMITTEE
HCO PL	10 July 65	LINES AND TERMINALS, ROUTING

The post of SERVICE PRODUCT OFFICER is hereby established in the Office of the CO/ED, Dept 19, of all Class IV and Sea Org orgs. His direct senior is the CO/ED.

Until such time as a SERVICE PRODUCT OFFICER is posted the responsibilities and duties are covered by the Service/Call-in Committee as fully laid out in HCO PL 9 Aug. 79 I, CALL–IN: THE KEY TO DELIVERY AND FUTURE INCOME and HCO PL 9 Aug. 79 III, SERVICE CALL–IN COMMITTEE.

The VALUABLE FINAL PRODUCTS of this post are (1) flawlessly serviced and completed paid pcs and students who re-sign up for their next service, and (2) high quality promotional items in the hands of volumes of public who come in, sign up and start an org service.

The main statistics for the SERVICE PRODUCT OFFICER are:

1. Number of pcs and students completed and re-signed on to their next service. (This includes those actually routed on to the next upper org for services and who do re-sign.)

2. Number of public in and started on to a service.

Completion: By completion is meant those actions completed and attested at C&A and accompanied by an acceptable success story.

Re-sign: By re-sign-ups are meant pcs and students who, after completion of a service, see the Registrar to sign up *again* for another service while in the org.

Promotional Items: Those items which will produce income for the organization. By promotional items are meant those things which make Scientology and our products known and will cause people to respond either in person or by written reply to the result of receiving Scientology commodities. These are: tours, book outlets, Sunday services, events, upstat image, fliers, info packs, handouts, books, ASR packs, specified service promotion, etc.

There are of course many other stats that reflect the SERVICE PRODUCT OFFICER'S subproducts and these are: VSD, TOTAL GI, INTENSIVES COMPLETED, BULK MAIL OUT, NUMBER OF PROMOTIONAL ACTIONS OF THE ORG IN, NUMBER OF FULLY AND PARTIAL PAIDS GOTTEN INTO THE ORG AND ON TO THEIR NEXT SERVICE. These are very important parts of the SERVICE PRODUCT OFFICER HAT, as they reflect his subproducts which lead to his valuable final product.

SERVICE PRODUCT OFFICER
RESPONSIBILITIES AND DUTIES

The purpose of an organization is to deliver service to the public. The primary functions which add up to delivery to the public are: promotion, sales, call-in, delivery itself and re-sign. The Service Product Officer is responsible for the flow of *products* through these areas. He is a *product officer.* He names, wants and gets products in these areas and thus ensures that the organization is accomplishing its purpose of service to the public.

The full technology of product officers is explained in the Flag Executive Briefing Course lectures, where the product–org officer system was developed. This system is still fully valid and is, in fact, the tech of the Service Product Officer. He is solely interested in products. When the Service Product Officer comes across a situation that requires organizing, he gets his organizing officer to handle it. The O/O (organizing officer) should actually be operating a few steps ahead of the Service Product Officer at all times — organizing for immediate production, per the product–org system. A full study of the product–org system, as contained in the FEBC tapes, the Org Series and AKH Series 33, 34 and 35, NAME, WANT AND GET YOUR PRODUCT is recommended in order to attain a thorough understanding of the actions of the Service Product Officer and his organizing officer.

The Service Product Officer is not a stopgap at any point of the promotion, sales, call-in, delivery and re-sign lines, where executives have failed to post and hat staff. This would be the responsibility of the Exec Establishment Officer per Esto Series 1. Establishment Officers see that short- and long-range establishment are occurring in the organization in the form of recruiting, hatting and training of staff. The Esto system is a necessary and very vital tool for the Service Product Officer and the organization and should definitely be in full use.

The Service Product Officer has the authority to directly order or work with any terminal involved in the promotion, sales, call-in, delivery or re-sign areas so long as he maintains direct liaison with their seniors.

The Service Product Officer must be fully aware of every post in the org and what their jobs consist of. He must know who handles what cycles and what cycles are on the lines. For instance, it is up to the Service Product Officer to be aware of all promotional actions occurring in the org and who is doing them, or if they aren't getting done. He must be aware of what public aren't getting serviced and he ensures those responsible get them serviced. He doesn't do this himself, as a serious goof of any product officer would be to go down the org board and do the job himself. The Service Product Officer *must* ensure others get the work done. Otherwise, he would wind up doing everyone's post and not getting anything done. It's actually pretty overwhelming to think of a Service Product Officer as responsible for doing everyone else's post duties. That's the surefire way to sink fast. Where a product isn't getting out the Service Product Officer debugs it using HCO PL 23 Aug. 79R I, DEBUG TECH, in order to get production. He is not interested in first finding the person's Mis-U or excuse, he is interested in getting production occurring now. Let the org officer and Qual worry about the staff member's Mis-Us.

Divisional Secretaries are the product officers for their division per the product–organizing officer system. The Service Product Officer sees that the product officers over the whole delivery cycle are getting their products. He coordinates the flow of products from division to division. A Service Product Officer doing his post fully and properly is, in fact, the person that makes the org board work. He sees that products aren't jamming up at one point of the line, but that they continue through the organization.

The Service Product Officer walks into the Tech Div and finds the Tech Sec sitting at his desk, shuffling paper and the pcs are piling high and complaining about no service. The last thing the Service Product Officer would do is start organizing the Tech staff around and scheduling the pcs. No sir, that's a serious offense. The first thing he would do is find out what can be produced RIGHT NOW, what auditors can be gotten into session right now and make the Tech Sec do it and GET IT DONE. This all takes about fifteen minutes and he gets the area flowing again and then,

WHAM! . . . he's out and into his next area. The Service Product Officer would not sit down and just start word clearing or doing Exchange by Dynamics on the Tech Sec. He would unstick the flows and get them moving. Then he would alert HCO and Qual to this serious problem of unhattedness and demand it be handled.

The basic sequence of the Service Product Officer on getting the products flowing off the lines is PUSH, DEBUG, DRIVE, NAME IT, WANT IT, AND GET IT. That's the only way you ever get a product. Products don't happen on their own.

This means he tells the Tech Sec to get Joe Blow there in session now! There is no general "audit these pcs." You'd never get a product that way.

The CO/ED has no authority to order the Service Product Officer to perform the total duties of any one post. The Service Product Officer must guard against being stuck into one post after another, doing it all himself. Nor is the Service Product Officer an "expeditor" for the CO/ED.

It is also very important that the Service Product Officer advise seniors that he is going into their areas so as not to create a Danger condition and wind up having to run the entire org. He also does this by getting the seniors to handle their juniors so a product is gotten. He does not walk in and cross-order the seniors of areas but works with them to see that products are produced.

The Service Product Officer is one who comes up with BIG IDEAS on getting public flooded into the org and being serviced swiftly. He is the one who thinks along the line of PRODUCTS, PRODUCTS, PRODUCTS. By spanning the divisions, he coordinates the product wanted and ensures each division is aware of its part in getting this product and that their actions are uniform. Where the Service Product Officer spots diversity, or lack of uniformity, he must alert his org officer or HCO. By doing the actions of coordination for a product and product demand, the product officer creates a team and more importantly sets the pace of the org's production and morale.

ORG LINES AND
THE SERVICE PRODUCT OFFICER

There are certain aspects of the organization which the Service Product Officer must be thoroughly trained in to do his job properly.

The Service Product Officer must be fully aware of all the Valuable Final Products (VFPs) of each department and each division of the org. Without this the Service Product Officer can create havoc, as he would be ordering Division 6 to recruit or the Reges to supervise. By not knowing cold the org VFPs, the Service Product Officer would certainly jam the flows throughout the org board.

A serious fault in any executive is not knowing the functions of terminals and the relation of one terminal to another. A key function of any executive is that of routing. An executive that misroutes communications and particles will tie his org in knots and wonder why no products are coming out. Therefore, a Service Product Officer must know cold every post function in the org and what particles belong on what lines.

He has got to know where a product comes from and where it goes in order to see it through the lines. A product officer's job is to name, want and get a product. However, he must first know where that product is to come from and where it is to go. This is an incredibly fundamental point.

In order for org lines to flow, routing forms (RFs) must be used. A routing form is a full step-by-step road map on which a particle travels. Every point a particle (which could be a student, a pc, mail, etc.) must go through to wind up at its destination must be listed on the routing form.

The Service Product Officer's Organizing Officer must ensure routing forms exist and are in use for each and every line in an org he deals in. Both he and the Service Product Officer must know these forms cold and be able to instantly spot when a line is being abused or ignored so as to slam in the correct routing.

A Service Product Officer must fully clay demo all the lines of an organization for each and every product. This must include each particle from entrance to the org and through all lines on which that particle would flow until it leaves the org. Lines are the most fundamental point of administration. To not have a full grasp of these lines would be detrimental to any product officer.

SERVICE PRODUCT OFFICER
SEQUENCE OF ACTIONS

It is very easy for the Service Product Officer to become wrapped up in one area while neglecting the others; however, this must not be done as, while products might be getting through in one area, they may well be seriously bogging in others.

The Service Product Officer is concerned with promotion, sales, call-in, delivery and re-sign. He begins his product officering in promotion and gets products out there or started and moves on to sales and gets them on to getting their products and so on through call-in and delivery and re-sign. He then returns to the beginning, promotion, and follows up on what he started there and gets even more production out. This is basically how the Service Product Officer moves through the org.

Daily, the Service Product Officer must plan and battle plan out his day. He must list those products he intends to achieve in each one of his areas and then get them.

The Service Product Officer is not an "information courier" or "data gatherer." He is ahead of the game and *knows* the data. He must know what public haven't been regged in the org yet, he must know who hasn't been taken into session that day, or who has been stuck in Ethics for three days, and ensure these things get handled. Therefore he must be quicker and faster than anyone else in the org and run run run.

PROMOTION

Promotion is the first action of the SERVICE PRODUCT OFFICER. He must ensure the many promotional pieces and actions are getting done. Some of these are:

1. Selling of books.

2. Staff selling books.

3. Books placed in public bookstores.

4. Selling of books to FSMs, missions, distributors, retailers and salesmen.

5. Books sold on each public contact.

6. Books advertised in mags, ads, posters, fliers, etc.

7. ASR packs.

8. Info packs.

9. Div 6 handouts for lectures and free testing.

10. Posters on major services in Div 6.

11. Promo to field auditors, FSMs, Gung-ho Groups, Dianetic study groups.

12. Org mags.

13. Flag shooting boards.

14. Promo for future events and tours.

15. *The Auditor* (for SHs).

16. *Clear News.*

17. *Advance!* mag (for AOs).

18. *Source* mag (FSO).

19. I Want to Go Clear Club promo (AOs).

20. SHSBC/NED/internships/NOTs/grades, etc., specified in promo.

21. Promo at points of public inquiry.

22. Free testing ads.

23. Fliers inviting people to buy Scientology books.

24. More Info Cards used in books.

25. Ads in newspapers.

26. Questionnaires to detect people's plans for training and processing.

27. Enough letters to public so they come in.

28. All promotional actions per HCO PL 20 Nov. 65RB I, THE PROMOTIONAL ACTIONS OF AN ORGANIZATION.

29. Book seminars, public campaigns and lectures.

30. Public Reception display (books, posters, handouts, etc.).

31. Tours and events, Sunday service.

32. Free testing line.

33. Handling of Gung-ho Groups, keeping FSMs well supplied and supervision of Dianetic study groups and FSMs.

34. Test Centers outside the org as an extension.

35. Radio and TV advertisements.

36. Dept 17 services.

37. Reception greeting, handling, routing, chasing up people for appointments and handling incoming calls with ARC and efficiency.

38. Formation of Dianetic Counseling Groups.

39. Weekly tape and film plays.

40. Promotes the org and standard tech to Auditors Association.

41. Contacts and sees any sign of ARC broken field and alerts Chaplain to clean up the field.

The first thing a Service Product Officer would want to do is get out a large volume of promo to at least get some activity occurring. This would entail Dissem getting any promo laying around the org dug up and sent out to students and pcs. They would get it out in letters and mailings, they would get it handed out to students and pcs, they would pick up the half-completed promo piece, have it fixed up and sent out. They would have promo placed in Reception, in any public inquiry, etc. In other words, the Service Product Officer ensures that the org fully utilizes what promo they do have. He would also have specific promo pieces done to enlighten the field on what services the org has. Where any of this bogged he would push — debug — drive — name it — want it — and get it.

The Service Product Officer, in trying to get in any promotional items, must review what resources he has. For example, is there a Dir Clearing, is there a Receptionist, etc.? He must concentrate on getting those terminals that already exist busy on promotional actions that will create the largest volume of inflow, while his organizing officer works on getting more immediate resources to increase the volume even further. It would be senseless to have the Dir Clearing running around trying to form up groups in an inactive field, single-handing, when he has FSMs that need to be gotten on to selecting and driving in new public. The Service Product Officer is concerned with priorities of promotional actions, so must be totally aware of all the promotional items and actions that an org can produce.

Actions such as "improved org appearance," "high ARC handling," and "correct and efficient routing of public" can be put in instantly. If he has two people in all of Dissem he still can and must get the particles flowing and products coming off the line.

SALES

The sales lines consist of enlightening the public, having lines to sign people up, getting public into the org and signed up for service.

The following gives you an idea of some of the sales actions and lines in an org:

1. Body Reg phones and schedules public to come in for interview.

2. Use of CF to produce business.

3. Reges who accept advance registrations.

4. D of T procurement of students.

5. D of P procurement of pcs.

6. Receptionist sells to public coming in.

7. SHs in communication with the Class IV org Tech Secs and Registrars and targeting them for public completing and routing on to the higher org.

8. AO's and SH's case consultant actions.

9. AO/SH events to Class IV org Academies to encourage upper-level auditor training.

10. Use of FSMs, Auditors Associations, personal contact, etc., to get public into the org and on to their next service.

11. Fast lines so public are not left waiting to see the Reg.

The lines of routing a public person to the Reg, or from the Reg to a service, must be tight so public aren't lost and the Reg is continuously kept busy with the public. Therefore, the Service Product Officer must police these lines and where he notices any lack of uniformity he gets his org officer onto it. Nonuniform or slow routing interferes with the product, so the Service Product Officer gets it speeded up now by push — debug — drive — name it — want it — and get it.

The first actions of the Service Product Officer in the sales area are to get all "in-the-org" public routed to the Reg on breaks or after course end to be further signed up for additional service. He can also have Dissem drilling done with Reges so as to increase sales in the org. His operating procedure is products, products, products, now, now, now. His org officer or HCO and Qual can worry about organize, organize, organize.

CALL-IN

Call-in is the action of getting fully paids into the org on to their next service. This also includes getting partially paids fully paid and on to their next service. These functions are of great concern to the SERVICE PRODUCT OFFICER as undelivered services to the public can mess up a field and increase the chance of refunds. The Service Product Officer should see to it that the Call-in Units are given stiff targets and that their production is not monitored by low auditor hours or low-producing training areas. The execution of needed programs to get Call-in Units fully operational is under the Service Product Officer per HCO PL 9 Aug. 79 I, CALL–IN: THE KEY TO DELIVERY AND FUTURE INCOME. This same policy also lists out the functions of the Call-in Units. Call-in falls between sales and delivery, as it deals with those either fully or partially paid and needing only to finish payment and be called in and gotten on to service.

DELIVERY

The Service Product Officer must ensure that the service lines of the org are fast and 100 percent standard, that pcs and students do complete quickly and don't get lost off the lines.

The Service Product Officer is to have an alert line with the public set up whereby if a student or pc's study or auditing is slowed, or if the public person is dissatisfied in any way, he can alert the Service Product Officer so it can be handled.

Some of the actions and lines to be product officered by the Service Product Officer are as follows:

1. Tech Services arranges housing, has the pc met when he is arriving and generally operates as the pc's host while in the org.

2. The many lines such as pc to Ethics, pc to Examiner, student to Ethics, student to Qual, C/S Series 25 line and pc to D of P line must be drilled so they are flawless and handled with ARC.

3. The most senior policy applied to this area is HCO PL 21 Nov. 68 I, SENIOR POLICY, "WE ALWAYS DELIVER WHAT WE PROMISE."

4. There must be an adequate amount of auditors, Tech Pages and FESers, Ds of P, Supervisors, Course Admins, etc.

5. The auditing line must be fast so no pcs wait to be serviced.

6. Use of all hands tech terminals in the org auditing when required to handle backlogged service.

7. Getting students through their courses and on to their internship at which point they can audit in the HGC.

8. Proper scheduling so every pc gets in 12½ hours a week minimum.

9. Recovering blown auditors, getting them fixed up and auditing.

The Service Product Officer ensures tech lines are fast. For instance, a pc's folder not getting C/Sed for days, or idle auditors and Ds of P "waiting" for pcs when they can be made to procure pcs, must be spotted and handled by the Service Product Officer.

The Service Product Officer must be kept briefed on what pcs and students arrive and how they are going to be handled. He must get around to these areas (Training and HGC) to ensure that there are no slows with public or anything that would get in the way of public receiving top-quality service.

Service to the public is the reason the org is there and service must be kept fast and 100 percent standard and plentiful. This is a primary duty of the Service Product Officer; he is there to ensure this occurs.

It is losses on service that keep public away, org income down and staff pay low.

RE–SIGN–UP

The re-sign-up line is also very key to an organization's prosperity. It brings further income, and proves conclusively that the last service received by the public person was of high quality. This is why the Service Product Officer must be very alert to the amount of re-signs. Some of the things that should be watched for are:

1. That the Reg is supplied with an upstat cert for his last completed service to present to the student or pc.

2. That the Reg knows fully how to handle the public person that won't re-sign (by sending them to Qual).

3. The Reg must be provided with tech estimates, Grade Chart information, etc., so he is aware ahead of time of what the student or pc's next action is.

4. Tech terminals are fully briefed and the line is in that every completion gets routed to the Reg. This must be drilled.

The public person should be serviced in your org until he/she requires upper-level service that your org cannot deliver, at which point they should be directed to the next higher org.

PITFALLS

The Service Product Officer can lose his effectiveness if he takes any "hey you" orders or gets stuck in at various points. He is not an expeditor. He is not an information and full-time coordinator terminal. He is an executive, a *product* officer, and he is there to ensure the entire machine runs.

He must be well versed on actions occurring in the org. He must also pay strict attention to completing actions he has started and to carrying a handling through to a done. Otherwise he can wrap himself around a pole with incomplete cycles which will ball up the line and prevent the service lines from flowing flawlessly.

Where the Service Product Officer post bogs it is undoubtedly due to a lack of an organizing officer, as with the speed in which a Service Product Officer demands products, he requires a fast-moving org officer. So it is essential this post be provided with an org officer as soon as possible.

Those personnel in the org who are responsible for organization, any Esto personnel, etc., are the people who put the units in the org there. It is not the duty of a Service Product Officer to man and hat the org. Therefore, it is a lot of sweat off the Service Product Officer's brow to have a fully functioning Esto team backing up his actions in getting the flow of products out of the organization.

SUMMARY

The Service Product Officer ensures all the actions of getting public into, through and out of the org are *accomplished* with high quality results.

It is extremely important that this post be manned in each and every org. It doesn't just make the difference between a poor, empty org and a good org. This post makes the difference between a good org and a booming org.

L. RON HUBBARD
FOUNDER

HCO POLICY LETTER OF 11 JUNE 1972

REMIMEO

ADMIN KNOW-HOW SERIES 38-1
ORG SERIES 39-1
ESTABLISHMENT OFFICER SERIES 37-1
PRODUCT OFFICERS

(Originally written by LRH for the *Apollo* OODs of 11 June 72.
Issued as an HCO PL on 21 Sept. 80.)

Worked last evening getting Tech to start shooting them through to completions.

The PL on Selling and Delivering Auditing (HCO PL 28 Sept. 71) tells why you have to audit a pc all at once, whole program. Dribbling it out means repairs due to life upsets before the guy made it.

So crowd it on and get a pc *through*. Then we'll have some products for our coins.

A product officer has to name, want and get his products.

This means one says, "You there. Joe Blow. Want him completed. All right get it DONE." Product by product. There is no general "Audit these pcs." "Get up the hours." Hell, you never get a product that way.

"You there, George Thunderbird. I want you through your Primary and onto and through course and classified. Get going, man, get going. Oh, you were told to weedle the toofle before you woofled by Dorance Doppler. Org Officer? Get that name — to Flag MAA, get the cross orders the hell off my lines. Now you George Thunderbird, I want you through your Primary and onto and through course by 1 July. You got it? You got it now! Good. Well, get with it. Get going!" Note on clipboard: Org Off to get cross order by Dorance Doppler invest and report. "There's your slip." Note on progress board. Geo Thunderbird HSDA 1 July. "Now you Tobler Tomias, what's the tale; how are you going? . . . Well, standing there smoking and looking at the scenery isn't going to do anything. If your girl doesn't like you anymore the thing to do is drown your sorrows in the Primary Rundown. . . . Okay, you are to be an Expanded Dianetics. All right, that's fine. I want you completed by 16 July. . . . I don't care if that's a 16-hour day. Let's see, Primary Rundown by _____ and Class IV Acad by _____ and _____. Yes, that's 16 July AT NOON. Man, to hell with your PTPs. Get going, man." And on the progress board. And from the board — "And here's Bill Coal. He should be off the Primary today, where is he? All right Bill — ah, you made it that far. Now you're on schedule. That's great. HSDA. Get with it, man. You completed Primary 20 minutes ago and aren't on the next course. Super! What the _____."

That's the way it goes for a Tech Prod Off. "We are finishing Agnes, Torp and Goshwiler today. Today. Yes today. Certified and off lines. Got it, D of T? Well, do it!"

Push, debug, drive. Name it, want it, get it.

That's the *only* way you ever get a product.

Sad but true.

They don't ever happen by themselves.

And all the public relations chatter in the world is not a product. I know this product officer beat.

It's a piece of cake.

But it has to be DONE.

L. RON HUBBARD
FOUNDER

HCO POLICY LETTER OF 14 FEBRUARY 1980

REMIMEO
EXEC HATS
ALL STAFF HATS

ORG SERIES 40
ESTABLISHMENT OFFICER SERIES 40
PRODUCT DEBUG SERIES 9

ORDER VERSUS DISORDER

Refs:

HCO PL	9 Feb. 74R	CONDITION BELOW TREASON
	Rev. 17.2.80	CONFUSION FORMULA AND EXPANDED CONFUSION FORMULA
HCO PL	30 Dec. 70	Personnel Series 15
		Org Series 20
		ENVIRONMENTAL CONTROL

I made a breakthrough recently, while investigating low production areas, and realized that a good deal more needs to be said on the subject of order and disorder.

Order is defined as a condition in which everything is in its proper place and performs its proper function. A person with a personal sense of order knows *what* the things in his area are, he knows *where* they are, he knows *what* they are for. He understands their value and relationship to the whole.

A personal sense of order is essential in getting out products in an area.

An orderly typist, for instance, would have all the materials requiring typing, she would have ample paper and carbons within arm's reach, she would have her correction fluid to hand, etc. With all preparatory actions done, she would sit down to type with an operational typewriter and would know what that typewriter was and what it was for.

She would be able to sit down and get her product, with no wasted motion or stops.

But let's say you had a carpenter who couldn't find his hammer and he didn't even know what a hammer was for and he couldn't find his chisel because when he picked it up he put it down and couldn't find it again and then he didn't know where his nails were. You give him a supply of lumber and he doesn't know what it's for, so he doesn't categorize it where he can put his hands on it.

How many houses do you think he would build?

The actual fact of the case is that a disordered person, operating in a disorganized area, makes a ten-minute cycle into a three-week cycle (believe it, this is true) simply because he couldn't find his ruler, lost his eraser, broke his typewriter, dropped a nut and couldn't find it again and had to send off to Seattle for another one, etc., etc., etc.

BASICS

In working with a group of nonproductive technicians recently, I discovered something interesting: out-basics. I actually found a lower undercut to what we generally think of when we say "basics."

These technicians had reportedly researched a key piece of equipment and had it all sorted out. But I found that they didn't even know the basic fundamental of what that machine was supposed to do and what they were supposed to be doing in their area!

That told me at once that they had no orderly files, no research data. They were losing things.

Now, if they were losing things, that opened the door to another basic: They couldn't have known where things were. They put down a tool over there and then when they needed it again they would have to look all over the place because they hadn't put it down where it belonged.

Their work was not organized so that it could be done and the tools were not known.

So I checked this out. Were they logging the things they were using in and out so they could find them again? Were they putting things away when they were done with them? No, they weren't.

This is simply the basic admin coupled with the knowledge of what the things one is working with are. It's orderliness and knowing what things are, knowing what they are for and where they are, etc. That's the undercut.

If people don't have a true knowledge of what the things they're working with are, if there are omitted tools, inoperational tools, if they don't know what their tools are supposed to do, if there are no files or if once used, files are not reassembled and put back in the file drawer, if things get lost and people don't know where things are and so on, they will be running around spending 3 or 4 hours trying to locate a piece of paper. That isn't production.

If a person can't tell you what the things he works with are, what they're for and where they are, he isn't going to get out any product. He doesn't know what he's doing.

It's like the carpenter trying to build a house without knowing what he's got to build it with, without understanding his tools and raw materials and the basic actions he must take to get his product. That's what was holding up production in the area: disorderliness. And the basics were out.

This is actually far *below* knowing the tech of the area — the actual techniques used to get the product. The person does not even know what his tools and equipment are or what they're supposed to do. He doesn't know whether they are operational or inoperational. He doesn't know that when you use a tool you return it to its proper place. When you have a despatch, you put it in a file where it can be retrieved. It undercuts even knowing the orders and PLs relevant to his hat.

What are the basics that are missing? The basics of sitting down to the table that one is supposed to sit down to, to do the work! The basics of knowing what the tools, materials and equipment he works with *are* and what he's supposed to do with them to get his product. Those are the basics that are missing.

We are down to a real reason why a person cannot turn out products.

That is what is holding up such a person's production. It is well below knowing the technique of his job.

Out-basics. Does the guy know where the file is? When he finishes with that file does he leave it scattered all over the place or does he put it back together and into the file where it can be found?

Now, a person who's working will have papers all over the place, but does he know where they are and is he then going to reassemble them and put them back in order or is he going to just leave them there and pile some more papers on top of them?

If you find Project No. 2 scattered on top of Project No. 1, you know something about that area. Basics are out.

This is a little piece of tech and with that piece of tech you've got insight. You would have to have an overall picture of what the area would look like when properly ordered and organized — how it would be organized to get optimum production.

Then you could inspect the area and spot what's going on. You would inspect on the basis of: How does the area compare with how it should be organized? You would find out if the personnel didn't know what the things in their area were or what they were for, you would see if they knew the value of things in the area or if there were altered importances, omitted files or filing, actions being done out of sequence, inoperational tools or equipment, anything added to the scene that was inapplicable to production, etc.

In other words, you can inspect an area by outpoints against this one factor of orderliness.

This sort of out-basics and disorderliness cuts production down to nothing. There just won't be any production at all. There will be no houses built.

What we are talking about here is an orderly frame of mind. A person with a sense of order and an understanding of what he is doing sits down to write a story or a report and he'll have his paper to hand, he'll have it fixed up with carbons and he'll have his reference notes to hand. And before he touches the typewriter he'll familiarize himself with what the scene is. He'll do the necessary preparatory work in order to get his product.

Now, someone else might sit down, write something, then dimly remember there was a note someplace and then look for an hour to find where that note was and then not be able to find it and then decide that it's not important anyway and then come back and forth a few times and finally find out he's typed it all up without a carbon.

———————

There is a handling for this. Anyone trying to handle an area who doesn't understand the basics of what they're dealing with and is in an utter state of disorder must get a firm reality on the fact that until the basics are learned and the disorder handled, the area will not produce satisfactorily.

The following inspection is used in determining and handling the state of such an area.

INSPECTION

This inspection is done in order to determine an area's knowledge of basics and its orderliness. It can be done by an area's senior for the purpose of locating and correcting disordered areas. It is also used as part of debug tech as covered in HCO PL 23 Aug. 79 I, Esto Series 38, Product Debug Series 1, DEBUG TECH. It is for use by anyone who is in the business of production and getting products.

The full inspection below would be done, clipboard in hand, with full notes made and *then* handlings would be worked out based on what was found in the inspection (according to the Handling section of this PL and the suggested handlings given in parentheses below).

1. **DOES HE KNOW WHAT ORGANIZATION, FIRM OR COMPANY HE'S IN? DOES HE KNOW WHAT HIS POST OR JOB IS?**

   This is a matter of does he even know where he is? Does he know what the organization or company he works for is, does he know what the post he is holding is?

   (If he is so confused and disoriented that he doesn't even know the company or org he's in or doesn't know what his post is, he needs to apply the Expanded Confusion Formula, HCO PL 9 Feb. 74R, and then work up through the conditions.

   Of course the person would also need to be instant-hatted on his post—the organization, his post title, his relative position on the org board, what he's supposed to produce on his post, etc.

   If he is doing this handling as part of his Expanded Confusion Formula, simply have him get the instant hatting and carry on with his Confusion Formula.)

2. **ASK THE PERSON WHAT HIS PRODUCT IS.**

   Does he know? Can he tell you without comm lag or confusion?

   You may find out that he has no idea of what his product is or that he has a wrong product or that he has confusions about his product. Maybe he doesn't even know he's supposed to get out products.

   (If this is the case, he must find out what his product is. If the person's product is given in policy references, he should look these up. If his product is not covered in tech or policy references, he'll have to work out what it is.)

3. CAN HE RATTLE OFF A LIST OF THE BASIC ACTIONS, IN PROPER SEQUENCE, NECESSARY TO GET OUT HIS PRODUCT OR DOES HE HEM AND HAW ON IT?

Does he know what to do with his product once it is completed?

He may try to tell you what he does each day or how he handles this or that and what troubles he's having with his post. You note this, but what you're interested in is does he know the basic actions he has to take to get out his product? And does he know what to do with the product once it is complete?

(If he can't rattle off the sequence of actions 1, 2, 3, then he'd better clay demo the basic actions, in proper sequence, necessary to get out his product and then drill these actions until he can rattle them off in his sleep. If he does not know what to do with his product once completed, then he'd need to find out and then drill handling the completed product.)

4. ASK HIM WHAT HIS TOOLS ARE THAT ENABLE HIM TO GET THIS PRODUCT.

Note his reaction. Can he name his tools at all? Does he include the significant tools of his area? Does he include his hat pack as a tool?

(If he doesn't know what his tools are, he'd better find out what he's operating with and what it does. A good workman knows his tools so well he can use them blindfolded, standing on his head and with one arm tied behind his back.)

5. ASK HIM TO SHOW YOU HIS TOOLS.

Are his tools present in the work area or does he have them out of reach, down the hall or in some other room?

(He may have to reorganize his work space to get his tools within easy reach and to get in some basics of organization. The purpose of such organization would be to make production easier and faster.)

6. ASK HIM TO TELL YOU WHAT EACH OF HIS TOOLS ARE.

Can he define them?

Does he know what each of them are and what they are for?

(If he doesn't know, he'd better find out.)

7. ASK HIM TO TELL YOU WHAT THE RELATIONSHIP IS BETWEEN EACH ONE OF HIS TOOLS AND HIS PRODUCT.

(If he can't do this, have him clay demo the steps he takes to get out his products with each tool he uses, so he sees the relationship between each tool and his product.)

8. ASK HIM TO NAME OFF THE RAW MATERIALS HE WORKS WITH. ASK HIM TO SHOW YOU HIS MATERIALS.

Does he know what his raw materials are? Are they in his work area? Are they in order? Does he know where to get them?

(He may have to find out what the raw materials of his post are [by defining them] and where they come from. He should drill procuring and handling them and then run Reach and Withdraw on them.)

9. **DOES HE HAVE A FILE CABINET? FILES? ASK HIM WHAT THEY ARE.**

Does he know what they are for? Does he know what a despatch is, etc.?

(He may have to be brought to an understanding of what files, file cabinets, despatches, etc., *are* and what they have to do with him and his product. He may have to clay demo the relationship between these things. He will have to set up a filing system. Ref: HCO PL 18 Mar. 72, Esto Series 10, FILES.)

10. **DOES HE HAVE A SYSTEM FOR LOCATING THINGS?**

Ask to see it. Check his files. Does he have logs? Does he log things out and correct the logs when he puts them back? Are the comm baskets labeled? Does he have a specific place for supplies? Ask him to find something in his files. How long does it take?

Does he have an orderly collection of references or a library containing the materials of his field? Is it organized so as to be usable?

(If he has no system for locating things, have him set one up. Have him establish a filing system, a logging system, label the comm baskets, arrange supplies, etc. Get a reference library set up and organized. Drill using the system he has.)

11. **WHEN HE USES AN ITEM, DOES HE PUT IT BACK IN THE SAME PLACE? DOES HE PUT IT BACK WHERE OTHERS CAN FIND IT?**

He'll probably tell you, yes, of course he does. Look around. Are objects and files lying about? Is the place neat or is it a mess? Ask him to find you something. Does he know right where it is, or does he have to search around? Is there an accumulation of unhandled particles around?

(Have him clay demo why it might be advantageous to put things back in the same place he found them. Drill him on putting things back when he's finished with them. Have him clean up the place, handling any accumulation of unhandled particles.)

12. **IF FEASIBLE, ACTUALLY GO WITH THE PERSON TO HIS PERSONAL LIVING AREA.**

Is the bed made? Is the area clean? Are things put away? How much dirty laundry does he have? Is it stowed in a bag or hamper or is it strewn about the place? People who had disorderly personal MEST, one for one were *not* getting out any products on post — they had no sense of order.

(If his personal quarters are a mess, have him — on his own time of course — straighten up his personal area and keep it that way on a daily basis. This will teach him what order *is*.)

HANDLING

Some areas, of course, will be found to be in excellent order and will pass the inspection. These will most likely be high production areas.

Other areas will be found to have only a few points out which would correct easily with the above handlings. These will probably be areas where some production is occurring.

Where personnel have a concept of what order is and why it is important, they will usually be eager to correct the points of disorder that have turned up on the investigation and may need no further urging, drilling or correction, but will quickly set about remedying outpoints. For many bright and willing staff members just reading this policy will be enough to get them to straighten out their areas right away.

There is, however, a sector which has no concept of order and may not have the slightest notion of why anyone would bother with it. You will most likely find them in apathy, overwhelm or despair with regard to their post areas. No matter what they do they simply cannot get their products out in adequate quantity and quality. They try and try and try but everything seems to be working against them.

When you find such a situation, know that the area is in Confusion. You are trying to handle an area which is in a confirmed, dedicated condition of Confusion.

Such an area or individual would require the application of the Expanded Confusion Formula (HCO PL 9 Feb. 74R) including the handlings above. So if these things confirm in an area, you must use the Expanded Confusion Formula and the handlings given above to full completion. Because, frankly, such an area or individual *is* in a condition of Confusion and will remain in Confusion until the Expanded Confusion Formula, including the full handlings from the inspection, are applied.

Once out of Confusion the person would have to be brought up through the rest of the conditions.

CAUTION

The condition of Confusion is a very low condition and should never be assigned where it is not warranted. Where one or two points on the above inspection were found to be out in an area, and where these corrected easily, there would be no purpose in assigning Confusion to that area. In fact, it may worsen an area to assign an incorrect condition.

But where you have a long-term situation of no or few products combined with a state of disorder, know that the area or individual is in a condition of Confusion and that the application of the Confusion Formula plus the handlings given in this PL will bring the area out of the muck and up to square one where it can *begin* producing.

NOTE: If the inspection is done on a person or area and some of the points are found to be out and handlings are done but no condition of Confusion is assigned, the area must be reinspected about a week later. This way you will detect if an actual condition of Confusion was missed, as the area will have lapsed back into disorderliness or will have worsened.

SUMMARY

A knowledge of the basics of an area and having orderliness in an area are essential to production.

When you find a fellow who is a light-year away from the basics and doesn't have a clue on the subject of order and he's flying way up in the sky someplace instead of just trying to put together what he's supposed to put together or do what he's supposed to do, you've got your finger on his Why for no production.

With the inspection and handlings given in this policy, we can now handle any degree of disorderliness and disorganization.

And order will reign.

Nonproductive areas become capable of producing.

Already producing areas increase their production.

And production will roll.

L. RON HUBBARD
FOUNDER

HCO POLICY LETTER OF 28 FEBRUARY 1980

REMIMEO

EXECUTIVE SERIES 21
ORG SERIES 41
FINANCE SERIES 17

PRODUCTION AND ONE'S STANDARD OF LIVING

Refs:

HCO PL	19 Mar. 71 II	Finance Series 6 BEAN THEORY, FINANCE AS A COMMODITY
HCO PL	9 Mar. 72 I	Finance Series 11 INCOME FLOWS AND POOLS PRINCIPLES OF MONEY MANAGEMENT
HCO PL	27 Nov. 71 I	Exec Series 3 Finance Series 6-1 MONEY
HCO PL	3 Dec. 71	Exec Series 4 Finance Series 6-2 EXCHANGE
FEBC Tapes		

(*NOTE:* I realize that management units, orgs and staffs are daily pounded with false economic data. The real facts of life collide with much false data. Such crippling data comes from many sources — school, advertisers, government, bankers, propagandists, even parents who insisted Johnny be a doctor so he could "live well" or set a horrible example themselves. Many have had a hand in messing up people's wits on the subject. It is a factor in inhibiting the individual prosperity of executives, staff members and orgs. Where an area is not prospering, this PL should be star-rated on its people and the false data they have on this subject stripped so that they then can prosper as they should.)

"Standard of Living" can be defined as the relative quality of a person's or group's possessions, quarters, food, equipment, tools and conditions of their area of work and existence. It is the state of the person's living, including working, environment. Where its potential continuance exists it is related to survival. It is a basic natural economic law that personal production of VFPs and one's standard of living are intimately related.

This applies to the individual as well as the team.

Where violations occur, inequities exist.

At a personal level one must produce in excess of his standard of living just to retain and maintain it.

Actually the "excess" means that because of overload, taxes, services, plant, utilities, raw materials, machine and other costs additional to his own work sphere, a person cannot expect to get the full value of his VFPs all to himself. That is not economically feasible. The "excess" varies from post to post and job to job but is never less than 5x minimum. In industry it is considered to be at least 10x to maintain company standards and solvency. The "excess" can be very high indeed in some industries. But in any case any idea that it should be one-for-one is fatal. People who know little of economics or management sometimes propose a worker should get the full value of his VFPs—but all work and all VFPs require support services and to neglect these would quickly bring on poverty. Even when working for oneself alone these "excess" factors exist and seldom drop below 5x as one still requires support services. Corrected gross income divided by staff has to be at least 5x the cost of the standard of living of the individual staff member for that standard to be barely maintained. This does not mean staff pay should be $^1/_5$ of that figure. It means that all the things (pay included) that go into maintaining their welfare and work environment would have to be covered by $^1/_5$ of that figure. A fairly efficient and prosperous org with a hatted, industrious, gung-ho staff can very easily maintain quite acceptable standards at $^1/_{10}$ that figure. The actual cash value of every piece of work done by a person can actually be calculated. It is intricate and tricky to do and much subject to over- and underestimation but it can be done. It is not vital to do this but one might just be curious about it. If so, do it for yourself. Thus VFPs can be priced against what they bring in as part of the overall scene even when they seem indirect. All the above figures are very rough and subject to variation but this gives you some idea of what is meant by "excess" in that law.

Where a number of people in a group or on a team do not produce VFPs in excess of their standard of living, they depress the standard of living of the group or team.

Where some in a group do not only not produce VFPs but produce overt products, they actively depress the standard of living of everyone in that group or on that team.

Many economists and theorists seek to avoid that law. They do it to gratify politicians or aggrandize some false philosophy whose true purpose is suppression under other colors. But the law remains and its violation breeds an epidemic of economic ills. Amongst such ills are inflation, superbureaucracy, chaos with the marketplace and a decay of the civilization.

When a whole society demands a high standard of living and yet doesn't concentrate on the personal production of VFPs, it is finished.

Products are the basis of a standard of living. They don't appear from midair. They come from work truly done. Not from hope or false data.

It is a druggie's dream that machines, computers, under the dictatorship will do it all. Machines can raise a standard of living by assisting in production. But they can't do man's living for him. Intelligently designed and used they permit, within limits, increases in population. But machines are just tools. They have to be thought up, designed, built, run and serviced and their raw materials and fuel have to be found and delivered and their products promoted, delivered, used and often in their turn serviced. The machine age was actually recognized as failed when world leaders first began to urge population reduction on the planet to "improve the individual standard of living." If machines were going to solve it all, why is the civilization now in such a steep decline? It took producing men *working* in and with a machine age to make the society go. Not idle mobs on welfare expecting a high standard of living while a few guys work their guts out. Pie in the sky is nice but did anyone ever get to eat it? This misinterpretation of the machine age was a heavy violation of the above economic law. But the real harm of the machine age was creating a false belief that one did not have to produce much to survive. This lowered people's estimate of how much they would themselves have to produce to survive, much less have a high standard of living. Factually one normally has to work fast and expertly and in high volume to bring about any acceptable standard of living for himself and his group. This is a point the machine age obscures. But it remains vividly and demonstrably true.

An executive who works hard yet wonders about his own low standard of living should look over his people to find those who are not producing VFPs or who produce even overt products while yet demanding a living. *They* are absorbing the potential raised standard of living of the group.

Where a group has a very low standard of living, it need only review the above law and its potential violations to understand why.

One cannot, in fact must not, increase the standard of living of a group in ways that violate the above law. It will eventually bring calamity on that group.

In a society led astray by crackpot economics, violations of the above law create a vast number of wrong examples. The rich (most of whom work like mad) are seen as idle or even criminals. The best way of life is made to appear to be idleness. One seems to be owed a living without any effort on his own part. The producing worker should be fined by higher taxation. These are not seen to be simply false data spread about to wreck the place but are held as "truths." And in their wake comes a funeral for that group or society.

There is even an economic theory spread about today called "equalitarianism." It declares everyone should get the same pay and have the same standard of living. It does not mention that anyone should do any work. It holds that the better worker should not be better rewarded. It would crash any society.

Then there is the "monetarist" who believes you can manipulate a whole society with money alone. And no thought of any production. His answer to production? (You won't believe this.) Decrease demand! In other words, reduce everyone's standard of living!

Basic economics eventually catches up with all these weird false pretenses. It may take time but, as in the law of gravity, the apple eventually falls. No matter how many crackpots advance theories to say it can't fall, will go up or vanish. Real basic economic laws are like that. They catch up. So don't wonder about inflation and depression and decayed civilizations. Basic economics caught up with the crackpots.

An executive has to pay attention to the basic law about a standard of living. If he doesn't pay close attention to it, the standard of living of himself and of his group will cave in.

He can be "a good fellow" and seek popularity by attempting to raise the standard above what is earned. He and his group will crash.

He can be foolish and seek to raise his own rewards above what he personally is earning in terms of VFPs. But both he and his group will fail.

He can ignore the real producers of the group and not see that their standard of living is comparable to their individual production. And he and the group will fail.

He can ignore the nonproducers and the overt product makers and, by so ignoring them, tear his own and the group's standard of living to bits.

He can listen to a bunch of PR from a staff member about how valuable that staff member is and surrender to it without ever really counting up the real VFPs that staff member is not producing (or even preventing). (It happens.) Only real VFPs count.

He can work himself half to death without demanding production from others and have his own standard of living crash.

There are swarms of false data flying about today on this subject. It is taught in schools, the very best schools; it is heard on the radio and seen on TV and in the papers. The civilization, as it caves in, is blinded by literally thousands of false ideas about what and how a standard of living occurs. These, where they conflict with the basic law, actively prevent one from prospering as they blind him to the truth of his scene.

In an org or management unit in Scientology, the real VFP is valuable fine people who produce valuable final products who then make up a valuable fine public. Every piece of work and duty in a management unit or an org contributes to that.

The standard of living of an executive, a management unit, an org or a staff member is determined by that one basic economic law: The personal production of VFPs for the group and one's standard of living are intimately related.

L. RON HUBBARD
FOUNDER

HCO POLICY LETTER OF 20 AUGUST 1982
ISSUE I

REMIMEO

ORG SERIES 42
ORGANIZATIONAL BASICS

An organization consists of coordinated purposes, lines and terminals. That is *all* it consists of.

To be viable, it must have a fair and valuable exchange with an area outside its perimeter in a volume adequate to its needs.

To expand, it must strengthen its purposes and increase its lines and terminals and multiply its exchange above the rate of its consumption.

When you have understood this fully you will understand all groups, companies, societies, civilizations, countries and empires.

Such rise or fall in direct relationship to how well they meet or fail to meet the first three paragraphs above.

And when you fully grasp the basic definition of organization and are trying to build, make viable and expand one, you will be very hard on anyone who is discoordinating or blunting the purposes, damaging or omitting the lines and is disestablishing the terminals. You will understand exactly what that person is doing. He is seeking to make the organization less viable and trying to contract and destroy it. So know your enemies.

And when you see somebody trying hard to build your organization up by following the first three paragraphs, you will know he is your friend and help him all you can.

It is very well to clear off all confusions by doing the first three paragraphs in clay. Then you will have, if you master it, many things clarified. And you can not only understand what makes a slum a slum, a good society a good one, why one area is poor and another opulent, you will also have acquired the potential of creating or helping to create a far better life for all.

L. RON HUBBARD
FOUNDER

HUBBARD COMMUNICATIONS OFFICE
SAINT HILL MANOR, EAST GRINSTEAD, SUSSEX

HCO POLICY LETTER OF 30 NOVEMBER 1982

REMIMEO
ALL ORGS
ALL EXECS
FBOS
D/FBOS

ADMIN KNOW-HOW SERIES 44
ORG SERIES 43
ESTABLISHMENT OFFICER SERIES 44
FINANCE SERIES 32

THE DEPUTY CO OR DEPUTY ED FOR DELIVERY AND EXCHANGE

Refs:

HCO PL	9 Aug. 79R II	AKH Series 38
	Rev. 19.11.79	Org Series 39
		Esto Series 37
		SERVICE PRODUCT OFFICER
HCO PL	10 Sept. 82	Finance Series 28
		EXCHANGE, ORG INCOME AND STAFF PAY
HCO PL	29 Jan. 71	Finance Series 1
		FLAG BANKING OFFICERS
HCO PL	10 Mar. 71R I	Finance Series 5
	Rev. 27.10.82	FBO HAT
HCO PL	27 July 82R	Finance Series 25
	Rev. 20.9.82	DEPUTY FBOs FOR MARKETING OF ORG RESOURCES FOR EXCHANGE (D/FBO FOR MORE)
HCO PL	3 Sept. 82	Finance Series 27
		DEPUTY FBO FOR MARKETING OF ORG RESOURCES FOR EXCHANGE (D/FBO FOR MORE) PURPOSE

(NOTE: The pilot for this post has been long and successful: it is the FCCI PO [Flag Case, Course, Internship Product Officer] whose duties were covered by the famous Bulldozer EDs issued on Flag. However, the FCCI PO also covers the post of what is now called D/FBO for MORE [D/FBO for Marketing of Org Resources for Exchange]. Without this post effectively manned, the FSO — Flag Service Org — collapses and any sag in its stats is instantly traced to the nonfunctioning of the FCCI PO post. The post once functioned well in the Office of the Staff Captain and has functioned less well in the Office of the CO FSO. Therefore, the D/CO [or D/ED] for Delivery and Exchange post is put in close liaison with the strong and powerful International Finance Office Network, while remaining under the authority of the CO or ED of the org.)

The Service Product Officer in any org should have D/CO or D/ED status.

His key function is to see that the org operates at the highest level of exchange. (Ref: HCO PL 10 Sept. 82, Finance Series 28, EXCHANGE, ORG INCOME AND STAFF PAY)

Therefore, his post is now retitled D/CO (or D/ED) for Delivery and Exchange and he is located in the Office of the CO/ED, Department 19, of all Class IV and Sea Org orgs.

He is the bridge between the D/FBO for MORE and the FBO.

This creates a flow:

You have the D/FBO whipping up business by seeing that the public is made aware of the org's products and services, and driving more business down on the org than it can waste.

The D/CO (or D/ED) for Delivery and Exchange makes sure this public gets SIGNED UP and SERVICED. He is a product officer who names, wants and gets promotion, sales, call-in, delivery itself and re-sign occurring.

The FBO, then, sees to the org's solvency by ensuring income is greater than outgo, that production is properly financed, that staff are well paid for their production and that Flag is recompensed for good management of the org. And all of this makes it possible for the org to then expand and deliver in greater volume.

The flow goes from public (D/FBO) to ⟶ the whole sign-up and service line (D/CO or D/ED for Delivery and Exchange) to ⟶ solvency and volume (FBO).

It is this incredibly workable lineup that takes an org stably up the conditions of exchange. (Ref: HCO PL 10 Sept. 82, Finance Series 28, EXCHANGE, ORG INCOME AND STAFF PAY)

But the line breaks down where there is no D/CO or D/ED for Delivery and Exchange posted. And where it breaks down most specifically and ruinously is in the area of CALL–IN.

If one wants call-in to occur and the org's exchange with its public kept in, the only way to do it and also expand the org is to get a D/CO or D/ED for Delivery and Exchange on post and functioning.

Public interest may be kindled, public reach may be occurring, public may be paying partially or in full for goods or services, but if goods and services aren't being delivered in full the flow is broken and the org is in a condition of only partial exchange. Delivery in full means calling in the person so the service CAN be delivered. In this way the org maintains "fair exchange" with each and every public on its lines.

So the answer for any org that is sitting in a condition of only partial exchange, or an org that is ANYWHERE below the fourth condition of exchange — exchange in abundance — is to immediately, at once and yesterday, and without ripping off some vital post, post a D/CO or D/ED for Delivery and Exchange.

The first and primary function of the D/CO (or D/ED) for Delivery and Exchange is CALL–IN and this means he personally gets call-in done all by his little lonesome. With his own hands and voice he himself begins to call in fully and partially paids. Call-in is his first duty and when he's got that going he posts a Call-in Officer to take over the hat which he has already begun and he then expands onto the other functions of his D/CO or D/ED for Delivery and Exchange post, as covered in HCO PL 9 Aug. 79R II,

SERVICE PRODUCT OFFICER. But he FIRST and PERSONALLY and BY HIMSELF gets call-in going and exchange occurring at once.

What is involved here is the administrative principle that in order to get something done that is an expanding function you give it to somebody and tell him to expand it.

A CO or ED, whose responsibility it is to see that the main functions of the org are getting done, also wears the planning and coordination hat for the whole of the org's activity. If he's going to get the show on the road he needs to delegate some of this responsibility. He needs a deputy — the Deputy CO (or D/ED) for Delivery and Exchange — and that deputy needs the authority and the clout to see that, through promotion, sales, call-in, delivery and re-sign, the main products of the org do get produced.

Getting this post filled competently enables the ED to fully wear his planning and coordination hat and makes it possible for the flow from D/FBO to D/CO (or D/ED) for Delivery and Exchange to FBO to occur.

As some orgs in recent times have experienced both external and internal suppression on the subject of calling people in and servicing them, the D/CO (or D/ED) for Delivery and Exchange is given the additional powers of immediate communication to the International Finance Office and the Inspector General Network without vias to report and get help to remedy internal and external situations in orgs which suppressively inhibit call-in, delivery or expansion whether by inattention, refusals to post vital posts, failures or refusals to contact or call in interested persons, theft of org prospects or business or outright rip-offs to the end of ensuring successful execution of his duties and the expansion of the org. A form for such a report will be provided but absence of a form or a supply of such forms must not inhibit such reports.

This IS the winning combination by which an org moves up to "fair exchange" with all of its public and from there up to the highest level of exchange.

And it is the highest level of exchange toward which the whole activity of the D/CO or D/ED for Delivery and Exchange is geared — exchange in abundance!

L. RON HUBBARD
FOUNDER

HUBBARD COMMUNICATIONS OFFICE
SAINT HILL MANOR, EAST GRINSTEAD, SUSSEX

HCO POLICY LETTER OF 19 DECEMBER 1982
ISSUE I

ALL ORGS
ALL EXECS
ALL STAFF
ALL DIV HEADS
LRH COMMS
HCO
DEPT 1 HATS
DEPT 3 HATS

PERSONNEL SERIES 32
ORG SERIES 44
"DOING A QUICKSILVER" FORBIDDEN

Refs:

HCO PL	19 Mar. 71 I	Personnel Series 20 PERSONNEL PREDICTION
HCO PL	24 June 70 II	PERSONNEL POOLS
HCO PL	7 Jan. 66 I	LEAVING POST, WRITING YOUR HAT
HCO PL	20 Apr. 69 II	HATS, NOT WEARING
HCO PL	20 Aug. 71 III	MUSICAL CHAIRS
HCO PL	11 Aug. 71 II	Personnel Series 22 DON'T UNMOCK A WORKING INSTALLATION
HCO PL	7 Mar. 65 III	OFFENSES AND PENALTIES
HCO PL	13 July 74 II	Org Series 34 WORKING INSTALLATIONS

There is a condition that can exist in orgs which differs slightly from "musical chairs" (the rapid transfer of personnel from post to post) but is akin to that and every bit as deadly.

We could call it a "quicksilver personnel" scene.

("Quicksilver" is another name for mercury, the silvery-white metallic element, liquid at room temperature, which is used in thermometers, barometers and similar instruments.)

Used figuratively, the term "quicksilver" means something that is quick-moving, unpredictable and as elusive as mercury, or "mercurial." Something that is mercurial is changeable, variable, volatile.

To anyone who has ever observed a drop of quicksilver, or mercury, in an open container or placed on a slab of glass, this will be real. One second it's here, the next second it's there. Just about all you have to do is breathe on it and it changes its position. And where it *was* a second ago there's now nothing.

It is miserable (if not impossible) for an executive or management body trying to run things with staff doing a quicksilver. One can hit up against some nasty surprises.

For example, an org's personnel scene may look great on the board, with posts filled, hats existing and known, production occurring and on the rise—all is looking good when suddenly the stats crash.

An initial check may show there haven't honestly been any post transfers, per se. But dig a bit further and you're likely to find a quicksilver personnel scene. The top delivery auditor is off on a two-week vacation. The Qual Sec has been fired on a recruitment tour. The Reg has gone out-ethics and been suspended, unreplaced, pending some ethics handling. The Chief Officer is off on maternity leave and the CO, holding her post from above, is being the guest speaker at an event in the next city.

It happens and it happens not only in Class IV orgs but in the higher service orgs and management units where tours are essential and missions need to be fired and other situations can crop up requiring personnel.

It has shown up drastically at times in several large orgs. In one, the head of a vital network went off on mission and, with no one left being the senior, the stats in the area crashed. In another, the sales manager took his leave, his routine functions were ignored and sales suffered severely. And in still another org, no less than *six* key delivery terminals were all found to be out on regging tours in one week, some of them over a period of several weeks, at a time when delivery of paid-in-full services was backlogged!

None of these terminals had been removed or transferred or promoted. And one could say the actions being done are all covered in some way in policy, are needed, and therefore justified. But these terminals were all off post unreplaced, weren't they?

That's a quicksilver personnel scene. It's unstable.

CONTRIBUTING FACTORS

Executives who issue orders that unmock working installations where production is occurring at "A" to get something done at "X" bring about such scenes.

Personnel who, like quicksilver, accommodatingly move off their assigned posts unreplaced to do something else at the first invitation or order, help to generate and sustain such scenes.

Seniors who permit or condone this are also a party to them.

Personnel can do a quicksilver for any of a number of reasons. For some, the chance to go off and see other people and new places may be an alluring prospect. Some are too timid to refuse a destructive order and so they comply, under protest. For others there is financial gain involved — there are often commissions or a bonus at stake.

Tours have been used by some, apparently condoned by executives, to take longer leaves (more time off on leave per year) by combining 4 to 6 or even 8 weeks of a "regging tour" with a "leave," with the org paying both the person's fare and living expenses and no clear distinction made between the period of "tour" and the period of the "leave." (While this is part of an unstable personnel scene, it is also a situation requiring a separate ethics handling in itself.)

Sometimes a staff member is made to feel, by a very convincing exec, that the action which calls for his suddenly going off post with no or inadequate replacement is actually more important than his job. Where this threatens production and there is no adequate replacement, this is almost always a falsehood.

It is true that missions need to be fired. Tours are vital to income and delivery. Staff sometimes do need to go off post temporarily for handling of one type or another. Events are valuable in terms of promotion, goodwill, PR and sign-ups, and for certain types of these, key personnel or trained tech delivery personnel may be required. Emergencies do arise. Personnel are entitled to annual leave. And speed of operations is important.

On the plus side, we do have capable and versatile staff who are willing to extend themselves, when needed, to make things go right. We have demanding, fire-breathing executives who are out to handle situations and open up new fields for delivery which, in itself, is a good thing. And many of these go about it standardly.

But the senior or exec at any level who endangers ongoing delivery and production and/or unstabilizes a producing personnel scene to get these things done is simply advertising to one and all that he can't predict and plan and organize or get others to do so. Control is lacking here as well as just plain common sense. The kindest thing one could say about such an exec is that he is shortsighted. And "quicksilver" is a rather mild term for the staff member who steps so easily off his post and leaves a hole in the lineup with no thought of the consequences.

One could say that everyone has personnel problems. BUT that is no Why.

HANDLING "QUICKSILVER PERSONNEL" SCENES

The first policies *missing in application* are those covering replacements and hat turnovers.

BECAUSE IT IS A *"TEMPORARY"* ABSENCE, NO ONE IS DEMANDING REPLACEMENT AND TURNING THE HAT OVER TO SOMEONE WHO CAN COVER THE POST *COMPETENTLY.*

But policies exist in abundance on this subject. HCO PL 29 Aug. 70 I, Personnel Series 1, PERSONNEL TRANSFERS CAN DESTROY AN ORG, points up the outnesses which can destroy an org faster than any others. HCO PL 7 Jan. 66 I, LEAVING POST, WRITING YOUR HAT, covers the staff member's responsibility for a post he is vacating under *any* circumstances. HCO PL 20 Apr. 69 II, HATS, NOT WEARING, emphasizes the staff member's responsibility for knowing that he *is* the Qual Sec, or Reg, or the post title for the post and functions he has accepted. HCO PL 11 Aug. 71 II, Personnel Series 22, DON'T UNMOCK A WORKING INSTALLATION, cites the main reason we have ever had slumps in orgs.

The personnel policies are there. But very often, where a "quicksilver personnel" scene is permitted, BECAUSE SOMEONE PULLS OFF A SUCCESS IN ONE AREA, EVEN THOUGH STATS IN HIS OWN AREA MAY CRASH, THE EXISTING ETHICS

POLICIES THAT COVER SUCH A CRASH OR THE COLLAPSE OF AN AREA MAY BE OVERLOOKED OR DELIBERATELY IGNORED.

So how do we handle "quicksilver personnel" scenes?

The answer is to add some teeth to the existing policies:

1. AN ABSENCE FROM POST FOR EVEN A TEMPORARY PERIOD OF AS LITTLE AS HALF A WEEK IS AN ETHICS OFFENSE, UNLESS SOMEONE IS NAMED AND THERE AS A REPLACEMENT WHO HAS HAD THE POST PROPERLY TURNED OVER TO HIM AND WHO CAN COVER THE POST *COMPETENTLY.*

2. IF SUCH ABSENCE WITHOUT COMPETENT REPLACEMENT OCCURS *AT ALL,* AN IMMEDIATE COURT OF ETHICS MUST BE CALLED ON THE STAFF MEMBER WHO LEAVES HIS POST UNFILLED OR INADEQUATELY COVERED, AS WELL AS ON THE SENIOR OR EXECUTIVE ORDERING, CONDONING OR PERMITTING IT.

3. IF IT OCCURS AND RESULTS IN STATS CRASHING IN A COURSE, A DIVISION, DEPARTMENT, SECTION, UNIT, AREA, ZONE OR ORG, A COMMITTEE OF EVIDENCE MUST BE CALLED WITH *ALL* INVOLVED NAMED AS INTERESTED PARTIES.

The charges are:

CONDONING OR CONTRIBUTING TO CIRCUMSTANCES OR OFFENSES CAPABLE OF BRINGING A COURSE, SECTION, UNIT, DEPARTMENT, ORG, ZONE OR DIVISION TO A STATE OF COLLAPSE

and

NEGLECT OF RESPONSIBILITIES RESULTING IN A CATASTROPHE EVEN WHEN ANOTHER MANAGES TO AVERT THE FINAL CONSEQUENCES.

With this policy made known and enforced, there *is* a cure for those who do a "quicksilver" and for executives and seniors whose out-planning and out-prediction bring about quicksilver personnel scenes.

L. RON HUBBARD
FOUNDER

HUBBARD COMMUNICATIONS OFFICE
SAINT HILL MANOR, EAST GRINSTEAD, SUSSEX

HCO POLICY LETTER OF 29 DECEMBER 1982RA
ISSUE II
REVISED 21 JANUARY 1991

REMIMEO
ALL ORGS
ALL EXECUTIVES
ALL MANAGEMENT
   PERSONNEL

ADMIN KNOW-HOW SERIES 45
EXECUTIVE SERIES 24
ORG SERIES 45
ESTABLISHMENT OFFICER SERIES 45

THE TOOLS OF MANAGEMENT

Refs:

HCO PL	11 Apr. 70 I	THIRD DYNAMIC TECH
HCO PL	28 July 72	Exec Series 16
		Org Series 32
		Esto Series 26
		ESTABLISHING, HOLDING THE FORM OF THE ORG
HCO PL	1 July 82	AKH Series 41
		MANAGEMENT COORDINATION

There is a simplicity to managing effectively. It begins with the basics of management.

Although it may appear so to some, successful management is not a highly complicated, esoteric activity. But, just as an auditor or a C/S must know and be able to use the exact tools of first dynamic tech in handling cases in order to achieve exact and standard results on a one-for-one basis, so must an executive or manager know and be able to use the exact tools of third dynamic tech in handling groups to achieve successful and exact results in every instance.

Within the wealth of data on third dynamic tech contained in HCO Policy Letters, the OEC Volumes and recorded LRH lectures and books on the subject, there are certain definite, specific *tools* a manager uses. These are the tools of management.

The difference between brilliant management and mediocre or no management, at any level, lies in:

1. Knowing what the *tools* of management are, and

2. Knowing how to use them.

Many people are not aware that, like a carpenter or any other workman, a manager uses specific and exact *tools*. Thus, we see people here and there who are doing the equivalent of using the handle of a chisel to drive nails into wet concrete.

299

It is a common fault with inexpert workmen to find them using their tools wrongly or not using them at all. They make a breakthrough when they discover what the specific tools are for.

One can see this in people who can't mix sound or can't become mixing engineers. They sit with all these knobs in front of them, reach out and grab this knob or that one, hoping hopefully something will happen to the sound. Yet every component they have in front of them is an exact tool to do an exact thing with sound!

There are a lot of comparisons one could make, but the point is that people in management positions have precise *tools* available to them in Dianetics and Scientology which happen to be far better tools than have ever been available on the planet.

One can have very good people on management posts who still can drown if they don't know and put to use the management tools.

But without these being specified as exact tools, one might not see the simplicity of it.

MANAGEMENT ECHELONS

Operating as it does into an expanding scene, Scientology has grown into the need for and use of various echelons of management.

In orgs, for some time we have had division heads and above them we have the Executive Council, headed by the CO or ED of the org.

Above the level of service orgs we have middle management and still above that we have the Senior Executive Strata of management. And each of these echelons must know the tools of management and how to use them.

The OEC (Org Executive Course) and the FEBC (Flag Executive Briefing Course) have long been established as the essential courses for training executives at service org level and above.

These courses, and the OEC and Management Series Volumes upon which they are based, teach the form of the org and how to use the parts and posts and functions that go to make up the whole. They give us executives who know how to correctly utilize staff and their assigned posts and duties. We call it "knowing how to play the piano" — it's a matter of knowing what key to hit when and which keys to use in combination to produce a desired result. (Ref: HCO PL 28 July 72, ESTABLISHING, HOLDING THE FORM OF THE ORG) In other words, it's a matter of knowing and using one's tools. The OEC and FEBC courses teach this data and much, much more.

While at this writing there are numerous OEC and FEBC grads and more in the making, thousands more will be needed to handle the current rate of expansion.

Meanwhile an executive at any level and whatever his training needs to know and use his management tools NOW if he is to function at all.

A div head must "know how to play the piano" within his division.

The posts of CO or ED, Chief Officer, Supercargo, Org Exec Sec and HCO Exec Sec require executives who are capable of "playing the piano" across the divisions of the entire org and using hats and posts and functions correctly in order to achieve immediate production from the org as a whole.

At middle management one is handling not one function nor only one org but many orgs and their functions, which requires "knowing how to play the piano" at that level.

And at the Senior Executive Strata of management, we get into the vital need for "knowing how to play the piano" across a much wider sphere, using the full scope of management tools and using them with high skill. One might be using the same tools as lower stratas of management but a higher level of expertise is required as one's planning, decisions and actions are influencing far, far broader areas.

What has brought this about is the rapid expansion of Scientology into wider zones of responsibility and therefore increased responsibility with a resultant increase in traffic. This naturally has to be handled by increasing efficiency. What it has done, in effect, is push some up from lower-level management status to upper-level management status, necessarily. Without realizing it, some executives have been climbing a status stairs in terms of influence and zones of control. And they can go only so high without being terribly precise in their use of tools. After that, without this acquired precision, they drown.

The obvious answer to all of this is an executive training program which instant-hats executives on the fundamental tools of management and provides Management Status checksheets through which an executive or manager raises his status by *becoming more and more expert with these and an even wider range of tools.* And such a program has now been developed!

MANAGEMENT STATUS CHECKSHEETS

The new executive training program consists of three status levels.

These levels are to be covered in a series of Management Status checksheets.

The Management Status One checksheet has a prerequisite of Staff Status II. It *instant-hats* an exec on the basic tools of management, such as:

The Admin Scale, target policy, strategic plans, programs, specific lines and org terminals, org boards, despatches and telexes, statistics and graphs, conditions, hats and hatting, files, personnel folders, ethics folders, etc. Each one is a specific tool.

The Management Status Two checksheet (with an OEC prerequisite) consists of a profound review of the basic management tools and study of the upper-level tools of management, which include:

Surveys, PR, pilots, review of past performance, general economics, finance systems, cost accounting, control through networks, admin indicators, morale, legal, goodwill, exchange, missions (Action missions), economical management and managing by dynamics.

The Management Status Three checksheet (with FEBC prerequisite) would be a more profound review of the basic *and* upper-level management tools, in addition to training on the twelve ingredients of expansion upon which the Senior Executive Strata operates.

Even an OEC or FEBC grad would do the Management Status checksheets as, when he comes out of an OEC or FEBC, all in the clouds, the Management Status checksheet is needed to bring him back down to earth and tell him he's dealing with tools which are very finite tools.

What is being communicated to executives by these checksheets is that they have tools, what the tools are exactly, and that they must use them.

EXECUTIVE STATUS LEVELS

There are specific requirements to be met by a manager to attain each of the three Executive Status levels.

Working up through these status levels, a manager not only becomes more proficient in handling an org, any org, but becomes fully certified to operate at middle or senior echelons of management.

The Executive Status levels are:

1. EXECUTIVE STATUS ONE: At this level, the person is simply thrown on post, the basic management tools are put into his hands via a brief, rat-a-tat-tat Management Status One checksheet and he gets on with it.

2. EXECUTIVE STATUS TWO: For one to be certified at this level, one must have completed the OEC, done the Management Status Two checksheet and have an adequate production record.

3. EXECUTIVE STATUS THREE: For one to be certified at this level, he must have completed the FEBC, done the Management Status Three checksheet and have a proven production record.

When the steps for Executive Status certification are complete, the exec must present adequate evidence of such to the Qualifications Division. After verification of the evidence, he is awarded the appropriate Executive Status certificate.

By use of these Executive Status levels, executives at management levels could see what executives they had (or not had). The designation "ES I" (Executive Status I) would tell them at once what they were dealing with, etc. Also, from the viewpoint of the individual, he would know where he had to go to get an upper-level rating.

Once these Management Status checksheets are issued, middle and central management personnel should not draw full pay or be bonus eligible until they have completed the Management Status One checksheet, as they will not be operating effectively until they have done this.

EXECUTIVE STATUSES AND STAFF STATUSES

The Exec Status levels do not replace Staff Status training. All staff and execs are programed and move up the Staff Statuses so as to have a better idea of the org as an org; these levels are also indicative of the training and experience of a staff member and show his promotion eligibility.

An executive should attain Executive Status One by completing the Management Status One checksheet as soon as possible upon assuming post, so he has the management tools available for his immediate application.

Once an exec attains Staff Status VI (Org Exec Course graduate), he can attain Executive Status Two by fulfillment of the requirements listed above. An FEBC graduate achieves Executive Status Three in a similar fashion.

SUMMARY

With the release of the new Management Status checksheets, precise and gradient training levels for all echelons of management will exist comparable to the precise and gradient training levels required for all echelons of technical delivery.

Quite an unbeatable combination!

One winds up with managers fully familiar with their exact tools, having the one-two-three of management tech at their fingertips, and "knowing how to play the piano" effectively across an org, a continent, a planet!

So the answer to current expansion is an action which is geared to bring about even further expansion. And that is the only way to go!

It begins with the basic tools of management.

L. RON HUBBARD
FOUNDER

Revision assisted by
LRH Technical Research
and Compilations

HUBBARD COMMUNICATIONS OFFICE

SAINT HILL MANOR, EAST GRINSTEAD, SUSSEX

HCO POLICY LETTER OF 31 JULY 1983R

ISSUE I

REVISED 21 JANUARY 1991

REMIMEO
ALL ORGS
ALL EXECS
ALL MANAGEMENT
 PERSONNEL

ADMIN KNOW-HOW SERIES 48
EXECUTIVE SERIES 26
ORG SERIES 46
ESTABLISHMENT OFFICER SERIES 47

BASIC MANAGEMENT TOOLS

Refs:

HCO PL	29 Dec. 82RA II	AKH Series 45
	Rev. 21.1.91	Exec Series 24
		Org Series 45
		Esto Series 45
		THE TOOLS OF MANAGEMENT
HCO PL	31 July 83 II	AKH Series 49
		Exec Series 27
		Org Series 47
		Esto Series 48
		MANAGEMENT TOOLS BREAKTHROUGH

The following is a list of the materials which, out of the many tools of management, comprise the BASIC MANAGEMENT TOOLS.

1. *ADMIN SCALE:* A scale for use which gives a sequence (and relative seniority) of subjects relating to organization. The scale, from the top down, includes: Goals, Purposes, Policy, Plans, Programs, Projects, Orders, Ideal Scenes, Statistics, Valuable Final Products. The scale is worked up and down until it is (each item) in full agreement with the remaining items. In short, for success, all these items in the scale must agree with all other items in the scale on the same subject.

2. *TARGET POLICY:* A series of policy letters which describe each type of target and how they are to be used by staff, executives and management personnel to get something *done*.

3. *STRATEGIC PLANS:* A STRATEGIC PLAN is a statement of the intended plans for accomplishing a broad objective and inherent in its definition is the idea of clever use of resources or maneuvers for outwitting the enemy or overcoming existing obstacles to win the objective. It is the central strategy worked out at the top which, like an umbrella, covers the activities of the echelons below it.

4. *PROGRAMS:* A PROGRAM is a series of steps in sequence to carry out a plan. Programs are made up of all types of targets coordinated and executed on time.

5. *PROJECTS:* A PROJECT is a series of guiding steps written in sequence to carry out one step of a program, which, if followed, will result in a full and successful accomplishment of the program target.

6. *ORDERS:* An ORDER is the direction or command issued by an authorized person to a person or group within the sphere of the authorized person's authority. It is the verbal or written direction from a lower or designated authority to carry out a program step or apply the general policy. Some program steps are so simple that they are themselves an order or an order can simply be a roughly written project. By implication an order goes from a senior to juniors.

   All orders of whatever kind by telex, despatch or mission orders must be coordinated with current written command intention. You can destroy an org by issuing orders to it uncleared and uncoordinated. Coordinate your orders! Clear your orders!

7. *COMPLIANCE REPORTS:* A COMPLIANCE REPORT is a report to the originator of an order that the order has been done and is a completed cycle. It is not a cycle begun, it is not a cycle in progress, it is a cycle completed and reported back to the originator as done.

   When an executive or manager accepts "done" as the single statement and calls it a compliance, noncompliance can occur unseen. Therefore, one must (1) require explicit compliance to every order and (2) receive the evidence of the compliance pinned to the compliance report. Such evidence might be in the form of copies of the actual material required by the order and procured, or photographs of it, ticket stubs, receipts, a signed note stating the time and place some action was carried out, etc. Evidence is data that records a "done" so somebody else can know it is done.

   It is up to LRH Comms, Flag Reps or execs to verify reports of dones or get dones done. True compliances to evaluated programs are vital.

8. *TERMINALS:* A TERMINAL is something that has mass and meaning which originates, receives, relays and changes particles on a flow line. A post or terminal is an assigned area of responsibility and action which is supervised in part by an executive.

   A fixed-terminal post stays in one spot, handles specific duties and receives communications, handles them and sends them on their way.

   A line post has to do with organizational lines, seeing that the lines run smoothly, ironing out any ridges in the lines, keeping particles flowing smoothly from one post to another post. A line post is concerned with the flow of lines, not necessarily with the fixed-terminal posts at the end of the lines.

9. *LINES:* A LINE is a route along which a particle travels between one terminal and the next in an organization; a fixed pattern of terminals who originate and receive or receive and relay orders, information or other particles.

A COMMAND LINE is a line on which authority flows. It is vertical. A command line is used upward for unusual permission or authorizations or information or important actions or compliances. Downward it is used for orders.

A COMMUNICATION LINE is the line on which particles flow; any sequence through which a message of any character may go. It is horizontal.

The most important things in an organization are its lines and terminals. Without these in, in an exact known pattern, the organization cannot function at all. The lines will flow if they are all in and people wear their hats.

10. *ORG BOARDS:* An ORG BOARD (ORGANIZING BOARD) is a board which displays the functions, duties, sequences of action and authorities of an organization. The org board shows the pattern of organizing to obtain a product. It is the pattern of the terminals and their flows. We see these terminals as "posts" or positions. Each of these is a hat. There is a flow along these hats. The result of the whole org board is a product. The product of each hat on the board adds up to the total product.

11. *HATS:* HAT is a term to describe the write-ups, checksheets and packs that outline the purposes, know-how and duties of a post. It exists in folders and packs and is trained in on the person on the post to a point of full application of the data therein. A HAT designates what terminal in the organization is represented and what the terminal handles and what flows the terminal directs. HATTING is the action of training the person on the checksheet and pack of materials for his post.

12. *TELEXES:* A TELEX is a message sent and received by means of telex machines at specific stations hooked up with one another. This is a fast method of communication, similar to a telegram or cable.

Use telexes as though you were sending telegrams. Positiveness and speed are the primary factors. Cost enters as a third. Security enters as a fourth consideration. All have importance but in that order.

Telexes must be of such clarity that any other person in the org can read and understand them. You must take responsibility for both ends of a communication line. Write your communication (telex) so that it invites compliance or answer without further query or dev-t. Entheta in telexes on a long-distance comm line is forbidden.

Don't use telexes when despatches will do. Nonurgent communications on telex lines jam them. Do NOT put logistics (supply) on a telex line. Telex lines should only be used for communications concerning operations.

13. *DESPATCHES:* A DESPATCH is a written message, particularly an official communication. When writing a despatch, address it to the POST — not the person. Date your despatch. Route to the hat only, give its department, section and org. Put any vias at the top of the despatch. Indicate with an arrow the first destination. Sign it with your name but also the hat you're wearing when you write it.

As with telexes, despatches must be written so clearly that any other person in the org can read and understand them, with the originator taking responsibility for both ends of the communication line. And, as with telexes, entheta in despatches on a long-distance comm line is forbidden.

14. *STATISTICS:* A STATISTIC is a number or amount *compared* to an earlier number or amount of the same thing. STATISTICS refer to the quantity of work done or the value of it in money. Statistics are the only sound measure of any production or any job or any activity. These tell of production. They measure what is done. Thus, one can manage by statistics. When one is managing by statistics they must be studied and judged alongside the other related statistics.

15. *GRAPHS:* A GRAPH is a line or diagram showing how one quantity depends on, compares with or changes another. It is any pictorial device used to display numerical relationships.

16. *CONDITIONS:* A CONDITION is an operating state. Organizationally, it's an operating state and oddly enough, in the MEST universe, there are several formulas connected with these operating states. The table of conditions, from the bottom up, includes: Confusion, Treason, Enemy, Doubt, Liability, Non-Existence, Danger, Emergency, Normal, Affluence and Power or Power Change. There is a law that holds true in this universe whereby if one does not correctly designate the condition he is in and apply its formula to his activities or if he assigns and applies the wrong condition, then the following happens: He will inevitably drop one condition below the condition he is *actually* in. One has to *do* the steps of a condition formula in order to improve one's condition.

17. *PERSONNEL FOLDERS:* A PERSONNEL FOLDER is kept in HCO for each person employed by the org. The folder is to contain all pertinent personnel data about the person: name, age, nationality, date employment started, address (if other than the org), next of kin, social security number, test scores, previous education, skills, previous employment, case level, training level, name of post, former posts held and dates held, production record on post(s), date employment ceased, copies of all tests, and any other pertinent data.

Copies of contracts, agreements or legal papers connected with the person are filed in the personnel folder. The originals of such papers are kept in the val doc files.

A personnel folder is used for purposes of promotion and any needful reorganization and so should contain anything that throws light on the efficiency, inefficiency or character of personnel.

Personnel folders are filed by division and department in HCO, with the personnel in separate folders filed alphabetically in their department. There should be two sections in the personnel files: (1) present employees and (2) past employees.

18. *ETHICS FOLDERS:* An ETHICS FOLDER is kept in HCO for each individual staff member. It is a folder which should include his complete ethics record, ethics chits, Knowledge Reports, commendations and copies, as well, of any

justice actions taken on the person, such as Courts of Ethics or Comm Evs, with their results.

Filing is the real trick of Ethics work. The files do 90 percent of the work. Ethics reports patiently filed in folders, one for each staff member, eventually makes one file fat. When one file gets fat, call up a Court of Ethics on the person and his area gets smooth.

19. *FILES*: A FILE by definition is an orderly and complete deposit of data which is available for immediate use. As FILES are the vital operational line it is of the GREATEST IMPORTANCE that ALL FILING IS ACCURATE. A misfiled particle can be lost forever. A missing item can throw out a whole evaluation or a sale. It is of vital interest both in ease of work and financially that all files are straight.

20. *DATA SERIES*: The tool to discover causes. The administrative technology described in these policy letters is applied to find what is logical by ferreting out what is illogical, using this to reveal the greatest outness which, when remedied, will resolve the scene.

There is considerably more data on each of these tools contained in the policy letters in the OEC Volumes and Management Series Volumes, *none* of it complicated or difficult to grasp.

The purpose of this policy letter is simply to advise the exec that these *are* his tools — his most fundamental and basic management tools. And that they are for USE and it is VITAL that he USE them.

Why? Because use of these simple, basic tools means the difference between a failing org and a flourishing one.

And we want organizations to flourish!

L. RON HUBBARD
FOUNDER

Revision assisted by
LRH Technical Research
and Compilations

HUBBARD COMMUNICATIONS OFFICE
SAINT HILL MANOR, EAST GRINSTEAD, SUSSEX

HCO POLICY LETTER OF 31 JULY 1983
ISSUE II

REMIMEO
ALL ORGS
ALL EXECS
ALL MANAGEMENT
    PERSONNEL

VITAL — IMPORTANT

ADMIN KNOW-HOW SERIES 49
EXECUTIVE SERIES 27
ORG SERIES 47
ESTABLISHMENT OFFICER SERIES 48

MANAGEMENT TOOLS BREAKTHROUGH

Refs:

HCO PL	29 Dec. 82R II	AKH Series 45
	Rev. 30.7.83	Exec Series 24
		Org Series 45
		Esto Series 45
		THE TOOLS OF MANAGEMENT
HCO PL	31 July 83 I	AKH Series 48
		Exec Series 26
		Org Series 46
		Esto Series 47
		BASIC MANAGEMENT TOOLS

THE FIRST THING AN EXECUTIVE OR MANAGER AT ANY LEVEL NEEDS TO KNOW IS THAT HE HAS *TOOLS* WITH WHICH TO MANAGE.

This applies to top levels of management, to middle management echelons and in every org from the CO or ED down through the Exec Council and every head of a division or department.

BREAKTHROUGH

This datum is the result of a recent, eye-opening breakthrough.

The breakthrough was not a matter of discovering or developing or improving the materials which make up the tools of management. Org boards, the Admin Scale, target policy, planning and programing, statistics, graphs and conditions (to name a few of these tools) have been a part of our technology, well defined, available for use and used for quite some years now.

THE BREAKTHROUGH WAS IN DISCOVERING THAT A GREAT MANY EXECUTIVES DID NOT LOOK UPON THESE AS *TOOLS*.

But unless one does recognize them as tools, unless one actually puts them in the *category of tools,* like rakes and shovels and wheelbarrows, he is apt to think of them as opinions or theories or something of the sort. He won't recognize that he does have actual *tools* with which to manage. And, not realizing this, he won't USE them in managing.

Such a scene could be compared to somebody building a house who didn't even know he was trying to build a house and, should this be pointed out to him, he would look at hammers and saws as if they were total strangers. He wouldn't wind up with a house.

Any activity has its tools. And if one is going to engage in an activity, he had better know what its tools are and that they are for use.

BASIC MANAGEMENT TOOLS

We are rich in management tools but the most fundamental of them, required for use at any executive level from the highest to the lowest, are these:

ADMIN SCALE

TARGET POLICY

STRATEGIC PLANS

PROGRAMS

PROJECTS

ORDERS

COMPLIANCE REPORTS

ORG TERMINALS

SPECIFIC LINES

ORG BOARDS

HATS AND HATTING

TELEXES

DESPATCHES

STATISTICS AND GRAPHS

CONDITIONS

PERSONNEL FOLDERS

ETHICS FOLDERS

FILES

DATA SERIES

Each of these fundamental tools is defined and covered briefly in HCO PL 31 July 83 I, BASIC MANAGEMENT TOOLS.

None of these are complicated. They are actually SIMPLE but VITALLY, VITALLY IMPORTANT.

One gets some terminals, gets them some lines, gets the channels of command and echelon worked out, gets in strategic planning and with that one can achieve some coordination.

But it is necessary to be able to conceive of purpose (which, in target policy, becomes objectives). And it is necessary to be able to write targets that will accomplish that objective or that purpose. To get the targets done one needs lines and terminals there. And to have lines and terminals, of course, one has to have an org board.

SIMPLE. But VITALLY IMPORTANT.

In laying out these tools we are laying out the fundamentals of organization as that, most definitely, is what these tools are. And these tools will give one an organization. Without them, you don't have an organization, you have a mob. And if one cannot figure out purpose or objectives or write targets and telexes and get hatting done and hats worn they'll just keep on being a mob. But correct use of just this basic list of management tools can turn a mob into a producing organization!

EXEC STATUS ONE CHECKSHEET

A fast, instant-hat type of checksheet called Exec Status One is being provided to swiftly train execs and managers at all levels on these tools.

This is not a substitute for an OEC or FEBC. But it is vital that an exec starts using these tools right now, instantly and at once yesterday, if he considers himself an executive or is in a position of handling an organization of any type, size or kind. Because if he doesn't use these tools, he's going to lay an egg.

ETHICS

Once the exec has passed this first checksheet, Exec Status One, it's an ethics offense to fail to use these tools properly. One would handle a first or second offense with cramming, but after that it's a Court of Ethics and, in the case of a person having trained on these tools continuing to misapply or not apply these tools, it becomes a matter for a Comm Ev.

SUMMARY

1. First, an executive or manager must know that actual TOOLS EXIST for his use in managing.

2. Second, he needs to know WHAT his tools are.

3. Third, he must realize that these tools are SIMPLE but VITALLY, VITALLY IMPORTANT, that they are for USE and he must *USE THEM*.

L. RON HUBBARD
FOUNDER

HUBBARD COMMUNICATIONS OFFICE
SAINT HILL MANOR, EAST GRINSTEAD, SUSSEX

HCO POLICY LETTER OF 18 JUNE 1985

REMIMEO
ALL EXECUTIVES
PRODUCT OFFICERS
ORG OFFICERS
ESTABLISHMENT OFFICERS
CRAMMING OFFICERS

EXECUTIVE SERIES 30
ORG SERIES 48

PRODUCT ORIENTATION

Refs:

HCO PL   14 Sept. 70 I   Org Series 2
                                  COPE AND ORGANIZE

Tape: 7011C17 SO   FEBC 1, "Welcome to the FEBC"

One of the primary duties of a product officer is to look around and find some production to do.

On an executive post, the formula one operates on is 50 percent production and 50 percent organize. When the organize is superlative and is very well done (while remaining only 50 percent of the time spent by the executive), it eventually gets up to 75 percent production and 25 percent organize. This is approximately the ideal scene.

OVER–ORGANIZE

Organization is a vital activity. However, when the amount of organize time starts outweighing the production time, it is an indicator of other outnesses. The purpose for organizing in the first place is so that *production* can occur. In an area of organize-organize-organize, one will always find crashing Mis-Us, false data, overts and withholds. In other words, these are the things which turn people into fiddle-fiddle organize.

Organize time should not exceed 50 percent of a person's post time. Cramming and drilling fall under the category of organize, and the 50-50 rule applies here as well. The solution to a flubbing staff member is not to put him onto full-time drilling or cramming. The person should do his correction actions for half a day and be put on the job in some capacity the other half of the day so that he stays accustomed to the scene. Otherwise, the person is liable to get stiff and have trouble getting back onto post when he does finish his correction. Study, and even cramming, is actually an award. What about the guys that are doing all the work? Wouldn't they like to have a full day of cramming too?

KEEPING PRODUCTION ROLLING

It is the responsibility of the executive to keep his staff busy producing.

Many people don't like to be executives because they always have to be ransacking around making sure staff are producing, and finding things for them to do. But personnel are actually put at risk when they aren't kept in production. A big company which suddenly dismisses a lot of personnel simply has shiftless executives who have not found things for the personnel to do.

Even if major production in a particular area is temporarily stopped for some reason, other related (or different) products and subproducts can be found for the staff to do which can be done with existing resources.

As an example of this, suppose one had a movie production company whose camera was out for repair. Though they wouldn't actually be able to put anything on film, there would still be cycles which could be done in the meantime. They could be rounding up props, rehearsing actors, and making sure all the other actions which will be needed to complete that film are done.

It is not a slight matter to overlook things like this because somewhere up the track, in the midst of heavy rush production, suddenly one of these overlooked cycles will pop into view and stall the whole line while it is done on an emergency basis.

SUMMARY

The trick of the product officer is to find blank periods and things to put in them. If one gets conditioned to thinking this way, it becomes a very easy job. Otherwise, it's all panic.

Product orientation is very important, as in the long run, it protects the worker and it gets the show on the road. One can't totally produce or totally organize at any given time. It takes an average between production and organize to keep things going. But the whole point is to keep things going, and keep products rolling out.

L. RON HUBBARD
FOUNDER

HUBBARD COMMUNICATIONS OFFICE
Saint Hill Manor, East Grinstead, Sussex

HCO POLICY LETTER OF 21 SEPTEMBER 1995

Remimeo
Estos
All Orgs
All Management
    Personnel

ADMIN KNOW-HOW SERIES 53
ORG SERIES 49
ESTABLISHMENT OFFICER SERIES 51
LOST TECH

(Written on 8 Nov. 79. Issued as
an HCO PL on 21 Sept. 95.)

Modifies: HCO PL 9 May 74   PROD–ORG, ESTO AND
                                OLDER SYSTEMS RECONCILED

I've just realized that the Esto and the prod–org system, both of which were successful in their day, have been totally dropped. One executive apparently had a confusion on the two systems and could not reconcile them and so stopped pushing both of them. That is my Why for some org failures.

The prod–org system was enormously successful and has been dropped. The Esto system had limited success and has been dropped. The reason for the failure of the Esto system was earlier isolated — the Supervisors let the Esto trainees fake their way through their study of the subject. They just didn't study the subject and then went around running into walls. This was true even though they were given heavy intensive training on it. They didn't do the training.

This comes up because of a cram done on this executive which states that he could never reconcile the two systems and has had a confusion on them. This definitely must have shown up during his tenure as an executive and it brings to mind right this minute that the prod–org system and the Esto system may never have been pushed in. This executive violated the normal actions of prod–org and org establishment. But this bares the fact that management and orgs may not be pushing either the prod–org system nor the Esto system and this could, in large measure, account for the fact that orgs in some cases became disestablished and ceased to produce and deliver.

The exact goof which this executive made is important to understand — he put the Service Product Officer over the Esto and made the Esto the org officer of the Service Product Officer, and hoped from this that his org would be established. Of course it wouldn't be established at all because a product officer's org officer normally specializes in disestablishment — org officers have tended mainly to tear up the org in the name of production. That is by our experience. An org having an Esto, recruits up an Esto corps. That is the only thing that will get posts filled and hatted.

These two systems must be represented on any org board. The product officer must be on those org boards, the product officer's org officer must be on those org boards. And the Executive Esto must be on those org boards. Otherwise these systems will continue to be submerged.

I mention this in order to get into action both the prod–org system and the Esto system. They must be called strongly to attention, otherwise they will go on being neglected.

This could be a major downfall of management and orgs if one just ceased to push these two successful points.

Thus I am calling to your attention the fact that you should use these systems so that we can recover this lost tech.

L. RON HUBBARD
FOUNDER

THE
ESTABLISHMENT OFFICER
SERIES

ESTO

HUBBARD COMMUNICATIONS OFFICE
SAINT HILL MANOR, EAST GRINSTEAD, SUSSEX

HCO POLICY LETTER OF 24 FEBRUARY 1972
ISSUE II

REMIMEO

ESTOs

(Originally written by LRH for the *Apollo* OODs of
24 Feb. 72. Issued as an HCO PL on 18 Sept. 80.)

An Esto has a definite job to do. He is not part of the division's lines. He hats, organizes, trains, sets up files, lines, and does all those establishment actions people need to *really* establish a division and maintain it.

If you want an Esto to go into gales of laughter, say "I am too busy to get hatted." Those papers and that enMEST show that a two hours of hatting a day save a year of dev-t nonproduction.

HCO over the world could not establish orgs. It can do its departmental functions. The answer is the Esto.

You'll be seeing a lot of this. Might as well know who these strange people are who keep insisting you find out about comm baskets and things.

L. RON HUBBARD
FOUNDER

HCO POLICY LETTER OF 7 MARCH 1972R
ISSUE I

REMIMEO

REVISED 13 APRIL 1972

ESTABLISHMENT OFFICER SERIES 1

THE ESTABLISHMENT OFFICER

PURPOSE

The Establishment Officer system evolved from the product–org system where it was found the HAS alone could not establish the org. The product–org officer system is entirely valid and is not changed. Tapes up to and including number 7 of the prod–org system (also called the FEBC tapes) are correct. From number 8 onward, the prod–org tapes are replaced by the Esto Series tapes. It is important to know that when the org officer is removed from a unit "because it now has an Esto" it will practically destroy the unit and crash its stats. Taking the org officer out of a division or org and making him the Esto is a guarantee of a crash. The Esto is an extension of the original HCO system as an Esto performs all the functions of HCO for the activity to which he is assigned *plus* his own tech of being an Esto.

The purpose of Establishment Officers is to ESTABLISH and MAINTAIN the establishment of the org and each division therein.

The term "Esto" is used for abbreviation as "EO" means Ethics Officer.

It has been found that the whole reason for any lack of prosperity of an org is INTERNAL. The surrounding area of the public has very little to do with whether stats are up or down. An org, by "delivering" out-tech and its own conduct, upsets its area but it can also straighten it out PROVIDING IT DOES ITS JOB. So this too is an internal cause.

Thus if an org is well established so that each staff member is doing his exact function, stats will go up and the org will prosper because it has been handled internally.

All booms and depressions of an org are due to its being expertly built up and then, having a peak period, is not maintained in that well-established condition and disintegrates.

In the vital flurry of getting the product and expanding, the org becomes disestablished.

In the product–org officer system of 1971 it was found uniformly that as soon as the org began to boom, the HAS was wholly unable to establish rapidly enough and the boom collapsed. HCO was too few to keep an org established even when the HCO was manned because THEY WERE NOT WORKING INSIDE EACH DIVISION.

The answer to these shortcomings is the Establishment Officer system. This preserves the best in the product–org system and keeps pace with product and expansion.

A well-trained, hard-working Esto in a division has proven to be the miracle of org prosperity.

The system has already been tested and is in successful operation.

Establishment consists of quarters, personnel, training, hatting, files, lines, supplies and materiel and all things necessary to establishment.

POSITION

The org board of Establishment Officers is:

Commanding Officer or Executive Director (coordinates)

Product Officer (operates org)
Org Officer (organizes for Prod Off)

Executive Establishment Officer (operates Estos)

Exec Esto Org Officer
Esto Establishment Officer
(Esto Course Supervisor) } Combined Hat

(Div secs are in charge of div and are product officers.)

7	1	2	3	4	5	6
LRH Comm	HAS	Dissem Sec	Treasury Sec	Tech Sec	Qual Sec	Dist Sec
Div 7 Esto	HCO Esto	DEO	Tr EO	TEO	QEO	PEO

CO or ED Foundation
Org Off Fdn

7	1	2	3	4	5	6
LRH Comm Fdn	HAS Fdn	Dissem Sec Fdn	Treas Sec Fdn	Tech Sec Fdn	Qual Sec Fdn	Dist Sec Fdn
Fdn Div 7	Fdn HCO	Fdn Dissem	Fdn Treas	Fdn Tech	Fdn Qual	Fdn Dist

(Same Esto covers same div Day and Fdn.)

PRODUCTS

To understand what the Esto system is you have to understand first and foremost the meaning of the word "PRODUCT." (The whole system breaks down where this one word is not understood and not understanding this one word and failing to get it understood has been found to be the barrier in most cases.)

PRODUCE (verb) = To bring into existence, make; to bring about; cause.

PRODUCT (noun) = Someone or something that *has been* brought into existence; the end result of a creation; something or someone who has been brought into existence.

If you really know that definition you can then look over HCO PL 29 Oct. 70 I, Org Series 10, THE ANALYSIS OF ORGANIZATION BY PRODUCT. In this we have (1) establishing something that produces (Product 1), (2) operating that which produces in order to get a product (Product 2), (3) repairing or correcting that which produces (Product 3), (4) repairing or correcting that which is produced (Product 4).

Now in order to get an org there and make money and eat and get paid and things like that, these things like products have to be understood and the knowledge USED.

If we try to operate an org that isn't there, or repair it, nothing happens. No stats. No money. The product officer and org officer have nothing to run. They're like a pilot and copilot with no airplane. They don't fly.

So an Establishment Officer is there to put the airplane there AND get the pilot and copilot to fly it well, without wrecking it, to everyone's benefit.

So, the Establishment Officers put the org there to be run and put the people there to run it so they run it well, without wrecking it, to everyone's benefit.

POSTS AND TITLES

The org is commanded by the Commanding Officer (SO orgs) or the Executive Director (non-SO orgs). In the triangular system of the Flag Executive Briefing Course (FEBC) (product–org officer system) the CO or ED *coordinates* the work of the product officer, org officer and Executive Esto.

In most orgs the CO or ED is also the PRODUCT OFFICER of the org which is a double hat with CO.

The product officer controls and operates the org and its staff to get production. Production is represented by the gross divisional statistics and valuable final products of the org.

The ORG OFFICER assists the product officer. He gets production lined up, grooves in staff on what they should be getting out and makes sure the product officer's plans are executed.

(The duties of CO or ED, product officer and org officer are covered in the FEBC tapes 1 to 7.)

The EXECUTIVE ESTABLISHMENT OFFICER is the one who puts the org there to be run. He does this by having Establishment Officers establishing the divisions, org staff and the materiel of the division. He is like a coach using athletes to win games. He sends them in and they put their divisions there and maintain them. They also put there somebody to *work* them.

The EXECUTIVE ESTABLISHMENT OFFICER ORG OFFICER (Esto Org Officer) is the E Esto's deputy and handles his programs and the personal side of Estos.

The ESTABLISHMENT OFFICER'S ESTABLISHMENT OFFICER (the Esto's Esto) is the one who trains and hats and checks out Estos and establishes the Esto system. He also runs the Esto course that makes Estos and is the Esto's Course Supervisor. In practice, the hats of Esto Org Officer (above) and Esto's Esto Officer are held as one hat until an org is very large. The person who holds this post has to be a very good Course Supervisor who uses study tech like a master as his flubs would carry through the whole Esto system.

An ESTABLISHMENT OFFICER IN–CHARGE is an Esto who has Establishment Officers under him in an activity that has five or less Estos, does duties comparable to an Executive Esto for that activity.

A CHIEF ESTABLISHMENT OFFICER + DIVISION is an Esto who, in a division, has Establishment Officers under him due to the numerousness of the division.

A LEADING ESTABLISHMENT OFFICER + DEPARTMENT is a departmental Establishment Officer who has section Estos under him due to the numerousness of the section.

An ESTABLISHMENT OFFICER + SECTION is an Establishment Officer of a section where there is a departmental and divisional Esto.

The divisional Establishment Officers are as follows. If they have other Estos under them in the division the title CHIEF is put in front of the title.

THE DIV 7 ESTABLISHMENT OFFICER (Div 7 Esto) for Division 7, the Executive Division. He is not "The Executive Esto." He carries out all the Esto duties for this division.

THE HCO ESTABLISHMENT OFFICER (HCO Esto) establishes and maintains HCO.

THE DISSEMINATION ESTABLISHMENT OFFICER (DEO) establishes and maintains the Dissem Division.

THE TREASURY ESTABLISHMENT OFFICER (Tr EO) establishes and maintains the Treasury Division.

THE TECHNICAL DIVISION ESTABLISHMENT OFFICER (TEO) establishes and maintains the Tech Division. This division amongst all the rest is most likely to have other Estos in the division.

THE QUALIFICATIONS ESTABLISHMENT OFFICER (QEO) establishes and maintains the Qual Division.

THE DISTRIBUTION ESTABLISHMENT OFFICER (PEO for Public Division) establishes and maintains the Distribution Division.

The Exec Esto and Esto Org Officer and the Esto's Esto and Esto course are org boarded as in Dept 21.

The Estos themselves are in their own assigned divisions.

The CO or ED, product and org officer are org boarded in Dept 19.

HEAD OF ORG

The head of the org is the Commanding Officer or Executive Director. He is usually also the PRODUCT OFFICER. He is senior to the Exec Esto.

DEPUTY CO OR ED

The CO's or ED's DEPUTY handles the programs functions of the CO or ED and is the org's org officer.

He ranks *with* the Exec Esto.

HEAD OF DIVISION

The head of a division is the DIVISIONAL SECRETARY. He is the PRODUCT OFFICER of his division. His boss is the CO or ED.

He is senior to the divisional Esto or Chief Esto.

He is *not* the divisional Esto's boss. The E Esto is.

DEPUTY DIVISION HEAD

The DEPUTY SECRETARY of a division is the org officer of that division.

He handles the programs of the division for the secretary.

He ranks with the divisional Esto or Chief Esto.

DEPARTMENT DIRECTOR

He is the PRODUCT OFFICER OF HIS DEPARTMENT.

The divisional Esto is senior to him.

The departmental director is senior to an Esto posted to his specific department.

SECTION OFFICER

The officer in charge of a section is the PRODUCT OFFICER of that section.

He is junior to all Estos except an Esto posted directly to his specific department.

STAFF

Staff members other than those who are Estos are all considered PRODUCT 2 and 4 PERSONNEL from the viewpoint of the Esto whose products are 1 and 3 (see above or Org Series 10, HCO PL 29 Oct. 70 I).

TEST

The test of the successful Esto is whether he increases QUANTITY and QUALITY of PRODUCT 2 PER STAFF MEMBER AND AN ABSENCE OF DEV-T (developed or unnecessary traffic).

SMALL ORGS

An Esto In-Charge in a small org (2 to 5 staff not counting Estos) would be one of two Estos. He would handle the Esto system for that org and Divisions 7, 1 and 2 and the other Esto, Divisions 3, 4, 5 and 6. He would also run the Esto course as well as work the Estos.

With trained Estos actually functioning, the production of this small org would increase and one would have an evolution leading to an Esto I/C, one Esto for 7, 1 and 2 and another for 3, 4, 5 and 6.

Further evolving there would be an Esto I/C, one for 7, 1 and 2, one for 3, 4 and 5 and another Esto for Div 6.

With additional expansion there would be an Esto I/C, one for 7, 1 and 2, one for 3 and 5, one for 4 and one for 6.

Additional expansion would have an Esto I/C, one for 7 and 1, one for 2, one for 3 and 5, one for 4 and one for 6. This reaches the stage of five Estos for one Esto I/C.

We now upgrade the system to an Exec Esto and a deputy and one Esto per division.

Almost at once Tech will need a Chief TEO and a TEO. Then a Chief TEO and three Leading Estos for 4.

The system goes on evolving. One Esto to ten staff is the maximum allowed at this stage.

BUREAUX

Where bureaux are combined with the service org the divisional Esto also has the duties of the bureaux establishment.

In such a case there is an OPERATIONS ESTABLISHMENT OFFICER in charge of the four Operations Bureaux which combined make up the Operations Bureaux. He, as expansion occurs, will shortly become a Chief Esto for Operations (or Chief Operations Esto) with an Esto in each bureau — the Action Leading Esto; the Data Leading Esto; the Management Leading Esto; and the Ext Comm Leading Esto.

RULE OF EXPANSION

The Esto system may not be expanded nor may the org be expanded without comparable expansion of GI, delivery completions and success statistics.

The quality and skill of Estos in acquiring personnel, training, hatting, supplying, FP conduct and other duties is directly reflected in statistical increase of GI, delivery, success and VIABILITY.

ESTO TRAINING

The EXEC ESTO (or Esto I/C) is responsible for the quantity of establishment done and the quality and performance of all his Estos. EXEC ESTOs or ESTO I/Cs are trained on Flag or as designated by Flag.

Exec Estos or Esto I/Cs are usually granted the right to train Estos. For this they must have the packs and equipment. The actual training is done by their Esto Org Officer or when one exists, the Esto's Esto.

The actual hatting and training of Estos comes under the Esto's Esto, the Esto Org Officer generally wearing this hat.

In a crush emergency in any one of the mentioned divisions the EXEC ESTO goes in on Divs 7, 1 or 2 and the Deputy Exec Esto goes in on Divisions 3, 4, 5 and 6.

An Esto usually works the full day less conference time and studies an additional five hours minimum.

Where there is a Foundation, the same Estos as the Day org cover the Foundation as well until both Day and Foundation are too large to be so handled, at which time a Foundation begins a separate Esto function under its own Esto I/C. When all Foundation divs are separately covered, the Foundation has its own Exec Esto.

TRAINING OUTLINE

A full training outline of the skills required in an Esto follows:

An Exec Esto should be ideally a full FEBC. This covers the OEC and the product–org officer system.

An Esto I/C would have to know the OEC.

In addition to the above would be added these specific requirements:

Primary Correction Rundown (HCOB 30 Mar. 72)

Word Clearer — able to handle a meter and do Method 2 and Method 4, assess prepared lists and do good TRs

Vol 0 OEC (if not done on the OEC)

Vol 1 OEC (if not done on the OEC)

Org Series PLs

Personnel Series PLs

Data Series PLs

PR Becomes a Subject (FEBC tapes)

Mini Course Super Hat (Full HPCSC for the Esto's Esto)

ARC triangle materials

Dianetics 55!

FP policy (finance pack)

PTS phenomena HCOBs

DB and SP HCOBs and PLs

Psychosis HCOBs

HCO investigatory tech

Establishment Officer tapes series

Establishment Officer Series PLs

LRH ED 174 Int (1972), STUDY AND TECH BREAKTHROUGH

HCO PL 9 Apr. 72, CORRECT DANGER CONDITION HANDLING

There is a difference in what the Esto himself has to know to be hatted and what he must teach in his division. These are TWO different bodies of knowledge.

The Esto must know all the hats and valuable final products of any division he is hatting.

He should know the Product–Org series tapes.

He should know quarters and housing materials.

He should know the operating manuals and how to operate any machine in the division he is establishing.

On ships he should know the FOs.

Any FOs, FSOs and CBOs that may apply in a bureau.

The Esto becomes totally proficient in his own hat and makes others proficient in theirs. He has to be able to read and pick up data on another's hat very rapidly.

CASE REQUIREMENTS
(Not necessarily in program order)

TRs the Hard Way

Admin TRs

OCA not below center line

Physically well

Case gain

C/S 53 to F/N on list

If drugs, full Drug RD

GF 40RR to F/N on list

The HAS Rundown

F/N on White Form

Study Correction List

W/C No. 1

HATTING CYCLE

The cycle of hatting of Estos and of staff members is HAT some and get production, hat more and get production, hat more and get production. Hat to total specialization, get production. Hat to more generalized skill and get production. Hat an activity until it can do own and everyone else's hat in the activity and get production.

Quarters, supply, equipment, space, all follow this same gradient. Get it in, get it producing, get more in, get it producing.

ESTO TRAINING

An Esto has two hats. (A) His own hat as an Esto in which he must be expert. (B) The hats and skills he is grooving in on others.

The most skilled Esto learns his own job and that of the other fellow rapidly and thoroughly.

These two hats are separate and must be kept separate.

INVOLVEMENT

The Esto may not involve himself in the production cycles of a post or division except to learn it himself so he can hat expertly or get the HCO PLs or tech applied to it understood by himself so he can hat and debug the post.

The Esto *must* be an *expert* on Word Clearing Method 3 tapes and then W/C Method 4ing them.

He, in Europe, MUST KNOW FOREIGN LANGUAGE TRANSLATED TAPE HCOBs, PLs AND EXPERTISE.

HCO

HCO performs its normal duties per policy. It is not called on to establish the whole org, however, but is to back up Estos.

Personnel is obtained through Department 1 by Estos but these do not have to depend only on that but must clear personnel and changes through it.

EXEC ESTO's MAA

The Executive Esto has a MASTER–AT–ARMS in a large org.

The MAA musters the crew, conducts any exercises, does ethics investigations as needful especially by the Exec Esto and helps hat the Ethics Officers of the org. He does not replace these. He does other duties assigned.

PRODUCT CONFERENCE

The PRODUCT CONFERENCE is conducted by the CO or ED (or his deputy). It consists of the divisional heads of the org as each of these is a PRODUCT OFFICER.

It sets and reports on targets.

As the CO or ED as PRODUCT OFFICER investigates and does evaluations and writes programs, some of the actions of the product conference are furnishing data to debug. The Data Series and the OEC and FOs are the tech used. (The primary reason for failures of such a conference will be found to be [A] operating on wrong Whys, [B] lack of knowledge of conference tech which is mainly do homework for the conference [CSW] before it begins, not during it and do not monopolize conference time.)

Therefore product conference success depends upon:

1. Finding and operating on correct Whys.

2. Getting targets for valuable final products of each div or department that exchange with the society around them in return for income.

3. Ensuring adequate preparation (intelligent programs).

4. Debugging production programs.

5. Getting DONES, not not-dones or half-dones as they will become hidden backlogs in the org.

6. Coming to conference prepared.

7. Not monopolizing conference.

8. Actually punctually holding them.

IT IS UP TO THE EXEC ESTO TO HAT AND GET THE PRODUCT CONFERENCE OPERATING AND COMPETENT.

ESTO CONFERENCE

The ESTABLISHMENT OFFICER CONFERENCE is held by the Exec Esto (or his deputy).

This conference handles Esto matters, debugs Esto targets worked out by the CO/ED or Estos' projects, gets in reports of divisions and their personnel, hatting, supply, spaces, quarters, etc.

The Esto conference handles financial planning using FP policy in which the Esto must be proficient. (FP must be approved by the Treasury Sec and the Flag Banking Officer. The org has to be run on FBO allocations.)

This conference is governed by similar guide rules as a conference to the product conference.

The PRODUCT conference is senior to the Esto conference but cannot overrule its FP.

PROGRAMS

Estos as well as PRODUCT OFFICERS run on programs.

These are in accordance always with Data Series 23 and 24.

AIDES COUNCIL

An Aides Council or A/Aides (or International Secretary or Assistant International Secretary) Council is held as:

1. A product conference or

2. A program conference or

3. An establishment conference.

But never two or three of these at the same time.

––––––––––

SUMMARY

The Esto system has already proven a success.

It will be successful in direct ratio to its:

1. Staying on policy;

2. Setting no independent policy;

3. Operating only toward production;

4. Its Estos continuing to train and be well trained;

5. Consistently staying in the division and actively working in it to establish and maintain, better establish and maintain;

6. Setting an excellent example to staff as competent, helpful executives and staff members.

L. RON HUBBARD
FOUNDER

––––––––––

HCO POLICY LETTER OF 9 MARCH 1972
ISSUE II

REMIMEO

ESTABLISHMENT OFFICER SERIES 2
HATTING THE ESTO

It will be found that hatting rules and procedures apply to the Esto himself.

In orgs while under training he himself is hatted and produces alternately, doing better and better.

He must NOT be let off hatting until he is *fully* hatted.

And he shouldn't, especially when being trained in an org by an Esto I/C, be let off establishing on the excuse he is not yet fully hatted.

IMPORTANCE OF ESTO HAT

It will be found that some Estos back off from an area because "they do not know all the tech lines and hats in that area."

The reason they give for this back-off is the wrong Why. They back off or fumble when they are not hatted as Estos! Not because they are not hatted on the area's hats.

Just like the housewife who criticizes her neighbor for a cluttered backyard while standing in a more cluttered one of her own, hatting begins at home.

If an Esto knows his business he could straighten up a huge corporation using the Esto system with never a whisper of their business!

It would be tough. But it shows where the importance lies.

There is Esto tech. When it is not known or used, then an Esto can just sink down into a division puzzled and apathetic, thinking *its* tech is what is bogging him.

He daily sees and talks to people swamped in dev-t, unsure, nervous and wide-eyed with problems and questions.

If an Esto does not at all times KNOW HE IS AN ESTO and ACT LIKE AN ESTO he can easily slide into these confusions and try to handle production-performance problems that are outside the Esto's line of duty.

FIRST, LAST AND ALWAYS IT IS THE ESTO HAT THAT MUST BE WORN IN ANY GIVEN SITUATION.

Thus the A (own hat) and B (div tech and hats) differences of hats is important to know.

It's great to know and one should know a division's tech and hats. But this is something one learns as he goes along.

It's a matter of THE MOST VITAL IMPORTANCE that the Esto wears his Esto hat.

That's the hat he has to have down cold.

Then he will find that org and division confusion is nothing to him.

HE HANDLES THINGS LIKE THAT!

HE IS AN ESTO!

L. RON HUBBARD
FOUNDER

HCO POLICY LETTER OF 9 MARCH 1972
ISSUE III

REMIMEO

ESTABLISHMENT OFFICER SERIES 3
DEV-T AND UNHATTEDNESS

The first thing an Esto runs into in an area that is not hatted is DEV-T (developed unnecessary traffic).

People in an org can be working frantically, totally exhausted and yet produce nothing of value. The reason is that their actions are almost totally dev-t.

The WHY of this is UNHATTEDNESS.

The people on the posts do not know their own hats or even if some do they are dealing in the "NOISE" of other people who don't know their own hats.

Few if any of these people know the other hats or duties of the org and so don't know where to go for service or who to approach or despatch for what.

So it's not an org or a division. It's a nonproductive chaos.

The answers are three:

1. Get dev-t understood and

2. Get the staff at least instant-hatted at once.

3. Chinese school (staff or div staff all together in front of a big org board chanting together the hats, duties and products of the org as visible on the org board).

In order to get anything done at all or even begin this, an Esto Ethics Officer function has to be in.

A schedule has to be posted including exercise, post time and study and staff has to be mustered and handled at these periods. This gets some awareness of the org group as a team of people with similar purposes.

DEV-T

Dev-t packs are made up. These consist of:

HCO PL	2 July 59 II	DEVELOPED TRAFFIC THE DELIRIUM TREMENS OF CENTRAL ORGS
HCO PL	19 Aug. 59 III	HOW TO HANDLE WORK

HCO PL	4 Sept. 59 I	COMPLETED STAFF WORK
HCO PL	17 Nov. 64 I	OFF–LINE AND OFF–POLICY YOUR FULL IN–BASKET
HCO PL	31 Jan. 65	DEV-T
HCO PL	8 Feb. 65	DEV-T ANALYSIS
HCO PL	13 Oct. 65	DEV-T DATA EXECUTIVE RESPONSIBILITY
HCO PL	5 Jan. 68 I	OVERFILLED IN–BASKET BAD NEWS
HCO PL	27 Jan. 69	DEV-T SUMMARY LIST
HCO PL	30 Jan. 69 II	DEV-T SUMMARY LIST ADDITIONS
HCO PL	27 Oct. 69 I	AKH Series 23 DEV-T
HCO PL	4 Nov. 69	DEV-T GRAPHED
HCO PL	23 July 71	TELEX COMM CLARITY (Dev-t Series)
HCO PL	25 Oct. 71 I	COMM ROUTING, HOW TO TIE UP A WHOLE ORG AND PRODUCE NOTHING
HCO PL	27 Feb. 72	Exec Series 9 ROUTING
HCO PL	29 Feb. 72 I	Exec Series 10 CORRECT COMM

These packs are issued to staff members and they are required to check out on them.

Each staff member keeps a dev-t log and writes down the name of anyone he is getting dev-t from and also issues Dev-t Chits.

HATTING

The staff at the least are instant-hatted at once—place on the org board, work space, supplies, what his title is and what it means, org comm system, what he is supposed to produce on his post.

He is gotten producing what he is supposed to produce in some volume at once.

Hat checklists and packs are verified as there or are gotten ready.

A full hat checkout can then begin.

Courses he needs are done in staff study time.

Actually hat study and checkout is done on the post a bit each day.

This is in fact "on-the-job training," as he is expected to go on producing while he is being hatted.

ORG BOARD

Org bds are rapidly gotten up or up-to-date in the org (in HCO) and (full org bd) in each division.

Each division is Chinese-schooled, first on its own org bd, then on the org as a whole, in such a way that they know the duties of divisions, departments and posts and the flow lines of the org.

Wherever an org or even a division falls apart or slows up, this campaign is repeated.

SAMPLE ORG ED

This is a sample Executive Directive (ED) giving a program written for an actual org where the above was done to cure dev-t and get the org hatted and producing:

ED _____   Date _____

TOP PRIORITY

Takes priority over all other EDs
(as they can then be gotten done!)

CORRECT COMM PGM

SITUATION:

It has been very difficult to handle the org.

DATA:

A long and intensive collection of data has finally culminated in discovering, through reports on comm and inspections by showing why the org appears fantastically busy and overworked while producing very little even when it was found the org was insolvent.

Ethics has been very heavy for some time and has not led to any spectacular recovery.

But the comm line reviews and analysis reveal

INVESTIGATION:

The org and all its units is drowning in DEV-T. HCO is even generating it. This makes an appearance of frantic action and overload while little is produced.

And an analysis has produced a

WHY:

The org is almost totally unhatted and untrained.

DEV-T comes only from AN UNHATTED UNTRAINED ORG.

STATS:

Out the bottom and below the briny bedrock of the sea so far as finished products per man-hours and as far as GI by reason of the org are concerned.

IDEAL SCENE:

A whole staff and the org fully hatted and producing only correct comm without dev-t and at work actually producing things of real value which will *exchange* for value.

HANDLING:

THE ESTO SYSTEM AND DEV-T PLs HANDLE THIS.

1. Admin Cramming and each Esto to be furnished with packs of dev-t policies at once including last Exec Series PL Routing and new dev-t PL Correct Comm.

    ALL HANDS DISSEM _____

2. FULL Esto setup to be gotten on post at once. They go on duty and part-time train.

    HAS _____

3. Existing Estos and those to be put on at once to hammer, hammer, hammer all posts on off-line, off-origin and other points of dev-t so they are UNDERSTOOD.

    EXEC ESTO _____

4. Big paper org bd with new complement to be gotten up at once in HCO.

    HCO ESTO _____

5. Big paper org bds from it to be gotten up in each div and the div Chinese-schooled on it. Specializing in the div but also covering the whole org so people know where they are and what each handles and where other terminals in the org are so they can properly route to or go to them for the exact service of that exact post.

    DIV ESTOs under EXEC ESTO _____

6. Straighten out the comm lines of each post.

    EXEC ESTO/DIV ESTOs _____

7. Report to his div Esto (see org bd) or Ethics Officer any person originating off-line, off-origin traffic or failing to originate from his post paper or body or remark. Report by "Dev-t Chit."

    EVERYONE IN THE ORG _____

8. Send flagrant offenders to Admin Cramming.

    EXECUTIVES _____

9. Put in:

1. Instruct, and if no improvement

2. Cram, and if no improvement

3. Retrain, and if no improvement

4. Offload

where hatting continues to fail to produce rapid comprehension of dev-t and/or persistent inability to actually DO his hat. Court of Ethics or Comm Ev on request to remedy any injustice.

ESTOs _____

10. Excuses concerning hatting and arbitraries like "only study hat in hatting college" to be wiped out and any barriers to getting on-policy, on-FO-FSO wiped out by Ethics action or Cramming.

ESTOs _____

11. Instant-hat every staff member.

DIV ESTOs _____

12. Chinese-school every division.

DIV ESTOs _____

LET'S MAKE THIS A CRACK ORG WE CAN BE PROUD OF!

EXECUTIVE DIRECTOR

_____

The above program can be completed in a few days.

It is followed by further programs to get in lines of the org, full hatting, and proper comm setups for each staff member, etc.

If the program falls out or dev-t flares again, (A) REHAT Estos and (B) do the program once more.

The org will come right and begin producing PRODUCTS WHICH EXCHANGE FOR VALUABLES.

The org will become solvent.

_____

Only the Esto system makes such a program possible.

We have long had the tech as you can see by the PL dates. Dev-t tech has existed since the mid-1950s. But it could not be gotten in swiftly enough to make a startling change in the org morale or stats until Estos were on post in an org.

If it does not go in rapidly even with Estos, then some of the Estos are not well enough or firmly enough hatted *as* Estos; and the answer of an Exec Esto or Esto I/C is to very rapidly cram his Estos or, following the (1) instruct, (2) cram, (3) retrain, (4) offload pattern, improve his Esto team.

Fully done, the program works like a beautiful breeze bringing peace and a cheerful staff.

L. RON HUBBARD
FOUNDER

HUBBARD COMMUNICATIONS OFFICE
Saint Hill Manor, East Grinstead, Sussex

HCO POLICY LETTER OF 10 MARCH 1972

Remimeo

Establishment Officer Series 4
EXEC ESTO HATTING DUTIES

An Esto I/C or Exec Esto has as his primary duty *the hatting and handling of ESTOs.*

It will be found that an Esto tends to get pulled into operating the division when (a) he is too new at it and (b) he fails to establish.

Such hatting actions usually require a repeat checkout or harder assertion of the PLs relating to HCO such as "musical chairs," "don't unmock a working installation." Such PLs cover the host of errors that HCOs and HASes have made.

Usually the Esto in training just doesn't know the material or even believes it's all "old" because it came before the Esto system. The prime cause of alter-is is just not knowing or understanding the material.

The system of (1) instruct, (2) cram, (3) retread applies to Estos in training.

WHYS

Like in auditing the situation may look so desperate that unusual remedies are thought to be needed.

The skill of an Esto in rapidly finding a Why (as in investigation tech and the Data Series) and quickly handling is what makes a real Esto.

Dreaming up new solutions not in policy usually comes from not really investigating and finding a Why.

Finding Whys is like seeing real gold for the first time. Until a person really finds a REAL Why that promptly unravels the whole knot he is like the tourist in the gold field who can be sold any yellow glitter as being gold. But when he sees real GOLD for the first time he never after can be fooled.

Usually first Whys an Esto I/T finds about a post or a class or a line are usually so shallow and so narrow that they are just dev-t. They would resolve nothing.

The Exec Esto will have to keep an Esto I/T at it, looking again, looking again, looking again.

An Esto I/T will first think of removals. Then he will think of doing musical chairs. Then he will think of having only the BEST people. He's going along the old worn

---

339

ruts of human prejudice and impatience. He is not really looking for a Why there in front of him but at his or another's dreams.

An Esto I/T usually buys whatever Why the person on the post gives him. He mistakenly believes "but he has more experience with the scene" and "I am so green on this scene that ..."

This piece of tech applies IF THE WHY THE PERSON OR AREA HAS WERE THE RIGHT WHY THERE WOULD BE NO TROUBLE THERE.

This comes from "the problem a pc thinks he has isn't the problem he has. If it were it would as-is and he wouldn't have it."

Whys are obtained by observing the obvious (obnosis) closely enough to find the biggest OUTPOINT that explains all the nearby outpoints (always a lack of production or low production per high man-hours).

Whys are traced back from the PRODUCT, its absence or lack of volume or quality.

So an Esto I/T has to be sent in again and again and again until he finds THE Why. And then the post unsnarls rapidly.

Example: TR Course product horrible, slow and upsetting the inflow of new people. Esto I/T was ordered to hat the TR Supervisor. After much blow-off, apathy, TR Super in tears, the Esto I/T said HE would take over the course. Wrong answer. It couldn't be more wrong. Esto I/T bypassed, an experienced Esto investigated students, Super and area and within about three hours found it. The Super was so unhatted that WHAT IS A COURSE? PL was wholly out. The TR students had no packs of their own, could not read those and weren't being supervised either and just struggled on with the unhatted Super falsely reporting how great the students were doing (while they didn't finish and wanted to blow).

Now what did this Esto I/T do wrong?

He didn't work out the product: successfully completed exultant students.

He didn't then start hatting the Super with just standard HCOBs about TRs and supervising.

He didn't check the course as a COURSE against WHAT IS A COURSE? PL to know what was missing on it.

Had he just done his job as an Esto he would have found the Why.

The course, of course, resolved at once and got the product.

BEWARE

A person training to be an Esto himself can be very guilty of dev-t to his senior Esto.

By *bringing a problem* to a senior without having resolved it, HE CAN GET HIS SENIOR UPSET, ALARMED, DESPERATE AND PULLED INTO THE DIVISION!

These solutions of "transfer this one or that," "comm ev this one or that," "this situation is so ghastly that (and there follows some wild solution that sounds like 'stand the pc on his head')" are simply abandonment of standard actions.

As the observation is bad, the Why is not found. Then the situation looks unusual. So unusual remedies are urged.

And a senior can be dragged right in!

CORRECT ACTION

Anyone handling Estos in training has to use the standard action of:

1. Get the packs of that post! (Or area or div he's trying to handle or proposes the unusual solution for.)

2. Look over the policy materials! (May include discard of "former occupant hat write-ups" and looking into PL or FO or files for the real materials about it. May include Word Clearing 4 or a clay demo or a Why as to why the Esto can't dig them.)

3. Work out the product of that post! (Or course or section or dept or div or even the org. May require getting the word PRODUCT understood or Word Clearing Method 4 on the Esto I/T, or even the "Management Power Rundown" or cram on products or any other standard action such as even finding Why he can't dig *products*.) (And it may require "detective" work on the materials of the post to find out what is continually talked ABOUT so one can figure out from *that* what the product would have to be.)

4. Be sure it is the major EXCHANGE product of that post! (Or dept or div or area. May require reviewing the Esto I/T on EXCHANGE, its PLs and the Esto tapes.)

5. Check it with the product officer! (The head of the dept or div or org and don't be startled if he has a cognition on it or if he violently disagrees with it while having his own product wildly nonexchangeable! Which opens up a whole new situation! Or he may simply suggest a revision of the wording. BUT THIS POINT HAS TO BE CLEARED or the Estos will find themselves going east while the product officers go west!)

6. Go to your area! (This may include making the Esto I/T do TR 0 on the area or running him on bodily reaching and withdrawing from it and other drills or even a third party investigation.)

7. Observe the scene! (Which may mean having to wait until it has traffic or action in progress. It may mean a microphone plant as on an auditor or a tape of an interview with a voice start–stop operated recorder to catch the traffic, but it generally means just looking and comparing what one sees to the key PL about it or an ideal scene as would have to be in order for a product to occur in it.)

8. Find the Why! (And that means investigation tech and the Data Series. It can be formally written up or just there it is!)

9. Get it accepted! (Which can mean argument or HE&R or violence or blows off post if it isn't the right Why or the person is just plain SP. The right Why brings in GIs almost always. It's usually as obvious as a bass drum in the middle of the floor once *seen*.)

10. Have (him, her or them) GET IT IN! (Which can mean a project written per Data Series 23 and 24 or it can be just "do it.")

11. Straighten up the (spaces, lines, materiel, personnel) indicated by the Why.

12. Hat the person (personnel) to get production! (Could mean begin to hat, wholly hat, could mean train further, could mean find the Why that stops him or them from being hatted, but it means get better hatting DONE.)

13. Review to find if production increased! (Means look it over again to be sure it was the right Why found as a Why must lead to a nearer approach to ideal scene. Usually means INCREASED STATS for the area.)

14. Train the Esto I/T better.

DOGGEDNESS

The protection of an Esto I/C or Exec Esto is his own insistence along the lines of the above.

The moment he comes off of holding this line of hatting his Estos and keeping them at it, the less successful he will be.

If he doesn't do this, the next thing he knows he will be in total exasperation with the *org* and will be pulled right into it himself.

AUDITORS

We've been through all this before training auditors in 55–58. Ds of P and I.

They often had unusual solutions. They also would say they had "already done that" so we had a trick—"*What* did you do?" And we'd hear some *other thing* than what was ordered.

We know all about that.

And today when we apprentice them in orgs, boy, they really come out as real auditors!

So we know all about getting standard actions really done.

And there IS a thing called standard tech.

And there is a thing called STANDARD ADMIN.

Above is the 1 to 14 of making a real Esto and thereby a real org. This is really third dynamic auditing for production.

RULE

The EXEC ESTO or his deputy must okay every major action any Esto means to take to be sure it is ON–POLICY, ON–LINES.

HOLD THE FORM

The one thing an Esto I/C or Exec Esto ALWAYS DOES is hold the form and lines of the org.

EQUIPMENT

An Esto I/C or Exec Esto should have a 1–14 checklist with a blank at the top for the Esto's name and date and time.

When a solution is brought in he enters the Esto's name and date and a note of it.

Then he or his deputy keeps tabs on it by checking off the dones.

Such an action as 1–14 takes little time, actually. Twenty-four hours is an AGE.

He will find that some of his Esto I/Ts can't complete them rapidly, a rare one can't complete at all. This needs a Why itself. And maybe a retread or, that failing, a replacement.

A policy and HCOB library like the Qual Library is a necessity. You can't hold the form of an org with no record of the form.

FAITH

Faith in the system comes first, then faith in the Esto I/Ts and then faith in the org will prevent a lot of shooting.

But a few right Whys then show that it usually isn't evil. It's just outpoints. AND THAT THESE CAN BE HANDLED. The real gold of REAL WHYS.

This restores one's faith. Rapidly.

SIGN

And on his desk, facing outward, the Exec Esto should have a sign:

THE ANSWER TO YOUR
OFF–POLICY SOLUTION IS "NO!"
FIND THE WHY.

HAT HAT HAT

An Esto is busy hatting staff, handling lines. He is being hit with weird solutions. Product officers talk to them about how it should really be established (while not themselves producing or getting anything produced).

Someone has to hold the Esto stable as an Esto.

That's the senior Esto of the org.

He hats Estos while they establish. He demands establishment! And he gets it if he hats, hats, hats Estos and keeps them establishing. He IS the real holder and expander of the form of the org. Via his Estos.

L. RON HUBBARD
FOUNDER

344

HCO POLICY LETTER OF 13 MARCH 1972

REMIMEO

ESTABLISHMENT OFFICER SERIES 5

PRODUCTION AND ESTABLISHMENT ORDERS AND PRODUCTS

The situation one often finds in an org, after one has to some degree conquered dev-t, is that PEOPLE REQUIRE ORDERS. For years I wondered why this was so. Well, I found it.

WHEN PEOPLE DO NOT CLEARLY KNOW WHAT THEIR PRODUCTS ARE THEY REQUIRE CONSTANT ORDERS.

To the Establishment Officer, this reflects most visibly in trying to get program targets DONE.

Some people have to be ordered and ordered and ordered and threatened and howled at. Then, in a bewildered way, they do a target, sometimes half, sometimes nearly all.

Behind this apparent blankness lies an omitted datum. When they're like that they don't know what their product is or what it adds up to. Or they think it's something else or should be.

That blankness can invite overts.

It is very seldom that malice or resentment or refusal to work lies behind the inaction. People are seldom that way.

They usually just don't understand what's wanted or why.

Because they don't know what a PRODUCT is!

A whole Ad Council of a downstat org was unable even to *define* the word.

They had required orders, orders, orders and even then didn't carry them out.

HAT SURVEY FOR ORDERS

A staff member who requires orders may also think that any order is a policy and lasts forever. If you look into hats you will even find casual "close the door" type of orders given on one occasion to fit one circumstance are converted over into STANDING (continued) ORDERS that forever keep a certain door closed.

An Esto surveying the hats of a unit may very well find all manner of such oddities.

It is a standard Esto action to survey hats.

In hats you will find despatches giving specific orders or quoted remarks preserved instead of notes on what one has to know to produce a product.

In auditors' hats, directions for *1* specific pc in 1960, never published and from no tape or correct source, held on to like death like it was to be applied to every pc in the world!

A dishwashing hat may have orders in it but not how to wash dishes rapidly and well.

This is all a symptom of a unit or activity that does not know what its products are.

DISESTABLISHMENT

Where you find lots of orders kicking around, you will also find disestablishment by bypass, command channels not held and staff members like to take their orders from anyone but those in authority—any passerby could give them orders.

This is rampant where an executive has not been well on post.

By counting such orders up and seeing who they are from one can determine the unhattedness of staff, their org bd weaknesses and principally their lack of knowledge of their products.

HATTING FOR PRODUCT

If an Esto is to hat so as to get the staff member to get his product out, then the Esto has to know how to clear up "products."

Now an Esto is an Establishment Officer. There are product officers. The product of an Esto is the establishment. Then what is he doing with products?

Well, if he doesn't *hat* so staff members get out products then the org will be a turmoil, unhappy and downstat.

Production is the basis of morale.

Hattedness is a basic of third dynamic sanity.

But if you don't HAT SO AS TO GET THE STAFF MEMBER YOU ARE HATTING PRODUCING YOU WILL HAT AND HAT AND IT WILL ALL BE IN VAIN. The person won't stay hatted unless he is hatted so as to be able to produce.

The product officer should be working to get the products out.

So if you don't hat for the product then the staff member will be torn between two sets of orders, the Esto's and the product officer's.

Only when you hat to get product will you get agreement with product officers.

346

If you are in disagreement with product officers, then the Esto is not hatting to get production.

RIGHT WAY TO

There is a right direction to hat. All others are incorrect.

1. CLEAR UP WHAT THE PRODUCT IS FOR THE POST. AND HAT FROM THERE.

2. HAT FROM THE TOP OF THE DIVISION (OR ORG) DOWN.

These are the two right directions.

All other directions are wrong.

These two data are so important that the failure of an Esto can often be traced to violation of them.

You can have a senior exec going almost livid, resisting being hatted unless you hat by first establishing what the *product* is. If PRODUCT is first addressed and cleaned up then you can also hat from the top down.

If this is not done, the staff will not know where they are going or why and you will get silly unusual situations like, "All right. So you're the Establishment Officer. Well, I give up. The division can have 2½ hours a day establishment time and then get the hell out of here so some work can be done . . . !" "Man, you got these people all tied up! Stats are down! Can't you understand . . ."

Well, if you don't *do* 1 and 2 above you'll run into the most unusual messes and "solutions" you ever heard of, go sailing off-policy and as an Esto wind up at your desk doing admin instead of getting your job done in the division. And an Esto who is not on his feet working in the division is worth very little to anyone.

So see where the basic errors lead and

Hat on product before doing anything else and

Hat from the top down.

STEPS TO CLEAR "PRODUCT"

This is a general rundown of the sequence by which *product* is cleared and re-cleared and re-cleared again.

This can be checklisted for any exec or staff member and should be with name and date and kept in the person's "Esto file folder" for eventual handing to his new Esto when the person is transferred out of the division or in personnel files if he goes elsewhere.

1. Clear the word PRODUCT. _____

2. Get what the product or products of the post should be. Get it or any number of products he has fully, fully stated, not brushed off. _____

3. Clear up the subject of *exchange*. (See HCO PL 27 Nov. 71 I, Exec Series 3, Finance Series 6-1 and HCO PL 3 Dec. 71, Exec Series 4, Finance Series 6-2.) _____

4. Exchange of the product internal in the org. For what valuable? _____

5. Exchange external of the valuable with another group or public. For what valuable? (Person must come to F/N VGIs on these above actions before proceeding or he goes to an auditor to get his Mis-Us and out-ruds very fully handled.) _____

6. Does he want the product? Clean this up fully to F/N VGIs or yourself get E/S to F/N or get an auditor to unsnarl this. _____

7. Can he *get* the products (in 2 above) out? How will he? What's he need to know? Get him fully settled on this point. _____

8. Will it be in volume? What volume? Is that enough to bother with or will it have to be a greater volume? Or is he being optimistic? What's real? What's viable? _____

9. What quality is necessary? What would he have to do to attain that? To attain it in volume? _____

10. Can he get others to want the product or products (as in 2 above)? What would he have to do to do this? _____

11. How do his products fit into the unit or section or department or division or the org? Get this all traced. _____

12. Now trace the blocks or barriers he may believe are on this line. Get what HE can do about these. _____

13. What does he have to have to get his product out? (Alert for unreasonable "have to have before he can do" blocks.) _____

14. Now does he feel he can get his product or products out? _____

_____

Signature of Esto
or Clearer

NOW he really can be hatted.

BRUSHOFF

Quickie handling is a very, very bad fault. "Quickie" means a brushoff "lick and a promise" like wiping the windshield on the driver's side when really one would have to work at it to get a whole clean car.

So don't "quickie" product. If this is poorly done then there goes the old balloon. Hatting won't be possible.

Orders will have to be poured in on this terminal. Dev-t will generate. Overt products will occur, not good ones. And it won't be worthwhile.

DISAGREEMENT

There can be a lot of disagreement amongst product officers and Estos on what products are to be hammered out.

In such a case, or in any case, one can get a Disagreement Check done in Dept of Personnel Enhancement (who should look up how to do one).

This is a somewhat extreme way to settle an argument and should only be a "when all else fails."

It is best to take the whole product pattern of the org apart with the person, STARTING FROM THE BIGGEST PRODUCT OF THE ORG AND WORKING BACK TO THE PERSON'S PRODUCT.

Almost always there will be an outpoint in reasoning.

An exec who *only* wants GI can be a trial as he is violating EXCHANGE. As an org is paid usually before it delivers, it is easy to get the org in trouble by backlogs or bad repute for nondelivery. An org that has credit payments due it that aren't paid maybe didn't deliver. But Div 3 may soften up collections for some reason like that and then where would the org be?

Vol 0 of the OEC Course gives an excellent background of how a basic org works. As one goes to higher orgs, lower orgs are depended upon to continue to flow upward to them. (See HCO PL 9 Mar. 72 I, Finance Series 11, INCOME FLOWS AND POOLS, PRINCIPLES OF MONEY MANAGEMENT.)

A study of Vol 0 OEC and a full understanding of its basic flows and adapting these to higher orgs will unsnarl a lot of odd ideas about product.

The Esto has to be very clear on these points or he could mis-hat a person.

Usually however this is very obvious.

PRODUCT OFFICERS

Heads of orgs and divisions have had to organize so long they get stuck in it.

They will try to order the Esto.

This comes about because they do not know their products or the Esto is not following 1 and 2 above and does not know his own product.

The product officer may try to treat the Esto as a sort of "organizing officer" or a "program officer" if

A. The Esto is not hatting to get production.

B. The product officer is not cleared on product.

So it comes back to the 1 and 2 first mentioned.

––––––––––

You can look over it now and see that if one is not doing these two things, dev-t, nonviability and orders will occur.

So where you have dev-t, down stats and orders flying around, you know one thing that will resolve it:

SOMETHING WILL HAVE TO BE IRONED OUT ABOUT *PRODUCT*.

When it all looks impossible, go to this point and get to work on 1 and 2.

L. RON HUBBARD
FOUNDER

HCO POLICY LETTER OF 14 MARCH 1972
ISSUE I

REMIMEO

ESTABLISHMENT OFFICER SERIES 6
SEQUENCE OF HATTING

1. The Executive Establishment Officer or Establishment Officer In-Charge hats and keeps Estos working in their areas.

2. The Estos work in their areas hatting and establishing.

3. The product officers get production.

In that way the org is built or expands stably. In that way the org is prosperous, the staff is happy.

If some other sequence is being tried or other things are happening then the org is likely to be slow, upset or nonviable.

When an org has both an Exec Esto and an Esto I/C or Chief Estos or Leading Estos the Exec Esto shall hat all the Estos and the I/C or Chief or Leading Estos especially until they can safely be trusted to become a 1A relay point in the above where 1 would be "The Exec Esto hats all Estos I/C, Chief and Leading Estos until they in turn can hat and handle their Estos as per 2."

SPEED

Power is proportional to the speed of particle flow. This applies to despatches, bodies, materiel and anything else that can be called a particle.

What then slows things down?

UNCERTAINTY.

Many things can cause uncertainty. Threats, transfers, rumors.

People want their posts. Leave one without one awhile and see what happens!

Firm establishment, unchanging orders give certainty.

Nothing however causes more uncertainty than what one's product is.

Or if he can get someone to get out a product.

As certainty becomes firm on the product of a post or org, the ability to get it out, then all else falls into place and establishment has occurred.

BYPASS

It is easy for an Exec Esto or Esto I/C or any Esto to imagine he could make it all right by just bypassing and doing the product job. If he does that he fails as an Esto and the staff becomes uncertain as they feel they can't get out the product.

SPEED UP

If you want to speed up an org just do the usual 1, 2, 3 as given above.

The org will become certain.

It will speed up.

ESTO DESKS

Estos who do lots of admin are not being Estos. They belong on their feet or at best sitting with a staff member hatting him.

When an Esto has given up he begins to do admin.

Of course one has to do org boards and CSWs for posting, lines and materials. And one does have despatches. But if these require more than a couple hours a day something is very wrong.

The Esto is the only one who MUST bring a body.

ASSISTANT MASTER–AT–ARMS

In a very large org there are at least two Esto Masters-at-Arms.

Both have crew mustering, exercise, etc. Their functions can interchange.

But the senior is the Exec Esto's MAA for investigation and finding Whys.

The Assistant MAA is the one who helps handle the Estos and cross-checks on them and helps them and acts as liaison between them and the Ethics Officer or HCO terminals of the org.

Estos do NOT go to the HCO Esto for HCO PRODUCTS. They go to the HCO terminals involved or, far better, put it via the Asst Exec Esto's MAA — "the Esto's MAA." And *he* does not go to the HCO Esto either but to the proper terminals in HCO.

The Assistant MAA should know at any given moment where to find any Esto in the org. This is so he can get them for the Exec Esto or locate them due to emergencies.

He is their personal troubles terminal.

He verifies their presence at any muster.

He is in fact keeping the lines in between the Exec Esto and the Estos.

It is all done by body traffic, not by any despatch.

In an exact division of duties the Senior Exec Esto MAA is responsible for the whole *staff* as people. And how they influence org form.

The Assistant Esto MAA is responsible for the Estos as Estos on post and as people. And how they influence the Esto pattern of operations 1, 2 and 3 above.

SUMMARY

Thus the pattern can be held.

If it is, the wins are fantastic.

It is an easy pattern to hold.

It can be done.

ORGS ARE BUILT OF PEOPLE.

ESTOs WORK DIRECTLY WITH PEOPLE.

And the pattern of the work is 1, 2 and 3 above.

L. RON HUBBARD
FOUNDER

HCO POLICY LETTER OF 14 MARCH 1972
Issue II

Remimeo

Establishment Officer Series 7

FOLLOW POLICY AND LINES

About the fastest way Estos can unmock an org is pursue the fatal course of org officers in the first product officer–org officer system.

These org officers bypassed all normal lines for personnel, materiel, spaces and supplies and by disestablishing in that fashion tore more org apart than they built. This made it almost impossible for the lonely HAS to establish anything.

An Exec Esto especially and any Esto must:

1. Get personnel on usual channels.

2. Get materiel only by proper procurement.

3. Get and use spaces only according to standard CSW to the authorities involved — usually the CO or ED.

4. Get supplies only by the exact purchase order and supply channels.

5. Follow the exact admin lines designed to achieve establishment.

For, after all, those lines ARE a major part of establishment.

If these lines are not in they must be put in.

If the Exec Esto and Estos cannot or do not follow the *exact* procedure required in policy or routing forms or admin patterns THEY WILL TEAR THINGS UP FASTER THAN THEY CAN BE GOTTEN IN.

Estos must be drilled on these lines until they are truly in and effective.

It is up to them to set the example to others.

LINES

Lines that cross from one division to another such as public lines are under the control of Dept 2 HCO.

They are dummy run by the Dir Comm under the guidance of the HCO Esto and with the cooperation of the Esto conference.

These lines are vital to an org.

This is also true of personnel *lines*, supply *lines* and routing forms for new staff or transfers or any other action that may involve two or more divisions.

Lines within a division are the business of the Estos of that division.

Where departmental Estos exist, the lines linking up departments are handled by the Esto conference of that division.

INVISIBLE

Lines are invisible to many people. They disregard them and chaos results.

Thus Estos of all people must see that edges are put on those lines, usually in the form of HCO routing forms and ethics actions for violations.

AN ORG WHOSE ADMIN OR BODY LINES ARE BEING VIOLATED WILL DISESTABLISH.

What is gained in sudden action is lost in disestablishment. The seized desk without permission, the grabbed space without proper allocation, the ripped-off supplies for lack of chits and supply lines, the suddenly transferred personnel all end up with a headache for somebody else and an unmocked area.

WORKING INSTALLATION

DO NOT DISESTABLISH A WORKING INSTALLATION!

Example: An exec spends months building up a producing Qual Div. The Qual Sec is suddenly ripped off without replacement and apprenticing the replacement. The div collapses. There went months of work. It was far more economical to have a Qual Sec In-Training under that Qual Sec for a month or two before the transfer.

Using the wrong personnel pools for want of proper recruiting and training is the downfall of most orgs.

Because it wrecks working installations.

This applies as well to org machinery. Don't wreck one machine to get a part for another. And don't ever take one apart that is running well.

OPERATIONAL

The definition of OPERATIONAL is running without further care or attention.

Anything that needs constant fiddling or working at to make it run is non-operational! It must be repaired fully or replaced.

Man-hours and time waste easily eat up any value of the inoperational machine.

Further, a machine that is forced to run that does not run well may then break down utterly and expensively. The time to repair is *soon*, the moment it cannot be run without great care or attention.

OPERATIONAL is a key definition that answers many problems.

It is also true of people. Those who need continual pushing around or rounding up cannot be considered operational. They can absorb time totally out of proportion to worth.

This is no license to shoot staff down. But it is a warning that where too much time is absorbed trying to make a staff member functional he cannot be considered OPERATIONAL.

If an Esto spent 100 percent of his time for weeks on just one staff member and let the rest go hang, he'd soon find he was rewarding a downstat as well as violating the definition of operational.

RIGHT TARGET

A working unit that is getting on well, has an already established activity even to internal training, is not the right target for an Esto to reorganize.

His whole activity should be to get it support and new trainees for it. His internal functions should be minimal so long as it runs well.

He helps it without hindering it.

Putting a unit there that is already there is a bit foolish.

The right thing to do is get it help and support!

Example: An exec who really turns out the production. Seven Esto should groove in his communicator and support lines and hat hell out of *them*.

Example: A Mimeo Section that runs like a bomb. The Esto recruits new in-trainings for it, eases its supply problems and better establishes the outside lines into it.

You keep what's established going.

New brooms may sweep clean. New Estos know their scene. And *then* establish what *isn't* established or its support lines. To do otherwise can hurt a working unit or activity.

––––––––––––

SUMMARY

Know what disestablishes.

Then you won't accidentally tear down faster than you build up.

The hallmark of the good Esto is

ESTABLISH AND MAINTAIN.

Sometimes he is unlucky and has disestablishing going on.

Sometimes he is very lucky and only has to maintain!

L. RON HUBBARD
FOUNDER

––––––––

HCO POLICY LETTER OF 16 MARCH 1972
ISSUE I

REMIMEO

ESTABLISHMENT OFFICER SERIES 8
LOOK DON'T LISTEN

An Establishment Officer who stands around or sits around just talking to people or seniors is dev-t.

If these people knew what was wrong the stats would be in Power. So if they aren't, why gab?

Questions, sharp and pointed, as in an investigation, yes.

But an Esto who just talks, no.

A GOOD ESTO LOOKS.

The scene is in the hats or lack of them. The scene is on the org board or lack of it.

THE SCENE IS RIGHT BEFORE ONE'S EYES.

It is moving or it is not.

Its graphs are rising or they are level or falling or they are false or don't reflect the product or they aren't kept or they aren't posted.

Products are appearing or they are not.

Overt products are occurring or good products.

The lines are followed or they aren't.

The MEST is okay or it isn't.

It is a SCENE. It is in three dimensions. It's composed of spaces and objects and people.

They are on a right pattern or they aren't.

A person is on post or he is moving onto one or moving off or isn't there at all or he is dashing in and out.

None of these things are verbal.

Few are in despatches. Quantities of despatches, types of despatches, yes. Content? Only good for investigation, not for adjusting the lines, types and volumes.

Example: Overloaded exec. Examine his traffic. Don't *talk* to him. Examine his traffic. Look to see if he has an in-basket for each hat he wears, a folder for each type or area. Find a WHY. It can be as blunt as he doesn't know the meaning of the word "despatch." Use the WHY. Handle. Hat his communicator on comm procedures. Hat him on comm procedures. Examine his org board. Find where it's wrong. Adjust it. Get his agreement. And the load comes off and product goes up.

Now there are moments in that example when one talks. But they are concerned with ACHIEVING THE PRODUCT OF AN ESTABLISHED PRODUCING EXECUTIVE.

If the Esto doesn't himself know, name, want and get and get wanted his Product 1 (an established thing) or Product 3 (a corrected establishment) he will talk, not look. (See HCO PL 29 Oct. 70 I, Org Series 10, THE ANALYSIS OF ORGANIZATION BY PRODUCT, for Products 1, 2, 3, 4.)

You can't know what's happening in a kitchen by talking to a cook. Because he's not cooking just then. You can't know how good the food is without tasting it. You don't know really how clean a floor is without wiping at it. You don't know how clean an icebox is without smelling it.

You don't know what a tech page is really doing without watching him.

You don't know how an auditor is auditing without listening to him, looking at the pc, the exam reports, the worksheets, the date and progress of the program. If you *listened* to him, wow, one sometimes hears the greatest sessions that you ever could conceive.

To adjust a scene you have to LOOK AT IT.

ADMIN

An Esto or Esto I/C or Exec Esto who tries to do it with admin will fail.

Admin is S-L-O-W.

A product officer acts very fast if he is producing. The flurry to get a product can tear the establishment apart.

You don't halt the flurry. That's exactly counter to the purpose of an Esto.

The right answer is to ESTABLISH FASTER AND MORE FIRMLY.

It takes quickly found RIGHT Whys to really build something up.

And it isn't done by admin!

"Dear TEO. I have heard that you are in trouble with the D of P. Would you please give me a report so I can bring it up at a meeting we are holding at the Hilton next week to see if we can get people to cooperate in sending us Whys about the insolvency of the org. My wife said to say hello and I hope your kids are all right. Drop around sometime for a game of poker. Seeing you sometime. Don't forget about the report. Best. Joe, Esto I/C."

Right there you'd have a Why of org insolvency. Not any meeting. But that it's on a despatch line. TOO DAMNED SLOW.

Already establishment is slower than production. It always is. And always will be. It takes two days to make a car on an assembly line and two years to build a plant.

BUT when you make establishing even slower, you lose.

Esto admin is a splendid way to slow down establishment.

Let me give you some actual times.

1. SITUATION: Overloaded exec. Three periods of looking, each 15 to 20 minutes. Time to inspect and find WHY, and handle Mis-U word 32 minutes. Time to write cramming orders on a communicator 17 minutes. Total time to totally Esto handle: 1 hr and 49 minutes over a period of 3 days.

2. SITUATION: Investigation of lack of personnel. Collection of past records 1 hour. Location of peak recruitment period by record study 7 minutes. Location of EDs and hats of that period 35 minutes. Study of what they did. 20 minutes. Location of Why (dropped out unit) 10 minutes. Orders written as an ED to reestablish unit. Approval 9 minutes. Total Esto time 2 hours and 21 minutes. Plus time to form unit by HAS. 1 day. Unit functioning in 36 hours and got first 3 products in 2 days.

3. SITUATION: Backlog on an auditor. Inspection of lines ½ hour. Of folders of all auditors and their times in session 2 hours. Finding WHY and verifying 25 minutes (other HGC auditors dumping their pcs on one auditor because he had a slightly higher class and "they couldn't do those actions"), investigation of D of T 32 minutes (not on post, doing admin, Supers doing admin). Writing pgm 35 minutes. Locating PLs on course supervision, 1 hour. Writing cramming chits on 6 auditors, Supers and D of T 1 hour 15 minutes. Total time 6 hours and 17 minutes. Check of Why 5 days later found HGC stats up and auditor not backlogged.

4. SITUATION: Stats I/C goofing, making errors. Meter action Method 4, 18 minutes. Found word "statistic" not understood. Total time 18 minutes. Check back in 3 days, Stats I/C doing well, taking on all the duties of the hat.

5. SITUATION: Pc Admin only instant hatted. Getting her mini-hatted. M4, demos, clay demos, 4 days at 1 hour per day and 15 minute check in late day to see if she is applying it to produce what it says, 5 hours.

6. SITUATION: Exec believes all his products are overt. Three hours and 15 minutes completing 14 steps of Esto Series 5 on him, locating only one product was overt. Twenty minutes clearing up how to unbug it. Three hours and 35 minutes.

These are typical Esto situations. They are not all the types of actions Estos do. They would be typical total required time involved if the Esto were right on his toes.

I do such Esto actions. They are very rapid and effective. So what I am writing is not just theory.

Not all actions are at once successfully resolved. I have been involved in efforts to find a WHY in a very broad situation for months before all was suddenly revealed.

But where in all this was writing despatches about it?

F/N VGIs

One knows he is right when he looks and when he finds the right WHY. It's always F/N VGIs. Gung-ho! ("Pull together.")

So one isn't only looking. He is looking to see the scene and find the WHY and establish.

If the Esto has spotted and named the product he wants, then he has a comparison with the existing scene.

He cannot compare unless he looks!

Product named and wanted. Is it here in this scene? One can only see by *looking*.

You start listening and you get PR, problems, distractions, 3rd partying, etc., etc. An Esto gets into a cycle of

Outpoint, handle, outpoint, handle, outpoint, handle.

He hasn't looked and hasn't found a Why. So the scene *will get worse*.

You have then a busy, frantic Esto with the walls of Jericho falling down all over him because he listens to people blowing their own horns.

When you see an Esto standing and listening. Okay. If you see it again elsewhere. What? What? This Esto is not doing his job.

If you see an Esto standing and watching, okay. If you see him pawing through old files, okay. If you see him sitting doing a checkout, okay. If you see him working with a meter on somebody, okay. If you see him with a pile full of hats gazing into space tapping his teeth, okay. If you see him running, okay. If you see him reading policy, okay.

If you see him sitting at a desk doing admin, no, unless it's "today's chits." As a habit all day, No No No No No No.

If you see him standing talking, standing talking, give him a Dev-t Chit. He's not being an Esto.

The real tale is told when a division or an org is established so that its stats RISE and RISE.

When the staff looks happier and happier.

When the public being served is bigger and bigger and more and more thrilled.

And the Esto achieves all that by LOOKING.

A good Esto has the eye of a hawk and can see an outpoint a hundred feet away while going at a dead run.

A good Esto can find and know a real WHY in the time it takes a human being to wonder what he'll have for dinner.

A good Esto LOOKS. And he only listens so he can look.

And like Alice he knows he has to run just to keep up and run like everything to get anywhere.

And so a good Esto arrives.

L. RON HUBBARD
FOUNDER

HCO POLICY LETTER OF 16 MARCH 1972
ISSUE II

REMIMEO

ESTABLISHMENT OFFICER SERIES 9
STUCK IN

An Esto, as well as being mobile, must not get "stuck in" on one point of a division or org.

Spending days hatting only *one* staff member and letting whole departments go is an example of what is meant by "getting stuck in."

This is why one "short cycles" an area. By that is meant doing a short start-change-stop that COMPLETES that action.

This is why one (a) instant hats, (b) gets production, (c) does a mini hat PL on the person, (d) gets production, (e) does another PL, (f) gets production.

The *produce* is a test to the Esto of whether or not he is winning on a post.

You cover your whole area as an Esto with short cycles you can complete on each person individually.

You do group drills of the whole group, little by little.

Gradient scales are at work here. (Look it up if you don't know it.)

Like, found one basic product for each in the div. Then handled other things. Then got product moved to Exchange on each one. Then did other things. Etc., etc.

The other things are find a Why for a jam area or handle a blow or any other Esto duty.

But don't spend 82 hours hatting Joe who then doesn't make it while the rest go hang.

Dev-t drops little by little and production rises IF you short cycle your actions.

Don't get "stuck in." "I've been working on Dept 1 and it is better now. Next month I go to Dept 2" is a wrong look.

Short cycles. Each staff member getting attention individually as well as a group.

If one man was totally hatted and all the rest not, they'd just knock his hat off anyway.

Don't get stuck in on a dev-t terminal. Instruct, cram, retread, dismiss is the sequence.

Short cycles work. They show up the good as well as the bad. This gives upstats a reward.

Never have a situation where a product officer can say to you, "I appreciate all the trouble you're taking getting Oscar hatted. Let me know someday when you've finished so I can stop holding the div together and get on with my product."

Little by little a whole group makes it. Drilled as a group as on org bds. Hatted on one product or a PL as an individual.

In between you work like mad to get up an org bd and groove in the new staff member or find the WHY the Exec Esto is so anxious to get.

If two days pass and a staff member has not had any individual attention, no matter how brief, from an Esto, that Esto has gotten "stuck in."

Stay unstuck!

Flow. Be mobile.

You can, you know. And be very effective too.

L. RON HUBBARD
FOUNDER

HCO POLICY LETTER OF 18 MARCH 1972

REMIMEO

ESTABLISHMENT OFFICER SERIES 10

FILES

The lowly and neglected item called FILES is the cause of more company downfalls than desks and quarters and sometimes even personnel.

Because files are looked upon as routine clerical work they seldom are given enough attention by executives. Yet the downfall of most executives is lack of information and FILES.

Files are often considered an area of overwork on the shoulders of one person or a part-time action. This is the most expensive "saving" an org can get itself into.

Example: One org (Joburg, early 1960s) did not have file cabinets or proper respect for files and kept losing their 6,500 Central Files of clients. The org remained in income trouble.

Example: Another org (SH 1960) would not file into its bills files or keep them up and routinely overpaid creditors. In 1964, for lack of these proper accounts files, it thought it owed £1,000 when it actually owed £22,000! And don't think *that* didn't cause management overwork!

Example: An org didn't have its CF straight and its Address was therefore incorrect and not tabbed for publics. (AOLA 1971–72) This cost thousands of dollars a week in (a) promo wasted to wrong addresses, (b) low returns, (c) insolvent cash-bills.

I could go on and on with these examples. FSM pgms broken down as Dept 18s had no proper FSM file or any real selection slip file. Inability to promote to correct publics because of no tabbed address plates. Inability to locate suppliers due to no purchaser files. No personnel obtained as personnel files nonexistent. And so on.

There are LOTS of files in an org. HCO PL 23 Feb. 70, THE LRH COMM WEEKLY REPORT,[*] lists the majority of these.

ORGANIZING FILES

The Establishment Officer will find all too often that in the flurry to get products, the file forming and maintenance function is bypassed. He will find files are being pawed through and destroyed by frantic staffs.

*[*Editor's Note:* HCO PL 23 Feb. 70, THE LRH COMM WEEKLY REPORT has been cancelled. The files to be kept by any division are covered in the OEC volume for that division.]

He will seldom find similar attention being given to files. He will even find local (and illegal) orders like, "They are spending too much time organizing and too little time producing. So just produce, don't organize."

Such people are getting this week's stats at the expense of all next year's income!

They even order files destroyed as "old" instead of setting up archives.

Half to two-thirds of an org's income comes from having a well kept Central Files and Address and FSM files and a lot of credit rating and correct payment comes from bills files. PL and HCOB files almost totally monitor training and processing and admin quality.

So files are FINANCIALLY VITAL TO AN ORG.

Efforts to block or cheapen files supplies and personnel must be countered. This is the first step of organizing files.

The next step is using a simple system that lets one recover things once they are filed.

The next step is collecting everything to be filed *while filing it*.

The next step is *completing* the files (usually by extra hands).

The final step is MAINTAINING the files by keeping people there to do it and having exact lines.

Independent files all over a division are liable to file out-of-date or lost. Therefore it is best to have DIVISIONAL FILES. These usually go in the last dept and section of the division. Usually every type of file in the div is kept there.

In this way you *can* keep a files person on the division's files.

A big deep FILES BASKET exists in the div comm center.

A log-out log-in book exists to locate where files have gone. This can be a large colored card that takes the place of the file.

A prefile set of boxes A–Z sits above the files and is used, so one isn't opening and closing file cabinets every time one files in one scrap of paper.

Files personnel HAVE TO KNOW THEIR ALPHABET FORWARDS AND BACKWARDS LIKE LIGHTNING. This is the biggest cause of slow or misfiling.

All hands of the division actions can be taken for an hour or two a day to catch a sudden inflow or backlog.

There are *no* "miscellaneous files" or catchall "that we put things in when we don't have another place for them."

Clerks must be able to get things out of files rapidly as well as file in.

The files location must not be so distant from the users (like Letter Reges or Accountants) that use of them is discouraged by the delay or the time lost. When this is true they start keeping their own independent files.

MEMORY

A person without memory is psychotic.

An org without files has no memory.

ESTOs

The Esto is responsible for organizing, establishing and maintaining files even when there is a Files I/C. The div head and dept heads are in command of files and their use and over files people. But this does not excuse an Esto from having the div's files established.

If an Esto only did this file action well, the increased income of an org and the decreased cost would cover his and the file clerk's pay several times over!

FILES ARE VALUABLE TO AN ORG.

L. RON HUBBARD
FOUNDER

366

HUBBARD COMMUNICATIONS OFFICE
SAINT HILL MANOR, EAST GRINSTEAD, SUSSEX

HCO POLICY LETTER OF 23 MARCH 1972

REMIMEO

ESTABLISHMENT OFFICER SERIES 11
FULL PRODUCT CLEARING
LONG FORM

Ref: HCO PL 13 Mar. 72   Esto Series 5
PRODUCTION AND ESTABLISHMENT
ORDERS AND PRODUCTS

MUST BE DONE ON AN ESTO
BEFORE HE DOES IT ON STAFF

If you ask some people what their product is, you usually get a DOINGNESS.

There are three conditions of existence. They are BE, DO and HAVE.

All products fall under HAVE.

The oddities you will get instead of a proper product are many.

Thus it is possible to "clear products" without any real result.

PRODUCT CLEARING FORM

Org

Person's Name

Date

Post

The 14 points of Esto Series 5 are done in this fashion, with a meter used to check words.

STEP ONE

DO NOT TAKE FOR GRANTED THAT THE PERSON KNOWS WHAT "PRODUCT" MEANS. GET IT AND EVERY WORD IN THE DEFINITION LOOKED UP.

a. Clear the word PRODUCT. Dictionaries give a variety of definitions. Make sure you get a usable definition that the person understands AND WHICH HE UNDERSTANDS ALL THE WORDS IN. He can be hung up on "that" or "is" in the definition itself believe it or not. _____

b. Have the person USE the word PRODUCT ten times in sentences of his own invention and use it correctly each time. _____

c. Now clear up BE, DO, HAVE, the conditions of existence. People often think a BE is a product or a DO. It is always something someone can HAVE.

   Clear the words BE, DO, HAVE by dictionary, especially HAVE. _____

d. Write these on a sheet of paper:

   BE

   DO

   HAVE

   Tell the person to name a product out in the world (a car, a book, a cured dog, etc.).

   Put an arrow into the word DO if he gives you a "do," into BE if he gives you a "be" instead of a HAVE.

   Mark HAVE with an arrow each time he gives a right HAVE product.

   When he can *rapidly* name a product that is something that one can HAVE, without a comm lag, go on to next step. _____

e. Clear up this question on a meter Method 4 (see HCOB 22 Feb. 72, Word Clearing Series 32, WORD CLEARING METHOD 4):

   Have I used any word so far you did not understand?

   Get it clean. _____

f. Now give the person a copy of HCO PL 29 Oct. 70 I, Org Series 10, THE ANALYSIS OF ORGANIZATION BY PRODUCT.

   Have him read the policy letter. _____

g. Clear by Method 4 Word Clearing this question:

   Are there any words in the policy letter you did not understand?

   Get it cleaned up. If there were any, have him reread the policy letter until he says he has it. _____

368

h. Drill the pc on Products 1, 2, 3 and 4.

Write:

Product 1   Product 2

Product 3   Product 4

on a sheet of paper. Let him retain and consult the HCO PL 29 Oct. 70 I, Org Series 10.

Put the point of your pen on one of the products (Product 1 or 2 or 3 or 4) and say, "Name a Product 1." "Name a Product 3." "Name a Product 4." "Name a Product 2." Do this until pc has it.

Now take the PL away from him and repeat the drill.

When your Product 1, etc., is all blacked up with ballpoint spots *and* the person is quick at it, thank him. Tell him he has it and go on to next step.   _____

STEP TWO

a. Look up the hat and org board of the post of the person being product cleared and get some idea of what the post's product would have to be to fit in with the rest of the scene. It won't necessarily be in former hat write-ups. What the post produces must be worked out. Write down what it possibly may be.   _____

b. Get the person to tell you what his post *produces*. Have him work the wording around until it is totally satisfactory to him and is not incorrect by Step 2a.

Be *very* careful indeed that you don't get a wrong product or you could throw the whole lineup of the org out.

Beware of "a high stat" or "a bonus" or "GI" as these are items received in exchange, not the person's produced product.

Once more resort to:

BE

DO

HAVE

to be sure he is not giving a doingness. And point this out until he actually has a HAVE.

Write down the product on the worksheet.   _____

c. Ask if there are any more products to the post. If the person is wearing several hats, he would have a product for each hat.

List each hat and get the product of each hat written after it.   _____

d. Now take the principal product of the post and see if it is really three products of different degrees or kinds. (Example: an auditor has [A] a well pc [one who has been gotten over a psychosomatic illness], [B] a person who is physically active and well and will continue to be well, and [C] a being with greatly increased abilities. A Super has [A] a trained student, [B] a course graduate, [C] a person who successfully applies the skills taught. Note: The above are rough wordings.)

The A, B, C you will notice fit roughly into (A) BE, (B) DO, (C) HAVE.

If the person has trouble with this, write BE, DO, HAVE on the worksheet.   _____

e. Find out if the person has had these confused one with another or if he is trying for A when his product was C, or any other mix-up.

See if he has to first get a BE, then a DO to finally achieve a HAVE.

When he has all this straight he should cognite on what product he is going for on his post, with VGIs.   _____

f. Tell the person that's it for the step and verify the products with a product officer. (Be sure it's a product officer who has had his Product Clearing. If this is THE product officer of the org, see if it compares to the valuable final products of an org [see HCO PL 8 Nov. 73RA, Rev. 9 Mar. 74, THE VFPs AND GDSes OF THE DIVISIONS OF AN ORG*].)

If the products are not all right check the person on a meter for Mis-Us and do Steps 1 and 2 again. If okay, proceed to Step 3.   _____

STEP THREE

a. Give the person HCO PL 27 Nov. 71 I, Executive Series 3, Finance Series 6-1, MONEY and HCO PL 3 Dec. 71, Executive Series 4, Finance Series 6-2, EXCHANGE. Have him read them.   _____

b. Return and do Method 4 on the PLs and clean up any misunderstood word. If these are found and looked up and used, then have the person read the PLs again.   _____

c. Now that the person has it, exchange objects with him.

Have him now explain exchange until he sees clearly what it is.   _____

*[Editor's Note: HCO PL 8 Nov. 73RA, Rev. 9 Mar. 74, THE VFPs AND GDSes OF THE DIVISIONS OF AN ORG was later cancelled and the data on VFPs can now be found on the org board provided with OEC Volume 0.]

a. Now write his product on the left-hand side of your worksheet and draw an arrow from it to the right:

His product ⟶

And one to the left below it ⟵

Have him tell you what, *internally* in the org, he could get in *exchange* for producing his product and getting it out.

Have him clear up why he might not get that. _____

b. Have him look at a worksheet picture:

        Overt Act ⟶ Injury

        Injury ⟵ Overt Act

SELF   No Product ⟶   OTHERS

        Nothing ⟵ Nothing

as a cycle. Be sure he grasps that. _____

c. Have him look at a worksheet picture:

        Overt Product ⟶ Upset

        Upset ⟵ Overt

And have him grasp that cycle. _____

d. Now have *him* draw various such cycles having to do with the products he has been getting out. Such as:

        Bad Product ⟶ Dissatisfied

        Bad Feelings ⟵ Ethics

But using various versions of products.

Do this until he has it untangled and feels good. _____

e. Have him write down his product on the left, arrow to the right, what comes back on the right and what occurs on the left.

If he has this now, tell him that's fine. _____

STEP FIVE
(All in Big Clay Demos)

a. Have him work out what theft is in terms of exchange, and arrows. _____

b. Have him show how his product contributes to the org's product. _____

c. Have him work out how the org's product as relates to his division is then exchanged with society outside the org and Scientology and what society exchanges back to the org.   _____

d. Have him work out how his product contributes to org's product outward and outside the org and Scn and then from the society outside back to the org and org back to him.

This may have more than two vias each way.   _____

e. Have him work out the combined staff products into an org product and then out into the society and then the exchange back into the org and to CLOs and upper management and to org staff.   _____

f. When the demos are all okay and BIG, tell him that's fine and go on to next step.   _____

STEP SIX
(Metered)

a. Find out if person wants his *product*? (not the exchange).

If not, find out who might suppress it? and E/S times.

Who might invalidate it? and earlier times.

Two-way comm it to F/N cog VGIs.   _____

b. Establish now if the person wants his product.   _____

(If bogs turn over to a C/S and auditor for ruds and completion.)

STEP SEVEN
(Metered)

a. Can the person get his product out?

Handle by two-way comm E/S to F/N.   _____

STEP EIGHT
(Metered)

a. What will his product be in volume?

Is that enough to bother about or will it have to be in greater volume?

What would be viable as to volume?

Clean up RUSHED or failures.

To F/N cog VGIs.   _____

STEP NINE
(Metered)

a. What quality would be necessary?

Get various degrees of quality stated.

What would he have to do to attain that quality?

What volume could he attain?

What would he have to do to attain that?

To F/N cog VGIs.   _____

STEP TEN
(Metered)

a. Can he get others to want the products he put out?

What would he have to do to attain this?   _____

STEP ELEVEN
(In BIG Clay)
(This is a progressive clay demo
added to at each step.)

a. How does his product or products fit into the framework of his
   section? Requires he work out the section product if his is not it.
   Then fit his to it.   _____

b. How does his product fit into the department? Requires he work out
   the department's product and fit his to it if his is not the dept's
   product.   _____

c. How does his product fit into the division's products? He will have to
   work out the div's product or consult HCO PL 8 Nov. 73RA, Rev. 9
   Mar. 74, THE VFPs AND GDSes OF THE DIVISIONS OF AN ORG.   _____

d. How does the division's product exchange with the public? And for
   what?   _____

e. What happens to the org on this exchange?   _____

STEP TWELVE
(In Big Clay)

a. What blocks might he encounter in getting out his product?   _____

b. What can HE do about these?   _____

STEP THIRTEEN
(Two-way Comm)

a. What does he have to have to get his product out? (Beware of too much have before he can do. Get him to cut it back so *he* is more causative.)

      _____

STEP FOURTEEN
(Written by Pc)

a. What is his product on the 1st dynamic — self?

How does it fit in with what he is doing?   _____

b. What is his product on the 2nd dynamic — family and sex?

How does it fit in with what he is doing?   _____

c. What is his product on the 3rd dynamic — groups?

How does it fit in with what he is doing?   _____

d. What is his product on the 4th dynamic — mankind?

How does it fit in with what he is doing?   _____

e. What is his product on the 5th dynamic — animal and vegetable kingdom?

How does it fit in with what he is doing?   _____

f. What is his product on the 6th dynamic — the universe of matter, energy, space and time?

How does it fit in with what he is doing?   _____

g. What is his product on the 7th dynamic — beings as spirits — thetans?

How does it fit in with what he is doing?   _____

h. What is his product on the 8th dynamic — God or the Infinite or religion?

How does it fit in with what he is doing?   _____

i. What is his post product?   _____

j. Can he get it out now?   _____

_____

Esto or Product Clearer

—————

Note this long form has to be run on leading executives and eventually on all staff. The short form in Esto Series 5, HCO PL 13 Mar. 72, PRODUCTION AND ESTABLISHMENT, ORDERS AND PRODUCTS, 14 points, serves as a rapid action.

Where there is any hang-up on the short form, send the person to an auditor. Where there is a hang-up on the long form, send the person to an auditor. The auditing action is to fly ruds on the RD and assess any key words the pc is upset about and do an 18 button Prepcheck *carrying* each prepcheck button to F/N.

TA

Where the TA is already high do not attempt the short or long form.

Where the person turns on a rock slam check for rings on the hands. If so, remove rings. Note if R/S continues.

In either case the person should be programed for TA trouble with C/S 53RRR and handled, and then given a GF 40RR Method 3 (F/Ning each question that reads) and then running the engrams with drugs run first.

Product Clearing is best done after Word Clearing No. 1 is successfully done.

An Esto who can use a meter and Method 4 W/Cing and knows clay demoing can do it.

HCO Bulletins are planned to be issued on this RD to handle it on rough ones or repair it as needed in the hands of an expert auditor.

L. RON HUBBARD
FOUNDER

HCO POLICY LETTER OF 1 APRIL 1972

EXECUTIVE SERIES 11
ESTABLISHMENT OFFICER SERIES 12
MAKING AN EXECUTIVE

FLOW LINES

If an executive has his flow lines wrong he will NEVER be a product officer but only a comm clerk.

For some poor reason executives get themselves onto all comm lines in their area. Probably it is an individual Why for each one. But the fact remains that they *do* do it!

And they promptly cease to be useful to anyone. While they "work" like mad!

Basically *they have confused a comm line with a command line.* These are two different things. A comm line is the line on which particles flow, it is horizontal. A command line is a line on which authority flows. It is vertical.

Here is an example of a divisional secretary who can get nothing accomplished while sweating blood over her "work."

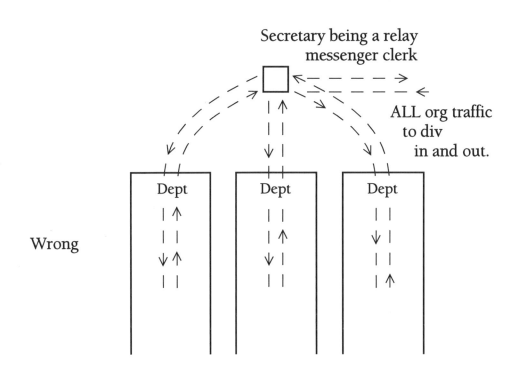

Now quite obviously this secretary is suffering from "fear of juniors' actions" or "having to know all." Exactly nothing will happen because the person is plowed under with paper. No real actions are taken. Just relays.

One such secretary of a division even acted as the relay point on all out and in BODY traffic. In short, just a divisional receptionist.

No product. Nothing happening at vast expense.

Here is another example. The correct one.

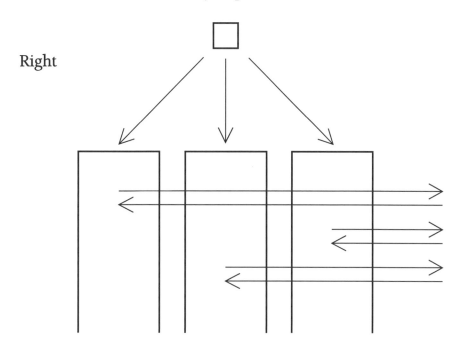

This is known as horizontal flow.

It is a fast flow system.

The correct terminals in each department are addressed by terminals outside the dept, directly. And are so answered.

Now we have a divisional secretary who is a PRODUCT OFFICER and whose duty is to get each department and section and unit producing what it is supposed to produce.

MISROUTE

So long as a command line is confused with the comm line an org will not produce much of anything but paper.

INFORMATION

It *is* vital that an executive keep himself informed.

The joker is, the despatch line does NOT keep him informed. It only absorbs his time and energy.

The data is not in those despatches.

The data an executive wants is in STATISTICS and REPORTS and briefings.

Statistics get posted and are kept up-to-date for anyone to look at, especially but not only the executive. They must ACCURATELY reflect production, volume, quality and viability.

Reports are summaries of areas or people or situations or conditions.

The sequence is (a) statistic goes unusually high, (b) an inspection or reports are required in order to evaluate it and reinforce it.

Or (a) the statistic dives a bit and (b) an inspection or reports are needed to evaluate and correct it.

Thus an executive is NOT dealing with the despatches or bodies of the division's inflow and outflow lines but the facts of the division's production in each section.

An executive makes sure he has comm lines, yes. But these are so he can make sure stats get collected and posted, so reports can be ordered or received and so he can receive or issue orders *about these situations*.

Despatchwise that is all an executive handles.

INSPECTIONS

Personally or by representative, an executive INSPECTS continually.

His main duties are:

OBSERVATION

EVALUATIONS (which includes handling orders)

and SUPERVISION.

All this adds up to the production of what the division is supposed to produce. Not an editing of its despatches.

A good executive is all over the place getting production done.

On a product he names it, wants it, gets it, gets it wanted, gets in the exchange for it.

He cannot do this without doing OBSERVATION by (1) stats, (2) reports, (3) inspections.

And he can't get at what's got it bugged without evaluation. And he can't evaluate without an idea of stats and reports and inspections.

Otherwise he won't know what to order in order to SUPERVISE. And once again he supervises on the basis of what he names, wants, gets, gets wanted and gets the exchange for.

THE SCENE

This *is* the scene of an executive.

If he is doing something else he will be a failure.

The scene is an active PRODUCTION SCENE where the executive is getting what's wanted and working out what will next be wanted.

ABILITY

An actual executive *can* work.

A real fireball can do any job he has getting done under him better than anyone he has working for him or under him.

He can't be kidded or lied to.

He *knows*.

Thus a wobble of a stat has him actively looking in the exact right place. And evaluating knowingly on reports. And getting the exact right WHY. And issuing the exact right orders. And seeing them get done. And knowing it's done right because he knows it can be done and how to do it.

Now that's an ideal scene for an exec.

But any exec can work up to it.

If he does a little bit on a lower job each day, "gets his hands dirty" as the saying goes, and masters the skill, he soon will know the whole area. If he schedules this as his 1400 to 1500 stint or some such time daily, he'll know them all soon. And if he burns the midnight oil catching up on his study.

And he *knows* he must watch stats and then rapidly get or do observations, so he can evaluate and find real Whys quickly and get the correction in and by supervision get the job done.

That's the ideal scene for the exec himself where he's head of the whole firm or a small part of it.

If he can't do it he will very likely hide himself on a relay despatch line and appear busy while it all crashes unattended.

An exec of course has his own admin to do but they don't spend hours at it or consider it their job for it surely isn't. Possibly an hour a day at the most handles despatches unless of course one doesn't police the dev-t in them.

Most of their evaluations are not written. They don't "go for approval" when they concern somebody's post jam. They are done by investigation on the spot and the handling is actual, not verbal.

A desk is used (a) to work out plans, (b) catch up the in-basket, (c) interview someone, (d) write up orders. Two-thirds of their time is devoted to production. Even if a thousand miles away they still only spend one-third of their time on despatches.

An executive has to be able to produce the real products and to get production. That defines even an Esto whose product has to do with an established person or thing.

Any department, any division, any org, any area responds the same way—favorably—to such competence.

ANALYSIS

To attain this ideal scene with an executive, one can find out WHY he isn't, by getting him to study this PL and then find WHY he can't really do it and then by programing him to remedy lack of know-how and other actions, increase his ability until he is a fireball.

If you are lucky you will have a fireball to begin with. But only the stats and *the truth of them* tell that!

Esto action: Can you do all this and these things? If the answer is no or doubtful or if the executive isn't doing them, find the Why and remedy.

L. RON HUBBARD
FOUNDER

HCO POLICY LETTER OF 3 APRIL 1972

ESTABLISHMENT OFFICER SERIES 13
DOING WORK

The basic Esto problem is getting somebody to do his job.

This is not just executives nor "bad staff." It tends to be rather prevalent in our modern culture.

The basic question really is, "Why can't you do what you are supposed to be doing?"

An Esto will find many people "busy," but really not doing their post hat.

As the Esto's own stat depends on people actually doing their jobs, and as the pay and well-being of those people also depend on it, it amounts to quite a problem.

You can do a Product Rundown to cognitions. But then in some cases nothing happens.

You hat and still nothing happens.

ABERRATION

To understand this you have to understand "aberration."

Get the idea of a being doing wholly what he is doing. You get this:

A.

⊖ Being

ı ı ı ı Task

It is a *straight* line of attention.

Now get the idea of somebody "doing a job that is not doing what he is doing."

We get

B.

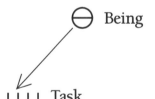

Being

ı ı ı Task

381

This is aberration. Which means "not in a straight line."

So in example (A), the person *does* what he is doing.

In example (B), he is doing but he is not doing what he is doing MENTALLY. Mentally he is doing something else while he is doing what he *seems* to be doing.

SCHIZOPHRENIA

The most prevalent "mental disorder" is supposed to be schizophrenia. This means "SCISSORS" or 2 plus "head." A two-head in other words. And in this case two heads are not better than one (joke).

You see this in institutions. A person is changing valences (personalities) click-click-click, one to the next.

But the condition is a gradient one that worsens between sanity and the bottom of the scale.

Midway, the condition is common but almost never noticed. It is so common today that it passes as normal humanoid.

The person is not doing what he is doing.

Examples of this are: people who do not like a job with responsibility because they "like to do mechanical things so they can dream of something else while working"; persons who "have to do something else before they can _____"; persons who are out of area; persons who continually make dev-t.

There is also the person who rams sideways into the work of others with "mistakes," "demands," and prevents them from doing what they are doing while himself not doing what he is doing.

One can't say these people are crazy. Not today. But one can say they make problems which are very difficult unless you know how to unlock the riddle.

BARRIERS

Study Series 2, HCOB 2 June 71 I, CONFRONTING, and the drills given in the Esto tape series can push their way through an astonishing mass of barriers.

For this is what the condition is — an effort to get through barriers.

The reason example (B) above occurs is that the person's attention is misdirected by mental barriers each time he tries to do (A) above.

Yet only if he can do (A) will he have any self-determinism and power.

It does not mean he is crazy. It means he is incapable of directing his attention straight. Each time he does, he hits something that deflects it (sends it off at an angle).

All this will seem very reasonable to him because it is the way it has always been. And like the little girl who never knew she had had a headache from the time of birth, and only knew it when it quit suddenly, such a person does not realize he cannot control his attention.

Such think about lots of other things while apparently thinking about what they are doing. And they do lots of other things.

MISUNDERSTOODS

Misunderstood words prevent them being in communication with materials or others. Thus they do not *read* or *listen*. They maunder (which means wander about mentally).

This is the inflow side of it.

The outflow side are barriers of odd fears and peculiar ideas.

Such people appear rather weak and dispersed. Or too heavy and stubborn to make up for it.

They have fixed ideas and other outpoints because their thoughts *detour* instead of running along a highway.

HAPPINESS

To get someone to actually do what he is doing when he is doing it will sound cruel to some people. That's because they find it painful to confront and would rather withdraw and maunder, sort of self-audit themselves through life.

They are not happy.

Happiness comes from self-determinism, production and pride.

Happiness is power and power is being able to do what one is doing when one is doing it.

COMPETENCE

When a person is competent, nothing can shake his pride. The world can yell. But it doesn't shake him.

Competence is not a question of one being being more clever than another. It is one being being more able to do what he is doing than another is.

Example (A) is competence.

Example (B) is incompetence.

MORE THERE

You could say a competent person was "more there." But this is really "more able to put his attention on what he has his attention on."

WHY

Anyone who is not a fireball on his post could be described by this WHY:

Unable to do his post for an individual WHY for each person.

Thus there are two ready remedies an Esto can use.

1. He can find the WHY a person cannot do his post, and then handle it.

2. He can do Esto drills on the person.

In finding the WHY, the observation itself that his stats are low may find the person a bit defensive.

It just could be that he *does* do what he is doing. But if so his stats would be high and he would be moving fast.

Thus one has to find his personal WHY. If it is the right one he should have very good indicators and speed up and do his job. If it is not quite the right one he may feel degraded or ashamed.

The test of any right WHY is does it raise the existing scene toward the ideal with existing resources.

Thus you can get a WHY that is not wholly acceptable until handled. But if you really are spot on it should blow a lot of the barriers.

Thus a real WHY blows a lot of the barriers, when handled, between the being and his job.

The drills then push it on through.

The drills sometimes blow through the WHY. The WHY sometimes blows right through any need of drills.

So these two actions interact.

If you see someone feeling very guilty after the WHY "is found," better check it over. It could be a wrong Why, and in this case, just find a new one.

THIRD ACTION

The Primary Rundown, HCOB 30 Mar. 72, should be done on a staff member thoroughly.

Otherwise he will remain to some degree out of comm. He will not be able to take in data quickly if he cannot communicate with words.

PROCESSING

Of course processing removes *all* the barriers eventually. But it is not necessarily aimed at doing a job.

Ability potential is enormously increased by processing.

But traditionally we do not rely on processing to handle staff.

We handle people and we handle cases.

But auditors and staff members, simply because we *do* handle people and cases, must not have cases on post. We do not admit that they have cases. This raises necessity level.

And it is quite amazing how high that necessity level can be raised and how a person can function despite his case.

If we admitted that staff had cases, we couldn't handle public cases. It's that simple.

So an Esto does not advise or use auditing on staff members as a post remedy nor accept case as a WHY.

Of course "case" is a Why. But when you accept it you retreat from example (A) above and at once get a (B).

You will be amazed how a person can begin to do what he is doing by finding his Why and doing drills.

And of course you also have to handle the fellows who jam in from the side at every turn and disperse the staff member's attention. He too (and especially) isn't doing what he is doing.

The same procedure (Why and drills) handles him as well.

In sum, if a staff member isn't doing what he is doing he is doing something else. They never do nothing.

Ask, "What is the reason you do not fully do your post?" or any such version. Find the real WHY. And handle the person.

That's the major part of an Esto's job.

And don't be surprised if you get a cheerful "but I am!" And find he is.

But his stats and speed tell the whole story.

L. RON HUBBARD
FOUNDER

HCO POLICY LETTER OF 4 APRIL 1972
ISSUE I

ESTABLISHMENT OFFICER SERIES 14
ETHICS

The normal level of an unhatted, dev-t, nonproducing org is out-ethics.

The reason you see so many heavy ethics actions occurring — or situations where heavy ethics actions should occur if they aren't — in such an org is that it has its EXCHANGE flows messed up.

It is important to know this fact as this factor alone can sometimes be employed to handle persons in the area whose ethics are out.

CRIMINALITY

Unless we want to go on living in a far nowhere some of the facts of scenes have to be confronted.

An inability to confront evil leads people into disregarding it or discounting it or not seeing it at all.

Reversely, there can be a type of person who, like an old-time preacher, sees nothing but evil in everything and, possibly looking into his own heart for a model, believes all men are evil.

Man, however (as you can read in HCOB 28 Nov. 70, C/S Series 22, PSYCHOSIS), is basically good. When going on some evil course he attempts to restrain himself and caves himself in.

The Chart of Human Evaluation in *Science of Survival* was right enough. And such people also can be found by the Oxford Capacity Analysis where the graph is low and well below a center line on the right.

This sort of thing can be handled of course by auditing but the Esto does not depend on that to handle his staff's problems.

Criminal actions proceed from such people *unless checked* by more duress from without not to do an evil act than they themselves have pressure from within to do it.

Criminality is in most instances restrained by just such an imbalance of pressures.

If you have no ethics presence in an org, then criminality shows its head.

Such people lie rather than be made to confront. They false report—they even use "PR," which means public relations, to cover up—and in our slang talk "PR" means putting up a lot of false reports to serve as a smoke screen for idleness or bad actions.

Unless you get ethics in, you will never get tech in. If you can't get tech in, you won't get admin in.

So the lack of ethics permits the criminal impulse to go unchecked.

Yes, it could be handled with tech. But to get money you have to have admin in.

Unless there is ethics and ways to get it in, no matter how distasteful it may seem, you will never get tech and admin in.

Of course there is always the element of possible injustice. But this is provided against. (See HCO PL 24 Feb. 72 I, INJUSTICE.)

When ethics is being applied by criminal hands (as happens in some governments) it can get pretty grim.

But even then ethics serves as a restraint to just outright slaughter.

Omitting to handle criminality can make one as guilty of the resulting crimes as if one committed them!

So criminality as a factor has to be handled.

It is standardly handled by the basic ethics PLs and the Ethics Officer system.

EXCHANGE

The unhatted, unproducing staff member, who is not really a criminal or psychotic, can be made to go criminal.

This joins him to the criminal ranks.

The ethics system also applies to him.

However there is something an Esto can do about it that is truly Esto tech.

This lies in the field of EXCHANGE.

If you recall your Product Clearing, you will see that exchange is something for something.

Criminal exchange is nothing from the criminal for something from another.

Whether theft or threat or fraud is used, the criminal think is to get something without putting out anything. That is obvious.

A staff member can be coaxed into this kind of thinking by

PERMITTING HIM TO RECEIVE WITHOUT HIS CONTRIBUTING.

This unlocks by the way an age-old riddle of the philosophers as to "what is right or wrong."

HONESTY is the road to SANITY. You can prove that and do prove it every time you make somebody well by "pulling his withholds." The insane are just one seething mass of overt acts and withholds. And they are very physically sick people.

When you let somebody be dishonest you are setting him up to become physically ill and unhappy.

Traditional Sea Org ethics labeled noncompliance as Liability and a false report as Doubt.

And it's true enough.

When you let a person give nothing for something, you are factually encouraging crime.

Don't be surprised that welfare districts are full of robbery and murder. People there give nothing for something.

When *exchange* is out the whole social balance goes out.

Every full scholarship ever given by an org wound up in a messy scene.

When you hire a professional pc who just sits around making do-less motions while people audit him and contribute to him DO NOT BE SURPRISED IF HE GETS SICKER AND SICKER.

He is contributing nothing in return and winds up in overwhelm!

Similarly if you actively prevented someone from contributing in return, you could also make him ARC broken and sick.

It is EXCHANGE which maintains the inflow and outflow that gives a person space around him and keeps the bank off of him.

There are numbers of ways these flows of exchange can be unbalanced.

It does not go same out as comes in. Equal amounts are no factor. Who can measure goodwill or friendship? Who can actually calculate the value of saving a being from death in each lifetime? Who can measure the reward of pride in doing a job well or praise?

For all these things are of different values to different people.

In the material world the person whose exchange factor is out may think he "makes money." Only a government or a counterfeiter "makes money." One has to produce something to *exchange* for money.

Right there the exchange factor is out.

If he gives nothing in return for what he gets, the money does not belong to him.

In Product Clearing many people it was found that some considered their food, clothing, bed and allowance were not theirs because they produced. They were theirs "just by being there." This funny "logic" covered up the fact that these people produced little or nothing on post. Yet they were the first to howl when not getting expensive (to the org) auditing or courses or tech!

Thus such a person, not hatted or made to produce, will get ill.

It is interesting that when a person becomes productive his morale improves.

Reversely it should be rather plain to you that a person who doesn't produce becomes mentally or physically ill. For his *exchange* factor is out.

So when you reward a downstat you not only deprive upstats, you also cave the downstat in!

I don't think welfare states have anything else in mind!

The riots of the ancient city of Rome were caused by these factors. There they gave away corn and games to a populace that eventually became so savage it could only enjoy torture and gruesome death in the arena!

A lot of this exchange imbalance comes from child psychology where the child is not contributing anything and is not permitted to contribute.

It is this which first overwhelms him with feelings of obligation to his parents and then bursts out as total revolt in his teens.

Children who are permitted to contribute (not as a cute thing to do but actually) make noncontributing children of the same age look like raving maniacs! It is the cruel sadism of modern times to destroy the next generation this way. Don't think it isn't intended. I have examined the OCAs of parents who do it!

So if a person is brought up this life with the exchange all awry, the Esto has his hands full sometimes!

He is dealing with trained-in criminality!

WHAT HE CAN DO

The remedy is rather simple.

First one has to know all about EXCHANGE as covered in the Product Clearing policy letters.

Then he has to specially clear this up with people who do not produce.

He should get them to work on it as it relates to ALL THEIR DYNAMICS IN RELATIONSHIP TO EVERY OTHER DYNAMIC.

That means he has to clear up the definitions of dynamics with *care* and then have the person draw a big chart (of his own) and say what he gives the first dynamic and what it gives him. Then what he gives the second dynamic and what it gives him. And so on up the dynamics.

Now, have him consider "his own second dynamic." What does his second dynamic give his first dynamic? What does his second dynamic give the second dynamic and what does it give him?

And so on until you have a network of these exchange arrows, each both ways.

Somewhere along the way, if your TRs are good and you have his attention and he is willing to talk to you, he will have quite a cognition!

That, if it's a big one, is the end phenomena of it.

And don't be surprised if you see a person now and then change his physical face shape!

CONDITIONS BY DYNAMICS

An ethics-type "action" can be done by giving the person the conditions formulas (pages 383, 438, 442, 443, 444, 445 of Vol 0, Basic Staff Hat. HCO PL 14 Mar. 68 — page 437 — gives one the table.)

Method 4 the person on the table of conditions and pick up any other misunderstoods.

Have the person study the *formula* of each of these conditions in the table so that he knows what they are and what the formulas are.

When he has all this now with no misunderstood words you must clear up the words related to his dynamics 1 to 8 and what they are.

Now you're ready for the billion-dollar question.

Ask him what is his condition on the first dynamic. Have him study the formulas. Don't buy any glib PR.

Don't evaluate or invalidate. When he's completely sure of what his condition really is on the first dynamic he will cognite.

Now take up the second dynamic by its parts — sex, family, children. Get a condition for each.

Similarly go on up each one of the dynamics until you have a condition for each one.

Now begin with the first dynamic again.

Continue to work this way.

You will be amazed to find he will come out of false high down to low and back up again *on each dynamic*.

Somewhere along the line he will start to change markedly.

When you have a person in continual heavy ethics or who is out-ethics (ethics bait, we say) and who is floundering around, you can do an S&D on him and quite often save his future for him.

When you have such a person you do this one first before you do the Exchange by Dynamics.

In other words, you use this on "ethics bait" and then when he's come out of such, you do Exchange by Dynamics on him.

SUMMARY

When all looks black, and you are getting false reports, and the things said done were not done and what was really being done were overt products and despite all your work the stats just *won't* go up, you still have three answers:

1. GET IN ETHICS ON THE ORG.

2. GET EXCHANGE DONE ON INDIVIDUALS.

3. GET IN CONDITIONS BY DYNAMICS ON THE ETHICS BAIT.

And after that keep a strong, just Division 1 Dept 3.

You'll be amazed!

L. RON HUBBARD
FOUNDER

HUBBARD COMMUNICATIONS OFFICE
SAINT HILL MANOR, EAST GRINSTEAD, SUSSEX

HCO POLICY LETTER OF 6 APRIL 1972
ISSUE I

REMIMEO

ESTABLISHMENT OFFICER SERIES 15
PRODUCT CORRECTION

If you find the wrong product for a post, you knock the staff member's hat off.

Example: Get the janitor a product of "a well-established business" and he's the Exec Esto!

When all the "products" have been "found" you can have bits of trouble here and there. This would be very mysterious unless you realize that a certain percentage of products found will be:

a. Incorrect,

b. Too few,

c. Incompletely worded,

d. Are doingnesses not havingnesses,

e. Can't be worked into a stat.

There will also be a certain small number who were upset by a poor Product Rundown and will have to have auditing to handle (usually the bypassed charge list L1C on the Product Rundown or what is called a Green Form or even a Word Clearing Correction List).

The majority probably will be all right, so that's a pluspoint.

But these flubbed rundowns become themselves a Why.

So let's see how to correct one.

1. **Did the product add up to a havingness?** _____

2. **Was it exchangeable?** _____

3. **Did it match the actual hat?** _____

4. **Were there more for the same post?** _____

5. **Is the person really wearing several hats, each of which has a product?** _____

6. If more than one found did they go together with each other? _____

7. Does it give the person a different hat? _____

8. Did it give the person somebody else's hat? _____

9. Were there misunderstood words in the rundown? _____

10. Does the person have contrary orders from some other person? _____

11. Was it just an exercise to the person? _____

12. Did doing the rundown make the person ARC broken or otherwise put ruds out? _____

13. Didn't the person agree with it? _____

14. Was the person really trying to do some other job? _____

15. Was the person about to leave present post or wanted to? _____

16. Was the Product Rundown really not done? _____

17. Is the person unhappy on post? _____

18. Is the person taking illegal orders? _____

19. Is the person connected to antagonistic people (PTS)? _____

20. Wrong post for the product? _____

21. Wrong org board? _____

22. Crossed over into another department? _____

23. Crossed over into another division? _____

The questions, assessed on a meter, should be handled if they read.

And when that is done (assessed and handled), the door is open to finding the Why called for in Esto Series 13. The above questions could be the Why or part of it but usually that's just a symptom of the real Why called for in Esto Series 13.

But in any event the questions correct the Product Rundown and it's vital to do that.

HATS AND ORG BOARD
EXISTING ORG BOARD

The routine action with a post is to get the person to list on separate cards WITH CORRECT EXACT WORDING each hat the person wears or has been wearing no matter how small. This is NOT copied from a PL. It's an honest "What hats do you really wear?"

393

The list may be as long as 35 or 40! The higher you go on the command channel, the more of these hats.

Having done that for every member in a division, you wind up with either:

1. Completely expressed division hats or

2. Woefully missing functions or

3. Badly adjusted workloads.

4. A totally cross-hatted scramble.

You put these cards (identified as whose by the writing) onto a blank org board. You now have AN EXISTING ORG BOARD.

NEXT ACTION

The following is an entirely separate action.

Now you take the 1965 org board or FEBC org board or whatever org board is a model and see if the "hats" you have go under the functions listed on the board.

You adjust the hats around to cover the actual functions of the division.

You write up cards to cover the missing functions.

You put these new cards on the org board.

FUNCTION BOARD

You write up the *functions* of the org board of the division by departments on a separate model and add the valuable final products per HCO PL 8 Nov. 73RA.*

This gives you the functions to get out the VFPs expected.

These functions will or won't get out the VFPs.

What *functions* are needed to get them out?

By blocking in these, you have now a FUNCTION ORG BOARD.

TITLES ORG BOARD

From this function org board you can now make up a TITLES ORG BOARD.

Each title has some of these functions. The functions must be of the same general type for the title.

When you have done this (with divisional secretary, divisional org officer and divisional Esto and department heads), you now have a TITLES ORG BOARD.

---

*[*Editor's Note:* HCO PL 8 Nov. 73RA, Rev. 9 Mar. 74, THE VFPs AND GDSes OF THE DIVISIONS OF AN ORG was later cancelled and the data on VFPs can now be found on the org board provided with OEC Volume 0.]

POSTING

The main failure in putting names on an org board is that people take the easy way out and try to put a different person's name on each title. This gives you a 100-person division "absolutely vital" while the production is about 5 man!

You take the names you have NOW in the division and post those to cover all the functions and titles.

You post from the top down. YOU NEVER POST FROM BOTTOM UP. And you NEVER LEAVE A GAP BETWEEN PERSONS ON LOWER POSTS AND HIGH POSTS. Either of these faults will raise hell in the division's functioning and are grave faults.

Having done this, you now have a POSTED ORG BOARD.

MATCHING

Now the hat lists you have are probably wildly different than your posted org board.

Take the cards of hats they were wearing and try to fit these onto your POSTED ORG BOARD.

You now at once "before your very eyes" will see what's wrong with your product and what might be right with it.

You will have one of these:

1. Completely expressed division hats

2. Woefully missing functions

3. Badly adjusted workloads OR

4. A function not on the POSTED BOARD but done by someone that is getting the product!

You will see that the board, made from the hat cards they wrote, doesn't usually compare with your posted org board!

AND THAT'S A POSSIBLE WHY YOU COULDN'T GET PRODUCT RUNDOWNS DONE!

Hats don't add up to product. Or the actions really being done are totally unproductive.

You now have it before your eyes.

CAUTION

By an excess of purity you can crash a division or an org by removing a key function someone is doing that's NOT on the posted org board *but* IS getting the product!

We had a Phone Reg recently removed because he wasn't allowed for on the org board and "had to be Dir Reg but wouldn't." When he was *forced* into line, the stats promptly crashed!

The stats recovered promptly when his removal was spotted and he was ordered back on post.

You don't juggle an org board lightly. You can destroy a division or unit by juggling hats.

The rule is DON'T DISMANTLE A WORKING INSTALLATION. NEVER!

You can build around it, support it, put in another one like it. But don't touch it!

It is heartbreaking to build a successful upstat division — takes months — and have somebody crash it by musical chairs, musical functions.

So always look at stats. And look at the PAST points of high stats of that div in past years and see what was its organization when it was *really* upstat.

You could do no better than to rebuild that old structure.

But if your div or activity was a working installation that was really getting out the product, don't monkey with it. Study it instead.

RECLEARING PRODUCT

If Product Clearing wasn't good, and the unit isn't doing well, then do the above org board exercises to see what gave.

And you probably will now see that you didn't have the right products.

Try to get your division or dept standard if its stats are low. Standard is your 1965 SH org board for a big org. That org really ran! Most policy is built on it.

But a little org builds up from "Org Program No. 1," LRH ED 49 Int, 9 Dec. 69. And can go through the 6-dept stage of London, LA and DC in their glory (56–62). They had an HCO, a Registration, Accounts, Training, Processing and a Department of Personnel Efficiency (public).

These did all the functions. There was an HCO Sec and an Association Sec. But Org Program No. 1 phases into it with a person in full charge of public.

Or a little org can build a big org from Org Program No. 1 right on into the 65 org board.

The *approximate* products of HCO PL 8 Nov. 73RA are being worked for. I say approximate as there may be more and the wording may be better adjusted.

When you have the hats getting out the subproducts (those necessary to make the VFPs of the org) you will get the VFPs.

CORRECTED ORG BOARD

You may find it necessary to correct your posted org board to get the VFPs.

Remember, it has the staff it has, plus any new ones it manages to get plus any field technical persons it can get in to go on staff.

YOU HAVE TO SET IT UP TO GET OUT THE VFPs NOW NOW NOW.

An org can't stand idle to be organized. It can die if it is halted just to establish.

So you post the people you have to do the functions that must be done.

Then you Product Clear.

You clear from the top down.

You HAT *to produce.*

There isn't anything more important than this step.

EASY WAYS

The easy way to do this is to do two of the short form steps quickly on EACH staff member from the top down.

Then take the next two on ALL the staff, each one.

If a Product Rundown has been done already but it isn't running well, correct it, with above list.

And do it with two steps and go on to the next staff member.

NEGLECTING TO CLEAR PRODUCTS

The biggest omission is not clearing products at all.

The next biggest omission is failing to clear from the top down.

The next is not clearing them all through the div two at a time.

The next is not clearing products on the new people coming into the div promptly.

CRISSCROSSING PRODUCTS

A div can be tangled by having the wrong products for the hats.

So product is always suspect when stats are down or lines tangle.

BIGGEST WHY

The biggest Why of products not getting cleared is an Esto I/C in a small org or an Exec Esto who does not run and train his Estos. If an Exec Esto listens to "but I can't use a meter," "my TRs are out," "she won't let me hat her," "I have Mis-Us on the PLs so don't read them" and does not handle his Estos the way a coach handles a hot football team, products won't get cleared.

Naturally if products are not cleared on an Esto I/C or an Exec Esto or if they aren't cleared on the Estos, they will flounder.

Once again it's a two-step at a time action round and round while getting other things done between each two steps.

EXAMPLE OF PRODUCTS

An example of Product Clearing that throws things out is crossing the hats of the Esto MAAs.

The Exec Esto's MAA is responsible for the schedule and getting to work and exercise and activities of STAFF MEMBERS.

The Assistant Esto MAA is responsible for Estos.

If their products are incorrectly cleared they will flounder around and their posts may look of little value.

The Exec Esto's MAA probably has a product like "effective post hours of each staff member." Each staff member on post one hour is a product. He also therefore has a welfare sort of function that leads to a lesser product that leads to the main one. Like "a staff member in good physical condition for the day." And this gives another lesser product, "a secure staff member for that day." And so it goes. This is not a list nor an exact wording of his products. But do you see that they all fit? They are ethics-type stats so they have *time* in them because they *preserve* and measure survival. They could not be graphed without *time* in them. They would not vary.

The Esto's MAA has "an Esto on post with ethics in that day." He has lesser products of "a defended or secure Esto that day" and "an Esto assisted with liaison with HCO." Do you see that the products mesh? If an Esto has out-ethics he can't be defended because he can be hit from above.

Also the Exec Esto's MAA has the staff and the Esto's MAA has the Estos so "both sides" are supported.

Now, if you product cleared the Exec Esto's MAA as having "a working Esto" as his product he would be at once the Exec Esto! While called "Esto's MAA." He wouldn't be able to make head nor tail of his post.

If the org's HCO Ethics Officer had the same products as the Esto MAAs (or, lord help us, all three had wrong products), whole zones of ethics would be missing in the org and out-ethics would occur. The Ethics Officer has several products but as HCO is a production division, he has "an out-ethics person whose ethic level has been made acceptable." It would not be "Ethics Orders issued" as that isn't the whole product of

---

398

the E/O nor would "people hit by Ethics" be a product because it isn't a product. The product would have to include *public* and if it didn't the whole public zone would be out. Students would get into an E/O section jammed with staff backlog and would be kept off course and maybe blow. Decent investigations couldn't be made. So ethics would go out in the area.

But an Esto having trouble with a staff member would know, if products were right and published, to send him to the Exec Esto's MAA!

And what of files? It's useless to duplicate files so HCO Ethics Files has *all* ethics files and the Exec Esto MAA's files and the Estos MAA files.

So, just with this example, you can see that products *can* be very neatly coordinated. AND MUST BE FROM STAFF MEMBER TO STAFF MEMBER in a section, a department, a division, an org. Then it all FLOWS. Somebody is in charge of each internal product in the org that it takes to make a VFP and in charge as well of that VFP loosely (incorrectly called) the GI (GI is really the valuable FINAL REWARD for which the VFPs are exchanged).

Thus, an org properly product cleared RUNS, PRODUCES VFPs in high volume and quality and is rewarded with GI and other things for which VFPs exchange.

And that's the org you want!

L. RON HUBBARD
FOUNDER

HCO POLICY LETTER OF 24 APRIL 1972
ISSUE I

REMIMEO

ESTABLISHMENT OFFICER SERIES 16

HATTING THE PRODUCT OFFICER
OF THE DIVISION

Estos have been told "hat from the top down."

Why? Because the head of a div or org or the product officer of the org is the one who gets other people to work.

If the product officer is not hatted to get people to work there will be no products, the stats will be very low and that Esto could be very mystified and look bad as an Esto.

For if he does not do this one thing first then whatever else he does will be wasted.

An Esto who gets drawn in and given orders by a div head or who cannot confront the div head will wind up withdrawing from the div or just being inactive.

The first major failure of an Esto would be a failure to hat the product officer of the org or div.

FIRST SITUATION: There is no head of div (or org). Correct action: Get a head of div (or org) *fast* and *rapidly* org board the div. The number of people in the div (or org) does not matter at this stage. First things first. Get a head of div (or org). And rapidly org board the place.

SECOND SITUATION: You have a head of div (or org). Correct action: Hat him with HCO PL 28 July 71, ADMIN KNOW–HOW No. 26. Tell him you will attend to the hatting IF he will get them producing. *He* is responsible for their production. Get him to know this PL. (Method 4 W/C.) Tell him he is in Phase I. So let's see some production.

THIRD SITUATION: The head of div or org flies about, looks busy or just sits there. He is not getting out production. He will tell you all about "not being hatted," "doesn't know the tech," on and on, excuses, excuses. But no production from him or staff. Correct action: He has to be made to understand that he isn't doing his job no matter how *busy* he looks or how many reasons he has. He probably has not noticed and does not know that he is faking work. People with low confront don't *see.* If he *is* really doing his job and getting out his products and forcing any staff to get out theirs, you have a pearl. Cherish him, and don't consider doing this third action on him. But one is easily fooled. Only real products tell the tale. A busy exec or division is not necessarily a producing exec or div. So if no products from him or staff for whatever reason, he's below Danger. You don't have a head of div or org if you don't have products coming off and exchange occurring. Only *these,* not excuses or motions, tell the tale. You can get "PR" and glowing (but false) reports. You can get all sorts of things. But where are the products? So you bait (tease) and badger (nag) the head of div (or org) to IMPINGE ON HIM (draw his attention) until he snarls or cries or screams AND SPITS OUT AN OUTPOINT. You don't ask him like repetitive commands "Why aren't you working?" You ask in many ways "Where are the products?" And he'll eventually tell you an outpoint. Like "But I can't get out any products because they aren't products until they are back home telling people how good we are so how can I _____." Or "I just keep running around here and nothing happens." Or some other nonsense that *is* nonsense. That's his Why. So you tell him, "Look, you don't get out products because you don't think you can!" Or "You are just trying to look busy so you won't be thought idle." And if you're smart and on the ball, that will be it. The exec will cognite and go into smooth two-way comm at once and you got him out of the Esto PL Series 13 state into a confront. This is "Bait and Badger" to get him broken out of nonconfronting. That's all that's wrong with him really. He doesn't look.

SITUATION FOUR: The exec won't let an Esto near him. Snaps, snarls. Don't avoid him. Correct action: Bait and Badger. He's already halfway through Situation Three above. Finish it up.

SITUATION FIVE: The exec goes into shock. This is a symptom of no confront. He won't fight back. He will propitiate. But he won't do anything either. Correct action: Get a new exec. Tame execs who won't fight and can't work will never get a staff to work. After getting a new exec, salvage the old one with processing. Do steps one to four on the new one.

SITUATION SIX: Having gotten the original or a new exec this far, you will find he is usually outpointy in his actions even if producing. Correct action: Run Confront in his area. Run Reach and Withdraw in his area. Then product clear him on every section and department he has as though he's the head of it.

SITUATION SEVEN: Gets out volume but quality suffers. This is a general nonconfront. Correct action: Bring him personally up through each dynamic, through the conditions per Esto Series No. 14. Get him in normal or higher on each dynamic. Now do Dynamic Exchange, Esto Series No. 14.

SITUATION EIGHT: He is active, producing but isn't forcing staff to produce. Correct action: Recheck him on HCO PL 28 July 71, ADMIN KNOW–HOW No. 26, and look for a Why that he can't pull himself out of Phase I into Phase II. Get this VGIed. Tell him, "Preach to them that dones come from effective doingness. If they don't do things that are effective they will not get a *done.* Demand DONES."

SITUATION NINE: He really doesn't know his job. Correct action: Begin to hat him. Don't start hatting him further than an instant hat before you have worked it up to Situation Eight. His *confront* will not be good enough to apply the material even if he knows it. So only at this stage do you start to really hat. And at this stage you hat by *observing* what he doesn't know that he needs to know and you look up and select PLs that fit his current state of unhattedness and check him out on only these. You keep a log of what he's checked out on so he gets credit for it.

SITUATION TEN: The executive skids back. He roller-coasters or gets ill. Correct action: Recognize this as a PTS situation. Get him interviewed by the D of P. Get the PTS situation HANDLED and don't buy "It's just the flu" or whatever. He's PTS and that's trouble. (See HCOB 17 Apr. 72, C/S Series 76, C/Sing A PTS RUNDOWN.)

SITUATION ELEVEN: The exec does not seem to remember what he's been checked out on or apply what he knows. He is glib or he is foggy. Correct action: Get him word cleared Method 1. Then word clear him Method 4 on the materials he has covered. (See Word Clearing Series HCOBs.)

HOW MUCH TIME

How much time do you spend with an exec?

Well, effective or not his time is valuable.

Do not use peak load post time or he'll be going mad with the PTP of unhandled actions needing to be done. So you won't get anywhere.

Try to do these actions on an exec during his *study time.*

Observe him on post to know what to do in his study time.

If he has no study time, you must get the Study Correction List (HCOB 14 Jan. 72, Study Series 7)* done on him and handled as in Situation Thirteen. An exec who can't study can't see either.

If this conflicts with your own study time, make other arrangements for that portion of yours. But get yours IN too.

SITUATION TWELVE: Has study time in addition to working hours but does not study. Correct action: See that study time is run per WHAT IS A COURSE? HCO PL 16 Mar. 71 I and WHAT IS A COURSE HIGH CRIME, HCO PL 16 Mar. 72 V and LRH ED 174 Int, STUDY AND TECH BREAKTHROUGH, 29 Mar. 72.

SITUATION THIRTEEN: Even though staff course exists does not study. Correct action: Have a Study Corr List, HCOB 14 Jan. 72, Study Series 7, done and properly handled.

REST OF STAFF

What do you do with the rest of staff?

These thirteen situations cover as well any staff member.

You could do no worse than do these things on each one as beginning actions.

There are many Esto actions that can be done but if you don't get these done you won't get far.

But on staff below dept head, Situations One, Two and Eight do not apply.

---

*[*Editor's Note:* HCOB 14 Jan. 72, Study Series 7, was later replaced by HCOB 4 May 81RA, Rev. 27 June 88, STUDY GREEN FORM.]

SITUATION ONE STAFF: Major post not posted. Correct action: Force a Dept 1 into existence via the Exec Esto and get it producing staff and get the post posted. (Don't do an incorrect action and use other parts of the org as personnel pools and dismantle working installations or rob Tech.) Get the org board up and the person on it.

SITUATION TWO STAFF: You have a person on the post. Correct action: Instant-hat him. Get him programed for training for post. Unbug his study time. See that he studies per program.

SITUATION EIGHT STAFF: He is active and producing but isn't moving his products or is backlogging and/or gets in jams. Correct action: Volume 0 of OEC Course, get in its comm sections, drill him on org board and show him the other terminals he is supposed to be in comm with. Make him follow his product physically through lines and then make him follow the routes of things that should come to him. While doing this you will find bugs in the lines or in his own lines. Smooth them out. Drill the person further.

THIS PL AS A CHECKLIST

You can use this PL as a checklist.

Get a cardboard folder. Put the person's name on it.

Write the person's name in at the top of this PL.

When each action is done, mark the dates it is being worked on in the margin beside the situation with your initial.

When fully done mark it DONE with date. Beware of NOT–DONES or HALF–DONES or BACKLOGS. (See AKH Series 29, Exec Series 5, both are HCO PL 26 Jan. 72 I, NOT–DONES, HALF–DONES AND BACKLOGS.)

Don't skip about on this one.

———

THE GENERAL WHY OF INACTIVITY OR NONPRODUCTION IS: LOW CONDITION ON ONE OR MORE DYNAMICS MAKING A NONALIGNMENT WITH OTHER DYNAMICS CAUSING AN INABILITY TO CONFRONT.

Most beings are not there as a being as they are below existence. As a being plus body they have social responses and can do orders or will do at something when attention is called to it. Otherwise they are blind with their eyes wide open. They are not malicious. They just don't SEE.

If they are not there they won't have to be responsible for what they do, will they? They do not think they have lived before or will live again, which is why the population is fixed on a one-life idea.

As a result the above situations *do* occur. And the handling has been tested and works.

Do not say, "Why haven't you seen _____" this or that outness. Say, "Do you see this _____" outness. And they will look in that direction. But sometimes have to be shown further evidence. Then they *see* it. Until the above situations are handled, you are working with social machinery.

When you have handled these situations as above correctly as noted, you will get toward full application of HCO PL 5 May 59, POLICY ON SEC EDs AND HATS, Vol 1 of OEC. Call the above "correct actions" the modern processes plus many other Esto actions and you *can* bring the exec to CAUSE so that he CREATES his post.

Until you have handled, using his social machinery as per the situation handlings above, he is *not* being bad, he just *can't see*.

This is how you get an exec functioning.

It is no overt act to get him functioning as only until you do will he have any morale at all.

SITUATION FOURTEEN: An exec or staff member may try to use the Esto as an org officer or to get the Esto to get involved in the division's products. BOTH are fatal Esto errors. Correct action: Explain Esto functions to them briefly so they know the Esto's product is THEM.

L. RON HUBBARD
FOUNDER

HCO POLICY LETTER OF 13 MAY 1972

ISSUE I

(Also issued as an HCOB, same date and title)

REMIMEO

ESTABLISHMENT OFFICER SERIES 17
STUDY SERIES 4

CHINESE SCHOOL

As very few westerners have ever seen a Chinese or Arab school in progress, it is very easy for them to miss the scene when one says "Chinese school."

The term has been used to designate an action where an instructor or officer, with a pointer, stands up before an assembled class and taps a chart or org board and says each part of it.

It is very funny to one who knows or has heard a real Chinese school to see the class sitting there silently. This is strictly a Western pattern. This is how a teacher does it in Omaha or Cornell. But never in Shanghai!

A Chinese class sings out in unison (all together) in response to the teacher. They *participate!*

The only Western near equivalent is a German beer hall where the audience choruses items sung out by the song leader.

Chinese school, then, is an action of class vocal participation. It is a very lively loud affair. It sounds like chanting.

In a real Chinese school the response is so timed that although spoken by many voices it is quite easy to tell what answer is being chorused.

It is essentially a system that establishes instant thought responses so that the student, given "2 x 2" thinks instantly "4."

For example, the instructor, tapping a big multiplication chart cries, "Two times two." The class in one voice cries, "Four." Instructor: "Five times two." Class: "Ten." And so on and on and on by the *hour*.

This gets more complex when, let us say, the maxims of good conduct or the Koran are being taught. In such cases the tablets or scrolls are on the wall. The teacher calls chapter and verse and the students chant it.

You could teach the Laws of Listing and Nulling, the Auditor's Code, Axioms and so on in this way.

The tools are the same — an instructor, a pointer, a chart or set of pictures or big scrolls, a class.

There are two steps in such teaching.

A. The instructor taps and says what it is. Then asks the class what it is and they chant the answer.

B. When the class has learned by being told and repeating, the instructor now taps with the pointer and asks and the class chants the correct answer.

DRILL

The instructor himself has to grasp the drill.

Here is how it would go on an org board.

A

Instructor taps Div 1. "This is Division 1 HCO Division."

Class chants, "Division 1 HCO Division."

Instructor taps Div 6. "This is Division 6 Distribution Division."

Class: "Division 6 Distribution Division."

And so on until all divisions have been named a few times.

B

Instructor taps Div 1. "What is this?"

Class: "Division 1 HCO Division."

Instructor taps Div 4. "What is this?"

Class: "Division 4 Tech Division."

And so on and on. The divisions are then considered trained-in on the class.

Next one would go to departments. Then to philosophic names of departments. Then to sections. Then one would go to the titles of each division head. Then to dept heads. Etc. Etc.

If one had a function org board of what each div and department and post *did* one would go on with the same thing.

A Chinese school drill run for a short period each day will eventually cover an enormous amount of org board.

Newcomers to the drill have to be schooled-in to catch up or join a new class.

Anything can be taught by Chinese school that is to be learned by rote. The parts and actions are always the same.

There is also a version that uses a text, preferably with a copy of it in each student's hands. It sounds the same.

One is limited only by what he can put on a chart or even in a text where each student has a copy of the text open before him.

Crude charts are easy to draw up with a felt (heavy ink) pen. The size of a chart is determined by the ability of the students furthest away to see it easily.

Cloud types, pictures to be named in a foreign language, even slides of airplane types, anything can be Chinese schooled that is to be learned verbatim. And you'd be surprised how many things should be. And if they aren't the person has a shaky foundation under the subject.

Care should be taken to define strange words. But it is not really a problem or exercise in Word Clearing. It is verbatim rote teaching.

And it works.

And is lots of fun.

L. RON HUBBARD
FOUNDER

HUBBARD COMMUNICATIONS OFFICE
SAINT HILL MANOR, EAST GRINSTEAD, SUSSEX

HCO POLICY LETTER OF 15 AUGUST 1978R
REVISED 31 OCTOBER 2000

REMIMEO
HCOs
ORG OFFICERS
ESTOS

ESTABLISHMENT OFFICER SERIES 17-1
CHINESE SCHOOLING AN ORG BOARD

Ref: HCO PL 13 May 72 I   Esto Series 17
Study Series 4
CHINESE SCHOOL

In a Chinese school the instructor stands up before the class, with a pointer, and taps each part of the chart or text being taught and says it. A Chinese class then chants in unison in response to the teacher.

This system of verbatim teaching is used in orgs to drill the org board.

There are two steps in Chinese schooling an org board.

A. The instructor taps the org board with a pointer and says what it is. Then asks the class what it is and they chant the answer.

B. When the class has learned by being told and repeating, the instructor now taps the org board with the pointer and asks, "What is this?" and the class chants the correct answer.

The top exec of the org (CO or Exec Dir) is the first one drilled, with other execs following suit, as they have to know the org board far better than the crew — otherwise they will run a "hey you" org board.

Chinese schooling an org board is never flattened. Once you get the org board itself and the names of the people on the posts well drilled, you start drilling the duties of each department and every post one by one, all the way down the org board and that takes weeks. Then you go back to whole org board drilling and so it goes.

L. RON HUBBARD
FOUNDER

Revision assisted by
LRH Technical Research
and Compilations

HUBBARD COMMUNICATIONS OFFICE
SAINT HILL MANOR, EAST GRINSTEAD, SUSSEX

HCO POLICY LETTER OF 12 JUNE 1972RA
REVISED 14 DECEMBER 2000

REMIMEO

DATA SERIES 26
ESTABLISHMENT OFFICER SERIES 18
LENGTH OF TIME TO EVALUATE

(Restored 14 Dec. 2000 to the original LRH text.)

It will be found that long times required to do an evaluation can be traced each time to AN INDIVIDUAL WHY FOR EACH EVALUATOR.

These, however, can be summarized into the following classes of Whys:

This list is assessed by a Scientology auditor on a meter. The handling directions given in each case are designations for auditing actions as done by a Scientology auditor and are given in the symbols he would use.

1. **MISUNDERSTOOD WORDS?** _____

   (Handled with Word Clearing [Method 1 and Method 4 of the Word Clearing Series].)

2. **INABILITY TO STUDY AND AN INABILITY TO LEARN THE MATERIALS?** _____

   (Handled by a Study Correction List HCOB 4 Feb. 72.*)

3. **OUTPOINTS IN OWN THINKING?** _____

   (Handled by what is called an HC [Hubbard Consultant] List, HCOB 28 Aug. 70.)

4. **PERSONAL OUT–ETHICS?** _____

   (Use PL 3 May 72, by an auditor. Has two Listing and Nulling type lists.)

5. **DOING SOMETHING ELSE?** _____

   (2-way communication or PL 3 May 72 or reorganization.)

6. **IMPATIENT OR BORED WITH READING?** _____

   (Achieve superliteracy. LRH Executive Directive 178 International.)

7. **DOESN'T KNOW HOW TO READ STATISTICS SO DOESN'T KNOW WHERE TO BEGIN?** _____

   (Learn to read stats from Management by Stat PLs.)

*[Editor's Note: HCOB 4 Feb. 72 was later replaced by HCOB 4 May 81RA, Rev. 27.6.88, STUDY GREEN FORM.]

8. **DOESN'T KNOW THE SCENE?**   ————
   (Achieve familiarity by direct observation.)

9. **READS ON AND ON AS DOESN'T KNOW HOW TO HANDLE AND IS STALLING?**   ————
   (Get drilled on actual handling and become Super-Literate.)

10. **AFRAID TO TAKE RESPONSIBILITY FOR THE CONSEQUENCES IF WRONG?**   ————
    (HCOB 10 May 72 on Robotism. Apply it.)

11. **FALSELY REPORTING?**   ————
    (Pull all withholds and harmful acts on the subject.)

12. **ASSUMES THE WHY BEFORE STARTING?**   ————
    (Level IV Service Facsimile triple auditing.)

13. **FEEL STUPID ABOUT IT?**   ————
    (Get IQ raised by general processing.)

14. **HAS OTHER INTENTIONS?**   ————
    (Audit on L9S or Expanded Dianetics.)

15. **HAS OTHER REASONS NOT COVERED IN ABOVE?**   ————
    (Listing and Nulling to blowdown F/N item on the list.)

16. **HAS WITHHOLDS ABOUT IT?**   ————
    (Get them off.)

17. **HAS HAD WRONG REASONS FOUND?**   ————
    (C/S Series 78.)

18. **NOT INTERESTED IN SUCCESS?**   ————
    (PL 3 May 72, and follow as in 14 above.)

19. **SOME OTHER REASON?**   ————
    (Find it by 2-way comm.)

20. **NO TROUBLE IN THE FIRST PLACE?**   ————
    (Indicate it to person.)

When this list is assessed one can easily spot why the person is having trouble with the Data Series or applying it. When these reasons are handled, one can then get the series restudied and word cleared and restudied and it will be found that evaluations are much easier to do and much more rapidly done.

L. RON HUBBARD
FOUNDER

HUBBARD COMMUNICATIONS OFFICE
SAINT HILL MANOR, EAST GRINSTEAD, SUSSEX

HCO POLICY LETTER OF 13 JUNE 1972

REMIMEO

ESTABLISHMENT OFFICER SERIES 19
PROGRAM DRILL

A majority of people cannot follow a written program. Yet all legal projects are in program form.

The reasons are various. But when programs are not understood they can be cross-ordered, abandoned, left half-done and the next thing you know you have a backlog (HCO PL 26 Jan. 72 I, NOT–DONES, HALF–DONES AND BACKLOGS).

There can be (and usually are) other situations that prevent the doing of a program. Out-ethics (PL 3 May 72, ETHICS AND EXECUTIVES), PTS or SP (PL 5 Apr. 72, PTS TYPE A HANDLING), lack of understanding of a product or exchange, an unmanned or undermanned area are the commonest reasons. But when all these have been handled, there can be two other reasons — the written project itself is bugged so it can't be done (needs special equipment or finance or is outpointy or doesn't apply) or THE PERSONS CONCERNED JUST CAN'T DO A PROJECT. The former of these reasons is seized upon all too often to excuse the latter WHICH USUALLY IS THE CASE. They can't execute a project and prefer cross orders because the orderliness of a project or what it is, is not understood. Therefore, to handle this we have the following project drills.

The person is just to do these, honestly, each one, from targets 1 on.

DUMMY PROJECT 1

PURPOSE: To learn to do a project.

MAJOR TARGET: To get it done.

PRIMARY TARGETS:

  1. Read this PL down to "Dummy Project 1."

  2. Check off each one when done.

VITAL TARGETS:

  1. Be honest about doing this.

  2. Do all of it.

411

OPERATING TARGETS:

1. Take off your right shoe. Look at the sole. Note what's on it. Put it back on.

2. Go get a drink of water.

3. Take a sheet of paper. Draw three concentric circles on it. Turn it over face down. Write your name on the back. Tear it up and put the scraps in a book.

4. Take off your left shoe. Look at the sole. Note what is on it. Put it back on.

5. Go find someone and say hello. Return and write a despatch to your post from yourself as to how they received it.

6. Write a despatch from your post to yourself in proper despatch form Volume 0 OEC correcting how you wrote the despatch in 5 above. File it in your hat.

7. Take off both shoes and bang the heels together three times and put them back on.

8. Write a list of projects in your life you have left incomplete or not done.

9. Write why this was.

10. Check this project carefully to make sure you have honestly done it all.

11. List your cognitions if any while doing this project.

12. Decide whether you have honestly done this project.

13. Hand all written papers including the scraps in the book over to your Esto or senior with a proper despatch on top Dummy Project No. 1 Completion.

END OF PROJECT

DUMMY PROJECT 2

PURPOSE: To learn about production.

MAJOR TARGET: To actually produce something.

PRIMARY TARGETS:

1. Get a pencil and five sheets of paper.

2. Situate yourself so you can do this project.

VITAL TARGETS:

1. Read an operating target and be sure to do it all before going on.

2. Actually produce what's called for.

OPERATING TARGETS:

1. Look very busy without actually doing anything.

2. Do it again but this time be very convincing.

3. Work out the valuable final product of your post. Get help from your Esto or senior as needed.

4. Straighten up the papers in your in-basket.

5. Take sheet 1 as per primary targets above. Write whether or not No. 4 was production.

6. Pick over your in-basket and find a paper or despatch that doesn't contribute in any way to your getting out your own product.

7. Answer it.

8. Take the second sheet called for in the primary target. Write on it why the action in 7 is perfectly reasonable.

9. Take the third sheet of paper and draw the correct comm lines of your post.

10. Get out one correct product for your post, complete of high quality.

11. Deliver it.

12. Review the operating targets and see which one made you feel best.

13. Take the fourth sheet of paper and write down whether or not production is the basis of morale.

14. Take the fifth sheet of paper, use it for a cover sheet and write a summary of the project.

15. Realize you have completed a project.

16. Deliver the whole project with papers to your Esto or senior.

END OF PROJECT

L. Ron Hubbard
FOUNDER

413

HCO POLICY LETTER OF 26 JUNE 1972

REMIMEO

ESTABLISHMENT OFFICER SERIES 20
SUPERVISOR TECH

Refs:

HCO PL	25 June 72	RECOVERING STUDENTS AND PCs
LRH ED 174 Int	29 Mar. 72	STUDY AND TECH BREAKTHROUGH
LRH ED 178 Int	30 May 72	SUPER–LITERACY

It should be very plain to an Esto that if the materials of Dianetics and Scientology are not available and not taught, all his work will be in vain.

The TRAINING and HATTING of Course Supervisors is not a product officer function. It belongs to HCO Dept 1 or the E Esto or his TEO.

A failure on course supervision (and Cramming Officer functions) will throw out the whole tech delivery of an org *and* staff and defeat everything an Esto is trying to do.

Public and staff courses are both of vital importance. After these come auditing. But where training fails, auditing won't occur as the auditors won't be able to audit.

Further, an Esto often trains and he should have these points down as well. And he should get them in on Supers NO MATTER WHAT DIVISION HE IS ESTOing.

If he doesn't, a training breakdown will defeat all his best laid plans. Bad Supers? So who gets trained?

MATERIALS

First and foremost is *materials*. If you don't have these on the course for that course, what course?

Always check the available materials and then move mountains to get them remedied where out or missing or too few.

SCHEDULES

Next is schedules.

These must be real and KEPT BY THE SUPER AS WELL.

PRESENCE

Next is the existence or presence of the Super.

There may be none, he may be there part time, he may be there but doing something else.

Get the Super on the course supervising the course, not doing admin or folders. (With a course co-auditing, the D of T whose job it is, dumps it on the Super or fails to get a C/S and then there's no Super.)

So get a Super supervising the course properly as his hat and duty.

SUPER ASSISTANCE

Two extremes can happen in course supervision:

1. *No* attention to the student.

2. Bothering the student and stopping his progress.

The point one has to grasp is "OBNOSIS." This is a coined (invented) word meaning OBSERVING THE OBVIOUS. There is no English or any other language precise equivalent for it.

Man just does not seem to observe the obvious. The reason for it is misunderstood words. Not understanding the symbol (word) the actual thing can become somewhat less visible.

The real job of the Course Supervisor is to get the puzzled or doping or bogged student going. And to *protect* the student who is flying from interference, including the Super's own.

To do this the Course Supervisor has to *observe the obvious.*

Is the student going okay?

Is the student bogged?

What *is* an F/Ning student? Is he chortling and gurgling and slapping his knee? No. He is just calmly going right along.

What *is* a bogged student? Is he stretched out on the floor snoring? No, he is groggy or puzzled or frowning or even emotionally upset by his Mis-U words. When not caught and handled he will go to sleep or just stare into space.

Should a student's fingers be wiggling? No, he should do demos fully and with full attention only when he has something to demo in order to grasp it. Should two students be chattering about a date they had? No. They are not F/Ning *students* even if they are F/Ning gossipers.

When the Super does not know the key words of his post, his power of observation is low. To remedy this one does Word Clearing Method 6 on him (HCOB 21 June 72 II, Word Clearing Series 39, METHOD 6).

And one gets him to look.

To keep from looking a Super can develop systems like, "Every 36 minutes I'll check up on every class member for it takes just 36 minutes to go around them all."

When an F/Ning student is interrupted by the Super he can be given a "withhold of nothingness." The student may say, "No, I've just been checked up" and the Super goes away. But the student now wonders, "Am I trying to hide something?" "Am I really doing all right?" Etc. A W/H of nothingness.

To keep students from blowing, BOTH these points have to be looked into.

OBNOSIS is the drill required on the Super.

And a Method 6 on the key words of his post.

And Product Clearing and his own study Why.

Study tech does work but must be applied!

A Supervisor must be a Super-Literate to be of real use.

Apply LRH ED 174 Int of 29 Mar. 72 and LRH ED 178 Int of 30 May 72.

BLOWN STUDENTS

See HCO PL of 25 June 72 RECOVERING STUDENTS AND PCs for check items of how to get students back on course.

SUMMARY

An Esto backed up by good courses and course supervision will eventually bring it all straight.

L. RON HUBBARD
FOUNDER

HCO POLICY LETTER OF 28 JUNE 1972

Remimeo

Establishment Officer Series 21
FILES ACCURACY

As files are the vital operational line it is of the GREATEST IMPORTANCE that *ALL FILING IS ACCURATE.*

A misfiled particle can be lost forever.

A missing item can throw out a whole evaluation or a sale.

Items get misfiled for four reasons:

1. Ignorance of the alphabet

2. Ignorance of geography

3. Ignorance of the vital role of the files

4. Personal out-ethics

The remedies therefore are:

1. ALL FILES PERSONNEL (a) MUST BE ABLE TO RATTLE OFF THE ALPHABET FORWARDS AND *BACKWARDS*. (b) They must be drilled then to be able to give the letter ahead of and behind each letter in the alphabet.

2. GEOGRAPHY must be known to files personnel, particularly the locations of orgs, cities, states and continents. This is done by drilling them on a map that has key locations related to files.

3. Method 6 W/Cing should be done on words connected with the post and action of filing. Then the value and purpose of the files they handle should be done by them.

4. Persons with out-ethics or on an ethics cycle should not be given filing as an amends as they are not drilled and are out of PT to say the least.

ETHICS ACTION

Anyone finding a misfiled particle should report it to the Ethics Officer or Master-at-Arms.

He must then quickly make every effort to locate who is misfiling and take rapid action.

The first action is to hat them as above.

Any repeat is an ethics offense handled by a Court.

If the E/O cannot find the person or does not act he himself must comb all files and straighten up the particles.

SUMMARY

It is of vital interest both in ease of work and financially that all files are straight.

L. RON HUBBARD
FOUNDER

HCO POLICY LETTER OF 14 JULY 1972

EXECUTIVE SERIES 14
ORG SERIES 30
ESTABLISHMENT OFFICER SERIES 22

ESTO FAILURES

For several months I have been studying the Esto system in operation and have finally isolated the exact points of any failures so they can be turned to successes.

PUTTING IN THE SYSTEM

An Esto returning to an org can crash it.

The exact reasons for this are:

A. The execs who heretofore did organizational work say, "Ah, here's the Esto system at last," and promptly drop their organizational and personnel actions.

Yet here is this lone E Esto, no divisional Estos, no one trained to support him.

The right answer is when an E Esto goes into an org where there are no Estos or only a TEO or QEO, he must gather up the execs and tell them it will take him weeks to recruit and train Estos and that THEY MUST CONTINUE ANY ORGANIZATIONAL ACTIONS THEY ARE DOING and that the HAS IS STILL ESTABLISHING THE ORG.

Otherwise they let go their lines.

B. The new E Esto takes key production personnel from the divisions to be Estos and they crash.

The answer to this is to RECRUIT the new Estos.

This is easier than it looks if you recruit idle area *auditors* to be Estos.

If you do this, remember that they went idle as auditors because they had out-ethics, were PTS, had misunderstoods and out-TR 0. To get them you do a 3 May 72 (ETHICS AND EXECUTIVES) PL, a 5 Apr. 72 (PTS TYPE A HANDLING) PL, Method 4 on their courses and make them do *real* TRs, especially zero. And they'll be ready.

You get a list of area auditors and contact them and do the above on them and you'll have Estos who are half-trained already.

Failing this or in addition to it just plain recruit.

C. The first post a new E Esto should take is Dept 1.

He does NOT "hat the HAS" or "just do programs." He rolls up his sleeves and WORKS as director of Dept 1.

He recruits, he posts up Dept 1. He hats the hell out of Dept 1.

He makes a Department 1 that really, really flows in personnel, puts up org boards and hats.

WHEN he has a Department 1 FUNCTIONING he can begin to recruit Estos as well as other org staff.

If he can't get a Dept 1 whizzing he has no business being an Esto, does he?

He does NOT put in Dept 2 or act as Dept 3. He makes the HAS handle these.

With a *strong, working* Dept 1, an Esto system can then go in.

D. Musical chairs is the commonest reason any org collapses.

A "new broom sweeps clean" complex will wreck any org.

An E Esto on arrival, taking over Dept 1, FREEZES ALL PERSONNEL TRANSFERS. He does not permit even one transfer.

The only exception would be where a musical chair insanity has just occurred. If this was followed by a stat crash then one REVERTS THE ORG TO THE UPSTAT PERIOD and *then* FREEZES PERSONNEL TRANSFERS.

But before one reverts one must evaluate the earlier period by stats to be sure it WAS the upstat period.

By freezing personnel one protects what he is building.

Almost all musical chairing is the work of a suppressive except when it is the work of an idiot.

E. Anyone trying to hold Dept 1 in a personnel starved org is holding a hot seat as any HAS or Personnel Director can tell you.

Body traffic to this dept in any medium-sized org defies belief.

It looks like Grand Central Station at the rush hour.

"I have to have _____," "Where is my Course Super _____?" etc., etc., etc., is the constant chant.

You can spend the whole day interviewing staff execs and get nothing done.

There is a right way to do all these things and a billion wrong ways.

Obviously the answer to all their problems is to get and train new people. Yet how can one in all the commotion?

Ninety percent of these requests are from people who are not hatting and using the people they already have.

The right way is on any new personnel demanded one gets Dept 3 to do an Inspection and Report Form for people in the area of the exec doing the demanding. You will find very often unhatted, untrained and wasted personnel and many outnesses.

You hold the line on personnel by saying: "Handle these unutilized or half-working staff or these outnesses. You are here on my procurement board as entitled to the (give priority, 3rd, 8th) person we hire or recruit."

And get industrious in recruiting, using all standard actions, for that is the only way things can be solved.

Most orgs would run better on less people because the personnel are not hatted or trained. One org, two years before this writing, made *four* times as much money on *half* the personnel it now has.

Unhatted, the staff is slow and uncertain. Unproducing, the div heads demand little.

But they sure can scream for more personnel!

No org ever believes it is overmanned.

F. Some divisions (like the usual Treasury or Dissem) can be undermanned. Key income posts most often are empty.

When one mans up an org one sets priorities of who gets personnel.

This is done by PRODUCTION paralleling. One mans up against production.

New people come in through Div 6. They are signed up by Div 2. Delivery is done by Div 4. Money is collected by Div 3. That gives you a sequence of manning up.

You man income and delivery posts with new hirings.

The E Esto is trying to get in a Dept 1 so of course he gives this a priority as well.

Until the income is really rolling in and the delivery rolling out, one does very little about other areas.

Having gained VOLUME, one now begins to man up for quality. This means a Cramming and a W/C Section in Qual. It means more HCO.

One now hits for future quantity by getting auditors in training, more upper execs in training.

When the org is so built and running and viable it is time the whole Esto system got manned up.

G. Every 5th person hired on an average should be put in Dept 1 as a *Dept 1* extra personnel who does Dept 1 duties and trains part time as an Esto.

This gives the E Esto additional personnel in Dept 1.

It also begins an Esto right.

His most essential duties as an Esto *are* Dept 1 type duties.

You eventually have a bulging Dept 1. You have a basic Dept 1 that functions well and will continue so. You have the Esto trainees who are working in Dept 1 as Dept 1 personnel. And you have of course some new people who are HCO Expeditors until they get in enough basics for real regular posting.

This makes a fat Dept 1 and proves one can Esto!

SUCCESS

If an E Esto introduces the Esto system exactly as above and in no other way, he will be a success.

Like an auditor varying processes or altering HCOBs, a new E Esto who varies the above will bring about disaster.

Where E Estos have gone into orgs other ways or where the system has been varied, stats have crashed.

By going in this way, as above, it can be a wild success.

How fast can you put in an Esto system? It takes months of hard work. It depends really on how good the E Esto is at recruiting, org boarding and hatting.

If he's good at these things the time does not stretch out to forever.

For comparison, it took half a year each to build DC, Johannesburg and SH to their highest peaks. They were all built from a Dept 1 viewpoint of recruiting, org boarding and hatting hard enough to get production.

So this is the oldest pattern we have — Dept 1 evolves the org.

When the org gets too big Dept 1 loses touch. You extend it into each div and you have the Esto system. And you have Estos.

L. RON HUBBARD
FOUNDER

HCO POLICY LETTER OF 23 JULY 1972RB
REVISED 11 JANUARY 1991

REMIMEO

EXECUTIVE SERIES 15
PERSONNEL SERIES 26
ORG SERIES 31
ESTABLISHMENT OFFICER SERIES 23

THE VITAL NECESSITY OF HATTING

On a graph analysis of past stats, my campaign on hatting where a hat was a checksheet and pack apparently introduced a steady rise of the International Gross Income.

Studying this further I discovered a new basic, simple fact:

HATTING = CONTROL

A person who is hatted can control his post.

If he can control his post he can hold his position in space — in short, his location. And this is power.

When a person is uncertain, he cannot control his post, he cannot control his position. He feels weak. He goes slow.

If he can control his post and its actions he feels confident. He can work effectively and rapidly.

The key is CONTROL.

Control is the ability to START, CHANGE and STOP.

When he is hatted he knows the tech of HANDLING things. Thus he can control them. He is at CAUSE over his area.

If you have an org composed only of weak wobbly posts, they tend to collapse in on each other. There is no POWER.

The org then cannot be CAUSE over its environment because it is composed of parts which are not cause. The whole is only the sum of its parts.

If all the parts are each one at cause, then the whole will be at CAUSE over its environment.

Only an org at CAUSE can reach and CONTROL.

Thus a fully hatted org can be at cause over its environment, can reach and control its fates and fortunes.

THUS THE PRIMARY TARGETS OF AN ESTO ARE:

A. ESTABLISHED ORG FORM and

B. FULLY HATTED PERSONNEL.

BASIC SEQUENCE OF HATTING

1. Recruited or hired. Signs contract.

2. Instant-hatted for the job assigned as an HCO Expeditor.

3. Staff Status 0.

4. Basic Study Manual (if the staff member has not previously done the Student Hat or Primary Rundown).

5. Staff Status I.

6. Staff Status II.

7. Posting as other than an HCO Expeditor.

8. Full hatting with a checksheet and pack fully done with M6, M7, M9, M3 and M4 Word Clearing.

9. Eligibility for study and auditing (OR for staff service or study).

10. Must have a stat and demonstrated he has produced on post.

11. Purification Rundown.

12. Objective Processes: CCHs, 8-C, SCS, Havingness, etc.

13. Scientology Drug Rundown (if required).

14. Method One Word Clearing, Student Hat.

15. Administrative or tech training (OEC or auditing).

Flag Orders in the Sea Org may change this lineup slightly but it is basically the same.

No one should have any other training, much less full-time training, before step 12 in the above.

After a staff member has completed Staff Status 0 he may receive PTS handlings and study the PTS checksheet and may have emergency assists. He may also be audited by students and TTC if he has rising stats.

There are time limits placed on how long it takes to do SS I and SS II. A person who can't make it is routed to Qual where he is offloaded with advice on how to get more employable. (In the SO it is Fitness Board.)

TIME–TESTED

The above is the route that has been tested by time and found good.

Other approaches have NOT worked.

Granting full-time training at once is folly. The person may get trained but he'll never be a staff member. This is the biggest failure with auditors — they don't know the org. Admin training with no org experience to relate it to is a waste of time.

This was how we built every great org. And when it dropped out the org became far less powerful.

Old-timers talk of these great orgs in their great days. And they will tell you all about the org boarding and hatting that went on. How the Hatting Officer in HCO and the Staff Training Officer in Qual worked as a team. And how fast the lines flew.

The above steps have stood the test of time and are proven by stats.

RECRUITING AND HIRING

You *never* recruit with a promise of free courses or free auditing. Not even HASes or HQSes. You recruit or hire somebody to be part of the team.

OPEN GATE

If *any* opinion or selection is permitted as to who is going to be let on staff, *all* recruitment and hiring will fail.

By actual stats when you let *anyone* say, "No! Not him! Not her!" the gate shuts, the flow stops. And you've had it.

Requirements and eligibility *fail*. The proof is that when they have existed in orgs, the org wound up with only PTSes and no-case-gains!

The right answer is FAST FLOW hiring. Then you have so many that those who can't make it drift low on the org board or off. You aren't trying to hold posts with unqualified people "who can't be spared."

In a short-staffed org "looking only for the best people" the guy nobody will have gets put in an empty "unimportant" department. He's now a Director!

It only happened because you didn't have dozens.

The answer is NOT lock the gate or have requirements. The answer is HAT.

An org that isn't hatted goes weak and criminal.

Don't be selective in hiring or recruiting. Open the gates and *HAT!*

Follow the steps given above and you have it.

Don't spend coins like training or auditing (or travel) on people until they have proven their worth. No bonuses or high pay for anyone until they have reached and attained step 10 (a good stat). The cost of such fast flow hiring is not then a big factor.

The only trouble I ever had with this was getting div heads to UTILIZE their staff. A FIRST JOB FOR AN EXECUTIVE IS TO GET THINGS FOR HIS PEOPLE TO DO. AND KEEP THEM BUSY AT PRODUCTIVE THINGS.

So I used to have to go through the org that did FAST FLOW HIRING regularly and get people to use their new people. And to move off those who could not work.

This was ALL the trouble I had with the system.

And until I enforced FAST FLOW HIRING there was always some effort by someone to close the gate.

ALL the great executives in Scientology came up in such orgs.

With a *flow* of people the best move on up. The worst, if any, drop off.

Only orgs with restricted hiring or recruiting give trouble.

IN A FAST FLOW HIRING ORG THE HAS AND ESTOs *MUST* BE ON THE BALL. THE BREAKDOWN OCCURS WHEN THEY DO NOT *HAT* AND KEEP ON TOP OF THE PERSONNEL SCENE.

Fast flow hiring only breaks down and gets protested where HCO and Estos are not doing a top job. They have to really *handle* the personnel, post them, hat them, keep the form of the org.

A fully formed org in a heavily populated location would need hundreds of staff. It would make hundreds of thousands.

But only if it is fast flow hiring, hatting, holding the form of the org, and only then could it produce.

L. RON HUBBARD
FOUNDER

Revision assisted by
LRH Technical Research
and Compilations

HCO POLICY LETTER OF 25 JULY 1972

REMIMEO

ESTABLISHMENT OFFICER SERIES 24

THE FORM OF THE ORG

You often hear that one should "hold the form of the org."

What is it?

Some people think it is making sure the command channel (junior to senior to senior's senior or on down). This is only a small part of an org form.

In any new group of a few people, each and every one wears all the hats. This is *not* an org form.

An org form is *that arrangement of specialized terminals which control and change the production and organization particles and flow lines of an activity.*

A *terminal* for this purpose is something that has mass and meaning which originates, receives, relays and changes particles on a flow line.

SPACE

To have any form at all, an org must have *space*.

The space must be located where it can have particles and flows or where the particles and flows with which it deals can easily be gotten to it and sent out from it and where it can conduct its activity without undue disturbance and at a velocity and volume with exchange that makes it viable.

There are a number of factors involved as noted in the above requirement: located, can have particles and flows, can get them in and out, no undue disturbance, velocity and volume, exchange and viability.

Although this looks complex, it is actually very simple as it involves *just those elements* and others are relatively unimportant. When you add aesthetics of building and grounds, and carpets and desks you can get too far off the definition of space requirement when these are given first priority. These are something you build up to. Clean and neat are closer to importance *after* the basic definition is met.

So one has a space. It has to be big enough for the traffic volume it has to handle to be viable. This is usually smaller than people think. The space is a building or other structure.

So we have a *space* as an essential of org form.

Potential Traffic Inflow

Departing Traffic

TRAFFIC GUIDE

Traffic, particles, flows have to be *guided.* They have to be pulled in (as per Div 6, Div 2 Reg, Div 2 Letter Reg, ASR, D of Tech Services, etc.). These are *reaches* out into the potential traffic that pulls it up to the space entrance point. In essence these posts work on the potential traffic and get it up to the door. So org form can start way out with a *general* approach, a magazine book ad, word of mouth, PR, an FSM, a ticket distributor, a book, etc. A specialized approach to specific names as per the Tour, the Letter Reg working CF, the Phone Reg, etc. One generally directs the whole "general public" toward the space and also specifically directs specific people in it toward the space.

This is the org form at work that functions outside the org space. If it doesn't function the org space itself gets no inflow.

Departing traffic must also be guided — and is too often neglected. An org without its CF up-to-date and used is neglecting its departing traffic.

England, for instance, loses a huge percent of its car sales business because it has no decent spare parts stockpiles (government taxes spare parts on the shelf). The customer who purchases often gets no follow-through.

Orgs that neglect departed traffic wind up with ARC broken fields.

So org form *must* include its own space *and* the spaces of its potential traffic and its departed traffic as they relate to the org's activity.

ROUTING

When particles arrive at the org space proper they must be routed AND MUST CONTINUE TO BE ROUTED FROM THE MOMENT THEY ENTER UNTIL THEY LEAVE THE ORG SPACE.

Thus there must be a Reception for bodies, for mail, for phone, for telexes and for messages in general.

There must also be an exit point for all these things and someone to send them on their way *out* of the org space.

Lack of a Reception that can and does route can break an org of any type or kind and has done so.

When bodies can't contact the org they assume the org is dead. And so it dies. The org can be so mislocated for its type of traffic that it can't get anyone in or out. Then, too, the org will seem dead.

No matter the INTERNAL form of the org, its external form can be so remote that success is impossible to maintain. Thus org form does not begin with reception and routing. This is an action that occurs after the external requirements are met.

But once the particle (body, despatch, raw materials, whatever) is at the door RECEPTION must establish the routing.

This is done usually with an each-step-signed-off ROUTING FORM that gives the full road map of the particle.

Without this, particles don't enter, jam up, get lost, go astray and DESTROY THE INTERNAL ORG FORM by making confusions.

Thus Reception has to have a very good idea of particle *types* and *org form* even to be able to issue the right routing form.

INTERNAL LINES

Routing forms often carry a particle into the org but not out.

This becomes a serious problem in getting anything *completed*. The start is on the form and not the exit. Thus the particle doesn't exit but piles up someplace.

When you see a mass of paper (in-baskets, pending, etc.) or a jam of bodies (Reg waiting room, DTS, etc.) or piles of unused pamphlets or unsold books you know two things at once:

A. Routing is unknown or not done or incomplete but in any event is faulty.

B. The internal org form is bad.

TERMINALS

To say internal lines are out, one must also be saying internal terminals are faulty.

Ideally, the internal org form is designed for flows with the target of production.

The internal space has to be so allotted and arranged that the lines flow.

The lines flow to terminals in the sequence of change required in each particle.

The principal particle, meaning the most important one for that org has the total priority for design of space and terminals.

If wheat were being processed, then the whole space and terminal allocation of the plant or org, to have *org form* would have to deal with *wheat*.

In a Scientology org it is public bodies. Thus the whole design of space and flows must deal with public bodies.

This is easily violated and when it is it makes a terrible confusion.

You have to trace such a flow with what is called a DUMMY RUN. This means going through the place pretending to be the principal particle.

When you first try this in most plants or orgs you really begin to wonder how *anything* happens ever.

The answer is correction of location, either of the whole space or the terminals in the space.

One can dummy run as anything. First dummy run the principal particle and lay that out by what has to be done to adjust the space and terminals to it. Then as a telex, then a despatch, then as a piece of money, then as an invoice, etc.

When you've done all these you'll really know what you're doing in terms of space and terminals. Until then it's all guesswork.

You will find you can't get in, you can't get handled, you can't stay in and you can't get out!

So you adjust space and terminals for the main particle and then for the lesser particles.

You will achieve a near optimum compromise.

Then you arrange it and drill it in on the terminals.

After that things will speed up and stats will go up.

HOLDING THE FORM

You now and only now have the FORM OF THE ORG.

It must be drawn up as org boards and flow plans and terminal location plans (three quite separate things). These three plans give you the form of the org.

Then you have to drill in EACH OF THE THREE PLANS usually with Chinese school.

You do the routing forms.

Now by HATTING you give each terminal control over his portion of the line.

The terminals will thereafter interact to bring about the needful flows.

And if your product is good and desired, the place will boom.

And that's what's really meant by the FORM OF THE ORG.

L. RON HUBBARD
FOUNDER

HCO POLICY LETTER OF 27 JULY 1972

REMIMEO

ESTABLISHMENT OFFICER SERIES 25
FORM OF THE ORG
AND SCHEDULES

Those parts of the org engaged upon similar functions must be on the same schedule.

In essence, you can't play a ballgame with different members of the team appearing at different times. It would look pretty silly to have a goalkeeper show up in the last third of the game. By that time it would be lost.

If over a 24-hour period people on public lines showed up, each one, at different hours, there would be no public line. Thus there would be no org form. For there could be no flow of the major particle.

If an activity is open for business at 0900, let us say, the persons on key posts would have to be there at 0830 or at least 0845 in order to "open for business" (which means open for flow) at 0900.

Precision of schedule is determined by the *type* of particle the org form is set up to handle.

A service org handles bodies. A management org handles messages as the principal flow particle. A refinery would handle crude oil. A flour mill wheat, etc.

Of all particle types bodies tend to be the most random and are most likely to erode or knock out org form.

Thus a service org handling bodies has to be established and hatted about a dozen times more than one which handles inert particles.

This is one of the reasons "standard business practices" do not work in setting up an org. They are not strong enough or fast enough.

Schedules become very important in orgs which handle bodies. The lines rapidly jam up and make considerable confusion wherever the line goes faulty.

As almost every part of an org requires internal cooperation from almost every other part of an org, lack of schedules, unreal schedules or failure to keep a schedule are, after hatting and line establishing, the most likely causes of confusion or nondelivery.

It is important to start as a team and it is also important to stop as one if there is a "next shift" as in a Foundation. As the staffs collide, the students collide and the space tangles.

Operating a number of schedules at the same time for different parts of the org can get complicated. Governments do this to ease off automobile and commuter traffic but then they (governments) do not produce much and it doesn't matter. Half a dozen daily schedules running at the same time for one org can cause a considerable confusion.

The best schedules are very simple ones. You can have a schedule that has so many times in it, so many musters, that it is a full day's work just to keep the schedule!

A grave fault in schedules is not allowing any slack between two time points. Example: Class ends 1600. Next class, three blocks away, begins at 1600! Either one class has to let out early or everyone is late to the next class!

Schedules commonly omit any time spaces to take care of things. Example: 0900 on post. 0900 public lines open. Well, it's going to take 15 minutes or more to get a post set up, so the schedule gets violated. Thus we have it saying 0900 when it can only be 0915! This makes schedules look unreal to people, so they drop out. A correct version would be 0840 on post. 0850 open for business checklist collected. 0900 public lines open.

CLOSING LINES

Closing of lines costs a great deal. An extreme example is closing an org for 2 weeks "so everyone can have a vacation." African orgs used to do this and would often lose their higher stats for months.

Closing orgs "during a congress" can cost. During one national congress, several missions closed for a week and had to fight crashed stats for months.

Closing an org at noon or for supper can ball up lines and can have a heavy effect on stats.

All this "closing" is simply saying "we're dead."

Lines have a tendency to keep flowing when flowing and remain stopped when they are stopped.

If an org began at 0900 and, with a Foundation or second and weekend shifts, ran continuously until 2300 seven days their general stats would improve out of proportion to the additional time open.

Management orgs run very raggedly on schedules as their traffic loads vary so greatly.

It takes good observation and skill to write a good schedule for an org. If an unreal schedule exists or if one is too complex, it will not be kept. Peak loads have to be taken into account and their approximate times have to be established. There are also no-load times and to cover these with a full org is to fail to have an adequate org there for the peak loads.

Careful, real study, on the ground, watching traffic flows, has to be done to make a real schedule that will be kept and which boosts production.

A schedule which does not boost production or a schedule just to have one, are a waste of everyone's time.

So select the principal particle the org handles. Use it to determine the times of peaks and no-loads, study what goes on in actual fact. And then write the schedule. And see that it is kept.

This will greatly improve org form.

L. RON HUBBARD
FOUNDER

HCO POLICY LETTER OF 28 JULY 1972

REMIMEO

EXECUTIVE SERIES 16
ORG SERIES 32
ESTABLISHMENT OFFICER SERIES 26
ESTABLISHING
HOLDING THE FORM OF THE ORG

If a person who could not play a piano sat down at a piano and hit random keys, he would not get any harmony. He would get noise.

If the head of a division gave orders to his staff without any regard to their assigned posts or duties, the result would be confusion and noise.

That's why we say a division head "doesn't know how to play the piano" when he knows so little about org form that he continually violates it by giving his various staff members duties that do not match their hats or posts.

But even if one could play the piano, one would have to have a piano to play.

SPECIALISTS

Each org staff member is a specialist in one or more similar functions. These are his specialties.

If he is fully trained to do these he is said to be HATTED.

The combined specialties properly placed and being done add up to the full production of an org.

The org form is then the lines and actions and spaces and flows worked out and controlled by specialists in each individual function.

These specialists are grouped in departments which have certain actions in common.

The departments having similar functions are grouped into divisions.

The divisions combine into the whole org form.

It is *far* less complex than it looks. It would be very complicated and confusing if there weren't divisions and departments and specialized actions. Without these you would get noise and very limited production and income, and at great strain.

Take a theater as an example. There are people who advertise it; these are the public relations people; they are hatted to get publicity and make people want to come to the play; call them the PR Division. There are the producers and directors; they are hatted to present a performance and make it occur; call them the Production Division. There are the actors and musicians; call them the Artists Division. There are the property men; they are hatted to get costumes and items needed; call them the Property Division. There are the stagehands and electricians and curtain and set men; call them the Stage Division. There are the ticket sellers and money handlers and payroll and bills payers; they are hatted on money and selling; call them the Finance Division. There are the people who clean the theater and show people to seats and handle the crowds; call them the House Division. And there are the managers and playwrights and score writers and angels (financiers); call them loosely the Executive Division.

Now as long as they know their org board, have their flows plotted out, are hatted for their jobs and do a good job, even a half-good play can be viable.

But throw away the org board, skip the flows, don't hat them and even a brilliant script and marvelous music will play to an empty house and go broke.

Why? Because an org form is not held. Possibly an untrained unhatted producer will try to make the stagehands sell tickets, the actors write the music, the financiers show people to their seats. If he didn't know who the people were or what their hats were he might do just that.

And there would be noise and confusion even where there was no protest. People would get in one another's road. And the general presentation would look so ragged to the public they'd stay away in droves.

ESTO ACTION

Now what would an Esto (or an Executive Director) have to do with, let us say, an amateur, dilettante theatrical company that was about to bog.

Probably half the people had quit already. And even if there were people in the company they would probably need more.

The very first action would be to Esto Series 16 the top men to make money quick.

The first organizing action would be to kick open the hiring door. This would begin with getting out hiring PR and putting someone there to sign people up who came to be hired (not to test and audition and look at references, but just to sign people up).

The next action would be to do a flow plan of public bodies and money. So one sees where the org form reaches. Then a schedule.

Next action would be to do an org board. Not a 3-week job. (It takes me a couple hours to sketch one with a sign pen for posting.) AND GET IT POSTED.

One then takes the *head* of each of these divisions and *hats* him on what his division is supposed to do and tell him to *do* it. NOW.

You make and post the flow plan, org bd and terminal location plan where the whole company can see them.

Chinese drill on a flow plan to show them what they're doing and what has to be done.

Chinese drill on the org board including introducing each person named on it and getting it drilled, what he does and who he is.

You Chinese drill the terminal locations where each of these persons (and functions) is to be found.

You get agreement on schedules.

You now have a group that knows who specializes in what and what's expected of each.

You get the head of the whole company to work with and hat the heads of his divisions.

Now you get the heads of divisions to hat their own staffs while you help.

And you get them busy.

You then put the polishing touches on your own Dept 1 (personnel PR, personnel hiring, personnel placement, org bds, hat compilations, hat library and hatting, hatting, hatting).

And by hatting and insisting on each doing his specialized job and getting seniors to HOLD THE FORM OF THE ORG by ordering the right orders to the right specialists and targeting their production and MAGIC! This amateur theatrical company gets solvent and good enough to wind up on Broadway. It's gone professional!

You say, yes, but what about artistic quality? What about the tech of writing music and acting . . .

Hey, you overlooked the first action. You kicked the door open on hiring and you hatted and trained. And you let go those who couldn't get a stat.

Eventually you would meet human reaction and emotion and would put in a full HCO and a full Qual particularly Cramming. But you'd still do that just to be sure it kept going.

Yessir, it can't help but become a professional group IF you, the Esto, established and made them HOLD THE FORM OF THE ORG and produce while they did it.

An Executive Director can do all this and produce too. The great ones do things like this. But here it is in full view.

A Scientology org goes together just like that. Which could be why, when we want to get something started, we say:

"Get the show on the road!"

But there is no show until it is established and the FORM OF THE ORG is held.

You are luckier than the amateur theatrical company's Esto. You have policy for every post and a book of it for every division and all the tech besides.

So there is no valid reason under the sun you cannot establish and then hold the form of the org.

L. RON HUBBARD
FOUNDER

HCO POLICY LETTER OF 21 AUGUST 1972

REMIMEO
HATTING OFFICER
  HATS

ESTABLISHMENT OFFICER SERIES 27
EFFECTIVE HATTING

Here is a report from the Ship Programs Chief on Flag of the results obtained from following my orders on how to get Estos to hat people.

It should be noted that the procedure laid down by my despatch on the second half of this PL was exactly how I operated to develop the data used for Esto Series 16. (HCO PL 24 Apr. 72 I, HATTING THE PRODUCT OFFICER OF THE DIVISION)

THE REPORT

"Dear Sir,

"We have been having trouble getting Hatting Officers in Dept 1 to actually produce. They don't complete cycles of action to a result, they don't hat from the top down or hat for production. They don't seem to understand *why* they are hatting and what are the results they should achieve in hatting.

"This was the same problem we had back in May of this year in getting Estos to do effective hatting.

"At that time you sent me the attached despatch addressed to the Exec Esto. I used it faithfully and, with it, actually got hatting to occur.

"The results are still evident on the ship. With the DEO hatting per this despatch the then Dissem Division came right up in production and is still producing very well as the PR and Consumption Bureau.

"The Treasury Division improved markedly. Some improvement was attained in the Steward's Dept, Electronics and Qual Div where all Estos hatted per this despatch.

"All of these Estos had big wins hatting because I *used* the data on this despatch and forced them to persist with a hatting action to a RESULT.

"I kept a big logbook with each hatting cycle noted down. I insisted the Esto kept at *that* cycle until it was complete.

"Each division had its own program for hatting from the top down.

"Each exec and staff member had his or her own personal hatting program kept by the Esto. These were followed and checked off as they were done.

"A number of the blue-chip FSO crew now so valuable for Flag stability were *made* by heavy hatting last spring.

"I know the data on your despatch *works* if it is *done*.

"The Estos under me at the time first had to be *forced* to hat and to continue hatting to a *result*. Apparently their lack of confront had to be overcome by a hard driving senior.

"Generally, once they started getting results, they no longer had to be forced. They knew that Esto tech worked and willingly went ahead and applied it with vigor.

"Their confront was improved as well by doing Esto No. 16 drills on each other and running TRs 6–9 on each other every evening for at least an hour.

"Only by applying the principles laid out by you on the attached despatch was I able to get real hatting done by others.

"As we are having the same problem now with Hatting Officers in Dept 1, I feel that if this data were released as policy I could force it into use and get the ship hatted up faster."

GETTING HATTING DONE

Here is the despatch I wrote to the Exec Esto on Flag back in May of this year:

Inspections do not show Estos being industrious in their divs. They are more active than they were.

They are not hatting from the top down and not hatting to get production.

Basically they do not parallel the current push. They do little cycles down the org board.

A general grasp of what's needed and wanted is missing. Thus Estos are actually in or below Non-Existence and have not achieved upgrade from a new post or new system condition.

They are getting individual results in some cases. They are not integrated into the scene with what they are doing.

They would have to upgrade their handlings about 500 percent in order to actually effect a marked change in the org.

Inspections show only a small percent of Estos do Esto actions for a small period of time each day. They have other fish frying or are acting a bit confused.

If you had that many auditors and found them auditing pcs as seldom as Estos are found doing Esto actions the HGC stat would be nearly zero WDAH.

I know what I'm talking about here because I am piloting the system to find out why it isn't producing marked changes. I find that, with two messengers a watch of six hours, working myself part time on it, I have been able to get areas working. They were NOT producing under the attention of existing Estos.

The difference is, I force those I find not working at the top to actually produce and demand production from their staffs.

In doing this I have never crossed or found an Esto working on it. I *have* found two div heads who were refusing to be gotten going. Both of these I later got going.

Thus from my viewpoint:

a. It can be done with untrained Esto Commodore's Messengers.

b. I find messengers who know little of a meter can use one without coaching or training.

c. Production *can* be achieved by getting people to work.

d. That Estos have to be run and exactly ordered to do exactly so-and-so.

e. That in running Estos one has to keep track of what one is doing with them so one doesn't get a lot of half-dones. One has to make up for a lack of persistence.

Therefore I conclude:

A. One has to know what he is trying to build.

B. One has to target and direct its building.

C. One has to force in a persistence.

I also conclude that training of Estos is secondary to getting them to DO and that "lack of training" is an excuse not to do.

This is what I am learning about the system from actually working it.

The current on-board application of the system lacks planning, direction and persistence, does not hat from the top down and does not hat toward production. It MUST *BEGIN*.

L. RON HUBBARD
FOUNDER

HUBBARD COMMUNICATIONS OFFICE
SAINT HILL MANOR, EAST GRINSTEAD, SUSSEX

HCO POLICY LETTER OF 4 OCTOBER 1972RA
REVISED 29 DECEMBER 2000

REMIMEO

ESTABLISHMENT OFFICER SERIES 28
HANDLING PTS AND OUT–ETHICS PERSONNEL

An Esto must know and be able to apply HCO PL 5 Apr. 72RD, PTS TYPE A HANDLING; HCO PL 3 May 72RA, Exec Series 12, ETHICS AND EXECUTIVES and HCOB 20 Apr. 72 II, C/S Series 78, PRODUCT PURPOSE AND WHY AND W/C ERROR CORRECTION.

I recently found an org where Division 2 and Division 6 refusals and inactivities were ruining GI. The Why behind this was a downgrade of importance of both divisions and a confusion between them. The Ethics Why was that SPs and PTSes were running "can't haves" of Scientology on the org and public.

An Esto must be able to spot out-ethics and PTS/SP phenomena and effectively deal with it.

L. RON HUBBARD
FOUNDER

Revision assisted by
LRH Technical Research
and Compilations

HCO POLICY LETTER OF 15 OCTOBER 1973

REMIMEO

ADMIN KNOW-HOW SERIES 31
ESTABLISHMENT OFFICER SERIES 29

ADMINISTRATIVE SKILL

An administrator is one who can make things happen at the other end of a communication line which result in discovered data or handled situations.

A very good administrator can get things handled over a very long distance. A mediumly skilled administrator has a shorter reach.

As this scale declines, we get people who can make things happen only at arm's length.

It is interesting that administrators are valued in direct proportion to the distance they can reach and get things handled over. Persons who can handle things only at arm's length are valued but not in proportion to a long-reaching administrator.

The complexity of situations and things handled is also a test of the administrator. If one began at the highest level of capability of handling things thousands of miles away and at the bottom of the scale handling things at arm's length, one would also find complexity entering the picture.

The artisan can, by means of heavy MEST communication lines and tools, make all manner of things occur but mostly within his visual sight line.

The day laborer who can only handle a shovel usually can only handle the simplicity of lifting a few pounds of dirt to a definite position.

One of the troubles PTS people have, as an example, is handling something over a long-distance communication line. One can tell them to handle the suppressive, but one must realize he may also be giving the order to someone to handle another person several thousand miles away. This is a high level of administrative skill and is usually no part of a PTS's ability, whatever other technical considerations may intervene.

Estimating situations thousands of miles away and handling them terminatedly is actually comparable to an OT ability.

There is no effort here to include artists and technicians who do work with their hands, for this is another class of activity requiring enormous technical skill and ability.

However, very few people understand the administrator or what he is or what he can do, yet the whole world is the effect of good or bad administrators.

The administrator has technology with which to discover and handle situations and if he is a very good administrator his handling is ordinarily constructive; but whatever it is, it is firm.

A skilled administrator therefore can be defined as ONE WHO CAN ESTABLISH AND MAINTAIN COMMUNICATION LINES AND CAN THEREBY DISCOVER, HANDLE AND IMPROVE SITUATIONS AND CONDITIONS AT A DISTANCE.

When you fully grasp this and realize it is the basic simplicity that is the basic all of an administrator's further complex technology, you can estimate an administrator's efficiency or effectiveness.

If you are engaged in administration, this basic truth will serve you very well if you fully understand it and use it.

L. RON HUBBARD
FOUNDER

HCO POLICY LETTER OF 22 NOVEMBER 1973

REMIMEO

ESTO SERIES 30

All persons doing Esto work may only use the title "Esto I/T" (In-Training) until he has successfully and honestly completed:

1. HCOB 21 Nov. 73, THE CURE OF Q AND A.

2. The PRD (Primary Rundown).

3. The OEC.

4. The Esto Series.

5. Has shown on post the ability to see situations and handle them terminatedly.

6. Gets staff members actually producing by increased stats.

Any reasons for failure of the Esto system anywhere have derived from (a) a dishonest "completion" of the PRD and (b) Qing and Aing instead of seeing and handling situations terminatedly.

An Esto must be at CAUSE.

L. RON HUBBARD
FOUNDER

HCO POLICY LETTER OF 7 AUGUST 1976
ISSUE I

REMIMEO
ALL EXECS
ALL PURCHASERS

ADMIN KNOW-HOW SERIES 33
ESTABLISHMENT OFFICER SERIES 31
PRODUCT–ORG OFFICER SYSTEM
NAME YOUR PRODUCT

The product–org officer system, covered fully in Flag Executive Briefing Course tapes, contains the key phrase for any product officer. This is:

NAME, WANT AND GET YOUR PRODUCT.

Breaking this down into its parts we find that the most common failure of any product officer or staff member or Purchaser lies in the first item, NAME YOUR PRODUCT!

On org boards and even for sections, one has products listed. Departments have valuable final products. Every staff member has one or more products.

IF PRODUCTION IS NOT OCCURRING, THE ABILITY TO NAME THE PRODUCT IS PROBABLY MISSING.

Misunderstood post titles were collected once on a wide survey. Whenever it was found a staff member did not seem to be able to do his job, it was checked whether he knew the definition of the word — or words — that made up his post title. It was found, one for one, that he could not define it even though no unusual or special definition was being requested. In other words, the first thing about the post could not be defined — the post title. This may seem incredible, but only until you yourself check it out on staff that habitually goof.

The ability to NAME the product required goes further than a mere, glib definition. Some engineers once drove a Purchaser halfway up the wall by glibly requesting "one dozen bolts." The Purchaser kept bringing back all different thicknesses and lengths and types of bolts. The Purchaser was going daffy and so were the engineers. Until the engineers were forced to exactly name what they were seeking by giving it ALL its name. The Purchaser trying to purchase could not possibly obtain his product without being able to FULLY name it. Once this was done, nothing was easier.

A product officer can ask, beg, plead, yell for his product. But maybe he isn't naming it! Maybe he isn't naming it fully. And maybe even he doesn't know the name of it. A product officer should spend some time exactly and accurately naming the exact product he wants before asking for it. Otherwise he and his staff may be struggling around over many misunderstood words!

When you see a staff whirling around and dashing into walls and each other and not producing a thing, calmly try to find out if any of them or their product officer can NAME what products they are trying to produce. Chances are, few of them can and maybe the product officer as well.

Handle and it will all smooth out and products will occur.

L. RON HUBBARD
FOUNDER

HCO POLICY LETTER OF 7 AUGUST 1976
ISSUE II

REMIMEO
ALL EXECS
ALL PURCHASERS

ADMIN KNOW-HOW SERIES 34
ESTABLISHMENT OFFICER SERIES 32

PRODUCT–ORG OFFICER SYSTEM
WANT YOUR PRODUCT

A product officer has to name, WANT and get his product.

Where no real or valuable production is occurring, one has to ask the question, does the product officer really WANT the product he is demanding? And does the staff member or members he is dealing with WANT the product?

The reason that a psychotic or otherwise evilly intentioned person cannot achieve anything as a product officer or staff member is that he does NOT want the product to occur. The intentions of psychos are aimed at destruction and not at creation.

Such persons may SAY they want the product but this is just "PR" and a cover for their real activities.

People who are PTS (potential trouble sources by reason of connections with people antagonistic to what they are doing in life) are all too likely to slide into the valence of the antagonistic person who definitely would NOT want the product.

Thus, in an org run by or overloaded with destructive persons or PTS persons, you see a very low level of production if you see any at all. And the production is likely to be what is called "an overt product," meaning a bad one that will not be accepted or cannot be traded or exchanged and has more waste and liability connected with it than it has value.

One has to actually WANT the product he is asking for or is trying to produce. There may be many reasons he does not, none of which are necessarily connected with being psycho. But if it is a creative and valuable product and assists his and the survival of others and he still does not want it, then one should look for PTSness or maybe even a bit of psychosis. And at the least, some withholds.

One does not have to be in a passionate, mystic daze about wanting the product. But one shouldn't be moving mountains in the road of a guy trying to carry some lumber to the house site either.

The question of WANT the product has to be included in any examination of reasons why a person or an org isn't producing.

L. RON HUBBARD
FOUNDER

HCO POLICY LETTER OF 7 AUGUST 1976
ISSUE III

REMIMEO
ALL EXECS

ADMIN KNOW-HOW SERIES 35
ESTABLISHMENT OFFICER SERIES 33
PRODUCT–ORG OFFICER SYSTEM
TO GET YOU HAVE TO KNOW HOW TO ORGANIZE

A product officer and ESPECIALLY an org officer has to know how to GET a product.

All science and technology is built around this single point in the key phrase "Name, want and get your product." Managers and scientists specialize in the HOW TO GET part of it and very often neglect the rest.

There are many product officers who do NOT know enough about organization to organize things so they actually GET their product. These, all too often, cover up their ignorance on how to organize or their inability to do so by saying to one and all, "Don't organize, just produce!" When you hear this you can suspect that the person saying it actually does not know the tech or know-how of organizing or how to put an organization together. He may not even know enough about organizing to shove aside other paper on his desk when he is trying to spread out and read a large chart — yet that is simple organization.

A bricklayer would look awfully silly trying to lay no-bricks. He hasn't got any bricks. Yet there he is going through the motions of laying bricks. It takes a certain economic and purchasing and transport tech to get the bricks delivered — only then can you lay bricks.

A manager looks pretty silly trying to order a brick wall built when he doesn't have any bricks or bricklayer and provides no means at all of obtaining either one.

A product officer may be great at single-handing the show. How come? He doesn't realize that building a show comes before one runs it. And even though economics demand at least a small show before one builds a large show, a very bad product officer who can't really organize either, will, instead of making the small show bigger, make the small show smaller by trying to run a no-show.

There is a HOW of organization. It is covered pretty well in the Org Series and elsewhere. Like you can't put in comm lines unless you put in terminals for them to connect with. Like you can't get particles flowing in a profitable way unless they have something for them to run *on*. That's simply the way things go in the universe in which you are operating. Now of course you could build a new universe with different laws but the fact is, that would require a knowledge of organization as well, wouldn't it?

The tech of how to produce something can be pretty vast. One doesn't have to be a total expert on it to be able to manage the people doing it, but one has to have a pretty good idea of how it goes and know enough NOT to stop the guys who do know how to make bricks when one wants bricks.

If the product is to get somebody to come in to see you, then you have to have some means of communication and some tech of persuasion to make him want to come in to see you. Brute force may seem okay to cops but in organization it seldom works. There is more tech to it than that.

If a product officer does not know there is tech involved in GETTING the product, then he will never make his staff study it or teach anybody to do it. And he will wind up with no product. So beware the product officer who won't give time off for hatting! He doesn't know one has to know the tech of getting his product. What do you think the OEC (Org Exec Course) Volumes and the technical bulletins are all about?

One has to spend some time organizing in many different ways—the organization itself, the hatting, the technical skill staff members would have to have, to get anywhere in GETTING a product.

Sure, if you only organize and never produce you never get a product either. But if you only produce and never organize, the only brick wall you'll ever see is the one you run into.

L. RON HUBBARD
FOUNDER

HCO POLICY LETTER OF 22 OCTOBER 1978R
REVISED 14 DECEMBER 2000

REMIMEO

ESTABLISHMENT OFFICER SERIES 34
MISTAKES

A new piece of Esto tech has come into view:

He who cannot be hatted will not learn by mistakes.

REPEATING MISTAKES

It isn't making mistakes that is actionable; it is failing to learn from them and repeating them.

We know in auditor training that we retread somebody who commits the same mistake twice but this is not true in any other area.

A failed student is apparently somebody who can't be hatted either and he is detected by somebody who makes the same mistake over and over and doesn't correct himself.

Thus it's possible to detect a failed student by somebody who makes the same mistake.

We are not unduly concerned with somebody who is unhatted. We are only concerned with people who cannot be hatted and these are easiest to detect by observing when they make the same mistakes without correcting themselves. This person is not only dangerous on lines but also frankly can't be utilized.

This could be classified as a new phenomenon, part of the cultural mess that has caught up with us.

For example, four people recently taken out of a Special Unit of a Filming Project not only couldn't apply tech standardly on which they were fully hatted but also couldn't learn from their mistakes. As a consequence their redone work contained the same mistakes that were originally made.

So this apparency of not being able to get anyplace with the unit was due to several people who could not learn by their mistakes as well as could not be hatted.

This is a new view of a failed student — it wasn't whether they studied, it was just that they couldn't be hatted and kept repeating the same mistakes, even some new ones, and they couldn't learn about their equipment.

This also connects with disassociation phenomenon in that the person does not connect the mistake he just made with the last time he made that mistake or why or what effect it created or how and why to prevent it occurring again.

SUMMARY

Where you have someone who does not learn from his mistakes and cannot be hatted, it is better to replace the person rather than just hope.

L. RON HUBBARD
FOUNDER

Revision assisted by
LRH Technical Research
and Compilations

HUBBARD COMMUNICATIONS OFFICE
SAINT HILL MANOR, EAST GRINSTEAD, SUSSEX

HCO POLICY LETTER OF 26 MARCH 1979RB
REVISED 2 SEPTEMBER 1979

(Also issued as an HCOB, same date and title)

REMIMEO

ESTABLISHMENT OFFICER SERIES 35
PRODUCT DEBUG SERIES 7
WORD CLEARING SERIES 60
MISUNDERSTOOD WORDS AND CYCLES OF ACTION

MISUNDERSTOOD WORDS AND NO PRODUCT

A misunderstood word can prevent a person from understanding the remainder of what is heard or written.

I have now discovered that: A MISUNDERSTOOD on any given subject CAN PREVENT THE COMPLETION OF A CYCLE OF ACTION related to that subject.

Therefore, those people who don't complete cycles of action on certain subjects have a misunderstood word on them.

This then results in no-product situations.

Therefore, when you are getting no product, look for the misunderstood word on the subject no matter how long and arduous it is. It's there. And when it's found the person can go on and complete a cycle of action and get a product.

CAUTION: Make sure the person actually does have an inability to complete a cycle of action *before* you get into handling him. You don't handle somebody who *is* completing cycles of action that result in production.

MISUNDERSTOODS AND PERCEPTION

Misunderstoods can also act as perception shut-offs. They can actually interrupt a person's perception.

It is quite astonishing that perceptions such as sight, sound and even touch can be shut off by Mis-U words.

This opens the door to the fact that people apparently do not see, hear, notice or handle outnesses when they have Mis-Us on them.

This also may open the door to people who have perceptic shut-offs, such as poor eyesight, deafness or other perception difficulties.

MISUNDERSTOODS AND COMPLEXITY

Misunderstoods lead to complexity. People who have Mis-Us in an area are inclined to develop vast complexities. They can generate confusions and complexities beyond belief.

People do this because, having misunderstoods, they do not confront and duplicate in the area and so get into a lot of think-think and unnecessary significance. Their ability to get things done in that area dwindles as a result. And at the bottom of all this is simply misunderstood words.

MISUNDERSTOODS AND TOTAL ORGANIZE

When you see an area that is organizing only, you know that area is loaded with misunderstoods.

When people have incomplete cycles due to Mis-Us, they get bogged down into organization.

You can tell when people have Mis-Us — they are totally involved in organize, organize, organize. They don't know what they are doing.

There is a level below this — they have overts and withholds which prevent even organizing.

Below that level people are PTS.

Lacking a sense of organization actually lies below this. It is below the level of Mis-Us, overts and withholds and PTSness — and you'd have to go north through PTSness and overts and withholds to even get to the Mis-Us.

MISUNDERSTOODS AND NO ORGANIZE

There can also exist a condition where someone does not organize any corner of his area or work or organizations or lines. This manifests itself by irrational demands to only produce and to prevent any organization so that production can occur. At the bottom of this you are very likely to find misunderstood words, particularly on the purpose of the production or why one is producing. It is in this sector that you get overt products most frequently.

HANDLING

The exact procedure for handling these Mis-Us is given in HCOB 17 June 79, CRASHING MIS-Us: THE KEY TO COMPLETED CYCLES OF ACTION AND PRODUCTS. Crashing Mis-U Finding is done as part of HCO PL 23 Aug. 79 I, DEBUG TECH. Additional data on the location of Crashing Mis-Us is found in HCOB 23 Aug. 79 I, CRASHING MIS-Us, BLOCKS TO FINDING THEM and HCOB 16 July 79, THE "ELUSIVE" MIS-U OR CRASHING MIS-U.

With this knowledge we can now handle all the factors that prevent the completion of cycles of action and products.

L. RON HUBBARD
FOUNDER

HUBBARD COMMUNICATIONS OFFICE
SAINT HILL MANOR, EAST GRINSTEAD, SUSSEX

HCO POLICY LETTER OF 7 AUGUST 1979
(Also issued as an HCOB, same date and title)

REMIMEO
SUPS
TECH
QUAL
EXECS
ALL STAFF

ESTABLISHMENT OFFICER SERIES 36
PRODUCT DEBUG SERIES 8
FALSE DATA STRIPPING

Refs:

The Study Tapes

DAB Vol 1, Nos. 1–2	STANDARD PROCEDURE
	(Tech Vol I)
DAB Vol 1, No. 3	HOW TO RELEASE A CHRONIC SOMATIC
	(Tech Vol I)

Book: *Notes on the Lectures,* Chapters 7 and 13

When a person is not functioning well on his post, on his job or in life, at the bottom of his difficulties will often be found *unknown* basic definitions and laws or *false* definitions, false data and false laws, resulting in an inability to think with the words and rules of that activity and an inability to perform the simplest required functions. The person will remain unfamiliar with the fundamentals of his activity, at times appearing idiotic, because of these not-defined and falsely defined words.

Verbal hatting is the main source of false definitions and false data. Someone who "knows" tells someone else a definition or a datum. The person now thinks he knows the definition (even though nothing in the field makes any sense to him). The word may not even read on the meter during misunderstood checks because the person "thinks he knows."

A politician is told by an adviser, "It doesn't matter how much money the government spends. It is good for the society." The politician uses this "rule" and the next thing you know inflation is driving everybody to starvation and the government to bankruptcy. The politician, knowing he was told this on the very best authority, does not spot it as false data but continues to use it right up to the point where the angry mobs stand him up in front of a firing squad and shoot him down. And the pity of it is that the politician never once suspected that there was anything false about the data, even though he couldn't work with it.

There is no field in all the society where false data is not rampant. "Experts," "Advisers," "Friends," "Families" seldom go and look at the basic texts on subjects, even when these are known to exist, but indulge in all manner of interpretations and even outright lies to seem wise or expert. The cost in terms of lost production and damaged equipment is enormous. You will see it in all sectors of society. People cannot think with the fundamentals of their work. They goof. They ruin things. They have to redo what they have already done.

You'll find people whose estimate of the environment is totally perverted to the point they're walking around literally in a fog. The guy looks at a tree and the reality of the tree is blurred by the "fact" that "trees are made by God" so he won't take care of the tree because he is convinced.

What we're trying to cure in people is the inability to think with data. This was traced by me to false data as a phenomenon additional to misunderstood words, although the misunderstood word plays a role in it and will have to be allowed for.

When a person is having difficulty in an area or on a post, when he can't seem to apply what he has "learned" or what he is studying or when he can't get through a specific drill or exercise in his training materials, you would suspect he has false data in that area or on those materials. If he is to use it at all effectively he must first sort out the true facts regarding it from the conflicting bits and pieces of information or opinion he has acquired. This eliminates the false data and lets him get on with it.

INABILITY TO HAT

We are looking here at a brand-new discovery I have made which is that it can be nearly impossible to hat anyone who is sitting on false data on the subject you are trying to hat him on. This is the *primary* reason people cannot be hatted, and False Data Stripping, therefore, enables a person to be hatted even though other approaches have failed. This is a very valuable discovery — it solves the problem of inability to hat or train.

SOURCES

False data on a subject can come from any number of sources. In the process of day-to-day living people encounter and often accept without inspection all sorts of ideas which may seem to make sense but don't. Advertising, newspapers, TV and other media are packed with such material. The most profound false data can come out of texts such as Stanislavsky (a Russian actor and director); and even mothers have a hand in it, such as "children should be seen and not heard."

Where a subject, such as art, contains innumerable authorities and voluminous opinions, you may find that any and all textbooks under that heading reek with false data. Those who have studied study tech will recall that the validity of texts is an important factor in study. Therefore, it is important that any Supervisor or teacher seeking to use False Data Stripping must utilize basic *workable* texts. These are most often found to have been written by the original discoverer of the subject and, when in doubt, avoid texts which are interpretations of somebody else's work. In short, choose only textual material which is closest to the basic facts of the subject and avoid those which embroider upon them.

It can happen, if you do False Data Stripping well and expertly without enforcing your own data on the person, that he can find a *whole* textbook false — much to his amazement. In such a case, locate a more fundamental text on the subject. (Examples of false texts: Eastman Kodak; Lord Keynes' treatises on economics; John Dewey's texts on education; Sigmund Freud's texts on the mind; the texts derived from the "work" of Wundt [Leipzig 1879 — Father of Modern Psychology]; and [joke] a textbook on "Proper Conduct for Sheep" written by A. Wolf.)

USE OF FALSE DATA STRIPPING

False Data Stripping should be used extensively in all hatting and training activities. Current society is riddled with false data and these must be cleared away so that we can hat and train people. Then they will be able to learn useful data which will enable them to understand things and produce valuable products in life.

False Data Stripping can be done on or off the meter. It can be done by an auditor in session, by a Supervisor, Cramming Officer or Word Clearer or by an exec, Esto or any administrator. Students and staff can be trained to do it on each other.

Not a lot of training is required to deliver this procedure but anyone administering it must have checked out on this HCOB/PL and have demoed and drilled the procedure. If it is going to be done on the meter (which is preferable), the person doing it must have an okay to operate an E-Meter.

GRADIENTS

It will be found that false data actually comes off in gradients.

For example, a student handled initially on false data on a particular drill will appear to be complete on it. He goes on with his studies and makes progress for a while and then sometimes he will hit a bog or slow in his progress. This is usually an indication that more false data has been flushed up (restimulated or remembered as a result of actually doing studies or drills). At that point more basic false data will come off when asked for. The reason for this is when you first give a student false data handling, he doesn't know enough about the subject to know false data from the true. When he has learned a bit more about the subject he then collides with more false data hitherto buried. This can happen several times, as he is getting more and more expert on the subject.

Thus, the action of stripping off false data can and must be checked for and used in any training and hatting. The rundown has to be given again and again at later and later periods, as a student or staff member may come up against additional faulty data that has been not-ised. It can be repeated as often as necessary in any specific area of training until the person is finally duplicating and is able to use the correct tech and *only* the correct tech exactly.

THEORY

There is a philosophic background as to why getting off false data on a subject works and why trying to teach a correct datum *over* a false datum on the subject does not work. It is based on the Socratic thesis-antithesis-synthesis philosophical equation.

Socrates: 470 B.C.–399 B.C. A great Greek philosopher.

A *thesis* is a statement or assertion.

Antithesis: opposing statement or assertion.

The Socratic equation is mainly used in debate where one debater asserts one thing and the other debater asserts the opposite. It was the contention of Socrates and others that when two forces came into collision a new idea was born. This was the use of the equation in logic and debate. However, had they looked further they would have seen that other effects were brought into play. It has very disastrous effects when it appears in the field of training.

Where the person has acquired a *false* thesis (or datum), the *true* datum you are trying to teach him becomes an antithesis. The true datum comes smack up against the false datum he is hanging on to, as it is counter to it.

In other words, these two things collide, and *neither one* will then make sense to him. At this point he can try to make sense out of the collision and form what is called a synthesis, or his wits simply don't function. (*Synthesis:* a unified whole in which opposites, thesis and antithesis, are reconciled.)

So you wind up with the person either:

a. attempting to use a false, unworkable synthesis he has formed, or

b. his thinkingness locks up on the subject.

In either case you get an impossible-to-train, impossible-to-hat scene.

GLIBNESS

Probably we have here the basic anatomy of the "glib student" who can parrot off whole chapters on an examination paper and yet in practice uses his tools as a doorstop. This student has been a mystery to the world of education for eons. What he has probably done in order to get by is set up a circuit which is purely memory. The truth of it is his understanding or participation is barred off by considerations such as "nothing works anyway but one has to please the professor somehow."

The less a person can confront, the more false data he has accumulated and will accumulate. These syntheses are simply additives and complexities and make the person complicate the subject beyond belief. Or the collision of false data and true data, without the person knowing which is which, makes him look like a meathead.

Therefore, in order to cure him of his additives, complexities, apathy and apparent stupidity on a subject, in addition to cleaning up misunderstood words, it is necessary to strip the false data off the subject. Most of the time this is prior to the true data and so is basic on the chain. Where this is the case, when that basic false data is located and stripped the whole subject clears up more easily.

FALSE DATA PRONE

Some people are prone to accepting false data. This stems from overts committed prior to the false data being accepted. The false data then acts as a justifier for the overt.

An example of this would be a student studying past Mis-Us on a subject, cheating in the exam and eventually dropping the subject entirely. Then someone comes along and tells him that the subject is useless and destructive. Well, he will immediately grab hold of this datum and believe it as he needs something to justify his earlier overts.

This actually gets into service facsimiles as the person will use the false data to make the subject or other people wrong.

So if you see someone who is very prone to accepting false data on a particular subject or in general, the answer is to get the prior overts pulled. Then the person will not need to justify his overts by accepting any false data that comes his way.

PROCEDURE

You may not easily be able to detect a false datum because the person believes it to be true. When False Data Stripping is done on a meter the false datum won't necessarily read for the same reason.

You therefore ask the person if there is anything he has run across on the subject under discussion which he couldn't think with, which didn't seem to add up or seems to be in conflict with the material one is trying to teach him.

The false datum buries itself and the procedure itself handles this phenomenon.

When the false datum is located it is handled with elementary recall based on 1950 Straightwire. Straight memory technique or Straightwire (so called because one is stringing a line between present time and some incident in the past and stringing that line directly and without any detours) was developed originally in 1950 as a lighter process than engram running. Cleverly used, Straightwire removed locks and released illnesses without the pc ever having run an engram.

Once one had determined whatever it was that was going to be run with Straightwire, one would have the pc recall where and when it happened, who was involved, what were they doing, what was the pc doing, etc., until the lock blew or the illness keyed out.

Straightwire works at a lock level. When overdone it can key in underlying engrams. When properly done it can be quite miraculous.

STEPS

A. Determine whether or not the person needs this procedure by checking the following:

    1. The person cannot be hatted on a subject.

    2. No Crashing Mis-Us can be found on a subject yet it is obvious they exist.

    3. The person is not duplicating the material he has studied as he is incorrectly applying it or only applying part of it, despite Word Clearing.

    4. He is rejecting the material he is reading or the definition of the word he is clearing.

    5. You suspect or the person originates earlier data he has encountered on the materials that could contain false data.

    6. The person talks about or quotes other sources or obviously incorrect sources.

    7. He is glib.

    8. The person is backing off from actually applying the data he is studying despite standard Word Clearing.

    9. He is bogged.

    10. He cannot think with the data and it does not seem to apply.

B. Establish the difficulty the person is having—i.e., what are the materials he can't duplicate or apply? These materials must be to hand and the person must be familiar with the basic true data on the subject being addressed.

C. If the action is being done metered, put the person on the meter and properly adjust the sensitivity with a proper can squeeze.

D. Thoroughly clear the concept of false data with the person. Have him give you examples to show he gets it. (This would be done if the person was receiving False Data Stripping for the first time.)

E. The following questions are used to detect and uncover the false data. These questions are cleared before they are used for the first time on anyone. They do not have to read on a meter and may not do so as the person will not necessarily read on something that he believes to be true.

    1. **Is there anything you have run across in** (subject under discussion) **which you couldn't think with?**

    2. **Is there anything you have encountered in** (subject under discussion) **which didn't seem to add up?**

    3. **Is there something you have come across in** (subject under discussion) **that seems to be in conflict with the material you are trying to learn?**

4. Is there something in (subject under discussion) **which never made any sense to you?**

5. Did you come across any data in (subject under discussion) **that you had no use for?**

6. Was there any data you came across in (subject under discussion) **that never seemed to fit in?**

7. **Do you know of any datum that makes it unnecessary for you to do a good job on this subject?**

8. **Do you know of any reason why an overt product is all right?**

9. **Would you be made wrong if you really learned this subject?**

10. **Did anyone ever explain this subject to you verbally?**

11. **Do you know of any datum that conflicts with standard texts on this subject?**

12. **Do you consider you really know best about this subject?**

13. **Would it make somebody else wrong not to learn this subject?**

14. **Is this subject not worth learning?**

The questions are asked in the above sequence. When an area of false data is uncovered by one of these questions, one goes straight on to step F—location.

F. When the person comes up with an answer to one of the above questions, locate the false datum as follows:

1. Ask, **"Have you been given any false data regarding this?"** and help him locate the false datum. If this is being done on the meter, one can use any meter reads one does get to steer the person. This may require a bit of work, as the person may believe the false data he has to be true. Keep at it until you get the false datum.

If the person has given you the false datum in step E, then this step will not be needed; just go straight on to step G.

G. When the false datum has been located, handle as follows:

1. Ask, **"Where did this datum come from?"** (This could be a person, a book, TV, etc.)

2. **When was this?**

3. **Where exactly were you at the time?**

4. **Where was** (the person, book, etc.) **at the time?**

5. **What were you doing at the time?**

6. If the false datum came from a person, ask, "**What was** (the person) **doing at the time?**"

7. **How did** (the person, book, etc.) **look at the time?**

8. If the datum has not blown with the above questions, ask, "**Is there an earlier-similar false datum or incident on** (the subject under discussion)?" and handle per steps 1–7.

Continue as above until the false datum has blown. On the meter you will have a floating needle and very good indicators.

DO NOT CONTINUE PAST A POINT WHERE THE FALSE DATUM HAS BLOWN.

If you suspect the datum may have blown but the person has not originated, then ask, "**How does that datum seem to you now?**" and either continue if it hasn't blown or end off on that datum if it has blown.

H. When you have handled a particular false datum to a blow, going earlier-similar as necessary, you would then go back and repeat the question from E (the detection step) that uncovered the false datum. If there are any more answers to the question, they are handled exactly as in step F (location) and step G (handling).

That particular question is left when the person has no more answers. Then, if the person is not totally handled on the subject under discussion, one would use the other questions from step E and handle them in the same way. All the questions can be asked and handled as above but one would not continue past a point where the whole subject has been cleared up and the person can now duplicate and apply the data he has been having trouble with.

I. *CONDITIONAL:* If False Data Stripping is being done in conjunction with Crashing Mis-U Finding, one would now proceed with the Crashing Mis-U Finding.

J. Send the person to the Examiner.

K. Have the person study or restudy the true data on the subject you have been handling.

END PHENOMENA

When the above procedure is done correctly and fully on an area the person is actually having difficulty with, he will end up able to duplicate, understand and apply and think with the data that he could not previously grasp. The false data that was standing in the road of duplication will have been cleared away and the person's thinking will have been freed up. When this occurs, no matter where in the procedure, one ends off the False Data Stripping on that subject and sends the person to the Examiner. He will have cognitions and VGIs and on the meter you will have an F/N. This is not the end of all False Data Stripping for that person. It is the end of that False Data Stripping on the person at that particular time. As the person continues to work with and study the subject in question, he will learn more about it and may again collide with false data, at which time one repeats the above process.

NOTE

False data buries itself as the person may firmly believe that it is true. Sometimes the person will have such faith in a particular person, book, etc., that he cannot conceive that any data from that particular source might be false. One artist being false data stripped had received some false data from a very famous painter. Even though the data didn't really add up and actually caused the artist tremendous problems, he tended to believe it because of where it came from. It took persistence on the part of the person administering the False Data Stripping to eventually blow this false datum with a resulting freeing up of the artist's ability to think and produce in the area.

MISUNDERSTOODS

Misunderstoods often come up during False Data Stripping and should be cleared when they do. One would then continue with the False Data Stripping. One person being false data stripped knew he had some false data from a particular source but the false datum was a complete blank—he couldn't remember it at all. It was discovered that he had a Mis-U just before he received the false data and as soon as this was cleared up, he recalled the false data and it blew. This is just one example of how Word Clearing can tie in with False Data Stripping.

REPEATED USE

False Data Stripping can be done over and over as it will come off in layers as mentioned before. If False Data Stripping has been done on a specific thing and at some later point the person is having difficulty with a drill or the materials, the stripping of false data should be done on him again. In such a case it will be seen that the person recognizes or remembers *more* false or contrary data he has accumulated on the subject that was not in view earlier. As he duplicates a drill or his materials more and more exactly, former "interpretations" he had not-ised, incorrect past flunks that acted as invalidation or evaluation, etc., may crop up to be stripped off.

CAUTIONS

CODE. False Data Stripping is done under the discipline of the Auditor's Code. Evaluation and invalidation can be particularly harmful and must be avoided. All points of the Code apply.

RUDIMENTS. One would not begin False Data Stripping on someone who already has out-ruds. If the person is upset or worried about something or is critical or nattery, then you should fly his ruds or get them flown before you start False Data Stripping.

OVERRUN. One must be particularly careful not to overrun the person past a blow of the false datum. The stress in recall is that it is a light action which does not get the person into engrams or heavy charge. Keep it light. If you overrun someone past the point of a blow, he may drop into engrams or heavy charge. Just take the recall step to a blow and don't push him beyond it.

DATE/LOCATE. Date/Locate is another way of getting something to blow. If a false datum does not blow on the recall steps despite going earlier-similar, then it could be handled with Date/Locate *in session* as ordered by the C/S. This would normally be done as part of a False Data Stripping Repair List. Date/locating false data would never be done except in session as ordered by the C/S or as directed by the False Data Stripping Repair List. The auditor must be totally star-rated on date and locating and practiced in it before he attempts it.

FALSE DATA STRIPPING REPAIR LIST. The False Data Stripping Repair List is used in session by an auditor when False Data Stripping bogs inextricably or the person is not F/N GIs at Exams or gets in trouble after False Data Stripping has been done. A bogged False Data Stripping session must be handled within twenty-four hours.

NEW STUDENTS. Students who are new to Scientology should not use this procedure on each other as they may be insufficiently experienced to deliver it competently. In this case the Supervisor or someone qualified would administer False Data Stripping to those students who need it.

SUMMARY

The problem of the person who is unable to learn or who is unable to apply what he learns has never been fully resolved before. Misunderstoods were and are a major factor and Word Clearing must be used liberally. Now, however, I have made a major breakthrough which finally explains and handles the problem of inability to learn and apply.

Man's texts and education systems are strewn with false data. These false data effectively block someone's understanding of the true data. The handling given in this HCOB/PL makes it possible to remove that block and enable people to learn data so they can apply it.

With the ability to learn comes stability and the production of valuable products. With stability and the production of valuable products comes the achievement of one's purposes and goals, high morale and happiness.

So let's get to work on stripping away the false data which plagues man, clogs up his ability to think and learn and reduces his competence and effectiveness. Let's increase the ability of individuals and the human race.

L. RON HUBBARD
FOUNDER

HUBBARD COMMUNICATIONS OFFICE
SAINT HILL MANOR, EAST GRINSTEAD, SUSSEX

HCO POLICY LETTER OF 9 AUGUST 1979RA
ISSUE II
REVISED 31 DECEMBER 2000

REMIMEO
ALL ORGS
ALL STAFF

ADMIN KNOW-HOW SERIES 38
ORG SERIES 39
ESTABLISHMENT OFFICER SERIES 37

SERVICE PRODUCT OFFICER

Refs:

Taped Lectures		The Flag Executive Briefing Course tape lectures
HCO PLs		The Org Series
HCO PLs		The Establishment Officer Series
HCO PL	9 Aug. 79 I	CALL–IN: THE KEY TO DELIVERY AND FUTURE INCOME
HCO PL	7 Aug. 76 I	AKH Series 33 Esto Series 31 PRODUCT–ORG OFFICER SYSTEM NAME YOUR PRODUCT
HCO PL	7 Aug. 76 II	AKH Series 34 Esto Series 32 PRODUCT–ORG OFFICER SYSTEM WANT YOUR PRODUCT
HCO PL	7 Aug. 76 III	AKH Series 35 Esto Series 33 PRODUCT–ORG OFFICER SYSTEM TO GET YOU HAVE TO KNOW HOW TO ORGANIZE
HCO PL	20 Nov. 65RB I Rev. 13. 3. 99	THE PROMOTIONAL ACTIONS OF AN ORGANIZATION
HCO PL	28 May 72	BOOM DATA PUBLICATIONS BASIC FUNCTION
HCO PL	15 Nov. 60R Rev. 4. 2. 91	MODERN PROCUREMENT LETTERS
HCO PL	14 Feb. 61 II	THE PATTERN OF A CENTRAL ORGANIZATION
HCO PL	21 Nov. 68 I	SENIOR POLICY
HCO PL	28 Feb. 65 I	DELIVER
HCO PL	23 Aug. 79R I Rev. 23. 8. 84	Esto Series 38 Product Debug Series 1 DEBUG TECH
HCO PL	23 Aug. 79R II Rev. 24. 6. 88	Esto Series 39 Product Debug Series 2 DEBUG TECH CHECKLIST
HCO PL	9 Aug. 79 III	AKH Series 39 SERVICE CALL–IN COMMITTEE
HCO PL	10 July 65	LINES AND TERMINALS, ROUTING

The post of SERVICE PRODUCT OFFICER is hereby established in the Office of the CO/ED, Dept 19, of all Class IV and Sea Org orgs. His direct senior is the CO/ED.

Until such time as a SERVICE PRODUCT OFFICER is posted the responsibilities and duties are covered by the Service/Call-in Committee as fully laid out in HCO PL 9 Aug. 79 I, CALL–IN: THE KEY TO DELIVERY AND FUTURE INCOME and HCO PL 9 Aug. 79 III, SERVICE CALL–IN COMMITTEE.

The VALUABLE FINAL PRODUCTS of this post are (1) flawlessly serviced and completed paid pcs and students who re-sign up for their next service, and (2) high quality promotional items in the hands of volumes of public who come in, sign up and start an org service.

The main statistics for the SERVICE PRODUCT OFFICER are:

1. Number of pcs and students completed and re-signed on to their next service. (This includes those actually routed on to the next upper org for services and who do re-sign.)

2. Number of public in and started on to a service.

Completion: By completion is meant those actions completed and attested at C&A and accompanied by an acceptable success story.

Re-sign: By re-sign-ups are meant pcs and students who, after completion of a service, see the Registrar to sign up *again* for another service while in the org.

Promotional Items: Those items which will produce income for the organization. By promotional items are meant those things which make Scientology and our products known and will cause people to respond either in person or by written reply to the result of receiving Scientology commodities. These are: tours, book outlets, Sunday services, events, upstat image, fliers, info packs, handouts, books, ASR packs, specified service promotion, etc.

There are of course many other stats that reflect the SERVICE PRODUCT OFFICER'S subproducts and these are: VSD, TOTAL GI, INTENSIVES COMPLETED, BULK MAIL OUT, NUMBER OF PROMOTIONAL ACTIONS OF THE ORG IN, NUMBER OF FULLY AND PARTIAL PAIDS GOTTEN INTO THE ORG AND ON TO THEIR NEXT SERVICE. These are very important parts of the SERVICE PRODUCT OFFICER HAT, as they reflect his subproducts which lead to his valuable final product.

SERVICE PRODUCT OFFICER
RESPONSIBILITIES AND DUTIES

The purpose of an organization is to deliver service to the public. The primary functions which add up to delivery to the public are: promotion, sales, call-in, delivery itself and re-sign. The Service Product Officer is responsible for the flow of *products* through these areas. He is a *product officer.* He names, wants and gets products in these areas and thus ensures that the organization is accomplishing its purpose of service to the public.

The full technology of product officers is explained in the Flag Executive Briefing Course lectures, where the product–org officer system was developed. This system is still fully valid and is, in fact, the tech of the Service Product Officer. He is solely interested in products. When the Service Product Officer comes across a situation that requires organizing, he gets his organizing officer to handle it. The O/O (organizing officer) should actually be operating a few steps ahead of the Service Product Officer at all times — organizing for immediate production, per the product–org system. A full study of the product–org system, as contained in the FEBC tapes, the Org Series and AKH Series 33, 34 and 35, NAME, WANT AND GET YOUR PRODUCT is recommended in order to attain a thorough understanding of the actions of the Service Product Officer and his organizing officer.

The Service Product Officer is not a stopgap at any point of the promotion, sales, call-in, delivery and re-sign lines, where executives have failed to post and hat staff. This would be the responsibility of the Exec Establishment Officer per Esto Series 1. Establishment Officers see that short- and long-range establishment are occurring in the organization in the form of recruiting, hatting and training of staff. The Esto system is a necessary and very vital tool for the Service Product Officer and the organization and should definitely be in full use.

The Service Product Officer has the authority to directly order or work with any terminal involved in the promotion, sales, call-in, delivery or re-sign areas so long as he maintains direct liaison with their seniors.

The Service Product Officer must be fully aware of every post in the org and what their jobs consist of. He must know who handles what cycles and what cycles are on the lines. For instance, it is up to the Service Product Officer to be aware of all promotional actions occurring in the org and who is doing them, or if they aren't getting done. He must be aware of what public aren't getting serviced and he ensures those responsible get them serviced. He doesn't do this himself, as a serious goof of any product officer would be to go down the org board and do the job himself. The Service Product Officer *must* ensure others get the work done. Otherwise, he would wind up doing everyone's post and not getting anything done. It's actually pretty overwhelming to think of a Service Product Officer as responsible for doing everyone else's post duties. That's the surefire way to sink fast. Where a product isn't getting out the Service Product Officer debugs it using HCO PL 23 Aug. 79R I, DEBUG TECH, in order to get production. He is not interested in first finding the person's Mis-U or excuse, he is interested in getting production occurring now. Let the org officer and Qual worry about the staff member's Mis-Us.

Divisional Secretaries are the product officers for their division per the product–organizing officer system. The Service Product Officer sees that the product officers over the whole delivery cycle are getting their products. He coordinates the flow of products from division to division. A Service Product Officer doing his post fully and properly is, in fact, the person that makes the org board work. He sees that products aren't jamming up at one point of the line, but that they continue through the organization.

The Service Product Officer walks into the Tech Div and finds the Tech Sec sitting at his desk, shuffling paper and the pcs are piling high and complaining about no service. The last thing the Service Product Officer would do is start organizing the Tech staff around and scheduling the pcs. No sir, that's a serious offense. The first thing he would do is find out what can be produced RIGHT NOW, what auditors can be gotten into session right now and make the Tech Sec do it and GET IT DONE. This all takes about fifteen minutes and he gets the area flowing again and then,

WHAM! . . . he's out and into his next area. The Service Product Officer would not sit down and just start word clearing or doing Exchange by Dynamics on the Tech Sec. He would unstick the flows and get them moving. Then he would alert HCO and Qual to this serious problem of unhattedness and demand it be handled.

The basic sequence of the Service Product Officer on getting the products flowing off the lines is PUSH, DEBUG, DRIVE, NAME IT, WANT IT, AND GET IT. That's the only way you ever get a product. Products don't happen on their own.

This means he tells the Tech Sec to get Joe Blow there in session now! There is no general "audit these pcs." You'd never get a product that way.

The CO/ED has no authority to order the Service Product Officer to perform the total duties of any one post. The Service Product Officer must guard against being stuck into one post after another, doing it all himself. Nor is the Service Product Officer an "expeditor" for the CO/ED.

It is also very important that the Service Product Officer advise seniors that he is going into their areas so as not to create a Danger condition and wind up having to run the entire org. He also does this by getting the seniors to handle their juniors so a product is gotten. He does not walk in and cross-order the seniors of areas but works with them to see that products are produced.

The Service Product Officer is one who comes up with BIG IDEAS on getting public flooded into the org and being serviced swiftly. He is the one who thinks along the line of PRODUCTS, PRODUCTS, PRODUCTS. By spanning the divisions, he coordinates the product wanted and ensures each division is aware of its part in getting this product and that their actions are uniform. Where the Service Product Officer spots diversity, or lack of uniformity, he must alert his org officer or HCO. By doing the actions of coordination for a product and product demand, the product officer creates a team and more importantly sets the pace of the org's production and morale.

ORG LINES AND
THE SERVICE PRODUCT OFFICER

There are certain aspects of the organization which the Service Product Officer must be thoroughly trained in to do his job properly.

The Service Product Officer must be fully aware of all the Valuable Final Products (VFPs) of each department and each division of the org. Without this the Service Product Officer can create havoc, as he would be ordering Division 6 to recruit or the Reges to supervise. By not knowing cold the org VFPs, the Service Product Officer would certainly jam the flows throughout the org board.

A serious fault in any executive is not knowing the functions of terminals and the relation of one terminal to another. A key function of any executive is that of routing. An executive that misroutes communications and particles will tie his org in knots and wonder why no products are coming out. Therefore, a Service Product Officer must know cold every post function in the org and what particles belong on what lines.

He has got to know where a product comes from and where it goes in order to see it through the lines. A product officer's job is to name, want and get a product. However, he must first know where that product is to come from and where it is to go. This is an incredibly fundamental point.

In order for org lines to flow, routing forms (RFs) must be used. A routing form is a full step-by-step road map on which a particle travels. Every point a particle (which could be a student, a pc, mail, etc.) must go through to wind up at its destination must be listed on the routing form.

The Service Product Officer's Organizing Officer must ensure routing forms exist and are in use for each and every line in an org he deals in. Both he and the Service Product Officer must know these forms cold and be able to instantly spot when a line is being abused or ignored so as to slam in the correct routing.

A Service Product Officer must fully clay demo all the lines of an organization for each and every product. This must include each particle from entrance to the org and through all lines on which that particle would flow until it leaves the org. Lines are the most fundamental point of administration. To not have a full grasp of these lines would be detrimental to any product officer.

SERVICE PRODUCT OFFICER
SEQUENCE OF ACTIONS

It is very easy for the Service Product Officer to become wrapped up in one area while neglecting the others; however, this must not be done as, while products might be getting through in one area, they may well be seriously bogging in others.

The Service Product Officer is concerned with promotion, sales, call-in, delivery and re-sign. He begins his product officering in promotion and gets products out there or started and moves on to sales and gets them on to getting their products and so on through call-in and delivery and re-sign. He then returns to the beginning, promotion, and follows up on what he started there and gets even more production out. This is basically how the Service Product Officer moves through the org.

Daily, the Service Product Officer must plan and battle plan out his day. He must list those products he intends to achieve in each one of his areas and then get them.

The Service Product Officer is not an "information courier" or "data gatherer." He is ahead of the game and *knows* the data. He must know what public haven't been regged in the org yet, he must know who hasn't been taken into session that day, or who has been stuck in Ethics for three days, and ensure these things get handled. Therefore he must be quicker and faster than anyone else in the org and run run run.

PROMOTION

Promotion is the first action of the SERVICE PRODUCT OFFICER. He must ensure the many promotional pieces and actions are getting done. Some of these are:

1. Selling of books.
2. Staff selling books.

3. Books placed in public bookstores.

4. Selling of books to FSMs, missions, distributors, retailers and salesmen.

5. Books sold on each public contact.

6. Books advertised in mags, ads, posters, fliers, etc.

7. ASR packs.

8. Info packs.

9. Div 6 handouts for lectures and free testing.

10. Posters on major services in Div 6.

11. Promo to field auditors, FSMs, Gung-ho Groups, Dianetic study groups.

12. Org mags.

13. Flag shooting boards.

14. Promo for future events and tours.

15. *The Auditor* (for SHs).

16. *Clear News.*

17. *Advance!* mag (for AOs).

18. *Source* mag (FSO).

19. I Want to Go Clear Club promo (AOs).

20. SHSBC/NED/internships/NOTs/grades, etc., specified in promo.

21. Promo at points of public inquiry.

22. Free testing ads.

23. Fliers inviting people to buy Scientology books.

24. More Info Cards used in books.

25. Ads in newspapers.

26. Questionnaires to detect people's plans for training and processing.

27. Enough letters to public so they come in.

28. All promotional actions per HCO PL 20 Nov. 65RB I, THE PROMOTIONAL ACTIONS OF AN ORGANIZATION.

29. Book seminars, public campaigns and lectures.

30. Public Reception display (books, posters, handouts, etc.).

31. Tours and events, Sunday service.

32. Free testing line.

33. Handling of Gung-ho Groups, keeping FSMs well supplied and supervision of Dianetic study groups and FSMs.

34. Test Centers outside the org as an extension.

35. Radio and TV advertisements.

36. Dept 17 services.

37. Reception greeting, handling, routing, chasing up people for appointments and handling incoming calls with ARC and efficiency.

38. Formation of Dianetic Counseling Groups.

39. Weekly tape and film plays.

40. Promotes the org and standard tech to Auditors Association.

41. Contacts and sees any sign of ARC broken field and alerts Chaplain to clean up the field.

The first thing a Service Product Officer would want to do is get out a large volume of promo to at least get some activity occurring. This would entail Dissem getting any promo laying around the org dug up and sent out to students and pcs. They would get it out in letters and mailings, they would get it handed out to students and pcs, they would pick up the half-completed promo piece, have it fixed up and sent out. They would have promo placed in Reception, in any public inquiry, etc. In other words, the Service Product Officer ensures that the org fully utilizes what promo they do have. He would also have specific promo pieces done to enlighten the field on what services the org has. Where any of this bogged he would push — debug — drive — name it — want it — and get it.

The Service Product Officer, in trying to get in any promotional items, must review what resources he has. For example, is there a Dir Clearing, is there a Receptionist, etc.? He must concentrate on getting those terminals that already exist busy on promotional actions that will create the largest volume of inflow, while his organizing officer works on getting more immediate resources to increase the volume even further. It would be senseless to have the Dir Clearing running around trying to form up groups in an inactive field, single-handing, when he has FSMs that need to be gotten on to selecting and driving in new public. The Service Product Officer is concerned with priorities of promotional actions, so must be totally aware of all the promotional items and actions that an org can produce.

Actions such as "improved org appearance," "high ARC handling," and "correct and efficient routing of public" can be put in instantly. If he has two people in all of Dissem he still can and must get the particles flowing and products coming off the line.

SALES

The sales lines consist of enlightening the public, having lines to sign people up, getting public into the org and signed up for service.

The following gives you an idea of some of the sales actions and lines in an org:

1. Body Reg phones and schedules public to come in for interview.

2. Use of CF to produce business.

3. Reges who accept advance registrations.

4. D of T procurement of students.

5. D of P procurement of pcs.

6. Receptionist sells to public coming in.

7. SHs in communication with the Class IV org Tech Secs and Registrars and targeting them for public completing and routing on to the higher org.

8. AO's and SH's case consultant actions.

9. AO/SH events to Class IV org Academies to encourage upper-level auditor training.

10. Use of FSMs, Auditors Associations, personal contact, etc., to get public into the org and on to their next service.

11. Fast lines so public are not left waiting to see the Reg.

The lines of routing a public person to the Reg, or from the Reg to a service, must be tight so public aren't lost and the Reg is continuously kept busy with the public. Therefore, the Service Product Officer must police these lines and where he notices any lack of uniformity he gets his org officer onto it. Nonuniform or slow routing interferes with the product, so the Service Product Officer gets it speeded up now by push — debug — drive — name it — want it — and get it.

The first actions of the Service Product Officer in the sales area are to get all "in-the-org" public routed to the Reg on breaks or after course end to be further signed up for additional service. He can also have Dissem drilling done with Reges so as to increase sales in the org. His operating procedure is products, products, products, now, now, now. His org officer or HCO and Qual can worry about organize, organize, organize.

CALL–IN

Call-in is the action of getting fully paids into the org on to their next service. This also includes getting partially paids fully paid and on to their next service. These functions are of great concern to the SERVICE PRODUCT OFFICER as undelivered services to the public can mess up a field and increase the chance of refunds. The Service Product Officer should see to it that the Call-in Units are given stiff targets and that their production is not monitored by low auditor hours or low-producing training areas. The execution of needed programs to get Call-in Units fully operational is under the Service Product Officer per HCO PL 9 Aug. 79 I, CALL–IN: THE KEY TO DELIVERY AND FUTURE INCOME. This same policy also lists out the functions of the Call-in Units. Call-in falls between sales and delivery, as it deals with those either fully or partially paid and needing only to finish payment and be called in and gotten on to service.

DELIVERY

The Service Product Officer must ensure that the service lines of the org are fast and 100 percent standard, that pcs and students do complete quickly and don't get lost off the lines.

The Service Product Officer is to have an alert line with the public set up whereby if a student or pc's study or auditing is slowed, or if the public person is dissatisfied in any way, he can alert the Service Product Officer so it can be handled.

Some of the actions and lines to be product officered by the Service Product Officer are as follows:

1. Tech Services arranges housing, has the pc met when he is arriving and generally operates as the pc's host while in the org.

2. The many lines such as pc to Ethics, pc to Examiner, student to Ethics, student to Qual, C/S Series 25 line and pc to D of P line must be drilled so they are flawless and handled with ARC.

3. The most senior policy applied to this area is HCO PL 21 Nov. 68 I, SENIOR POLICY, "WE ALWAYS DELIVER WHAT WE PROMISE."

4. There must be an adequate amount of auditors, Tech Pages and FESers, Ds of P, Supervisors, Course Admins, etc.

5. The auditing line must be fast so no pcs wait to be serviced.

6. Use of all hands tech terminals in the org auditing when required to handle backlogged service.

7. Getting students through their courses and on to their internship at which point they can audit in the HGC.

8. Proper scheduling so every pc gets in 12½ hours a week minimum.

9. Recovering blown auditors, getting them fixed up and auditing.

The Service Product Officer ensures tech lines are fast. For instance, a pc's folder not getting C/Sed for days, or idle auditors and Ds of P "waiting" for pcs when they can be made to procure pcs, must be spotted and handled by the Service Product Officer.

The Service Product Officer must be kept briefed on what pcs and students arrive and how they are going to be handled. He must get around to these areas (Training and HGC) to ensure that there are no slows with public or anything that would get in the way of public receiving top-quality service.

Service to the public is the reason the org is there and service must be kept fast and 100 percent standard and plentiful. This is a primary duty of the Service Product Officer; he is there to ensure this occurs.

It is losses on service that keep public away, org income down and staff pay low.

RE–SIGN–UP

The re-sign-up line is also very key to an organization's prosperity. It brings further income, and proves conclusively that the last service received by the public person was of high quality. This is why the Service Product Officer must be very alert to the amount of re-signs. Some of the things that should be watched for are:

1. That the Reg is supplied with an upstat cert for his last completed service to present to the student or pc.

2. That the Reg knows fully how to handle the public person that won't re-sign (by sending them to Qual).

3. The Reg must be provided with tech estimates, Grade Chart information, etc., so he is aware ahead of time of what the student or pc's next action is.

4. Tech terminals are fully briefed and the line is in that every completion gets routed to the Reg. This must be drilled.

The public person should be serviced in your org until he/she requires upper-level service that your org cannot deliver, at which point they should be directed to the next higher org.

PITFALLS

The Service Product Officer can lose his effectiveness if he takes any "hey you" orders or gets stuck in at various points. He is not an expeditor. He is not an information and full-time coordinator terminal. He is an executive, a *product* officer, and he is there to ensure the entire machine runs.

He must be well versed on actions occurring in the org. He must also pay strict attention to completing actions he has started and to carrying a handling through to a done. Otherwise he can wrap himself around a pole with incomplete cycles which will ball up the line and prevent the service lines from flowing flawlessly.

Where the Service Product Officer post bogs it is undoubtedly due to a lack of an organizing officer, as with the speed in which a Service Product Officer demands products, he requires a fast-moving org officer. So it is essential this post be provided with an org officer as soon as possible.

Those personnel in the org who are responsible for organization, any Esto personnel, etc., are the people who put the units in the org there. It is not the duty of a Service Product Officer to man and hat the org. Therefore, it is a lot of sweat off the Service Product Officer's brow to have a fully functioning Esto team backing up his actions in getting the flow of products out of the organization.

SUMMARY

The Service Product Officer ensures all the actions of getting public into, through and out of the org are *accomplished* with high quality results.

It is extremely important that this post be manned in each and every org. It doesn't just make the difference between a poor, empty org and a good org. This post makes the difference between a good org and a booming org.

L. RON HUBBARD
FOUNDER

HCO POLICY LETTER OF 11 JUNE 1972

REMIMEO

ADMIN KNOW-HOW SERIES 38-1
ORG SERIES 39-1
ESTABLISHMENT OFFICER SERIES 37-1
PRODUCT OFFICERS

(Originally written by LRH for the *Apollo* OODs of 11 June 72.
Issued as an HCO PL on 21 Sept. 80.)

Worked last evening getting Tech to start shooting them through to completions.

The PL on Selling and Delivering Auditing (HCO PL 28 Sept. 71) tells why you have to audit a pc all at once, whole program. Dribbling it out means repairs due to life upsets before the guy made it.

So crowd it on and get a pc *through*. Then we'll have some products for our coins.

A product officer has to name, want and get his products.

This means one says, "You there. Joe Blow. Want him completed. All right get it DONE." Product by product. There is no general "Audit these pcs." "Get up the hours." Hell, you never get a product that way.

"You there, George Thunderbird. I want you through your Primary and onto and through course and classified. Get going, man, get going. Oh, you were told to weedle the toofle before you woofled by Dorance Doppler. Org Officer? Get that name — to Flag MAA, get the cross orders the hell off my lines. Now you George Thunderbird, I want you through your Primary and onto and through course by 1 July. You got it? You got it now! Good. Well, get with it. Get going!" Note on clipboard: Org Off to get cross order by Dorance Doppler invest and report. "There's your slip." Note on progress board. Geo Thunderbird HSDA 1 July. "Now you Tobler Tomias, what's the tale; how are you going? . . . Well, standing there smoking and looking at the scenery isn't going to do anything. If your girl doesn't like you anymore the thing to do is drown your sorrows in the Primary Rundown. . . . Okay, you are to be an Expanded Dianetics. All right, that's fine. I want you completed by 16 July. . . . I don't care if that's a 16-hour day. Let's see, Primary Rundown by _____ and Class IV Acad by _____ and _____. Yes, that's 16 July AT NOON. Man, to hell with your PTPs. Get going, man." And on the progress board. And from the board — "And here's Bill Coal. He should be off the Primary today, where is he? All right Bill — ah, you made it that far. Now you're on schedule. That's great. HSDA. Get with it, man. You completed Primary 20 minutes ago and aren't on the next course. Super! What the _____."

That's the way it goes for a Tech Prod Off. "We are finishing Agnes, Torp and Goshwiler today. Today. Yes today. Certified and off lines. Got it, D of T? Well, do it!"

Push, debug, drive. Name it, want it, get it.

That's the *only* way you ever get a product.

Sad but true.

They don't ever happen by themselves.

And all the public relations chatter in the world is not a product. I know this product officer beat.

It's a piece of cake.

But it has to be DONE.

L. RON HUBBARD
FOUNDER

HUBBARD COMMUNICATIONS OFFICE
SAINT HILL MANOR, EAST GRINSTEAD, SUSSEX

HCO POLICY LETTER OF 23 AUGUST 1979R
ISSUE I
REVISED 23 AUGUST 1984
(Also issued as an HCOB, same date and title)

REMIMEO
PRODUCT OFFICERS
ORG OFFICERS
EXECS
ALL STAFF
PROGRAMS CHIEFS
PROJECT OPERATORS
MISSION OPERATORS
MISSIONAIRES
FLAG REPRESENTATIVES
LRH COMMUNICATORS
CRAMMING OFFICERS
REVIEW

ESTABLISHMENT OFFICER SERIES 38
PRODUCT DEBUG SERIES 1
DEBUG TECH

Refs:

LRH ED 302 Int		DEBUG TECH BREAKTHROUGH
HCO PL	23 Aug. 79 II	Esto Series 39
		Product Debug Series 2
		DEBUG TECH CHECKLIST
HCOB	23 Aug. 79 II	Product Debug Series 10
		PRODUCT DEBUG REPAIR LIST
HCOB	17 June 79	Product Debug Series 3
		Word Clearing Series 61
		CRASHING MIS-Us: THE KEY TO COMPLETED
		CYCLES OF ACTION AND PRODUCTS
HCOB	7 Aug. 79	Esto Series 36
		Product Debug Series 8
		FALSE DATA STRIPPING
HCO PL	26 Mar. 79RB	Esto Series 35
	Rev. 2.9.79	Product Debug Series 7
		Word Clearing Series 60
		MISUNDERSTOOD WORDS AND
		CYCLES OF ACTION
HCOB	23 Aug. 79 I	Product Debug Series 6
		Word Clearing Series 65
		CRASHING MIS-Us, BLOCKS TO FINDING THEM
HCOB	9 Feb. 79R	KSW Series 23
	Rev. 23.8.84	HOW TO DEFEAT VERBAL TECH CHECKLIST

When I wrote LRH ED 302 Int, DEBUG TECH BREAKTHROUGH, in February of this year, I promised that there would be a policy letter issued covering the tech more fully. Well, there have been further breakthroughs in the area of debugging production. The tech given in that LRH ED has been acclaimed by hundreds to be miraculous. This policy reissues that tech and brings it up-to-date with the new discoveries.

HISTORY

Recently I noticed quite a few programs were not progressing rapidly. I found many targets bugged. Project operators did not seem to know what to do and were getting losses and becoming frustrated. Their targets were "bugged."

"Bugged" is slang for snarled up or halted.

"Debug" means to get the snarls or stops out of something.

I had always been given to believe somebody had developed and written up debug tech. People would often tell me they had debugged this or that, so of course I assumed that the tech existed and that issues and checksheets existed and were in use. Yet here were people operating projects who couldn't get the targets done by themselves or others.

I didn't recall ever having written any policy letter containing the tech of debugging programs or targets.

So I called for the various "debug checksheets" and "debug issues" they were using and found something very astonishing. None had any real tech on them to debug something. They just had various quotes that did not necessarily apply.

I did a study of the subject based on what people trying to debug should be doing and what they were not doing and developed a fast, relatively simple system. Some project operators were located in very bugged areas which had brought them to apathy and even tears of frustration. The new debug tech was put into their hands and they came streaming back in wild excitement. It worked! Their areas were rolling!

I am releasing this tech to you as it is vital that programs are quickly executed and that production occurs.

This debug tech is tested, fully valid and for *immediate* use.

Debug tech is a vital executive tool. Anyone who is responsible for getting targets and programs executed, getting production out, turning insolvency into solvency and generally making a better world frankly can't live without it.

Debug tech is used to debug program targets, programs, a lack of completion of the cycles of action which lead to production and, in short, whenever there is *any* insufficiency of viable products coming from an area, org or individual.

THE TECH

I. *INSPECTION*

The first action in debugging an area is an inspection to see what is going on in terms of production. In inspecting the area you do the following:

1. You look for what products have been gotten out in the past.

2. You look for products that are there completed.

3. You look for what products can be attained in the immediate future.

---

4. You look for the value of the products produced as compared to the overall cost of the production organization.

5. You look for overt products or cycles where products continuously have to be redone, resulting in no or few products.

The full volume of data on how to do an investigation is given in the Investigations Checksheet of *The Volunteer Minister's Handbook*.*

When you first inspect an area for products, you just look. Policies on "Look Don't Listen" apply (HCO PL 16 Mar. 72 I, LOOK DON'T LISTEN). Don't listen to how they are going to get 150 products; just look and walk around with a clipboard.

If you don't see 150 products waiting to be shipped or invoices showing they have been, they don't exist. If you don't see receipts for 150 shipped products, they don't exist and never have. The product is either there or there is ample shipping or departure or finance evidence that they have just left or been shipped. Products that are only in people's heads don't exist.

Dreams are nice — in fact they are essential in life — but they have to be materialized into the physical universe before they exist as *products*.

The most wide trap the debugger can fall into is "But next week . . . ," since experience will tell you that next week's production may never arrive. The definition of product is something that can be exchanged for a valuable product or currency. They have subproducts. These are necessary. A subproduct can also be an overt product and block final products.

When you have done your product inspection, you then look over the period of time from a viewpoint of time and motion. This is to answer the question "Are things arranged so that there is no time wasted in useless motions which are unnecessary?" This includes poor placement of materiel on a flow line or tool sheds five miles from the site of work so that one has to go there every time one wants a hammer, out-of-sequence flows or waits.

One counts up the amount of wasted time simply because of the disorganization of a place. It isn't enough to say a place is disorganized. How is this disorganization consuming time and motion which is not resulting in a higher quantity of production? Examples of this are quite gross.

When you have done this study, during which of course you have made notes, you will have the raw materials necessary to make an estimation of the area.

If there is not an adequate and even spectacular record of products getting out and if products have to be redone or if no products are coming out, you proceed as follows:

II. *PERSONAL HANDLING*

Find a product that *can* be gotten out, any product, and insist that it and products like it or similar cycles be gotten out flat out by the existing personnel.

*[*Editor's Note*: This data is now covered in *The Scientology Handbook* chapter on "Investigations."]

Do not let this debug act as an excuse for them not to produce. The first step of this handling *is* to demand production.

When you have gotten them on that, you enter in upon a second stage of debug. This consists essentially of finding if the place is knowledgeable enough and able enough to produce what is actually required and what is actually valuable or being needed from it.

This is accomplished as follows:

(Note: You should not attempt to find Crashing Mis-Us, etc., until the above inspection and the steps A to I below have been done.)

A. **WHERE ARE THE ORDERS RELATING TO THIS TARGET (OR PROJECT OR PRODUCTION AREA)?** (Can include policies, directives, orders, bulletins, issues, despatches, tapes, valid texts and previous debugs and any and all files.)

Handling: Collect up all of the orders relating to this target (or project or production area). This includes the orders and policies the person is operating off of as well as all those he should be operating off of. At this point you may need to employ the "How to Defeat Verbal Tech Checklist":

1. If it isn't written it isn't true.

2. If it's written, read it.

3. Did the person who wrote it have the authority or know-how to order it?

4. If you can't understand it, clarify it.

5. If you can't clarify it, clear the Mis-Us.

6. If the Mis-Us won't clear, query it.

7. Has it been altered from the original?

8. Get it validated as a correct, on-channel, on-policy, in-tech order.

9. IF IT CAN'T BE RUN THROUGH AS ABOVE *IT'S FALSE!* CANCEL IT! And use HCOB 7 Aug. 79, FALSE DATA STRIPPING, as needed.

10. Only if it holds up this far, force others to read it and follow it.

B. **HAVE YOU READ THE ORDERS?**

Handling: If he has not read them, then have him read, word clear and star-rate them.

Ca. **DO YOU HAVE MIS-Us ON THESE ORDERS?**

Handling: Get the orders word cleared using M4, M9 or M2 Word Clearing— whatever Word Clearing *is* needed to fully clear any Mis-Us he has.

Cb. **DO YOU HAVE FALSE DATA ON THESE ORDERS?**

Handling: Strip off the false data per HCOB/PL 7 Aug. 79, FALSE DATA STRIPPING.

Handle this step (Ca and Cb) until the person has duplicated the orders and issues relating to this production area.

D. **ARE THERE FINANCIAL OR LOGISTICS PROBLEMS ON THEM?**

Handling: Debug using HCO PL 14 Mar. 72 II, FOLLOW POLICY AND LINES, and Flag Divisional Directive of 25 Aug. 76, FINANCIAL PLANNING MEMBER HAT CHECKSHEET. Debugging this may require getting the whole FP Committee through the FP pack.

E. **ARE THERE PERSONNEL PROBLEMS?**

Handling: Debug this using HCO PL 16 Mar. 71 IV, LINES AND HATS, and the Personnel Series, as given in the *Management Series*.

It may be necessary to do this debug on the HAS or any person responsible for getting the products of staff members who produce.

F. **ARE THERE HATTING PROBLEMS?**

Handling: Handle this using full Word Clearing and False Data Stripping and get the scene debugged using HCO PL 29 July 71 I, WHY HATTING? and HCO PL 22 Sept. 70, HATS, and HCO PL 27 Dec. 70, HATS PROGRAM PITFALLS.

Hatting problems may include the total and utter lack of a hatting course for the staff or a hatting course where WHAT IS A COURSE? PL is flagrantly not in, and if you find this, you have gotten to the root of why you are working hard debugging all over the place and it had better be handled quick.

It may also be that the area senior doesn't make sure his staff puts in study time off production hours, and in this you may find the senior is a failed student himself and this you would also have to handle.

Note: A person who *cannot* be hatted at all has false data. The handling would be to strip off the false data.

G. **IS THERE EXTERIOR INFLUENCE STOPPING THE PRODUCTION WHICH CANNOT BE HANDLED IN THE PRODUCTION AREA?**

Handling: Handle using HCO PL 31 Jan. 72, THE WHY IS GOD, and HCO PL 25 May 73, SUPPLEMENTARY EVALUATIONS, and HCO PL 30 Dec. 70, ENVIRONMENTAL CONTROL.

When told that these exterior influences exist, the wise debugger immediately verifies. The simplest way to verify is to ask the person who is supposed to be putting stops on the line if he has issued such orders. You commonly find out he hasn't. But if he has, then you have started to locate your area to handle.

You commonly run into verbal tech at which moment you use the "How to Defeat Verbal Tech Checklist."

H. **WHAT OTHER EXCUSES EXIST?**

Handling: As per HCO PL 31 Jan. 72, THE WHY IS GOD; HCO PL 19 May 70, SANITY; HCO PL 30 Sept. 73 II, SITUATION FINDING; and HCOB 19 Aug. 67, THE SUPREME TEST.

And once any obvious ones in the above have been handled, and production *still* isn't rolling, you have:

I. **ROUTINE FINDING OF MIS-Us PER WORD CLEARING SERIES.**

J. **CRASHING MIS-U TECH PER HCOB 17 JUNE 79, CRASHING MIS-Us: THE KEY TO COMPLETED CYCLES OF ACTION AND PRODUCTS.**

Crashing Mis-U Finding is done exactly per this HCOB. Crashing Mis-Us can be buried or suppressed as covered in HCOB 23 Aug. 79 I, CRASHING MIS-Us, BLOCKS TO FINDING THEM. The factors as listed in that HCOB which can cause a Crashing Mis-U to remain hidden and unknown may have to be handled before the Crashing Mis-U appears.

K. **DO THEY HAVE ANY IDEA AT ALL THAT THEY SHOULD BE GETTING OUT ANY PRODUCTS? OR DO THEY PRETEND TO BUT DON'T?**

Handling: Simply two-way comm on why the guy is there. It might come as a startling realization that he is supposed to get out products. This can be backed up with Exchange by Dynamics, HCO PL 4 Apr. 72 I, ETHICS, and Short Form Product Clearing, HCO PL 13 Mar. 72, PRODUCTION AND ESTABLISHMENT, ORDERS AND PRODUCTS, or HCO PL 23 Mar. 72, FULL PRODUCT CLEARING LONG FORM.

There is also such a thing as a person who will not complete a cycle of action. This is normally true of what we call a "suppressive person" or even an insane person.

Handling: Get the person's case looked into by a competent C/S and also by the Ethics Officer for background.

But as PTS people are in suppressive persons' valences, he may only be PTS.

Handling: See section P below for de-PTSing.

L. **WRONG STAT.** The person has been given a stat that has nothing to do with what he is supposed to produce.

Handling: Get the right stat figured out so that it agrees with what he is supposed to produce and actually measures his actual production.

M. **WRONG VFP OR WRONG PRODUCT? DO THEY HAVE THE IDEA OF VFP RIGHT?** (Or does the org think it's the award rather than the product, i.e., GI rather than an audited paying pc or a trained paying student?)

It of course can occur, amazingly, that the person or department, etc., is trying to turn out a product that has no exchange value. This can occur because what they do produce is so flubby as to be called "an overt product" which nobody can use further on up the line or even at the end of the line.

You handle this by coming down on their sense of fitness of things. Overt products waste resources and time and personnel and are actually more destructive than on first glance. They cannot be exchanged but they also waste resources as well as lose any expected return. You can remedy this sort of thing by improving their tech so they do turn out something decent and useful.

They can also be turning out a type of product nobody wants—such as 1819 buggy whips in a space age. They may be great buggy whips but they won't exchange because nobody wants them.

They may also be getting out products of excellent quality but never tell anybody they have or do them. This can apply as narrowly as one worker who doesn't tell anybody he is having or doing them or a whole organization which, with complete asininity, never markets or advertises their products.

It is also possible that a combination of all three things above may be found.

It also may be they have all sorts of products they could get out but they never dreamed of getting them out, yet their lifeblood may depend upon it.

Handling: HCO PL 24 July 78, SUBPRODUCTS, HOW TO COMPILE A SUBPRODUCT LIST, which tells how to compile a subproducts list and attain VFPs. Exchange by Dynamics per HCO PL 4 Apr. 72 I, ETHICS, and Full Product Clearing Long Form on the correct and actual VFP (as well as any other products the person or area may have), as well as marketing and PR tech.

N. **NEVER FIGURED OUT WHAT THEY WOULD HAVE TO DO TO GET A PRODUCT?**

Handling: Handle this using HCO PL 7 Aug. 76 I, II and III, AKH Series 33, PRODUCT–ORG OFFICER SYSTEM, NAME YOUR PRODUCT; AKH Series 34, PRODUCT–ORG OFFICER SYSTEM, WANT YOUR PRODUCT; AKH Series 35, PRODUCT–ORG OFFICER SYSTEM, TO GET YOU HAVE TO KNOW HOW TO ORGANIZE; HCO PL 24 July 78, SUBPRODUCTS, HOW TO COMPILE A SUBPRODUCT LIST; and HCO PL 14 Jan. 69 I, OT ORGS.

O. **OUT–ETHICS?**

Handling: Determine the situation and handle with O/W write-ups or auditing and ethics conditions or correction of past conditions and the ethics policies that apply.

P. **IS THE AREA OR INDIVIDUAL CREATING PROBLEMS AND DEMANDING SOLUTIONS TO THEM?**

Handling: Give the person PTS handling as per ethics policies. If and when available, get the personnel de-PTSed using Clay Table De-PTSing as per HCOB 28 Aug. 79 I, PTS CLAY TABLE HANDLING, THEORY AND ADMINISTRATION. (Note: Clay Table De-PTSing can only be done on someone by a person who has had the step himself.)

Q. **TOTAL ORGANIZE? (IS THE AREA ORGANIZING ONLY?)**

Handling: This is an indicator of many misunderstoods in the area, especially on the part of its senior. The senior and the personnel in the area need full Word Clearing on the materials to do with the production area, including Crashing Mis-U Finding as in J (Ref: HCO PL 26 Mar. 79RB, MISUNDERSTOOD WORDS AND CYCLES OF ACTION) off production hours and meanwhile make them produce what they can.

R. **ORGANIZATION ADEQUATE TO GET THE PRODUCT?**
   INADEQUATE ORGANIZATION?

Handling: Debug the organization per HCO PL 13 Sept. 70 II, BASIC ORGANIZATION; HCO PL 14 Sept. 70 I, COPE AND ORGANIZE; HCO PL 14 Sept. 70 II, HOW TO ORGANIZE AN ORG; HCO PL 8 Oct. 70, ORGANIZING AND PRODUCT; HCO PL 29 Oct. 70 I, THE ANALYSIS OF ORGANIZATION BY PRODUCT.

NO ORGANIZATION?

Handling: This is the situation where someone does not organize any corner of his area or work or organizations or lines. This manifests itself by irrational demands to only produce and to prevent any organization so that production can occur. The handling is to clear the misunderstoods (including Crashing Mis-Us) in the area, particularly on the purpose of the production and why one is producing.

LACKING A SENSE OF ORGANIZATION?

Handling: Lack of a sense of organization lies below the level of Mis-Us, overts and withholds and PTSness — and you have to go north through PTSness and overts and withholds to even get to the Mis-Us.

The handling would be de-PTSing as in step P. Then handle any overts and withholds and then clear the Mis-Us in the area being addressed (including Crashing Mis-Us).

Debug tech is laid out as a checklist in HCO PL 23 Aug. 79R II, DEBUG TECH CHECKLIST. It is a very useful checklist, as the points of debug can be assessed on a meter by an auditor (or any person trained to use an E-Meter) or be administratively used by anyone wishing to debug an area.

HCOB 23 Aug. 79R II, PRODUCT DEBUG REPAIR LIST, is for use by an auditor to repair someone who has been messed up by somebody trying to debug his area. As faulty debugging can mess a person up, this repair list has been written to remedy that, should it occur.

Normally, in an area that is very bogged and not producing, the first question or two will deliver the reasons right into your hands. They are trying to produce blue ruddy rods but the order they finally dig up after a fifteen-minute search says specifically and directly that green finglebums are what are wanted here and that blue ruddy rods are forbidden. It is usually outrageous and large. As you go down the list, you will find out that you are running into things which open the door to justification. So you take very good care to notice the justifications which are being used. The handling of justifications is indicated in HCOB 23 Aug. 79 I, CRASHING MIS-Us, BLOCKS TO FINDING THEM, and HCOB 21 Jan. 60 I, JUSTIFICATION.

WHAT TO HANDLE

Handling of course is indicated by what you find and the above references. But handling must always be in the direction of at least 50 percent production. Even while debugging, do not go for an all-organize handling. Also do not go for an all-production handling.

A person, once trained on the data as contained in this PL, Crashing Mis-U tech, False Data Stripping and Product Clearing, will be able to get almost any area debugged and producing. It is important to remember that debug tech applies from the very small expected action to the huge expected project.

THE EP OF DEBUG

The above debug actions are never carried on past the point where the target or area or individual or org has been debugged.

Once production has been debugged and desirable products are now being gotten for real in adequate quantity, the debug has been accomplished.

This could occur at any one of the above steps. And when it does, you let the area get on with producing the products they are now able to produce.

EVALUATION AND PROGRAMING

There is a whole different technology called evaluation. The full tech on how to evaluate and program is contained in the Data Series and the Data Series Evaluator's Course and the Target Series HCO PLs: 14 Jan. 69 I, OT ORGS; 16 Jan. 69, TARGETS, TYPES OF; 18 Jan. 69 II, PLANNING AND TARGETS; 24 Jan. 69 I, TARGET TYPES; 24 Jan. 69 II, PURPOSE AND TARGETS; and HCO PL 14 Dec. 73, TARGET TROUBLES. One is expected to know how to evaluate. But even after you have evaluated, evaluations contain targets. And targets get bugged. So you will need debug tech even when you are an accomplished evaluator.

———————

With the debug tech and the added steps of Crashing Mis-U Finding, overts and withholds, False Data Stripping, Product Clearing, etc., you will be able to crack the back of the most resistive nonproducing areas and get them into roaring, high-morale production.

Between February 79 and 23 August 79, I have spent a great deal of development time on the technology needed to completely debug people, projects, targets and production. A very large number of missions, researches and pilots were undertaken to discover and polish up this tech. It can now be considered a completed development cycle.

The above IS the tech.

USE IT!

L. RON HUBBARD
FOUNDER

HCO POLICY LETTER OF 17 NOVEMBER 2000

REMIMEO

ESTABLISHMENT OFFICER SERIES 38-1
STOPPING PRODUCTION LINES

(Originally issued 4 Oct. 79 as LRH Executive Training Instructions.)

I just figured out how some secretly ill-intentioned persons could go about totally stopping a production line. They could pretend to be busy and doing something while actually creating chaos and overt products and pretending to reform and reassuring people it was all going along, and so involve the actual producers in the area in complexities and problems to a point where nothing could be completed.

This would come from an extremity of PTSness or secret revenge, but it could be developed into a system which would effectually stop production without seeming to.

The clue that this might be going on is the consistent use of orders and policy to stop and pretended false data. It's a kind of a trap they would get one into.

L. RON HUBBARD
FOUNDER

HUBBARD COMMUNICATIONS OFFICE
SAINT HILL MANOR, EAST GRINSTEAD, SUSSEX

HCO POLICY LETTER OF 23 AUGUST 1979R
ISSUE II
REVISED 24 JUNE 1988

REMIMEO
TECH/QUAL
ALL EXECS
ALL STAFF
PROGRAMS CHIEFS
PROJECT OPERATORS
MISSION OPERATORS
MISSIONAIRES
DEPT OF SPECIAL AFFAIRS
LRH COMMS
FRS

ESTABLISHMENT OFFICER SERIES 39
PRODUCT DEBUG SERIES 2
DEBUG TECH CHECKLIST

Refs:

HCO PL	23 Aug. 79R I	Esto Series 38
	Rev. 23.8.84	Product Debug Series 1
		DEBUG TECH
HCOB	23 Aug. 79R II	Product Debug Series 10
	Rev. 14.6.88	PRODUCT DEBUG REPAIR LIST
The Product Debug Series		

(This checklist is clarified by HCO PL 23 Aug. 79R I,
DEBUG TECH, and is used in conjunction with that PL.)

Production is the basis of morale. People who don't get products have low morale.

Executives and responsible people have the task of getting out products. When they don't get them out, the unit or organization fails.

It is extremely upsetting and puzzling to a staff member and to his seniors when he can't get out the products expected of him. I have seen an executive going around in circles for weeks trying to guess why such and such a staff member couldn't get out the products of his post area. I have seen staff members actually in tears because they were unable to achieve the products of their post. I have also seen people busy, busy, busy and totally unaware of the fact that they were producing absolutely nothing.

LRH ED 302 was a breakthrough. It has now been written into HCO PL 23 Aug. 79R I, DEBUG TECH, and contains a considerably expanded tech on how to debug products. People have had very great success in applying it.

To give them even greater successes, I have rewritten LRH ED 302-1 into this PL. The whole object of this checklist is to debug a lack of products and accomplishments of an org or post.

USE OF THIS CHECKLIST

This Debug Checklist is used in conjunction with HCO PL 23 Aug. 79R I, DEBUG TECH. It gives the person doing the debug a list of things that could be standing in the way of production. The sequence of handling is as laid out in the Debug Tech PL. The first action is an inspection of the area. Then come the personal handling steps.

This sequence must be followed in any debug action. For instance, if you haven't done the inspection, then how would you know what it is you are trying to debug?

This checklist can be assessed on a meter or be administratively used (off the meter) by Mission Operators, Program Operators, Project Operators, Evaluators, executives and anyone else needing to debug a cycle of action or lack of products, including any staff member or student himself. The only restriction on the administrative use of the list is that Sections O (out-ethics and O/Ws), P (PTS) and S (drugs) must be turned over to a qualified auditor who checks them using an E-Meter. They are *not* checked without using a meter. This is to ensure that reads and withholds don't get missed on these sections.

When assessed on a meter, each reading line is taken to F/N by doing the handling given for that line. In many cases the full handling of a reading line will involve steps done off the meter or in another session. Where this is the case, the person being debugged is put back on the meter when all the handling steps for that question are done, to ensure that he is F/Ning and VGIs and satisfied that that point is now handled.

Though the checklist is often done with the use of a meter, its purpose is not to sort out a person's *case* considerations or difficulties. Some of its questions and handlings involve case-handling actions such as rudiments and PTS handlings, but the purpose of the list is to get stalled production *unstalled* and production occurring.

When doing this checklist the individual should have the issues and references he may need to carry out the handlings along with him. He must also have a copy of HCO PL 23 Aug. 79R I, DEBUG TECH, with him for ready reference.

Anyone using this checklist must be checked out and drilled on it and on HCO PL 23 Aug. 79R I, DEBUG TECH.

THE EP OF DEBUG

Debug actions are never carried on past the point where the target or area or individual or org has been debugged.

Once production has been debugged and desirable products are now being gotten *for real in adequate quantity,* the debug has been accomplished.

This could occur at any one of the steps. And when it does, you let the area get on with producing the products they are now able to produce. But don't neglect to keep an eye on the area to make certain it is actually and stably debugged, and don't drop any incomplete action (such as PTS handling or False Purpose RD) because production is now occurring.

PRODUCT DEBUG REPAIR LIST

In case of a bog or trouble on the following checklist use HCOB 23 Aug. 79R II, PRODUCT DEBUG REPAIR LIST, to repair the person so he can continue with the debug actions.

INSPECTION

00. The first action in debugging an area is an inspection to see what is going on in terms of production.

    THIS ACTION IS *ALWAYS* DONE AS THE FIRST STEP IN ANY DEBUG. IT IS NOT OMITTED OR SKIMPED OR BRUSHED OFF.

    In inspecting the area you do the following, making notes on what you find and checking off each step as it is completed:

___ 1. You look for what products have been gotten out in the past.

___ 2. You look for products that are there completed.

___ 3. You look for what products can be attained in the immediate future.

___ 4. You look for the value of the products produced as compared to the overall cost of the production organization.

___ 5. You look for overt products or cycles where products continuously have to be redone, resulting in no or few products.

    Full data on how to do this inspection is given in HCO PL 23 Aug. 79R I, DEBUG TECH.

0. Find a product that *can* be gotten out, any product, and insist that it and products like it or similar cycles be gotten out flat out by the existing personnel.

THE CHECKLIST

Section A:

A1. **NO ORDERS?** _____

    (Find out if [a] he's needing orders due to not knowing his hat, [b] he's not getting any direction or guidance from his senior or [c] if he never received the orders. Handle [a] by getting him hatted or [b] by doing this checklist on his senior or [c] by having him get the orders and handle any cut line that isn't relaying the orders.)

A2. **CROSS ORDERS?** _____

    (Find out what and handle per HCO PL 13 Jan. 79, ORDERS, ILLEGAL AND CROSS.)

A3. **ILLEGAL ORDERS?** _____

    (Find out what and handle per HCO PL 13 Jan. 79, ORDERS, ILLEGAL AND CROSS.)

A4. **VERBAL TECH?** _____

   (Find out what and handle per the "How to Defeat Verbal Tech
   Checklist" in HCO PL 23 Aug. 79R I, DEBUG TECH, and with False
   Data Stripping.)

Section B:

B1. **HASN'T READ THE ORDERS?** _____

   (Have him read, word clear and star-rate the orders.)

B2. **AVOIDANCE OR NEGATION OF POLICY?** _____

   (Get his O/Ws off per HCOB/PL 2 Mar. 84R, O/W WRITE–UPS,
   or with Sec Checking. Then clear up his Mis-Us on the relevant
   policy.)

B3. **POLICY UNKNOWN?** _____

   (Determine what applicable policy is unknown to him and have him
   read, word clear and star-rate it.)

B4. **LACK OF TECH?** _____

   (Have him get familiar with the exact problem he's encountering
   and make him work out a solution that will handle it.)

B5. **NEVER LOOKED OVER AND READ UP ON THE EXACT
   MATERIALS YOU ARE SUPPOSED TO BE USING IN THIS
   PROJECT OR ACTION?** _____

   (Have him read and word clear the exact materials he needs to know
   to get out the products.)

B6. **NEVER MEMORIZED THE BASIC STABLE DATA AND LAWS OF
   THE AREA?** _____

   (Have him dig up and memorize the stable data and laws of his field
   or area. Note that this applies to admin and other type personnel
   quite in addition to technical people.)

Section C:

C1. **MISUNDERSTOODS?** _____

   (Find and clear the Mis-Us.)

C2. **MISUNDERSTOODS ON THE ORDERS?** _____

   (Find and clear the Mis-Us.)

C3. **DOESN'T UNDERSTAND THE ORDERS?** _____

   (Handle with Word Clearing and False Data Stripping.)

C4. **FALSE DATA ON THE ORDERS?** _____

   (Handle with False Data Stripping.)

C5. OUT OF AGREEMENT WITH THE ORDERS? _____

(Get any out-ruds handled. Then handle with Word Clearing and False Data Stripping. If needed, get C/S okay and do a Disagreement Check per HCOB 22 Mar. 72RA, DISAGREEMENT CHECK.)

C6. NO INTEREST? _____

(Find out if it's out-ruds or Mis-Us or past failures and handle accordingly.)

C7. LACK OF VALUE OF THE CYCLE OF ACTION ITSELF? _____

(Find his Mis-Us and handle. Have him demo out the cycle of action.)

Section D:

D1. FINANCE BUGS? _____

(Find out what the bug is and get it debugged by using this checklist and finance policy on it. If it amounts to that, get the whole FP Committee through the FP pack.)

D2. LOGISTICS PROBLEMS? _____

(Find out what it is and handle with HCO PL 14 Mar. 72 II, FOLLOW POLICY AND LINES, and any other debug tech needed.)

D3. ARE YOU MISSING ANY EQUIPMENT? _____

(Find out what is needed and if it *is* really needed; if so debug it per D1 and D2 above so it is gotten. Remember that there are enormous percentages of people who absolutely have to have before they can possibly do and use that usually as an excuse not to produce.)

Section E:

E1. SCARCITY OF PERSONNEL? _____

(Indicate it. Then investigate and handle HCO, which is usually up to its ears in personnel requests and busy on them instead of putting an HCO there that properly recruits, hats and utilizes personnel. This may mean doing this Debug Checklist on the HAS or any person responsible for that division or activity because they aren't getting the products of staff members who produce.)

E2. SOME OTHER PROBLEM WITH PERSONNEL? _____

(Debug this using HCO PL 16 Mar. 71 IV, LINES AND HATS, and the Personnel Series, Org Series and Esto Series.)

F1. **ABSENCE OF HATTING?** _____

(Find out if it's [a] lack of a hatting course for the staff, [b] a hatting course where What Is a Course? PL is flagrantly not in, [c] the area's senior doesn't make sure his staff put in study time off production hours or [d] some other reason why the person does not go to study. Handle according to what comes up and HCO PL 23 Aug. 79R I, DEBUG TECH.)

F2. **DOESN'T ATTEND STUDY?** _____

(Find out if it's [a] lack of a hatting course for the staff, [b] a hatting course where What Is a Course? PL is flagrantly not in, [c] the area's senior doesn't make sure his staff put in study time off production hours or [d] some other reason why the person does not go to study. Handle according to what comes up and HCO PL 23 Aug. 79R I, DEBUG TECH.)

F3. **ABSENCE OF DRILLING?** _____

(Get any needed drilling on equipment and actions done.)

F4. **ABSENCE OF CRAMMING?** _____

(Get the subject cramming is needed on and send him to Cramming.)

F5. **FAULTY CRAMMING?** _____

(Get what occurred. If it doesn't clean up immediately, then send the data in to the C/S, who will program for handling, e.g., with a Cramming Repair List.)

F6. **A DISASSOCIATION BETWEEN THE THEORY OF WHAT IS SUPPOSED TO BE DONE AND THE PHYSICAL UNIVERSE?** _____

(Get the specific area of disassociation and have him demonstrate — in clay if necessary — and give real examples of the application of the theory. Program for the Hubbard Key to Life Course and Super Power.)

F7. **FALSE DATA ON THE HATTING MATERIALS?** _____

(Handle with False Data Stripping.)

F8. **LACK OF TECHNICAL KNOW–HOW?** _____

(Locate the area of technical know-how he is lacking in and get him studying and drilling the tech on it.)

F9. **UNABLE TO BE HATTED?** _____

(Strip off the false data in the area with False Data Stripping. If this does not fully handle, send the person's folder to the C/S for programing; the program can include Student Rehabilitation List, Study Green Form, False Purpose RD, etc., as applicable.)

Section G:

G1. **EXTERIOR INFLUENCE STOPPING THE PRODUCTION WHICH CANNOT BE HANDLED IN THE PRODUCTION AREA?**   _____

(Handle per Section G of HCO PL 23 Aug. 79R I, DEBUG TECH.)

Section H:

H1. **OTHER EVENTS OR REASONS?**   _____

(Find out what and handle per HCO PL 23 Aug. 79R I, DEBUG TECH.)

H2. **HUGE PRODUCTION BUG?**   _____

(Find out what and use full debug tech to handle.)

H3. **TIME?**   _____

(Find out if there's just NOT ENOUGH time to do what he has to do or if he's wasting time by not being organized or is being dev-ted. Handle with HCO PL 14 Feb. 80, ORDER VERSUS DISORDER, study and application of dev-t PLs, etc., as applicable.)

H4. **TROUBLE WITH COMM LINES?**   _____

(Find out what the trouble is. It could include W/Hs, Mis-Us, unfamiliarity with the comm lines, an incomplete or omitted Non-Existence Formula, an absence of functioning comm lines. Handle what is found as applicable per ethics policies, Word Clearing tech and the Org and Esto Series.)

H5. **INABILITY TO COMMUNICATE?**   _____

(Pull his W/Hs. Make him do Reach and Withdraw on the people and objects of his area. Program him for a TRs course and the Hubbard Key to Life Course.)

H6. **ABSENCE OF ALTITUDE?**   _____

(Have him read HCO PL 4 Oct. 68 II, ETHICS PRESENCE, and Exec Series 1 and 2. Have him demo how he can use them and then drill their use.)

Section I:

I1. **MISUNDERSTOODS OR CONFUSIONS IN THE PRODUCTION AREA?**   _____

(Routine Word Clearing per the Word Clearing Series.)

I2. **MISUNDERSTOODS OR CONFUSIONS ON WHAT IS SUPPOSED TO BE DONE?**   _____

(Routine Word Clearing per the Word Clearing Series.)

Section J:

J1. **CRASHING MISUNDERSTOOD?** _____

(Crashing Mis-U Finding per HCOB 17 June 79, CRASHING
MIS-Us: THE KEY TO COMPLETED CYCLES OF ACTION AND
PRODUCTS.)

J2. **TROUBLE COMPLETING CYCLES OF ACTION IN THE
PRODUCTION AREA?** _____

(Crashing Mis-U Finding per HCOB 17 June 79, CRASHING
MIS-Us: THE KEY TO COMPLETED CYCLES OF ACTION AND
PRODUCTS.)

Section K:

K1. **NO IDEA AT ALL THAT PRODUCTS SHOULD BE GOTTEN OUT?** _____

(Simply two-way comm on why the guy is there. It might come
as a startling realization that he is supposed to get out any products.
This can be backed up by Exchange by Dynamics per HCO PL
4 Apr. 72 I, ETHICS, and Product Clearing per HCO PL 13 Mar. 72,
PRODUCTION AND ESTABLISHMENT, ORDERS AND
PRODUCTS, or HCO PL 23 Mar. 72, FULL PRODUCT
CLEARING LONG FORM.)

K2. **PRETENDING TO KNOW THAT PRODUCTS SHOULD BE
GOTTEN OUT BUT DOESN'T GET THEM OUT?** _____

(Simply two-way comm on why the guy is there. It might come
as a startling realization that he is supposed to get out any products.
This can be backed up by Exchange by Dynamics per HCO PL
4 Apr. 72 I, ETHICS, and Product Clearing per HCO PL 13 Mar. 72,
PRODUCTION AND ESTABLISHMENT, ORDERS AND
PRODUCTS, or HCO PL 23 Mar. 72, FULL PRODUCT
CLEARING LONG FORM.)

K3. **WON'T COMPLETE A CYCLE OF ACTION?** _____

(Get the person's case looked into by a competent C/S and an Ethics
Officer for background. If you are dealing with a suppressive or
insane person, handle per ethics policies. If it is PTSness, get the
person de-PTSed; if it is pretended PTSness as per HCOB/PL 28
Feb. 84, PRETENDED PTS, get the person programed for the False
Purpose RD.)

Section L:

L1. **WRONG STAT?** _____

(Get the right stat figured out per policy on stats and stat
management so that it agrees with what he is supposed to produce
and actually measures his actual production.)

L2. **DOES THE STAT HAVE NOTHING TO DO WITH WHAT IS SUPPOSED TO BE BEING PRODUCED?** _____

(Get the right stat figured out per policy on stats and stat management so that it agrees with what he is supposed to produce and actually measures his actual production.)

Section M:

M1. **WRONG VFP?** _____

(Use HCO PL 24 July 78, SUBPRODUCTS, HOW TO COMPILE A SUBPRODUCT LIST, Exchange by Dynamics and full Product Clearing Long Form on the correct and actual VFP — as well as any other products the person or area might have.)

M2. **WRONG PRODUCT?** _____

(Use HCO PL 24 July 78, SUBPRODUCTS, HOW TO COMPILE A SUBPRODUCT LIST, Exchange by Dynamics and full Product Clearing Long Form on the correct and actual VFP — as well as any other products the person or area might have.)

M3. **UNSURE OF WHAT THE PRODUCT IS?** _____

(Get a complete and accurate statement of the correct product and product clear him on it. See also HCO PL 7 Aug. 76 I, PRODUCT–ORG OFFICER SYSTEM, NAME YOUR PRODUCT.)

M4. **THINKING IT'S THE AWARD RATHER THAN THE PRODUCT?** _____

(Use HCO PL 24 July 78, SUBPRODUCTS, HOW TO COMPILE A SUBPRODUCT LIST, Exchange by Dynamics and full Product Clearing Long Form on the correct and actual VFP — as well as any other products the person or area might have.)

M5. **OVERT PRODUCTS?** _____

(Handle any W/Hs connected with this. Then handle per HCO PL 23 Aug. 79R I, DEBUG TECH, Section M.)

M6. **NO MARKETING OR ADVERTISING OF THE PRODUCT?** _____

(Handle any W/Hs connected with this. Then handle per HCO PL 23 Aug. 79R I, DEBUG TECH, Section M.)

Section N:

N1. **NEVER FIGURED OUT WHAT WOULD HAVE TO BE DONE TO GET A PRODUCT?** _____

(Handle per HCO PL 23 Aug. 79R I, DEBUG TECH, Section N.)

Section O:

Note: Section O is to be done only by a qualified auditor using an E-Meter. It is not to be done off the meter.

Each question in Section O must be prefaced so that the questions are limited to the person's current post, position or the immediate cycle that is being debugged (e.g., "Concerning the production of ruddy rods, _____," "As dishwasher, _____" or "On the target to plant potatoes, _____," etc.).

O1. **OUT–ETHICS?**   _____

(Handle as a W/H, E/S to F/N. Then get the person sorted out by application of ethics conditions, Sec Checking, etc., as applicable per ethics policies. May require repair of past ethics conditions per HCO PL 19 Dec. 82R II, REPAIRING PAST ETHICS CONDITIONS.)

O2. **ACTIVE COUNTER–INTENTION?**   _____

(Handle as a W/H, E/S to F/N. Locate and clear the person's Mis-Us in the area of the counter-intention. C/S to program for False Purpose RD. In any case, watch him and remove him if he remains CI.

If it is CI on the part of others, then find out who and handle any agreement he has with their CI as a W/H, E/S to F/N. Get the person or persons who have CI handled on their O/Ws and get their Mis-Us found. C/S to program them for False Purpose RD. In any case, watch them and remove if they remain CI.)

O3. **OTHER–INTENTIONEDNESS?**   _____

(Handle the other-intentionedness as in O2.)

O4. **ARE YOU WITHHOLDING SOMETHING FROM ME?**   _____

(Pull it, E/S to F/N.)

O5. **HAVE YOU DONE THINGS YOU COULD BE HIT FOR?**   _____

(Handle as a W/H, E/S to F/N.)

O6. **ARE YOU BEING CRITICAL OF OR MALICIOUS ABOUT OTHERS?**   _____

(Pull all overts and withholds connected with this, each E/S to F/N. Note for handling of any black PR campaign he may be running on others. C/S to program for the False Purpose RD if applicable.)

O7. **HAVE YOU LISTENED TO CRITICAL OR MALICIOUS STATEMENTS ABOUT OTHERS?** _____

(Pull all overts and withholds he has connected with this, each E/S to F/N. False data strip the area of the critical or malicious statements to EP. Note for investigation and handling of any black PR campaign that may be occurring. C/S to program for the False Purpose RD if applicable.)

O8. **IS THIS NOT A POST OF YOUR OWN CHOOSING?** _____

(Handle the dishonesty of accepting a post with no intention of doing it and go E/S on times he's done that, to F/N. C/S to program for Sec Checking and/or False Purpose RD, as applicable.)

O9. **DO YOU KNOWINGLY DO THINGS THAT CAUSE OVERT PRODUCTS?** _____

(Get what he has done specifically and handle each thing done as a W/H, E/S to F/N. C/S to program for False Purpose RD.)

O10. **WHEN PRODUCTS ARE NOT COMING OUT RIGHT, DO YOU NOT CROSS–CHECK TO MAKE SURE YOU LOCATE ALL THE ERRORS?** _____

(Handle as a W/H, E/S to F/N.)

O11. **HAS ANY EQUIPMENT BEEN REMOVED OFF THE LINES?** _____

(Get the data. Handle any overts and withholds connected with it, E/S to F/N.)

O12. **HAVE YOU DAMAGED ANY EQUIPMENT?** _____

(Handle as a W/H, E/S to F/N.)

Section P:

Note: Section P is to be done only by a qualified auditor, using an E-Meter. It is not to be done off the meter.

P1. **LOTS OF UNSOLVABLE PROBLEMS IN THE AREA?** _____

(Get the data, noting all meter reads and route it to the C/S. The person will need PTS handling per ethics policies. Other personnel in the area must also be checked for PTSness and handled as found necessary.)

P2. **CONNECTED TO SOMEONE OR SOMETHING ANTAGONISTIC?** _____

(Get the data, noting all meter reads and route it to the C/S. The person will need PTS handling per ethics policies.)

P3. **PTS?** _____

(Get the data, noting all meter reads and route it to the C/S. The person will need PTS handling per ethics policies.)

P4. **ACCIDENTS?** _____

(Get the data, noting all meter reads and route it to the C/S. The person will need PTS handling per ethics policies.)

P5. **ROLLER–COASTERING?** _____

(Get the data, noting all meter reads and route it to the C/S. The person will need PTS handling per ethics policies.)

Section Q:

Q1. **ORGANIZING ONLY?** _____

(Handle his Mis-Us in the area, including any Crashing Mis-Us.)

Q2. **TOTAL ORGANIZATION?** _____

(Handle his Mis-Us in the area, including any Crashing Mis-Us.)

Section R:

R1. **IS THE AREA DISORGANIZED?** _____

(If this is the case, do the inspection and handling steps of HCO PL 14 Feb. 80, ORDER VERSUS DISORDER. Also get done any needed study, Word Clearing, Crashing Mis-U Finding, etc., as per Section R of HCO PL 23 Aug. 79R I, DEBUG TECH, so that the area is understood and gotten organized and productive.)

R2. **IS A LOT OF TIME SPENT TRYING TO FIND THINGS?** _____

(Handle as in R1.)

R3. **ARE THINGS NOT FILED BUT JUST PILED AROUND THE AREA?** _____

(Handle as in R1.)

R4. **IS THERE NO SYSTEM OF LOCATING THINGS?** _____

(Handle as in R1.)

R5. **ARE THINGS NOT LOGGED IN AND OUT WHEN THEY ARE USED?** _____

(Handle as in R1.)

R6. **DOESN'T UNDERSTAND THE THINGS BEING USED WELL ENOUGH TO ORGANIZE THEM?** _____

(Handle as in R1.)

R7. **PUZZLED ABOUT HOW TO ORGANIZE THE AREA?** _____

(Handle as in R1.)

R8. **LACKING A SENSE OF ORGANIZATION?** _____

(Get the person through PTS handling per ethics policies. Next handle any overts and withholds on the area with Sec Checking, then clear the Mis-Us and Crashing Mis-Us in the area being addressed.)

R9. **NO GRASP OF THE CONCEPT OF ORGANIZATION?** _____

  (Handle as in R8.)

Section S:

  Note: Section S is to be done only by a qualified auditor, using an E-Meter. It is not to be done off the meter.

S1. **HAVE YOU EVER TAKEN DRUGS, MEDICINE OR ALCOHOL?** _____

  (Let him tell you about it, noting any reads. Get the data to the C/S so that he can be programed for full drug handling and/or FES and repair of past drug handlings.)

S2. **ARE THERE PEOPLE IN THE PRODUCTION AREA WITH UNHANDLED DRUGS?** _____

  (Get the data and how he feels this may be affecting production in the area. Any unhandled drug cases must be gotten through the Purification RD and full drug handling.)

L. Ron Hubbard
FOUNDER

*Revision assisted by
LRH Technical Research
and Compilations*

HCO POLICY LETTER OF 14 FEBRUARY 1980

REMIMEO
EXEC HATS
ALL STAFF HATS

ORG SERIES 40
ESTABLISHMENT OFFICER SERIES 40
PRODUCT DEBUG SERIES 9

ORDER VERSUS DISORDER

Refs:

HCO PL	9 Feb. 74R	CONDITION BELOW TREASON
	Rev. 17.2.80	CONFUSION FORMULA AND EXPANDED CONFUSION FORMULA
HCO PL	30 Dec. 70	Personnel Series 15
		Org Series 20
		ENVIRONMENTAL CONTROL

I made a breakthrough recently, while investigating low production areas, and realized that a good deal more needs to be said on the subject of order and disorder.

Order is defined as a condition in which everything is in its proper place and performs its proper function. A person with a personal sense of order knows *what* the things in his area are, he knows *where* they are, he knows *what* they are for. He understands their value and relationship to the whole.

A personal sense of order is essential in getting out products in an area.

An orderly typist, for instance, would have all the materials requiring typing, she would have ample paper and carbons within arm's reach, she would have her correction fluid to hand, etc. With all preparatory actions done, she would sit down to type with an operational typewriter and would know what that typewriter was and what it was for.

She would be able to sit down and get her product, with no wasted motion or stops.

But let's say you had a carpenter who couldn't find his hammer and he didn't even know what a hammer was for and he couldn't find his chisel because when he picked it up he put it down and couldn't find it again and then he didn't know where his nails were. You give him a supply of lumber and he doesn't know what it's for, so he doesn't categorize it where he can put his hands on it.

How many houses do you think he would build?

The actual fact of the case is that a disordered person, operating in a disorganized area, makes a ten-minute cycle into a three-week cycle (believe it, this is true) simply because he couldn't find his ruler, lost his eraser, broke his typewriter, dropped a nut and couldn't find it again and had to send off to Seattle for another one, etc., etc., etc.

BASICS

In working with a group of nonproductive technicians recently, I discovered something interesting: out-basics. I actually found a lower undercut to what we generally think of when we say "basics."

These technicians had reportedly researched a key piece of equipment and had it all sorted out. But I found that they didn't even know the basic fundamental of what that machine was supposed to do and what they were supposed to be doing in their area!

That told me at once that they had no orderly files, no research data. They were losing things.

Now, if they were losing things, that opened the door to another basic: They couldn't have known where things were. They put down a tool over there and then when they needed it again they would have to look all over the place because they hadn't put it down where it belonged.

Their work was not organized so that it could be done and the tools were not known.

So I checked this out. Were they logging the things they were using in and out so they could find them again? Were they putting things away when they were done with them? No, they weren't.

This is simply the basic admin coupled with the knowledge of what the things one is working with are. It's orderliness and knowing what things are, knowing what they are for and where they are, etc. That's the undercut.

If people don't have a true knowledge of what the things they're working with are, if there are omitted tools, inoperational tools, if they don't know what their tools are supposed to do, if there are no files or if once used, files are not reassembled and put back in the file drawer, if things get lost and people don't know where things are and so on, they will be running around spending 3 or 4 hours trying to locate a piece of paper. That isn't production.

If a person can't tell you what the things he works with are, what they're for and where they are, he isn't going to get out any product. He doesn't know what he's doing.

It's like the carpenter trying to build a house without knowing what he's got to build it with, without understanding his tools and raw materials and the basic actions he must take to get his product. That's what was holding up production in the area: disorderliness. And the basics were out.

This is actually far *below* knowing the tech of the area — the actual techniques used to get the product. The person does not even know what his tools and equipment are or what they're supposed to do. He doesn't know whether they are operational or inoperational. He doesn't know that when you use a tool you return it to its proper place. When you have a despatch, you put it in a file where it can be retrieved. It undercuts even knowing the orders and PLs relevant to his hat.

What are the basics that are missing? The basics of sitting down to the table that one is supposed to sit down to, to do the work! The basics of knowing what the tools, materials and equipment he works with *are* and what he's supposed to do with them to get his product. Those are the basics that are missing.

We are down to a real reason why a person cannot turn out products.

That is what is holding up such a person's production. It is well below knowing the technique of his job.

Out-basics. Does the guy know where the file is? When he finishes with that file, does he leave it scattered all over the place or does he put it back together and into the file where it can be found?

Now, a person who's working will have papers all over the place, but does he know where they are and is he then going to reassemble them and put them back in order or is he going to just leave them there and pile some more papers on top of them?

If you find Project No. 2 scattered on top of Project No. 1, you know something about that area. Basics are out.

This is a little piece of tech and with that piece of tech you've got insight. You would have to have an overall picture of what the area would look like when properly ordered and organized — how it would be organized to get optimum production.

Then you could inspect the area and spot what's going on. You would inspect on the basis of: How does the area compare with how it should be organized? You would find out if the personnel didn't know what the things in their area were or what they were for, you would see if they knew the value of things in the area or if there were altered importances, omitted files or filing, actions being done out of sequence, inoperational tools or equipment, anything added to the scene that was inapplicable to production, etc.

In other words, you can inspect an area by outpoints against this one factor of orderliness.

This sort of out-basics and disorderliness cuts production down to nothing. There just won't be any production at all. There will be no houses built.

What we are talking about here is an orderly frame of mind. A person with a sense of order and an understanding of what he is doing sits down to write a story or a report and he'll have his paper to hand, he'll have it fixed up with carbons and he'll have his reference notes to hand. And before he touches the typewriter, he'll familiarize himself with what the scene is. He'll do the necessary preparatory work in order to get his product.

Now, someone else might sit down, write something, then dimly remember there was a note someplace and then look for an hour to find where that note was and then not be able to find it and then decide that it's not important anyway and then come back and forth a few times and finally find out he's typed it all up without a carbon.

There is a handling for this. Anyone trying to handle an area who doesn't understand the basics of what they're dealing with and is in an utter state of disorder must get a firm reality on the fact that until the basics are learned and the disorder handled, the area will not produce satisfactorily.

The following inspection is used in determining and handling the state of such an area.

INSPECTION

This inspection is done in order to determine an area's knowledge of basics and its orderliness. It can be done by an area's senior for the purpose of locating and correcting disordered areas. It is also used as part of debug tech as covered in HCO PL 23 Aug. 79 I, Esto Series 38, Product Debug Series 1, DEBUG TECH. It is for use by anyone who is in the business of production and getting products.

The full inspection below would be done, clipboard in hand, with full notes made and *then* handlings would be worked out based on what was found in the inspection (according to the Handling section of this PL and the suggested handlings given in parentheses below).

1. **DOES HE KNOW WHAT ORGANIZATION, FIRM OR COMPANY HE'S IN? DOES HE KNOW WHAT HIS POST OR JOB IS?**

   This is a matter of does he even know where he is? Does he know what the organization or company he works for is, does he know what the post he is holding is?

   (If he is so confused and disoriented that he doesn't even know the company or org he's in or doesn't know what his post is, he needs to apply the Expanded Confusion Formula, HCO PL 9 Feb. 74R, and then work up through the conditions.

   Of course the person would also need to be instant-hatted on his post — the organization, his post title, his relative position on the org board, what he's supposed to produce on his post, etc.

   If he is doing this handling as part of his Expanded Confusion Formula, simply have him get the instant hatting and carry on with his Confusion Formula.)

2. **ASK THE PERSON WHAT HIS PRODUCT IS.**

   Does he know? Can he tell you without comm lag or confusion?

   You may find out that he has no idea of what his product is or that he has a wrong product or that he has confusions about his product. Maybe he doesn't even know he's supposed to get out products.

   (If this is the case, he must find out what his product is. If the person's product is given in policy references, he should look these up. If his product is not covered in tech or policy references, he'll have to work out what it is.)

3. **CAN HE RATTLE OFF A LIST OF THE BASIC ACTIONS, IN PROPER SEQUENCE, NECESSARY TO GET OUT HIS PRODUCT OR DOES HE HEM AND HAW ON IT?**

Does he know what to do with his product once it is completed?

He may try to tell you what he does each day or how he handles this or that and what troubles he's having with his post. You note this, but what you're interested in is does he know the basic actions he has to take to get out his product? And does he know what to do with the product once it is complete?

(If he can't rattle off the sequence of actions 1, 2, 3, then he'd better clay demo the basic actions, in proper sequence, necessary to get out his product and then drill these actions until he can rattle them off in his sleep. If he does not know what to do with his product once completed, then he'd need to find out and then drill handling the completed product.)

4. **ASK HIM WHAT HIS TOOLS ARE THAT ENABLE HIM TO GET THIS PRODUCT.**

Note his reaction. Can he name his tools at all? Does he include the significant tools of his area? Does he include his hat pack as a tool?

(If he doesn't know what his tools are, he'd better find out what he's operating with and what it does. A good workman knows his tools so well he can use them blindfolded, standing on his head and with one arm tied behind his back.)

5. **ASK HIM TO SHOW YOU HIS TOOLS.**

Are his tools present in the work area or does he have them out of reach, down the hall or in some other room?

(He may have to reorganize his work space to get his tools within easy reach and to get in some basics of organization. The purpose of such organization would be to make production easier and faster.)

6. **ASK HIM TO TELL YOU WHAT EACH OF HIS TOOLS ARE.**

Can he define them?

Does he know what each of them are and what they are for?

(If he doesn't know, he'd better find out.)

7. **ASK HIM TO TELL YOU WHAT THE RELATIONSHIP IS BETWEEN EACH ONE OF HIS TOOLS AND HIS PRODUCT.**

(If he can't do this, have him clay demo the steps he takes to get out his products with each tool he uses, so he sees the relationship between each tool and his product.)

8. **ASK HIM TO NAME OFF THE RAW MATERIALS HE WORKS WITH. ASK HIM TO SHOW YOU HIS MATERIALS.**

Does he know what his raw materials are? Are they in his work area? Are they in order? Does he know where to get them?

(He may have to find out what the raw materials of his post are [by defining them] and where they come from. He should drill procuring and handling them and then run Reach and Withdraw on them.)

9. **DOES HE HAVE A FILE CABINET? FILES? ASK HIM WHAT THEY ARE.**

Does he know what they are for? Does he know what a despatch is, etc.?

(He may have to be brought to an understanding of what files, file cabinets, despatches, etc., *are* and what they have to do with him and his product. He may have to clay demo the relationship between these things. He will have to set up a filing system. Ref: HCO PL 18 Mar. 72, Esto Series 10, FILES.)

10. **DOES HE HAVE A SYSTEM FOR LOCATING THINGS?**

Ask to see it. Check his files. Does he have logs? Does he log things out and correct the logs when he puts them back? Are the comm baskets labeled? Does he have a specific place for supplies? Ask him to find something in his files. How long does it take?

Does he have an orderly collection of references or a library containing the materials of his field? Is it organized so as to be usable?

(If he has no system for locating things, have him set one up. Have him establish a filing system, a logging system, label the comm baskets, arrange supplies, etc. Get a reference library set up and organized. Drill using the system he has.)

11. **WHEN HE USES AN ITEM, DOES HE PUT IT BACK IN THE SAME PLACE? DOES HE PUT IT BACK WHERE OTHERS CAN FIND IT?**

He'll probably tell you, yes, of course he does. Look around. Are objects and files lying about? Is the place neat or is it a mess? Ask him to find you something. Does he know right where it is, or does he have to search around? Is there an accumulation of unhandled particles around?

(Have him clay demo why it might be advantageous to put things back in the same place he found them. Drill him on putting things back when he's finished with them. Have him clean up the place, handling any accumulation of unhandled particles.)

12. **IF FEASIBLE, ACTUALLY GO WITH THE PERSON TO HIS PERSONAL LIVING AREA.**

Is the bed made? Is the area clean? Are things put away? How much dirty laundry does he have? Is it stowed in a bag or hamper or is it strewn about the place? People who had disorderly personal MEST, one for one were *not* getting out any products on post — they had no sense of order.

(If his personal quarters are a mess, have him — on his own time of course — straighten up his personal area and keep it that way on a daily basis. This will teach him what order *is*.)

HANDLING

Some areas, of course, will be found to be in excellent order and will pass the inspection. These will most likely be high production areas.

Other areas will be found to have only a few points out which would correct easily with the above handlings. These will probably be areas where some production is occurring.

Where personnel have a concept of what order is and why it is important, they will usually be eager to correct the points of disorder that have turned up on the investigation and may need no further urging, drilling or correction, but will quickly set about remedying outpoints. For many bright and willing staff members just reading this policy will be enough to get them to straighten out their areas right away.

There is, however, a sector which has no concept of order and may not have the slightest notion of why anyone would bother with it. You will most likely find them in apathy, overwhelm or despair with regard to their post areas. No matter what they do they simply cannot get their products out in adequate quantity and quality. They try and try and try but everything seems to be working against them.

When you find such a situation, know that the area is in Confusion. You are trying to handle an area which is in a confirmed, dedicated condition of Confusion.

Such an area or individual would require the application of the Expanded Confusion Formula (HCO PL 9 Feb. 74R) including the handlings above. So if these things confirm in an area, you must use the Expanded Confusion Formula and the handlings given above to full completion. Because, frankly, such an area or individual *is* in a condition of Confusion and will remain in Confusion until the Expanded Confusion Formula, including the full handlings from the inspection, are applied.

Once out of Confusion the person would have to be brought up through the rest of the conditions.

CAUTION

The condition of Confusion is a very low condition and should never be assigned where it is not warranted. Where one or two points on the above inspection were found to be out in an area, and where these corrected easily, there would be no purpose in assigning Confusion to that area. In fact, it may worsen an area to assign an incorrect condition.

But where you have a long-term situation of no or few products combined with a state of disorder, know that the area or individual is in a condition of Confusion and that the application of the Confusion Formula plus the handlings given in this PL will bring the area out of the muck and up to square one where it can *begin* producing.

NOTE: If the inspection is done on a person or area and some of the points are found to be out and handlings are done but no condition of Confusion is assigned, the area must be reinspected about a week later. This way you will detect if an actual condition of Confusion was missed, as the area will have lapsed back into disorderliness or will have worsened.

SUMMARY

A knowledge of the basics of an area and having orderliness in an area are essential to production.

When you find a fellow who is a light-year away from the basics and doesn't have a clue on the subject of order and he's flying way up in the sky someplace instead of just trying to put together what he's supposed to put together or do what he's supposed to do, you've got your finger on his Why for no production.

With the inspection and handlings given in this policy, we can now handle any degree of disorderliness and disorganization.

And order will reign.

Nonproductive areas become capable of producing.

Already producing areas increase their production.

And production will roll.

L. RON HUBBARD
FOUNDER

HUBBARD COMMUNICATIONS OFFICE
SAINT HILL MANOR, EAST GRINSTEAD, SUSSEX

HCO POLICY LETTER OF 17 DECEMBER 1981

ESTABLISHMENT OFFICER SERIES 41
POST PURPOSE CLEARING REVIVED

(Originally issued as an HCO Bulletin of same date, same title.)

Ref: HCOB 4 Aug. 71R   POST PURPOSE CLEARING
Rev. 26.11.74

Recently some new technology, known as Deoppression, was developed for and is being used on orgs. (Deop is part of mission tech and is the subject of Flag Orders.)

There is a piece of good technology that has fallen out of use: It is Post Purpose Clearing. It is quite successful in raising the general tone level and production of orgs. All by itself it produces an increase in production.

It should be undertaken, for sure, after a Deoppression of an org is done. And, factually, it should be done in any case.

The tech of it is contained in the reference HCOB. But to that HCOB could be added additional steps.

PPC 12A. One asks, "What is your intention toward your post?" One takes this to F/N.

PPC 12B. One asks, "What is your post product?" One takes this to F/N.

PPC 12C is done, "What is your intention in getting out that product?" To F/N.

PPC 12D. "What volume of product do you intend to get out?" To F/N.

PPC 12E. "What degree of quality do you intend your products to have?" To F/N.

PPC 13 and PPC 14 are as given in the reference HCOB.

There is an added note to Post Purpose Clearing. It probably accidentally got swept aside when some Quals abused What, How and Why in questions and got org staff snarled up because these were listing questions. Qual was arbitrarily forbidden to use such listing questions and this may have influenced this action of Post Purpose Clearing, so necessary to orgs, and the tech got lost. The result has been, in some cases, confused and unproductive staffs.

Also, some seniors, not knowing how their own departments or divisions were supposed to run, tended to knock off hats and put people on posts doing the wrong things, resulting in a "hey you" org board.

The remedies for these two errors are quite plain.

1. When any step results in a BD F/N result, indicate it to the pc. In case of any bog, treat the two-way comm pc statements as though they were L&N items. Any bog can be repaired with an L4B.

2. In the case of executives and seniors, clear them on the various posts over which they have command, using the OEC Volumes for reference. This will tend to make them hold the form of the org.

Various outnesses will be found by any Qual attempting to do this on an org. They may discover, for instance, that the org has no hats: But this should not stop them, although it should be remedied fast as well.

By adding the intention step, Qual is certainly going to collide with a few rock slams regarding products or the org. But this is all to the good: we don't want rock slammers messing up products or the org. Any plants or people of evil intentions will show up, though PPC is not intended as an ethics cycle.

PPC is an organizing step and should not be used to stop production. But, at the same time, it should not be forbidden because it is an organizing step.

The speed with which a PPC can be done is not forever. At PPC 2, if the person is set up to have one as in this step, the PPC should, for most posts, simply sail along like a June breeze. With a VGIs at the end.

QUAL'S OBJECT IN GETTING THIS DONE ON A STAFF AND NEW STAFF MEMBERS IS TO IMPROVE THE QUALITY OF PRODUCTION OF THE ORG AND TO INCREASE THE PRODUCTION OF THE ORG.

It is quite true that the pay of the org depends upon the individual quality and volume productivity of each individual org member. A PPC well done throughout an org inevitably should raise, by making a better org, org income and pay.

Remember that orgs which have had the highest stats were those orgs which ran closest to OEC policy. This is an historical fact, borne out time after time. So in all Post Purpose Clearing, your main reference is green-on-white, the policy letters, and these should be handy and referred to in any case where the duties of the staff member are unclear.

It will also come about that you are handling someone who holds two or three posts. In that case, clear all of them but add a step PPC 12F, "Is there any conflict with your other hats and posts?" If it reads, "What are the conflicts?" and "How are you going to resolve that?"

All cautions and directions in the reference HCOB apply in doing any Post Purpose Clearing.

L. RON HUBBARD
FOUNDER

HUBBARD COMMUNICATIONS OFFICE
SAINT HILL MANOR, EAST GRINSTEAD, SUSSEX

HCO POLICY LETTER OF 26 DECEMBER 1981

REMIMEO

ESTABLISHMENT OFFICER SERIES 42
POST PURPOSE CLEARING
FOR MANAGEMENT TEAMS AND EXECUTIVES

(Originally issued as an HCO Bulletin of same date, same title.)

Refs:

HCO PL	17 Dec. 81	Esto Series 41
		POST PURPOSE CLEARING REVIVED
HCOB	4 Aug. 71R	POST PURPOSE CLEARING
	Rev. 26.11.74	

The two necessary ideas a management team or executive must have:

1. That a long-term view, as well as immediate remedies, is vital.

2. That an increase in stats and betterment of organization health is desirable.

Management staff members or executives who do not have these concepts or intentions have no business on a management team or on post as these two basics are why they are there.

A member of management or an exec can always shortsightedly operate for a quick profit (i.e., get lots of service sold but none delivered; buy a cheap machine that will look good on an FP but will break down in a month; do a fast, bad job to get up stats and then involve others for months trying to handle the botch; falsely reassure seniors that all is well when, in a short time, a crash will expose them; operate on short-term stats and ignore the gradual drift down over the months).

When only short-term views are taken, disaster is being courted.

A betterment of the organization and its prosperity has to be intended by management or an executive in order to bring it about. When a management team or an executive has other-intentioned items at work, they harm or destroy not only the organization but also themselves (i.e., not have to work so hard; be powerful personally; get even with others; have more time for the family; keep up with my golf; live better; wear better clothes; escape the Ethics Officer; and, of course, simply intending to do the place and staff in).

Upper-echelon intentions bring about the state of the division, org or network not only in the present but in the future. If they *intend* to make things go right, they will, of course, observe their area and study successful policies and actions of proven worth and apply them.

The state of stats, long term, of an executive or management team gives a definite revelation of their real intentions.

SUMMARY

Where any management team or executive is failing, it will be found that their view is very short term and they are other-intentioned on post.

In management and executive Post Purpose Clearing, one has to keep these two things in view.

A good manager or executive works hard hour by hour to keep the show on the road but always with a long-term view as well. And he intends that org and staff will prosper.

The auditor in Post Purpose Clearing will get a lot of glib answers. The stats, the honest ones, and the true long-term performance of the executive, measured by the health of his zone of responsibility, tell the tale and should be consulted when in doubt.

The Post Purpose Clearing auditor must be sure these two principles above are really the case and, if not, handle the executive so that they are.

L. RON HUBBARD
FOUNDER

HCO POLICY LETTER OF 29 MARCH 1982

PERSONNEL SERIES 30
ESTABLISHMENT OFFICER SERIES 43
PERSONNEL POLICY

We are building strongly for the future.

Scientology is going to go on for a VERY long time.

The way to build a strong future is to build a strong organization.

Internally, the only way we have been held back is by out-ethics and nonproduction. This does not build a strong organization or a strong future.

Therefore, we have no room on staffs for those who do not produce — or worse, are extravagant and produce overt products — or (which goes with poor production) are out-ethics.

We need productive people who keep their ethics in.

Individuals, and above all execs, are the building blocks of organizations.

To build strongly for the future, keep the above points in mind where appointing, promoting or handling personnel.

Personnel of that caliber belong outside orgs — they are the pcs and cases. Do not recruit them, appoint them or leave them on post when found.

One can mend people. But one cannot build a new world with broken straws.

It takes the ethical few to handle the many. And these are what our orgs must be built with now. The strong within only then can handle the weak outside.

Make it easy in the future for all of us. We have a long way to go. The speed we get there is measured by the ethical quality of persons on exec posts and on staffs. It is fine to be big brother to all the world — so long as we keep our staffs the top people. Be them.

L. RON HUBBARD
FOUNDER

HUBBARD COMMUNICATIONS OFFICE
SAINT HILL MANOR, EAST GRINSTEAD, SUSSEX

HCO POLICY LETTER OF 30 NOVEMBER 1982

REMIMEO
ALL ORGS
ALL EXECS
FBOS
D/FBOS

ADMIN KNOW-HOW SERIES 44
ORG SERIES 43
ESTABLISHMENT OFFICER SERIES 44
FINANCE SERIES 32

THE DEPUTY CO OR DEPUTY ED FOR DELIVERY AND EXCHANGE

Refs:

HCO PL	9 Aug. 79R II	AKH Series 38
	Rev. 19.11.79	Org Series 39
		Esto Series 37
		SERVICE PRODUCT OFFICER
HCO PL	10 Sept. 82	Finance Series 28
		EXCHANGE, ORG INCOME AND STAFF PAY
HCO PL	29 Jan. 71	Finance Series 1
		FLAG BANKING OFFICERS
HCO PL	10 Mar. 71R I	Finance Series 5
	Rev. 27.10.82	FBO HAT
HCO PL	27 July 82R	Finance Series 25
	Rev. 20.9.82	DEPUTY FBOs FOR MARKETING OF ORG RESOURCES FOR EXCHANGE (D/FBO FOR MORE)
HCO PL	3 Sept. 82	Finance Series 27
		DEPUTY FBO FOR MARKETING OF ORG RESOURCES FOR EXCHANGE (D/FBO FOR MORE) PURPOSE

(NOTE: The pilot for this post has been long and successful: it is the FCCI PO [Flag Case, Course, Internship Product Officer] whose duties were covered by the famous Bulldozer EDs issued on Flag. However, the FCCI PO also covers the post of what is now called D/FBO for MORE [D/FBO for Marketing of Org Resources for Exchange]. Without this post effectively manned, the FSO—Flag Service Org—collapses and any sag in its stats is instantly traced to the nonfunctioning of the FCCI PO post. The post once functioned well in the Office of the Staff Captain and has functioned less well in the Office of the CO FSO. Therefore, the D/CO [or D/ED] for Delivery and Exchange post is put in close liaison with the strong and powerful International Finance Office Network, while remaining under the authority of the CO or ED of the org.)

The Service Product Officer in any org should have D/CO or D/ED status.

His key function is to see that the org operates at the highest level of exchange. (Ref: HCO PL 10 Sept. 82, Finance Series 28, EXCHANGE, ORG INCOME AND STAFF PAY)

Therefore, his post is now retitled D/CO (or D/ED) for Delivery and Exchange and he is located in the Office of the CO/ED, Department 19, of all Class IV and Sea Org orgs.

He is the bridge between the D/FBO for MORE and the FBO.

This creates a flow:

You have the D/FBO whipping up business by seeing that the public is made aware of the org's products and services, and driving more business down on the org than it can waste.

The D/CO (or D/ED) for Delivery and Exchange makes sure this public gets SIGNED UP and SERVICED. He is a product officer who names, wants and gets promotion, sales, call-in, delivery itself and re-sign occurring.

The FBO, then, sees to the org's solvency by ensuring income is greater than outgo, that production is properly financed, that staff are well paid for their production and that Flag is recompensed for good management of the org. And all of this makes it possible for the org to then expand and deliver in greater volume.

The flow goes from public (D/FBO) to ⟶ the whole sign-up and service line (D/CO or D/ED for Delivery and Exchange) to ⟶ solvency and volume (FBO).

It is this incredibly workable lineup that takes an org stably up the conditions of exchange. (Ref: HCO PL 10 Sept. 82, Finance Series 28, EXCHANGE, ORG INCOME AND STAFF PAY)

But the line breaks down where there is no D/CO or D/ED for Delivery and Exchange posted. And where it breaks down most specifically and ruinously is in the area of CALL–IN.

If one wants call-in to occur and the org's exchange with its public kept in, the only way to do it and also expand the org is to get a D/CO or D/ED for Delivery and Exchange on post and functioning.

Public interest may be kindled, public reach may be occurring, public may be paying partially or in full for goods or services, but if goods and services aren't being delivered in full the flow is broken and the org is in a condition of only partial exchange. Delivery in full means calling in the person so the service CAN be delivered. In this way the org maintains "fair exchange" with each and every public on its lines.

So the answer for any org that is sitting in a condition of only partial exchange, or an org that is ANYWHERE below the fourth condition of exchange — exchange in abundance — is to immediately, at once and yesterday, and without ripping off some vital post, post a D/CO or D/ED for Delivery and Exchange.

The first and primary function of the D/CO (or D/ED) for Delivery and Exchange is CALL–IN and this means he personally gets call-in done all by his little lonesome. With his own hands and voice he himself begins to call in fully and partially paids. Call-in is his first duty and when he's got that going he posts a Call-in Officer to take over the hat which he has already begun and he then expands onto the other functions of his D/CO or D/ED for Delivery and Exchange post, as covered in HCO PL 9 Aug. 79R II,

SERVICE PRODUCT OFFICER. But he FIRST and PERSONALLY and BY HIMSELF gets call-in going and exchange occurring at once.

What is involved here is the administrative principle that in order to get something done that is an expanding function you give it to somebody and tell him to expand it.

A CO or ED, whose responsibility it is to see that the main functions of the org are getting done, also wears the planning and coordination hat for the whole of the org's activity. If he's going to get the show on the road he needs to delegate some of this responsibility. He needs a deputy—the Deputy CO (or D/ED) for Delivery and Exchange—and that deputy needs the authority and the clout to see that, through promotion, sales, call-in, delivery and re-sign, the main products of the org do get produced.

Getting this post filled competently enables the ED to fully wear his planning and coordination hat and makes it possible for the flow from D/FBO to D/CO (or D/ED) for Delivery and Exchange to FBO to occur.

As some orgs in recent times have experienced both external and internal suppression on the subject of calling people in and servicing them, the D/CO (or D/ED) for Delivery and Exchange is given the additional powers of immediate communication to the International Finance Office and the Inspector General Network without vias to report and get help to remedy internal and external situations in orgs which suppressively inhibit call-in, delivery or expansion whether by inattention, refusals to post vital posts, failures or refusals to contact or call in interested persons, theft of org prospects or business or outright rip-offs to the end of ensuring successful execution of his duties and the expansion of the org. A form for such a report will be provided but absence of a form or a supply of such forms must not inhibit such reports.

This IS the winning combination by which an org moves up to "fair exchange" with all of its public and from there up to the highest level of exchange.

And it is the highest level of exchange toward which the whole activity of the D/CO or D/ED for Delivery and Exchange is geared—exchange in abundance!

L. RON HUBBARD
FOUNDER

516

HUBBARD COMMUNICATIONS OFFICE
Saint Hill Manor, East Grinstead, Sussex

HCO POLICY LETTER OF 29 DECEMBER 1982RA
Issue II
Revised 21 January 1991

Admin Know-How Series 45
Executive Series 24
Org Series 45
Establishment Officer Series 45

THE TOOLS OF MANAGEMENT

Refs:

HCO PL	11 Apr. 70 I	THIRD DYNAMIC TECH
HCO PL	28 July 72	Exec Series 16
		Org Series 32
		Esto Series 26
		ESTABLISHING, HOLDING THE FORM OF THE ORG
HCO PL	1 July 82	AKH Series 41
		MANAGEMENT COORDINATION

There is a simplicity to managing effectively. It begins with the basics of management.

Although it may appear so to some, successful management is not a highly complicated, esoteric activity. But, just as an auditor or a C/S must know and be able to use the exact tools of first dynamic tech in handling cases in order to achieve exact and standard results on a one-for-one basis, so must an executive or manager know and be able to use the exact tools of third dynamic tech in handling groups to achieve successful and exact results in every instance.

Within the wealth of data on third dynamic tech contained in HCO Policy Letters, the OEC Volumes and recorded LRH lectures and books on the subject, there are certain definite, specific *tools* a manager uses. These are the tools of management.

The difference between brilliant management and mediocre or no management, at any level, lies in:

1. Knowing what the *tools* of management are, and

2. Knowing how to use them.

Many people are not aware that, like a carpenter or any other workman, a manager uses specific and exact *tools*. Thus, we see people here and there who are doing the equivalent of using the handle of a chisel to drive nails into wet concrete.

It is a common fault with inexpert workmen to find them using their tools wrongly or not using them at all. They make a breakthrough when they discover what the specific tools are for.

One can see this in people who can't mix sound or can't become mixing engineers. They sit with all these knobs in front of them, reach out and grab this knob or that one, hoping hopefully something will happen to the sound. Yet every component they have in front of them is an exact tool to do an exact thing with sound!

There are a lot of comparisons one could make, but the point is that people in management positions have precise *tools* available to them in Dianetics and Scientology which happen to be far better tools than have ever been available on the planet.

One can have very good people on management posts who still can drown if they don't know and put to use the management tools.

But without these being specified as exact tools, one might not see the simplicity of it.

MANAGEMENT ECHELONS

Operating as it does into an expanding scene, Scientology has grown into the need for and use of various echelons of management.

In orgs, for some time we have had division heads and above them we have the Executive Council, headed by the CO or ED of the org.

Above the level of service orgs we have middle management and still above that we have the Senior Executive Strata of management. And each of these echelons must know the tools of management and how to use them.

The OEC (Org Executive Course) and the FEBC (Flag Executive Briefing Course) have long been established as the essential courses for training executives at service org level and above.

These courses, and the OEC and Management Series Volumes upon which they are based, teach the form of the org and how to use the parts and posts and functions that go to make up the whole. They give us executives who know how to correctly utilize staff and their assigned posts and duties. We call it "knowing how to play the piano" — it's a matter of knowing what key to hit when and which keys to use in combination to produce a desired result. (Ref: HCO PL 28 July 72, ESTABLISHING, HOLDING THE FORM OF THE ORG) In other words, it's a matter of knowing and using one's tools. The OEC and FEBC courses teach this data and much, much more.

While at this writing there are numerous OEC and FEBC grads and more in the making, thousands more will be needed to handle the current rate of expansion.

Meanwhile an executive at any level and whatever his training needs to know and use his management tools NOW if he is to function at all.

A div head must "know how to play the piano" within his division.

The posts of CO or ED, Chief Officer, Supercargo, Org Exec Sec and HCO Exec Sec require executives who are capable of "playing the piano" across the divisions of the entire org and using hats and posts and functions correctly in order to achieve immediate production from the org as a whole.

At middle management one is handling not one function nor only one org but many orgs and their functions, which requires "knowing how to play the piano" at that level.

And at the Senior Executive Strata of management, we get into the vital need for "knowing how to play the piano" across a much wider sphere, using the full scope of management tools and using them with high skill. One might be using the same tools as lower stratas of management but a higher level of expertise is required as one's planning, decisions and actions are influencing far, far broader areas.

What has brought this about is the rapid expansion of Scientology into wider zones of responsibility and therefore increased responsibility with a resultant increase in traffic. This naturally has to be handled by increasing efficiency. What it has done, in effect, is push some up from lower-level management status to upper-level management status, necessarily. Without realizing it, some executives have been climbing a status stairs in terms of influence and zones of control. And they can go only so high without being terribly precise in their use of tools. After that, without this acquired precision, they drown.

The obvious answer to all of this is an executive training program which instant-hats executives on the fundamental tools of management and provides Management Status checksheets through which an executive or manager raises his status by *becoming more and more expert with these and an even wider range of tools*. And such a program has now been developed!

MANAGEMENT STATUS CHECKSHEETS

The new executive training program consists of three status levels.

These levels are to be covered in a series of Management Status checksheets.

The Management Status One checksheet has a prerequisite of Staff Status II. It *instant-hats* an exec on the basic tools of management, such as:

The Admin Scale, target policy, strategic plans, programs, specific lines and org terminals, org boards, despatches and telexes, statistics and graphs, conditions, hats and hatting, files, personnel folders, ethics folders, etc. Each one is a specific tool.

The Management Status Two checksheet (with an OEC prerequisite) consists of a profound review of the basic management tools and study of the upper-level tools of management, which include:

Surveys, PR, pilots, review of past performance, general economics, finance systems, cost accounting, control through networks, admin indicators, morale, legal, goodwill, exchange, missions (Action missions), economical management and managing by dynamics.

The Management Status Three checksheet (with FEBC prerequisite) would be a more profound review of the basic *and* upper-level management tools, in addition to training on the twelve ingredients of expansion upon which the Senior Executive Strata operates.

Even an OEC or FEBC grad would do the Management Status checksheets as, when he comes out of an OEC or FEBC, all in the clouds, the Management Status checksheet is needed to bring him back down to earth and tell him he's dealing with tools which are very finite tools.

What is being communicated to executives by these checksheets is that they have tools, what the tools are exactly, and that they must use them.

EXECUTIVE STATUS LEVELS

There are specific requirements to be met by a manager to attain each of the three Executive Status levels.

Working up through these status levels, a manager not only becomes more proficient in handling an org, any org, but becomes fully certified to operate at middle or senior echelons of management.

The Executive Status levels are:

1. EXECUTIVE STATUS ONE: At this level, the person is simply thrown on post, the basic management tools are put into his hands via a brief, rat-a-tat-tat Management Status One checksheet and he gets on with it.

2. EXECUTIVE STATUS TWO: For one to be certified at this level, one must have completed the OEC, done the Management Status Two checksheet and have an adequate production record.

3. EXECUTIVE STATUS THREE: For one to be certified at this level, he must have completed the FEBC, done the Management Status Three checksheet and have a proven production record.

When the steps for Executive Status certification are complete, the exec must present adequate evidence of such to the Qualifications Division. After verification of the evidence, he is awarded the appropriate Executive Status certificate.

By use of these Executive Status levels, executives at management levels could see what executives they had (or not had). The designation "ES I" (Executive Status I) would tell them at once what they were dealing with, etc. Also, from the viewpoint of the individual, he would know where he had to go to get an upper-level rating.

Once these Management Status checksheets are issued, middle and central management personnel should not draw full pay or be bonus eligible until they have completed the Management Status One checksheet, as they will not be operating effectively until they have done this.

EXECUTIVE STATUSES AND STAFF STATUSES

The Exec Status levels do not replace Staff Status training. All staff and execs are programed and move up the Staff Statuses so as to have a better idea of the org as an org; these levels are also indicative of the training and experience of a staff member and show his promotion eligibility.

An executive should attain Executive Status One by completing the Management Status One checksheet as soon as possible upon assuming post, so he has the management tools available for his immediate application.

Once an exec attains Staff Status VI (Org Exec Course graduate), he can attain Executive Status Two by fulfillment of the requirements listed above. An FEBC graduate achieves Executive Status Three in a similar fashion.

SUMMARY

With the release of the new Management Status checksheets, precise and gradient training levels for all echelons of management will exist comparable to the precise and gradient training levels required for all echelons of technical delivery.

Quite an unbeatable combination!

One winds up with managers fully familiar with their exact tools, having the one-two-three of management tech at their fingertips, and "knowing how to play the piano" effectively across an org, a continent, a planet!

So the answer to current expansion is an action which is geared to bring about even further expansion. And that is the only way to go!

It begins with the basic tools of management.

L. RON HUBBARD
FOUNDER

Revision assisted by
LRH Technical Research
and Compilations

HCO POLICY LETTER OF 30 JANUARY 1983

REMIMEO

ESTABLISHMENT OFFICER SERIES 46
KEEPING SCIENTOLOGY WORKING SERIES 28
YOUR POST AND LIFE

A vital datum has emerged in my recent whole track research.

IF ONE KNOWS THE TECH OF HOW TO DO SOMETHING AND CAN DO IT, AND USES IT, HE *CANNOT* BE THE ADVERSE EFFECT OF IT.

This applies in many, many ways and is in fact a key point of life — a fundamental that may underlie all others.

And it applies to you directly on a post and in life.

If you know the tech — and that includes policy — of your post and apply it, you cannot be the adverse effect of it. FACT!

This has many ramifications:

1. A hatted staff member is not only at cause over his post, he is safe.

2. A well-trained auditor gets no adverse reaction from auditing others.

3. A well-trained Supervisor has no adverse reaction from students.

4. A fully trained and functioning staff can get no real adverse reaction from superiors or even an enemy.

5. An SP confronted by someone who knows and can use all the tech concerning SPs would shatter.

The list could go on and on since the datum pervades all sectors of life itself. In fact, it is almost mystical!

There is a corollary: If one is experiencing an adverse effect on a post or in life, then he does not know or has not applied the tech or policy covering it.

There is also a limiting factor: The full benefit of the datum is not sweepingly realized in all sectors until one is all the way up the Bridge. *BUT* the datum is so powerful that it can be applied and will manifest itself even in small things like opening cans, much less doing a post.

And knowing that one datum can save you enormous trouble and grief and put you on the road to OT doing what you're doing and right where you are!

Nice, eh?

L. RON HUBBARD
FOUNDER

HCO POLICY LETTER OF 31 JULY 1983R
ISSUE I
REVISED 21 JANUARY 1991

ADMIN KNOW-HOW SERIES 48
EXECUTIVE SERIES 26
ORG SERIES 46
ESTABLISHMENT OFFICER SERIES 47

BASIC MANAGEMENT TOOLS

Refs:

HCO PL	29 Dec. 82RA II	AKH Series 45
	Rev. 21.1.91	Exec Series 24
		Org Series 45
		Esto Series 45
		THE TOOLS OF MANAGEMENT
HCO PL	31 July 83 II	AKH Series 49
		Exec Series 27
		Org Series 47
		Esto Series 48
		MANAGEMENT TOOLS BREAKTHROUGH

The following is a list of the materials which, out of the many tools of management, comprise the BASIC MANAGEMENT TOOLS.

1. *ADMIN SCALE:* A scale for use which gives a sequence (and relative seniority) of subjects relating to organization. The scale, from the top down, includes: Goals, Purposes, Policy, Plans, Programs, Projects, Orders, Ideal Scenes, Statistics, Valuable Final Products. The scale is worked up and down until it is (each item) in full agreement with the remaining items. In short, for success, all these items in the scale must agree with all other items in the scale on the same subject.

2. *TARGET POLICY:* A series of policy letters which describe each type of target and how they are to be used by staff, executives and management personnel to get something *done.*

3. *STRATEGIC PLANS:* A STRATEGIC PLAN is a statement of the intended plans for accomplishing a broad objective and inherent in its definition is the idea of clever use of resources or maneuvers for outwitting the enemy or overcoming existing obstacles to win the objective. It is the central strategy worked out at the top which, like an umbrella, covers the activities of the echelons below it.

4. *PROGRAMS:* A PROGRAM is a series of steps in sequence to carry out a plan. Programs are made up of all types of targets coordinated and executed on time.

5. *PROJECTS:* A PROJECT is a series of guiding steps written in sequence to carry out one step of a program, which, if followed, will result in a full and successful accomplishment of the program target.

6. *ORDERS:* An ORDER is the direction or command issued by an authorized person to a person or group within the sphere of the authorized person's authority. It is the verbal or written direction from a lower or designated authority to carry out a program step or apply the general policy. Some program steps are so simple that they are themselves an order or an order can simply be a roughly written project. By implication an order goes from a senior to juniors.

All orders of whatever kind by telex, despatch or mission orders must be coordinated with current written command intention. You can destroy an org by issuing orders to it uncleared and uncoordinated. Coordinate your orders! Clear your orders!

7. *COMPLIANCE REPORTS:* A COMPLIANCE REPORT is a report to the originator of an order that the order has been done and is a completed cycle. It is not a cycle begun, it is not a cycle in progress, it is a cycle completed and reported back to the originator as done.

When an executive or manager accepts "done" as the single statement and calls it a compliance, noncompliance can occur unseen. Therefore, one must (1) require explicit compliance to every order and (2) receive the evidence of the compliance pinned to the compliance report. Such evidence might be in the form of copies of the actual material required by the order and procured, or photographs of it, ticket stubs, receipts, a signed note stating the time and place some action was carried out, etc. Evidence is data that records a "done" so somebody else can know it is done.

It is up to LRH Comms, Flag Reps or execs to verify reports of dones or get dones done. True compliances to evaluated programs are vital.

8. *TERMINALS:* A TERMINAL is something that has mass and meaning which originates, receives, relays and changes particles on a flow line. A post or terminal is an assigned area of responsibility and action which is supervised in part by an executive.

A fixed-terminal post stays in one spot, handles specific duties and receives communications, handles them and sends them on their way.

A line post has to do with organizational lines, seeing that the lines run smoothly, ironing out any ridges in the lines, keeping particles flowing smoothly from one post to another post. A line post is concerned with the flow of lines, not necessarily with the fixed-terminal posts at the end of the lines.

9. *LINES:* A LINE is a route along which a particle travels between one terminal and the next in an organization; a fixed pattern of terminals who originate and receive or receive and relay orders, information or other particles.

A COMMAND LINE is a line on which authority flows. It is vertical. A command line is used upward for unusual permission or authorizations or information or important actions or compliances. Downward it is used for orders.

A COMMUNICATION LINE is the line on which particles flow; any sequence through which a message of any character may go. It is horizontal.

The most important things in an organization are its lines and terminals. Without these in, in an exact known pattern, the organization cannot function at all. The lines will flow if they are all in and people wear their hats.

10. *ORG BOARDS:* An ORG BOARD (ORGANIZING BOARD) is a board which displays the functions, duties, sequences of action and authorities of an organization. The org board shows the pattern of organizing to obtain a product. It is the pattern of the terminals and their flows. We see these terminals as "posts" or positions. Each of these is a hat. There is a flow along these hats. The result of the whole org board is a product. The product of each hat on the board adds up to the total product.

11. *HATS:* HAT is a term to describe the write-ups, checksheets and packs that outline the purposes, know-how and duties of a post. It exists in folders and packs and is trained in on the person on the post to a point of full application of the data therein. A HAT designates what terminal in the organization is represented and what the terminal handles and what flows the terminal directs. HATTING is the action of training the person on the checksheet and pack of materials for his post.

12. *TELEXES:* A TELEX is a message sent and received by means of telex machines at specific stations hooked up with one another. This is a fast method of communication, similar to a telegram or cable.

Use telexes as though you were sending telegrams. Positiveness and speed are the primary factors. Cost enters as a third. Security enters as a fourth consideration. All have importance but in that order.

Telexes must be of such clarity that any other person in the org can read and understand them. You must take responsibility for both ends of a communication line. Write your communication (telex) so that it invites compliance or answer without further query or dev-t. Entheta in telexes on a long-distance comm line is forbidden.

Don't use telexes when despatches will do. Nonurgent communications on telex lines jam them. Do NOT put logistics (supply) on a telex line. Telex lines should only be used for communications concerning operations.

13. *DESPATCHES:* A DESPATCH is a written message, particularly an official communication. When writing a despatch, address it to the POST — not the person. Date your despatch. Route to the hat only, give its department, section and org. Put any vias at the top of the despatch. Indicate with an arrow the first destination. Sign it with your name but also the hat you're wearing when you write it.

As with telexes, despatches must be written so clearly that any other person in the org can read and understand them, with the originator taking responsibility for both ends of the communication line. And, as with telexes, entheta in despatches on a long-distance comm line is forbidden.

14. *STATISTICS:* A STATISTIC is a number or amount *compared* to an earlier number or amount of the same thing. STATISTICS refer to the quantity of work done or the value of it in money. Statistics are the only sound measure of any production or any job or any activity. These tell of production. They measure what is done. Thus, one can manage by statistics. When one is managing by statistics they must be studied and judged alongside the other related statistics.

15. *GRAPHS:* A GRAPH is a line or diagram showing how one quantity depends on, compares with or changes another. It is any pictorial device used to display numerical relationships.

16. *CONDITIONS:* A CONDITION is an operating state. Organizationally, it's an operating state and oddly enough, in the MEST universe, there are several formulas connected with these operating states. The table of conditions, from the bottom up, includes: Confusion, Treason, Enemy, Doubt, Liability, Non-Existence, Danger, Emergency, Normal, Affluence and Power or Power Change. There is a law that holds true in this universe whereby if one does not correctly designate the condition he is in and apply its formula to his activities or if he assigns and applies the wrong condition, then the following happens: He will inevitably drop one condition below the condition he is *actually* in. One has to *do* the steps of a condition formula in order to improve one's condition.

17. *PERSONNEL FOLDERS:* A PERSONNEL FOLDER is kept in HCO for each person employed by the org. The folder is to contain all pertinent personnel data about the person: name, age, nationality, date employment started, address (if other than the org), next of kin, social security number, test scores, previous education, skills, previous employment, case level, training level, name of post, former posts held and dates held, production record on post(s), date employment ceased, copies of all tests, and any other pertinent data.

Copies of contracts, agreements or legal papers connected with the person are filed in the personnel folder. The originals of such papers are kept in the val doc files.

A personnel folder is used for purposes of promotion and any needful reorganization and so should contain anything that throws light on the efficiency, inefficiency or character of personnel.

Personnel folders are filed by division and department in HCO, with the personnel in separate folders filed alphabetically in their department. There should be two sections in the personnel files: (1) present employees and (2) past employees.

18. *ETHICS FOLDERS:* An ETHICS FOLDER is kept in HCO for each individual staff member. It is a folder which should include his complete ethics record, ethics chits, Knowledge Reports, commendations and copies, as well, of any

justice actions taken on the person, such as Courts of Ethics or Comm Evs, with their results.

Filing is the real trick of Ethics work. The files do 90 percent of the work. Ethics reports patiently filed in folders, one for each staff member, eventually makes one file fat. When one file gets fat, call up a Court of Ethics on the person and his area gets smooth.

19. *FILES:* A FILE by definition is an orderly and complete deposit of data which is available for immediate use. As FILES are the vital operational line, it is of the GREATEST IMPORTANCE that ALL FILING IS ACCURATE. A misfiled particle can be lost forever. A missing item can throw out a whole evaluation or a sale. It is of vital interest both in ease of work and financially that all files are straight.

20. *DATA SERIES:* The tool to discover causes. The administrative technology described in these policy letters is applied to find what is logical by ferreting out what is illogical, using this to reveal the greatest outness which, when remedied, will resolve the scene.

There is considerably more data on each of these tools contained in the policy letters in the OEC Volumes and Management Series Volumes, *none* of it complicated or difficult to grasp.

The purpose of this policy letter is simply to advise the exec that these *are* his tools — his most fundamental and basic management tools. And that they are for USE and it is VITAL that he USE them.

Why? Because use of these simple, basic tools means the difference between a failing org and a flourishing one.

And we want organizations to flourish!

L. RON HUBBARD
FOUNDER

Revision assisted by
LRH Technical Research
and Compilations

HCO POLICY LETTER OF 31 JULY 1983

ISSUE II

REMIMEO
ALL ORGS
ALL EXECS
ALL MANAGEMENT
  PERSONNEL

VITAL — IMPORTANT

ADMIN KNOW-HOW SERIES 49
EXECUTIVE SERIES 27
ORG SERIES 47
ESTABLISHMENT OFFICER SERIES 48

MANAGEMENT TOOLS BREAKTHROUGH

Refs:

HCO PL	29 Dec. 82R II	AKH Series 45
	Rev. 30.7.83	Exec Series 24
		Org Series 45
		Esto Series 45
		THE TOOLS OF MANAGEMENT
HCO PL	31 July 83 I	AKH Series 48
		Exec Series 26
		Org Series 46
		Esto Series 47
		BASIC MANAGEMENT TOOLS

THE FIRST THING AN EXECUTIVE OR MANAGER AT ANY LEVEL NEEDS TO KNOW IS THAT HE HAS *TOOLS* WITH WHICH TO MANAGE.

This applies to top levels of management, to middle management echelons and in every org from the CO or ED down through the Exec Council and every head of a division or department.

BREAKTHROUGH

This datum is the result of a recent, eye-opening breakthrough.

The breakthrough was not a matter of discovering or developing or improving the materials which make up the tools of management. Org boards, the Admin Scale, target policy, planning and programing, statistics, graphs and conditions (to name a few of these tools) have been a part of our technology, well defined, available for use and used for quite some years now.

THE BREAKTHROUGH WAS IN DISCOVERING THAT A GREAT MANY EXECUTIVES DID NOT LOOK UPON THESE AS *TOOLS*.

But unless one does recognize them as tools, unless one actually puts them in the *category of tools,* like rakes and shovels and wheelbarrows, he is apt to think of them as opinions or theories or something of the sort. He won't recognize that he does have actual *tools* with which to manage. And, not realizing this, he won't USE them in managing.

Such a scene could be compared to somebody building a house who didn't even know he was trying to build a house and, should this be pointed out to him, he would look at hammers and saws as if they were total strangers. He wouldn't wind up with a house.

Any activity has its tools. And if one is going to engage in an activity, he had better know what its tools are and that they are for use.

BASIC MANAGEMENT TOOLS

We are rich in management tools but the most fundamental of them, required for use at any executive level from the highest to the lowest, are these:

ADMIN SCALE

TARGET POLICY

STRATEGIC PLANS

PROGRAMS

PROJECTS

ORDERS

COMPLIANCE REPORTS

ORG TERMINALS

SPECIFIC LINES

ORG BOARDS

HATS AND HATTING

TELEXES

DESPATCHES

STATISTICS AND GRAPHS

CONDITIONS

PERSONNEL FOLDERS

ETHICS FOLDERS

FILES

DATA SERIES

Each of these fundamental tools is defined and covered briefly in HCO PL 31 July 83 I, BASIC MANAGEMENT TOOLS.

None of these are complicated. They are actually SIMPLE but VITALLY, VITALLY IMPORTANT.

One gets some terminals, gets them some lines, gets the channels of command and echelon worked out, gets in strategic planning and with that one can achieve some coordination.

But it is necessary to be able to conceive of purpose (which, in target policy, becomes objectives). And it is necessary to be able to write targets that will accomplish that objective or that purpose. To get the targets done one needs lines and terminals there. And to have lines and terminals, of course, one has to have an org board.

SIMPLE. But VITALLY IMPORTANT.

In laying out these tools we are laying out the fundamentals of organization as that, most definitely, is what these tools are. And these tools will give one an organization. Without them, you don't have an organization, you have a mob. And if one cannot figure out purpose or objectives or write targets and telexes and get hatting done and hats worn they'll just keep on being a mob. But correct use of just this basic list of management tools can turn a mob into a producing organization!

EXEC STATUS ONE CHECKSHEET

A fast, instant-hat type of checksheet called Exec Status One is being provided to swiftly train execs and managers at all levels on these tools.

This is not a substitute for an OEC or FEBC. But it is vital that an exec starts using these tools right now, instantly and at once yesterday, if he considers himself an executive or is in a position of handling an organization of any type, size or kind. Because if he doesn't use these tools, he's going to lay an egg.

ETHICS

Once the exec has passed this first checksheet, Exec Status One, it's an ethics offense to fail to use these tools properly. One would handle a first or second offense with cramming, but after that it's a Court of Ethics and, in the case of a person having trained on these tools continuing to misapply or not apply these tools, it becomes a matter for a Comm Ev.

SUMMARY

1. First, an executive or manager must know that actual TOOLS EXIST for his use in managing.

2. Second, he needs to know WHAT his tools are.

3. Third, he must realize that these tools are SIMPLE but VITALLY, VITALLY IMPORTANT, that they are for USE and he must *USE THEM*.

L. RON HUBBARD
FOUNDER

HUBBARD COMMUNICATIONS OFFICE
SAINT HILL MANOR, EAST GRINSTEAD, SUSSEX

HCO POLICY LETTER OF 27 MARCH 1984

REMIMEO
EXECS
ESTOS
ALL NETWORKS
SENIOR HCO
HCOS
QUALS
HCO BOARDS OF REVIEW
MISSIONAIRES

ESTABLISHMENT OFFICER SERIES 49

THREE CLASSES OF PEOPLE

Refs:

HCO PL	19 Sept. 58	A MODEL HAT FOR AN EXECUTIVE
HCO PL	23 Feb. 78	LRH Comm Network Series 19 BOARD OF REVIEW
HCO PL	24 Feb. 72 I	INJUSTICE
HCO PL	29 Mar. 82	Personnel Series 30 Esto Series 43 PERSONNEL POLICY

People generally fall into three types:

1. Those who go along handling life,

2. Those who get into bad situations occasionally and have to be pulled out of them, and

3. Those who are incorrigibly making sure that nothing ever gets anywhere.

This is a very high generality but it has some workability in application.

Those in category 1 don't need any correction and are self-correcting.

Those in category 2 can be corrected and will then fly right.

Those in category 3 are simply dedicated losers and will continue to be dedicated losers until they have been put through an extensive program of Sec Checking and PTS checking for nonsurvival considerations and evil purposes on all dynamics.

It usually depends on the person's track record but mostly whether the person has actually been productive or counterproductive as a way of life.

This data is especially relevant to execs, HCOs and Quals.

Boards of Review also should know this data as sometimes people in the middle category are unjustly removed or dismissed when they should have simply been corrected. Sometimes people in the first or second category are gotten rid of by people in the last category. So this too must be watched for.

In investigating along these lines, your target is simply justice or injustice.

L. RON HUBBARD
FOUNDER

HUBBARD COMMUNICATIONS OFFICE
SAINT HILL MANOR, EAST GRINSTEAD, SUSSEX

HCO POLICY LETTER OF 2 JULY 1984

REMIMEO
ALL EXECS
ALL STAFF
ESTOS
HATTING OFFICER
SSO
MAAS/ETH OFFS

EXECUTIVE SERIES 29
ESTABLISHMENT OFFICER SERIES 50
HATTING AND THE ENVIRONMENT

There is a single difference I have spotted between past environments I have hatted people in and the current environment. The sea, war, expeditionary wilds are all very dangerous places and a person either gets hatted or he kicks the bucket most gruesomely, not because some senior will clobber him, but because the environment will not only wipe him out but torture him in the bargain.

Now, suppose you had a junior who was always sending problems to you. He never handled them or recommended any handling or tried to prevent them. He even invented them. What would you think of a staff member who did that? Charitably, you could say that he is just green or untrained or deaf or blind or that he has lots of Mis-Us. In some cases these may account for this type of behavior. But there is also this other factor of the environment.

I have taken illiterate crews who were the dregs of the docks and hatted them up into a crack crew very quickly. These guys weren't just illiterate, they were even in awe of someone who could read because they couldn't. Yet, they could be hatted and rapidly. The difference between this and training staff in our orgs is that these guys had to be able to operate in an environment which would have no mercy on them if they failed. They were forced by the environment to know their hats and wear them if they wanted to survive.

A senior in an org can bring duress on his juniors to get the job done. However, this duress, or even threat, is only coming from a senior, not from the environment. A staff member might feel that he has nothing to lose if he doesn't get hatted. He won't get tortured or killed. He'll just have some senior a bit mad at him which is really a bit mild.

In other words, we are apparently trying to hat people in a totally safe space with no threat to them whether they get hatted or don't. After all, someone will pick up all the pieces and pay all the bills, or they can blow and go back to their pot.

Factually, the environment we live in could eat us up. There is more threat to a staff member personally in not doing his job right now than the sea or war or anything like that. The threat to us if we don't make it is eternity.

One could ask a staff member that refuses to get hatted how he would like to spend all of the coming eternity blind, in the dark and in pain. He would probably say he wouldn't like that. But if we don't make it, that's what we've got and that's what he is condemning this planet to.

This probably would sound quite mad to some, yet is the most stark truth I have ever uttered.

A staff member who refuses to get hatted and get out real products does not know what we are trying to do. He doesn't realize that he himself, next life, is for it if we don't make it.

If a sailor didn't get hatted, he only died once in his estimation. If staff in our orgs don't get hatted, they're condemning themselves and the planet to death a thousand times over.

So understand that no matter how mild the environment might appear to you, we are actually fighting a full-scale war against ignorance and enslavement. But we *do* have the tech to win.

L. RON HUBBARD
FOUNDER

HCO POLICY LETTER OF 21 SEPTEMBER 1995

Remimeo
Estos
All Orgs
All Management
    Personnel

Admin Know-How Series 53
Org Series 49
Establishment Officer Series 51

LOST TECH

(Written on 8 Nov. 79. Issued as
an HCO PL on 21 Sept. 95.)

Modifies: HCO PL 9 May 74   PROD–ORG, ESTO AND
                                       OLDER SYSTEMS RECONCILED

I've just realized that the Esto and the prod–org system, both of which were successful in their day, have been totally dropped. One executive apparently had a confusion on the two systems and could not reconcile them and so stopped pushing both of them. That is my Why for some org failures.

The prod–org system was enormously successful and has been dropped. The Esto system had limited success and has been dropped. The reason for the failure of the Esto system was earlier isolated — the Supervisors let the Esto trainees fake their way through their study of the subject. They just didn't study the subject and then went around running into walls. This was true even though they were given heavy intensive training on it. They didn't do the training.

This comes up because of a cram done on this executive which states that he could never reconcile the two systems and has had a confusion on them. This definitely must have shown up during his tenure as an executive and it brings to mind right this minute that the prod–org system and the Esto system may never have been pushed in. This executive violated the normal actions of prod–org and org establishment. But this bares the fact that management and orgs may not be pushing either the prod–org system nor the Esto system and this could, in large measure, account for the fact that orgs in some cases became disestablished and ceased to produce and deliver.

The exact goof which this executive made is important to understand — he put the Service Product Officer over the Esto and made the Esto the org officer of the Service Product Officer, and hoped from this that his org would be established. Of course it wouldn't be established at all because a product officer's org officer normally specializes in disestablishment — org officers have tended mainly to tear up the org in the name of production. That is by our experience. An org having an Esto, recruits up an Esto corps. That is the only thing that will get posts filled and hatted.

These two systems must be represented on any org board. The product officer must be on those org boards, the product officer's org officer must be on those org boards. And the Executive Esto must be on those org boards. Otherwise these systems will continue to be submerged.

I mention this in order to get into action both the prod–org system and the Esto system. They must be called strongly to attention, otherwise they will go on being neglected.

This could be a major downfall of management and orgs if one just ceased to push these two successful points.

Thus I am calling to your attention the fact that you should use these systems so that we can recover this lost tech.

L. RON HUBBARD
FOUNDER

ABOUT
THE AUTHOR

ABOUT
THE AUTHOR

No more fitting statement typifies the life of L. Ron Hubbard than his simple declaration "I like to help others and count it as my greatest pleasure in life to see a person free himself from the shadows which darken his days." Behind these words stands a lifetime of service to mankind and a legacy of wisdom that enables anyone to attain long-cherished dreams of happiness and spiritual freedom.

Born in Tilden, Nebraska on 13 March 1911, L. Ron Hubbard's road of discovery and dedication to his fellows began early in life. By the age of nineteen, he had traveled more than a quarter of a million miles, examining the cultures of Java, Japan, India and the Philippines. He had even gained access to forbidden Buddhist lamaseries in the Western Hills of China. Yet for all the celebrated traditions of the East, he found much that troubled him: ignorance, poverty and wanton disregard for suffering. "And amongst this poverty and degradation," he later wrote, "I found holy places where wisdom was great, but where it was carefully hidden and given out only as superstition."

Returning to the United States in 1929, Ron resumed his formal education and enrolled in George Washington University the following year. There, he studied mathematics, engineering and the then new field of nuclear physics — all providing vital tools for his continued philosophic research. To finance that research, Ron embarked upon a literary career in the early 1930s, and soon became one of the most widely read authors of popular fiction. Yet never losing sight of his primary goal, he continued his mainline research through extensive travel and expeditions.

With the advent of World War II, he entered the United States Navy as a lieutenant (junior grade) and served as commander of antisubmarine corvettes. Left partially blind and lame from injuries sustained during combat, he was diagnosed as permanently disabled by 1945. Through application of his theories on the mind, however, he was not only able to help fellow servicemen, but also to regain his own health.

After five more years of intensive research, Ron's discoveries were presented to the world in *Dianetics: The Modern Science of Mental Health*. The first popular handbook on the human mind expressly written for the man in the street, *Dianetics* ushered in a new era of hope for mankind and a new phase of life for its author. Ron did not, however, cease his research, and as breakthrough after breakthrough was carefully codified through late 1951, the applied religious philosophy of Scientology was born.

With the ever-increasing popularity of Dianetics and Scientology came the need for an administrative and managerial technology to keep pace with expanding organizations around the world. Through the following six years LRH researched existing organizational systems, theories and managerial methods, all to come to the conclusion that "We are starting with known data. A word, *organization*, exists. That's known data. The rest of it's wilderness."

And so, Ron embarked upon a fully original path of discovery—specifically, "to shake out all the basic fundamentals of business and organization so they exist as laws." What eventually followed from that "shake out" are those organizational policies and patterns fundamental to every Scientology organization.

All told, the fruition of his research spanned more than 30 years of work and resulted in the largest cohesive statement on the subject of organization from any single author. Here is what LRH quite correctly describes as an actual philosophy of administration drawn from natural laws embracing the whole of the subject.

As he wrote, "Administration is third dynamic auditing. And just like auditing, has its standard processes for standard situations." This is the technology contained within the eight volumes of the Organization Executive Course. It is a technology representing the natural laws governing all organizational and group endeavors—a technology stripped from the very "woof and warp" of the material universe.

Particularly in the name of third dynamic auditing, L. Ron Hubbard provided the Management Series—with tools for the building and running of organizations in ways that entirely parallel the precision of auditing technology. The three volumes of the Management Series provide eleven essential managerial subjects containing the laws and principles governing organizations.

All told, L. Ron Hubbard's works on Dianetics and Scientology total forty million words of recorded lectures, books and writings. Together, these constitute the legacy of a lifetime that ended on January 24, 1986. Yet the passing of L. Ron Hubbard in no way constituted an end—for with over a hundred and ten million of his books in circulation, millions of people and thousands of groups and organizations daily applying his technologies for betterment, it can truly be said the world still has no greater friend.

INDEX

ALPHABETICAL LIST
OF TITLES

E

F

G

H

I

L

M

O

P

R

S

T

V

W

Y

CHRONOLOGICAL LIST
OF TITLES

1970

1972

SUBJECT INDEX

A

aberration

counter-policy and group aberration, 186

description, 381

overt product and, 169

scale of lines and terminals and, 214

social aberration at work, 230

stat pushing is, 248

Acting

application for Acting status of executive, 110

activity

has sequence of actions, 117

admin

Esto and, 352, 358

ethics, tech and, 387

order and basic admin, 280

solutions in, 209, 210

squirrel administrators and, 209, 211

standard admin, why sometimes not used, 210

success in, 210, 212

train admin people for admin, 8

transferring tech personnel to admin post, 3

administration, *see* **admin**

administrator

basic of tech used by, 443

description, 442

distance over which one can get things handled, 442

few understand administrator, 442

skilled administrator, definition of, 443

technology used by, 443

test of, 442

value of long-reaching administrator, 442

Admin Scale

basic management tool, 310

debug, use of Admin Scale to debug orders, projects, 189

definition of, 304

description, 187

first true group technology, 190

group mores aligned to, 188

items in, should be in full agreement, 188

management and, 188

morale and, 204

points of group sanity must be in line with, 191

universe as a trap and, 190

valuable tool of organization, 188

advertising

promotion and, 199

Aides Council

functions of, 330

allocation board

manning up of org and, 254

alter-is

prime cause of, 339

anarchy

failure of, reason for, 180

antithesis

definition of, 457

apprenticeship

continual apprenticeship system, 197

economic limitations of, 197

Oporto wine industry and, 197

point of success or failure in
organization, 191, 192, 197

required for permanent posting, 110

artisan

effects of, 442

artist

producing a reaction, 199

auditing

program done all at once, not dribbled
out, 277

auditor

admin post and, 130

Esto, idle area auditor recruited as, 234

idle area auditor, handling for, 234

loss of, in org, 10

post hat and, 130

awareness

scale of lines and terminals and, 213

B

bait and badger

description, 401

barrier

being, 382

basics

order, disorder and, 281

production and, 283

basic staff hat

how basic org works, 349

beingness

correct sequence of action and, 164

doingness, havingness and, 368

engineer, beingness of, 147

list of, subproducts and, 260

thetan considers any beingness better than
no beingness, 28

valuable, 28

blow

heavy workload and, 28

bogged student

description, 415

book

don't give away, 136

broken straws

cannot build a new world with, 102

bugged

definition of, 478

bureaux

Esto duties in, 325

business

failure in, reasons for, 164

C

call-in

D/ED for Delivery and Exchange and, 293

description, 273

Service Product Officer and, 273, 293

Call-in Officer

D/ED for Delivery and Exchange's first duty
and, 293

camouflaged hole

definition of, 19

executive post as, 20

can't-have

definition of, 89

PTSes and SPs running can't-have on org
staff, 441

capitalism

cannot cope with squad mentality, 176

case

personnel not handled as, 18

cause
Esto must be at, 444
knowledge and, 522

chaos
creation of, by ill-intentioned persons, 487

Chart of Human Evaluation
out-ethics people and, 386
tool to use in evaluation of personnel, 18

checksheet
hat and, 127

Chief Esto, *see* **Establishment Officer**

child
not permitted to contribute, effects of, 389
production in life and, 164

Chinese school
charts used in, 407
description, 333, 405, 408
learning by, 406
org board Chinese school is never
flattened, 408
org board drilling and, 406
steps in Chinese schooling org board, 408
steps in teaching, 406

Christians
success over Romans, reason for, 141

command, *see* **executive**

command channel
description, 427

Commanding Officer
see also **Executive Director**
head of SO org, 322

command line
confusion of comm line with, 376
definition of, 306, 376

Committee of Evidence
crashed stats due to absence without
competent replacement, grounds
for, 298

transfers and recruiting, when grounds
for, 100

communication
has to have terminals, 224
HCO and, 224

communication line
confusion of command line with, 376
definition of, 306, 376
jamming of, 163

communism
based on squad mentality, 176

company
collection of small org boards, 119
transfer policies of, why unworkable, 19

competence
ability to control environment and, 205
pride and, 383
respect and, 232
success and, 212

complement
assigning complement, 80
definition of, 80
organization, complement for every separate
org, 81

completion
definition of, 267

compliance report
basic management tool, 310
definition of, 305

conditions
basic management tool, 310
definition of, 307

Conditions by Dynamics
procedure for, 390

confidence
has to be earned, 232
hatting and, 230

cycle of action

be, do, have and, 164

misunderstood word and, 452

D

Data Series

basic management tool, 310

description, 308

locating and isolating situations in organization and, 219

Date/Locate

False Data Stripping and, 462

debug

definition of, 478

end phenomena of, 485, 489

first action, inspection of area, 478, 490

handling must be at least 50 percent production, 485

Product Debug Repair List, 484, 490

second stage of, 480

subproducts and, 260, 262, 263

debug tech

checklist for use in, 489

assessment of, on meter, 489

vital executive tool, 478

D/ED for Delivery and Exchange

see also **Service Product Officer**

bridge between D/FBO for MORE and FBO, 293

call-in and, 293

Call-in Officer posting and, 293

exchange in abundance and, 294

Executive Director and, 294

flow of public through the org and, 293

functions of, 292, 293

main products of the org and, 294

powers of immediate communication to International Finance Office and Inspector General Network, 294

delivery

D/ED for Delivery and Exchange and, 293

Esto system and, 326

failure in, 193

money can prevent, 202

most susceptible to breakdown in any organization, 200

point of success or failure in organization, 191

posts operating on irreducible minimum and, 201

Service Product Officer and, 274

success in, 200

valuable final product and, 201

delusion

scale of lines and terminals and, 214

democracy

nation of Clears and, 161

department

director of, product officer of his department, 324

Department 1

Esto system and, 237

every 5th person hired goes into, 237

evolves the org, 237

first post of Exec Esto, 235

functions of, 244

no study time and, 8

personnel starved org and, 235

Department 3

not inspecting, results of, 8

Department 13

no study time and, 8

Department 14

recruitment and, 9

deputy

ED's deputy, duties of, 324

every key post should have, 76

rule regarding, 197

system of, 197

economy

booms and depressions of national
economy, 207

false data of, in society, 289

ills of, and production of OPs, 288

education

decline of, 192

effect

cannot be adverse effect if one knows
tech, 522

E-Meter

tool to use in evaluation of personnel, 18

enforced overt-have

definition of, 89

engineer

beingness, doingness and havingness of, 147

hat and, 126

enthusiasm

vital ingredient in organization, 172

environment

see also MEST

control of

begins with oneself, 205

competence and, 205

dangerousness of, 534

hatting and, 534

nineteenth-century psychologist preached
that man had to adjust to, 205

one's standards and control of, 205

equalitarianism

description of, 289

equipment

must be utilized, 198

establishment

consists of, 321

lines are major part of, 354

slower than production, 359

Establishment Executive International

issues directives on approval lines for Acting
status, 110

Establishment Officer

see also Executive Establishment
Officer

ability of, to spot out-ethics and PTS/SP
phenomena and effectively deal with
it, 441

actions of, 440

admin work and, 352, 358

agreement of, with product officer, 346

application of PTS, ethics and correction
tech by, 441

availability of Dianetics and Scientology
materials and, 414

back-off due to not being hatted as Esto, 331

basic problem of, 381

busy hatting staff, handling lines, 344

case requirements of, 327

Chief Esto, duties of, 323

concern of, 358

Correct Comm Program and, 337

criminality, exchange and, 387

cycle of hatting of, 328

Disagreement Check, use of by Esto, 349

drilling of lines by, 354

duties and functions
of, 319, 323, 346, 351, 354

encounters dev-t in unhatted area, 333

establish faster and more firmly, 358

Esto conference and, 329

Esto I/C, duties of, 323

Esto's Esto, duties of, 323

Esto system

evolved from product–org system, 320

failures, reason for, 234, 314, 400

Foundation org and, 326

putting in, 234

success of, 330

extension of original HCO system, 320

fast flow hiring and, 241

finding Whys and, 339

good courses, course supervision and, 416

group drills done by, 362

guilty of dev-t to senior Esto, 340

hallmark of, 356

has to be held stable as an Esto, 344

hatting of staff and, 400, 439

hat to be worn in any given situation is Esto hat, 331

HCO and, 319, 328

importance of, 321

involvement of, in production of an area, 328

Lead Esto, duties of, 323

learning from mistakes, hatting and, 450

looks, not just talks, 357

major part of job of, 385

must be at cause, 444

must not get "stuck" in, 362

operating division, 339

organizing files and, 364

org board of, 321, 324

people requiring orders on program targets and, 345

primary targets of, 239

prod–org system and, 314

production is a test to, 362

product of, 346

product officer trying to use as org officer, handling for, 404

products are Product 1 and 3, 325

purpose of, 320

puts the org there, 322

quality and skill of, 326

reaction of, to staff member who is too busy to get hatted, 319

recruitment of idle area auditors as, 234

remedies used by, on staff unable to do post, 384

responsibility of, for tech delivery, 414

right target for, 356

runs on programs, 330

skill of, 339

standard actions to handle Estos In-Training, 341

test of successful Esto, 325

time spent with executive, 402

training of, 326, 331, 440, 444

two hats of, 328

typical Esto situations, 359

undermanned divisions, handling of by, 236

unmock of org and, 354

using key personnel as, 234

works directly with people, 353

Esto conference

function of, 329

Esto I/C, *see* **Establishment Officer**

Esto's Esto, *see* **Establishment Officer**

Ethics

filing is real trick of, 308

first target of, 87

Personnel and, how they work together, 30

staff member goofs, Ethics target for, 28

ethics

Admin Scale alignment and, 188

Conditions by Dynamics and, 390

exchange and out-ethics, 386

Exchange by Dynamics and, 389

failure to organize and, 124

filing not to be done by person on ethics cycle, 417

harsh ethics periods and HCO, 86

hats went out when ethics came strongly in, 122

heavy ethics and lack of hatting, 30

remedy for handling out-ethics in group, 391

role of, 122

serves as restraint, 387

tech, admin and, 387

ethics folder

basic management tool, 310

definition of, 307

evaluation

executive and, 378

length of time to do, 409

tech of, contained in Data Series, 485

evidence

description, 305

F

repair list for, 463

use of, 456

false definitions, *see* **false data**

fast flow system

communication and, 377

field Scientologist

should have a hat, 131

file

all hands actions on divisional files, 365

basic management tool, 310

basics and, 280

definition of, 308

disorder and, 284

divisional files, 365

Ethics inspection and, 308

expensive, 364

importance of, 417

lowly and neglected item, 364

miscellaneous files, there are none, 365

misfiling in, 417, 418

organization of, steps in, 365

org without, has no memory, 366

out-ethics person not to do filing, 417

final valuable product, *see* **valuable final product**

finance

concept of money and, 202

correct viewpoint for, 202

failure in, 193

greatest aberration of, 203

other factors in scale of sanity and, 202

point of success or failure in organization, 191

PTS people on finance lines, 89

success in, 202

financial planning

knowledge of VFPs and, 183

transactions of an organization, 202

unusual pay arrangement, 96

Flag Banking Officer

D/ED for Delivery and Exchange and, 293

functions of, 293

income and, 293

production and, 293

staff member and, 293

Flag Executive Briefing Course

essential course for executive, 300

lectures of, product/org officer system developed in, 267

training on, will increase stats, 22

Flag Representative

duties of, 305

flow

see also **traffic**

horizontal flow, 377

org board and, 118

power and particle flow, 351

public flow through org, 293

space and particles and, 427

stable terminals and, 224

F/Ning student

description, 415

foreman, *see* **executive**

Foundation

org schedule and, 432

fraud

description, 221

FSM commission

rules regarding, 136

function

duplicate functions

effects of, 208

handling for, 208

irreducible minimum and, 144

left off org board, results of, 132, 143

function org board, 394

G

genius
organizational genius, 120

George Thunderbird, 277

glib student
false data and, 457

goal
definition of, 189

government
people versus, 142

gradient
false data comes off in, 456

gradient scale
definition of, 127
organizing and, 127

graph
basic management tool, 310
definition of, 307

gross divisional statistic
subproducts and, 256, 259

group
see also **organization**
agreement factor in, 215
antigroup members, handling for, 189
composed of individual members, 207
economics of, 182
interchange factor and, 222
jams and random or counter-purposes of, 190
low standard of living and, 289
organization and, 232
outward signs of a badly organized group, 232
overall test for, 146
right way to handle is narrow but strong, 209
sequences and programs of, 139
source of confusion in, 215

survival of, 207
20 percent of members of any group are antigroup, 189

gung-ho
description, 360

H

happiness
comes from self-determinism, production and pride, 383
power and, 383

HAS, *see* **HCO Area Secretary**

hat
see also **hatting, post hat, staff hat, tech hat**
adjust to cover functions, 394
any hat is better than no hat, 131
auditor must have post hat as well, 130
basic management tool, 310
basket for each, 144
checksheet for, 127
comparison of hat lists to posted org board, 395
content of, 126, 129
cope sort of hat, 128
counter-effort and, 138
definition of, 24, 126, 130, 147, 306
determining existing org board and, 393
development of, 126
engineer, hat of, 147
Esto has two hats, 328
Esto must wear Esto hat in any given situation, 331
every hat has a product, 126
expert also needs full post hat, 129
field Scientologist must have, 131, 196
fully hatted personnel and Esto, 239
goofiness occurs as result of hats not being grooved in, 125
gradient scale of hats, 127
inability to, 455
lack of, results, 131

main outnesses about, 69

major organizational factor, 219

neatness of quarters is part of, 162

omitted hat, 144

org board and, 139

Personnel has vested interest in hats being complete, 101

post, each post is a hat, 145

production and, 346, 395, 397, 440

proper utilization includes hats, 130

right direction to, 347

staff member responsibility for, 162

study of, done on post a bit each day, 334

survey of, by Esto, 346

training and, 196

turnover of, in temporary absence, 297

United States government and, 128

went out when ethics came strongly in, 122

write-up of, 20, 127

wrong products for, 397

hatting

alter-is and, 339

answer to not having recruitment restrictions, 240

basic errors in, 347

basic of third dynamic sanity, 346

begins after Situation Eight, 401

cause and, 238, 522

control and, 238, 534

Course Supervisor hatting, 414

criminal and, 230

done from top down, 347, 400

Esto and, 319

HCO and, 224

heavy ethics and, 30

laws regarding importance of, 229

level double-hatting, 264

mistakes and, 450

org form and, 243

org trouble and, 25

post performance and, 230

product officer, hatting and, 400

rules and procedures of, apply to Esto, 331

sequence of, 239

verbal hatting main source of false definitions and false data, 454

vertical double-hatting, 264

Hatting Officer

pitfalls of hats to be aware of, 70

havingness

beingness, doingness and, 368

correct sequence of action and, 164

list of, subproducts and, 260

HCO

see also **Hubbard Communications Office**

establishing division, 225

HCO Area Secretary

fast flow hiring and, 241

functions of, 225

hey you! org board

description, 143

executive knowledge of org board and, 408

production and, 143

seniors knocking off hats, resulting in, 509

HFA

common on org boards, 264

don't condone too much, 264

means held from above, 264

hiring

see also **personnel, recruit, recruitment**

every 5th person hired goes into Dept 1, 237

failure in, 192

fast flow, 240

breakdown of, 241

point of success or failure in organization, 191

requirements for retaining staff, 96

success in, 194

honesty

road to sanity, 388

horizontal flow

description, 377

Hubbard Communications Office

backlogs in, 85

Dept 13 works with, to get programing done, 7

elementary actions of, 224

establishment and, 225, 226, 227

Estos and, 319, 328

functioning of, 86

functions of, 224

harsh ethics periods and, 86

nonfunctional, handling for, 85

PTS people in registration or on finance lines; 89

puzzles in org

HCO must solve not make them, 87

reason they won't resolve, 86

recruitment, 224

responsibility of, for external lines, 225

smooth, producing HCO can and must exist in every org, 87

Hubbard Consultant

skills and procedures of testing contained in checksheet for, 16

human beings

no perfect human beings, 15

I

I&R Form 1

authorization for transfers or assignments from, 72

personnel demands and, 72

ignorance

insanity and, 206

impossibility

behind every impossibility lies some great big Why, 5

in-charge

duties of, 115

vertical double-hatted, actions to take, 265

income

files and, 365

GDSes and, 13

income tax, 91

indicator

pushing of, result, 248

industrialist

dream of, 15

inflation

moonlighting and, 38

injustice

possible injustice provided against, 387

insanity

acts that are insane are not unintentional, 206

common denominator in insanities is desire to succumb, 193

definition of, 193

end product of, 193

ignorance and, 206

motive is key factor in determining, 221

overts, withholds and, 388

percentage of planet's population who are insane, 206

product, not behavior, determines, 206

sign of, 84

inspection

importance of, 8

personnel demands and inspection of the area, 27, 72, 101

time and motion study and, 479

Inspections and Reports

demands for personnel and, 72

Inspector General Network

confirmation of Permanent posting of executive by, 110

instant hat

description, 334

interchange
principles of, 222

irreducible minimum
law of, 201

J

jam
reasons for, 429

justice
effort to bring equity and peace, 204

handling of, by man, 204

point of success or failure in
organization, 191

success in, 203

task of, 204

juvenile delinquency
be, do, have and, 164

K

knowledge
cause and, 522

L

labor
management versus, 142, 176, 179

lawyer
post hat of missing, results, 129

leader
election of, how to elect, 161

Lead Esto, *see* **Establishment Officer**

Liability
noncompliance labeled as, 388

lines
basic management tool, 310

command line, 306

communication line, 306

definition of, 305

design of, 217, 218

drilling of
by Esto, 354

dummy run and dummy bullbait serve
as, 216

importance of, in organization, 306

major organizational factor, 219

new actions piloted before being added
to, 246

organization and, 215, 291

scale concerning terminals and, 213
cause for lower positions on, 214

standard production line, 246

violation of, will disestablish org, 355

LRH Communicator
divisional recruitment disputes and, 97

duties of, 305

M

machine
human beings versus, 15

man
basically good, 386

basic nature is social, not antisocial, 17

not a savage beast, 17

management
see also **executive**

basics of, 299

basic tools of, 304, 310

brilliant and mediocre, difference
between, 299

description, 188

Esto system and prod–org system and, 315

ideas management must have, 511

intention of, to improve scene in divisions,
orgs, networks, 511

comes from lack of personnel programs based on predictions, 79

definition of, 247, 295

description, 3

org collapse and, 235

solution to, 100

work of a suppressive or idiot, 235

N

Napoleon
defeat of, 141

NCG
means no case gain, 89

Nero
fall of Roman Empire and, 141

network
divisional recruitment and, 96

noise
overt products and, 167

nonproduction
general Why of, 403

O

obnosis
definition of, 415

observing the obvious, 340

omitted datum
blankness and, 345

omitted hat
commonest fault in programs and org boards, 144

O/O, *see* **organizing officer**

operational
definition of, 355

key of machinery and people, 355

order
basic management tool, 310

definition of, 176, 178, 279, 305

disestablishment and, 346

disorder versus, inspection of area to determine, 282

people who don't know what their product is require orders, 345

policy and, 174, 177

staff member who requires, 345

org, *see* **organization**

organization
see also **third dynamic**

actions of, fall under particle motion and change, 159

Admin Scale
relating to, 187

valuable tool of, 188

altered sequence of action and, 164

answer to sane org, 230

apprenticeship and a total working organization, 197

bad repute of Earth organizations, reasons for, 170

basic principles of, 119

basic training is vital for every member of, 196

basic words of, not understood, 171

building blocks of, 102

building of, 351, 353

call-in and, 293

certain personalities don't want organization to succeed, 210

checklist of twelve factors regarding products of, 154

clearing of, actions to take in, 187

closing of lines of, effects, 432

conditions of when staff may be transferred out, 97

confusion and, 282

consists of, 143, 215, 291

cope and, 120, 125

course of exclusion, things which set organization on, 195

cutative prices and, 136

result of, is a product, 145

salvage of, 133

shows pattern of organizing to obtain product, 145

situations encountered with, 395

terminals only on, results, 118

titles org board, 394

typical army org board, 118

viability of products, hats and, 148

Org Executive Course

essential course for executive, 300

Org Series

covers tech of how of organization, 448

OT ability

long-distance comm line and, 442

out-basics

disorderliness and, 281

files, research and, 280

out-ethics

exchange and, 386

filing not done by person with out-ethics, 417

outpoint

cope and, 122

outpoint-correct

right Why versus, 360

out-reality

breeds out-comm and out-affinity, 188

out sequence

commonest fault in programs and org boards, 144

overrun

False Data Stripping and, 462

overt

blankness can invite, 345

false data acting as justifier for, 458

insanity and, 388

product as, 167

overt product, 447

ill-intentioned persons and, 487

Oxford Capacity Analysis

out-ethics people and, 386

tool to use in evaluation of personnel, 18

P

participation

achievement of, 29

particle

see also **traffic**

flows in sequence, 116

organization and, 215

space and particles and flows, 427

people

ability to confront, is high ability, 206

three classes of, 532

perception

shut-offs of, misunderstood word and, 452

permanent status

entitled to training or auditing, 96

Personal Enhancement, *see* **Personnel Enhancement**

Personnel

Ethics and, how they work together, 30

hatting and training, vested interest in, 101, 130

prediction of, how to determine, 76

unutilized people are backlog on lines of, 78

personnel

see also **recruit, recruitment, staff member, training**

actions to reduce heavy turnover in, 11

appointing, promoting or handling, factors in, 102

aren't personnel until they are utilized, 79

control of, complement and, 81

cycle of not training and utilizing, effect on, 28

demand for handling, 236

demands for, 27, 72, 101, 236

enhancement of, Dept 13 created to permit, 7

errors in handling, 4

    results of, 4

factors which underlie failure of, on post, 19

four general classes of, 15

full-time training of, qualifications for, 10

green personnel not cause of org upset, example of, 16

handling for unhattedness of new staff, 14

heavy turnover in, 10

human beings versus machines, 15

keeps orgs manned and trained up, 13

knowledge of VFPs and personnel assignment, 183

lack of complement and, 80

loss of high-level personnel, 10

madmen amongst, results, 17

major organizational factor, 219

man up of, parallels production, 236

moonlighting and, 38

most common way to overload an area, 29

new personnel create dev-t, 14

not doing well on post

    reasons for, 20

    remedy, 20

not handled as cases, 18

open gate of hiring of, 240

operational, 355

pitfalls in hats of, 69

policies anyone hiring should be familiar with, 16

precise tools used to evaluate personnel, 18

prediction on, 76, 77, 78

problems with procurement internally created, 4

public relations personnel, 40

quicksilver personnel scene, 295

solutions to procurement and utilization of, 5

taking key production personnel as Estos, 234

testing procedures and, 16

transfer of, 3, 25

utilization of, 28, 130

without purpose, 29

Personnel Enhancement

scope of, 196

personnel folder

basic management tool, 310

description, 307

personnel programing

Dept 13 must work out, 7

purpose of Personnel Programer, 88

remedy for org problems, 9

right way to do it, 7

workable personnel programs drawn up by Personnel Programer, 88

planning

Executive Director and, 294

"play the piano"

executive ability to, 242, 300

know how, 261

policy

authorized policy must be made available, 187

basis of group agreement, 174

bugged projects and, 187

counter-policy

    effects of, 186

    varieties of, 186

definition of, 175

illegal policy, effects of, 186

orders and, 174, 177

purpose and, 186, 189

random or counter-policy, when to look for, 189

set by top management, 179

so many meanings it has become confused, 174

statistics and, 510

using policy to stop, 487

post

see also **terminal**

can be made untenable, 28

cause over, 522

clearing purpose of, 178

estimate existing scene of, by looking at product of, 167

failure on, factors underlying, 19

fixed-terminal post, 305

importance of, 229

judgment and decision needed on, 160

line post, 305

misunderstoods on title of, 445

nonproduction and transfer, 21

not doing post, reasons for, 20

people hate to lose, 229

purpose of, and hat write-up, 20

status regarding and performance on post, 20

tends to dwindle down to, 144

trouble in training up for, ordinarily lack of adequate material, 21

trust and crusade, 163

valuable final product and, 166

value of, 28

post hat

definition of, 24

posting

drilling of post holders when postings change, 216

executive posting, 109, 110

expected rapidity of, 111

top down, 395

Post Purpose Clearing

added note to, 509

additional steps, 509

bog on, handling for, 510

done on org, 510

double or triple hatted person and, 510

glib answers in, 512

intention step and rock slams in, 510

listing questions and, 509

main reference used in, green-on-white, 510

management and executive, intentions and long-term view of, 512

organizing step, 510

seniors cleared on posts over which they have command in, 510

speed of, 510

successful in raising general tone level and production of orgs, 509

potential trouble source

administrative skill and, 442

communication lines and, 442

dramatizes, 89

has no business in PR, 40

key post with, results of, 90

staff member, PTS handling of, 239

tools for handling of, 90

power

happiness and, 383

hatting and, 238

holding position in space and, 229

proportional to the speed of particle flow, 351

PR

see also **public relations**

definition of, 387

pricing

costing versus, 200

cutative prices, 136

pride

competence and, 383

happiness and, 383

Primary Rundown

Establishment Officer tool, 384

problem

solving of, 219

processing

personnel and, 17

removes barriers, 385

training and, 197

prod–org system

Esto system and, 314

handle backlogs and omissions in products, 228

HAS and, 320
valid system, 320

produce
definition of, 322

product
basis of a standard of living, 288
bogs in trying to debug, Product Debug
  Repair List used, 484
confusion and, 282
coordination of, 399
correction of, 392
definition of, 322
difference between sane and insane and, 206
disordered person and ability to get, 279
don't assume person knows meaning of, 367
engineer, product of, 147
estimate existing scene of a post by looking
  at, 167
Esto product, 346, 358
Esto system and, 322
every hat has a, 126
falls under have, 367
four basic products, 151
inspection for, 479
laws of, 159
low in quantity and quality
    handling for, 167
    reasons for, 167
name the exact product, 446
no product, debug of by subproduct
  lists, 262
org product, factors regarding, 153
overt act, product as, 167
overt product, cause of, 169
personal sense of order and, 279
post product and beingness, doingness and
  havingness, 370
pride of workmanship and, 168
push, debug, drive and, 278
quality of, 146, 148
quality of delivered product determines
  demand, 6
represented as statistic, 126
situations that may be found with, 392

statistics and, 252
three major factors governing every
  product, 151
tools and, 280
total product comes from product of each
  hat, 145
twelve major points regulating, 152
unclear, results of, 345
want the product, 447

Product 1
definition of, 151, 322
org and, 153

Product 2
definition of, 151, 322
org and, 153

Product 3
definition of, 151, 322
org and, 153

Product 4
definition of, 151, 322
org and, 153

product clearing
best done after Method 1 Word
  Clearing, 375
biggest Why for not getting done, 398
correction of, 392
easy way to do all staff on, 397
example of, 398
long form procedure for, 367
omissions in, 397
reclearing of product and, 396
short form, 374
    procedure for, 347

product conference
conducted by CO or ED of org, 329
success of, 329

production
ability to name product and, 445
chain of all production sequences, 199
completed cycles of action, 248
debug of, 489

impeding of product distribution to
potential consumers, 193

perversion of finance, 193

prevent production, 192

refusal to employ people, 192

substitute of violence for reason, 193

unreal or nonfactual promotion, 192

psychotic

does not want production to occur, 447

PTS, *see* **potential trouble source**

public relations

confront and, 40

delusory requirements, 41

organizing and, 40

personnel in PR, characteristics for, 40

potential trouble source has no business
in, 40

promotion and, 199

work and, 40

purpose

can be strangled, 29

definition of, 189

group jams and, 190

morale and, 204

organization and, 291

personnel without, can commit crimes, 29

policy and, 186

post purpose and hat write-up, 20

post purpose uncleared, 170, 171

random, counter or illegal policy, purpose
and, 189

revolt and lack of, 29

senior to policy, 189

Q

Qual, *see* **Qualifications Division**

Qualifications Division

classes of people and, 533

quarters

neatness of, 162

quickie

definition of, 349

quicksilver

definition of, 295

examples of, 296

handling for quicksilver personnel
scene, 298

quota

doable, 261

subproducts and, 261

R

racial degeneration

environmental control and, 205

raw materials

disorder and, 283

reasonableness, 16

recruit

absence of, Why for, 122

any organization or activity has to, 15

divisional secretary may recruit or hire
divisional staff, 96

excess, recruit in, 10

failure to, 30, 100, 197

making one replace himself in private
business is moonripping, 103

never recruit with promise of free courses or
auditing, 240

new recruits, effects of, 206

recruitment

see also **hiring**

beginning cycle of, 16

disputes arising on divisional recruitment
are to be resolved by the Continental
LRH Comm, 97

doesn't just happen, 15

down statistics and lack of, 24

Establishment Officer and, 234

handling of, 14

inefficiency in org and, 25

linear versus simultaneous, 12

network representatives and divisional
    recruitment, 96

open gate and, 240

prediction in, 76

remedy for org problems, 9

vital necessity, 14

registration

PTS people on registration lines, 89

research

basics and, 280

re-sign

D/ED for Delivery and Exchange and, 293

definition of, 267

revolt

reasons for, 29, 146

sympathy winds up in, 155

rip-off

definition of, 103

Rome

exchange factor in ancient Rome, 389

Nero and destruction of, 141

route

agreed upon procedure, 160

routing

organization and, 428

routing form

description, 270

org form and, 429

rudiments

False Data Stripping and, 462

S

sales

actions and lines of, 273

D/ED for Delivery and Exchange and, 293

failure in, 193

point of success or failure in
    organization, 191

success in, 199

sanity

making things go right and, 206

motive is key factor in determining, 221

scale

Sanity Scale, 191, 204

schedule

course schedules, 414

Foundation org and, 432

grave fault in, 432

handling dev-t and, 333

importance of, in organization, 431

includes exercise, post and study, 333

operating a number of different ones at same
    time, 432

organization and, 431

precision and, 431

production and, 433

schizophrenia

definition of, 382

scholarship

rules regarding, 136

Sea Org member

full-time auditor or admin training, 97

promotion of, 97

security

post and, 229

self-determinism

happiness and, 383

senior

overload of, 217

responsible for hatting of juniors, 129

training officer, 25

Senior Executive Strata

above middle management, 300

Senior HAS International

responsibility for approval lines of executive status, 110

service

importance of, 275

no free service or materials, 137

Service/Call-in Committee

Service Product Officer and, 267

service facsimile

false data and, 458

Service Product Officer

see also **D/ED for Delivery and Exchange**

actions and lines to be product officered by, 274

authority of, 268

call-in and, 273

delivery and, 274

duties of, 267, 268

Esto system and, 314

first action of, is promotion, 270

organizing officer and, 267, 270, 275

post of, 266

re-signs and, 275

sales and, 273

sequence of actions of, 269, 270

service and, 275

Service/Call-in Committee and, 267

statistics for, 267

status of, 292

VFPs and, 267, 269

short cycle

definition of, 362

significance

organization and, 215

single-handing

comes from failure to man in sequence, 255

definition of, 140

executive trains his staff while, 142

missing elements when this occurs, 140

unhatted, untrained staff and, 140

situation

administrator and complexity of, 442

estimating situations thousands of miles away, 442

society

answer to sane society, 230

common methods of handling organizational trouble in, 170

coordination between social disorder and no-hat or no-training, 30

effect of good or bad administrators, 442

exchange and, 388

false data rampant in, 290, 455

lack of training, effect on society, 30

nightmare when insane rise to positions of power, 203

personal production of VFPs and, 288

secret of a turbulent society, 29

slave society, 160

social decline, reasons for, 29

stress on time in, is an aberrated factor, 196

structure, 249

successful organization will be fought by rulers or enemies of, 212

tends to confuse and unstabilize people with its hectic pace, 229

source

false data, any number of sources for, 455

SP, *see* **suppressive person**

space

factors involved in space of org, 427

knowledge of VFPs and space allocation, 183

must be utilized, 198

squirrel

administration and, 209

stability
    hatting and, 230
    quicksilver personnel scene and, 296

stable datum
    confusion and, 127

staff hat
    contents of, 127
    definition of, 24

staff member
    considered Product 2 and 4, 325
    cycle of hatting of, 328
    despatch system and, 163
    Esto Series 16 situations and, 402
    full-time training and, 240
    gets job done of his own post, his
        department and the whole org, 162
    looking, 382
    most common failure in, 445
    necessary to have and know org board, 135
    operational, 356
    part of flow line, 263
    personnel program for, 88
    product clearing, long form on, 374
    refusal of, to get hatted, 535
    responsibility of, 162
    specialist in one or more similar
        functions, 242
    subproduct lists and, 262
    two stable data on which to operate, 162

Staff Status
    Exec Status levels and, 303
    following procedure of, grooves staff in, 16
    handling for hatting of new staff, 14

Staff Status I
    time limit on, 239

Staff Status II
    time limit on, 239

standard of living
    definition of, 287
    one must produce in excess of, 287
    products and, 288

standards
    definition of, 205

stat faker
    description, 250

statistics
    always look at, 396
    basic management tool, 310
    definition of, 307
    description, 252
    down statistics, reasons for, 24
    effects of trained and untrained executive
        on, 22
    indicator of scene, 248, 251
    management of, 252
    posted and kept up-to-date, 378
    products represented as, 126
    social acceptability versus, 6
    subproducts and GDS, 256, 259

stat push
    examples of, 249
    skilled management and, 250
    specialized actions in, 249
    varieties of, 250
    what it is, 248
    wrong target and, 248

status
    considerations about, post performance
        and, 20
    cycle of attaining and losing status, 30

Straightwire
    description, 458

strategic plan
    basic management tool, 310
    definition of, 304

stuck in
    Establishment Officer must not get, 362

student
    bogged student, 415
    failed student, mistakes and, 450
    F/Ning student, 415

study

    executive, handling for no study time, 402

subproduct

    assessing list of, to find why no VFP, 260

    assessment of subproduct list, 262

    be-do-have breakdown and subproduct list, 260

    example of list of, using cup of coffee, 260

    GDSes and, 256, 259

    incomplete list of, 263

    list of

        accomplishment of VFPs and, 260

        assists understanding of what an area is supposed to produce, 262

        debug and, 262

        informative, 262

        test of, 263

        used as basis for issuing orders, 261

    necessary to make VFPs of org, 396

    quotaing of, 261

    wrongly worked out, result, 263

success

    competence and, 212

succumb

    insanity and, 193

Supervisor, *see* **Course Supervisor**

suppressive person

    deprives PTS or enforces unwanted things on PTS, 89

    knowledge of tech and, 522

    staff member as, results, 16

survival

    organization and, 233

    toughness and, 232

    VFPs and basic survival, 222

sympathy

    morale destroyer, 156

    winds up in revolt, 155

synthesis

    definition of, 457

T

target

    policy on

        basic management tool, 310

        stating of desired product and, 166

target policy

    definition of, 304

tech

    administrative technology, 443

    ethics, admin and, 387

    keep tech trained people in tech, 8

    transferring tech personnel to admin post, 3

Tech Division

    as personnel pool, 3

tech hat

    definition of, 24

technology

    subdivision of personnel and hats, 219

telephone

    use of, 163

telex

    basic management tool, 310

    definition of, 306

    despatch versus, 306

    primary factors in sending, 306

terminal

    basic management tool, 310

    communication and, 224

    definition of, 305, 427

    flows and stable terminals, 224

    importance of, in organization, 306

    organization and, 215, 291

    org form and, 429

    scale concerning lines and, 213

        cause for lower positions on, 214

testing

    Hubbard Consultant checksheet and, 16

    personnel and, 16

Management Cycle and, 19

nonproduction on post and, 21

rapid transfers, result of, 3

solution to, 100

triangular system

FEBC system, 322

U

unawareness

scale of lines and terminals and, 214

uncertainty

slows things down, 351

understanding

ceases on going past a misunderstood word or concept, 169

unmock

description, 247

utilization

see also **personnel**

big subject, 199

factors that send one off utilization, 198

failure in, 192

if you've got it, use it, 198

includes people, equipment and space, 198

personnel aren't personnel until utilized, 79

point of success or failure in organization, 191

requires knowledge of what VFPs are, 198

success in, 198

V

valuable final product

acceptance of, 199

agreed upon and issued, 183

basic survival and, 222

combined products of all members of the org, 168

definition of, 221

delivery and, 201

educational institutions VFP not stated, 181

establishment of character of, 179

ethics, morale and, 222

example of, using cup of coffee, 260

exchangeability of, 221

exchange value of, 185

finance and, 203

flaws in delivery and, 200

man has planet as, 198

nonproduction and/or nondelivery of, repair earlier steps of production, 200

precisely listed, 180

producer and, 223

production of, and sales, 200

promotion and, 199

Scientology org VFP, 290

Service Product Officer VFP, 267

subproducts and, 260, 262, 396

survey of, 179, 184

top management responsibility for, 182

training VFP, 201

Verbal Tech Checklist

use of, 480

veteran

adequate replacement of, 97

ordering of, to Flag, 97

viability

Esto system and, 326

overall test for group, 146

vocabulary

key vocabulary of organization, 172

W

welfare state

be, do, have and, 165

crime and, 29, 388

executive ability and, 198

pays people not to work, 29

SCIENTOLOGY CHURCHES, MISSIONS AND CENTERS

CHURCHES

UNITED STATES

ALBUQUERQUE

Church of Scientology
8106 Menaul Boulevard NE
Albuquerque
New Mexico 87110

ANN ARBOR

Church of Scientology
2355 West Stadium Boulevard
Ann Arbor, Michigan 48103

ATLANTA

Church of Scientology
1611 Mt. Vernon Road
Dunwoody, Georgia 30338

AUSTIN

Church of Scientology
2200 Guadalupe
Austin, Texas 78705

BOSTON

Church of Scientology
448 Beacon Street
Boston, Massachusetts 02115

BUFFALO

Church of Scientology
47 West Huron Street
Buffalo, New York 14202

CHICAGO

Church of Scientology
3011 North Lincoln Avenue
Chicago, Illinois 60657-4207

CINCINNATI

Church of Scientology
215 West 4th Street
5th Floor
Cincinnati, Ohio 45202-2670

CLEARWATER

Church of Scientology
Flag Service Organization
210 South Fort Harrison Avenue
Clearwater, Florida 33756

Church of Scientology
Flag Ship Service Organization
c/o *Freewinds* Relay Office
118 North Fort Harrison Avenue
Clearwater, Florida 33755

COLUMBUS

Church of Scientology
30 North High Street
Columbus, Ohio 43215

DALLAS

Church of Scientology
Celebrity Centre Dallas
1850 North Buckner Boulevard
Dallas, Texas 75228

DENVER

Church of Scientology
3385 South Bannock Street
Englewood, Colorado 80110

DETROIT

Church of Scientology
321 Williams Street
Royal Oak, Michigan 48067

HONOLULU

Church of Scientology
1146 Bethel Street
Honolulu, Hawaii 96813

KANSAS CITY

Church of Scientology
3619 Broadway
Kansas City, Missouri 64111

LAS VEGAS

Church of Scientology
846 East Sahara Avenue
Las Vegas, Nevada 89104

Church of Scientology
Celebrity Centre Las Vegas
1100 South 10th Street
Las Vegas, Nevada 89104

LONG ISLAND

Church of Scientology
99 Railroad Station Plaza
Hicksville, New York
11801-2850

LOS ANGELES AND VICINITY

Church of Scientology
4810 Sunset Boulevard
Los Angeles, California 90027

Church of Scientology
1277 East Colorado Boulevard
Pasadena, California 91106

Church of Scientology
1451 Irvine Boulevard
Tustin, California 92680

Church of Scientology
15643 Sherman Way
Van Nuys, California 91406

Church of Scientology
American Saint Hill
Organization
1413 L. Ron Hubbard Way
Los Angeles, California 90027

Church of Scientology
American Saint Hill
Foundation
1413 L. Ron Hubbard Way
Los Angeles, California 90027

Church of Scientology
Advanced Organization of
Los Angeles
1306 L. Ron Hubbard Way
Los Angeles, California 90027

Church of Scientology
Celebrity Centre International
5930 Franklin Avenue
Hollywood, California 90028

LOS GATOS

Church of Scientology
2155 South Bascom Avenue,
Suite 120
Campbell, California 95008

MIAMI

Church of Scientology
120 Giralda Avenue
Coral Gables, Florida 33134

MINNEAPOLIS

**Church of Scientology
 Twin Cities**
1011 Nicollet Mall
Minneapolis, Minnesota 55403

MOUNTAIN VIEW

Church of Scientology
2483 Old Middlefield Way
Mountain View, California 94043

NASHVILLE

**Church of Scientology
Celebrity Centre Nashville**
1204 16th Avenue South
Nashville, Tennessee 37212

NEW HAVEN

Church of Scientology
909 Whalley Avenue
New Haven, Connecticut
06515-1728

NEW YORK CITY

Church of Scientology
227 West 46th Street
New York, New York
10036-1409

**Church of Scientology
Celebrity Centre New York**
65 East 82nd Street
New York, New York 10028

ORLANDO

Church of Scientology
1830 East Colonial Drive
Orlando, Florida
32803-4729

PHILADELPHIA

Church of Scientology
1315 Race Street
Philadelphia, Pennsylvania
19107

PHOENIX

Church of Scientology
2111 West University Drive
Mesa, Arizona 85201

PORTLAND

Church of Scientology
2636 NE Sandy Boulevard
Portland, Oregon 97232-2342

**Church of Scientology
Celebrity Centre Portland**
708 SW Salmon Street
Portland, Oregon 97205

SACRAMENTO

Church of Scientology
825 15th Street
Sacramento, California
95814-2096

SALT LAKE CITY

Church of Scientology
1931 South 1100 East
Salt Lake City, Utah 84106

SAN DIEGO

Church of Scientology
1330 4th Avenue
San Diego, California 92101

SAN FRANCISCO

Church of Scientology
83 McAllister Street
San Francisco, California 94102

SAN JOSE

Church of Scientology
80 East Rosemary Street
San Jose, California 95112

SANTA BARBARA

Church of Scientology
524 State Street
Santa Barbara, California 93101

SEATTLE

Church of Scientology
601 Aurora Avenue North
Seattle, Washington 98109

ST. LOUIS

Church of Scientology
6901 Delmar Boulevard
University City, Missouri 63130

TAMPA

Church of Scientology
3617 Henderson Boulevard
Tampa, Florida 33609-4501

WASHINGTON, DC

**Founding Church of
 Scientology of
 Washington, DC**
1701 20th Street NW
Washington, DC 20009

PUERTO RICO

HATO REY

Church of Scientology
272 JT Piñero Avenue
Hyde Park, Hato Rey
San Juan, Puerto Rico 00918

CANADA

EDMONTON

Church of Scientology
10206 106th Street NW
Edmonton, Alberta
Canada T5J 1H7

KITCHENER

Church of Scientology
104 King Street West, 2nd Floor
Kitchener, Ontario
Canada N2G 2K6

MONTREAL

Church of Scientology
4489 Papineau Street
Montreal, Quebec
Canada H2H 1T7

OTTAWA

Church of Scientology
150 Rideau Street, 2nd Floor
Ottawa, Ontario
Canada K1N 5X6

QUEBEC

Church of Scientology
350 Bd Chareste Est
Quebec, Quebec
Canada G1K 3H5

TORONTO

Church of Scientology
696 Yonge Street, 2nd Floor
Toronto, Ontario
Canada M4Y 2A7

VANCOUVER

Church of Scientology
401 West Hastings Street
Vancouver, British Columbia
Canada V6B 1L5

WINNIPEG

Church of Scientology
315 Garry Street, Suite 210
Winnipeg, Manitoba
Canada R3B 2G7

UNITED KINGDOM

BIRMINGHAM

Church of Scientology
8 Ethel Street
Winston Churchill House
Birmingham, England B2 4BG

BRIGHTON

Church of Scientology
Third Floor, 79-83 North Street
Brighton, Sussex
England BN1 1ZA

EAST GRINSTEAD

**Church of Scientology
Saint Hill Foundation**
Saint Hill Manor
East Grinstead, West Sussex
England RH19 4JY

**Advanced Organization
 Saint Hill**
Saint Hill Manor
East Grinstead, West Sussex
England RH19 4JY

EDINBURGH

**Hubbard Academy of Personal
 Independence**
20 Southbridge
Edinburgh, Scotland EH1 1LL

LONDON

Church of Scientology
68 Tottenham Court Road
London, England W1P 0BB

**Church of Scientology
Celebrity Centre London**
42 Leinster Gardens
London, England W2 3AN

MANCHESTER

Church of Scientology
258 Deansgate
Manchester, England M3 4BG

PLYMOUTH

Church of Scientology
41 Ebrington Street
Plymouth, Devon
England PL4 9AA

SUNDERLAND

Church of Scientology
51 Fawcett Street
Sunderland, Tyne and Wear
England SR1 1RS

AUSTRIA

VIENNA

Church of Scientology
Schottenfeldgasse 13/15
1070 Vienna, Austria

**Church of Scientology
Celebrity Centre Vienna**
Senefeldergasse 11/5
1100 Vienna, Austria

BELGIUM

BRUSSELS

Church of Scientology
rue General MacArthur, 9
1180 Brussels, Belgium

DENMARK

AARHUS

Church of Scientology
Vester Alle 26
8000 Aarhus C, Denmark

COPENHAGEN

Church of Scientology
Store Kongensgade 55
1264 Copenhagen K, Denmark

Church of Scientology
Gammel Kongevej 3–5, 1
1610 Copenhagen V, Denmark

**Church of Scientology
Advanced Organization Saint
 Hill for Europe**
Jernbanegade 6
1608 Copenhagen V, Denmark

FRANCE

ANGERS

Church of Scientology
6, avenue Montaigne
49100 Angers, France

CLERMONT-FERRAND

Church of Scientology
6, rue Dulaure
63000 Clermont-Ferrand
France

LYON

Church of Scientology
3, place des Capucins
69001 Lyon, France

PARIS

Church of Scientology
7, rue Jules César
75012 Paris, France

**Church of Scientology
Celebrity Centre Paris**
69, rue Legendre
75017 Paris, France

SAINT-ÉTIENNE

Church of Scientology
24, rue Marengo
42000 Saint-Étienne, France

GERMANY

BERLIN

Church of Scientology
Sponholzstraße 51–52
12159 Berlin, Germany

DÜSSELDORF

Church of Scientology
Friedrichstraße 28
40217 Düsseldorf, Germany

**Church of Scientology
Celebrity Centre Düsseldorf**
Luisenstraße 23
40215 Düsseldorf, Germany

FRANKFURT

Church of Scientology
Kaiserstraße 49
60329 Frankfurt, Germany

HAMBURG

Church of Scientology
Domstraße 12
20095 Hamburg, Germany

Church of Scientology
Brennerstraße 12
20099 Hamburg, Germany

HANOVER

Church of Scientology
Odeonstraße 17
30159 Hanover, Germany

MUNICH

Church of Scientology
Beichstraße 12
80802 Munich, Germany

STUTTGART

Church of Scientology
Hohenheimerstraße 9
70184 Stuttgart, Germany

HUNGARY

BUDAPEST

Church of Scientology
1399 Budapest
VII. ker. Erzsébet krt. 5. I. em.
Postafiók 701/215.
Hungary

ISRAEL

TEL AVIV

College of Dianetics
12 Shontzino Street
PO Box 57478
61573 Tel Aviv, Israel

ITALY

BRESCIA

Church of Scientology
Via Fratelli Bronzetti, 20
25125 Brescia, Italy

CATANIA

Church of Scientology
Via Garibaldi, 9
95121 Catania, Italy

MILAN

Church of Scientology
Via Lepontina, 4
20159 Milan, Italy

MONZA

Church of Scientology
Largomolinetto, 1
20052 Monza (MI), Italy

NOVARA

Church of Scientology
Via Passalacqua, 28
28100 Novara, Italy

NUORO

Church of Scientology
Via Lamarmora, 102
08100 Nuoro, Italy

PADUA

Church of Scientology
Via Ugo Foscolo, 5
35131 Padua, Italy

PORDENONE

Church of Scientology
Via Dogana, 19
Zona Fiera
33170 Pordenone, Italy

ROME

Church of Scientology
Via del Caravita, 5
00186 Rome, Italy

TURIN

Church of Scientology
Via Bersezio, 7
10152 Turin, Italy

VERONA

Church of Scientology
Corso Milano, 84
37138 Verona, Italy

NETHERLANDS

AMSTERDAM

Church of Scientology
Nieuwezijds Voorburgwal
    116–118
1012 SH Amsterdam
Netherlands

NORWAY

OSLO

Church of Scientology
Lille Grensen 3
0159 Oslo, Norway

PORTUGAL

LISBON

Church of Scientology
Rua da Prata 185, 2 Andar
1100 Lisbon, Portugal

RUSSIA

MOSCOW

Hubbard Humanitarian Center
Boris Galushkina Street 19A
129301 Moscow, Russia

SPAIN

BARCELONA

Dianetics Civil Association
Pasaje Domingo, 11–13 Bajos
08007 Barcelona, Spain

MADRID

Dianetics Civil Association
C/ Montera 20, Piso 1° dcha.
28013 Madrid, Spain

SWEDEN

GÖTEBORG

Church of Scientology
Värmlandsgatan 16, 1 tr.
413 28 Göteborg, Sweden

MALMÖ

Church of Scientology
Porslinsgatan 3
211 32 Malmö, Sweden

STOCKHOLM

Church of Scientology
Götgatan 105
116 62 Stockholm, Sweden

SWITZERLAND

BASEL

Church of Scientology
Herrengrabenweg 56
4054 Basel, Switzerland

BERN

Church of Scientology
Muhlemattstrasse 31
Postfach 384
3000 Bern 14, Switzerland

GENEVA

Church of Scientology
12, rue des Acacias
1227 Carouge
Geneva, Switzerland

LAUSANNE

Church of Scientology
10, rue de la Madeleine
1003 Lausanne, Switzerland

ZURICH

Church of Scientology
Freilagerstrasse 11
8047 Zurich, Switzerland

AUSTRALIA

ADELAIDE

Church of Scientology
24–28 Waymouth Street
Adelaide, South Australia
Australia 5000

BRISBANE

Church of Scientology
106 Edward Street, 2nd Floor
Brisbane, Queensland
Australia 4000

CANBERRA

Church of Scientology
43–45 East Row
Canberra City, ACT
Australia 2601

MELBOURNE

Church of Scientology
42–44 Russell Street
Melbourne, Victoria
Australia 3000

PERTH

Church of Scientology
108 Murray Street, 1st Floor
Perth, Western Australia
Australia 6000

SYDNEY

Church of Scientology
201 Castlereagh Street
Sydney, New South Wales
Australia 2000

**Church of Scientology
Advanced Organization
   Saint Hill Australia,
   New Zealand and Oceania**
19–37 Greek Street
Glebe, New South Wales
Australia 2037

JAPAN

TOKYO

Scientology Tokyo
2-11-7, Kita-otsuka
Toshima-ku
Tokyo
Japan 170-004

NEW ZEALAND

AUCKLAND

Church of Scientology
159 Queen Street, 3rd Floor
Auckland 1, New Zealand

AFRICA

BULAWAYO

Church of Scientology
Southampton House, Suite 202
Main Street and 9th Avenue
Bulawayo, Zimbabwe

CAPE TOWN

Church of Scientology
Ground Floor, Dorlane House
39 Roeland Street
Cape Town 8001, South Africa

DURBAN

Church of Scientology
20 Buckingham Terrace
Westville, Durban 3630
South Africa

HARARE

Church of Scientology
404-409 Pockets Building
50 Jason Moyo Avenue
Harare, Zimbabwe

JOHANNESBURG

Church of Scientology
4th Floor, Budget House
130 Main Street
Johannesburg 2001
South Africa

Church of Scientology
No. 108 1st Floor,
   Bordeaux Centre
Gordon Road, Corner Jan
   Smuts Avenue
Blairgowrie, Randburg 2125
South Africa

PORT ELIZABETH

Church of Scientology
2 St. Christopher's
27 Westbourne Road Central
Port Elizabeth 6001
South Africa

PRETORIA

Church of Scientology
307 Ancore Building
Corner Jeppe and Esselen Streets
Sunnyside, Pretoria 0002
South Africa

ARGENTINA

BUENOS AIRES

**Dianetics Association of
   Argentina**
2169 Bartolomé Mitre
Capital Federal
Buenos Aires 1039, Argentina

COLOMBIA

BOGOTÁ

Dianetics Cultural Center
Carrera 30 #91–96
Bogotá, Colombia

MEXICO

GUADALAJARA

**Dianetics Cultural
   Organization, A.C.**
Avenida de la Paz 2787
Fracc. Arcos Sur, Sector Juárez
Guadalajara, Jalisco
C.P. 44500, Mexico

MEXICO CITY

**Dianetics Cultural
   Association, A.C.**
Belisario Domínguez #17-1
Villa Coyoacán
Colonia Coyoacán
C.P. 04000, Mexico, D.F.

**Institute of Applied
   Philosophy, A.C.**
Municipio Libre No. 40
   Esq. Mira Flores
Colonia Portales
Mexico, D.F.

**Latin American Cultural
   Center, A.C.**
Rio Amazonas 11
Colonia Cuahutemoc
C.P. 06500, Mexico, D.F.

**Dianetics Technological
   Institute, A.C.**
Avenida Chapultepec 540
   6° Piso
Colonia Roma, Metro
   Chapultepec
C.P. 06700, Mexico, D.F.

**Dianetics Development
   Organization, A.C.**
Avenida Xola #1113 Esq. Pitágoras
Colonia Narvarte
C.P. 03220, Mexico, D.F.

**Dianetics Cultural
   Organization, A.C.**
Calle Monterrey #402
Colonia Narvarte
C.P. 03020, Mexico, D.F.

VENEZUELA

CARACAS

**Dianetics Cultural
   Organization, A.C.**
Calle El Colegio, Edificio
   El Viñedo
Sabana Grande
Caracas, Venezuela

VALENCIA

**Dianetics Cultural
   Association, A.C.**
Avenida 101 No. 150-23
   (Atrás Fiat. Bolívar Norte)
Urbanización La Alegría
Valencia, Venezuela

MISSIONS & CENTERS

UNITED STATES

ALASKA

Church of Scientology
Mission of Anchorage
1300 East 68th Avenue
Suite 208A
Anchorage, Alaska 99502

CALIFORNIA

Church of Scientology
Mission of Antelope Valley
22924 Lyons Avenue
Suite 204, 205
Newhall, California 91322

Church of Scientology
Mission of Auburn
17740 Crother Hills Road
Meadow Vista, California 95722

Church of Scientology
Mission of Berkeley (Bay Cities)
2975 Treat Boulevard, Suite D-4
Concord, California 94518

Church of Scientology
Mission of Beverly Hills
9885 Charleville Boulevard
Beverly Hills, California 90212

Church of Scientology
Mission of Brand Boulevard
143 South Glendale Avenue
Suite 103
Glendale, California 91205

Church of Scientology
Mission of Buenaventura
180 North Ashwood Avenue
Ventura, California 93003

Church of Scientology
Mission of Burbank
6623 Irvine Avenue
North Hollywood
California 91606

Church of Scientology
Mission of Capitol
9915 Fair Oaks Boulevard, Suite A
Fair Oaks, California 95628

Church of Scientology
Mission of the Diablo Valley
610 West 4th Street
Antioch, California 94509

Church of Scientology
Mission of Escondido
326 South Kalmia Street
Escondido, California 92025

Church of Scientology
Mission of the Foothills
2254 Honolulu Avenue
Montrose, California 91020

Church of Scientology
Mission of Los Angeles
5408 Carpenter Avenue #204
North Hollywood
California 91607

Church of Scientology
Mission of Marin
1930 4th Street
San Rafael, California 94901

Church of Scientology
Mission of Palo Alto
3505 El Camino Real
Palo Alto, California 94306

Church of Scientology
Mission of Redwood City
617 Veterans Boulevard, #205
Redwood City, California 94063

Church of Scientology
Mission of River Park
1010 Hurley Way, Suite 505
Sacramento, California 95825

Church of Scientology
Mission of San Bernardino
5 East Citrus Avenue, Suite 105
Redlands, California 92373

Church of Scientology
Mission of San Francisco
701 Sutter Street, 3rd Floor
San Francisco, California 94109

Church of Scientology
Mission of San Jose
826 North Winchester
Boulevard, Suite 1
San Jose, California 95128

Church of Scientology
Mission of Santa Clara Valley
2718 Homestead Road
Santa Clara, California 95051

Church of Scientology
Mission of Santa Rosa
850 2nd Street, Suite F
Santa Rosa, California 95404

Church of Scientology
Mission of Sherman Oaks
13517 Ventura Boulevard,
Suite 7
Sherman Oaks, California 91423

Church of Scientology
Mission of West Valley
21010 Devonshire Street
Chatsworth, California 91311

Church of Scientology
Mission of Westwood
12617 Mitchell Avenue #4
Los Angeles, California 90066

COLORADO

Church of Scientology
Mission of Alamosa
511 Main Street, Suite #6
Alamosa, Colorado 81101

Church of Scientology
Mission of Boulder
1021 Pearl Street
Boulder, Colorado 80302

Church of Scientology
Mission of Roaring Fork
827 Bennett Avenue
Glenwood Springs
Colorado 81601

DELAWARE

Church of Scientology
Mission of Collingswood
PO Box 730
Claymont, Delaware 19703-0730

FLORIDA

Church of Scientology
Mission of Clearwater
100 North Belcher Road
Clearwater, Florida 33765

Church of Scientology
Mission of Fort Lauderdale
660 South Federal Highway
Suite 200
Pompano Beach, Florida 33062

Church of Scientology
Mission of Palm Harbor
565 Hammock Drive
Palm Harbor, Florida 34683

Church of Scientology
Mission of West Palm Beach
1966 South Congress Avenue
West Palm Beach, Florida 33406

HAWAII

Church of Scientology
Mission of Honolulu
6172 May Way
Honolulu, Hawaii 96821

ILLINOIS

Church of Scientology
Mission of Champaign-Urbana
312 West John Street
Champaign, Illinois 61820

Church of Scientology
Mission of Chicago
6580 North NW Highway
Chicago, Illinois 60631

Church of Scientology
Mission of Peoria
2020 North Wisconsin
Peoria, Illinois 61603

KANSAS

Church of Scientology
Mission of Wichita
3705 East Douglas
Wichita, Kansas 67218

LOUISIANA

Church of Scientology
Mission of Baton Rouge
9432 Common Street
Baton Rouge, Louisiana 70806

Church of Scientology
Mission of Lafayette
104 Westmark Boulevard,
   Suite 2A
Lafayette, Louisiana 70506

MAINE

Church of Scientology
Mission of Brunswick
2 Lincoln Street
Brunswick, Maine 04011

MASSACHUSETTS

Church of Scientology
Mission of Merrimack Valley
142 Primrose Street
Haverhill, Massachusetts 01830

Church of Scientology
Mission of Watertown
313 Common Street #2
Watertown, Massachusetts 02472

MICHIGAN

Church of Scientology
Mission of Genesee County
423 North Saginaw
Holly, Michigan 48442

Church of Scientology
Mission of Rochester Hills
850 Lakewood Drive
Rochester Hills, Michigan 48309

NEBRASKA

Church of Scientology
Mission of Omaha
843 Hidden Hills Drive
Bellevue, Nebraska 68005

NEVADA

Church of Scientology
Mission of Las Vegas
2923 Schaffer Circle
Las Vegas, Nevada 89121

Church of Scientology
Mission of Sierra Nevada
1539 Vassar Street, Suite 201
Reno, Nevada 89502-2745

Church of Scientology
Mission of Vegas Valley
7545 Bermuda Road
Las Vegas, Nevada 89123

NEW HAMPSHIRE

Church of Scientology
Mission of Greater Concord
Suite 3C-4 Bicentennial Square
Concord, New Hampshire 03301

NEW JERSEY

Church of Scientology
Mission of Elizabeth
339 Morris Avenue
Elizabeth, New Jersey
07208-3616

Church of Scientology
Mission of New Jersey
1029 Teaneck Road
Teaneck, New Jersey 07666

NEW YORK

Church of Scientology
Mission of Middletown
21 Mill Street
Liberty, New York 12754

Church of Scientology
Mission of Queens
56-03 214th Street
Bayside, New York 11364

Church of Scientology
Mission of Rochester
45 Edgerton Street
Rochester, New York 14607

Church of Scientology
Mission of Rockland
11 Holland Avenue, White Plains
Westchester, New York 10603

PENNSYLVANIA

Church of Scientology
Mission of Pittsburgh
220 Nazareth Drive
Belle Vernon
Pennsylvania 15012

SOUTH CAROLINA

Church of Scientology
Mission of Charleston
8334 Witsell Street
North Charleston
South Carolina 29406

TENNESSEE

Church of Scientology
Mission of Memphis
1440 Central Avenue
Memphis, Tennessee 38104

TEXAS

Church of Scientology
Mission of El Paso
1120 North El Paso Street
El Paso, Texas 79902

Church of Scientology
Mission of Harlingen
1214 Dixieland Road, Suite 4
Harlingen, Texas 78552

Church of Scientology
Mission of Houston
2727 Fondren, Suite 1-A
Houston, Texas 77063

Church of Scientology
Mission of San Antonio
5119 Fort Clark Drive
Austin, Texas 78745

VIRGINIA

Church of Scientology
Mission of Piedmont
Sage Building, Box 15
115 Jefferson Highway
Louisa, Virginia 23093

WASHINGTON

Church of Scientology
Mission of Bellevue
15424 Bellevue-Redmond Road
Redmond, Washington 98052

Church of Scientology
Mission of Burien
15216 2nd Avenue SW
Seattle, Washington 98166

Church of Scientology
Mission of Seattle
1234 NE 145th Street
Seattle, Washington 98155

Dianetics Center
Mission of Spokane
1810 North Ruby
Spokane, Washington 99207

WISCONSIN

Church of Scientology
Mission of Milwaukee
710 East Silver Spring Drive,
   Suite E
Whitefish Bay, Wisconsin 53217

AFRICA

Église de Scientologie
Mission de Kinshasa
BP 1444
7, rue de Fele
Kinshasa/Limete, Zaire

Church of Scientology
Mission of Lagos
16 Moor Road
Off University Road, Yaba
Lagos, Nigeria
West Africa

Church of Scientology
Mission of Norwood
18 Trilby Street
Oaklands, Johannesburg 2192
Republic of South Africa

Church of Scientology
Mission of Soweto
PO Box 496 Kwa-Xuma
1868 Soweto
Republic of South Africa

AUSTRALIA

Church of Scientology
Mission of Inner West Sydney
4 Wangal Place
Five Dock, New South Wales
Australia 2046

Church of Scientology
Mission of Melbourne
55 Glenferrie Road
Malvern, Victoria
Australia 3144

CANADA

Église de Scientologie
Mission de Beauce
11925, 1ᵉ avenue
Ville de St-Georges
Beauce, Quebec
Canada G5Y 2C9

Church of Scientology
Mission of Calgary
Box 22
Site 2 RR1
Millerville, Alberta
Canada T0L 1K0

Church of Scientology
Mission of Halifax
2589 Windsor Street
Halifax, Nova Scotia
Canada B3K 5C4

Church of Scientology
Mission of Montreal
1690 A, avenue de l'Église
Montreal, Quebec
Canada H4E 1G5

Church of Scientology
Mission of Vancouver
2860 West 4th Avenue
Vancouver, British Columbia
Canada V6K 1R2

Church of Scientology
Chinese Mission of Vancouver
304-7260 Lindsay Road
Richmond, British Columbia
Canada V7G 3M6

Church of Scientology
Mission of Victoria
2624 Quadra Street
Victoria, British Columbia
Canada V8T 4E4

COMMONWEALTH OF INDEPENDENT STATES

BELARUS

Borisov Dianetics Center
Borisov
2nd pereulok Turgeneva 19
Belarus

Dianetics Center of Minsk
Minsk
Cherviakova 57-121
Belarus

Scientology Mission of Mogilev
212011 Mogilev
8th March Street 54
Belarus

GEORGIA

Dianetics Mission of Tbilisi
Tbilisi
Ul. Ushangi Chkheidze 8
Georgia

KAZAKHSTAN

Dianetics Center of Almaty
Almaty
Ul. Abaja, ugol Mate-Zalki 4A
Kazakhstan

Dianetics Center of Karaganda
Karaganda
Erzhanova 10/2
Kazakhstan

Scientology Mission of Pavlodar
Pavlodar
Lomova 135/1
Kazakhstan

Scientology Mission
of Semipalatinsk
Semipalatinsk
Naimanbayeva 10-311
Kazakhstan

KYRGYZSTAN

Scientology Mission of Bishkek
Bishkek
Ul. Zhukeeva-Pudovkina 73
AB box 2023
Kyrgyzstan

MOLDOVA

Kishinev Dianetics Center
MD 2028, Kishinev
AB box 1145
Moldova

RUSSIA

Scientology Mission of Arbat
Moscow
Tzvetnoy blvd. 26
Russia

Scientology Mission of Barnaul
Barnaul
Malakhova 85-183
Russia

Scientology Mission of Bryansk
241037 Bryansk
Ul. Dokuchaeva 15-72
Russia

Scientology Mission
of Chelyabinsk
Chelyabinsk
Ul. Vorovskogo 23B
Russia

Scientology Mission of Chelny
423810 Naberezhnie Chelny
AB box 27
Russia

Dianetics Center of
Dimitrovgrad
Ulyanovskaja Obl.,
Pr. Dimitrova 14
Russia

Scientology Mission of
Ekaterinburg
620077 Ekaterinburg
Ul. Papanina 9, 8th floor
Russia

Scientology Mission of
Khabarovsk
Khabarovsk
Per Garazhniy 3-38
Russia

Dianetics Center of Ivanovo
153000 Ivanovo
Ul. 3rd Internationala 41-11
Russia

Scientology Mission of Izhevsk
Izhevsk
Millionnaya 3
Russia

Scientology Mission of
Kaliningrad MR
141070 Kaliningrad MR
Moscow Region, Korolev MR
Ul. Frunze 24-13
Russia

Scientology Mission of
Kalininskaya
St. Petersburg
Ul. Vekeneeva 4-42
Russia

Dianetics Humanitarian Center
of Kaluga
Kaluga
M. Zhukova 18
Russia

Scientology Mission of Kazan
420089 Kazan
Ul. Latyshskih Strelkov 33-171
Russia

**Scientology Mission
of Kislovodsk**
357746 Kislovodsk
Ul. Telmana 3-6
Russia

Dianetics Center of Krasnoyarsk
663080 Divnogorsk
Ul. Naberezhnaya 41-27
Russia

Scientology Mission of Kursk
Kursk
Magistralny proezd 12-2
Russia

Scientology Mission of Kushva
624300 Kushva
Sverdlovsk Region
Krasnoarmeiskaya 13-18
Russia

**Scientology Mission of
Ligovskaya**
St. Petersburg
Ligovskaya
Rizhski pr. 8
Russia

**Dianetics Center of
Magnitogorsk**
455000 Magnitogorsk
AB box 3008
Russia

Dianetics Center of Mitishi
141007 Moscovskaja
    Obl. Mitischi
2-oj Shelkovsky proezd 5/1-62
Russia

Scientology Mission of Moscow
103030 Moscow
2nd Uzhnoportoviy proezd 27
Russia

**Dianetics Center of Moscow
Central**
Moscow
Ul. Argunovskaya 18-117
Russia

Dianetics Center of Murmansk
183071 Murmansk
Per. Sviazi 3
Russia

Dianetics Mission of Nazran
Ingushetia, Karabulak
Ul. Chkalova 38
c/o Mayor's Office
Russia

**Scientology Mission
of Nizhnekamsk**
Tatarstan, Nizhnekamsk
Ul. 30 Let Pobedy 5A
AB box 357
Russia

**Dianetics Center of
Nizhny Novgorod**
Nizhny-Novgorod
Blvd. Mira 12
Russia

**Scientology Mission of
Novgorod I+II**
173001 Novgorod
AB box 120
Russia

**Scientology Mission of
Novokuznetzk**
654917 Novokuznetzk Obl.
Kemerovo Region
Rostovskaya 13
Russia

**Dianetics Center of
Novosibirsk**
Novosibirsk
Petropavlovskaya 17
Russia

**Scientology Mission of
Novy Urengoy**
626718 Tiumenskaya Obl.
Novy Urengoy
Ul. Youbuleynaya 1-41
Russia

**Hubbard Humanitarian Center
of Omsk**
644043 Omsk
AB box 3768
Russia

Dianetics Center of Omsk II
644099 Omsk, Glavpochtamt
AB box 333
Russia

Dianetics Center of Orenburg
Orenburg
Cheluskintsev 14
Russia

Scientology Mission of Oriol
Oriol
Moskovskaya, 155
Russia

Scientology Mission of Penza
440061 Penza
Ul. Tolstogo 8A
Penza, Russia

Dianetics Center of Penza II
440056 Penza
Ul. Riabova 6C
Russia

Dianetics Center of Perm
614000 Perm
AB box 7026
Russia

**Scientology Mission of
Perovskaya**
Moscow
Electrodny proezd 14-1
Russia

**Scientology Mission of
Petropavlovsk-Kamchatskiy**
Petropavlovsk-Kamchatskiy
Karla Marxa 29
Russia

Dianetics Center of Samara
443041 Samara
Karla Marxa 40
Russia

Dianetics Center of Saratov
410601 Saratov
AB box 1533
Russia

**Scientology Mission of
Solnechnogorsk**
141500 Solnechnogorsk
Ul. Podmoskavnaya 27-46
Russia

**St. Petersburg Scientology
Center & St. Petersburg
Scientology Center II**
St. Petersburg
Ligovsky Prospect 33
Russia

**Dianetics Humanitarian
Center of Surgut**
Surgut
M. Karamova 86
Russia

Scientology Mission of Tambov
Tambov 32
AB box 12
Russia

**Dianetics Humanitarian
Center of Tolyatti**
445050 Samarskaya Obl., Tolyatti
AB box 14
Russia

Dianetics Center of Troitsk
142092 Troitsk
Sirenevaya 10-87
Russia

Scientology Mission of Tula
300000 Tula
Krasnoarmeysky Prospect 7-127
Russia

Dianetics Center of Ufa
Ufa
Ul. Zemtzova 70
Russia

Scientology Mission of Ulan-Ude
670009 Ulan-Ude
Ul. Nevsky 11
Buryatia, Russia

Scientology Mission of Uljanovsk
Uljanovsk
Gagarina 34-613
Russia

Scientology Mission of Vladivostok
Vladivostok
Primorski Krai
Borisenko 33-10
Russia

Dianetics Humanitarian Center of Volgograd
400075 Volgograd
AB box 6
Russia

Scientology Mission of Voronezh
Voronezh
Druzhinnikov 2
Russia

Scientology Mission of Zheleznogorsk
662990 Krasnoyarski Region
Zheleznogorsk-2
Ul. Komsomolskaya 37-19
Russia

UKRAINE

Dianetics Humanitarian Center of Kharkov
61052, Kharkov
AB box 53, Ukraine

Scientology Mission of Kremenchug
Kremenchug
60 Let Oktiabria 45-24
Ukraine

Scientology Mission of Melitopol
Melitopol
Ul. Grizodubovoy 42-18
Ukraine

Scientology Mission of Nikolayev
54056 Nikolayev
Artilleriyskaya 18
Ukraine

Dianetics Center of Uzgorod
294000 Uzgorod
Ul. Dobrianskogo 10-9
Ukraine

EUROPE

ALBANIA

Church of Scientology Mission of Tirana
Rr "Bardhyl" PL. 18 shk: 2
   AP: 3
Tirana, Albania

AUSTRIA

Scientology Mission Salzburg
Rupertgasse 21
A-5020 Salzburg, Austria

Scientology Mission Wolfsberg
Wienestrasse 8
9400 Wolfsberg, Austria

CZECH REPUBLIC

Dianeticke Centrum
Jindrisska 7
110 00 Prague 1
Czech Republic

DENMARK

Church of Scientology Mission of Aalborg
Boulevarden 39 st.
9000 Aalborg, Denmark

Church of Scientology Mission of Copenhagen City
Rathsacksvej 1 st. th.
1862 Frederiksberg C
Denmark

Church of Scientology Mission of Lyngby
Sorgenfrivej 3
2800 Lyngby, Denmark

Hubbard Dianetik Center Odense
Ove Gjeddes Vej. 27
5220 Odense
Denmark

Church of Scientology Mission of Silkeborg
Virklundvej 5, Virklund
8600 Silkeborg, Denmark

FINLAND

Church of Scientology Mission of Helsinki
Peltolantie 2 B
01300 Vantaa, Finland

Church of Scientology Dianetiikka-keskus
Hämeenkatu 11 D
15110 Lahti, Finland

FRANCE

Église de Scientologie Mission de Bordeaux
41, rue de Cheverus
33000 Bordeaux, France

Église de Scientologie Mission de Marseille
2, rue Devilliers
13005 Marseille, France

Église de Scientologie Mission de Nice
28, rue Gioffredo
06000 Nice, France

Église de Scientologie Mission de Toulouse
9, rue Edmond de Planet
31000 Toulouse, France

GERMANY

Scientology Mission Bremen e.V.
Stolzenauer Str. 36
28207 Bremen, Germany

Dianetik Göppingen e.V. Scientology Mission
Geislingerstraße 21
73033 Göppingen, Germany

Scientology Heilbronn Mission der Scientology Kirche e.V.
Am Wollhaus 8
74072 Heilbronn, Germany

Mission der Scientology Kirche
Karlstraße 46
76133 Karlsruhe, Germany

Scientology Mission Pasing
Landsbergstraße 416
81241 Munich, Germany

Scientology Kirche Bayern e.V.
Gemeinde Nuremberg
Färberstraße 5
D-90402 Nuremberg, Germany

Scientology Mission e.V.
Heinestraße 9
72762 Reutlingen, Germany

Scientology Mission Ulm e.V.
Eythstraße 2
89075 Ulm, Germany

Scientology Wiesbaden Mission der Scientology Kirche e.V.
Mauritiusstraße 14
65183 Wiesbaden, Germany

GREECE

Greek Dianetics and Scientology Centre
Patision 200
11256 Athens, Greece

HUNGARY

Church of Scientology Mission of Baja
6500 Baja
Galamb u. 13.
Hungary

Church of Scientology Mission of Belvarosi
1052 Budapest
Karoly krt. 4. III/10.
Hungary

Church of Scientology
Mission of Bonyhad
7150 Bonyhad
Bartok B. ut 56/a
Hungary

Church of Scientology
Mission of Debrecen
4031 Debrecen
Derek u. 181. IV/12.
Hungary

Church of Scientology
Mission of Dunaujvaros
2404 Dunaujvaros, Pf.: 435
Gorkij u. 3/A fsz/1.
Hungary

Church of Scientology
Mission of Eger
3300 Eger
Vallon u. 11. 9/27.
3301 Eger, Pf.: 215
Hungary

Church of Scientology
Mission of Esztergom
2500 Esztergom
Budapesti ut 30.
Hungary

Church of Scientology
Mission of Gyor
9026 Gyor
Dozsa Gyorgy rakpart 1/4.
Hungary

Church of Scientology
Mission of Kalocsa
6300 Kalocsa
Alkotas u. 20. II/7.
Hungary

Church of Scientology
Mission of Kaposvar
7400 Kaposvar
Bajcsy-Zs. u. 38. 1/1.
Hungary

Church of Scientology
Mission of Kazincbarcika
3700 Kazincbarcika
Egressy ut 11. 3/8.
Hungary

Church of Scientology
Mission of Keszthely
8360 Keszthely
Sopron u. 41.
Hungary

Church of Scientology
Mission of Kiskunfelegyhaza
6101 Kiskunfelegyhaza, Pf.: 63
Hungary

Church of Scientology
Mission of Mezokovesd
3400 Mezokovesd
Dr. Lukacs Gaspar u. 5.
Hungary

Church of Scientology
Mission of Miskolc
3530 Miskolc
Szechenyi u. 34. I. em.
Hungary

Church of Scientology
Mission of Nyiregyhaza
4400 Nyiregyhaza
Vasvari Pal ut. 14.
Hungary

Church of Scientology
Mission of Ozd
3600 Ozd
Sarlitelep
Hungary

Church of Scientology
Mission of Paks
7030 Paks, Pf.: 10
Kodaly z. ut. 30.
Hungary

Church of Scientology
Mission of Pecs
7621 Pecs
Rakoczi ut 73/C
7602 Pecs 2, Pf.: 41
Hungary

Church of Scientology
Mission of Sarospatak
3950 Sarospatak
Andrassy 57. II/3.
Hungary

Church of Scientology
Mission of Sopron
9401 Sopron, Pf.: 111
Frankenberg u. 2/b
Hungary

Church of Scientology
Mission of Szazhalombatta
2440 Szazhalombatta, Pf.: 69
Hungary

Church of Scientology
Mission of Szeged
6722 Szeged
Honved u. 5/B
6701 Szeged, Pf.: 1258
Hungary

Church of Scientology
Mission of Szekesfehervar
8001 Szekesfehervar, Pf.: 176
Moricz Zs. u. 36.
Hungary

Church of Scientology
Mission of Szekszard
7100 Szekszard, Pf.: 165
Ady E. u. 14.
Hungary

Church of Scientology
Mission of Tatabanya
2800 Tatabanya
Dozsakert 49. III. Lepcsohaz I/1.
2801 Tatabanya, Pf.: 1372
Hungary

Church of Scientology
Mission of Tiszaujvaros
3580 Tiszaujvaros
Teleki Blanka u. 2.
Hungary

Church of Scientology
Mission of Veszprem
8200 Veszprem
Volgyhid ter 3.
Hungary

ITALY

Chiesa di Scientology
Missione di Aosta
Corso Battaglione, 13/B
11100 Aosta, Italy

Chiesa di Scientology
Missione di Asti
Corso Alfieri, 51
14100 Asti, Italy

Chiesa di Scientology
Missione di Avellino
Via Fratelli Bisogno, 5
83100 Avellino, Italy

Chiesa di Scientology
Missione di Barletta
Via Cialdini, 67/B
70051 Barletta (Bari), Italy

Chiesa di Scientology
Missione della Bergamasca
Via Roma, 85
24020 Bergamo, Italy

Chiesa di Scientology
Missione di Bologna
Via Angelo Custode, 66/2
40141 Bologna, Italy

Chiesa di Scientology
Missione di Bolzano
Via Al Boschetto, 7
39100 Bolzano, Italy

Chiesa di Scientology
Missione di Cagliari
Via Sonnino, 177
09127 Cagliari, Italy

Chiesa di Scientology
Missione di Cantù
Via G. da Fossano, 40
22063 Cantù (Como), Italy

Chiesa di Scientology
Missione di Carpi
Via due Ponti, 102
41012 Carpi (Modena), Italy

Chiesa di Scientology
Missione di Castelfranco
Via 8/9 Maggio, 59
Cornuda (Treviso), Italy

Chiesa di Scientology
Missione di Como
Via Torno, 12
22100 Como, Italy

Chiesa di Scientology
Missione di Conegliano
Via Manin, 9
31015 Conegliano (Treviso), Italy

Chiesa di Scientology
Missione di Cosenza
Via Duca degli Abruzzi, 6
87100 Cosenza, Italy

Chiesa di Scientology
Missione della Franciacorta
Via de Gasperi, 6
Nigoline di Cortefranca
25100 Brescia, Italy

Chiesa di Scientology
Missione di Lecco
Via Mascari, 78
22053 Lecco, Italy

Chiesa di Scientology
Missione di Lucca
Viale G. Puccini, 425/B
S. Anna, 55100 Lucca, Italy

Chiesa di Scientology
Missione di Macerata
Via Roma, 13
62100 Macerata, Italy

Chiesa di Scientology
Missione di Mantova
Viale dei Caduti, 2
46100 Mantova, Italy

Chiesa di Scientology
Missione di Merate
Via Paolo Arlati (Ang. via Roma)
23807 Merate, Lecco, Italy

Chiesa di Scientology
Missione di Milano
Via Domenichino, 16
20149 Milano, Italy

Chiesa di Scientology
Missione di Modena
Via Giardini, 468/C
41100 Modena, Italy

Chiesa di Scientology
Missione di Olbia
Via Gabriele D'Annunzio, 13
Centro Martini
07026 Olbia (Sassari)
Italy

Chiesa di Scientology
Missione di Palermo
Via Mariano Stabile, 139
90100 Palermo, Italy

Chiesa di Scientology
Missione di Ragusa
Via Caporale degli Zuavi, 67
97019 Vittoria (Ragusa)
Italy

Chiesa di Scientology
Missione di Romano (Clusone)
Via Pesenti, 17
24048 Treviolo (Bergamo)
Italy

Chiesa di Scientology
Missione di Treviglio
Via Bicetti, 8
24047 Treviglio (Bergamo)
Italy

Chiesa di Scientology
Missione di Trieste
Via Matteotti, 5
34138 Trieste, Italy

Chiesa di Scientology
Missione di Vicenza
Viale Milano, 38D
c/o Complesso Polialte
36075 Montecchio Maggiore
(Vicenza), Italy

Chiesa di Scientology
Missione di Vicenza Centro
Via Camisana, 278
Lerino-Torri di Quartesolo
36040 Vicenza, Italy

MACEDONIA

Hubbard Center for Dianetics
and Scientology
Mission of Skopje
Bul. Parizanski Odredi Br. 21/1
Kompleks Porta Bunjakovec A 2/3
1000 Skopje
Republic of Macedonia

ROMANIA

Church of Scientology
Mission of Szekelyudvarhely
4150 Odorheiu Secuiesc
Str. Rozei Nr 2
CP: 28
Romania

SLOVENIA

Dianetics Centre of Koper
Za Gradon 22, S10
Koper, Slovenia

SPAIN

Centro de Eficiencia
Personal Dianética
C/Hermanos Rivas, 22-1-1A
46018 Valencia, Spain

Centro de Mejoramiento
Personal
C/Viera y Clavijo, 33-2 Planta
35002 Las Palmas de Gran Canaria
Spain

Centro de Mejoramiento
Personal
Urbanización Los Mirtos, 65
41020 Sevilla, Spain

Centro de Mejoramiento
Personal de Cercedilla
Cambrils, 19
28034 Madrid, Spain

Misión de la Moraleja
Cuesta Blanca, 213
28100 Madrid, Spain

SWEDEN

Dianetik Huset
Finnbodavägen 2, 4th
13131 Nacka, Sweden

SWITZERLAND

Chiesa di Scientology
Missione di Lugano
Via Campagna, 30A
6982 Serocca D'Agno
Switzerland

Dianetik and Scientology
Luzern Mission
Zentrum für
Angewandte Philosophie
Sentimattstrasse 7
6011 Luzern, Switzerland

Mission der Scientology Kirche
Regensbergstrasse 89
8050 Zürich, Switzerland

GREAT BRITAIN

Dianetics and Scientology
Mission of Bournemouth, Ltd.
42 High Street
Poole, Dorset, England
BH15 1BT

Church of Scientology
Mission of Hove, Ltd.
59A Coleridge Street
Hove, East Sussex, England
BN3 5AB

HONG KONG

Church of Scientology
Mission of Hong Kong
Flat D, 21/F, Tower 3
Laguna Verde, Hung Hom
Kowloon
Central, Hong Kong

INDIA

Scientology Counseling Centre
24 Sampooran Lodge
Ajit Nagar, Punjab 147001
India

**Dianetics Center
of Ambala Cantt**
6352 Punjabi Mohalla
Ambala Cantt 133001
India

IRELAND

**Church of Scientology
Mission of Dublin, Ltd.**
62/63 Middle Abbey Street
Dublin 1, Ireland

LATVIA

**Dianetics Center of Riga
Latvia, Humanitarian Centrs**
"Dianetika"
A. Briana 9/1-15
Latvia

LITHUANIA

Dianetics Center of Vilnius
Centrinis paštas 2000, p.d. 42
Vilnius, Lithuania

LATIN AMERICA

COLOMBIA

**Asociación Dianética
Bogotá Norte**
Avenida 13, No. 104-91
Bogotá, Colombia

**Fundación para el
Mejoramiento de la Vida**
Calle 70A, No. 12-38
Bogotá, Colombia

**Iglesia de Cienciología
Misión de Medellín**
Carrera 13, No. 19-23
La Ceja, Antioquia, Colombia

CHILE

Centro de Tecnología Hubbard
Jorge Washington, No. 338
Santiago de Chile
Chile

**Centro Hubbard
Misión de Chile**
Nuncio Laghi, 6558
La Reina, Santiago, Chile

COSTA RICA

**Instituto Tecnológico
de Dianética**
300 Mts. sur de auto mercado
en Los Yoses C.R.
Apdo: 1245700-1000
San José, Costa Rica

DOMINICAN REPUBLIC

Dianética Santo Domingo
Condominio Ambar Plaza II
Bloque II, Apto. 302
Avenida Núñez de Cáceres Esq.
Sarasota
Santo Domingo
Dominican Republic

ECUADOR

**Iglesia de Cienciología
Misión de Guayaquil**
Avenida Fco. de Orellana,
No. 218
Guayaquil, Ecuador

GUATEMALA

**Asociación de Cienciología
Aplicada Dianética
de Guatemala**
21 Avenida "A," 32-28
Zona 5, Guatemala

MEXICO

**Centro de Dianética Hubbard
de Aguascalientes A.C.**
Hamburgo, No. 127
Fraccionamiento del Valle 1A Sec.
C.P. 20080 Aguascalientes, Ags.
Mexico

**Instituto de Filosofía
Aplicada de Bajío**
Boulevard Adolfo López Mateos
507 Oriente
Zona Centro Entre Libertad y
República
Leon Gto.
C.P. 37000, Mexico

Mission Chihuahua
Ortiz del Campo, 3309 Frace
Colonia San Felipe, Chihuahua
Chihuahua, Mexico

Centro Hubbard de Dianética
Tecamachalco
#314 Prsdo. Norte
Lomas de Chapultepec
Mexico, D.F. Mexico

Instituto de Dianética
Monterrey A.C.
Tulancingo, 1262, Col. Mitras
Monterrey
N.L., Mexico

Misión de Satelite
Calle Alamo, #93-3er Piso –
Local B
Santa Monica, Tlalnepantla
Edo. de Mexico, 54040
Mexico

Misión de Tijuana
Calle Balboa, #5284
Lomas Hipódromo
Tijuana B.C.
C.P. 22480 Mexico

Misión de Valle
Juárez, 139
San Pedro Garza García
N.L. Monterrey, 66230 Mexico

NEW ZEALAND

**Church of Scientology
Mission of Christchurch**
PO Box 1843
Christchurch
New Zealand

PAKISTAN

Dianetics Centre
A-3 Royal Avenue
(opposite Urdu College
Block 13C)
Gulshan-E-Iqbal Karachi
Pakistan

TAIWAN

**Church of Scientology
Mission of Capital**
3F No. 200, Fu-Hsing S. RD
Section 1
Taipei, Taiwan

**Church of Scientology
Mission of Kaohsiung**
85 Tong-shin Road
Shin-Shin District
Kaohsiung, Taiwan

**Church of Scientology
Mission of Taichung**
82-2 Wu-Chuan-5th Street
Taichung, Taiwan

**Church of Scientology
Mission of Taipei**
1F, No. 16, Lane 63
Sung-Chang Road
Taipei, Taiwan

THAILAND

**Church of Scientology
Mission of Bangkok**
325/329 Silom Road
11th Floor
Bangkok, Thailand 10500

To obtain any books or cassettes by L. Ron Hubbard which are not available at your local organization, contact any of the following publishers:

Bridge Publications, Inc.
4751 Fountain Avenue
Los Angeles, California 90029

Continental Publications
  Liaison Office
696 Yonge Street
Toronto, Ontario
Canada M4Y 2A7

NEW ERA Publications
  International ApS
Store Kongensgade 55
1264 Copenhagen K
Denmark

ERA DINÁMICA Editores,
  S.A. de C.V.
Pablo Ucello #16
Colonia C.D. de los Deportes
Mexico, D.F.

NEW ERA Publications
  UK, Ltd.
Saint Hill Manor
East Grinstead, West Sussex
England RH19 4JY

NEW ERA Publications
  Australia Pty Ltd.
Level 1, 61–65 Wentworth
  Avenue
Surry Hills
New South Wales
Australia 2000

Continental Publications
  Pty Ltd.
6th Floor, Budget House
130 Main Street
Johannesburg 2001
South Africa

NEW ERA Publications
  Italia S.r.l.
Via Cadorna, 61
20090 Vimodrone (MI)
Italy

NEW ERA Publications
  Deutschland GmbH
Hittfelder Kirchweg 5A
21220 Seevetal-Maschen
Germany

NEW ERA Publications
  France E.U.R.L.
105, rue des Moines
75017 Paris
France

NUEVA ERA DINÁMICA
  S.A.
C/ Montera 20, 1° dcha.
28013 Madrid, Spain

NEW ERA Publications
  Japan, Inc.
3-4-20-503 Sala Mita
Minato-ku, Tokyo
Japan 108

NEW ERA Publications
  Group
Ul. Kasatkina, 16, Building 1
129301 Moscow, Russia

"I AM ALWAYS HAPPY TO HEAR FROM MY READERS."
–L. RON HUBBARD

These were the words of L. Ron Hubbard, who was always very interested in hearing from his friends and readers. He made a point of staying in communication with everyone he came in contact with over his fifty-year career as a professional writer, and he had thousands of fans and friends that he corresponded with all over the world.

The publishers of L. Ron Hubbard's works wish to continue this tradition and welcome letters and comments from you, his readers, both old and new.

Additionally, the publishers will be happy to send you information on anything you would like to know about L. Ron Hubbard, his extraordinary life and accomplishments and the vast number of books he has written.

Any message addressed to Author's Affairs Director at Bridge Publications will be given prompt and full attention.

BRIDGE PUBLICATIONS, INC.
4751 Fountain Avenue
Los Angeles, California 90029
USA

KEEPING SCIENTOLOGY WORKING THROUGH STANDARD ADMINISTRATION

SCIENTOLOGISTS AROUND THE WORLD know the true benefits of Scientology—spiritual freedom and immortality—are assured only with 100 percent Standard Tech. Thus they take to heart the responsibility for keeping Scientology working.

Yet purity of application applies not just to auditing technology—but also to administrative technology.

"Just as there is STANDARD TECH, so is there STANDARD ADMIN. The fact is that any organization can be seen to fail when standard administrative policy is not known and used by its people. And every successful organization will be found to be composed of people who DO know and DO apply the basic principles found in our policy letters."

L. RON HUBBARD

HCO PL 10 July 86 III

The purpose of Religious Technology Center is to keep Scientology working by safeguarding the proper use of the trademarks, protecting the public and making sure the powerful technologies of Dianetics and Scientology remain in good hands and are properly used. Where LRH administrative technology is applied standardly, it invariably results in expansion.

Do your part to maintain the purity of the technology so the Bridge to Total Freedom will always be there for you and all mankind. Keep Scientology working through Standard Administration.

RELIGIOUS TECHNOLOGY CENTER
HOLDER OF THE DIANETICS & SCIENTOLOGY TRADEMARKS
1710 IVAR AVENUE, SUITE 1100
LOS ANGELES, CALIFORNIA 90028, USA

Learn to Think

"The ability to evaluate puts one at cause over both the mad and ideal. It places a being at a height it is unlikely he has ever before enjoyed in the realm of commanding the situations of life. Evaluation is a new way to think. It is very worthwhile to acquire such an ability as it is doubtful if it ever before has been achieved."

– L. Ron Hubbard

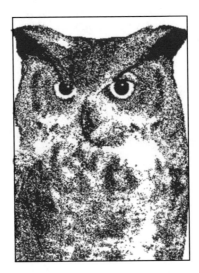

For thousands of years philosophers failed to discover the answer to logic and rational thought.

With the development of the Data Series that discovery has been made— *the* greatest thinking breakthrough in man's history, unlocking the entire field of logic.

Learn to think!

Master the technology of evaluation. Gain the ability to locate *exact* cause behind any situation every time.

This is a course that will change your life. On it, you will:

• Learn the basics of logic and how to think

• Learn how to recognize the difference between fact and opinion

• Drill how to investigate and find the right Why that opens the door to achieving an ideal scene

• Drill recognizing pluspoints and outpoints so that you know them cold

• Drill on how to spot situations

• Learn how to analyze data

• Learn how to investigate and get to the bottom of any situation

• Learn how to establish the ideal scene for any activity

Do the Hubbard Elementary Data Series Evaluator's Course.
Your own survival depends on Your Ability to Think.

FLAG EXECUTIVE BRIEFING COURSE

The Class VIII Course of Admin Technology

"The exact intention of the Flag Executive Briefing Course is to bring executive action up to the high level of precision now only attained in auditing."
– **L. Ron Hubbard**

Learn 3rd dynamic auditing technology by becoming a Class VIII Auditor of Admin tech.

A Class VIII Auditor is a flawless, flubless, smooth as silk specialist in standard tech who can handle *any* case with ease. And for the administrator, the "case" is the organization itself.

The FEBC brings administrative tech to the level of Class VIII auditing—<u>precision</u> with exact predictable results every time. Gain the skills to run *any* organization, handle *any* situation, organize *any* area and make it expand and flourish — as a flubless 3rd dynamic auditor.

> *"Administration is third dynamic auditing. And just like auditing, has its standard processes for standard situations." – LRH*
>
> Those standard processes are learned to perfection on the FEBC with:
>
> - an exhaustive study of the powerful Management Series,
> - rough, tough administrative drills on the key organizational skills,
> - the landmark lectures LRH personally delivered aboard the *Apollo* to the first students on the FEBC and those training as Establishment Officers.

Become a Class VIII Auditor—on the 3rd Dynamic.
ENROLL ON THE FLAG EXECUTIVE BRIEFING COURSE

YOUR GUARANTEE OF FREEDOM.

INTERNATIONAL ASSOCIATION OF SCIENTOLOGISTS

The purpose of the International Association of Scientologists is: "To unite, advance, support and protect the Scientology religion and Scientologists in all parts of the world so as to achieve the aims of Scientology as originated by L. Ron Hubbard."

All great movements have succeeded because of the personal conviction and dedication of their members. And no members are as dedicated as those of the IAS, the group which is winning the war against suppression around the world.

Even if you're not directly involved in the fight, it *is* your war. You have a stake in what kind of world this is — and will become.

Become a member of the International Association of Scientologists.

Help guarantee your route to full OT as well as freedom for the millions.

WRITE TO THE MEMBERSHIP OFFICER

INTERNATIONAL ASSOCIATION OF SCIENTOLOGISTS

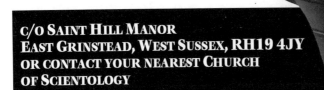

C/O SAINT HILL MANOR
EAST GRINSTEAD, WEST SUSSEX, RH19 4JY
OR CONTACT YOUR NEAREST CHURCH
OF SCIENTOLOGY

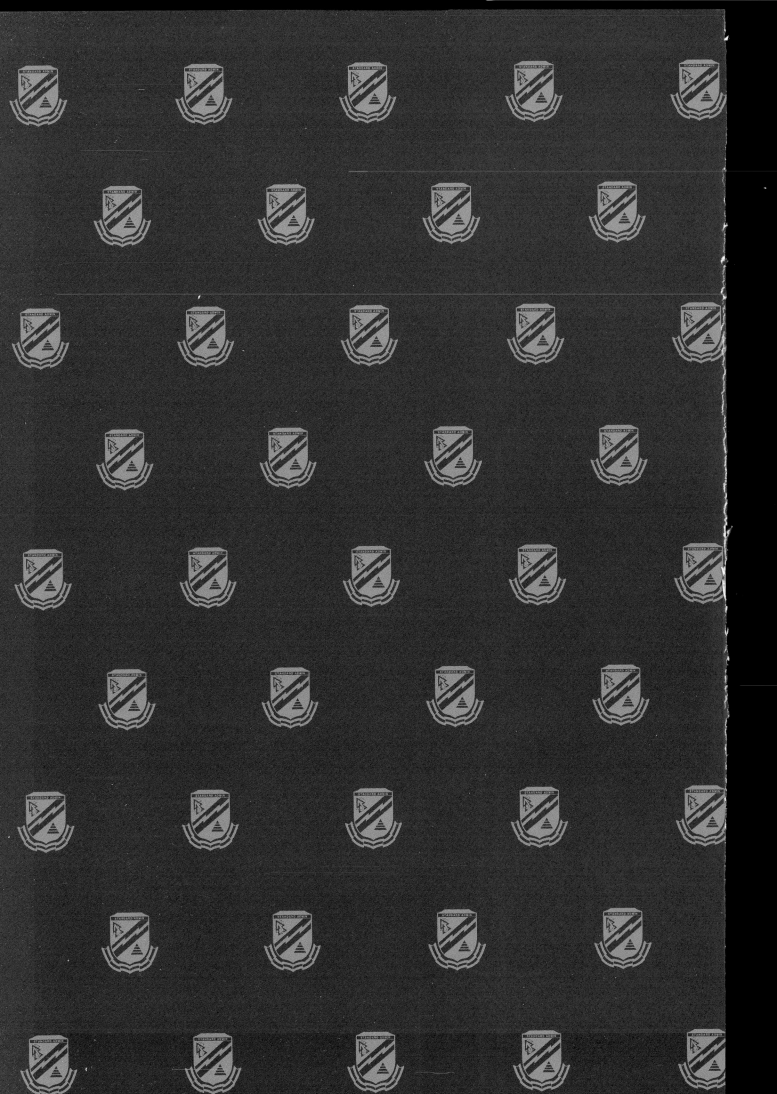